A CULTURAL HISTORY OF THE
MODERN AGE

A CULTURAL HISTORY OF THE MODERN AGE

BY EGON FRIEDELL

TRANSLATED FROM THE GERMAN BY CHARLES FRANCIS ATKINSON

ALFRED · A · KNOPF · PUBLISHER

A CULTURAL HISTORY OF THE MODERN AGE

THE CRISIS OF THE
EUROPEAN SOUL

FROM THE BLACK DEATH
TO THE WORLD WAR

BY

EGON FRIEDELL

Translated from the German

by

CHARLES FRANCIS ATKINSON

VOLUME III.

BOOK FOUR—Romanticism and Liberalism: from the Congress of Vienna to the Franco-German War

BOOK FIVE—Imperialism and Impressionism: from the Franco-German War to the World War

EPILOGUE—The Collapse of Reality

NEW YORK · ALFRED · A · KNOPF · 1932

Originally published as
Kulturgeschichte der Neuzeit

"... *that all this is true in a way precisely because it is false in a way.*"

AUGUSTINE

TABLE OF CONTENTS

BOOK V: IMPERIALISM AND IMPRESSIONISM

From the Franco-German War to the World War

CHAPTER I: *Black Friday*

CHAPTER II: *Gone to the Devil*

EPILOGUE: *The Collapse of Reality*

ix

BOOK IV: ROMANTICISM AND LIBERALISM

From the Congress of Vienna to the Franco-German War

CHAPTER I

THE DEPTH OF EMPTINESS

" Our yearning sets for home
And yet we know not whither."
Eichendorff

We have reached the third part of our trilogy. The first eve- *The inmost circle of hell* ning's performance showed us the *birth* of the man of the Modern Age, the second the *flowering* of this peculiar historical variety, and the theme of the last evening is the *death* of the Modern Age. The " incubation-time " in which the poisonous fruit of modern thought was developed we could only see in the pale gleam of a chill winter night. The world of the Renaissance had for us the unreality of a glittering and godless fever-dream, and the mankind of Reformation times had reality indeed, but only the reality of a dull gnarled woodcut. The life of the Baroque spoke to us like the strange grimacings of a stiff marionette-play, and the soul of the Rococo as the distant echo of a tired autumnal evensong. Even the familiar *milieu* of our Classicism was seen as the half-light of the declining afternoon, and the French Revolution, that followed so hard upon it, as in the spectral beam of a magic lantern. But with the fall of the last fairy-tale king that Europe has seen, that magic effect of distance, the misty disembodying brilliance drops away from persons and courts, and all becomes intimate, familiar, compact, and concrete. The heroes who carry on the play of world-history are no longer queer stories, dark legends, silhouettes projected by the world-spirit upon a mysterious background; they transform themselves into private existences, people holding down jobs, people you meet in the street, people who will answer when you question them, for they are made of the same material as we ourselves are. With the Congress of Vienna begins the history of the Present.

Now, one hears it said, often and with emphasis, that our existence is becoming greyer, indeed, and more humdrum, but on that very account more reasonable, more livable, more human, more comfortable. This is not true. The nineteenth century is the inhuman century *par excellence*. The "triumphant career" of technics has completely mechanized us, which is as much as to say, made us stupid; the worship of gold has impoverished mankind thoroughly and irredeemably; and a world without God is not only the most immoral but the most uncomfortable that the imagination can conceive. With his entry into the Present, Modern Man reaches the inmost infernal circle of that path of suffering which is as absurd as it is necessary.

The unreal Present It might be supposed that at least we have more accurate, more trustworthy, clearer information about this phase in the evolution of the world's course than about its predecessors. But no, there is not even this consolation — if consolation it were. We have compared the "two-souled" men, with whom the Modern Age begins, to a *fractional* number, one that is no longer unitary, but still fully comprehensible; and the men of the Baroque to an *irrational* number, the value of which can only be expressed approximately by means of an unending decimal. If we were to continue the analogy, we should have to regard the man of the nineteenth century as an *imaginary* number of the type $\sqrt{-1}$, which is simply not real at all and cannot be reached by any mental operations whatsoever. The whole of our attempt to present history started from the premiss that history is not a science, and if the work of rigorous research is highly problematical in the case of the past, in that of the present it is quite hopeless. History of the past is scarcely possible, but history of the present is impossible, for the very simple reason that it deals with the existing, visible, and corporal present. For there is nothing more unintelligible than the moment, and nothing more unreal than physical existence. The mist of uncertainty, instead of clearing, thickens with every day that brings us nearer to this Now, and we have practically as accurate a picture of times, persons, and events that "belong to us" as we have of our nearest relatives, with whom we deal in terms of love (or, since Freud, hate), but never of knowledge.

Poetical, historical, and journalistic truth The will to history, which exists elementally in every "posterity" — the historians are merely its more or less conscientious executive agents — works out a progressive process of distillation. That which lies very far away is invested already with the silvern nimbus of poetry and appears before our face with that irrefutable authenticity that it alone possesses: it has become completely "true." That which lies some way back has been sifted, sorted, pruned, and purified and has attained to probability: it has be-

4

come " historical." But the history of the Present is still in the uncertain state of a trial in which only the juggling attorney, the bullying prosecutor, the candid or uncandid expert, the lying or prejudiced, shy or brazen-faced witnesses say their say. If, as I tried to show in the Introduction to this work, all history of the past is only legend, all history of the present is only reporting; that is, the most unscientific, the cheapest, the most suspect form of human narrative. When history is old enough to have crystal- lized into pure poetry, then out of it there speaks to us, directly, the web of the world-spirit that cannot lie, the word of God; and in this sense the Bible is not only the noblest but also the most trust- worthy historical work that we have. When the history is some- what more recent, what speaks out of it is the spirit of the people, which is local and of earthly origin indeed, but yet guided by the sure instinct of the genus. The history of the present, however, has for its mouthpiece merely the spirit of the " editor," a sly parti- san creature, armed with an iron courage for lying, who serves only himself and his party dogma; it matters not whether what he edits is a school-book, a blue-book, a diplomatic note, a general-staff appreciation, or, for that matter, a journal, all " contributions " to the history of the present have the truth-value of the newspaper.

Consequently, in order to attain to historical truth, one has only to preserve, unvaryingly and incorruptibly, three things — a believing reverence for the sanctity of poetical history, a ready trustfulness towards the sure fact of traditional history, and a profound mistrust in the short-sightedness and false coinage of " contemporary history." The content of it all can be summarized in the concise phrase of an English writer: " Very nearly every- thing in history very nearly did not happen." If not so laconically, yet just as unambiguously Nietzsche says: " A historian has to do, not with what actually happened, but only with what was supposed to have happened. . . . His theme, world-history so called, con- sists in suppositions concerning supposed happenings and the supposed motives thereof. . . . All historians relate things that have never existed save in the imagination."

One must ask oneself — it need be only once, but it must be squarely — what the materials are that serve as the foundation of what is called the science of history. These are, firstly, " docu- ments " and " originals " such as records of trials and debates, proclamations and orders-in-council, dossiers and contracts, fis- cal and cadastral returns, minutes and dispatches, and other such

The ghost-
stream

5

relics of various sorts; the study of these constitutes the field of Diplomatic. Secondly, there are the " memorials," particularly inscriptions, with which Epigraphy deals, and the coinages, which are the province of Numismatics. Thirdly, there are the evidences of " tradition," which attempt consciously and of set purpose to fix historical recollections; in this class fall chronologies and genealogies, annals and chronicles, diaries and memoirs, biographies and histories. Even these " sources," all of them — and we are not considering those which are unfixed or unfixable — become historical documents only through being regarded and evaluated as such by the man who examines them; otherwise they are merely chaotic masses of interpolations, discoveries, self-deceptions, and fortuitous accuracies. It is he who first puts them in their place — and very often the wrong place. It is he who links them into a system and so makes of them a history. They are mere signs and symbols for facts, and these facts themselves are neither true nor false, for they are both — all equally untrue (for they were only true, in the sense of natural science, in the moment of their happening) and all equally true (for as the expression of this and that specific movement of life it is impossible for them to be " false "). They become permanent phenomena only through being taken into a historical consciousness, and, further, it does not matter what historical consciousness this is, for error can make them just as immortal as knowledge.

Strictly speaking, the data which the historian has are only indicative. " One is deceiving oneself," says Hermann Paul (*Prinzipien der Sprachgeschichte*), " if one thinks that the simplest historical fact can be established without a supervening element of speculation. For man speculates, even if unconsciously, and it is some happy instinct that we have to thank when we hit the mark." Nature, it is said, is stupid in contrast to man, but for the researcher the exact opposite is the case, for nature gives him answers, and man none, or (what comes to the same thing) too many — to each a different one. Jakob Burckhardt observes, in his *Weltgeschichtliche Betrachtungen:* " The sources are inexhaustible, for they present a different face to every reader and every century, even to every different age-phase of the same individual. . . . And this is not in the least a misfortune, but simply a consequence of continuously living communication." So far from being a misfortune, indeed, it is a blessing, for the charm and value of history lie precisely in the fact that it never deals with

6

"natural" things that can be subjected to calculation and experiment, but always and only with things of the spirit; that is, with living things that change ceaselessly and at every time and every place speak a different language. A Stygian ghost-stream flows, eternal and subterranean, from that which *was* to that which *is;* we call it world-history. It is the collective work of the myriad-headed poet-guild that is called humanity. All memory that man possesses he can only store in the form of poetry. Every song that springs from mouth to mouth, every anecdote that leaps from ear to ear, every hastily scribbled report, nay, every individual word is already a poem. And every poem is by its nature a thing of a thousand meanings. Poems, received, enhanced, compacted, condensed, distorted, enriched by other poets — this contact of poetic forces constitutes " historical knowledge."

Schopenhauer observes, not without harshness: " Besides this incompleteness of history there is the fact that Clio, the Muse of History, is as permeated with lies as a street-whore with syphilis. The new, or critical, historical research goes to considerable trouble indeed to cure her, but with its local remedies it can only deal with individual symptoms that break out here and there — and not a little quackery, too, finds its way into the process, which makes matters worse than ever." This clumsy, pretentious, and not infrequently dishonest quackery reached its apogee in the school of Ranke — a historical genius, but it was not " scientificness " that made him so — and in its working-out contributed not a little to making history the pet aversion of the second half of the nineteenth century. " Scientific " history was merely the result of the increasing dearth of imagination and of talent, the extinction of the natural creative instincts. The old-fashioned historians invented speeches and situations that they regarded as *characteristic,* with all possible light-heartedness, wholly unconscious of committing forgery, for they started from the sound feeling that the more pregnant the fact is — the deeper it etches the furrow in the memory, the more portrait-like the etching — the truer it is. They sought for their living artistic shape, and not for their dead scientific description. The Iliad was looked upon by the Greeks, not as " literature," but as a history-source. It was the same with the Middle Ages and their heroic poems, whereas their chronicles, with their effort materially to preserve crude facts, constitute even thus early a primitive attempt to write history " exactly." And yet even these chronicles — and, for that matter, numerous works of

" Critical "
history-
writing

7

the Renaissance — make no fundamental distinctions between the symbolical truth of the saga and the reporter's truth of the " real " narrative. Far into the eighteenth century, in fact, one finds writers (and many of them) who, in the handling of their material, yield to the human inclination for fable and adornment, and whose forms in consequence approach those of rhetoric and story-telling. The historians of the Enlightenment, even, were phantasts to this extent, that they held certain chosen tendencies in honour and illuminated them by brightly and variously colouring the facts. This sort of historiography consisted in seeing a piece of history through a temperament, and thus was not so far removed from theological historiography as one would suppose — did not Montesquieu charge Voltaire with writing " like a monk for his Church "? But in our " critical " study of history philology has dominated poetry as thoroughly as the modern Alexandrinism had already dominated it in the study of literature. The essence of this school (which was regarded for several decades as the only legitimate one, the supreme triumph of the " historical century ") consists simply in this, that in it the childish reverence for anything written and printed — which differs only in degree from the superstitious belief of the unlettered in the newspaper — has become a *methodology*. Henceforth the more " proofs " could be drummed up to support a fact — that is, the more letters had been used in handing it down — the more certain it was, whereas, surely, the very multiplication of evidences must lead to confusion if they differ, and increase the risk of error if (through being, as they usually are, copied one from another) they agree. Presently, indeed, opinion went so far as to allow validity only to " original sources " — that is, practically, the so-called " diplomatic " archive-material — and so quite happily landed itself in the dark hell-circle of lies. From this it was a perfectly logical development of the system to go to the newspaper, which indeed not a few conscientious historians, in their unwillingness to debase their serious and responsible calling to the feuilleton level by arbitrary philosophical systemizations and shallow psychological guessings, came to regard as the worthiest source of history.

All that can be " exactly " ascertained from all these reports, dispatches, notes, bulletins, circulars, and memoranda is that their authors were either damnable liars or feckless idiots, for either they distort the facts or else they do not grasp them. Consequently the only thing that a truly critical mind could extract from

8

this documentation would be that *nothing at all* happened — except knavery and stupidity. We can only prove that events have happened " just so " in the past when we can equally prove that these same events will happen again and again " just so." I can, for instance, show scientifically — that is, unambiguously and with complete precision — that Jupiter and Mars are in opposition, that in a bath of copper sulphate an electric current separates out a precise quantity of copper, that a particular projectile has described its trajectory with a mean velocity of five hundred foot-seconds, that a swarm of infusoria has under the stimulus of light moved to the lighted edge of a drop of water. All these, however, are mere processes, which can and indeed must repeat themselves. Given the same conditions, we have as rock-like a belief in their future existence as we have in their past. But with regard to a historical event we cannot even *imagine* that it should experience a repetition, much less be convinced of such a thing, for at bottom it is an individual event or (what means the same thing) a spiritual event. Spiritual processes include no duplicates; not for the future, and not for posterity. There is no science of spiritual processes — for they are not physical, but metaphysical facts — and anyone who denies this, himself possesses no soul, or, rather, has forgotten that he possesses one. Nay, even in respect of natural things, the exact method fails as soon as we attempt to reconstruct instead of merely reimagining them. If, for example, I wish to create within myself the image of a certain oak with which I am personally very friendly, two possibilities are open to me. I can go to it and carry out researches " at the source," examining it, conscientiously setting it down in every detail; or I can let its well-remembered portrait arise before the inward vision of my memory. In the first case I am proceeding " philologically," in the second " historically." And for me, without the slightest doubt, the second has the better claim to " truth."

The Italian philosopher and historian Benedetto Croce, one of the wisest and most candid thinkers of the present day, says on this subject of " philological " history-writing: " If one applies the method of evidences in all strictness, one finds that there is no evidence that cannot be tainted or deprived of cogency . . . if one arbitrarily invests particular evidences with validity, on account of outward marks, then there is nothing so perverse that one can refuse to accept it, for there is nothing so perverse that it has not the authority of sensible, clean, and intelligent men on its side.

History is invented

9

Under the philological criteria, one cannot even reject miracles, since these rest upon just as reliable evidences as do wars and peace treaties." And on the subject of historical " criticism " he observes: " Hypercriticism is the natural extension of criticism, criticism itself. . . . No authorities are 'more reliable' or 'less reliable,' but all are alike unreliable. And with an unreliability, moreover, that is graded in a wholly external and arbitrary way. Who can protect us against the falsehood that an otherwise exact and conscientious witness sets up in some moment of absent-mindedness or temporary passionate excitement? "

As, then, all evidences are dubious — and, incidentally, all equally usable, since even the most obvious errors and lies and nullities are material (often very telling and convincing material) for the historian — how is historical truth to be determined? The answer is, we do not know; it is a mystery like everything else. In the course of history certain events, figures, and ideas slowly become true, certain others become false — or, to speak more correctly, some become historically existent, some historically non-existent. They may change their rôle even in the recollections of their followers, they may start up as unexpectedly as a coral reef and be smothered like a Vesuvian town. They are *births*, and, as such, secrets. But the notion that their existence depends upon the activity of the collating and compiling archive-grubber, paper-sapper, bookworm, is as scandalous a fallacy as the idea of Mr. Chanticleer that his crowing causes the sunrise, whereas in fact he merely announces it — an activity useful on occasions, even if annoyingly overloud and out of tune, but unfortunately not limited to those occasions, for he is apt to regard his cock-a-doodle-doo as an end in itself. In all circumstances the function of science is that of a midwife, who takes no part in the birth itself, but merely makes it more comfortable, or of a collector of botanical specimens, who " preserves " a radiant flora by first killing it and then bottling it in his vulgar spirit.

History is *invented*, and every day newly found, newly quickened, reinterpreted according to the needs of the world-structure as it stands at each moment. Here, once again, we meet that law which has more than once been expressed in this work: namely, that the spiritual is the primary, and the actual only its projection and materialization. America sprang out of the ocean in the moment when European man turned his attention from the secrets of his own soul to the enigmas of his earthly dwelling-place. In the moment when he wanted to know, no longer about God, but about the world, the Babel-tower of the telescope reared itself up, its giant eye directed upon the structure and movements of the remotest stars. And after he had made up his mind to become a machine-being, his planet filled up with mere dead replicas of this new mankind, with the tumult of chugging piston-rods and rattling wheels, screeching cranks and crossing belts and the unending mist and smell of steam and oil. When Renaissance Italy suddenly became enthusiastic about its Roman past, the " sacred soil " opened of itself and cast antiquities by the hundred before the delighted connoisseurs. When the Germans around Goethe sought with their souls for the land of the Greeks, that land emerged magically from centuries of dark mist into the full sunlight. And how else should they have sought it but with their souls? And today we see with amazement a whole continent that hitherto we have called " dark " coming into the light and, touched by the rays of our desire, beginning like the Memnon statues to give forth sound. The moment comes, and the " historical evidences " are there! They are there because the spirit of conception that shapes them is there. All " historical facts " exist, but most of them lie dead, or seemingly dead in a magic sleep, waiting for their re-awakening. History is not something that *is*, as naïve science imagines, but something that continuously *becomes*, every day new, changing, reversing, re-forming, rejuvenated, negatived, developed, and thrown back — just as every man is every day new for himself and for others.

In the year 1919 there appeared a very remarkable book by Theodor Lessing: *Geschichte als Sinngebung des Sinnlosen,* an effort of Lucifer boldness, captivating in its pale nocturnal beauty and ice-clear logic — perhaps the first attempt that has been made to think out to its end the question: " What *is* history, really and truly? " He has carried out the task with the keenness, and indeed two-edged keenness, that comes of such an irreverent and self-sufficient beginning. Yet he arrives in the philosophy of history at the same result as Spinoza did in the philosophy of nature: that is, at *nothingness*. It is a cold Pyrrhic victory of the intellect, which celebrates its last and most sophisticated triumph in suicide. It is a work to which we may well apply this saying of another Lessing: " grand and full of poisonous mephitic gases, and only without grave dangers when in the hands of a prudent transcriber like myself." His basic idea is implicit in the title itself: it is, namely, that

History promoted in rank

causal connexions through history and evolution through time do not manifest themselves immediately and without human extrapolation. " But history is the charter of this meaning, the settlement of this connexion, the discovery of this evolution. It does not find the meaning of the world ready to hand, but gives it." History is *logificatio post festum*. The notion of actuality, says Lessing, is not so simple as is supposed by the historian who only regards as historical that which " can be proved by documents " and treats all else as mere saga. Men will one day come to see that " outside mechanics, no exact science whatever is probable, and life in particular can only be experienced livingly, never determined. . . . Finally, myth possesses essential truth of a metaphysical sort, compared with which historical actuality appears as thoroughly untrue and falsified. . . . The effort of all history is to begin with the fact and to end with the symbol," which is true, whereas the fact is merely actual. If we apply this most illuminating principle to the present, we shall have to say that its facts are not yet even actual. Says Lessing in another part of his work: " It is only when memory has gathered several millennia into a whole that we are definitely sensible of the poetical force of history. . . . The great is only recognized, as God was recognized by Moses, when it has passed." Humboldt, too, a century earlier, had remarked in his essay *Über die Aufgabe des Geschichtschreibers:* " If one tries to narrate the most insignificant facts, and yet rigorously limits oneself to that only which has actually come to pass, one very soon notices how . . . falsehoods and uncertainties occur. . . . Hence nothing is rarer than a literally exact relation. . . . Hence historical truth more or less resembles the clouds, which only take shape for the eye at a distance ; and hence the facts of history, as linked by their various settings, are little more than results of tradition and research that it has been agreed to regard as true." But the way in which these cloud-forms gather themselves together in their glory and greatness to astonish, to please, and to elevate the later world is a transcendent process. The spirit of God weaves this web, " which we only know after it has passed over us."

The knowledge that history is poetry has indeed never quite faded out of human consciousness, but it is proper to our own day in a greater degree than it is to many earlier periods, and especially that which immediately preceded it, which was afflicted with a blind superstition for actuality, and in history, as in every other domain, hunted for facts. This phase, however, in no wise amounted to a dethronement of history; it detached history from a sham throne to invest it with a grander crown than it had ever hitherto worn. The historiography of the last generation, which styles itself "positivist," was in reality negativist to the last degree, destructive, sceptical. And it suffered the fate that the "sense of actuality" met with in all domains, in that it was made to learn that its more intensive knowledge of certain subaltern sections of experience had to be paid for by the loss of all others, and that this "sense" is not a keener and a richer, but an infinitely duller and poorer sense. Or, to express it with all brevity, the fact that the author of a historical work is not a historian will not nowadays disturb anybody but a historian.

Dumas *père* made the witty remark on Macaulay that he "raised History to the rank of Romance." But it did not need Macaulay to bring about this promotion, for, given a certain lapse of time, it comes to pass of itself. The fact that we describe the age that is two to three thousand years *younger* than our own as "Antiquity" proceeds from the same naïveté of vision as makes us look upon our grandfather not only as being but as always and in all circumstances having been an old gentleman, whereas he was doubtless younger — that is, warmer, less complicated, more child-like — than ourselves. The man of the past, whether of Merovingian or of Medicean times, is younger than we are, just as, in comparison with rodents, lizards and fish are younger — nay, infantile — although, or rather because, they existed earlier. And therefore ancient history is history in a higher, more genuine, purer sense than modern and even present-day history, since the history of our childhood and youth is truer than the history of our ripe and over-ripe years. Everyone has the feeling, indisputable though incapable of proof, that his life then was more real, more affirmed, stronger, more existent, even though the flow of the "sources" is more spasmodic, scantier, more turbid, and "evidences" are almost non-existent. Hence, again, the enthusiasm which Antiquity has released, in all periods, as an object of the passion for history, in contrast with the coolness that envelops the recording of present conditions. And yet these times too will one day become youth and shine with truth and beauty. Every age becomes in its turn the Golden Age in the golden light that we throw on it; only it must have passed away sufficiently long ago. For it, too, is truly present in the one place where things can become present: namely, in the spirit.

13

The Present, on the contrary, which is made grey and impenetrable by the mist of nearness, is inevitably as destitute of colour as it is of clarity. On it falls only the glassy stare of idiosyncrasy.

What is Romanticism?

Already, at its very beginning, the first part of the period that we are dealing with here — namely, the half-generation lying between 1815 and 1830 — the Congress of Vienna and the July Revolution — is subject in a very remarkable degree to the law of historical unfairness. It is usually called the era of *Restoration* or of *Reaction,* and in this dual nomenclature itself there is implicit the whole controversy that has gone on, and still goes on, between opposite valuations of it. If one treats it as reactionary and reversing, one can only see in it a Satanic attempt to put back the clock of history by force and to conjure up anew all the darkness, madness, and corruption of periods that had been overcome. If one treats it as restorative and re-establishing, one can only see in it the return of the order, reason, and morals that had been dethroned. But history only apparently, never really, steps backwards. And, in fact, during this phase the European spirit only went back in the way that a leaper runs back in order to get a start for his leap. The Restoration is merely the picture of an immense Pan-European Revolution that reploughed, not merely the political field, but all fields of human existence, which went far deeper, spread far wider, and lasted far longer than the French.

The most appropriate name for this decade and a half is the age of *Romanticism*. I have already, in the first volume of this work, shown that it is at bottom inaccurate to speak of an English or a French Renaissance, or of a Danish or a Polish Reformation, for in the strict sense the only Renaissance was the Italian, and the only Reformation the German. In the same way, it is unsound to speak of any Romanticism prior to the Vienna Congress or posterior to the July Revolution. As we shall see later, the so-called French Romanticism, which only set in about 1830, amounted really to a complete reversal and dissolution of the Romantic idea; and on the other hand, as I have already tried to show at the end of my second volume, the so-called Early Romanticism was only a differently coloured variety of the archaistic feeling which monopolized the period, a mere offshoot of Classicism, and, like it, the child of Rationalism and Hellenism. We have, therefore, even at the risk of presenting things as less mixed and more orderly than they were in reality, to draw a sharp line of demarcation between " Early " and " Late " Romanticism, and regard only the latter as

14

the genuine Romanticism; although naturally, for convenience and intelligibility, we shall still employ without qualms the accepted terminology " Early Romanticism " for the older or Jena kind, and "Late" for the younger or Heidelberg kind. (These places are regarded as the " capitals " of the two schools, but actually Berlin was the centre in both cases.) If we regard Romanticism as a linear progression from, say, 1790 to 1830, we are up against the difficulty that the first school, which was really something late — namely, the last, over-ripe, and even worm-eaten fruit of the Enlightenment — has to be regarded as the period of flowering, and the second school, which was something new — a birth — as the period of decadence; as Ricarda Huch regards it in her two-volume work, which in other respects is a most kindly and understanding effort of feminine empathy.

We are, however, not in a position to offer any reasonably inclusive and unambiguous definition of the concept " Romanticism " and must practically be content to presume that everyone knows what is meant anyhow, and console ourselves, if we may, with the thought that no one — neither adherents nor opponents, neither contemporaries nor successors — has ever arrived at a clear paraphrase of the Romanticist's essence. Probably, indeed, this is inherent in the concept itself. Ludwig Tieck, who is considered as the founder of the first Romantic school, said to Köpke about the middle of the nineteenth century, long after Romanticism was over: " If I were challenged to give a definition of Romanticism, I could not do it. I cannot make out any difference whatever between the Romantic and the poetic in general." This wide formulation of the idea, which is not peculiar to Tieck, would entitle us, without more ado, to call any intensification of world-feeling Romantic and to count among the Romantics Ibsen and Zola, Kalidasa and Homer. Further, it should be observed that the Romantics, although they all felt as, and tried to be, a self-contained intellectual group and to form a militant literary party, never designated themselves as the " Romantic school." This label first appears between 1810 and 1820, and it was invented by their *opponents*.

The " Late " Romantic, of which the very first heraldings appeared about the turn of the century, and which advanced to full domination in the period which we are discussing, can — in spite of the fact that it is a particularly homogeneous and even a Pan-European movement — only be properly characterized in a

The " Organic "

negative way: namely, as reaction, and this time meaning by the word, *throw-back*. Early Romanticism, as we have said, was still precisely as rationalistic as the French Revolution, Napoleon, the Empire style, the Classical drama, the Kantian and post-Kantian idealism, and all other significant phenomena of the pre-Waterloo period. The Late Romanticism, on the contrary, took as its central concept Irrationalism, or, in its own favourite phrase, "the Organic," the grown, the become, life in all its incalculability and incomprehensibility, power and sanctity, in opposition to the mechanical, which can be reduced to rational formulæ. Consequently the Romantic is a supporter of tradition in all its branches (for tradition is universally the expression of a slow evolution ripened in the dark womb of Time, a work, not of arbitrarily deciding reason, but of mysteriously working life). And so he looked with reverence upon all unconscious and earth-wedded, upon Nature and upon "the people" (who for him were not a social but a natural-historical phenomenon), upon the folk-born myth, upon Woman as springing from the subterranean realm of the "Mothers." And so he felt (was, in truth, the first to feel) historically above all, and he conceived history not pragmatically, as a chain of human motivations and actions, but (again) organically, as an evolutionary series of emanations from the "spirit" that ruled in it, each in its own way complete and justified. The Enlightenment had judged the past in relation to the present, or to the future, which was an idealized present — based for the Classicists on the Antique, and for the early Romantics on the Middle Ages. All alike took their position and view-point outside history and treated it dogmatically, whereas Late Romanticism looked upon each people and each age as an organism which, in that it was the actualization of the form and idea determined for it, represented an absolute value — therein, as in many other respects, taking up afresh the short-lived movement that had set in so hopefully in the early 1770's, the ideas of Herder, Hamann, and the "*Geniezeit*." Everything which they regarded from this new standpoint they sought ultimately to bring under the super-concept of "the Totality," regarding all life-functions and their interrelations — politics, religion, art, language, morals — as the workings-out of this mysterious Totality. This concept of Totality and the Organic poses, and at the same time resolves, all the contradictions contained in the world of Romanticism; it is at once catholic and national, mystic and naturalistic, evolutionary and conservative.

16

Although this " second " Romanticism had nothing about it of the doctrinaire and arbitrarily schematic punctilio of the older school, it was none the less, from its inevitable character of intermezzo and the forced renunciation of its time and its world to which it was committed, an unhealthy movement. Clemens Brentano, with his great gift of self-knowledge, expressed it thus: " Every man has a poetry in his body, just as he has a brain, a heart, a stomach, a spleen, a liver, and so on. But whoever overfeeds misfeeds, and disproportionately uses one of his members . . . has lost his balance, and an over-large goose's liver, however nice it tastes, always presupposes a sick goose." This period, especially its most representative personalities, suffered without a doubt from hypertrophy of the poetical organs. It entirely lacked harmony, and in the absence of all external activity everything struck inwards. Every exaggeration indicates a deficiency that tries to compensate for itself, and everything can be exaggerated, even the intellectual. Says Nietzsche: " Sufferers are of two sorts, those who suffer from *excess of life* and those who suffer from *impoverishment of life,* those who seek rest and quiet and calm seas, and release from self in art and knowledge — and, on the other hand, those who seek intoxication, spasm, deafness, madness. It is from the dual needs of the *latter* that all Romanticism, both in art and in knowledge, springs." And with this we come face to face with the profoundest meaning of the word " Reaction " that is applied to this period — it is a reaction against the forced impoverishment of life, stricken by the self-deepening of intoxication-spasm or by sclerosis.

Rahel Levin described the state of society then as " the infinite depth of emptiness," and no less competent an observer than Metternich called this remark " an inspiration of real genius."

This state of society was artificially created by the Congress of Vienna. " Europe," wrote one of its delegates, " has sent here the brilliance of its thrones and courts, the prestige of its states, the heads of its political and military power, the finest flower of its society, even the fairest flowers of its elegance and beauty, art and taste." And in truth there was collected in Vienna during those months practically everything that, rightly or wrongly, in the good sense or the bad, had a European reputation. Among the potentates who found themselves there were two Emperors and four Kings, whose activities were thus resumed and surveyed in a *bon mot* that circulated at the time: " The Emperor of Russia loves for

17

them all, the King of Prussia thinks for them all, the King of Denmark speaks for them all, the King of Bavaria drinks for them all, the King of Württemberg eats for them all, and the Emperor of Austria pays for them all." Besides these figures there was a crowd of minor rulers, among them Karl August of Saxe-Weimar, and round them were the beauties and the celebrities — Archduke Charles and Wellington, Stein and Hardenberg, Metternich and Gentz, Jakob Grimm and Wilhelm von Humboldt, the sculptor Dannecker and the painter Isabey — in short, everybody that was anybody, even to the " divine " danseuse Bigottini (who eavesdropped for Talleyrand as a side-line), and good old Jahn with his long beard and the thick boots which his democratic principles made him wear even at the most elegant soirées and which were always muddy (in fact, malicious gossip asserted that they were artificially kept so).

All these guests were lavishly entertained. Kaiser Franz, exceptionally economical at other times, spared no expense on this occasion, and the whole nobility of Austria and Hungary followed his example. The entire Congress period was nothing but an uninterrupted festival of extraordinary brilliance. Every known sort of entertainment and display was arranged in the handsomest and most elegant fashion. Fabulous balls and suppers, public feasts for the crowd, monster concerts of a thousand performers, " carrousels " (which in those days meant something different and much more costly than today: namely, cortèges and mounted evolutions of the utmost pomp), excursions by sledge, tableaux vivants, races, hunts, illuminations. Beethoven conducted his Battle Symphony, " Wellington's Triumph of Vitoria," before five thousand people, including the notabilities of the Congress, and his *Fidelio*, which ten years earlier had been a failure, brought down the house at the Kärntnertortheater. At the Leopoldstädter Theater Ignaz Schuster played his *Staberl* more than a hundred times; the Cathedral of St. Stephen was a theatre of another sort with Zacharias Werner's sermons, which were listened to by immense congregations; there were operas or comedies daily in the Burgtheater, ballets in the Wiedener Theater, farces in the Josefstädter Theater, gala dances in the Apollosaal. Day and night the streets were filled with equipages, soldiers, dandies, liveried servants, bands of music, cocottes, and linkmen. There was nothing to remind people that they had a twenty years' world-war behind them.

The soul of this Congress — to which the results of the " Hundred Days " made no essential difference — was the Duc de Talleyrand. It cannot be pretended that this diplomat could look back upon a career of consistency. He had participated in four different forms of French government, and he had succeeded in obtaining a leading place in each of them. He had been a bishop under the Bourbons, an ambassador under the Girondins, Grand Chamberlain under Napoleon; and he was now officiating under the Bourbons again as Foreign Minister to the restored Louis XVIII. He even lived to transfer his allegiance once more to the " bourgeois monarchy " of Louis Philippe, and that without forfeiting anything of public esteem. He himself, with his witty cynicism, said that he never abandoned any government before it abandoned itself, but did so just a little earlier than other people, as his watch was a little fast. It was he, too, who tossed into the Congress that fateful word " legitimacy," which Gentz with equal cleverness and unscrupulousness took up and exploited. A man who could sail safely between *ancien régime* and guillotine, between Bonapartism and Holy Alliance, between Restoration and July Revolution, and never be at a loss for his bearings, must certainly have had no common powers of trimming, suppleness, and tact. And with these gifts he got what he wanted even in the precarious position in which he found himself at the Vienna Congress, for at first the others were not inclined to admit a French envoy, and even later he was regarded with the greatest mistrust, it being suspected that he had come to set up mutual discontents among the powers and so to win advantages for himself. The suspicion was abundantly justified, but it did not prevent Talleyrand from completely achieving his aims; he *did* set up discord and he *did* get advantages.

The aims that he pursued, and in his position as French envoy necessarily pursued, were two. He had to try to get France through the Congress without loss of territory or prestige, and to prevent Germany from reaching the rank of a great power to which her geographical position, her historical evolution, and her military and cultural achievements entitled her. As everyone knows, he succeeded fully in both objects. For Germany the Congress of Vienna opened a fifty years' period of complete impotence and impoverishment and a century of torturing uneasiness in the presence of an arrogant and insatiable neighbour, who herself — though she had been decisively defeated by her external enemies and was hopelessly disorganized within — emerged from this world-war undiminished and victorious.

The new map

The two questions on which controversy was bitterest and most prolonged were the partition of Poland, which Russia, and that of Saxony, which Prussia wanted to swallow whole. Tempers rose to such a pitch that the Tsar on one occasion nearly challenged Metternich to a duel and openly threatened war, saying again and again: " I have occupied Poland with two hundred thousand men and I will see if anybody can drive me out of it." The Austrian Kaiser for his part declared: "The King of Saxony must have his land again, or I shoot." Although only hazy rumours of these dangers reached the outside world, the long duration of the Congress itself aroused scorn and bitterness in the public, which was intensified by the increase of prices due to the presence of the numerous delegates and their suites — a multitude that the city found it very difficult to feed and house — and to the overpaying for goods and supplies by wealthy foreigners. Wood, meat, and beer soared to such heights that many firms were able to amortise their whole capital during the Congress. The intrigues of the diplomats became day by day more involved and hopeless. What made an end of all this was Napoleon, returning from Elba.

The decisions of the Vienna Congress constituted a retrogression to the worst times of dynastic cabinet-politics. Neither in respect of internal organization nor in the territorial formation of the new states was any regard paid to the wishes of the populations. Even so, it was not possible completely to restore the pre-Revolutionary map. The most important changes were that Austria lost Belgium and received Venetia instead; that Prussia obtained Swedish Pomerania and about three fifths of the kingdom of Saxony and was greatly extended in the west; and Russia in the " Fourth Partition " obtained what was called " Congress Poland ": namely, the greater part of the Napoleonic Grand Duchy of Warsaw; Prussia for her part regaining the Grand Duchy of Posen, and Austria the southern part of Galicia, while Cracow was set up as a " Free State." England secured to herself Heligoland, the Cape, Ceylon, Malta, and the Ionian Islands. Sweden and Norway were joined under a personal union. Holland and Belgium were made into a " Kingdom of the Netherlands." Piedmont, augmented by Nice and Genoa, fell to the house of Savoy again; Parma was given to Marie Louise, Napoleon's consort and the Austrian Emperor's daughter, Tuscany to a son of Leopold II,

Modena to a nephew of Maria Theresa. In Naples, Spain, Portugal, and the Papal States the old governments were reinstated. Germany, unlike the former Holy Roman Empire, became a union of princes, the "Germanic Federation," with, as common organ, the Federal Diet at Frankfurt am Main, which was an assembly of all the envoys of the various states under Austrian presidency. Austria, however, was outside the system in respect of her Hungarian, Polish, and Italian possessions, while on the other hand the King of England as King of Hanover, the King of Denmark as Duke of Holstein and Lauenburg, and the King of the Netherlands as Grand Duke of Luxemburg were princes of the Federation. Paragraph 13 of the Act of Federation was a lie: "In every state of the Confederation there shall be a constitution of Estates for the land." Obviously, these were, almost without exception, the arbitrary dispositions of monarchs. Peoples that had disliked one another for centuries, like the Dutch and Belgians, the Swedes and Norwegians, were forcibly amalgamated. Free states of historic power and standing like Poland, Venice, and Genoa were brutally annexed. The whole Romance south was subjected to the old and detested alien régimes, and Germany — "a child of force and forceps, brought into the world dead, finished before it was born," as Görres expressed it in the *Rheinische Merkur* — was made into a political monstrosity, clumsier, more chaotic, and absurder even than the Holy Roman Empire. The victor over Europe, as in all world-wars of modern times, was England.

Shortly before the Congress dissolved, there was formed at the suggestion of the Tsar — a queer Slavonic compound of mystic and realist-statesman, pietist and autocrat, "half-fool, half-Bonaparte," as England called him — the Holy Alliance of Russia, Prussia, and Austria, in the text of which one reads amongst other things that "Their Majesties solemnly declare . . . their unshakable resolution . . . to take as their sole rule the precepts of holy Religion, precepts of righteousness, Christian love, and peace. . . . Consequently, Their Majesties have agreed, conformably to the words of Holy Writ which command all men to regard one another as brethren, to remain united by the bonds of a true and indissoluble brotherhood, and to help one another like fellow-countrymen in all conditions and all cases. Towards their peoples and their armies they will behave as fathers to their families, and they will guide them into the same spirit of brotherliness as that

The Holy Alliance

21

which inspires themselves. . . . The three allied sovereigns feel themselves but the plenipotentiaries of Providence for the Government of three branches of the same family. . . . All powers that solemnly subscribe to these principles will be joyfully received into this Holy Alliance." And in fact all the European potentates did adhere to it, with the exception of the Prince Regent of England, who declared that it was incompatible with the constitution of his country; the Pope, who considered that he was already, from time immemorial, in possession of Christian truth; and the Sultan, who of course did not recognize this Christian truth at all. Consequently, on the same day as the Second Peace of Paris, England concluded with Russia, Prussia, and Austria the Quadruple Alliance, the object of which was the " maintenance of the existing state of things "; in other words, balance of power externally, order and quiet within.

The importance of this Holy Alliance has been vastly overrated. It rested on no real guarantees of peace, but on mere romantic phrases, which might or might not be made good. As early as 1816 Gentz, that keen and illusionless observer, said that " it is a political nullity and will never lead to serious results; it is a piece of stage scenery invented in a spirit of misplaced devoutness, or of pure jealousy; for Alexander it is nothing but an instrument with which to exercise the influence that is a principal object of his ambition." Metternich, too, regarded it as *un verbiage*. In fact the Tsar, with his pathological jealousy, regarded it only as a pretext under which to set himself up as the arbiter of Europe and to justify himself as " Plenipotentiary of Providence," in tolerating no will but his own in his dominions. As far as words went, indeed, there is no more complete political program than that of the Holy Alliance, for it is laid down in the draft treaty that " a Christian people can in truth have no other ruler than Him to whom alone belongs power, in that in Him alone abides the treasure of love, knowledge, and truth: namely, God, our divine Redeemer Jesus Christ." But few ideals have advanced so little beyond rhetoric as this did. That the Saviour should rule the earth has been, from the moment of His appearing on it, the desire and dream of all Christians, but for the fulfilment thereof cold-hearted Habsburg emperors, megalomaniac tsars, narrow-souled Hohenzollern kings, and cynical princes of lying of the Metternich kind are scarcely the right instruments. With the fine idea of being fathers to their peoples, they turned Europe into a nursery, and although,

22

to judge by their chastisements, their love must have been very great, their paternal régime produced nothing but an immense Œdipus-complex.

In spite of all, there was no major war in Europe for nearly forty years. But the reason for this did not lie in the Holy Alliance — which was blown up within ten years by the Liberal policy of the English Minister Canning — but elsewhere. It is, in fact, a chief characteristic of these decades that in them *internal* politics played the chief part. The history of the preceding century had been determined principally by motives of external policy and, essentially, by the great conflict between France and the house of Habsburg. The development of this began even with the Reformation, and it dominates the periods of the Thirty Years' War, Louis XIV, the Revolution, and Napoleon. Seen in broad lines, Europe is in the permanent condition of having two fronts, an eastern and a western, which are sharply distinguished from one another amid all the continuous modifications of form that they undergo — sometimes extending, sometimes contracting, sometimes again fusing (as in the Seven Years' War, when they combined in the effort to destroy Prussia, and under Napoleon, who sought to turn the whole power of the Continent against England). But after the Congress of Vienna the European system of states formed a single connected front turned inwards. The opposition was no longer between Eastern and Western powers, but between government and people. And so, strictly speaking, the united governors of Europe, even after Leipzig, were still fighting Napoleon — the spirit of the Revolution that through him had spread itself over the Continent.

One of the first governmental acts of the restored King of Spain was to reintroduce the Inquisition. In several countries the wearing of the pigtail, the symbol of the Counter-Revolution, was once more obligatory, and even decades later *codino* (wearer of the tail) was a synonym to " reactionary " in upper Italy. In Piedmont illiteracy became in a measure the subject's duty, for permission to learn reading and writing was restricted to persons with an income of fifteen hundred lire and above. In Lombardy and Venetia the Austrian stick—*il bastone tedesco* — ruled, and the old Austrian specialties in the way of censorship, domiciliary visits, violations of the secrecy of the post, secret surveillance by " *Spitzel* " and " *Vertraute*," were the ordinary thing, not merely in the Habsburg lands, but in Prussia also — where not only *Egmont,*

23

Wilhelm Tell, Die Räuber, but even Fichte's *Reden an die deutsche Nation* and the *Prinz von Homburg* were banned. Here bureaucracy was for a time more petrified than in Austria, and Stein remarked that " we are ruled by paid, book-learned, uninterested bureaucrats of no personal status. These four words contain the essence of our own and other soulless governmental machines . . . they draw their pay from the Treasury and they write and write and write, in the quiet bureau with its well-shut doors, unknown, unobserved, undistinguished, and they bring up their children in turn to be similar efficient writing machines, and they die unlamented." Even in free England one Tory ministry followed another, and the leading statesman Castlereagh — the " spiritual eunuch," as Byron called him — suppressed by emergency laws every attempt at self-help, until his active persecution-mania changed to a passive one and drove him to suicide. The English merchant marine in 1815 was about one and a quarter times as large as that of the entire European continent, but the economic *floraison* was obtained at the cost of monstrous misery for the disinherited. It was regarded as a great step in progress when the minimum age for children in factories was fixed at nine, and the hours of working at twelve (though even then overtime was allowed), and in the first quarter of the century the penalty for theft was still death. It was in England, broadly speaking, that the Romantic theory of the State (upon which the Reaction based itself) originated: its founder is Edmund Burke, who in his *Reflections on the Revolution in France* (1790) put forward the thesis that the State is not a mechanism, but an organism inspired by mystical forces to which the State Church gives the consecration of religion.

In France, Louis XVIII, the brother of Louis XVI — an unornamental and gluttonous man, but neither stupid nor malevolent — had given the country a moderate constitution after the English model. But, although he himself — with his wits sharpened by the sufferings of the Revolution — was not genuinely a reactionary, he was unable to resist the pressure of the insolent and brainless " Ultras " who remigrated, and particularly in the south the " White terror " raged indifferently against Protestants, Bonapartists, and republicans. The Constitutional Charter became less important year by year; the King (as Saint-Simon put it) was the " prisoner of the ancient nobility," and matters became worse still from 1824, when his brother Charles X followed him on the throne. This King established a hypocritical priest-government and so obviously aimed at absolutism that even Metternich, in view of the situation, felt himself compelled to say that " the Legitimists are legitimizing the Revolution." And in all this, though France had been treated tenderly enough in the peace treaties and had not even had to give up Alsace-Lorraine, the clamour for the left bank of the Rhine never ceased; a fashionable coiffure was called "*à la chemin de Mayence*."

Against this dark background the magic figure of *l'Empéreur* acquired new and enhanced splendour. His autocratic will to annihilate, the two million men that he had sacrificed to his insane greed for power, the iron barrack-gate within which he had confined the French genius, were no longer thought of. All that men recalled was his democratic urge to progress, the legendary victories that he had won with his citizen armies, the unhampered career that his wisdom had opened to talent of all sorts, the sovereign genius with which he had rejuvenated and reorganized all things. For twenty years he had turned the Continent into an inhuman battlefield, but he had given the world its long-overdue spectacle of a being of superhuman powers of mind and force of rulership — two million dead, but dead heroes; France a barracks, but full of air and light. His fall was a " judgment from God," but it was that of a fallen angel, and the instruments of the fall were not men, but shadows, puppet kings and soulless dwarf princes. The victory of mediocrity over genius is never particularly elevating, even if the genius is dæmonic, and when his course had fulfilled itself, it was clear that he too was a Horseman of the Apocalypse who had been sent by God to fulfil some inscrutable purpose. He had himself said that "great men are like meteors, they shine and consume themselves to illuminate the world." Like a bloody comet he appeared in the terrestrial night, threatening and lighting, fearful and amazing, and millennia will not forget his trail.

Napoleon's prophecy in the Chamber of the " Hundred Days," — " You will come to weep bitter tears over me " — fulfilled itself. Every word that he had, or had not, spoken was treasured. Busts and engravings, market stalls and children's playbooks, walking-stick heads and snuff-boxes displayed his features everywhere, and his relics became sacred. Men did not hesitate to liken St. Helena to Golgotha, and Letitia to the Mater Dolorosa. He was called " the Man," and it was enough. Thiers brought about the translation of his remains to the Dome of the Invalides, and in brilliant

25

histories created that Napoleonic legend which has remained more or less classical in France to this day. Béranger's songs fashioned an immortal genre-figure, the plain soldier-Emperor with his grey redingote and his cocked hat, whose heart belonged to the people. Painting immortalized the deeds and sufferings of the Grand Army. Victor Hugo hailed him as the "Mahomet of the West," and even Beyle-Stendhal, the arch-sceptic and inexorable piercer of human masks, declared that "Beyle respected one man alone — Napoleon." Nay, men everywhere believed that he was not dead. The mountain folk of Sicily expected his return, the Arabs fused him into one figure with Alexander the Great and told one another tales of the reappearance of Iskander, the Sultan of the Franks; in Thuringia men said that no longer Barbarossa but Napoleon sat in the Kyffhäuser Cavern. But how completely he had already become a myth is best shown by a phenomenon that is the direct opposite to these: namely, the effort of a certain Pérès — one does not know whether to regard the book as the product of imbecility, irony, or pedantry — to prove that Napoleon was nothing but a personification of the Sun, that the name *Napoleon* meant *Apollo,* who was both destroyer and sun-god; his mother's name was Letitia, which could mean both Joy and Dawn; his four brothers were the four seasons; his twelve marshals the twelve signs of the zodiac, which are under the rule of the Sun; the twelve years of his reign the twelve hours of the day; and his path from Corsica to St. Helena began in the east and ended in the west like the sun's. Here we have an excellent example of what incorruptible historical criticism can lead to — and not so extraordinary an example either, when one remembers that the distinguished French scholar Sénart regarded the whole Buddha tradition as a solar myth, how the Karlsruhe philosopher Arthur Drew (he at any rate in full possession of his senses) attempted to derive the history of Jesus from "astral ideas," and how a whole group of strict researchers has declared that Bacon wrote the dramas of Shakspere — the latest among them indeed crediting him with *Don Quixote* as well, for the sake of simplicity.

The " Alt-teutschen " Germany, still under the quickening impulse of the Wars of Liberation, began by regarding the alien suppressor with Teutonic hatred. The political slogans were "freedom," "unity," and "Germanism." But it soon became evident that not all tyrants were "*Welsch.*" In 1815 the first German *Burschenschaft* was founded in Jena, to be followed three years later by the *Allgemeine Deut-*

26

sche Burschenschaft, "founded on the relation of German youth to the coming unity of the German people " — for the students at least were going to try to set up a united German front. Its colours, taken from those of the Lützow Free Corps, were black, red, and gold. " Content with what the tailor gave them in the way of Germanism," in Immermann's words, these students' unions especially affected the *" Wichs,"* a costume which called itself "old Teutsch " — a closed coat fastened with loops, usually black, broad open shirt-collar, coloured scarf, plumed cap of black, red, or violet silk with gold braid and cockade, and (to complete the picture) long hair and a republican dagger with death's-head pommel. They called the grey-haired *Nachburschen,* the professors *Lehrburschen,* the Fatherland the *Burschen's* gymnasium, the university the gymnasium of reason. They renounced brawling, drunkenness, and dancing, and despised women and Jews. When they met a foppishly or otherwise un-Germanly dressed man, they formed a half-circle round him and shouted: " Eh! Eh! " At a celebration that was held at the foot of the Wartburg on October 18, 1817 — the anniversary of the Reformation and of the battle of Leipzig — they set up a bonfire and ceremonially burned therein a Hessian pigtail, an Austrian corporal's stick, a Prussian guardsman's corset, and some reactionary books. Even this sufficed to arouse serious fears in the Governments and was taken up by the Congress of the Powers at Aachen. On March 23, 1819 a more serious event happened. A student named Karl Ludwig Sand forced his way into Kotzebue's house at Mannheim and crying: " Here, thou traitor to the Fatherland! " stabbed him to the heart. Kotzebue was a Russian state councillor and, as such, held conservative opinions of which in his journal, the *Literarische Wochenblatt,* he made no concealment, and the only justification, if any, for killing him would have been in the badness and cheapness of his dramas. It could not be proved that Sand was a member of any conspiracy. All the same, the Holy Alliance seized the opportunity at another conference of ministers to frame the notorious " Karlsbad Resolutions," bringing books and newspapers under censorship, putting the universities under strict supervision, and forbidding all student unions and gymnastic societies. And thereupon began the cruel persecutions of popular leaders of which the " Central Commission of Inquiry " at Mainz was the organ. It struck at everyone who had supported the German National movement. A stainless patriot like " Father Jahn " was dragged for six years

27

from one fortress prison to another. Ernst Moritz Arndt, a monarchist to the bone, was deprived of his professorship, and the great biblical scholar de Wette met with the same fate for having written a letter of consolation to Sand's mother. In the end, everything was suspect — democratic moustaches, Carbonaro felt hats, Revolutionary horizontal-bar exercises, and even a *sand*-coloured cloth.

The unreasoning and inhuman rigour with which " disturbances " were suppressed throughout the area of the Germanic Federation can only be explained as the consequence of a sort of fear-neurosis that had seized upon the governing circles. Gentz, for example, trembled when in a social gathering he noticed a beard, and, on his own confession, could faint at the sight of a naked knife. On top of this there was their superior disdain of the hobbledehoy inelegances of Jahn's young men. All this — wrong and folly, lying, even crime — mankind could forgive, but one thing is unforgivable to governors, and that is tactlessness.

The liberation of South America and Greece Withal, the Revolution simmered on below ground, among the Jacobin *" Exaltados "* in Spain, the radical-republican *" Unbedingten "* of Giessen, the Carbonari in Italy (the " charcoal-burners " who " assembled to rid the woods of wolves "), the *Hatairia Philike,* which aimed at re-establishing the old Hellenic freedom, the " National Patriotic Society " that demanded a free and united Great Poland.

The first open outbreaks occurred in the north and the south of Italy — Piedmont and Naples. The Congresses of Troppau and Laibach empowered Austria to march in, and she crushed the movement at once. Shortly afterwards Spain rose against the treacherous and cruel Ferdinand VII, but here, too, absolutism was restored by foreign troops, in this case the French, who were mandated to that end by the Congress of Verona. But " sects cannot be destroyed by cannon " — that Napoleon himself had had to realize, with resignation, in listening to the youth Staps, who had planned to assassinate him. In Russia the accession of the new Tsar was marked by the revolt of the Dekabrists (" Men of December "). The first successor of Paul I had been his eldest son, Alexander I, and after his death the legitimate successor was the second son, Constantine; he, however, had resigned in favour of the third son, Nicholas. But the fact that Constantine's resignation had not been " official " was used by part of the officer-corps and the Guard to promote a *coup d'état,* which, however, failed; the people had so little idea of what it was all about that

28

the " Constitution " that the malcontents championed was taken to be Constantine's wife.

The first tangible success of the revolutionary movement was won on the other side of the Atlantic. All the Spanish possessions on the American continent fell away one by one. In 1810, first Uruguay and then Paraguay declared their independence; next year it was Venezuela, in 1816 Argentina, in 1819 Colombia, in 1820 Chile, in 1821 Peru, in 1822 Ecuador, in 1825 Bolivia. The Portuguese colony of Brazil, too, constituted itself an independent empire in 1822. In Central America General Don Agustín de Iturbide was invited to become Emperor of Mexico, which, however, two years later adopted the republican form. The other five states of Central America — Guatemala, Honduras, Salvador, Nicaragua, Costa Rica — likewise shook themselves free, and the whole continent south of the United States (with the exception of the coastal strips of British, French, and Dutch Guiana on the Spanish Main and the tiny district of British Honduras on the Isthmus) was freed from European domination. The soul of this emancipation movement was the Creole, Simon Bolivar, whose far-sighted purpose was the federation of all the newly-formed republics as a United States of South America. To this end he summoned a Congress to meet at Panama, but against the parochial jealousies and political immaturity of the narrow Spaniards and the spiritually indifferent half-castes he could achieve nothing, and thereafter the history of South America has been an almost unbroken series of popular *émeutes*, military revolts, and border forays.

The South Americans would probably not have succeeded so readily in wrenching themselves free but for the support of the two Anglo-Saxon powers. The Holy Alliance would have wished to uphold " order " in the New World as well as the Old, but the United States of North America proclaimed in 1823, by the mouth of their President, the fateful " Monroe Doctrine," which declared that no interference of Europe in the political relations of America would be tolerated, while the Liberal minister Canning (the successor of Castlereagh) recognized the new free states in the name of England, being led to this step partly by public opinion, but still more by trade interests. Canning also assisted the second successful revolutionary movements of this period, the eight years' struggle of the Greeks for freedom. This, long prepared for in secret, began openly in 1821; all the Classicist and Romantic sympathies

29

of Europe speeded it, although these modern Greeks had by then but a very distant affinity with the countrymen of Plato and Polycletus. The terrible blood-bath of Chios, the heroic defence of Missolonghi excited universal enthusiasm. " Philhellene " volunteers hurried to the scene from Germany, France, and Italy. Wilhelm Müller wrote his songs of Greece, Byron landed with two ships' companies and found his death in the fevers of the Ætolian marsh-air. The Governments, with their policy of maintenance, followed the struggle at first with disapproval, and it was the new Tsar who first gave a lead. On Canning's invitation England, France, and Russia formed an alliance for the protection of the Greeks and staged a naval demonstration before Navarino harbour; this, however, without either side's having actually intended it, turned into one of the most murderous sea-fights of modern history, and the Turco-Egyptian fleet was entirely destroyed. Russian land forces occupied the Danubian Principalities and Adrianople, as well as, in Asia, Kars and Erzerum. In the Treaty of Adrianople, Turkey consented in advance to the decisions of the London Conference, in which the protecting powers declared the independence of Greece and set up the son of the King of Bavaria as Otto I, King of the Hellenes.

The Austrian infection

But in this war, though outwardly victorious, the Holy Alliance declared its own principle to be bankrupt. Gentz, the author of the Karlsbad Resolutions, saw this at once when the Greek War of Independence broke out. "I have always been well aware that in the long run the spirit of the times would prevail . . . and that the forces of diplomacy were just as powerless as violence to put a spoke in the world's wheel." And yet he, too, was the prey of the Austrian infection, and shared this fate with all the rest of Europe. For the master of the Continent in this period was the Emperor Francis, in whom, a whole generation before the Congress of Vienna, his uncle Joseph II had noted " a good memory, but a barren one," " a sensitive fear of the truth," "irresolution, laziness, nonchalance in thought and action," "incapacity for great affairs." He was the hall-marked type of the Austrian narrowness that never saw beyond any but the nearest and concretest things, and to add to this he was behind the times — for, like all his countrymen, he stuck with a heavy and anxious obstinacy to reality, and reality is always obsolete. His dry and exceedingly apt witticisms — which marked him as the countryman and contemporary of Nestroy — concealed his treacherousness and nar-

30

row-heartedness from his countrymen, who will forgive everything for a good joke. The executioner of his will was Prince Metternich, the " physician to the great world-hospital," as he called himself. Strange though it seems to admit it, Metternich was one of the heroes of the age. For he was perfectly clear in his mind that the inroad of national and liberal ideas would necessarily lay the Habsburg monarchy in ruins, and therefore, sometimes by order and sometimes by counsel, he imposed his reactionary policy on the adjacent countries. A country was nothing but "a geographical expression," and its inhabitants an aggregate of subjects. As Chancellor of the Austrian state he, probably, had to act as he did. But at the bar of History — which happily is not the same thing as Austrian history — his system stands convicted as an insane effort to turn a set of buildings into a hospital because an inhabitant of one of them was sick. And the insane thing about it is that it succeeded.

Fundamentally, his view of the State was an after-fruit of the Enlightenment, in which indeed lay his own spiritual origins. A government must proceed, not according to symptoms, but according to dogma; it does not examine, but prescribes. It is the absolutism of the eighteenth century, but this time with a minus sign — instead of forced progress, forced regression, an anti-Josephine Josephinism. His political outlook was anti-Romantic to the last degree, in that he looked upon aggregates of men, not as living beings carrying their laws within themselves and developing organically, but as machines to be regulated, stopped, and started at will. And it was a fateful lie in the soul of many political theorists who called themselves " Romantic " that they deliberately refused to face the fact of this antagonism.

Psychologically considered, his passion for " stability " was simply mental indolence. He wrote once to Countess Lieven: " I detest every New Year's Day. I am so prone to prefer what I know to what I must learn that this trait applies even to the four figures that I am accustomed to write." Talleyrand went further and called him a " politician of the week." His system was summarized by Gentz, his most intimate collaborator, in the famous phrase " Metternich and I are still holding on." And yet it cannot be denied that to carry out this system in practice called for a high degree of intellect and shrewdness, finesse and inventiveness. " The great world-comedy," wrote Albert Sorel, " the high-grade plot (intrigue) of the European theatre, has never found so fertile an author or so perfect an actor." And he was one of the most complete embodiments of the spirit of Vienna that there has been. Ferdinand Kürnberger, one of the finest connoisseurs of the Austrian soul, says: "You may be doing this city a real and undeserved injustice when you measure it by the German standard and claim it as a German city. On the other hand everything is perfectly bright and clear, comprehensible and understandable, just and easy, if you take Vienna as what it is — a European-Asiatic frontier city. . . . Austria then ceases to be incomprehensible; it has to be comprehended as a sort of Asia. But in this meaning, 'Europe' and 'Asia' are quite clear and indeed hard-edged conceptions — Europe is law, and Asia is arbitrary will; Europe is duty, and Asia mood; Europe is strictly factual, and Asia purely personal; Europe is the man, and Asia the child and old man." This was the soul of Metternich — arbitrariness as law, fulfilment of caprice as doing of duty, the personal desire made into an affair of the world, an infantile and irresponsible playing with today, a senile and unimaginative sticking to yesterday — in short, the essence of him was *complete frivolity*.

The "modern ideas"

All through his life Metternich set before himself the image of an invisible host of enemies, which filled him with longing to exterminate them; he called these foes "the modern ideas." But how can anyone who professes to be a statesman, anyone indeed who professes to think, fight ideas as "modern," seeing that they are the *only* ideas in the particular period, whatever this may be, and that all others not merely are powerless against it, but do not in truth exist at all, save in wry-necked, short-sighted, and worm-eaten heads — and such are not heads at all? As every thinking man and, above all, every statesman ought to know, there is but *one* victorious force, the Idea, and it is mere hopeless quixotism to fight against it. If at all, it must be fought earlier or, again, later, and with sure discernment. At one and the same stage of historical evolution there are never two ideas, but always one which alone is able and entitled to live, and another, or more than one other, which is not. Legitimacy and Divine Right are truly noble ideas, perhaps the noblest that we know! But, always and everywhere, the only thing that is legitimated by inward truth, and the only thing invested with Divine Right as a stage in the inscrutable process of man's education, is "the modern idea."

In all periods the "modern" — or whatever equivalent phrase was used — has meant for mankind the ruling spirit of the age —

32

or rather the spirit that was beginning to strive for that rulership — and the term has always carried both a laudatory and a pejorative sense. Always there have been some who regarded it as subversive of the surest foundations of ethical, spiritual, and social life, as absurd, false, vicious, ugly, trivial, perverted — in a word, pathological. And always there have been others who said that it *was* morale, it *was* art, reform, the future — in short, the definitive Ideal. And both have been wrong. So also the costume prevailing at a particular time is called " the fashion " in a dual sense, admiringly by those for whom it is the summit of beauty and suitability to purpose, contemptuously by others for whom it is the acme of tastelessness and folly — and again both are wrong. For the phenomenon of fashion is quite incapable of being brought under æsthetic, or even logical, categories; it would be just as absurd to judge this and that flora or fauna from such standpoints and say, for example, that the shape of the kangaroo is tasteless, the petals of the sea anemone smart, or the appearance of the giraffe finicking. Every fashion is reasonable. As the outwardly visible distillate of particular ideals and concepts of beauty, expressed in the arrangement, the fit, the concealments and emphases of outward appearance, it resembles what in natural history is called a creature's " habit." And with this is connected the fact that every generation — unconsciously, for these characters become distinct only after it is dead and gone — possesses a pose and attitude special to itself alone. We have already discussed this point somewhat more closely in connexion with a particular case: namely, that of Baroque man and his secret ideal of the marionette; in our own time it is no less a person than the photographer who is the executant of this " will to pose." Never yet has a " good society " behaved itself naturally, and yet every such society has imagined that it was doing so, and regarded things as " unnatural " only when they came into conflict with its laws. In the same way, anyone who sets himself up against the laws of fashion in costume produces an effect of the ridiculous, and this for a deeper reason than is generally imagined. For while he believes that he is combating certain " senseless externals and accidents of the day," he is really fighting against the *spirit* of the day, and fighting a spirit is always rather comic. For this reason women, who in general are on a much more intimate footing with the *Zeitgeist* than men, almost never struggle against fashion. For they know that it is not made by the tailor or, for that matter,

33

by any single individual; appearances may seem to indicate the contrary, but in reality the *arbiter elegantiarum* is ever a mere intelligent mandatory of the *Zeitgeist*. The proof is evident when fashion becomes historical, becomes " costume." *Then* it emerges that it was no arbitrary dictature of snobbism, or of commercial speculation, but purely and simply *the style of the time*. We may regard costume as beautiful or ugly, as pleasing or not " suiting " (though even this predicates an error of vision), but in the whole of human history from the Pyramids to our eighties there has never been " styleless " costume.

The Mephistopheles of Romanticism

How, then, did it come about that a fine connoisseur of men, a subtle arguer, a realist from the cradle, like Metternich did not recognize such simple connexions, and in all sincerity believed to the very end that he was right — thereby exposing himself to the derision of the Court of History? Simply because he was incapable of comprehending the world and its essence with the heart, because he was the absurdly complete embodiment of the sterile intelligence, the pure reason that understands nothing at all. And for that reason he may be called the Mephistopheles of Romanticism, for that likewise is the tragedy of mere brain, of a gifted self-seeking and radical scepticism that is always bound to succumb. Like Mephistopheles, he was a finished gentleman and witty conversationalist — an educated and well-bred devil, an eighteenth-century devil. He fought over the Romantic soul of Europe, dragged it down into the abyss, and lost the game.

Romantic science

The great conquests of Romanticism, as a matter of fact, lay rather in the domain of science than in those of poetry and the arts. Almost every one of the intellectual sciences was reinvigorated by original and fruitful ideas. Not a few disciplines, indeed, came into being then for the first time — for example, jurisprudence with Karl Friedrich Eichhorn, who was the first to present German law as a unitary whole developed in the people. His teacher was Friedrich Karl von Savigny, the founder of the " historical " school of jurisprudence, whose basic doctrine was that all law arises " in the way that the prevailing linguistic usage, as a customary law, indicates for it . . . by inner, stilly working forces and not by the arbitrary will of the legislator." First there is custom, popular belief, the self-evident, axiomatic, and undemonstrable sense of right; only afterwards and as a late product comes the codification, in law-books and juridical forms and formulæ, of what has long been in existence. Thus regarded law appears as something that has grown up more or less out of the soil, as the natural flower and fruit of the folk-soul, and so as falling within the same circle as poetry, cult, ethic, and language. In the same way Adam Müller regarded the State as a living organism and individuality, as a " totality of human affairs." The State " is not a mere factory, farm, insurance office, or mercantile society, but the intimate bond making all parts of the inward and outward life of a nation into a great, energetic, infinitely mobile, and living whole." This, however, may easily lead to the apotheosis of the State and the sanctioning of all its commissions and omissions, and in fact it did so, as evidenced by Karl Ludwig von Haller, who ruled that all kings and princes were holders of power, and that it was the divinely ordained and willed order of nature that power should be obeyed; they were not " servants of the State," but independent masters, and the State was their property just as a household belongs to the father of the family; he admitted no essential difference between public law and private law. Adam Müller even wrote on " the necessity of a theological foundation " for economics. Now, all this was no mere Tartufferie. Indeed, the spirit of the time was deeply religious as was shown, for instance, in the great rapprochement that took place between the various Christian confessions; there were not a few pious Catholics whose whole lives were dominated by pietism, and pious Protestants who spoke to a certain extent in the language of Catholicism. On the occasion of the third centenary of the Reformation Frederick William III tried — and at first with some success — to bring Lutherans and Calvinists together in the " Evangelical Union." While Haller lauded the patriarchal régime of the Middle Ages as divinely ordered, Raumer in his (somewhat leathern) *Geschichte der Hohenstaufen* extolled the old German inwardness, and Niebuhr in his epoch-making work on *Roman History* the agrarian Middle Ages of ancient Rome: "When Rome's burghers were peasants and looked after their fields themselves, their State embodied the Ideal from which it has so far departed since."

A wholly new science was founded by Karl Ritter, who in his *Erdkunde im Verhältnis zur Natur und zur Geschichte des Menschen* exhibited the form and evolution of the State as a function of geographical conditions, slow and quiet workings of which the laws could only be penetrated by approaching them with " an equally quiet soul." The field of history was widened in a quite startling degree. Georg Heinrich Pertz, on the suggestion of Stein, founded the *Monumenta Germaniæ historica,* a comprehensive collection of sources for the history of the German Middle Ages. August Böckh edited, under the auspices of the Berlin Academy of Sciences, the *Corpus inscriptionum Græcarum.* Grotefend, a German schoolmaster, deciphered by means of Persian royal names the cuneiform that had long been thought to be a mere decoration. Champollion solved the riddle of the hieroglyphs, which had hitherto been regarded as a picture-writing; by means of a stone of the Ptolemaic period that contained an inscription in Egyptian and Greek he succeeded in reconstructing the alphabet, translating numerous texts, and even laying down the elements of a grammar. "One man," as the Egyptologist Adolf Erman says, "in one decade restored a whole people to the history of the world." And the history of the East in general came into the very foreground of interest. "Towards the lands of the morning, the banks of Indus and Ganges, our spirits feel drawn as by a secret compulsion," wrote Görres, who brought out a history of the myths of the ancient world based on Persian linguistic studies. Friedrich Schlegel's work *Sprache und Weisheit der Indier* gave the impetus for the most profound and fruitful studies of Sanskrit. Rückert translated — often in a masterly way — poetry of China and Persia, India and Arabia; and Goethe wrote his *Westöstliches Diwan* as "a collection of German poems with a constant relation to the East." He also, like the brothers Grimm, Chateaubriand, and other outstanding contemporaries, was keenly and sympathetically interested in the discovery — or rather the invention — of the national literature of Bohemia by Wenzeslaus Hanka, the editor of the "Königinhof Manuscript," a collection of Czech poems and epic fragments which he asserted had been found in the vault of the church-tower of Königinhof. Their spuriousness, which is even now denied by ultra-patriots, was only definitely established some seventy years later.

The folk-spirit as poet

The "song-theory" which Karl Lachmann built upon the Homeric researches of the famous old philologist Friedrich August Wolf was a product of hypercriticism. Long before this the Abbé d'Aubignac — whose work *Conjectures académiques ou dissertation sur l'Iliade* appeared as early as 1715 (and even this was considerably after his death) — had maintained that no one of the name of Homer had ever existed, and that the Iliad was a collection of individual pieces put together without any general scheme by an editor. Wolf did not indeed go as far as this, though denying that it had an original unity or a single author. But Lachmann pledged himself to the extreme view that there was no sort of connexion between the individual songs of the Homeric epos, and he showed that they contained certain topographical and psychological discrepancies — as though the avoïdance of such errors was the chief virtue in a poet and Baedeker exactitude the chief requisite in an epic. In Lachmann we have the reverse side of the Romantic theory of the " poetic folk-spirit," a theory which certainly implied a deepened understanding of certain phenomena, but, when handled without flair, cannot but destroy the very idea of the " work of art," since under it everything not historically verifiable must be regarded simply as a poetry that has come into being of itself. Wolf's chief argument, repeated by Lachmann, was the testimony of Antiquity itself that Pisistratus collected the so-called Homeric poems (that is, obviously, individual lays). But he only reassembled them. The rhapsodists were in the habit of reciting individual pieces, or, as we should say today, books and chapters of the work, and these were brought together in Athens into a sort of new edition, so that at most one can speak of a reconstruction. Nevertheless, the poet, with his essentially Greek technique of relief, did make of each song a rounded-off work of art, as indeed was necessary since they were communicated far more by recitation than by reading and could not therefore depend upon the audience's having a constantly present idea of the work as a whole. But the numerous allusions, retrospects, and prophecies worked into the fabric point unmistakably to such unity, and later research has in fact thrown overboard the over-clever scepticisms of the *Liedertheorie* and believes again in a poet Homer of Smyrna, the mightiest epic genius of all time, who composed the Iliad about 700 B.C. But it is not the philological and archæological evidences that are decisive in this question — for all the industry, scholarship, and finesse that have been displayed in assembling and interpreting them — but the fact that every healthy and unprejudiced person feels beyond challenge that this work can owe its birth only to a great artist. In every age there have been " profound minds " who look behind any and every simple matter of fact for something that has still to be " discovered " or " elucidated." They uncover this supposed background, interpret this undermeaning attributed to the facts; and thereupon the whole matter becomes hopelessly unintelligible to everyone. The Homeric " saga-cycle," indeed, existed before Homer, but, unfortunately, without Homer. The building-stones were there, but not the builder, the genius that makes cosmos out of chaos. Shakspere, from the chaos of his predecessors' store of bold but dark and fantastic figures, made the cosmos of his drama-world. Homer made out of the rhapsodic fragments of unconscious poets the conscious and meaningful light-world of his Iliad — and instead of being astounded at the achievement of this light-bringer they say that he never existed! We might as well be asked to believe that the Zeus ascribed to Phidias was made by a committee of stone-cutters and colour-grinders. And if, some day, all exact information about Goethe were to vanish, there would probably be found some keen scholars who claimed that his name was the personification of a lost tribe and that *Faust,* with its numerous contradictions and the lack of unity even in the central figure itself, was gummed together out of pieces of this Gothic folk-poetry which had been erroneously called Goethic.

Consequently, the second of Lachmann's theories, that concerning the Nibelungenlied, does not inspire us with much more confidence than the first, even though science still accepts it in part. Here again he maintained that it was merely a compilation of romantic lays, twenty in number, which he cleanly separated one from another. But Wilhelm Scherer, who, dutifully following him, declared with decision that the " poet of the Nibelungenlied is undiscoverable," felt himself obliged to supplement this by the remark: " since our poem does not merely pick out episodes from the mass of material, but exhausts it, it possesses outwardly a higher degree of unity than the Iliad." But in whom can that unity exist but in a great poet? The main argument of Lachmann and his school here (it was not applicable to Homer) was that the Nibelungenlied contains " botched " passages. But this could easily happen through the corruption of tradition, and in any case it proves nothing, since an artist is not a factory for turning out excellences — indeed, inequality is precisely what distinguishes him from a man of talent; there are more failures in Schiller than there are in Wieland, and so bad a theatre piece as Maeterlinck's *Le Bourgmestre de Stilmonde* would never have been written by Ludwig Fulda. Jakob Grimm very aptly characterized Lachmann as the born editor, who took notice of the content of a work only in so far as he could evolve from it rules and new dodges for his textual criticism; if all philologists, he added, could be divided into those who busied themselves with words for the sake of things, and those who busied themselves with things for the sake of words, Lachmann would unmistakably belong to the latter class.

The brothers Grimm were men of quite another stamp. In them the warmest introjection of themselves into the object and the subtlest ear for the stimuli of speech were united with the most patient care and a microscopic strictness. Their " veneration of the insignificant," at which Friedrich Schlegel laughed, was not pedantry or pettiness, but something of artistic, nay, religious origin. In his *Deutsche Grammatik* Jakob Grimm investigated the psychology of language-formation with the most delicate appreciation, and in *Deutsche Rechtsaltertümern* and the *Deutsche Mythologie* he dug deep into the dark strata of the national life. Wilhelm Grimm tackled the heroic sagas of Germany, and edited old Danish ballads, *Freidank*, the *Rosengarten*, the *Rolandslied*, and much else. Jointly the brothers edited the famous *Kinder- und Hausmärchen*, stories of Irish elves, and vanished poems of the homeland like the *Hildebrandslied* and *Der arme Heinrich*, and began the gigantic enterprise of the *Deutsches Wörterbuch*. To Görres, the philosopher of Ultramontanism, the " Catholic Luther," the public owed its acquaintance with the *Deutsche Volksbücher*, and Uhland — greater here almost than in his poems — plunged with delighted affection into the poetry of the French troubadours and Walther von der Vogelweide.

The word by which that epoch hoped to break all seals was " comparison." What this meant was an attempt to extend to all history the method that Cuvier, in his *Anatomie comparée*, had so fruitfully applied to the objects of natural history. By comparing the conjugation-forms of all the ancient languages accessible to him, Franz Bopp discovered the derivation of Persian, Greek, Latin, and Gothic from Sanskrit and so became the creator of general comparative philology. Jakob Grimm founded the comparative philology of German; Friedrich Diez the comparative historical grammar of the Romance languages, for which he proved a common origin in Latin; and Wilhelm von Humboldt, on the basis of comprehensive studies that extended even to Chinese and the Kavi language of Java, produced, in his *Über die Verschiedenheit des menschlichen Sprachbaues und ihren Einfluss auf die geistige Entwicklung des Menschengeschlechts*, the philosophical distillate of the philological researches of the Romantic period. Karl Ritter (to whom we have already alluded) created comparative geology, Johannes Müller (of whom also the reader

The magician's wand of analogy

39

has heard) the comparative psychology of the senses, and Niebuhr became the Cuvier of Roman history, drawing from the evidences of the preserved conclusions as to the lost and thus reconstructing the fossil world of hoary Antiquity. As with languages, so with the other products of the human collective soul. All were subjected to " comparative " treatment. For example, constitutions ancient and modern, considered not as the edifices of legislators, but the creation of the local soul; and the Aryan and Semitic mythologies, not as conventions of cunning priests, as the Enlightenment had thought, nor yet as crystallizations of folk-poetry, as Herder had suggested, but as recollections of real historical conditions and of the life-forms of vanished ages. In short, it was the " magician's wand of analogy " that everywhere caused new springs of human understanding to flow.

As we see, the historical eye of the period was by no means exclusively fixed on the Middle Ages, with which alone Romanticism is commonly supposed to have associated itself. Among the wide public, however, this interest was undoubtedly dominant. Raumer's *Geschichte der Hohenstaufen* owed its great success most of all to its subject. Raupach, with his sure flair for the theatre, realized that these peep-show figures would do very well on the stage too, and he dramatized Raumer in a cycle of sixteen performances, which sold the house out in Berlin. He even planned to work out, in conjunction with others, the whole of German history from Henry I to the Peace of Westphalia. And even the gifted Grabbe was not above writing a *Friedrich Barbarossa* and a *Henry VI*, Immermann was the author of a *Frederick II*, Eichendorff of an *Ezzelin*, and in the forties Rethel — powerfully, suggestively, and with a unique combination of historical empathy and sense of actuality — painted the frescoes which, in the Coronation Hall at Aachen, tell the story of Charles the Great.

Birth of Romantic poetry

If one were to attempt to characterize the decisive works in the poetry of this time, one might perhaps say that they had depth, but that it was pictorial depth. The representative poets were able — some of them amazingly so — to create profound characters, but they themselves were not profound. The " depth of emptiness," in fact.

In the first year of the new century there appeared the first poem which can be called Romantic in the legitimate sense of the word, Chateaubriand's *Atala*. This is an Indian story in which flame-coloured exotic nature-pictures, sweet and melancholy eroticism, and Catholic piety were skilfully mixed — not one of the three genuine, the background landscape a grandiose stage-setting, the love and the religion artificial opiates. But it immediately went to the heads and hearts of everyone, primitives and decadents alike; it was dramatized, illustrated, parodied, and presented as a waxwork show. Two years later followed the story *René*, the centre of which was a secret love of brother and sister — a theme favoured by that period and actually lived by its eponymous hero, Byron. (His love-romance with his half-sister Augusta, which was probably the reason for his divorce and flight from England, only became known decades after his death and caused an immense sensation. Then again for decades it was relegated by the worthy historians of literature to the gutter of base scandal, and now, under the influence of the fashionable psychoanalysis, it is brought up again. The facts in so ticklish a business can never be established by "documentation," but only by characterology, and one's instinctive feeling is that incest is, so to say, mythologically appropriate to a titanic demigod-nature like Byron's.) In *René* was created the type of the *esprit romanesque*, which, at odds with itself and the world, delicate and ironic, full of yearning for love and faith, but without the strength for either, reaches for every fruit and sees the worm in it — " all," says René, " preaches to me of dissolution." In the art of Chateaubriand, which culminates in Byron, literature becomes *poisonous*, a splendid greeny-gold growth, glittering and seductive, but filled with intoxicating saps that corrode.

There was also within Romanticism, however, an essentially harmless fraction which contented itself with mere colour. Its most important representatives were, in England, William Wordsworth, leader of the " Lake school," which drew inspiration from the beauty of the rich green hills and the picturesque lakes of Westmorland; and in Italy Count Alessandro Manzoni, head of the *romanticismo* and author of the celebrated *Promessi Sposi*, a history which (he declared, in order to heighten the illusion) he worked up from an old seventeenth-century Milanese manuscript of the Spanish time. The literary organ of the Italian Romantic was the Milan *Conciliatore*, that of the English Lake school the *Quarterly Review* (the mouthpiece of the Tory Party), to which the Lakists, originally haters of tyrants, became converted when one of their leaders, Southey, was appointed Poet Laureate. Apart from those stood Shelley — the *cor cordium*, as his tombstone calls him — whose poetry is an excited Midsummer Night's dream, pantheistic and even atheistic, misanthropic and yet all feeling, through and through — Charles Lamb, a poetic-humorous genius of the line of Laurence Sterne, and the splendid Leopardi, who rejected the world in verse of such moving beauty that he was converted to it. Among the authors of world-importance who wrote in English we must also count the American Fenimore Cooper, whose Leatherstocking Tales will still stir young hearts when the Lake school has long been forgotten.

In 1814 there began to appear the Waverley series, which continued with unflagging vigour for eighteen years and filled the fancy of the Western world with its splendid colour-printing; not only in book-form, but as play, opera, ballet, costume-pageant. Scott's romances derive visibly from the ballad, a form in which he himself had originally practised and which he only gave up because of the irresistible competition of Byron. His works are a mixture of human and kindly and naïvely refined sentiment and humour, Tory outlook and love of the people, folk-lore and Meiningerism. They exhibit, as the penetrating insight of Carlyle perceived at once, only the skin and never reach to the heart.

With the year 1806 the German Romantic sets in. In that year appeared *Des Knaben Wunderhorn*, edited by Clemens Brentano and Achim von Arnim, who later became brothers-in-law through Bettine, "the Sibyl of literary Romanticism." Immermann said of this whole school of poetry that it was "nourished on shades and tones," and of its leader, the wild, capricious, and charming Brentano, Eichendorff remarked that he was not really a poet, but a poem. The widest popularity fell to Fouqué — whose *Undine* is one of the most beautiful of romantic stories and whose many chivalry-romances established for half a century the cliché of a Middle Ages in shining armour — and to Uhland, clear, forceful, but wholly unproblematical. Of Fouqué, Brandes remarks (as maliciously as penetratingly) that his men are nothing but stuffed suits of armour, and that the only beings that he has psychologically mastered are the horses; and Heine, still more unkindly and still more cleverly: "His knights consist of nothing but iron-cased sentiment, they have neither flesh nor reason." When Uhland in 1815 published the first edition of his poems, which began with the words: "*Lieder sind wir. Unser Vater schickt uns in die offene Welt*" ("Songs are we," etc.), an unfortunate misprint occurred in the first word, so that the phrase read: "*Leder sind wir* " (" Leather are we "). But this criticism on the part of the imp of the type-fount is a little too severe and must be softened at least to the extent of allowing that the leather is handsomely stamped and gilt, even if a little frayed from the outset. The genius of the school, the Novalis of late Romanticism, comparable with him in purity, delicacy, and originality if coming nowhere near him for depth and universality, was Eichendorff. While Brentano and Arnim collected anonymous folk-songs and tried to elevate them into a literature, Eichendorff's poems took the opposite way; from being artificial products they became songs of all the world, which the people sang as if they had made them. Wherein, then, lies the genius of Eichendorff and his immortal " *Taugenichts* "? It consists in a pious sense of the holiness of doing nothing, in a pleasure, at once humble and buoyant, in God's creations — a truly German, and probably uniquely German, sort of giftedness. Thomas Mann has expressed it in words strangely beautiful and clairvoyant: " He is a man, and so verily a man that he neither cares to be nor has the power to be anything besides; and it is just that that makes him the *Taugenichts*. For one is manifestly ' no good ' if one sets out to be no more than just a man." In the story of the *Taugenichts,* too, there lives already a wholly new Italy — not the Classical Italy, the master-land, the pattern-land of closed form, but the romantic Italy of dissolved and disjointed, crumbled and exploded form, the " land of ruins and flowers," as Zacharias Werner called it, the enchanted and picturesque Italy, heavy of soul and light of spirit, the Italy of handsome lovers, of blue sea and moonlight, of decaying churches and emptied piazzas, of scented wild gardens and shadowed bubbling fountains, of still days and bright nights — the sleeping dreaming Italy of the ruins.

Is there a Romantic drama as well? This question suggests first of all the so-called " destiny-drama," Zacharias Werner's *Vierundzwanzigste Februar* and its much inferior copies, Müllner's *Schuld* and *Neunundzwanzigste Februar,* Houwald's *Bild* and Grillparzer's *Ahnfrau,* and that clever skit on it, Platen's *Verhängnisvolle Gabel.* The literary historians have decreed that the *Vierundzwanzigste Februar* is an artificial absurdity, and for a hundred years each has been telling the other so. In fact, it is probably one of the most powerful and suggestive one-act plays in the world's literature and has a power of creating atmosphere approximating to Maeterlinck's; its action, however, does not

Grillparzer and Raimund

43

conform to the laws of a bourgeois calculus of probabilities. Werner's comprehensive drama *Die Söhne des Thals* too, which portrays the catastrophic fall of the Templar Order, is, in all its sentimentality and chaos, its sweetness and perversity, narcotic with the enchantment of the coulisses. And even Raupach's notorious *Müller und sein Kind* does not in all probability deserve the disdain of the professors who do not go to the theatre; a piece that has for a hundred years made the gallery and the stalls shudder cannot be quite destitute of dramatic qualities.

The drama of Grillparzer belongs to Romanticism only in respect of a few quite external characteristics; it is really a subtle and no longer quite viable after-growth of the Weimar Classicism. Even in his choice of metre Grillparzer was not altogether happy. The trochaic, which he originally took over from Calderón, is easily handled in German, but equally easily descends to banality and even bathos. He was still more unfortunate in his titles. *Woe to him who lies* might serve for a Blumenthal farce, *A True Servant of his Lord* for a novel by Sacher-Masoch, *King Ottokar's Fortune and Fall* for the tale of strolling players, while so comic a title as *Waves of the Sea and of Love* has probably seldom been printed. And, be it observed, in dramatic creation in particular, the title is anything but a subsidiary and external detail; the spirit of the whole work is most expressively heralded in the finding of the right title. Ibsen, for example, was a genius in this regard; one would be hard put to it to find more telling labels for the whole problem than *A Doll's House, Pillars of Society,* and the Norwegian title of *The Pretenders* (untranslatable, but meaning something like " Material of Kings " or " The Clay of which Kings are Fashioned ") and *Ghosts* (a rough translation, really " Spirits that Return ") ; and a title like *The Wild Duck* is unfathomably grandiose. And not one of these is abstract, not one of them wholly unambiguous and exhaustive, but each is drama, is theatre — compact and at the same time unreal.

The only trait of the Romantic in Grillparzer, and that was Austrian rather, was his flight from reality. The story is that he possessed an uncommon intensity of sensibility and outlook, but was without a corresponding store of intellectual energy. In reality it was just the reverse, his understanding was extraordinary, but it was nourished by no adequate power of feeling. In plain language, he lacked courage in himself. The last word was said about him two days after his death, in Kürnberger's essay *Grill-*

parzers Lebensmaske: "While they are making Grillparzer's death-mask, I should like to say a word on his life-mask. . . . This is the life-mask of Grillparzer: sent out like a flaming tempest to clear the Austrian air, he has passed over Austria like a damp grey cloudlet, tinged a little at the edges with purple. And the cloudlet sinks . . . ! His strong passions, his great capacities called to him: 'Send plagues over Egypt; go before Pharaoh, speak for thy people, lead it into the Promised Land! . . .' But in a corner of his heart the Austrian in him began to sigh and to lament: 'Lord, send another, I am afraid. . . . Let me rather be Pharaoh's councillor. . . .' A phenomenon without parallel, and only possible in Austria. For the psychology of Austria the biography of Grillparzer is indispensable. The biography will of course be written in any case, but — may the hand wither that will not tell its *whole* truth!"

Ferdinand Raimund, notwithstanding that all his life he looked up to Grillparzer as an unattainable ideal, was really the stronger. He too was not truly rooted in Romanticism, but in an older art-world, in his case the Baroque. His fairyland is made of sugar icing and terracotta and reminds one of the cheap wares hawked by figurine-sellers in his native city, or the sweet glittering creations of the confectionery business to which in his youth he was bound, but all the same he moves us with his delicious suburban naïveté, and his comic characters — intensified and transfigured types of his mother soil, popular heroes out of a sort of Vienna Valhalla — are unsurpassable. Scenes like that of " old age " in *Bauer als Millionär,* the doubling of Rappelkopf in *Alpenkönig und Menschenfeind,* the beggar in *Verschwender,* as he follows Flottwell in his boat over the sea, are of Shaksperian cast.

The most powerful dramatic genius of the age, perhaps of Germany in any age, Heinrich von Kleist, we should have to call a Romantic in the fullest sense were it not that he was also the keenest psychological naturalist that the theatre possessed, from Lessing to Ibsen; and it is precisely in this paradoxical mixture that his gigantic uniqueness lies. There is in all his dramas (as has frequently been remarked) an irrational and even pathological element — somnambulism in the *Prinz von Homburg,* the sadism of Thusnelda and Penthesilea, hallucination in Käthchen and the Graf vom Strahl — and even when they abstain from direct miracle, they have the character of staged mysteries. Kleist's most

Kleist

45

thoroughly Romantic theme is the "confusion of feelings." At the same time — and the fact is in no way a contradiction — he was the first to stage the modern man, with all his infinite differentiation and heterogeneity, as a problem of "psychology of the deeps." We need illustrate this only by one case, the way in which he creates so relatively simple a figure as the Elector in the *Prinz von Homburg*. Schiller would presumably have displayed him as a hard soldier-Prince who is softened in the end, and Goethe as a sovereign with the ideal of duty. Kleist, on the contrary, presents him as the victim of a "Brutus-complex." Naturally, this Elector had not the slightest idea of posing as a Brutus in jack-boots, but we may say nevertheless that if Brutus had never existed, the Elector would have acted differently. And the Prince certainly did him an injustice when, at one splendid point of the drama (which shows incidentally how in the mouth of a poet the most trivial words can rise to the most dynamic passion), he exclaims: "And when at such a moment he confronts me, a sheer embodiment of the Classic Age, I am sorry for him and needs must pity him." But the Brutus idea lived in him as a submerged memory of his childhood, his dreams, nay, his father and forefathers, and appears to us as the strongest motif of his action.

How eminently modern, even in form, Kleist was can be seen in *Robert Guiscard*, of which Wieland said: "If the spirits of Æschylus, Sophocles, and Shakspere united to create a tragedy, it would be just that which Kleist's death of the Norman Guiscard supplies, if the whole is anything like the part which he let me hear at the time. From that moment on, it was settled once and for all for me that Kleist was born to fill the great gap in our literature, the gap that, in my opinion at least, even Goethe and Schiller did not completely fill." As everyone knows, it has only been preserved as a fragment. Kleist burned the manuscript and then wrote the first ten scenes anew four years later. Yet it is no fragment, but a complete work of art, and this precisely because it was not "complete" in the classical sense of the word, but pointed beyond itself. In these few scenes of this torso one experiences the tragedy of utter disintegration of feeling, and one can well understand why Kleist destroyed the "complete" drama, not in an "uprush of despondency," but because he was an artist.

It is understandable that Goethe neither could nor wished to follow this trend; manifestly, what annoyed him in Kleist's poetry was exactly that which makes its uniqueness: namely, its psychopathic clairvoyance, its will to irrationality in form and content, and its more than life-scale size. The literary modes by which men turn life into form work out in three ways. Most remain *below* life, and their personalities are emptier, more foolish, less personal than actuality. This is not because they cannot see rightly (that they can do this is shown by dreams; no dream ever contains a badly drawn figure). They merely lack the gift of translation — and it is solely in respect of this that poetry ranks as an " art." Does anyone behave so inanely and boringly as do the characters of an operetta or a provincial newspaper serial? Then there are the artists whose fancy transforms men into megatheria, fabulous monsters of superhuman size and spiritual capacity; think of Dante, Æschylus, Shakspere, Michelangelo! And lastly there are creators who succeed in the most self-evident, and the rarest, quality, that of re-creating life to scale. To this category Goethe belongs, and that is why it took him so long to bring himself to approach Schiller and why he was necessarily repelled by Kleist as much as by Kotzebue — two opposite poles between which he found himself at the golden mean of the life-size that was natural to him.

In any case, after Schiller's disappearance Goethe's main interest was no longer poetry. Writing poetry was henceforth insufficient, for he had become a compendium of the whole world. The second part of *Faust* is no longer a drama, but rather a universal epic; and yet again the notion of a " work of art " is too limited for it. It is a biography of humanity, a world-panorama, a philosophical cathedral, an encyclopædia of the soul, and even, not infrequently, a work of reference. But if Goethe had been asked what he considered the chief work of his old age, he would probably have named the *Farbenlehre*. "By it," he said, " I have attained to a culture that I should scarcely have made for myself by any other way." The historical part of this work is a grandiose presentation of the essence and transformation of the nature-idea from primitive times to the present; the theoretical part created the foundations of a new science: namely, physiological optics. Here Goethe explored, with the subtlest understanding, the properties of the eye; for instance, the nature of the sensation of contrast, which arises from the fact that light is asked for when dark is offered, and vice versa, and that every colour has its counter-colour — to yellow violet, to orange blue, to red green. What he described was, as he says in his preface, the " deeds and sufferings

" Farbenlehre " and " Vergleichende Sinnesphysiologie "

47

of Light." And yet he did not push his theory to its last, and almost inevitable, conclusion, for he continued to regard colours as " natural phenomena " and not as sensations of the eye. To take this step he would have had to be a Kantian, like Schopenhauer, who was one of the earliest and most ardent admirers of the *Farbenlehre,* and took that step in his essay *Über das Sehen und die Farben,* which Goethe disowned. It was the same in this case as in that of Kleist — Goethe *would* not understand, for a dissolution of the whole coloured world of the light into mere effects of the retina would have turned his world-picture and world-feeling, which was *objective* in the highest degree, topsyturvy. His researches were rejected as a matter of course by the professional scientists, but there were a few gifted minds that realized their epoch-making significance, among them Purkinje, the founder of experimental physiology, and Johannes Müller, who in his *Zur vergleichenden Physiologie des Gesichtssinnes des Menschen und der Tiere* (1826) declared: " I for my part do not hesitate to confess how much I owe to the stimulus of the Goethe colour-theory, and I can say indeed that without several years' study of this the present investigations could never have been." This essay contains the theory of the so-called " specific sense-energies."

At the end of the nineteenth century a Munich journal took a plébiscite of its readers on the question, what was the most important phenomenon of the century in Germany. The answers were numerous : some said *Faust, Zarathustra, Tristan,* the *Ninth Symphony,* and the majority said Kaiser Wilhelm. It is remarkable that not one thought to name Johannes Müller, for his discovery of " specific sense-energies " signified nothing less than the experimental proof of Kantian philosophy. By a series of most ingenious experiments Müller arrived at two surprising fundamental propositions : firstly, that one and the same stimulus produces different sensations when it affects different nerves; and, secondly, that different stimuli produce the same sensation when applied to the same sensory nerve. In the case of the sensitivity of the eye, for example, it is a matter of entire indifference whether it is struck by a blow, by an electric current, or by an ætheric wave — in all three cases it answers with light-sensations. It is the same with the ear, whose reaction to any conceivable stimulus can only be sound. On the contrary, the same ætheric waves will produce on the skin sensations of heat, and in the eye sensations of light (varying in colour with the wave-length), just as one and the same disturbance of the air is felt by the hand as warmth and by the ear as sound (of low or high pitch according to wave-length again). The purely quantitative difference between the wave-lengths of ætheric and sound waves is converted by the receiving apparatus into a far-reaching qualitative difference. And therefore " the generation of light in the eye is not to be thought of as the generation of physical light therein by friction or the like. Such stimuli in the eye can never generate what would be recognized as light by an outside observer, however strong that observer's own sensitivity to light in his own eye may be. . . . It is thus incorrect to say that bodies would shine even without the sensitive organ, as though light existed ready-made outside and was only waiting to reach a membrane to be felt as such. We must accept the warning, that light, dark, colour, tone, heat, cold, the various scents, the taste, everything that our five senses offer us in the way of general sensations, are not the truths of outward things, but the qualities of our senses." This is not a denial that something " outside " exists — nor indeed did Kant deny this — but as to what this something is, every guess fails us.

Johannes Müller would not have been able to carry out these experiments with such exactitude or in such variety had it not been that a magnificent research-instrument was at his disposal in the electric current. It was in fact in this period that the theory of electricity started on its way to becoming the central theory of physics. In 1820 the Dane Hans Christian Oersted, Professor of Physics at Copenhagen, found that the electric current causes the needle of a magnet to deviate, even when water, wood, clay, stone, and metal intervene, and thus discovered electro-magnetism. And his discovery was amplified by Gay-Lussac, who proved that the current magnetizes a non-magnetized steel needle, and by Ampère, who found the " swimmer " rule: namely, that if one imagines oneself swimming in the direction of the electric current, with one's face turned towards the magnet, one sees the north pole of the needle move to the left. In 1823 Seebeck achieved the discovery of thermo-electricity, by showing that two strips of different metals soldered together at their two ends constituted a thermo-element in which, if one of the strips was heated and so brought to a different temperature from the other, an electric current flows in the closed circuit formed by them; and, thus, that electricity can be produced by heat. In 1827 Ohm laid down the law that bears his name, resting on the two equations: " Current

49

equals electro-motive force divided by resistance " and " Resistance equals specific resistance multiplied by length and divided by cross-section " — that is, the strength of an electric current (measured by the magnitude of its magnetic effect) stands in a direct ratio to the driving force that causes it to flow, and in inverse ratio to the resistance that it finds before it, this resistance being itself greater in proportion as the specific resistance of the material through which the current passes is higher, its length greater, and its cross-section smaller. And with this, electrical phenomena became for the first time exactly measurable, and electricity joined the ensemble of the natural sciences on an equal footing.

In 1828 Karl Ernst von Baer published his work *Über die Entwicklungsgeschichte der Tiere,* which, uniting in truly scientific fashion the " observation " and the " reflection " of which its sub-title speaks, laid down the fundamental lines of all embryology. The gifted optical researcher Fraunhofer created, by the discovery of the dark lines in the solar spectrum which bear his name, the preconditions for spectrum analysis, and so decisively improved the construction of the telescope that his tombstone could justly bear the inscription: " *Approximavit sidera* " (" he brought the stars closer to us "). The Frenchman Dutrochet and the Englishman Graham investigated the laws of diffusion, the mixture of gases in juxtaposition (establishing the law that velocities of diffusion are inversely proportional to the square roots of specific weights) and the phenomenon of " osmosis ": that is, the complete exchange of two fluids through a porous partition, a process of outstanding significance since the metabolism in the cells of plants, animals, and men alike depends on continuous osmotic action. In the winter of 1827–8 Alexander von Humboldt's Berlin lectures on physical descriptive geography made a sensation and led to his *Kosmos,* an astounding work such as had never been written and is not likely to be written again very soon. This is nothing more or less than a canvas of the world, a universal history of Nature, of all that is visible and examinable from peat-beds to star-clusters, from a stone to a human brain, in which, beautifully interlinked, we have the results of the life of a world-traveller who was at the same time a philosopher, and which with its combination of critical taste, popular character, and pure plastic of description is no less entitled to figure in literary history than in scientific. The work was translated into eleven languages, and for a whole generation Humboldt was regarded as Germany's greatest title to fame.

Chemistry, meantime, was investigating a number of very peculiar problems. Klaproth, professor at the newly-founded University of Berlin, discovered polymorphism — the fact that bodies of like chemical composition could appear in quite different forms. He observed this first in the case of Iceland spar and aragonite, which both consist of calcium carbonate ($CaCO_3$). The best-known and most striking instances are that of diamond and graphite, the hardest and the softest of minerals, and that of vinegar and sugar, which for our human taste are radically different substances, but possess chemically the same constitution. The young Liebig similarly discovered that the dangerous fulminate and the harmless cyanate of silver are chemically identical. The Swedish researcher Berzelius, the teacher of Klaproth and of Liebig, and the leading chemist of his age, sought to explain the strange phenomenon of dimorphism (also called, in the case of simple elements, allotropy) by supposing that, as between outwardly different bodies, similarity of inward constitution was only *relative*, the individual molecules being built of different numbers of atoms; the expression he invented for this is " polymerism." There were also, however, cases in which dimorphic substances were found to be *absolutely* like (that is, their molecules contained the same number of atoms), and for these Berzelius set up the hypothesis of differences of disposition of the atoms in the molecules, which are called " metamerism." In experiments in this field of isomerism — which is Berzelius's name for the whole group of such phenomena — a third pupil, Friedrich Wöhler, arrived, however, at a still more remarkable result, for he succeeded in making out of inorganic materials ammonium cyanate, $(NH_4)CNO$, which is isomeric with urea, $(NH_2)_2CO$, so that he was able to write to Berzelius: " I must tell you that I can make urea without using kidneys or anything whatever from the animal." And thus the frontier between organic and inorganic chemistry was abolished. It was, however, an altogether premature jump from this (and numerous like homunculus-pastimes) to the conclusion that they amounted to a refutation of Vitalism, with its axiom that to give rise to the material products of an organism a separate vital force is necessary. The very fact of isomerism, indeed, should have indicated that the " becoming phenomenal " (whether for geologists and chemists or for theologians and

51

philosophers) is something simply incomprehensible, for ammonium cyanate is definitely not urea. And the structure hypothesis is in truth a mythology of the nineteenth century; that is, an effort poetically to interpret the miracle of actuality in the current terms of the age.

Homœopathy   The doctrine which assumes that the soul is located at one definite point in the brain — though Vitalism by no means stands and falls by it — was refuted by Franz Josef Gall, whose work in cerebral anatomy laid the foundations of the modern " localization theory "; he showed that particular parts of the brain surface have particular functions. The jealousy and stupidity of professional colleagues, however, conspired against him so successfully that even today his doctrine is branded in certain circles with the stigma of charlatanism, though it must be admitted that the spirit of arbitrary fancifulness in which he tried to build up his system lent to this condemnation a certain colour of justification. The same may be said of homœopathy, which Samuel Hahnemann founded with his *Organon der rationellen Heilkunde* (1810). Against Galen's principle of " *contraria contrariis* " he set up that of " *similia similibus* " : " In every case of sickness, choose, if you would get better easily, quickly, and permanently, a medicine that can evoke the same suffering (*homoion pathos*) as that which it is called upon to cure." In support of this he brought forward numerous examples — such as the treatment of frost-bitten members with snow, of mild burns with hot cloths, the curing of headaches by (headache-producing) coffee, the prevention of smallpox in man by inoculation with cow-pox. He came to the conclusion, further, that medicaments should only be administered in extremely weak solutions. These he called "potencies," and to each of them he assigned a set of effects, the numbers sometimes reaching the thousand — thus, salt at the thirtieth potency causes disinclination for work (No. 40), impatient scratching of the head (No. 45), a twitching of the earlap (No. 287), love-dreams (No. 1,240). Applying the " *similia similibus* " principle, he ranged against each complaint the means of dealing with it, so that remedies were provided for everything — jealousy, concupiscent dreams, unhappy love, clumsiness, proneness to writing poetry. He carried the attenuation-idea to extremes, and often a mere scent was held to suffice. But with all this, homœopathy was based on a sane and profound idea. " Medicaments," said Hahnemann, " are not dead substances in the usual sense; in their real essence they are purely dynamic spirit — that is, simply, force — and the homœopathic act of healing consists in bringing out these spirit-like curative forces for its own purposes." The materialistic medicine which dominated the nineteenth century saw in the human body only chemistry and mechanism — that is, at bottom, something dead — and correspondingly looked to purely physical potencies in its remedies, whereas homœopathy saw in it a magical play of forces of will and purpose and correspondingly looked upon therapy as a spiritual intervention; hence "*similia similibus*," mysterious relations and affinities to be summoned to the rescue in the battle for healing, sickness to be cured by creating sickness as an enhanced and abnormal condition in which the organism brought into action its last reserves of energy and force-relations. It was no accident that homœopathy was the contemporary of Novalis and Kleist, Fichte and Schelling, for it is a *Romantic* medicine.

But it was only in music, naturally, that the Romantic spirit found its full expression, for music alone was capable of providing the vessel for its will to irrationality. In many of the operas this applies even to the choice of material. Mysterious nature-forces, even spirits of the underworld, are used as heroes; Marschner composed *The Vampire* and *Hans Heiling*, Konradin Kreutzer a *Melusina*, Meyerbeer *Robert le Diable*, Lortzing (whose real talent lay rather in the direction of the comic opera) an *Undine*. Many songs took the same path as Eichendorff's poems, and from being opera pieces became folk-songs; for instance, "*Ein Schütz bin ich*" from Kreutzer's *Nachtlage von Granada*, "*Du stolzes England, freue dich*" from Marschner's *Templer und Jüdin*, "*O selig, ein Kind noch zu sein*" from Lortzing's *Zar und Zimmermann*, Weber's "*Du Schwert an meiner Linken*" and "*Das ist Lützows wilde verwegene Jagd*," Schubert's *Haideröslein* and *Das Wandern*, and Hans Nägeli's "*Freut euch des Lebens*" enjoyed an immense popularity, and as for Friedrich Silcher's songs, we can say that it is only they, and not their long-forgotten composer, that live in everyone's mouth — "*Ich weiss nicht, was soll es bedeuten*," *Annchen von Tharau*, "*Morgen muss ich fort von hier*," "*Ich hatt' einen Kameraden.*"

It is customary to speak of Rossini as the initiator of the Romantic music, although in fact in his first period he belongs still to the Rococo and in his second to the French Romantic. At its first performance at Rome in 1816 *The Barber of Seville* was

Rossini, Weber, and Schubert

hissed off the stage; after the performance his friends hastened to his house, but found him already asleep — either because his intellectual sovereignty was proof against a fiasco or because he was too thoroughly convinced of the ultimate success of the work to mind — and, indeed, already on the following evening he was roused by the alarming uproar of hundreds who had come to give him a wild ovation. It was not an accident that Rossini was one of the greatest cooks that ever lived — as composer also he is the supreme gourmet, savourer, host, and compounder. Into his music, which for delicacy and fullness, grace and lightness comes near Mozart's, he put also the kindly *gauloiserie* and self-seeing irony that distinguished him in life. True, there is a good deal of justification for the verdict of that fine cultural historian Riehl, that Rossini's music consisted entirely of slumber-songs to make one sleep and dream. But in his *Tell* he showed that he had the power to create something more than " charming and lascivious sleep-songs."

E. T. A. Hoffmann, that astonishing discoverer of the pathology of the everyday and the unreality of the philistine, the strange universal genius who belongs to the history of music, painting, and literature alike (for he was draughtsman, caricaturist, decorator, conductor, music-teacher, and music-critic and composed twelve operas, a symphony, and much else), declared, in accord with almost all Romantic theorists of musical æsthetics, that it was not music's business to represent concrete fact, or even specific feelings. From the Romantic standpoint this was theoretically entirely correct, but the practice never carried out the theory in full — one of the most important composers of the age, Louis Spohr, drove program-music to extremes even in his symphonies.

The greatest historian — indeed, the greatest painter and lyrist — of Late German Romanticism was Karl Maria von Weber. But for a long time he was obscured by the grandiose but also bombastic figure of Gasparo Spontini, who was at first the pet of Napoleon (resembling Napoleon, indeed, in his dashing rat-catcher quality and Latin purposefulness, in his mixture of theatrical passion and *Realpolitik*) and afterwards — in spite of being the very embodiment of the typical French tradition of " heroic opera " — Director-general of Music and court composer at Berlin, in which capacity he enjoyed a dictature of such prestige that the censorship forbade criticism of him. Weber, who was a superlative example of what Nietzsche called a " dancer," was

54

lame — like Byron, the winged and fiery soul, like Talleyrand, the insinuating eel and lightning thinker, and like many another example of the " compensatory plus-value " discussed in our two first volumes, the left-handed Leonardo, the stuttering Demosthenes, the phthisical Watteau. *Freischütz* and even *Oberon* are best characterized perhaps by calling them inspired song-plays. In them the hunter's horn, the harp, the viola, the clarinet, the oboe began to sound mysterious, intoxicating, new, decisive. His overtures, pot-pourris only in appearance, are whole dramas, character-pictures, plastic creations that anticipated what was to come. The first production of *Freischütz,* in 1821, opened a new chapter in German musical history. Men realized with amazement that the German forest, alike in its ghostly darkness and jubilant sunniness, in its soft dreaming meadows and wicked lurking ravines, was suddenly beginning to sing, to laugh and cry, to yearn and fear, to be a body and spirit wakened to immortal life. In *Freischütz* and *Oberon* it is Nature herself that sings, the magic root of all being from which men grow up only as dark or bright flowers. These had, of course, been " Higher Powers " in the Classicist music-drama also, but there their interventions had been of the Antique kind — personal, mechanical, corporeal — whereas here they are romantic — cosmic, dynamic, spirit-like.

Weber and Schubert have it in common that they are the purest Romanticists and the most German musicians that can be conceived of. But whereas even in poverty and obscurity Weber was always the baron and cavalier, Schubert was all his life the Eichendorff wastrel, the lazy village Hans who gladly paid for freedom with poverty. And like that " *Taugenichts,*" he was essentially anything but lazy, but on the contrary very industrious, though not consciously so, for he was always singing, and hence — half a thousand songs! An awkward spectacled oaf of a suburban teacher with the *Heurige* as his only friend and world — and when he appeared, humanity discovered for the first time what a song is. Just as the brothers Grimm created (which means, not invented, but raised to the rank of art) the German fairy-tale, so Schubert ennobled the folk-song and set it as an equal by the side of the highest tone-creations. His song was not as a rule handled by stanzas, but *durchkomponiert,* and the accompaniment was emancipated from the voice and almost became the chief element — two epoch-making enrichments and deepenings of musical expression. In another way, too, Schubert stands evidenced as an

55

absolute genius — in the fact that he never gives one the impression of anything queer or out of the ordinary. A genius, in fact, is related to other people as normal beings to an abortion, it is *they* that are the " exceptions," and he the rule. If all were well with the world, every man should have the world-grasp of a Bismarck, the brain of a Kant, the humour of a Busch, should understand life as fully as Goethe did and sing as many songs as Schubert. In all these men there is not a trace of " art." No one can detect their dodges, for they used none. A blissful instrument of God like a bird of the fields, Schubert let his songs sound, an invisible grey lark in a ploughed field, darting up from the earthy furrow, sent into the world for a summer to sing.

Biedermeier   One of the round table gathered about Schubert was Moritz von Schwind, who was akin to him in delicacy and warmth of musical feeling, and to Weber in devotion to the German forest. With pencil and brush, ever in the same key, yet with inexhaustible variety, he told the full story of the German life of his time — and not merely the external, but the inner life, as this worked itself out in the shapes of the people's dreams and fancies. The same thing was done, but even more simply and unpretendingly, by Ludwig Richter. He did not, like the " Heidelbergers," imitate childishness with a refined artistry, nor painfully twist himself back into infantilism like the " Nazarenes," but just *was* a child. For eighty years. And even when he is empty, he has that endearing emptiness of the child's eyes — he had neither an " art-will " nor a " style," but simply gossiped about a world with no problems, atavistic and yet eternal. He sees the peasant and his family not sociologically, nor even ethnographically, but as people straight out of a fairy-story, timeless, idyllic, unreal, and yet growths of the German soil. Over his pictures there lies the charm of a village fair or an afternoon show in a small town, that inviting scent of coffee-cups and tobacco-pipes, of wax-bespattered Christmas-tree and crackling firewood, freshly ironed linen and freshly baked tarts, that is conjured up by the word " Biedermeier."

Heinrich Heine thus characterized this culture: " People practised renunciation and modesty, bowed before the invisible, snatched at shadow kisses and 'blue flower' scents, resigned themselves, and laughed wryly." This resignation was due not merely to political but to economic causes. The overpowering competition of England, in which country immense masses of

56

goods had accumulated during the Continental embargo, reduced German industry to a sort of powerless homecraft. Further, the British Government had, for the protection of its home agriculture, set up a high tariff against imported grain, and thus there was no outlet for the surplus agrarian produce of northern and eastern Germany. The consequence was that the bourgeois culture of Germany was sensibly narrowed in mode of living and in horizon and threw back to the forms of existence of the pre-Classicist period; and its spiritual attitude — washed out, plaintive, affected, concentrated on the cultivation of private feelings — reminds one of that of the era of " Sensibility." The symbol of the age was the night-watchman, the sources of its education were the reading-circle and the theatre. The favourite reading of the middle class was the childlike moralizings of Christoph von Schmid, the pathetic lies of Julius Lafontaine, the imbecilities — regarded by the age as piquancies — of Claurens, and the kitchen novels of Spindler. On the stage Kotzebue and Iffland reigned, until in 1828 Birch-Pfeiffer had her first tremendous success with the *Pfefferrösel*, and from then on fed the public from her dusty rag-fair with the cheap luxury-emotions for which it pined.

In costume the general enforced simplicity was evidenced in a good-hearted tendency to " discretion." For the frock-coat quiet colours were preferred — light grey, dark blue, bottle-green (the *Rock*, which corresponded essentially to the present-day frock-coat, was not yet *de rigueur* in the street and in company) — and the only point of men's clothing in which individual taste could develop itself was the silk waistcoat. The jabot gave way slowly to the cravat, the elegant tying of which was not easy and, indeed, formed the subject of special lessons. The footwear consisted of half-boots (for journeys) and shoes cut away to show bright-coloured stockings, the tight pantaloons reached only to the ankle; " *en escarpin* " — that is, in knee-breeches, stockings, and buckled shoes — one now only appeared at court or on gala occasions in conservative society. An indispensable part of the dandy's outfit was the lorgnette with its silk ribbon. The beard was despised, or at most a thin line on the cheeks was tolerated. The *arbiter elegantiarum* was George Bryan Brummell, who set up the revolutionary theory that the essence of elegance consisted in being *not* striking and was expressed only in cut and fit, points to which he devoted the greatest imaginable care; he kept three hairdressers, one for the back of his head, one for the brow-locks, and one for the cheeks, and he had the thumbs and the fingers of his gloves made by different tradesmen. Through him London achieved that primacy in masculine fashions that it has kept to this day.

As regards the ladies, tight lacing set in again after 1815, and the waist-line, which under the Empire had been fixed close under the bosom, returned to its natural position. (Men also frequently wore corsets, which, indeed, in the Prussian Guard were considered indispensable to a faultless turn-out.) After 1820 women's sleeves assumed monstrous forms, such as " leg of mutton " and " elephants," which could only be kept in shape by the aid of whalebones. A variety of nuances came into being, however, and there was choice of "shot," *moiré, ombré,* damascene, flowered, and checked material, especially for the ribbons that were lavished on the bonnets, hats, and coats. True mantles became impossible with the gigantic sleeves, and so people took to lace collars, the so called " berthas," shawls of every possible material — cashmere or crêpe-de-Chine being preferred, and, towards the end of the period, the fur boa. Quite as fantastic as the sleeves were the poke-bonnets, a sort of horse's hat, very large and unpractical, which so buried the face in blinkers as to interfere with both vision and hearing; nevertheless this form of headgear held its own longer than any of its predecessors or successors. Besides this were worn large caps and, when the East became fashionable, turbans; after the conquest of Algeria the burnous of that country also came into favour via France. As Louis XVIII was fond of comparing himself with Henri IV (who, he considered, had come to the throne with a political situation like his own to deal with), neckwear and feather-caps *à la Henri Quatre* prevailed awhile in Paris and elsewhere; another reminiscence of that period was the *ferronière,* a precious stone set in a thin gold chain as a brow-band; and in still other respects there was a fondness for striking ornaments, such as long ear-rings, huge brooches and girdle-clasps, and broad bracelets worn above the elbow.

In furniture the Biedermeier style was of excellent taste — still simpler than the Empire, but not as dry and twisty. It took over from its predecessor the smooth surfaces, straight lines, and simple motifs, while avoiding its parvenu richness of decoration. Thus, whereas Empire had been a cold forced opera-Spartanism and tortured archaistic artifact, here there emerged a real style, an organic and fit expression of the inward life and spiritual attitude of the whole period.

In Berlin at that time there were working two artists of true Prussian stock and spirit, plain and dour and yet of a veiled warmth of heart and having a strict sort of charm — Rauch and Schinkel. Rauch has stamped the figures of Frederick the Great and Queen Luise, of Yorck and Scharnhorst, of Blücher and Gneisenau for ever in the German popular mind. Schinkel was a man of Michelangelesque spaciousness, in whom the complete plan of an entirely new city could dwell; the crampedness of the times prevented the realization of the most and the best of it, and there is only the Schauspielhaus, with its pure and dignified bareness and its instinctive elegance of proportions, to afford us a modest sample of powers that were far greater. The other German architects were more of the stamp of Klenze, the creator of the Regensburg Valhalla, which is a Doric temple, and of numerous other ornamental buildings in the " Hellenic " style which alone he considered as genuine, others being mere "ways of building." Of Cornelius, another whom Ludwig I of Bavaria drew to his court, that King remarked that " he can't paint "; Genelli also could not and was proud of it. Nevertheless the boldly conceived thought-poems of the former, which are so deep that they send one to sleep, were pure drama — only unfortunately they were merely a book-drama. Josef Anton Koch's nature-studies have something touching about them, reminding us a little, with their tidy composition and sober ear for details, of those patterns which make such charming lampshades. Just as one observes in John Flaxman's dry illustrations to Homer and Dante the fact that he was originally a sculptor, so one's impression of Preller's Odyssey landscapes is that they are pretty dull and void of temperament, and the same may be said of Rottmann's " reminiscence landscapes " of historically important sites such as Marathon, the intention of which was picturesque suggestion, but the inspiration merely literary. This "historical " or " heroic " was in general the favourite genre — a landscape art in a style that worked back to the feeling of an ancient key that was imagined as essentially monumental, and of which the content was, not Nature in her simplicity as taken in (that would have been too crude and inartistic for them), but an " idea." Of course, in practice what came out was not a thought (since it is in painting particularly that the " thought " must consist in the presentation of the object), but an abstraction.

The habit of regarding Rome as the capital of art and the source of all stimuli remained, but the " *Deutschrömer* " divided into two camps, the one continuing with the archaistic orientation, and the other being those Romantics who (at first derisively) were called the " Nazarenes." These constituted a sort of order of painters who lived as a " brotherhood of St. Luke " in the Monastery of St. Isidore that Napoleon had dissolved; they slept in the monks' cells and took their meals together in the refectory. Their leader was Friedrich Overbeck, and their essential principle was the voluntary renunciation of all the progress that the art of seeing had made in the past three centuries. Their ideal was the " Primitives " of the Late Middle Ages in Germany and the Early Renaissance in Italy — Perugino, early Raphael, Hans Memling, and Lochner. But this reversion, being artificially brought about and programmatically willed, lacked the convincingness and the magic of the originality that distinguishes every true primitive. All that lay between the Primitives and themselves they despised, and it was then that the term " pigtail (*Zopf*) " for the Rococo came into vogue and the word " Baroque " acquired the connotation of senseless, tasteless, pretentious, overloaded. In this the Romantics were entirely at one with the Classicists, whom in other respects they fought with bitterness. At bottom, indeed, these two were brothers at enmity, alike to the point of being indistinguishable in lack of temperament and in the bloodlessness of their art of pale imaginings and cold premisses — media in which was enacted yet again the typical drama of killing one's own life by accepting a " renaissance." Since the Middle Ages still believed in God, the Nazarenes demanded " piety " of the artist, but meant thereby merely a sweet and empty worthiness. The greatest popular success amongst them was Julius Schnorr von Carolsfeld, with his thoroughly album-like woodcuts that were to be seen in every bourgeois household — not unnaturally, since their world was a gilt-edged world. In genre painting the leaders were the " Düsseldorfers," who purported to create from life, but actually ran alongside it, in that what they invented was lying picture-sheets so philistine that in the long run the school-name sank to the level of a term of abuse in art circles, much as in our own day the term " Meininger " has become. The only genre, however, that really counted as dignified was the " History " — that is, the narrative (and, where possible, tendentiously narrative) representation of this or that accepted scene of history.

But already there were appearing in France the first signs of an art wholly opposed to this. In 1819 Théodore Guéricault exhibited his " Raft of the *Medusa* " — shipwrecked creatures on the ocean, on the point of being devoured by the waves when at the last moment the rescuing sail appears on the distant horizon. In 1822 Delacroix painted the "Dante bark" which put Dante and Virgil over the Styx, while the damned clung desperately to the gunwales, and in 1824 the " Massacre of Chios," an event of the most recent past — as, for that matter, the " Raft " had been, for it was in 1814 that the frigate *Medusa* went aground on the African coast, and the survivors drifted twelve days on the improvised raft. Thus there also were " historical " pictures, but their essence was different — nothing of sentimental or scholarly "reminiscence," but the most brutal present, the most passionate actuality, the most foaming and fiery realism. Of the " Massacre of Chios " it was contemptuously remarked that it was a massacre of art, but it was more, it was a massacre of the whole Romanticist world-picture; in Guéricault and Delacroix the July Revolution was already boiling up.

Guéricault died as early as 1824, and we may apply to him the phrase of Lao-tse: " When a noble man comes at his time, he rises, but if he does not come at his time, he vanishes like a plant in an inundation." It may be applied to Saint-Simon and Stendhal also. Count Claude Henri de Saint-Simon — descendant of Charlemagne, grandson of the duke who immortalized the court of Louis XIV in his memoirs, and pupil of d'Alembert — was the inventor of modern Socialism. He took as his starting-point the concept of the *"Industriel."* What is an industrial? A man who works to create or to make accessible resources for the satisfaction of human needs or pleasures. Consequently *everyone* who works is an industrial. But what rank do these industrials hold in society? The lowest. And which ought they to occupy? The highest, for no one is so important as they. Their opposite is the "bourgeois," the possessors of the unearned income, the nobles of today, and so long as these rule, the Revolution is incomplete and Freedom not achieved. This can only come about with the " industrial régime," *the command of the state-power by labour.* These notions of a " social physics " were further worked out by Charles Fourier, who himself came from prosperous bourgeois stock. For all development, all freedom, said Fourier, the indispensable prerequisite is wealth. This wealth does not happen of itself, however, but must be acquired, and acquired by work. Now, if we assume that each one manages to produce only so much as he himself needs, then if a third of the community merely consumes, another third must go short of its needs. This is the basic error of civilization. Freedom is impossible so long as men are the slaves of their wants, and anyone who desires to see the reign of freedom must desire wealth for *everyone,* or at any rate what he called the "minimum": namely, that measure of goods which secures full material independence. This aim is only realizable through the partnership of labour and capital, for only so is it possible to reach the high productivity that is required if everyone is to be rich. In general, let everyone work, but everyone as he will, for it is a fact that every human being takes pleasure in work of some sort. These views of Saint-Simon and Fourier coincided, indeed, with Communism and with what came later to be understood by Socialism, in their philosophical foundations, but they differed from these in important points, for, firstly, they allowed of the continued existence of private property; secondly, they knew nothing of the concept of the "proletariat," but recognized only that of the "worker," who need not by any means be a manual worker; and, thirdly, they expected everything to come from the goodwill of the governors, the insight of the possessors, and the peace indispensable to development.

As for Stendhal, he was the complete living embodiment of the type of the "passed-over" so beloved of the literature of the time. He prophesied that he would "only be understood in 1900," and the prophecy came out almost to the day. Much could be said of him that could be said of Lichtenberg and Goya. In common with Lichtenberg's, the basic feeling in his creativeness is that of a sort of roused-spectator passion; in common with Goya he prefigures the coming Impressionism; and he shared with both the fate of being regarded by his contemporaries as a mere caricaturist and oddity. He himself considered that his chief affinity was with Pascal — though in reality his astounding psychological flair and analytical keenness of intellect only link him to one side of Pascal, that which was turned towards earth. Stendhal is one of the subtlest and maturest masters of soul-anatomy, a gifted vivisector, with the coldness and cruelty that this calling demands. His whole object is the raw truth — *" la vérité, l'âpre vérité! "* He shares with his French discoverer, Taine, his passion for the *" petits faits,"* for strict and unadulterated description, and his belief in the *milieu* — the sociological view-point. With his German discoverer, Nietzsche, he shares his impetuous scepticism, his belief in the aristocracy of culture, and his admiration of the men of prey of the Renaissance.

The eponymous hero of the age, however, as we have already said, is Lord Byron. Just as a famous picture distributes itself among mankind in thousands of reproductions, coarse and fine, cheap and costly, exact and careless, so Europe was populated with innumerable copies of Byron which with more or less success, more or less exactly, more or less superficially, tried to reproduce the essence of this extraordinary creature. The soul-life of the whole epoch bore his stamp, and all the coins, big and little, including counterfeits and mere play-counters, bore the countenance of Byron.

The eponymous hero of the age

Everyone knows that Byron was the inventor of "*Weltschmerz*," the sorrow that suffers from the world and is therefore incurable, for only the abolition of the world could remove it. This sorrow would necessarily lead to the denial of life were it not that it is itself an enjoyment; and hence it is not so easy as it seems to answer the question whether Byron, who counts as the classic type of the unhappy man and poet, was really unhappy — the question has two solutions, as the quadratic equation has its positive and negative roots. When in Rome Thorwaldsen had finished his bust, Byron exclaimed indignantly: "No, that's nothing like me, I look far unhappier than that!" But *one* happiness at any rate he had throughout his life, perhaps the highest that can come the way of an artist, that which the French call "*la vie à grande vitesse*." His existence was one continuous drama or, one might better say, film — filled with abrupt reversals, tensions, crises, hunts, heroic deeds, and drawing-room conquests, adoration and scandal. Rarely have such intensities of feeling been directed towards a human being. An English lady fainted when he unexpectedly appeared at Madame de Staël's; another fell in love with him ten years after his death and killed herself. He awakens ideas of Achilles and Alexander, those other beautiful tragic youths, and he too had his fateful heel. Macaulay says of him: "All the fairies save one had been bidden to his cradle. All the gossips had been profuse of their gifts. One had bestowed nobility, another genius, a third beauty. The malignant elf who had been invited came last and, unable to reverse what her sisters had done for their favourite, had mixed up a curse with every blessing. . . . He was sprung from a house, ancient indeed, and noble, but degraded and impoverished by a series of crimes and follies. . . . The young poet

63

had great intellectual powers; yet there was an unsound part in his mind. . . . He had a head which statuaries loved to copy and a foot the deformity of which the beggars in the street mimicked." Yes, he had his Achilles' heel, and we do not mean by this his club-foot. The vulnerable spot of this hero lay in his soul, and it was the sickness of his time — in enjoyment he pined, in " to be " he scented " not to be," Faust and Hamlet in one person. A life full of fame, love, wealth, and beauty turned him into a despiser of the world. It is a matter of entire indifference what Fate brings to a man, for only that happens to him which is bound to happen to him. The rain-worm swallows soil and flourishes on it, for it knows how to find the nourishing substance that it needs even in the dead earth, and equally he who *needs* joy will find joy even in death and darkness. Every human organism is, so to say, attuned to a specific quantum of joy and sorrow. The cow makes milk and dung out of everything, the bee wax and honey, the artist beauty, the melancholic tragedy. And the genius makes out of everything something new — with nothing left over.

One might, under the reservation that nothing contemptuous is meant by the term, describe Byron's whole life as a gigantic feuilleton. In his action he is never very inventive, action being merely the incidental scaffolding on which his splendid fireworks are let off. The astounding and unprecedented thing was his palette, and the subject that he paints is always the same George Gordon Noel, Lord Byron, the brilliant tragic Lion of the Romantic. He has frequently been reproached for painting men and things in too deep a black, but if this be true, he must have turned the laws of optics topsyturvy, for never has an artist managed to induce the dark to emit so many gleaming nuances. His own customary reply to such reproaches was: " I feel that you are right, but I feel that I am sincere." He knows that knowing is killing, that the Tree of Knowledge is poisonous, that " sorrow is knowledge." How different this sounds from the ringing triumph-cry of another Englishman, three hundred years before him: " Wisdom is power "! Between Bacon and Byron lies the path of knowledge of modern Europe. For him, thought is the " rope of sand " of life, " and know, whatever thou hast been, 'tis something better not to be." Goethe characterized him in the fine phrase, that his being had consisted in " rich despair." It is well known that Euphorion, the child of Faustian world-urge and Hellenic beauty, is Byron. At the point where Euphorion falls to earth from the

64

heavens, one reads the enigmatic stage-direction: " In the dead the spectators think they recognize a well-known form." Euphorion is Modern Poetry, Icarian, non-viable, and yet filled with life, " naked, genius without wings, faun-like without animality."

The age was literally infected with Byronism, and his shadow even threw forward. Already we find Chateaubriand's René saying: " Everything wearies me; painfully I drag my boredom about with me, and so my whole life is a yawn." In 1804 appeared Sénancour's *Obermann,* with which the figure of the " passed-over " made its entry into French literature, a sort of Werther that, like the other, led many a reader to suicide, although this one denies life only in his thoughts. In contrast to René, and more honest than René, he is an atheist. His basic feeling is *le désenchantement de la vie,* disillusionment about life. Numerous similar novels followed; their heroes are all (as Benjamin Constant said of his Adolphe) " victims of a mixture of egoism and sensibility," and their philosophy is the Leopardian " Sorrow and ennui is our being, and dung is the earth — nothing more." Wherever one looks, no meaning and no fruit: " *uso alcuno, alcun frutto indovinar non so.*" Slavonic literature, too, took possession of the " superfluous " idea — Mickiewicz with his *Pan Tadeusz,* Pushkin with his *Eugene Onegin,* Lermontov with his modern ballad of *A Hero of Our Time.* Even Metternich knew whole cantos of *Childe Harold* by heart; the whole world was in the grip of the " *maladie du siècle.*" There were literally epidemics of suicide. The eighteen-year-old Charlotte Stieglitz stabbed herself in order that her husband, out of so terrible an experience, might develop into a great poet; the experiment failed, of course, and, as Relling prophesied of Hjalmar Ekdal, " scarce three quarters of a year, and she is for him only a fine declamation-theme." Other romantic women did not go so far as this and contented themselves with saying that they did not belong to this world — a sentiment they implemented by frequent fainting, constant headaches, and abstention from all bodily exertions and pleasures. Eating, particularly, was regarded as unromantic. Byron worked out a hunger-diet of his own, in order to seem all spirit, and a marchesa in whom he was interested was dropped at once when he perceived with what appetite she enjoyed a veal cutlet. Shelley lived on bread and water, and his friend the Countess Guiccoli did not eat at all. Now, nothing happens twice in history, and this second " Sensibility," as compared with the first, was on the one hand far less original, and on the other far more honest — being, in fact, purely literary and honestly nihilistic — a mixture that makes it much more complicated than its predecessor. " It is," says Immermann in his *Epigonen,* " as though humanity, tossed about in its little bark by an overwhelming ocean, is suffering from a moral seasickness of which the outcome is hardly to be foreseen."

The self-consciousness of the age

Byronism's only competitor for the rulership of the age was, it must be considered, Hegelianism, though this only developed its full power in the disciples' time and not in the master's. The philosophy that Hegel himself taught was not, as is so often maintained, the extreme antipole of Romanticism, but touched it at several points, in its conservatism, its emphasis on the evolution-idea, its theological colouring, and its historicism. We might say that Hegel stands to the Romantic as Socrates to the Sophists, in that he was at once their opponent and their fulfilment. Late Romanticism has no representative philosopher of its own — Oken, Schubert, Baader cannot be named in the same breath with Fichte, Novalis, and even Schelling, for their disjointed, eclectic, wild, and epigone conceptions, nourished chiefly on artificial and obscure analogies, are throughout second-rate — " a porridge of thoughts from all sources," as Hegel called them in his *History of Philosophy.* What a German philosopher can do when he gets the chance, we see in Karl Christian Friedrich Krause, who, finding the existing terminology not clear and not German enough, invented a complete new vocabulary with such terms as " *Vereinsatzheit,*" " *Inbeweg,*" " *Sellbilden,*" " *das Ordarzulebende,*" " *Seinheitureinheit,*" " *vollwesengliedbaulich,*" " *eigenleburbegrifflich.*" When he says, somewhere or other : " The word ' *Eindruck* ' is a translation (*Übersetznis*) of ' *impressio* ' and is to be taken to mean ' onworkedness (*Angewirktnis*),' " no doubt everyone who has racked his brains over the rare and difficult word " impression " will welcome with joy this illuminating explanation, and only lament that the author did not live long enough to do the same for " Impressionism," for which he would no doubt have discovered a still clearer translation. But when, elsewhere, he remarks that " a new word must be self-explanatory," we feel obliged to ask whether formations like " *Vereinselbstganzweseninnesein* " and " *Orendeigen-Wesenahmlebheit* " entirely fulfil this desideratum.

Every age demands its *doctor universalis,* a spirit both rich enough and concentrated enough to mirror its self-consciousness. This is what — each at his very different level of height and depth, but each completely right for his age — Aristotle, St. Thomas Aquinas, Nicolaus Cusanus, Bacon, Leibniz, Voltaire, Nietzsche did, and this is what Hegel was for the first half of the nineteenth century. His system rested on the assumption of the identity of thought and being: it is logocratic and also (as it fully affirmed a government of the world) in a sense theocratic. Seen from this angle, it must be called an extreme Rationalism, for it taught that concepts do not merely *correspond to* the essence of things, but *are* their essence. Nevertheless, Hegel's famous — or notorious — remark that " what is real is reasonable, and what is reasonable is real " is usually misunderstood. By this phrase — which was exploited by the Reaction to its own advantage — he naturally did not mean a simple assertion that every phenomenon, by the fact of its existing at all, has the legitimacy of reality — which would explain every stupidity, lie, and injustice — but exactly the opposite: namely, that all reality is reasonable only at the particular historical point of time at which it actually rules existence (so that, in fact, the Reaction stands convicted of un-reality and consequently unreason) and that, only the reasonable being real, the unreasonable is a sham existence, a nonent, a μή ὄν, as Plato and the Platonists called matter. If we were to take the sentence literally, it would involve the nonsensical position that all unreasonable is reasonable. Nay, one might even say that every reality, in the moment when it becomes known and therefore rea-sonable, has ceased to exist. For humanity, as a rule, begins to take reality seriously only when it should not be taken so; namely, when it has been incorporated — which is as much as to say, lived out — and become an institution — which means when it is be-hind the times, for institutions are always behind the times. Hegel himself, in his *History of Philosophy*, says emphatically that to know the *Zeitgeist* is to dethrone it; when the riddle of the Sphinx is answered, the Sphinx falls over the cliff. And in his *Rechtsphi-losophie* he says, in one of his most beautiful and sublime pas-sages: " When philosophy paints her grey on grey, then a shape of life has become aged. With grey on grey one cannot rejuvenate, but only know, and the owl of Minerva flies forth only when the dusk sets in."

Hegel's method, as subtle as it is fruitful, is the so-called " dia-lectical "; it rests on the assumption that the motive force in world-evolution is contradiction. The two antithetical ideas which together form a contradiction are " *aufgehoben* " — in all senses

The dialectical method

67

of the word: namely, *negatived, elevated,* and also *preserved* to live on as valid motives, though each containing but half the truth — by a third which is more comprehensive, higher, and truer. In front of this super-concept, then, arises another opposite so as to form a still richer synthesis, and thus each stage is only a transitional point, and, moreover, the movement is *self-effecting,* in that every concept contains inherently the tendency to turn itself into its opposite, and every contradiction the tendency to be reconciled in a unity which Hegel called the " more concrete," since it cannot generate further contradictions out of itself. But there he was to go wrong.

His methodology, the path to absolute knowledge, Hegel laid down in the *Phänomenologie des Geistes,* which he concluded at the midnight before the battle of Jena. It bears this title because it deals with the " modes of appearance " of the knowledge, the evolutionary stages of consciousness from the lowest to the highest. On this foundation he built up a doctrinal structure that is spacious, cleanly ordered, and embellished with strict and solid ornamentation, and of which the main departments or storeys are logic, natural philosophy, the philosophies of law, history, art, and religion, and the history of philosophy.

In the second half of last century Hegel was regarded as the classic example of a philosopher who cannot be enjoyed. This is not quite correct, for large parts of his work, especially the purely historical, are very enjoyable reading indeed. But it must be admitted that his main work, the *Phenomenology,* is scarcely readable; further, in the *Natural Philosophy* he had not full command of the material. Electricity he defined thus: " It is the aim of the form that liberates itself from it, the form that begins to resolve its indifference; for electricity is the immediate outcome, the being that proximately emerges from the form and is still conditioned by it — but not yet the resolution of the form itself, but the superficial process of differences leaving the form while yet having this as their condition and not being as yet independent of it." The example is maliciously chosen, of course, but it cannot be denied that in the high vapours that constitute the atmosphere of Hegel's elevated thought-world the reader is very often dizzy. At bottom, Hegel was one of the clearest of thinkers. It was only in his diction, and particularly in the obscure professional jargon which he could not shake off, that he was unclear. Very often it is almost an impossibility to follow the very exactly cut but endless screw-thread of his logical borer. In general, clarity in the expression of thought seems to be a matter far more of artistic than of philosophical gifts. It would be a pretty shallow and, indeed, a false thesis-antithesis to credit the artist with the power of dark but creative vision, and the philosopher with the gift of keen, clarifying, and illuminating conception. The reverse is rather the case, for the true artist is the master of fulfilled thought, in that he has succeeded in completing it by bringing it into standard form, whereas the out and out philosopher's domain is rather in the unexpressed, the inexpressible, the *mere conception and no more* of new and deep thoughts. All great philosophers are inclined to mysticism, and all philosophers to ambiguity and obscurity; the very earliest Western philosopher of world-importance, Heraclitus, was nicknamed "the dark" (ὁ σκοτεινός). The "exceptions" whom one can call to mind — Montaigne, Pascal, Lessing, Lichtenberg, Schopenhauer, Nietzsche — were all far more artists than philosophers. On the contrary, almost all poets of a size to span the generations have been distinguished by the purest transparency and sharpest outlining of the structure of their thought. This, too, is perfectly natural; the more one loses oneself in pure thinking, the more one gets into abysses, darknesses, and windings, whereas the closer and closer approach to the picture means a process of elucidation, ordering, and interpretation. Always the philosophers only have the new ideas, and the artists make the clear picture of them.

Hegel was anything but an artist in his style, and even his oral lectures, according to contemporaries, lacked all smoothness; he made his hearers the witnesses of his wrestlings with thought, and put the results before them in a raw and unprepared form. And yet out of the darkness of his thoughts there often flashes some most beautiful jewel; sometimes, too, he is positively witty. His remark that the well-known proverb: "No man is a hero to his valet," is true "not because the hero is not a hero, but because the valet is a valet," has become famous because, unknown to him, Goethe has said it before him, and Carlyle copied it from Goethe. His observation in the *Religionsphilosophie* that it is not philosophy's business to make religion into a subject he elucidates by the analogy: "This would be as preposterous as to attempt to put intellect into a dog by giving him printed matter to chew." Of Schelling's Absolute, which its author had defined as "the total indifference of subjective and objective," he said that it was the night, in which all cows are black. Of the French Revolution, that "since the sun had stood in the firmament and the planets had circled, it had never happened before that man had stood on his head — that is, his thoughts — and built up actuality accordingly." Of the Kantian philosophy, that it tested the constitution and the limits of our faculties of knowing, as to whether and how far these were capable of fathoming the nature of things, after the fashion of the Schoolman who would not enter the water before he had learnt to swim (whereon Kuno Fischer has commented, still more cleverly, that if knowing is to be compared with swimming, Kant's relation to it was not that of the Schoolman, but that of Archimedes). All these *bons mots,* certainly, are a little frosty and remind us of the teacher who here and there in his lessons makes a joke, but will not allow the class to laugh.

Hegel's Historical Philosophy

The distillate of Hegel's philosophy is contained in his *Philosophy of History,* a grandiose panorama of the course of human destiny from the beginnings of China to the July Revolution, always driving down from the variegated surface to the "idea," the *Zeitgeist,* which is often tidied up a little at the expense of the facts — but, after all, what intellectual construction does not do this? The ruling motif of the work lies in the proposition that "the only thought that philosophy brings with her as dowry is the simple idea of reason," that reason therefore rules the world, and that consequently the history of the world has proceeded reasonably. This thesis, however, is not a preconceived dogma prejudging the subject to be approached, but merely the anticipated result of his review of world-history; if one regards the world as reasonable, then it looks reasonable to one. The divine wisdom, the reason, that imbues everything is the same in great and small, and, in so far, history is a theodicy, a justification of God. It is the expansion of the spirit, and as the substance, the essence, of the spirit is freedom, it is simply progress in the consciousness of freedom. "It is the exegesis of spirit in time, as the Idea as Nature expounds itself in space." Philosophy seeks to grasp this spirit and is concerned, as Hegel so finely says, at the conclusion of his work, "only with the splendour of the Idea that is mirrored in world-history."

Hegel's theodicy is, however, far too deep to be regarded as an affair of "happiness." By progress he in no wise means that shallow Liberal notion of betterment, the greatest happiness of the greatest number, as his contemporary Bentham expressed it.

World-history is not in fact the soil of happiness. "The periods of happiness are empty pages in it, for they are the periods of agreement, of the missing antithesis." Nor is it merely the theatre of the good, it is rather that of guilt (*Schuld*); and, indeed, "the seal on man's absolutely high mission" is the fact that he knows what good and bad are, that he can feel responsibility (*Schuld*), "not only as to this and that and the other thing, but in respect of the good and evil belonging to his individual freedom." Only the animals are truly irresponsible-innocent (*unschuldig*). Man in his history is a religious phenomenon. "Religion is the place wherein a people gives itself the definition of what it regards as truth"; the idea of God constitutes the common foundation of a people; and as this is, so will the State and its constitution be. It determines also progress in the consciousness of freedom. World-history proceeds from East to West, "for Europe is merely the end of world-history, and Asia its beginning." The East knows only that *one* is free, the world of Greece and Rome that *some* are free, the Germanic world that *all* are free. The first form is despotism, the second democracy and aristocracy, the third monarchy. Hegel's *Religious History* is a variant of the same basic theme, for religion and philosophy have the same object: namely, eternal truth, "God, nothing but God and the explanation of God." Philosophy is not worldly wisdom, but knowledge of the unworldly, "not knowledge of external measures, of empirical being and living, but knowledge of what the eternal is, what God is, and what flows from God's nature." The *History of Philosophy* follows the same scheme as his *Philosophy of History;* it consists in the development of the self-knowledge of the human spirit, in which the numerous historical philosophies are the individual stages — all equally transient, but all equally necessary in the process of reason's becoming ever more and more conscious of itself. "Every stage has its own form in the true system of philosophy, nothing is lost, all principles are preserved, since the final philosophy is the totality of the forms." This final philosophy, the totality of the forms, is, however, not, like Kant's completed realm of knowledge, a goal of our spirit, unattained and unattainable and only to be striven for by endless approximation, but has appeared incarnate in Georg Wilhelm Friedrich Hegel.

But Hegel's philosophy ought to hold good in Hegel's own case, since its rights should be valid even against himself. And it emerged that there is no final synthesis, but only, time and again,

Amortisation of Hegel by Hegel

71

a thesis that is destined to transform itself into its opposite. He originated a school that called itself Hegelian, but was in reality what he himself had called an " imitation in inversion." The generation that took the lead about the end of the twenties fulfilled the antithesis that, long pent up, burst out with all the wilder energy. It turned against all Romanticism and Reaction in State, faith, art, and mode of life, against the world of " shadow-kisses " and shadow-kings, against the whole theatre of shadow-figures that had led its ghostly existence in the shadow of the Holy Alliance, against the shadowy conceptions of the German Romanticism of Ideas, whose last and greatest master was Hegel. He was overthrown — and in the name of Hegel.

CHAPTER II

THE DISCORDANT SONG

> "*At present the immensity of political interests has swallowed all else — a crisis in which everything that has otherwise been valid seems to be being made into a problem.*"
>
> *Hegel*

The second stage of the nineteenth century begins with the July Revolution of 1830 and ends with the February Revolution of 1848. This division offers itself so self-evidently that there could hardly be found a history-book in which it was not applied. The slogan of the Romantic had been: " Away from reality, from the present, from politics ! " but now the catchword is " Realism." The thought and feeling of the age crystallized emphatically and exclusively upon questions of the day, and the European soul intoned a million-voiced political chant. This noisy battle-song *had* to happen, filling the whole Continent and outsinging all others, and the fact that it arose was the work, above all, of the very people who, by means as unwise as they were inhuman, had sought to suppress it. In it sang Fate, but discordantly.

In this period Europe became for the first time ugly. We remarked in the first volume that every historical era is tinctured with a definite light of day or night; this world had for the first time an artificial light: namely, gas, which was already flaming up in London in the days when Napoleon's star was declining, and entered Paris almost at the same moment as the Bourbons, conquering slowly and obstinately every street and public place. By about 1840 it burned everywhere, even in Vienna. In this clear and murky, sharp and flickering, prosaic and spectral light, there lived and moved fat, fussy cockroaches of tradesmen, whose preposterously ill-made clothing cannot penetrate to our consciousness simply because our own is derived from it. The upper part of the body was fitted into the flapping tube of the *Gehrock* (which drove the *Frack* into its present rôle of a full dress for evening), and the neck into the grotesque horse-collar. The *triste* and impersonal black became more and more dominant, till presently everyone

The world in gaslight

73

who wished to be regarded as a serious person made a point of looking like a notary or an undertaker. Apart from black, the only tolerated colours were dirty brown and grey, and at most the waistcoats were allowed to be gorgeous in designs of all sorts — mostly tasteless. The trousers were ridiculously wide, made of horrible checks for choice, the extremities being, as in riding-pantaloons, drawn over the shoe, which made the shape of them quite impossible. Above the coat arose the " parricide " — to this day part of the stock-in-trade of the provincial comedian — with the stiffened and pleated shirt-front, in which were two quite purposeless gold buttons, and the formless broad black or white stock, to which two pins connected by a short chain added barbarity. Add to this the hair hot-ironed into hairdressers' curls with already, in the case of the young man, a variety of unpleasant forms of face-hair, cake beards, seaman's beards, seal beards, goat's beards, *Henri Quatres*. Another novelty (at any rate in popularity) was the rimmed monocle on a preposterous wide ribbon, indispensable to every dandy. The " cigarro," in reality the original form in which the Mexican enjoyed his tobacco, became now for the first time, with the introduction of the covering leaf, a successful competitor to the pipe; in Prussia it was at first forbidden in public, and then permitted by police regulation if enclosed in a wire case (" on account of the danger of fire ") ; Byron sang it, Heine rejected it, Schopenhauer vilified it. It stood to the pipe in the same relation as the nerves of the new rapid-thinking age to the comfort and reflectiveness of the old; one finds it difficult to imagine a present-day stockbroker without a fat cigar, but impossible to think of him with a pipe. Further, with the cigar smoking was for the first time admitted to the drawing-room, and steadily displaced the snuff-taking which had hitherto been regarded actually as an elegance.

Women's costume, too, was characterized by a number of distinctly unbecoming innovations — first among them the ugly hooped petticoat which was called " crinoline " from the coils of horsehair (*crin*) which kept it in position, and of which the solid effect was enhanced by the three- and four-fold flounces. It was not a bizarre but engaging weapon of flirtation like the " hencoop " of the Rococo, nor yet an aid to stiff but stylish *grandezza* like the " virtue's guard " of the Counter-Reformation ; but, in the new bourgeois and materialistic world, it was insolent, suggestive, and loud. Next came, gradually, the dowdy button-boots and the glacé gloves which then for the first time began to supplant natural leather, for although the French invention of enamelling leather had been spread over Europe by Huguenot refugees as early as 1700, its general introduction awaited the day of the parvenu who wanted expression for his primitive delight in showiness. The hair was peaked up flatly and without charm and secured by monstrous combs that were called " Chinese," or else worn in thick plaited or crimped coils right and left, about the ears (which style was called the " Greek ") ; often, too, long curls hanging down on either side of the head were the fashion. Yet, taking it all in all, women's costume was not nearly so repellent as men's, and, quite generally indeed, one may say that it never is so distinctive of its age as men's, for the simple reason that, as Weininger says, woman is created by man; a proposition strikingly confirmed by (among other things) the fact that man determines the prevailing erotic ideal, and with it the costume, while the rôle of woman is merely that of executant; hence, too, the variations disclosed by the history of her costume are surprisingly small and do not amount to much more than a juggling with a few rapidly changing but also rapidly recurring nuances, such as the length of the train, the height of the coiffure, the shortness of the sleeves, the bulging of the skirt, the exposure of the bosom, the position of the waist-line. Even radical revolutions like the short boyish hair of today are only " eternal recurrences of the like," for " page's " hair was not unknown to the Italian and Burgundian ladies of the fifteenth century, not to mention the Egyptian of the Old Kingdom — the Sphinx was bobbed. In fact, when one's historical fancy tries to conjure up the style of a past period, it always settles first on the costume of the men because this is the more physiognomic and because in fact it works its way through bolder and more characteristic changes. In the Thirty Years' War, for example, it was everyone's ambition to look like a dashing landsknecht or a raffish provocative student; fifty years later the wild blade had become a thoughtful and respectable government official or university rector ready at any moment to read a will or conduct a disputation; fifty years later again he has become a fragile and æsthetic youth that appears to think of nothing but amours. If with these we compare the corresponding women's costumes, the differences in the latter are much smaller and sometimes only discoverable by an expert; the cardinal differences, indeed, only turn on the use of powder and the wig — both male inventions.

75

Looking at these " sons of the time " " with spectacles instead of eyes, as the result of thinking with a cigar in the animal mouth, and a sack on their back instead of a coat " — as Schopenhauer severely but quite justly characterized them — clothed with a tastelessness that only the following period surpassed, we have nevertheless to admit that they had a most pregnant and significant style, not merely because (as we have remarked in the previous chapter) no such thing as styleless costume has ever existed, but because they were being truly themselves — putting forth a special energy in the shaping of their external life-forms. It is costume as a *haute bourgeoisie*, arriving at supremacy, conceives it: factual routine, untheatrical and therefore tiresome, undecorative and void of fancy, like everything that the financier does outside his office, practical, plebeian, of animal seriousness, a costume for employés, accountants, and commercial travellers who live in smoke and soot, for tradesmen and journalists, quick coarse agents of goods-exchange or news-getting. Dressing has sunk to the level of clothing.

Locomotive No. 1

But, as men make not only their clothes but the whole countenance of their lives, even to the contour of their gestures and the profile of their landscapes, everything else likewise changed towards the useful and ugly. In amongst the beauties of nature the hurrying black giant snakes began to wind themselves, belching evil vapours from their mouths. Innumerable factory chimneys reared their grey throats into the heaven, and soon endless wires, whispering their dubious financial information, were to disturb its peace. Stephenson had built his locomotive in 1814, but the discovery was not of practical importance till the rolling of rails was invented, in 1820. Five years later, between Stockton and Darlington, two little towns in the county of Durham, the first railway line was opened, and even today " Locomotive No. 1 " is to be seen on Darlington Station, the mother of a million progeny of land monsters. Five years later the steam train was running between Manchester and Liverpool. On the Continent at first only short stretches of line were laid down, such as would equally well have been covered by horses, or even on foot — between Nürnberg and Fürth in 1835; between Leipzig and Dresden, and Paris and Saint-Germain in 1837; between Berlin and Potsdam, Vienna and Wagram in 1838. The novelty was regarded in fact as an entertaining curiosity. But in America in 1839 the first sleeping-car was running between Baltimore and Philadelphia, and it was on the

76

other side of the Atlantic, too, that the first steamboat appeared, the *Clermont,* which from 1807 plied between New York and Albany, and the first seagoing steamship, the *Phoenix,* which worked between New York and Philadelphia. The first ocean-going steamer was the *Savannah,* also American, which in 1818 crossed from New York to Liverpool in eighteen days. England did not lag behind; in the period between the Congress of Vienna and the July Revolution the number of her passenger steamers increased from twenty to more than three hundred, and in 1833 she built the first steam warship. But on the Rhine it was only in 1825 that the first steamers came into service, though already in that same year a British steamer was on its way to India. It was the discovery of the screw propeller that made the new mode of communication universal. This was successfully achieved by Joseph Ressel of Trieste as early as 1829, but the Austrian police forbade the trials. Britain took up the experiments afresh in the later thirties, and it was there that, ten years after Ressel's fiasco, the first screw steamer was launched. Then Germany slowly followed. In 1842 a regular steamship service was opened between Bremen and New York, and in 1847 the Hamburg-Amerika company was founded. But it was only in the second half of the century that the steamer ousted the sailing ship everywhere; till then it had had to fight against the conservatism of the public and the inertia of governments. The railway encountered still greater resistance. When in Bavaria the first German line was projected, the medical faculty of Erlangen gave the opinion that the operation of public steam vehicles should be forbidden; the swift motion would infallibly lead to cerebral troubles, and even the sight of a train rushing past might do so; at the very least the track must be shielded by a hoarding five feet high on both sides. In opposition to the second German railway, that between Dresden and Leipzig, a miller alleged that the trains took his wind away, and when powers to drive a tunnel were sought, the doctors declared that the sudden change of air-pressure might easily cause a stroke to an elderly person. (The opposite standpoint to this was taken by the Austrian Emperor Ferdinand, who obstinately insisted on a tunnel, since a railway without a tunnel was not really a railway.) In Prussia the Postmaster-General Nagler advised against the construction of a line between Berlin and Potsdam, on the ground that the coach which he ran on this route four times a week was already half-empty, and even the King thought it no particular

77

advantage that one could get to Potsdam a few hours sooner than before. Tieck, summoned to an audience there, refused to use the railway and travelled by coach alongside it. Ludwig Richter was another opponent of the railway, and Thiers prophesied that no important consequences would follow from its introduction, while Ruskin observed that railway journeys are not journeys at all, since one is simply conveyed from place to place like a package. The Prince of Anhalt-Cöthen, on the contrary, was so enthusiastic a supporter of the new invention that he swore he must have a railway in his principality too, " even if it cost a thousand dollars." Still, by 1845 railways and steamers were fairly general in Europe; the new modes of conveyance were lauded in speech and poetry, and a veritable travel-fever set in, which expressed itself in literature as well as in practice; travel pictures, travel letters, travel stories became the favourite genre for writers and public alike. The increased density, speed, and capacity of traffic which was made possible by steam power did not, as most experts had foretold, mean the ruin of other methods of transport, but indirectly benefited them; in Germany in particular they led to the construction of a system of first-class roads such as France had enjoyed since Richelieu. The third great event in the field of technics, and one at least equal in importance to the invention of locomotives and steamships, was the introduction of anthracite — a discovery by which England once more was the chief gainer, since she both possessed the largest deposits and was the first to recognize their value. As she had from the beginning taken the first place in the development of machinery, so now she had the most successful equipment for the winning of the new energy-sources, and a reciprocal action set in, the more and more numerous machines demanding more and more coal, and the coal permitting the construction of more and more powerful machines. The inventors of the steam plough (Heathcoat, 1833) and of the steam hammer (Nasmyth, 1845) were British.

The high-speed press

    The most important machine, however, that was born in this period was the high-speed printing press, which automatically performed the operation hitherto done by the hand press, and at a rate many times as fast. It was used for the first time in 1814 — in England, of course, though the inventor was a German, Friedrich König. The first newspaper that needed no human hand for its production was *The Times,* and it was this alliance with the machine that first gave the newspaper its character of universal

78

power; a word, true or false, flies into the great, silent, expectant drum of the machine, which sucks it in, prints it, multiplies it a thousandfold, and vomits it into wherever human beings dwell, into the morning room of the bourgeois, the tavern of the rustic, the barrack-room, the palace, the basement, and the attic. And this word becomes a spell.

Slowly the triumphal march of the press passed from west to east. From the British Isles France was the first to receive it; there its mightiest potentate was Louis François Bertin, for forty years editor of the *Journal des Débats*, Bourbonist under Louis XVIII and Orleanist under Louis Philippe, whose portrait, preserved for posterity by the genius of Ingres, ought to bear the title "The Power of the Press"; and who should be remembered for yet another reason, that it was in his journal that Berlioz, with his keen sword of analysis and polemic, established the program of modern music. Another grand master of the press was Émile de Girardin, of *La Presse*, who in the middle of the thirties introduced three decisive innovations. Firstly, selling by individual copies, instead of by expensive yearly subscriptions as heretofore, made the newspaper for the first time the universal daily habit and peculiar penetrative power that it is. Secondly, by developing the advertisement business it allied itself with the other great power of the day, mercantilism. And thirdly, with the serial feuilleton, the press fused with literature. In fact, almost all French, and many British, novelists of note have begun their productive career in this form, and not seldom they have continued in it all their lives. This involved them, indeed, in the temptation to crude tensions and scaffold-pole structures and was without doubt a degradation of the story-teller's art, but on the other hand it exercised on them a benevolent pressure in the direction of popularity and gave them a peculiar *élan;* the incomparable freshness of the sketches in Thackeray's famous *Book of Snobs*, for instance, is certainly, in part at least, the result of their having been written for *Punch*.

In this field of development, too, Germany lagged behind. There there was only the semi-official press — and even that was a French invention (the prototype being Napoleon's *Moniteur*), which gave, under a mask of objectivity, only such news and views as the Emperor's Government held to be useful. This institution was further built up by Metternich, who created in all the capitals newspapers ostensibly independent, but really inspired from above, and managed, partly by chicanery and partly by bribery, to draw into his service much of the publicist talent of the time. Apart from these imposed politics, the papers contained only futile gossip of the day. Hoffmann von Fallersleben satirized the typical contents of the gazette of the time in verses that in their dull harmlessness are just as typical themselves. " An ensign is promoted to the rank of lieutenant, a court preacher receives an order, the lackeys receive silver braid, the leaders of society go north, and spring is here on time — how interesting, how interesting! God bless the dear Fatherland! " With the coming of the poetic school of " Young Germany," however, the newspaper began, even in the Germanic Federation, and in spite of pressure and emasculation, to spread that spirit of actuality and political interest which is characteristic of the time, and to become the ubiquitous and inevitable companion that we know, forcing itself under every door and into every pocket, as intolerable and indispensable to the Modern Man as Mephistopheles to Faust.

Lithography   For the illustrated journal lithography had somewhat the same importance as the machine press had for printed matter. Its inventor, Aloys Senefelder, originally had in mind merely the easier production of facsimiles of manuscripts, and the processes published in his *Vollständige Lehrbuch der Steindruckerei* (1818) have that object. It was others who developed his idea into a technique of lithography as such. It allowed of a speed of drawing which almost equalled that of writing, and consequently it had from the first a character of improvisation, of writing down, of dialogue, of literature; and at the same time, with its actuality and its cheapness, it was democratic, a journalism of the drawing-pen that expressed the rapid, pointed, materialistic spirit of the time as completely as the woodcut had expressed the spirit of the Reformation, and the engraving that of the Rococo — and, indeed, it is symbolic that the woodcut, which carried here, there, and everywhere the spirit of an awakening and upstriving age is a process of raised printing surfaces, whereas the engraving, which embodied the feelings of a dying and introvert epoch, is a process of hollows, and lithography a process of the flat. Incidentally, woodcut technique was at this time radically improved by the Englishman Thomas Bewick's invention of " wood-engraving," and it is significant that this was the favourite method of reproduction in harmless Germany; the *Fliegende Blätter* (1845) and the *Münchener Bilderbogen* owe their birth to it. Towards the end of the period, too, multiplication by photography was already beginning.

In those days lithography had in its service no less artists than Goya, Guéricault, Delacroix, Schwind, and Menzel, and comic journals of a week's immortality such as the *Caricature*, founded by Philipon immediately after the July Revolution — greatly feared and finally suppressed — and the *Charivari*, another product of Paris. This was fashion journal, pamphlet, and chronicle in one, a razor-keen, witty, now malicious and now kindly, but never flattering mirror of life, and its illustrations ranged through the whole gamut of expression open to the draughtsman, from the naïvely narrative to the devastatingly satirical. It knew its age through and through, in work and pleasure, in friendship and love, in poverty and climbing, court and proletariat, advocate and politician, financier and *petit bourgeois*, bureaucrat and dandy, cocotte and critic, to the last wrinkle and gesture. Gavarni, who has been called the Raphael of caricature, delighted in models with feminine and very charming manners; he is, in fact, rather a depicter of manners than a critic. Daumier, on the other hand, drew his world in with the fiery pen of a Dante. When Daubigny stood for the first time in the presence of Michelangelo's Sistine ceiling, he murmured: "Daumier." These things are no longer caricatures, but nightmares and visions of hell before which people forget to laugh, twitching flashlight shots made monumental by a dæmonic fist. In these fevered goblins technics already grins its triumph, while man bewails his lost soul. And as in a scene of Apocalyptic horror Paris, *la ville lumière,* appears as the radiating focus of all culture, beauty, and intellectual power, and the world about it as a fat, snuffling money-bag. We have observed in the previous volume that the Dutch artists achieved the *tour de force* of creating a mythology out of the commonplace. Daumier completed their work, but two centuries later — more intellectual and nervous by far than they, the atheist of the big city.

Hegel says in his *Religionsphilosophie:* "Our age is distinguished by knowing about anything and everything, an infinite multitude of objects — only, nothing about God. Formerly it was the highest interest of the spirit to know about God and to fathom His nature. . . . Our age has hushed up this need, and all the pains and struggles belonging to it, and it is done with. . . . A condition like this must be regarded as the lowest stage of man's degradation, and yet, more arrogantly than ever, he regards this

81

degradation as a peak and believes his attainment thereof to be the achievement of his true mission." But this age no longer needed to know about the Christian God, for it already possessed a god of its own: namely, Money. It will be remembered from our first volume that one of the great events that brought on the Modern Age was the decline of the economics of kind and the rise of the economics of money — or, more accurately, of gold, although there was long a certain uneasiness of conscience about gold business. Gradually, indeed, this uneasiness wore away, yet as late as the Rococo the ruling caste still knew only landownership, and its relation to money was merely that of paying it out or owning it, while even in other social strata the art of making money remained infantile, amateurish, and rudimentary. We have also alluded to the fact that the introduction of coin levelled the souls of men, in that it identified their possessions and performances by specifying these in terms of uniform metal products that could be exchanged amongst themselves at will. But a minted gold piece is still a reality, if only a very low one, and what happened now was that its place was taken by something still more soulless, the bank-paper, which is nothing but an empty fiction of a number. And it was before this nullity without essence that all mankind bent the knee, and to the winning of these papers went not merely an eased conscience, but restless ambition, passionate love, and religious fervour.

Paper money had of course long existed (we need only mention the Law catastrophe), but it was only now that it became the hero of the day and the age. Henceforth, thinking in goods was in the same relation to thinking in money as handiwork (work of the hand, the greatest artist in the world) to factory production (work of the machine, the most impersonal of all producers, which makes " numbers "), as living likeness to dead equality, as the analogy-logic of the artist of the Middle Ages, who by physiognomic insight grasped the organically-linked, to the inductive logic of the scientist and the modern era, which from mechanically juxtaposed individual cases calculates a common measure — in a word, as quality to quantity. Money is the greatest of the enemies of private property, for it is completely relationless; for that reason the very Communists do not desire to abolish it, but only to " nationalize " it, and for that reason, too, the peasant (the profoundest of the Communist's enemies), for all his avarice, nurses a deep mistrust of paper and looks even at his coins with an eye to their material and not their minting. Money strips all objects of their symbolism; suppositing itself as a common denominator, it robs each of its uniqueness and its soul. Money is plebeianism's most effective vehicle, for it is obtainable by all, without distinction of status or talent. Money is the milliform characterless Proteus which can turn itself into anything and necessarily therefore became the symbol and idol of a mankind that can worm its way into anything, but is itself nothing, describes everything and loves nothing, knows everything and believes nothing.

There is, further, a close interconnexion between money-economy and exact physical science, or, for that matter, modern science in general. In both there is at work the aptitude and desire to think " calculatingly " and to express everything possible in abstractions and general formulæ of world-validity. This demand for a formula such that simply everything can be brought into its scope money satisfies in the highest degree; and that is why its world-wide rule is one of the greatest triumphs — or apparent triumphs — of Rationalism. All values and realities, even the most inward and intensive, like happiness, personality, gifts, can be expressed arithmetically in money terms (or does the richest man not now count as the happiest and most admirable, and did perchance Balzac and Daumier regard their works as beyond price?). We have already, and frequently, emphasized the fact that every Culture makes, not only its own poetry and ethic, strategy and garden-art, jurisprudence and erotic, but also its own natural science; there is, therefore, a deep affinity between the plutocracy, or, rather, the plutolatry, that sprang up in this period and the contemporary rise of the doctrine of the Conservation of Energy, which asserts that light, heat, motion, electricity, and even the phenomena of life are only forms of one and the same neutral energy and can therefore be transformed into each other — in other words, that qualities are only quantities. And in truth, from the moment that one admits that all values are expressible in money, all the spiritual relations of men and all their destinies of happiness and sorrow, triumph and fall, bliss and damnation, are reducible to transformations of a money-force of which the sum, like the total energy-capital of the universe, is a fixed amount.

Georg Simmel says in his thoughtful (but unhappily rather unreadable) work *Philosophie des Geldes:* " For many people, money definitively concludes the teleological series by giving them

83

a measure which brings all interests together uniformly, a measure of abstract supremacy, sovereign above the particulars of life, which weakens in them the need of finding intensification of these satisfactions in the courts of religion." As man cannot at the same time believe both in God and in money, money replaces God; and precisely because it is a super-real principle, the object of a religion, it has the tendency to become an aim in itself. Men no longer pray to it, as primitives pray, in order to obtain something from it; they pray to it because it is worthy of reverence, because it is the godhead. The truly pious money-worshipper does not worship it because it can buy everything, but because it is his tribunal of highest appeal, his pole-star, that which gives meaning to his existence. It must be conceded that this is no material and crude superstition like that of the fetish-worshipper and the pilgrim, but an idolatry endowed with the highest powers of sublimation; it is no simple materialism, but prostration before an *immaterial* principle — such as in fact the Devil is. And at once there arise in the cities mighty chief temples called bourses, and crowds of smaller temples called banks, where they pray to something magic, almighty, omnipresent, but invisible; priests, reputedly initiate (though mostly ignorant or fraudulent) declare Its will and innumerable devotees gladly offer their all, murmuring in pious terror the unintelligible spell-formulæ of an alien language. Creed has become Credit.

Balzac   Nothing was more interesting to the humanity of that period than money. Even the artists liked to depict financial situations such as pawnings, bankruptcies, gaming scenes, the pedlar with his bale of goods; and Comte places the bankers at the head of the worldly government of his State of the future. The Song of Songs and Homeric epos of money's might, however, was sung by Balzac. In him everything revolves around money, it is the hero of all his creation, and he himself and all his figures are veritable satyrs of its train. With a magic hand the pulse-stopping shadow that this evil giant throws upon souls is painted on the wall. And since the poet is nothing but the megaphone of his time, he could not but proclaim, from his lonely nocturnal watch-tower, this devil's doctrine; nay, he was forced to live it himself. A poet, not unworthy to stand beside Shakspere and Rembrandt in the power of creating men, but become the troubadour and prophet of money — Mammonism could achieve no higher triumph than this!

84

In almost every chapter he whispers of figures, chances, prices, percentages, of dowries and heritages, transactions and lawsuits, all handled in detail and with professional knowledge. He himself spent his life in taking up every enterprise that fancy could conceive, all of which failed — pineapple-growing, printing, type-founding, popular editions of French classics, experiments on a new paper-pulp, the exploitation of Sardinian silver mines, the recovery of buried treasures in the Seine. Physiologically, too, he had the constitution of a financier. It has been mentioned in the previous volumes that Schiller introduced the motif of work into the art of poetry. But whereas Schiller's "work" was the quiet and almost unconscious industry of a librarian or a bridge-builder, Balzac worked with the panting desperate fury of a big speculator who keeps the market reports ever before his eyes by day, and broods feverishly over his accounts by night. For his books *were* his "books"; he worked on his texts with so persistent a file that sometimes scarcely a syllable of the first draft remained. His corrections were the terror of the compositors, he demanded five, six, seven pulls. He himself said: " If the artist does not leap into the abyss like a Curtius and does not work in it like a trapped miner, he is committing suicide with his talent. And therefore the same prizes, the same laurels, beckon to the poet as to the commander." He was no priest as the poet of older times was, no secretary to the world-spirit as even his contemporary Goethe still was, no wakeful dreamer of the night as the poet will ever be, grasping the secret of actuality with clairvoyant intuition, but an alchemist seeking to conjure it by magical formulæ, to squeeze it out of retorts, a strategist trying to surround it by chess-genius. His truths are not oracles for which he has been made God's vessel (for he has no God), but triumphs of energy, of calculation, of science, of persistent underground shovelling. He wrote sixteen and even three-and-twenty hours a day, by candle-light behind closed shutters (for the study, for this poet, was a laboratory), drinking the while as many cups of coffee as Voltaire did. But whereas for the hero of the Rococo mocha was a fine-tasting stimulant that made his wit more piquant, fresher, and more penetrating, it was for the hero of the Bourse Age only a cruel elixir to whip up the last reserves of his overstrained organism. In Voltaire's case it ministered to a playful self-satisfaction, in Balzac's to dull industrialism. Voltaire was an aristocrat, Balzac a plebeian; and yet this very fact constitutes a part of his greatness, for it was precisely his plebeian qualities — massive vitality, freedom from inhibitions, senses sharpened by innate mistrust and a hard lot — that fitted him to be a portrayer of life such as had never been seen before.

In Balzac the machine-age was boiling and smelling. He himself was nothing but a giant machine of marvellous construction, that untiringly steamed and stamped and ground, and out of matter made matter. Genius has turned into the *perpetuum mobile*! Balzac's gigantic factory rolls out men, of all sizes and qualities, without pause and *en masse*, and spews them on to the market. He is the manager of a human manufactory. His products are imposing, but, like all the rest of the " marvels of technics," depressing and not profoundly convincing. They are not images of God, but competitors of Nature. All the same, Balzac is a Romantic (though strictly in the French sense), for he has an art of vision which is intensified in one direction to nightmare and in the other to caricature. In this he is the true pendant to Daumier.

Balzac's own wish was not to be a Romantic, but a historian and even a natural-historian. In the preface to his *Comédie humaine*, which in nearly three thousand characters and over a hundred stories covers the whole life of the period (*La Vie privée, La Vie parisienne, La Vie de province, La Vie de campagne, La Vie militaire, La Vie politique*, with, in addition, the *Études philosophiques* and *Études analytiques*), Balzac says that his intention is to accomplish for human society what Buffon did for the animal kingdom. " Soldiers, workmen, advocates, scholars, statesmen, merchants, sailors, poets, beggars, and priests are just as distinct from each other as wolves, lions, ravens, sharks, and lambs." He might, in fact, have mentioned his contemporary Comte, whose sociology aimed at the same ideal of a comparative natural-history of human society, the establishment of its types and laws. The plan was indubitably a grandiose one, and its execution, given the limits set by human imperfection, was marvellously successful. But the fact that it could be conceived at all has its roots in the dual Rationalism that marks Balzac both as a Frenchman and as a man of the nineteenth century; the conviction that there is some system into which actuality will go without remainder, that life is a problem of mechanics and the rules of permutation. On one occasion Balzac set himself in comparison with Napoleon by writing on the statuette of the Emperor that stood in his room: "What he could not accomplish with the sword, I will bring to pass with the pen. Honoré de Balzac." And the prophecy was correct. He brought Europe under his yoke, and from the Seine to the Volga men obeyed the magic pen. That the sword could never have achieved. His world existed first in fancy and only later became actual, but this would have been impossible had not the fancy been from the outset something more real than reality itself. One day, when Balzac was working — as a matter of fact, on *Eugénie Grandet* — Jules Sandeau, just back from a journey, was telling him of all sorts of novelties; Balzac listened awhile and then said: "That is all very interesting, my dear fellow, but let's get back to reality, and talk about Eugénie." I have already remarked, in the Introduction to this work, that the great men of action in world-history are one and all simply artists that have missed their vocation and become entangled in life. Nero had to set fire to Rome, which was a dangerous, costly, and thoroughly rotten idea; Dante with his flaming brush set alight a whole hell, the fire of which burned inextinguishably for centuries. Napoleon's fancy stuck fast in realities and hence had to make his hopeless attempt to conquer it with soldiers.

Sainte-Beuve tells us that it was the ambition of everyone to dress " according to Balzac " (which incidentally meant without taste, overdone, Sunday-best, *bourgeois gentilhomme,* being of the essence of the time as well as of Balzac), but this was only one of the many ways in which Balzac's works were livingly effective. Only in a time such as this could so paradoxical and indeed so lamentable a " sport " of a poet be born as that which lived in Balzac, and only out of Balzac could the age, in turn, give form to its ultimate impulses, its intellectual legitimation and its inner life. And so, once more, we are faced with the question, does the poet make reality, or reality make the poet?

The phrase " Bourgeois monarchy " was a very apt description of this era. The King was nothing more than the first citizen, and in reality it was the citizen who was king. The July Monarchy was the creation of a revolution that lasted only three days and was carried through chiefly by workmen, students, and Napoleonic veterans. Its immediate cause was a set of ordinances in which Charles X declared the results of the last election (which returned the opposition) invalid, introduced a new and reactionary electoral law, and abolished the freedom of the press; and thus was justified Louis XVIII's *bon mot* on his brother, that " he has conspired against Louis XVI and against me, and one day he

87

will conspire against himself." The whole city became rigid with barricades, everyone armed himself with a musket or a paving-stone, and Marmont, the royal Commander-in-Chief, was obliged to report that every house had become a fortress and every window a loop-hole. The troops, whose mood was already indifferent, retired after a brief street-fight, the King abdicated in favour of his nephew — whose father had fallen a victim to assassination ten years before — and departed to England. But the peers and deputies decided to raise a member of the younger line of the house of Bourbon, Louis Philippe, Duke of Orleans, to the throne, following therein the example of the English Revolution of 1688, which, while deposing the old dynasty, yet set up in its place a semi-legitimate line: namely, that with the next-best claim. The old Lafayette, who had led the National Guard forty years before, was persuaded to the view that this was the only way in which France could be saved from republicanism, but the result was that the Fourth Estate, which had carried the Revolution through, was cheated of its fruits. The new King was a man of exceptional prudence and complete freedom from prejudice; politically he was not compromised, in that he had never borne arms against his country, and indeed had fought for her at Valmy and Jemappes. In other respects also his previous life recommended him for the rôle now assigned to him; as an *émigré* he had always kept in the background, pushing himself only in ways befitting a citizen, and even during the Restoration he had not returned to feudal habits, but continued in the bourgeois way of life. And so the stout um-brella which he was accustomed to carry in his walks became the symbol of the new monarchy. In order that the cleavage with the old régime should be marked outwardly in the clearest possible way, he called himself, not Louis XIX or Philip VII, but Louis Philippe; his title was, not *roi de France*, as under the Bourbons (who had in this wise asserted a sort of property in the country), but *roi des Français*, as a king elected by the French, to whom he swore the Constitutional oath; and he put aside the fleur-de-lis standard in favour of the Tricolour. But, as he owed his crown to a league of wealthy bankers, energetic journalists, and influen-tial party men, he had no alternative but to remain in alliance with these three powers; that is, with corruption, which in those days reached a height that had never been seen since the heroic days of the Greek and Roman republics. Over the gateway of this era stood the notorious mottoes: " *juste milieu* " and " *enrichissez-*

88

vous." For all his outstanding diplomatic talents, he was never able entirely to establish his position, and he never lost sight of the fact for one instant. For the Republicans and the Bonapartists he was a usurper and enemy of the people, for the royalists and the conservative courts of other countries an illegitimate parvenu. The Tsar was only prevented from armed intervention by the Polish Revolution, which broke out in the same year. On two occasions Louis Napoleon, the nephew of Napoleon I, who was to become Napoleon III, attempted an insurrection, and throughout Louis Philippe's reign there were attempts at assassination by pistol, dagger, "infernal machine," and in one instance (that of the Corsican Fieschi) a machine-gun built up of twenty-four barrels — so that in the end he hardly dared to go out.

An immediate consequence of the July Revolution was the insurrection in Belgium. The artificial union of Holland and Belgium had shown itself to be completely untenable. The Walloons, who inhabit the southern half of Belgium, are Latins and speak French, but even the Germanic Flemings, who live in the northern half, are divided from the Dutch by their Catholic faith, and in their large towns French is the prevailing tongue. Further, Holland was predominantly a trading and seafaring country, Belgium one of industry and agriculture. Consequently the Flemings, although (as we have said in the previous volume) they are almost identical with the Hollanders in descent and character, have always gravitated towards Belgium. Hatred of the union was so strong that clericals and liberals made common cause in the Revolution. This broke out in Brussels during a performance of the opera *La Muette de Portici* — which, as everyone knows, describes the insurrection of the Neapolitans under the leadership of the fisherman Masaniello — and swiftly spread over the whole country. The London Conference of the Great Powers accorded recognition to the declaration of independence made by the Belgian National Congress, and to the choice of Prince Leopold of Saxe-Coburg as King. Thus called to the throne, Leopold managed matters with the greatest wisdom and prudence, governing strictly according to the Constitution, reconciling parties, and promoting the economic interests of the country, in particular by the construction of a railway network that is even today the pride of Belgium. Further, the country was declared for ever neutral under the treaty of guarantee of the great powers, though the point of this neutrality was then still directed against France.

89

Close upon the Belgian insurrection came the Polish, which, like it, began in the capital. The native portion of the army joined it, and the newly-formed provisional Government declared the deposition of the Tsar and demanded the frontiers of 1772. General Diebitsch, the conqueror of Adrianople, invaded Poland with a Russian army and after some indecisive engagements was victorious at Ostrolenka. Shortly afterwards, however, he died of cholera. Abroad the Polish outbreak evoked lively sympathy, the songs of Poland followed the songs of Greece that had so lately been popular, and Lafayette demanded that France should declare war. But the superiority of the Russian artillery and the division of the people into an aristocratic and a democratic party led to the fall of Warsaw and shortly afterwards to the complete collapse of the movement. The " Organic Statute " deprived Poland of her constitution and reduced her to the status of a Russian province. Army, religion, administration, were forcibly Russified with true Muscovite brutality. In 1846 there was a fresh Polish outbreak, this time in Posen and Cracow, which resulted in the latter's losing its freedom and being incorporated in Austria.

In this year of revolutions 1830 the Swiss also rose, overthrew all their aristocratic governments, and transformed them into democratic. From that time Switzerland has been the European refuge of all the political martyrs or malcontents, and in impotent anger Metternich had to see the " fortified sewer " (around which he would have liked to draw a " sanitary cordon ") become the focus of every sort of revolutionary poison. After movements in Parma, Modena, and the Romagna had been suppressed by the aid of Austrian forces, the young Mazzini, who had been the soul of them, founded at Berne the secret society of " Young Europe," with its branches " Young Italy," " Young Poland," " Young Germany." In Saxony, Electoral Hesse, Hanover, and almost all other parts of Germany disturbances flamed up, and only Prussia and Austria remained quiet. In May 1832, at the ruins of Schloss Hambach in the Palatinate, in the presence of more than two thousand persons, a high-sounding " popular declaration " for democracy and the emancipation of women was adopted; whereat Metternich revived the Karlsbad Resolutions. As the literary school of " Young Germany " also had an undisguised political orientation and ardently, if with entire vagueness, championed the " modern ideas," their members (with the exception of Börne, who in fact was the only dangerous one of them all) were at Metternich's instigation outlawed by the Federation in 1835; several of them were imprisoned, their works, not merely existing, but even future, were banned, and their very names were forbidden to be printed, whether by way of praise or disapproval. It was their ill luck to be identified with the political secret society above mentioned, though they had nothing whatever to do with it and were not even aware of its existence. It was a purely superficial coincidence that Laube's first novel bore the title *Das junge Europa,* and that Wienbarg opened his *Ästhetische Feldzüge* with the phrase: " To thee, the young Germany, I dedicate these words, and not to the old," and in any case it was the persecutors who grouped them as a " school," for its members not only had no program in common, but could not endure one another and were in a continuous state of feud and ill will. Five years later King Frederick William IV, on ascending the throne, a hundred years after Frederick the Great and two hundred years after the Great Elector, granted a general amnesty.

This ruler was intelligent, enterprising, magnanimous, warmhearted, and unquestionably a personality. That he had a noble character and an interesting mind, even his opponents have not been able to dispute; but that clarity was lacking to his thought, and energy to his will, even court historians like Heinrich von Treitschke have had to admit. His figure, inclining to embonpoint, but yet not inelegant, his slack and yet lively features, his impetuous and yet sensitive impressionability, gave him an unsoldierly but kindly stamp. He resembled the first King of Prussia, Frederick I, in his naïve love of display, Frederick the Great in his satirical disposition and his intensive interest in all contemporary intellectual movements, and William II in his irrepressible love of making speeches, which came out not only in private, but on every possible public occasion — sometimes, indeed, very impressively — and also in his temperamental and finger-in-every-pie dilettantism. He was in close friendship with Alexander von Humboldt and Ranke, brought Rückert and Schelling, Schlegel and Tieck, Mendelssohn and Cornelius and many another coryphæus to Berlin, and even received Herwegh, the poet of the German revolution, in audience. Numerous *bons mots* from his lips were current in Berlin; on one occasion, leaving his box at the theatre, he found one of the lackeys asleep and remarked: " This fellow has evidently listened." On another he said: " At first the Berliners liked me so much that they wanted to eat me, now they are sorry they didn't "; and this indeed was the truth, for the rousing speeches and enthusiastic promises were followed by deep disillusionment, when it became clear that it had all been a matter of impulsive phrases, and that the new King was in no wise prepared to reform the State on up-to-date lines, but was filled with nebulous, half-poetical reminiscences of mediæval life-forms — patriarchal government, aristocratic hierarchy, vassal-loyalty, Christian State, and suchlike romantic properties that the age had long ago relegated to the dust of the antique-shop. Thus the King, tirelessly conceiving more and more plans and making more and more speeches, very soon ceased to be taken seriously, and Berlin humour turned his favourite phrase: "*das gelobe und schwöre ich*" ("that I vow and swear"), into: "*das globe ich schwerlich*" ("that I find it hard to believe"). Following Gutzkow's drama *Nero*, which showed Ludwig I of Bavaria as a Romantic tyrant who sacrificed his people to his art-mania, David Friedrich Strauss wrote on the Emperor Julian (" the Romantic on the throne of the Cæsars ") an *ouvrage à clé* that was modelled on Friedrich Wilhelm. The parallel was insipid, philistine, and distorted, like everything else by this author, since one could hardly select two more unlike persons and situations — but the name stuck to the King. And if by the term " Romantic " we mean quite generally any man who lives continuously in fancy, then Frederick William IV was the very type of a Romantic. " My situation," he wrote to Metternich shortly after his accession, " appears to me like a dream, from which I long to awake." From that dream he never awoke.

The year of his accession is memorable for another reason, for it was filled with a diplomatic conflict that almost led to a great European war. Mahemet Ali, an Albanian officer of great gifts, had succeeded in making Egypt completely independent of the Porte, which, moreover, ceded to him Crete as the price of his intervention in the Greek War of Independence, and Syria as the result of being completely defeated by his son-in-law Ibrahim. In 1839 there was a new conflict, the Egyptians were victorious at Nisib, the opposing fleet went over to their side, and the existence of Turkey seemed to be in peril. Consequently England, Russia, Austria, and Prussia concluded in the following year a Quadruple Alliance to preserve the integrity of the Turkish Empire, while France took the side of Mahemet Ali. The latter, however, had to give way before superior force and to retrocede Crete and Syria. But this the French felt as a humiliation, and in their anger revived the demand for the Rhine frontier. The alarm of war continued for a whole winter. The French, who must always revenge themselves for something or other, raised the cry: " Revenge for Waterloo! " Thiers caused Paris and Lyon to be fortified (with the double aim of protection from without and within — hence the Radicals' phrase *l'embastillement de Paris*). Hoffmann von Fallersleben wrote "*Deutschland, Deutschland über alles,*" Lamartine a " Marseillaise of Peace," Arndt " *All Deutschland in Frankreich hinein,*" Schneckenburger the "*Wacht am Rhein,*" Becker the Rhine song "*Sie sollen ihn nicht haben,*" which evoked from Musset a rejoinder in the far more artistic " *Nous l'avons eu, votre Rhin allemand,*" and from Ludwig I of Bavaria a cup of honour with the inscription " From this gilded, silvern cup, presented by me, drink often, singing the while ' *Sie sollen ihn nicht haben.*' " Even the republican poet Georg Herwegh sang " Strike in, strike in! The Rhine, the Rhine, shall ever German be," although with the cosmopolitan supplement " were it only for its wine." Of the tragic fact that France is the political madhouse of Europe and that provocation is second nature to her, there can hardly be stronger evidence than the events of 1840. For no one can pretend that this scramble of fellaheen was a reason for threatening the Palatinate. Louis Philippe, however, was far too prudent not to see the danger of his situation between two fires — the prospect of the Tsar starting a legitimist crusade of the Eastern powers, and the fact that the Republicans would seize the occasion of a war to bring about a revolution.

In this crisis England once more showed herself definitely as the leading power. It was in London that the Quadruple Alliance and the Turco-Egyptian peace were concluded. There likewise, in 1841, was signed the important Straits Agreement, to which all five of the great powers adhered, and which provided that no foreign warship might pass the Bosporus and the Dardanelles in peace time. It was directed against Russia, who eight years previously had extorted from Turkey the opening of the Bosporus for all Russian and the closing of the Dardanelles to all other vessels. In 1837 the young Queen Victoria followed her uncle on the throne, and the personal union with Hanover — where female succession did not run — was dissolved. In 1839 England occupied Aden, the key of the Red Sea, and thus provided herself with a strategic counter-pole to Gibraltar. In 1840 she waged the scandalous Opium War with China, forcing her to permit the import

Manchester

93

of Indian opium and to cede the island of Hongkong. Already she was spreading over the west and south of Australia and had subjected part of Farther India, and in the forties she also conquered the Punjab region in India proper, so obtaining a priceless sally-port against Afghanistan and Russia. We have already seen to what an astonishing extent she had outpaced the Continent in machine industry, railway-building, and steam navigation. Even then fairy-tale things like matches, wax candles, and steel pens had long been in use, and in 1840 Rowland Hill introduced the adhesive stamp and the penny post, which conveyed a letter throughout the Kingdom at a flat rate of one penny, whereas within the Prussian frontiers it still cost ten to twenty *Silbergroschen*. It was almost at the end of the forties that the main part of the German states followed this new system, and Mecklenburg-Strelitz did not do so till 1863. The conquest of vast areas of extreme fertility, combined with the development of technique, had naturally very beneficial economic consequences — though of course only for the possessing classes. The English scientist William Draper, besides being a first-rate physiologist and a pioneer in the development of photography, was Professor of " Philosophy " in New York and published a history of the American Civil War, as well as his once widely read work *History of the Intellectual Development in Europe,* which, in the Buckle manner and with the scientist's superstition, glorified the progress of the European intellect, telling the world that already in 1833 the length of the yarn spun in England in one year would have girdled the earth more than two hundred thousand times, adding: " Men have accomplished works that seem almost godlike."

The Reform Bill of 1832 secured to the industrial classes participation in Parliamentary elections. In the following year slavery was abolished in the British Colonies, less from humanitarian than from economic motives. The embitterment of the Fourth Estate broke out in tumultuary refusals to work — the organized strike was not yet known — of which the most terrible was that at Birmingham in 1839, where the workmen devastated the whole city, plundered the houses, and reduced the factories to ashes. The Duke of Wellington, who suppressed the outbreak, declared in the Upper House that he had often seen cities captured, but never witnessed horrors like this. It is inexplicable that a people so distinguished for political wisdom, a people with an experience of the problems of practical life so much richer than that of others, refused to see that the class to which it owed its entire prosperity must be adequately cared for. But it would be unfair not to mention that at all times the British cultural area has produced high-hearted idealists who have made it their business to stir the conscience of their countrymen. One of these was Richard Cobden. He recognized that the main cause of the misery in the great towns was to be found in the high cost of bread, and that this in turn was traceable to the import duties, to which the Upper House, consisting, as it did, almost entirely of great landowners, clung with short-sighted selfishness. He therefore founded the Anti-Corn-Law League (to which even the manufacturers adhered, though *their* aim was to lower wages even further when the price of bread should fall), and after a ten years' struggle he succeeded in effecting the repeal of the corn-laws. In consequence of his doctrines and demands, there developed in Manchester, the centre of the cotton industry, a new national-economic current — the so-called Manchester school — which declared for Free Trade — that is, the entire abolition of protective tariffs. In alliance with this school were the leaders of Chartism, who under the banner of the " People's Charter " championed the right of the people to a decisive share in the government; and attached to these in turn were the Irish separatists, who fiercely and tirelessly, sometimes by peaceful and sometimes by warlike means, agitated for separation from England (" repeal of the Union "). These three movements, strengthened and accelerated by energetic and skilful agitators like O'Connell and O'Connor, kept England during the thirties and forties in a state of continuous ferment. In Parliament, Tories succeeded Whigs and vice versa without either party being able to effect anything that was generally satisfactory. The Chartists demanded universal and equal franchise, secret voting, and annual elections; the Anti-Corn-Law Leaguers the abstention of the State from all interference in trade and industry; while the Irish were not far removed from anarchist principles. In these confusions Sir Robert Peel stood out as by far the most penetrating, unprejudiced, and far-seeing mind; originally a strict Tory, he had gradually taken up a Liberal attitude, and with his astounding adaptability to facts, he was able to steer a middle course between the extreme desires and demands of the parties. The fact that he frequently altered his program — although opponents denounced it as weakness and inconsistency — sprang from his healthy sense of reality, which preferred to be guided by the circumstances and conditions of each situation instead of by rigid party doctrines. In this way he succeeded in managing the Irish question so as at least to avoid a catastrophe, in guiding the Chartist movement into Parliamentary forms, and in pushing the cause of Free Trade to victory in the most important cases.

The Social Question

The first practical experiments in the field of social service were made (without state support of any kind) by the noble Robert Owen, whose works, further, made the word " Socialism " world-famous, though its actual inventor was the Saint-Simonist Pierre Leroux. His Socialism, however, was a socialism from above, just as Liberalism from above had been the ideal of the Emperor Joseph II. He shortened the hours in his workshops, which employed over two thousand souls; he introduced unemployment aid, provided hygienic work-rooms and free treatment of sickness, he built houses, schools, and mess-rooms and worked up a vigorous agitation for improved factory legislation and the organization of the workers. He also attempted to formulate a scientific theory of Communism. Proudhon also was regarded as a Communist, on account of his famous saying: " Property is theft," but it is important to note that this remark was directed against inactive State-protected *property* — that is, dividends and interest, house-rents and land-rents, sinecures and privileges and the like — and not against private *possessions*. Property, he said, is the source of all abuses, but possession (consisting simply in the use of what one has produced or worked up) excludes every possibility of abuse; possession is the condition, property the suicide, of human society, the former is lawful, the latter unlawful. Far from thinking that private possession should be abolished, he regarded it as the necessary spur to effort, the basis of the family and the source of all progress, and he desired that every man should be a private possessor. Communism, for him, was only an inverted kind of property, an exploitation of the strong by the weak just as its predecessor had been one of the weak by the strong, and both are theft. True justice rests not on equality of possessions, but on equality of service, on " mutualism." Naturally, therefore, Marx called him a bourgeois. Actually, Proudhon is the first representative of logical anarchism, for he regarded the power of the State as the principal criminal and would have liked it abolished in every form. The Free Trade school found an enemy in Louis Blanc, who proclaimed that free competition was just what favoured exploitation, and that therefore the State must make itself the master of all production. From Switzerland Wilhelm Weitling, a tailor's apprentice of Magdeburg, sent out a stream of Communist pamphlets with a Christian colouring, and those were widely read by the workers in Germany. In 1844 there occurred the rising of the Silesian weavers which Hauptmann made the subject of his "*Schauspiel aus den Vierzigerjahren.*" The conditions that led to this despairing outburst are described by the economist Alfred Zimmermann in his book *Blüte und Verfall des Leinengewerbes in Schlesien:* " No children played in the streets, for the children had to add their weak efforts to the work of their parents. Even the barking of dogs, once heard in every village, was stilled, for the people had no food for them and were glad themselves to devour these faithful guardians. . . . Most families never saw meat . . . it was a glad event when a peasant brought his family some buttermilk or potato peelings." One June day the weavers invaded and demolished the house and factory of the Zwanziger firm in Peterswaldau. " The work of revenge was accomplished in a deep silence, broken only by the crashes of breaking furniture and machines." Two companies of infantry, which meantime arrived on the scene, fired first over the heads of the assailants. These replied with a shower of stones, and thereupon the troops fired a second volley, killing some of the workmen. But the mass was not in the least cowed by this, and fresh showers of stones drove the troops to retreat. After some more buildings had been destroyed, however, the outbreak suddenly died away and everything was as before. All that remains of that day is the queer song *Das Blutgericht,* which then circulated among the masses (" You rascals all, you Satan's spawn, you demons of hell, you devour the poor man's all, and curses shall be your reward "), and Heine's *Weberlied* (" Curse the King, the rich man's King, who could not milden our misery, but squeezes the last penny out of us and shoots us like dogs. We weave, we weave ") . It was at this time, too, that there began the great current of emigration which was directed especially towards North America, and the newly-coined phrase " tired of Europe " became the motto of large numbers of the people. The only public institution of Germany in which some progress could be shown was the school. In 1841 Fröbel started the first kindergarten, and Johann Friedrich Herbart, Professor of Philosophy of Königsberg, founded a " training school for teaching," at which was taught his new educational method, based not on mere knowledge, but on character-formation, on

97

ethics as assigning the aim, and on psychology as determining the method; this was in conformity with his philosophy, which deduced all spiritual processes from the reciprocal action of ideas — their fusion, linkage, or mutual interference, their passing from the evident to the latent state and vice versa, their " rise " and " fall " — and just as physical motions are capable of mathematical representation, so Herbart attempted to establish a series of formulæ for his psychological mechanics.

Friedrich List

While the " Red International " had, for the time being, little success to show, with the " Golden International " it was the very reverse. One of its manifestations was the formation of extended customs unions. The Manchester school aimed at nothing less than a Pan-European customs union. In France all internal tolls had long been abolished, and at the beginning of the forties there were considerable negotiations towards a Franco-Belgian customs union, which would have succeeded but for the French industrialists' fear of Belgian competition. The German Zollverein was in essence the work of Friedrich List. When he submitted to the Diet a bill for the abolition of all internal tariffs, he was condemned to imprisonment and only amnestied on promising to emigrate to America. In Pennsylvania he discovered a coal-field, the exploitation of which made him a prosperous man. But to him, as he said himself, Germany was as a crippled child to its mother — the more infirm her child, the greater her love. He settled in Leipzig as American Consul, and there worked unwearyingly for the two ideas nearest his heart, the economic unification of Germany, and the development of a railway system, to which he sacrificed his energies, his health, and his money. The theory from which he started was that a nation's economy passes through three stages; at first rural economy prevails, then agriculture and industry, and lastly agriculture, industry, and trade. In the first stage, free dealing is natural, for rural economy must export its raw material and import the craft-products it needs without hindrance; in the second stage, the State must protect the young industries as one protects children and growing orchards and vineyards, and here consequently he recommends the tariff system, though it must only be as a system of education to be dispensed with in the third stage. In List's view, Spain and Portugal were at that time in the first, Germany and the United States at the second, and England in the third. Therefore, he concluded, the European nations must unite against the mercantile supremacy of

England, and the Continental embargo must be revived in a peaceful form until England had realized that she could only be a first among equals. In spite of this hostile attitude, List was better understood and appreciated in England than in Germany; and when he visited London, he was treated by the leading statesmen and by Parliament with distinction. However, the Zollverein eventually came into being in spite of all. Its beginnings go back to the year 1818, in which the internal and economic union of the Prussian possessions was effected; the Prussian enclaves joined in, then Hesse-Darmstadt, Anhalt, Hesse-Cassel, Bavaria and Württemberg, Saxony and Thuringia, which, after concluding agreements partly amongst themselves and partly with Prussia, eventually drew all together into the Prussian-German Zollverein. At the stroke of midnight on the memorable New Year's Eve of 1833, the customs barriers were thrown open throughout four fifths of Germany amidst universal jubilation. List's ideas, however, went much further still; he desired the adhesion, not only of the Hanse towns, but of Belgium and Holland as well, for, he said, a German Zollverein without the mouth of the Rhine was like a house whose door belonged to a stranger; he also pointed to the possibilities of its eastward extension, through Austria and Hungary and Turkey, and he called for the creation of a German fleet, for a nation without shipping was like a bird without wings, a fish without fins, a lion without teeth. But the general incomprehension, the malicious attacks continually made upon him, financial worries, and torturing nervous headaches so embittered him that he shot himself at Kufstein in 1846.

In literature the social note was struck first and most strongly in England. The master in it was Charles Dickens, who described the scandals of the factory system, the school system, the poor-law system, and class justice with a simplicity rooted in knowledge of life, and a humour rooted in compassion. His attacks, from the very fact that they were wholly without gall and purely poetic, made a profound impression at the time and have retained an imperishable freshness. Other great poets have their ups and downs in the esteem of later generations, but this noble child will for ever remain one of mankind's darlings. And yet even this angelically pure spirit paid honour to the dæmon of his age, in that he let himself be persuaded into gold-digging in the form of lucrative lecture tours, which wore out too soon his splendid vital energies. In these years of confusion, however, there appeared the strongest moral potentiality that the Anglo-Saxon race has ever brought forth, Thomas Carlyle.

It is uncommonly easy to criticize Carlyle, and it is uncommonly difficult to praise him. Anyone who has read even part of his works can without difficulty discover in him a whole series of mistakes and inadequacies. He repeats himself, he contradicts himself, he exaggerates, he writes obscurely and fantastically, his passion is overheated, his tempo unsteady, his thought unordered and baroque.

All these defects and many more can be discovered and exactly specified right away, whereas when one sets out to say, with an equal brevity, what virtues should be set against them, one is in difficulties. If, for instance, we were to say that Carlyle had temperament, keenness of thought, fine psychological sensitiveness, the gift of plastic character-portrayal, that he was quaint, thrilling, and ingenious, we should have said nothing about him that really matters, or got any nearer to him. Quite probably all this is true, but it is irrelevant. Everyone who knows his Carlyle feels inevitably that one cannot arrive at Carlyle by firing such attributes at him, for they all glance off him.

We are baffled even by the central problem of putting him in this or that category of writers. Is he a philosopher, or a historian, a critic, a sociologist, a biographer, an æsthetic, a romancer? Is he all these together, or is he perchance none of them? Is he, for that matter, even a writer? He himself answered this question in the negative, saying that literature was the thing above all for which he was least fitted, and that he would have been a better and happier man if he had been taught even the simplest practical activity. This self-judgment by a man whose books have circulated in hundreds of thousands may at first blush be surprising, but as soon as one looks into it more closely, one finds some truth in it. That is, if by a writer one means a human being who has the gift of fluently and brilliantly presenting his observations and sensations, who has learnt how to give out, evidently and easily, everything that is in him — in a word, one who is thoroughly able to express his impressions — then most assuredly Carlyle was no writer. Literary work, for him, was never anything but a torture, and no man ever suffered more from inhibitions and resistances to production. When he was full of material, he felt as though he were walking under a heavy load, he experienced nothing but an intolerable pressure. The joy of creation was entirely lacking to him. And even finished work, in his case, bears the traces of his struggle with the material. The basic character of his style is a strange combination of vividness and heaviness; it is a style that makes one doubt at every instant whether it should be called ardent or crabbed. It carries the reader away and yet is ever painfully wrestling with itself; now stumbling over itself with vigour, now lame-footed and hanging back, formless and formal, and with its innumerable interpolations, qualifications, references back, sudden parentheses, tied-on supplements, and disrupting interjections it is the despair of many a reader. But this precisely is what gives Carlyle's prose its unique rhythm.

If we were to try to describe Carlyle's nature in one word, we might perhaps, drawing on his own vocabulary, call him a Hero as Thinker. What Carlyle attempted and achieved was to discover the various manifestations of heroism in all human activities. One form of it only he overlooked, the Hero as Thinker, and for the very simple reason that he himself was its embodiment. And yet this one is precisely the most effective and comprehensive of them all. The thinker is, so to say, the universal hero, comprising all the Carlylean forms within himself. He is prophet, poet, priest, writer, organizer, in one person. His influence lasts longest and strikes deepest. And he is not only the mightiest form of heroism, but also the purest, the humanly greatest, for the very reason that he does not seek his goal in concrete action. Every action presupposes a certain amount of limitedness, blindness, injustice; always its content is only a definite given and momentary truth. But the thinker wills the whole, he understands, sees through, sees into everything, he cognizes everything in terms of its individual justification.

This does not, however, imply that the Thinker must from indifferentism and lack of temperament admit validity for anything and everything. On the contrary, every genuine Thinker is also a passionate reformer, and consequently the tone in which he speaks is very frequently uncompromising and arbitrary. It is not enough for him to have discovered truths for himself, he wants to make them the possession of the whole world, to bring them to it whether it wills or no. He carries things in his heart that imperiously drive him outwards, things that he would like to shout into everyone's ear, to write on every door-post, to placard at every street-corner.

These traits determined Carlyle's creativeness. He felt himself not as the author of books, but as the vessel of a mission. The form was a matter of indifference to him. He repeats his key-phrases again and again like refrains, for he knows that one must proclaim a truth a hundred times before one man will believe it. He is as immoderate in praise and blame as a crude and good-natured school-teacher. He *always* goes too far, and with intent. But, after all, are not all genuine and profound feelings " exaggerated," hyperbolical, hypertrophied — and for that very reason productive? We could almost say that all truly live feelings are more than life-sized. Carlyle's technique consisted simply in willingly letting himself be carried away by every strong impression, right to its last and extreme consequence or inconsequence — the technique of *every* great artist. Withal, Carlyle was not wanting in the balancing element of self-irony; a close observer can sometimes detect him in laughing at himself behind it all.

His utterances, for all that they are so subjective in form, are founded upon the most sensitive feeling for the right that can be imagined. The fact that he so often contradicts himself is only the natural consequence of his love of truth. He would sooner contradict himself than the facts. These are his one and only guide, for this extreme idealist and ideologue is at the same time the most practical, shrewd, and factual realist. His gifts of vision are extraordinary. Although he always starts from certain abstractions, he never writes in the least abstractly; nay, he has the capacity for so vivifying ideas that they become actual entities, personal friends and enemies. He himself possessed in the highest degree the quality that he was accustomed to call " vision." Always and unerringly he hits the heart of everything, whatever the domain to which it may belong.

In such a mind all things had necessarily to join together of themselves in a world-picture. Facts have an irresistible affinity for facts and fit themselves together automatically. The decisive element is that mysterious gift of " vision "; we might say that this by itself already constituted a complete world-view, if not, indeed, the only world-view worthy of the name.

The seer of souls To understand Carlyle's unique position in English literature we must bear in mind that he was a Scotsman, and moreover from the Lowlands, where the Celtic admixture is much smaller than in the Highlands, and the Lower German element is stronger even than it is in the English. Although he did not write in the special dialect of his home, as his countryman Burns had done, but in the ordinary literary English, it would be clumsy to call him an English author. What is truly un-English is his whole way of looking at things; in his thought it is the Scottish national character that speaks, with its contradictions and enigmas, its strange combination of dreaminess and day-shrewdness, moody irritability and sturdy resistance, melancholy and humour, selfishness and adaptability, aloofness and sociability. All these are found in Carlyle, and often in that queer magnification with which men of genius embody the characteristics of their peoples.

Finally, we must not forget that Carlyle came of a people that is credited with the gift of " second sight." This faculty may or may not be demonstrable, but that Carlyle possessed it, in another and higher sense, admits of no doubt; if one tried to summarize his essence and significance in the shortest possible way, one would call him a seer of souls.

The first half of Carlyle's life was devoted to German literature. He read Goethe and Schiller, Novalis and Jean Paul, recognized at once that here was an entirely new world of thought and creation as apart from and as far above the English as the heavens, and determined to reveal these new values to his countrymen. In this, however, he met with the greatest resistance. In England the new German literature was regarded as an attempt to give a new validity to view-points that had long been abandoned. Goethe appeared to most people as a man who had lost himself in abstruse mysticism; few of his works were known, and there was no desire to widen the acquaintance. In William Taylor's history of German literature, the only existing book on the subject, its development was stated to culminate in Kotzebue. Not that there was little interest in historical and æsthetic questions; the number of serious reviews that prospered proves the contrary. But the art-form which these cultivated was wholly unlike Carlyle's, it was in fact chattiness dignified by scientific accuracy and tasteful presentation. The most important and popular representative of this form was Lord Macaulay. His continued vogue is explained primarily by the fact that he combined two qualities that would have been self-evident in a Classical author, but are extremely rare in a modern: namely, the possession of wide knowledge and the power of imparting it to others. His lessons are as nourishing as they taste nice, and his works are entertaining in the best sense of the word. Everything, however tough or dry, became under his hands enjoyable and salubrious, and that without the slightest

Only a lord

derogation on his part. The fineness of his education and the sureness of his eye for men, astonishing as these were, never obtruded themselves. His method of investigation was all-round, penetrating, calm, and dignified. And with all this his intellect had an exceptionally wide range, for his studies embraced philosophy, religious history, manners and customs, war, politics, economic history, philology, æsthetics, biography, and literary criticism and covered half a millennium of the European Culture. It is hard to decide which of Macaulay's works is the best, since each one of them shows his rare qualities in union — his immense and always ready memory, his brilliant gift of combination, his art of grouping endless sets of facts in broad lines and of making intricate linkages plain, his faculty of turning thousands of little details into bright and multi-coloured mosaics.

Few thinkers have been as prudent as Macaulay, and almost none so distinguished for manners. He was always the lord, in dress as in other things, well-groomed, courteous, full of tact and good form — probably the most elegant author that ever wrote in the English language, but with an elegance that consisted above all in noble simplicity. Everything was " just right "; had attitude and style in it; every word was in its right place, he never said too much or too little, and the ensemble floats in a benevolent aura of beautiful sincerity — which, however, sprang not so much from breadth or warmth of heart as from a fine and well-ordered intellect and is therefore only apparent and assumed, for just as it is precisely in the best salons that one hears the most poisonous stupidities, so behind the literary good breeding of Macaulay there lurks often the malice and partiality of a fanatical Whig.

In truth, as has already been indicated, Macaulay's way of seeing the linkages of things was, for all its breadth and insight, juridical. It is true that as a rule (though not always) he disdained to confront men or events in the manner of an advocate or public prosecutor; on the contrary, he was at pains to play the objective rôle of the presiding judge. But as we all know, even the presiding judge represents a definite outlook on society and can never be wholly objective; he is and remains the mouthpiece and defender of certain definite and extremely one-sided laws. Even apart from that, Macaulay's conception of world-history as a trial-at-law to be decided by the enlightened judgment of the " present time " satisfies neither the needs of an artistic view of the world nor the demands of a higher ethic; what speaks in it is the complacent, narrow-browed, disputatious morality of the second class, which is the hall-mark and stigma of all bourgeois periods. We can see him, the just and enlightened Liberal, proud of civilization, elevated by the possession of artificial manures and steam engines, free press and free vote, and passing judgment as he calls up Past, Present, and Future before his register.

Macaulay was very fond, on occasion, of putting poets and poetry in their places like a schoolmaster; for instance, he says of eighteenth-century English literature that "it contained no poetry of the very highest class, and little which could be placed very high in the second class," and of the Latin poems that have been written in modern times: "None of those poems can be ranked in the first class of art, or even very high in the second." If one were to attempt a succinct judgment upon Macaulay, one would probably have to say precisely the same, using the same terms, but with a variation in his favour: namely, that he does not belong to the first class of men who have chosen the pen as their medium of expression, but in the second class he stands very high up. One sees this at once when one compares him with Carlyle, the rough peasant's son from Annandale, for whom form is nothing and feeling everything, whose sentences shoot forth as the water of a mountain stream over stones and bushes, whose thoughts violently discharge outwards like the red-hot eruptions of a volcano, who was never prepared to serve any other cause but the thing which he had to describe, and who by criticism never understood blame, but inspired re-experience, for, in his own phrase, before we reproach a man for what he is not, we had better make it clear what he is. This phrase contains Carlyle's whole criticism. Even his essay on Voltaire, whom he felt as his very antipodes, became for him, insensibly, an artist's portrait of the great Revolutionary of literature.

With Carlyle's removal to London began, not merely outwardly, but inwardly as well, a new phase of his life. Hitherto his intellectual creativity had been predominantly directed to literature; it was from the world of books that he had expected to get certainties and consolations; and the particular guides that he had chosen, the German poets and thinkers of the eighteenth century, necessarily had the effect of confirming him in this direction towards pure theory. Like Faust, he began as a scholar monologuing in the study. But now his spiritual evolution took a decisive turn towards life. And although the roots of this decision

Carlyle's faith

105

lay deep in his nature, and it had long been maturing below the surface, yet it did mean an entire reversal of the principles, methods, and aims that governed his intellectual activity.

He lived now in the largest, most vigorous, and most modern city of Europe and was forced to come to a working compromise with the actualities that surrounded him. For him it was impossible henceforth to make a clean division between theory and practice, to devote himself wholly to his own inward perfection and leave the work of perfecting the outer world to others, to live the quiet life of a thinker or artist and create merely in parallel with life. He saw the abuses, and he felt himself compelled and in duty bound to speak of them. In all strata of society he saw the indications of degeneracy. Modern life seemed to him one monstrous system of deception, to which even the most honest and worthy had unconsciously to adapt themselves. This hostility to the present — which on the Continent only found its representatives much later, because the pace of economic development there was slower — forms the thoroughbass in all that Carlyle wrote during the next decades. The peculiarity of the position that he took up (which at the time only very few rightly judged) was the entire absence of partisanship and party spirit in it. He has been called a Tory, because he fought against the democratic dogma of equality; a Whig, because on occasion he declared the aristocracy to be parasitic idlers, and the established Church a hypocritical institution; a Peelite, because he was in harmony with Peel; a Chartist, because he stood for the uplifting of the working classes; a Radical, because he wrote against the corn-laws; a black reactionary, because he described the abolition of slavery in the Colonies as a useless piece of sentimentality. And in fact, if one must apply such labels, he was a little of all these things. His criterion was, everywhere and always, the truth, and whoever seemed to have the truth in him, to him and his party Carlyle was attracted. But the public wants a definite label for every public phenomenon, and such a capacity as Carlyle's for adaptation to things only confuses and disillusions it.

The leitmotiv of his political writings is protest against flabby Liberalism and its desire to level down, its *laissez faire*, its platform volubility and phrase-making. The fundamental offences of the time, for him, were Jesuitry, general dishonesty and make-believe; the doctrines of Loyola had outwardly been repudiated, but inwardly had become the creed of almost every Englishman, and a subtle poison of lies had permeated the whole of society. The remedy he saw, not at all in parliamentary reform, universal suffrage, or the like, but in a wise and humane government which regarded the worker not as a mere tool, but as something to be cared for in soul and in body; for the very fact of its social independence had put the proletariat in a wretched position of dependence upon the employers, its freedom being little more than a freedom to starve. In his *Past and Present*, basing himself on an old monkish chronicle of the twelfth century, he describes the monastic life of that age, not with a Romanticist halo, but as the practising of a healthy realism. These men of the Middle Ages still knew what honest work, honest obedience, and honest governance meant. They willingly let themselves be ruled by better and stronger men. The relation between sovereign and subject, lord and vassal, master and serf, was primarily a moral relation, based on reciprocal loyalties, and not a mere material one based on exploitation. The relations of men were regulated, not by the law of supply and demand, but by the law of God. The practical application of all this to the present did not at all imply that we ought to return to the conditions of those days, but we could perfectly well take over what was good in them into our own. Two things, above all, these men of old could teach us: their belief in higher things, and their sanctification of work. Inequality is the natural state; it is only right and convenient that the wiser and more capable should rule over the rest. Work is not something that can be bought with pieces of money; honest work is something that concerns God: *laborare est orare*.

In his *The French Revolution: a History*, his object was to warn his countrymen by example. He saw in this "immense conflagration" a sort of divine judgment upon false rulers and priests who, without the justification of real superiority, had made laws to suit themselves against the rest; he showed the extremity at which man arrives when misled and embittered by intolerable injustice. The form of presentation is unique. The rich background is the technique of a genius of decorative painting, and in front of it performs, under flickering beams of light, an unreal puppet-world. Twenty years later Carlyle published the first two volumes of his *Frederick the Great*. He did not, certainly, idealize Frederick as one of the great men of faith, but he did look upon him as one who, in the middle of a century of false coinage and windy emptiness, never lied to another unless he had to do so, and never in any case to himself, and who, by his self-sacrificing loyalty to duty, his tireless working power, and his gift of seeing things just as they really were, built up Prussia as a great power. "You have," said Bismarck to Carlyle, "given us Germans our great Prussian King in his full stature. You have presented him as a living column-statue." In truth, not only for England, but for Germany also, Carlyle created the first real portrait of Frederick. And it is a memorial not only of Frederick, but of his whole period; the numerous figures grouped about him appear in the ensemble; he works them out, each according to his rank and significance, carefully or sketchily, on a large scale or a small, in the round, high relief or low relief, but he forgets none of them. Much in the work appeared later as prophetic, for only a year after this the Hohenzollern State made its reckoning with the "Habsburg chimera."

Carlyle's most representative work is his *On Heroes, Hero-Worship and the Heroic in History*. It rests upon a single great thought, around which all the rest order themselves unforcedly and yet imperatively, and, as in all significant and fruitful books, this thought is quite simple and almost obvious. Hitherto a hero had been imagined as something splendid and even processional, a stock pageant-figure. Carlyle, however, demonstrated that what distinguishes the hero above the rest is precisely his simplicity, his unvocal, unselfish activity in the service of an idea that fills him and leads him mysteriously onward. His principal characteristic is that he always speaks the truth, always stands on facts; all other characteristics are secondary. He is the bravest man, but his bravery has nothing dazzling or theatrical about it: he engages in no wondrous adventures with dragons and sorcerers, but fights the far more difficult fight with actuality.

This, more or less, is the unique discovery of Carlyle. Superficially it is self-evident to the point of being commonplace, but underneath it signifies a complete inversion of ideas as to the nature and activity of great men. It consists, to sum it up in a sentence, in the clear and resolute divorce of the Germanic from the Latin ideal of hero. The hero as the Latin imagination conceives him is the knight, the cavalier. He carries his feelings on his tongue, and his courage on the end of his sword. He is highly sensitive to the point of honour, but less so to the point of duty. He knows how to bear himself nobly, to talk wittily and hold intercourse with ladies. He is very precise in things of good breeding and picturesque nobility, but less so in things of moral uprightness.

His whole life is a novel, exciting, brilliant, full of feeling, and not always true. He is a luxury product. The Germanic hero is the reverse of all this; he is a real, an unadorned, and often an unattractive necessity.

Carlyle's ethical demand can be summarized in a very short formula, as belief in the God-given truth of facts. This commandment includes all the rest in itself. He who follows it will of himself be a religious and a moral man, a gifted and effective man, an upright and brave and wise man. He will lead a beautiful and a useful life, in harmony with destiny, nature, and men.

It is an acid test of souls: on it are decided the destinies of the individual and the nation. They can confess the simple and clarifying faith of Carlyle. Or they can agree with Napoleon III, who with a like simplicity and clarity said: " Carlyle is mad."

Carlyle is one of those thinkers who, because he has no other system but that of his humanity, can never age, whereas the greatest contemporary effect is usually obtained by the systematics. Such a systematic, and one ranking among the highest, was Hegel. When he died, in 1831, his world-dominance was compared with that of Alexander, and the parallel holds to this extent, that, like Alexander's, it fell to pieces at once at his death and was fiercely disputed among his Diadochi. His proposition that all actual was reasonable, and all reasonable actual, admitted of a double interpretation. If the first half only is taken, the result is a sort of mystical conservatism, while if the emphasis be placed on the second half, we come out at revolutionary Rationalism. Further, Hegel regarded philosophy and religion as in essence identical, which could be interpreted in the orthodox and supra-naturalistic sense, but at the same time he declared that they were expressions of the same content in different languages, and that what the believer looked upon as a unique historical fact and concrete dogma was for the philosopher only a timeless symbol and universal idea; and this view might well be the starting-point for the disintegration of all positive religion. Consequently the school of Hegel divided into two hostile parties, which David Friedrich Strauss was the first to call the " Right " and the " Left." The first, or " Old Hegelians," entrenched themselves in the ideas of the fading Romantic and the ecclesiastical and political Restoration, while the second, or " Young Hegelians," fought for " progress in the consciousness of freedom." They found their central organ in the *Hallische Jahrbücher für Wissenschaft und Kunst,* founded by Ruge and

Echtermeyer in 1838, and they launched the famous "Manifesto against Romanticism." The centre of the leftward theology was the " Tübingen school "; its head was Ferdinand Christian Baur, the creator of scientific dogma-history, who in his work on the first three centuries of Christianity presented the growth of the Catholic Church as the synthesis resulting from the two antitheses of Judaic proto-Christianity and Pauline pagan Christianity, of Messianism and Universalism, and in his *Kritik des Johannesevangeliums* established the late origin and derivative character of the fourth Gospel. 1835, the year of the reappearance of Halley's comet and of the celebrated " comet vintage," was signalized in Germany by some events of deep importance; it saw the first German railway, the catastrophe of " Young Germany," Wilhelm Vatke's *Religion des Alten Testaments*, and *Das Leben Jesu, kritisch bearbeitet,* of David Friedrich Strauss. The first of these two books, which was the foundation of modern historical criticism of the books of the Old Covenant, attracted little or no attention, although it was far more serious and profound than Strauss's. The latter, on the contrary, excited an unparalleled amount of notice. It produced about fifty rejoinders — among them a parody entitled *La Vie de Strauss écrite en 2839,* which appeared in Paris in 1839 and dealt with Strauss's own life as a myth. The basic idea of the Life of Jesus, developed in some fifteen hundred pages — rather on the lines of searching dialectic than of historical narrative — was once more Hegelian. The myth-idea which it introduced was regarded as a synthesis of the two elucidations previously attempted: namely, the supernatural, which stuck to the miracles and the direct divine interventions, and the rationalistic, which tried (by means of hypotheses so tortured and sophistical as to verge on the imbecile) to explain all the events of the Gospel story by natural causes — the healings, for example, by suggestion, the raisings from the dead by coma, the walking on the water by mist-illusion, the miraculous feedings of the multitude by the introduction of wealthy disciples, the changing of water into wine by the supposition of secret stores. According to Strauss, the Gospels were neither revelation nor history, but products of the folk-soul, off-spring of the common consciousness, myths such as every religion possesses; a myth is " any unhistorical tale, however it may have arisen, in which a religious community is conscious of some particular part of its own sacred foundations; in fact, an absolute expression of the thoughts and feelings constitutionally belonging to it." " The key to all Christology is to put, as subject of the predicate which the Church attaches to Christ, not an individual, but an idea — a real idea, however, and not a Kantian unreality. Imagined as embodied in an individual, a God-Man, the properties and functions ascribed to Christ by ecclesiastical dogma are mutually contradictory, but in the idea of the genus they fuse. *Humanity itself* is the union of the two natures, the God become Man, the infinite resigned to the finite, and the finite spirit mindful of its infiniteness. It is child of the visible Mother and the invisible Father, spirit and nature. It is *miracle-worker,* inasmuch as in the course of human development the spirit more and more fully masters nature (in himself and in his ambiance), which is subordinated to him as powerless material for him to work upon. It is *sinless,* in that the course of its evolution is without reproach, for uncleanness adheres only to the individual and does not exist as regards the genus and its history." The result of all this soothing micro-analysis — which assumes that the Early Christian community had sat at the feet of Professor Hegel — is of course that humanity, in virtue of its evolution " without reproach," is itself the sinless God-Man, which was no doubt an immense relief to the Strauss-reading public of stock-jobbers, newspaper-liars, and mishandlers of workmen. The degree of comprehension which Strauss had of the phenomenon of the Saviour will be gathered from the following characterization, which appears in one of his later works: " Everything relating to love of God and love of one's neighbour, to individual purity of heart and life, was completely developed in him, but even *the life of man in his family* takes a subordinate place for this teacher without a family; his relation to the State appears as a wholly passive one: business is not only declined as regards himself, as a career, but also openly spurned, and everything whatever relating to *art and enjoyment of the beauty of life* lies completely outside his field of view . . . and it is a vain undertaking to try to determine the activity of man as citizen, or his efforts to enrich and beautify life by business and art, from the precepts or example of Jesus." In truth, such an undertaking *is* quite futile.

The immense effect of Strauss's work is one of the curiosities of literary history. It would be more readily understandable if it had been an amusing piece of *belles lettres* or piquant polemic, but in fact it was nothing but an essay in pedantic scholarship swollen to gigantic proportions. The attempt has been made to account for its success by Strauss's "classic" style, but the few examples given above will have already shown the reader that even in this regard he is not specially attractive, or, for that matter, faultlessly clear. Strauss's stylistic merits are much more conspicuous in his later works, *Christliche Glaubenslehre, Das Leben Jesu, für das deutsche Volk bearbeitet;* the same may be said of *Der alte und der neue Glaube* (to be dealt with presently), though on the other hand it far surpasses his first work in complacent banality and hidebound cocksureness. In these he employs a slow and unmusical, but yet transparent and powerful, style, and his pictures are precise and clean, even though dry and, often, all too deliberately calculated; as regards presentation, they are about on the level of an exceptionally successful school-anniversary address.

Catholic theology   In Catholic theology too, there were new tendencies. Adam Möhler, who died as dean of Würzburg Cathedral when only forty-one, produced in his *Symbolik oder Darstellung der dogmatischen Gegensätze der Katholiken und Protestanten* (1832) an apologia of Catholicism, critical and yet kindly, by far the strongest, subtlest, and worthiest work of its kind in the nineteenth century, in which, incidentally (as is frequently the case with such gifted natures), he justified neither party without reserve, neither the Protestants nor the strict Catholics — who accused him in consequence of heresy. Truth, in fact, is apt to occupy a middle place and to find itself there solitary or with one companion at most. On both sides a vigorous controversy set in, though, as Karl von Hase admits in his *Handbuch der protestantischen Polemik gegen die römisch-katholische Kirche,* none of the rejoinders to Möhler's work came anywhere near it in weight. In England, about the middle of the thirties the so-called "Oxford Movement" began, with as its aim the Catholicizing of the Anglican Church. Of this Anglo-Catholicism — called also Puseyism from its founder, Ritualism from its attempt to reintroduce the ritual, and Tractarianism from the tracts which spread its doctrines — the outstanding representative was John Henry Newman, who was originally a no-popery Methodist and later entered the Roman Church and became a Cardinal, but always championed the cause of Union, striving in numerous writings to prove the Catholic validity of Anglicanism and to emphasize the nobility of the Roman tradition.

Kierkegaard and Stirner   A theologian in his way, too, was the Dane Sören Aaby Kierkegaard, one of the most original and remarkable writers of his time, a " *Janus bifrons,*" as he himself said, sceptic and *homo religiosus,* sentimentalist and cynic, melancholic and humorist. The character of his spirit is shown in this aphorism of his: " Ask me about anything you like, but do not demand reasons! You forgive a young girl if she is unable to produce reasons, because, as they say, she lives on feelings. But with me it is different. I have so many and usually so contradictory reasons that for this reason I can give no reasons." In his bizarre and many-faceted writings, in which he mystified himself and the rest of the world alike — even in his titles, in which he sometimes went so far as to call himself the editor of an editor, and with a pseudonym to boot — he hid and revealed a profound and gentle heart. " From my youth upward," he said, " I have been stirred by the thought that in every generation there are two or three who are sacrificed to the rest, in that they discover with terrible anguish something by which the rest profit; and sorrowfully I found that the key to my own being was that I was destined to be one of these." He was not one of those who, as he says elsewhere, " reach a life's result like schoolboys who get behind the teacher and write down the answer to their sums without having worked them." He bought his psychological knowledge by great sufferings, which were less of an external than of an inward sort. His craving to disentangle every spiritual emotion and find the last secrets of its structure made him permanently unhappy, though this did not prevent him from now and then producing masterpieces of playful irony and good humour. His fight for Christian thought in the midst of an era of empty façade-belief and imbecile anti-religion is tragic. " Luther had ninety-five theses; I should have only one, that Christianity does not exist." " So much is true, for, if the state of the Church in those days was Christian, then the New Testament could no longer serve as the Christian guide, because the axiom on which it is based — namely, conscious opposition to the world — has gone," but " men have always from of old managed to find a way of ridding themselves of the burden of weighty problems, the simple way — be a chatterer, and lo, all difficulties vanish! "

Quite off the main line, too, stands Johann Kaspar Schmidt, who under the pseudonym of Max Stirner (a nickname given him as a student, from his conspicuously high forehead) published in 1845 *Der Einzige und sein Eigentum.* At first it was taken so little seriously that even the authorities declined to confiscate it, as it was " too absurd " to suppose that it could ever be dangerous; and even today it is widely misunderstood. Some regard Stirner as a charlatan, others — such as his most meritorious biographer and editor, John Henry Mackay — as one of the great geniuses of philosophy. The first among later writers to draw attention to the *Einzige* was Eduard von Hartmann, who went so far as to say that the work "in point of style was in no way inferior to Nietzsche's writings, and in philosophical content towered above them." It is quite correct that the Stirner-renaissance of the last decades is connected with the rise of the Nietzschean philosophy, although the connexion is only a very superficial one. Nietzsche himself, it is patent, never read Stirner; otherwise, with his love for all literary "outsiders," he would certainly have mentioned him more than once. Nor does it admit of doubt that the *Einzige*, with its rich and vivid dialectic and its captivating power of thinking things to a finish, is one of those conceptions that contain a whole class of thought in themselves alone. According to Stirner, only the isolated individual exists, the "*Einzige*," and all else is his property, his "*Eigentum*." This leads to the negation in principle of all religious, ethical, political, and social obligations. "My cause is neither God's nor man's, but just mine." This clever fancy, for it is no more, is then applied in the most ingenious, boldest, and most logical fashion to all fields of life and knowledge, only to emerge — and herein lies its splendid inconsequence — in a new altruism. For to the question whether one should therefore livingly participate at all in the person of another he replies: "On the contrary, I can gladly sacrifice innumerable satisfactions to him, I can forgo innumerable things to heighten *his* pleasure and cast away things that to me without him would be the dearest of all, my life, my welfare, my freedom. For it constitutes my pleasure and my happiness to bask in his pleasure and his happiness. But *me, myself*, I do not sacrifice to him, but remain an egoist — and enjoy him." Moreover, in numerous other passages he expresses a sublime spiritualism: "The Christian has spiritual interests, for he permits himself to be a spiritual man. These interests, in their purity, the Jew does not understand in the least, because he does not permit himself to attribute *no value at all* to things. . . . Their *soullessness* alienates the Jews for ever from the Christians. The Classical acuteness and penetration is as remote from the soul and spirituality of Christianity as earth from heaven. He who feels himself a free spirit is not oppressed and worried by the things of this world, for he does not regard them. If one feels their burden, it is because one is still limited enough to attach *weight* to them. . . . The Classical civilization as it drew to a close won for the first time its property in the world by having broken down the world's power and 'divinity' and recognized its impotence and 'jealousy.' It is the same with the *spirit*. When I have reduced it to a *ghost*, and its power over me to a scarecrow, then it is to be regarded as dethroned, deconsecrate, dedivinized, and I *use* it, just as unconcernedly as one uses Nature." So Stirner, for all his caricature-like exaggeration, comes very near to the " magic idealism " that Novalis preached.

The founder of the so-called wish-theology was Ludwig Feuerbach, son of the famous criminologist Anselm, Ritter von Feuerbach. He began as a pupil of Hegel, but soon diverged from him, in that he regarded the " Absolute Spirit " as the departed spirit of theology still hovering ghostlike around the Hegelian philosophy, and the latter as only apparently the negation of theology and in reality just theology over again. His principal works are *Das Wesen des Christentums* (1841) and the *Vorlesungen über das Wesen der Religion,* which he delivered at Heidelberg in the winter of 1848–9 and shortly afterwards published in book-form. His basic idea, repeated with tiresome tirelessness in all his works, is contained in the sentence: " As the kernel of natural religion is Nature, but Nature as object and essence of human wishes and human imagination, so the kernel of spiritual religion, of Christianity, is Man, but Man as object and essence of human wishes, imagination, and abstraction." *Homo homini deus est.* God did not create men after His image, but men created God and gods after their image. Man is the beginning, the mid point, and the end of religion, and the secret of theology is anthropology. An idea of idiotic simplicity, that solves every enigma at one blow and brings Feuerbach to the declaration that " in the domain of Nature there is still plenty that is incomprehensible, but the secrets of religion, which have their source in men, can be known to their deepest foundations."

The ethic that flows from this new theology is something like this: As the poet no longer calls on the Muse, as the sick man no longer hopes for healing from prayer, but from the doctor, so in time men will cease to regard the laws of conduct as God's laws. The place of belief in God will be taken by belief in ourselves (here emerges the Straussian equation, the Son of Divinity is Humanity). In the beginning the wonders were worked, in the belief of

Ludwig Feuerbach

115

men, by God, but in the end man himself works them in virtue of his command over nature; humanity's only providence is its education, its culture. Christianity is " an *idée fixe* which stands in flagrant contrast to our fire and life insurances, our railways and steamships, our galleries of painting and sculpture, our military and commercial schools, our theatres and natural-history cabinets." Obviously, theology gives way to anthropology, religious edification to lessons in ballistics and machine design, churches to picture galleries and the collections of may-bugs, Providence to the pointsman and the insurance agent.

These platitudinous products of a leathern half-education (a judgment that may sound paradoxical in view of Feuerbach's many-sided learning, until one reminds oneself that learning and education are not the same thing) culminate in the coarse-grained sensualism of " Truth, actuality, and sensuality are identical "; " Only sensualism is sun-clear, it is the secret of immediacy of knowing "; " The only gospels we should study are the gospels of our five senses "; and above even these the famous phrase: " Man is what he eats (*Der Mensch ist, was er isst*)." And their aim, as Feuerbach himself says, at the conclusion of his Heidelberg lectures, is to make men " from friends of God into friends of man, from suppliants into workers, from candidates for the Beyond into students of the Here, from Christians (who by their own confession are *half beasts* and *half angels*) into men, whole men." As there is a depth of emptiness, so there is an abyss of shallowness, and in his case an unfathomable one.

Neptune, Actualism, stereoscope, and electroplating

Meantime the study of Here made continued progress. After the discovery of Uranus by Herschel in 1781, unaccountable variations were found in its orbit. Leverrier came to the conclusion that only a planet could be the cause of these disturbances, and that this planet must lie beyond Uranus. After long and close investigations he succeeded in exactly locating the supposed star for a given date, and when in September 1846 he asked the observer at Berlin to search for the planet, it was found on the very same day in the predicted position. It was a triumph of pure speculative reasoning; " with the point of his pen," as the famous scientist Arago put it, Leverrier had discovered a new heavenly body. Neptune, as it was named, has a " year " of almost a hundred and sixty-five terrestrial years and until recently has been thought to be the outermost of the sun's satellites; there are, however, certainly many others still more distant, in which the astronomers

116

disbelieve for no better reason than that it is their peculiarity to identify the relations of the universe with the efficiency of their optical instruments. By Schleiden's discovery of the plant cell in 1838 and Schwann's of the animal cell in the following year, it was revealed that all living things are built up of very similarly constituted elements. Both these investigators were able, even thus early, to distinguish the principal parts of the cell, the membrane, the fluid content, the nucleus, and a special granular substance which executed most peculiar movements and was named by the eminent botanist Hugo von Mohl (who carried out more exact researches into it) by the significant name of *protoplasm*.

In the year of the July Revolution Charles Lyell refuted Cuvier's doctrine of terrestrial revolutions, by reducing the geological changes of the past to causes that were still effective in the present, " actual causes." If we assumed that we could embrace in one glance the earth's history during the last five thousand years, with all the volcanic craters, all the eruptions, sinkings, and risings, all the new gulfs and peninsulas that happened in it, and then imagined these metamorphoses taking place within a single year, we should conclude that we were in the presence of one continuous catastrophe; and this had been the mistake of the geologists; they "worked in centuries where it was really a matter of millennia, and with thousands of years when the language of nature pointed to millions." In 1838 Wheatstone constructed his mirror stereoscope, which enabled him to study the laws of binocular vision more closely; in this two different images of the same object were shown, for the right eye the image which presented the object in perspective as it would be seen from the standpoint of that eye, and for the left eye the image as it would appear to it. In this way we have the illusion of a corporeal and three-dimensional object before us, the experience of the third dimension only arising from dual vision, and it is for this reason that a painting, which only reproduces the view-point of one eye, can never evoke the illusion of full actuality. Faraday in 1831 discovered and studied the phenomenon of *induction*, the production of electric currents by others (voltaic induction) or by magnetism (magneto-induction). This was an inversion of the phenomenon, already observed, that an electric current magnetizes an iron bar temporarily and a steel bar permanently, and Faraday therefore came to the much more fundamental conclusion that magnetism is a universal property of matter, and that all materials, even fluids and gases, could be magnetized. He enunciated a theory of electrolysis. As this was in the main observed in the case of salts dissolved in water, and as every salt consists of a metal and the so-called acid residue (namely, what remains when in an acid hydrogen is replaced by a metal), he called the two constituents into which the current was able to break up the fluid, *ions,* wanderers, the ions which went to the *anode* (the plate of the element connected with the positive pole of the source of current) being called *anions,* " wanderers to," and those which attached themselves to the *kathode* (the plate connected with the negative pole) *kations,* " wanderers away." The theory he propounded was that in every electrolysis the metal detaches itself to the kathode and is always a kation, while the acid residue (salt minus metal), which goes to the anode, is always an anion. This led Jacobi in 1837 to the discovery of electro-plating; as the activity of the electric current gives the kathode a coating of metal, it is possible to " plate " any article placed there with copper, silver, gold, or nickel, according to the metallic salt chosen (copper sulphate, nitrate of silver, chloride of gold, etc.).

The Law of Energy   Faraday was also the first to assert that light, heat, electricity, and magnetism were only different manifestations of the same natural force, and this led to the discovery, already alluded to, of the law of energy. It was formulated first in 1842 by Robert Mayer, then in the following year by the Dane Colding and about the same time by the Englishman Joule, without any of the three knowing each other. But (as we have already said in the Introduction to this work) the question of priority is only of importance in connexion with patent rights, whereas in respect of ideas we are concerned only with the question of who formulates them most acutely, who elucidates them most clearly, and who applies them most comprehensively. Here the merit, in this sense, belongs unquestionably to Hermann von Helmholtz, one of the most fruitful researchers, most suggestive savants, and best German writers of his century — one, in fact, who, unlike Strauss, could advance real claims to classical style. Eugen Dühring, in two empty volumes characterized by his crude and second-hand manner, has tried to represent Robert Mayer as a martyr and " the Galileo of the nineteenth century." Now, even that martyrdom of Galileo is (as we have shown in our first volume) a melodramatic schoolbook story, and the supposed persecution of Mayer by professional science is a pure invention of malicious sophistry, for after the statutory period that any new knowledge needs for its acceptance had passed, he was not only overwhelmed with academic honours, but actually honoured with the personal title to nobility — which, as governments are on principle behind the times, is a sufficiently marked proof of the fact that he was anything but neglected. And Helmholtz himself, in his unmasking of Dühring's plagiarisms, was the first to acknowledge Mayer's priority, and that though he himself had arrived at the same results independently.

The Law of Energy states that the sum of forces that exist in the universe represents a constant quantity, which can be neither increased nor diminished, and that energy, when it seems to vanish or to appear suddenly, is merely passing from one phenomenal form to another, living energy (or energy in action) being continually transformed into potential energy (or energy in tension) and vice versa. Further, all forms of energy are capable of being turned into each other. The steam engine creates mechanical work out of heat, and mechanical processes like impact or friction generate heat. Every thermal unit corresponds to a definite equivalent of work, the quantity of heat which raises the temperature of one pound of water by one degree, the force necessary to lift one pound 425 metres. If I wind up a cross-bow, I invest work-capital in it, which remains latent, and when I shoot, this capital passes into the bolt. In the fall of a body the work that was required to raise it is transformed into motion. In water-mills the gravitational energy of the water provides the motive power, in clocks the gravity of the weight. In the passage of gaseous bodies into the liquid state, or of liquids into the solid aggregate, heat is set free, and in the reverse case it is locked up. In chemical processes, too, heat is either used up or manifested. Energy, in fact, can be neither annihilated nor newly formed, but when one entry is cancelled, an exactly equivalent entry appears somewhere or other else. This conception, which forms Nature into one gigantic ledger, with " load " on one side of the account and " manifestation " on the other, could only have emerged in an age in which the bourgeoisie was supreme.

In the period with which we are dealing, Science also recorded some practical achievements that were very much in the spirit of the time. Justus von Liebig, who founded the first chemical laboratory and in 1844 published his *Chemische Briefe* (a masterpiece of language which evoked the admiration even of Jakob Grimm), was the creator of agricultural chemistry. It starts from the consideration that plants needed, in order to flourish, not merely certain general conditions such as light, humidity, and

Guano, hydrotherapy, Morse key, and daguerreotype

warmth, but also an appropriate soil which contained the nutritive elements they require. If these are not present, they must be added in the form of manure. While ammonia is necessary in all cases, certain plants needed also calcium, others potassium, yet others phosphoric acid. And as all of these could be produced in the laboratory, agricultural research stations at once sprang into existence and a manure industry developed. For the phosphoric acid a phosphate reservoir was found in Chile in guano, bird droppings which were accumulated in huge quantities there. And just as Liebig conjured up beautiful flowers from filth, so Friedrich Ferdinand Runge, who in 1834 discovered aniline in coal-tar, turned smuts into glorious colours.

One Vinzenz Priessnitz, observing a shot deer healing its wound in a spring, conceived the idea of curing illnesses simply by cold water, hot damp compresses, air, and diet and founded the first therapeutic establishment of this kind in his native town of Gräfenberg. His neighbour, a mortal enemy, Johann Schroth of Lindeweise, was furious at this, and jealousy inspired him to promote a still more primitive and rational method; he merely made his patients do without food and drink, and with the greatest success, for in fact many of our illnesses do come from eating and drinking. Professional medicine does not like to be reminded of these two peasants.

The two characteristic inventions of the age, however, were telegraphy and photography. The first persons to communicate telegraphically between themselves were two famous German savants, the Göttingen professors Gauss and Weber, who interconnected their laboratories by wire. Then Steinheil accidentally discovered that it was quite unnecessary to lay two wires, as the earth provided the return path. The decisive achievement, however, only came in 1837 with Morse, the inventor of the writing telegraph, the principle of which was that the current excited an electro-magnet at the receiving station, the armature of which, being drawn in, pressed down a pencil, the movement serving to impress signs on a strip of paper as it rolled past; if the current was of very short duration, a dot, and if somewhat longer a dash, was produced, and so arose the Morse alphabet of dots and dashes. The telegraphic stations which were consequently erected were at first only of an experimental character, but from the middle of the forties, thanks to substantial improvements that had meantime been introduced, they began to multiply with great rapidity.

The process of photography or, as it was originally called, daguerreotypy, was first published by the Paris scene-painter Louis Jacques Mandé Daguerre, who had discovered it in conjunction with Nicéphore Niepce; they first produced their pictures on silver plates. The discoverer of paper photography was Henry Fox Talbot, who coated sheets of paper with nitrate of silver. In his report to the Royal Society he observes that the thing which has become the proverbial symbol of all that is evanescent and momentary, the shadow, could now be fixed for all time in the position which had seemed to appertain to it for a mere instant. In 1835, with a camera obscura, he took views of his villa, which, he said, was the first of its kind to draw its own portrait, and shortly afterwards he discovered a fixing process.

It was wholly appropriate that this age of realism, photography, and world-travel should also produce that greatest of nineteenth-century German historians, Leopold von Ranke. He has frequently been claimed for Romanticism, but he touches it in only a few of his principles of historical philosophy. According to his penetrating and well-considered doctrine, the special character of each historical epoch consists in its " Idea," a " spiritual potentiality " that forms and guides its life in a quite definite way and from which alone, indeed, the inward unity of the epoch arises. But " the ideas by which human conditions are founded include the divine and eternal from which they gush forth, without, however, ever being complete in themselves. . . . When the time is fulfilled, there arise, above the cracking structure of the past, new efforts of a wider-reaching spiritual content that destroy it utterly. These occurrences are God's dispensations in the world." The ideas cannot be expressed in concepts, but must be perceived intuitively. " There are forces, and spiritual forces, forces that bring forth life, creative forces," " moral energies." Capable of definition and formulation they are not, but we can evoke in ourselves a sympathetic consciousness of their existence. In them resides the secret of world-history, and the task of the historian is to recognize the work of God. Still, Ranke's theory of ideas is not the essential in him. The rare qualities that enabled him to create a wholly new type of historiography — his sovereign objectivity, his razor-keen political judgment, his gift of realist psychology, his capacity for weighing historical material to fractions of an ounce and setting it all out for the reader — place him in the anti-Romantic camp. His aim, as he himself once said, was " simply to wipe himself

Ranke

out." It is questionable, or rather it is not questionable, whether this ought to be the historian's ideal, and in any case he did not attain it — on the contrary, his writing is quite traceably impregnated with his personality — but that he could formulate it at all is characteristic of his mind. It is a modern, natural-science, ideal, the conquest of the outer world by way of exact methods and empirical observation. It signified a transplantation to history of the physicist's faith in the conquering force of accumulated facts, an attempt to make respect for facts and documents the exclusive driving force in the writing of history. Moreover, the almost complete politicizing of history (which Ranke again put back into that domain) was highly un-Romantic and, equally, highly post-Romantic. His creation of " diplomatic " history was certainly a decisive fact in scholarship, and an advance to purer and richer knowledge; but to some extent he was himself the victim of his professionalism, in that his constant intercourse with dead ambassadors and ministers and political correspondents tinctured him somewhat with their colour and made him a diplomat himself, always dignified, courteous, accomplished in forms, and decorated with invisible orders, in fact with just a little too much of " perfectly understanding " about him. And, broadly speaking, he not only limited himself to political history, but, even within that field, concentrated in the main on the history of governments, whose doings were almost always right in his eyes. No unprejudiced reader will fail to sense that it was not mere " objectivity " that was at work here, but a permanent habituation to the air of courts. Once again we see that even the superior intellect pays its tribute to the *Zeitgeist* — a historian who could match Schiller as a psychological portraitist, Jakob Grimm as a master of language, and Hegel as a historical thinker, and who for historical intuition stands unrivalled, was necessarily, in the age of politics, a historian of the State.

The French Romantic

" I see myself in an age of transition," said Stendhal, " and that means, in an age of mediocrity." Against this mediocrity there stepped into the ring the young painters and poets of the French Romantic school. Their challenge began even with externals, with their Polish frogged coats, green trousers, loud waistcoats, sugarloaf hats, and flame-coloured " Calabrians." Yet they were just as much an expression of their time as a protest against it, and this makes them a very complicated phenomenon. First of all, we must not be misled by names. French Romanticism was anti-Romantic.

The only Romantic feature with which they can be credited is their passion for the picturesque, but this is a trait common to all the French, which remained true to itself even in periods of extreme anæmia in life, poetry, and thought — think, for instance of the age of Louis XIV with its love of magnificent music, decoration, and rhetoric; or of the high colour of the literature of the Enlightenment — and had only to order its expression logically and architecturally to be wholly compatible with Rationalism.

Superficially the new tendency harked back to the Middle Ages. But what really matters is never the choice of subject, but solely the apperception-form. The equations are not so simple that one can just label all art-currents with a set towards the ancient as Classicist, all that take an interest in the Middle Ages as Romantic, and all that deal with the present as Realist. The word "Romantic" sounds as though it were akin to "Romance," but nevertheless no "Romance" Romantic ever existed — there has only been a single case of a true Romantic in French literature, that of the handful who centred on Maeterlinck, and they were Germanic Flemings to a man.

The prime phenomenon from which all human life-expressions derive is the relation to God. The Romantic is religious, while the Romance, the Latin, is clerical or else atheistic. Of course, there have at all times been clericals and atheists on Slavonic and Germanic soil also, but these have never risen to representative national importance. On the other hand, religious figures like Luther and Bach, Fichte and Carlyle, Dostoievski and Nietzsche are unimaginable as Romance products.

We have several times already alluded to the fact that every Frenchman is a Cartesian and every Frenchman a Latin, and this statement is not in the least less valid for the Romantics than for others. They passionately turned against Classicism, but this was only the strict Classicism of Boileau's court etiquette, against the three unities and the sharp separation of tragedy and comedy, against the linguistic tyranny of the Academy and the absolutism of the Lully tradition, against geometrical picture-composition and salon landscape, against the *Versailles of art*, which even then was not yet dead. The movement was revolutionary in form — in that it went over from the classically closed to the "open" form (so far as anything open is possible to a Frenchman) in material — in that it preferred the pathological, the gruesome, the harsh, the disharmonious — but, above all (in contrast to

123

the German Romanticism), in politics. Or, to put it more accurately, the French Romantic alone was directionally political, and the German was totally unpolitical. For nothing is so unromantic as politics, and this fact alone would suffice to show that the French movement was no true Romanticism. It was, in simple truth, being a hot and bubbling elemental expression of the *Zeitgeist*, a Realism — although naturally (like every other artistic Realism) it was a transposed and emphasized one. Victor Hugo in his preface to *Hernani* put it with all desirable clarity when he remarked that " Romanticism is in poetry what Liberalism is in the State "; and Delacroix said, still more simply and distinctly: " *Qui dit romantisme, dit art moderne.*"

Hugo, Dumas, Scribe, Sue The birthday of the Romantic school in France is taken as the 25th of February 1830. On this day, five months before the July Revolution, took place the memorable first performance of *Hernani*, which — like almost every decisively important first night — was an immense theatrical scandal. Théophile Gautier wore his famous red silk waistcoat, as a symbol of his artistic hatred of convention and his political Radicalism. But already, three years earlier, Hugo had formulated his conception of the Romantic in his *Cromwell* preface, of which Gautier said that " it shone before our eyes like the tables of the law on Sinai." The Romantic is actual, but the actual arises from a crossing of the sublime and the grotesque, and so the Romantic " *drame* " is a union of tragedy and comedy. He did not, however, genuinely fuse these — that was left to the end of the century to accomplish in Ibsen and his school — but juxtaposed them. Yet this very taste for literary manifestoes discloses the Gallic love of program and regularity, and this rationalism (for which the passion for shriek and bizarrerie, the unnatural and the insane, is only a mask) expresses itself still more clearly in Hugo's cool, clear composition and his conscious — self-conscious — insistence on being tendentious. Hugo spent his whole life in nailing up theses, and in the second half of it he rose to the rank of national prophet. In him at the same time the French decorative genius reached its apogee; his poems are glowing tapestries, bewitching colour-schemes, grandiose studio feasts, masterly scores. His dramas are the most enthralling libretti that were ever written, and at the very first glance invite orchestration, although in reality they are already beyond the need of it. Their stars are those eternal figures without which opera cannot live: the noble outlaw who lives *against* society and revenges its misdeeds, the honourable trollop who *shares* his life and whose great love ennobles her. The action conforms to opera-logic, the humour is that of *opéra comique*. In his novels the world appears as a madhouse, as in Shakspere and yet wholly differently; his vision is more subjective and monomaniac, it is a sadistic fever-vision.

With Hugo, the elder Dumas, Scribe, and Sue achieved the greatest popularity. The distance between him and these was not felt in France as strongly as we feel it. There literary æsthetic was not made by the professors — who are never poets and seldom even writers — but by artists and society. Consequently the standards ruling there were different; a drama was appreciated according to its stage effectiveness, and a book according to its power of hypnotizing its readers. Dumas wrote more than a quarter of a thousand books — hollow pageantry, no doubt, but filled with delicate bonbons. Scribe wrote the most effective opera libretti in the world — *La Muette de Portici, Fra Diavolo, La Juive, Robert le Diable, Le Prophète, L'Africaine* — and became an absolute virtuoso of the modern intrigue-play, the "*pièce bien faite.*" He possessed the paradoxical gift of seeing the world, not in the natural light of sun and moon, but in the artificiality of insistent searchlights and many-coloured lanterns, and of seeing men not as natural beings, but as wearers of powder, wigs, and false beards. Further, he was one of the first who treated their dramas as commercial articles. He was nothing but the extraordinarily prudent and inventive chief of a *galanterie*-manufactory in which all the departments worked and interlocked with precision. Very many of his pieces are company-productions, one man inventing the characters, another the complications, a third the dialogue, and a fourth the smart sayings. In such conditions it goes without saying that money is always the mid point of the plot, though his heroes are conceived much more innocently and unprofoundly than Balzac's, and money is represented merely as the irresistible seducer to which all must succumb. As for the notorious Eugène Sue, he possesses (as we have already pointed out in our second volume) a certain similarity to Schiller — not merely in his liking for the criminalistic and sensational and for the technique of straight black and white, but also in his tendency to ethical and social moralizings. Yet even in his case it is only through the reading-glass of the school essay that he comes in for condemnation; Balzac and Hugo for their part regarded him as a rival. On the other hand, the sickly colour-prints in which Murger portrayed the *vie de Bohème* of Paris are today scarcely tolerable to any taste but the French.

Delacroix   The French painting of the period is the exact counterpart of the literature. Delacroix took as his motto: "The ugly is the beautiful," and correspondingly his art substituted a riot of colour for the more graphical correctness of Classicism and gave preference to the horrible, the degenerate, the nasty, over what was "fit for the drawing-room." Even in his materials he loved the exotic. The capture of Algiers, an event of no very great significance at first, either politically or economically, had an instant effect artistically. Not very long after Hugo had written his *Orientales*, Delacroix discovered the Orient for painting. This involved a reversal of existing practice in the representation of biblical characters, for painters began to see that their models should be sought for, not among Flemish peasant girls or Florentine princesses, but among Africans. Further, Delacroix found in Africa, where the sunlight endowed objects with far stronger reflecting-power and emphasized colour-contrasts far more sharply, the confirmation of his colouristic outlook on the world. It was his habit to group his colours first of all, before beginning on the drawing, and it was not for nothing that his favourite painter was Rubens, who surpasses him, indeed, in technical mastery, colouristic force, and elemental vitality, but falls short of him in problem-posing intellect, vibrant passion, and dæmonic originality.

Among the other painters of the new school there was none who came near Delacroix, but it was nevertheless filled with bubbling life, rich and varied in ideas; bold and triumphant in its will to revolt, and withal — true heir both of its race and of the Classicist spirit — never tasteless and always in full control of its means. It was filled with a marked predilection for figures out of the Chamber of Horrors (partly out of perversity, partly with the idea of making the bourgeois sit up); it was propagandist and agitatorish (there is the fanfaron in every Frenchman), play-acting and theatrical (but in the key of high artistry), morbid and neurasthenic (even, according to Ingres, epileptic), but with all this, in its delight in, and powers of, building and ordering and grading, essentially Cartesian. In the feeble genre of historical painting Delaroche was the most powerful; his paintings can be set in parallel with the ingenious historical novels of Dumas *père*, the sentimental anecdote being for him always the main thing. Horace Vernet depicted the African campaign, the Napoleonic legend, the story of *La Gloire*, the *Grande Armée*, very successfully and with a minute professional accuracy in matters of uniform and armaments, strategy and tactics. Ingres falls quite outside the period — a Classicist, but not with the Latin art-feeling, but the Greek, which in general is wholly alien to the French make-up; a master of splendid line and pure proportion, of unforced nudity and true (namely, ideal) naturalness.

The music of French Romanticism began in 1828 with the *Muette de Portici* of Auber, who had already made himself known for comic operas of variegated and witty piquancy. It was not merely the idea, as original as it was happy, of making a dumb girl the heroine of an opera that made *La Muette* the success that it was, but also the revolutionary passion that darted from it like fire from a match. In this period, in fact, there occurred the paradox of music, of all things, becoming political. The *Muette* not merely anticipated the July Revolution, but (as mentioned above) actually touched off the Belgian. And in the numerous " operas of Freedom" that followed, Liberalism conquered the orchestra. The two most famous examples of this genre are Bellini's *Norma*, of 1832, which depicts the struggle of the Gauls against Roman domination, and Rossini's *Tell*, of 1829, in which heroic passion for liberty and idyllic landscape were magnificently combined. Meyerbeer (who won his first great success in 1831 with *Robert le Diable*), heretical though it may seem to say so, is a musical Victor Hugo in his passion for the picturesque, the intensified, and the intoxicatingly effective. Though born in Berlin, he was French through and through — like his predecessor in Berlin and Paris, the Italian Spontini, from whom he learnt his extravagant use of both orchestra and stage equipment for the production of crushing effects, but whom he far surpassed in richness of expedient and subtlety of orchestration. The German author and æsthetic critic Robert Griepenkerl said of Meyerbeer's operas that in them one felt " the tone of this iron century," which is a very accurate judgment, if not as flattering as it was meant to be, for in Meyerbeer the steely will to success, hard-hearted to the point of indecency, is made music. The other half of Hugo's soul, his pleasure in the abnormal, the illogical, the grim-grotesque, is embodied in Berlioz, a genius of the chromatic in whom a feeling for sound is hypertrophied almost to the pathological, who saw sounds almost bodily. His " *Symphonie fantastique*" *Épisode de la vie d'un artiste*, which was performed for the first time in 1830, and its sequel, *Le Retour de la vie*, mark the foundation of modern program-music. His subject is the narcotic dreams of a young artist whom an unrequited love has brought to attempt suicide by opium — the dominance of the motif is, by ingenuity of suggestion, emphasized to the point of morbidity and *idée fixe*. Chopin, born near Warsaw of a French immigrant and a Polish mother, is for dance music proportionately what Schubert is for song, in that he made high art out of a genre that before now had served only for entertainment. His polonaises and mazurkas sang in the ears of Europe the lament of violated Poland. He lived in Paris, one of the most celebrated of celebrities, admired as virtuoso pianist no less than as composer. Liszt and Berlioz, Heine and Balzac were his friends, and for years he had a liaison with George Sand — that ugly suffragette of literature whom Musset (also one of her lovers) called the " very type of an educated blackbird," and Nietzsche, still more plainly, " a writing cow." On the violin the greatest phenomenon of the age and perhaps of all ages was Paganini, whose contagiously passionate playing and unparalleled technical mastery bewitched men and women even to intoxication. He was of dæmonic ugliness, and already legendary even in his lifetime. The most melodramatic stories were related of him — that he had murdered his mother, strangled his fiancée, and acquired all the points of virtuosity in prison by playing on one string — and he was in all seriousness suspected of magic.

Mendelssohn and Schumann

The German music of this period lived and moved in the circle of feeling of the German Romantic and has consequently, with all its high qualities, something rear-guard, behind-the-time, yesterdayish, about it, like Frederick William IV, who greatly admired and promoted it ; it is a pendant neither to the Romantic music of France nor to the contemporary literature of its own country. As everyone knows, its two chief representatives were Mendelssohn and Schumann. Mendelssohn, the grandson of the philosopher, rescued the *Matthew Passion* from oblivion by a perfect rendering in Berlin, elevated opera — in Düsseldorf as a pupil of Immermann and in Berlin as the King's favourite — to new heights, conducted frequently and with immense success in London, and as conductor of the Gewandhaus concerts made Leipzig the musical capital of Germany. He was a delicate and ingenious water-colourist like Heine (whom, indeed, he loved to set to music), and no unique giant. Still, influenced though he was in his oratorios by Handel and Haydn, in his *Midsummer Night's Dream* and *Waldlieder* by

Weber, in his piano music by Schubert, he was a deep and original personality — capricious and graceful, sentimental and gay, indeed almost witty, highly educated (in fact, almost too highly for a musician), and imbued with a pure and genuine piety, neither ossified nor artificial, that in those days was something of a rarity. Robert Schumann, almost of the same age, but far more individual, founded (likewise in Leipzig) the society of the " Davidsbündler " to fight philistinism in music, and the *Neue Zeitschrift für Musik* to champion Berlioz, Chopin, and the young Brahms against Meyerbeer. It was his marriage to the celebrated pianist Klara Wieck that brought him out as a song-writer, in which capacity he showed himself a " *Gelegenheitsdichter* " in Goethe's sense and a lyrist of the purest type. This was stamped on his every trait: he was feminine and childlike, with the somnambulist's melancholy; greatest as a pure piano-composer, a master of free accompaniment and instrumental ending, prelude, and interlude, which with him never sank to mere ornament, but were rather the most intimate element in the expression of mood; weakest in opera. In him the German Biedermeier found a late and wondrously melodious echo, which sings like a stray note of the violin even to our own day.

As we have already observed, the writers of " Young Germany " by no means regarded themselves as members of one literary school. Nevertheless they had a number of traits in common, and indeed it could not very well be otherwise. There can hardly have been many intellectual movements that in their beginnings and aims, their leading ideas and expression-means, were less artistic than this. First of all, the trade-mark that they chose for themselves was most inappropriate, for they were no more " young " than the first Romantic school had been " romantic." They included, indeed, poets who had not yet passed their thirtieth year, but nearly all of them were stone-old when they came into the world — superior, learned, deflagrated to an extent that only grey hairs can be in this world. They had an unanswerable, penetrating, devouring — in short, an intolerable — cleverness about them. They took nothing on trust in any domain whatever, religion or politics, art or philosophy. They unmasked this, that, or the other as fraudulent or infantile, till nothing was left but a compact materialism. And all this, from their very beginnings, with a cleverness and worldly wisdom, a fund of experience and manipulative skill, a literary sureness and propagandist energy that are certainly not the usual properties of youth. And yet, with nothing more than unsympathetic or inferior characteristics, they could not have achieved the great spiritual successes that they quite unquestionably did. To what, then, did they owe their widespread and profound effect?

The question carries its own answer — they were the voice of the time. They expressed what everyone, tacitly or in whispers, loudly or mutedly was feeling; though they did so in a purely negative form, they set themselves against the indescribable boredom, inertia of feeling, and rigidity of mind in which their epoch was spellbound. They tore apart the grey atmosphere that lay over the world and brought light and clarity into human relations. Certainly, it was nothing but the clarity and obviousness, the ordinary commonplace enlightenment, of everyday wisdom, but it eased and it liberated. For what good to the German burgher was all the previous Mysticism and Romanticism, which only confused him, or his eminent Hegel, so rich and so profound, of whom he understood not a word? And now, all at once, appeared men who, although they wrote for print, at any rate wrote entirely in his own language, fluently, simply, and engagingly; and yet again not just in that language, but with piquancy, wit, and variety — which was a second reason for their success. *Esprit* had hitherto been regarded as a French import-article, hard to come by, but now he had it in his own country — the good joke that one could retail at the beer table, the little literary gossip to go with the morning coffee — in short, the feuilleton, from which we have never since been able to free ourselves.

The "Zeitgeist" We have many times alluded to the fact that almost every period possesses a catchword that it blindly follows, a cipher that it regards as the key to all secrets. For "Young Germany" this magic catchword was "*Zeitgeist*." "The Time is the poet's Madonna," sang Herwegh. The Time, however, was merely the Day. This was what they meant by the "realism" to which they had subscribed and which itself meant the particular brand of actuality-worship represented by the newspaper, a realism of words which presumed reality in phrases, which reiterated its untruths or half-untruths long and intensively enough for them to become effective *and therefore true*. Nor, in fact, did they even manage this feuilleton genre with real mastery; this only came later, reaching the last state of fulfilment in point of style with Speidel, of content with Kürnberger, and of both style and content with Bahr. In our previous volume we found ourselves compelled to reject the view that Schiller is the ancestor of modern journalism, but Young Germany certainly is this. In every normal writer, and in general every normal man, the word develops out of the thing, but in these authors it was the reverse. Always the metaphor is there first, and only then the idea, and even the metaphor consists in mere words, which make it in most cases badly drawn or forced and in all hopelessly pedestrian. This is true even of the best stylist of the school, Ludwig Börne: when, for example, he cries: " The free stream of public opinion, whose waves are the daily papers, is the German Rubicon," he has achieved a *locus classicus* of hollow and oblique rhetoric, and when Ludolf Wienbarg says of Schiller that " sentimental, understanding, good-humoured, eloquent, he was adapted to the very worthy audience that dislikes the tragic dagger being set against its breast unless it can see that it has previously been rendered harmless by the pommel of beautiful phrase and style," it is just pure quibbling. Above all, however, what spoilt their style was its laborious tastelessness. The same Wienbarg says in the dedication, already quoted, of his *Ästhetische Feldzüge:* " University air, court air, and other such bad and vitiated atmospheres, that separate themselves from the free and sunny daylight of the peoples, must either be avoided altogether or at least only breathed for short periods. On these occasions scent-bottles fitted with bitter-satirical vinegar such as Börne, for example, distils in Paris are not to be despised." And on the July Revolution he sang thus: " Let the Frank sing the *Marseillaise* and sip the champagne of his songs that, too big for its bottle, blows out its cork right to the Neva." Theodor Mundt described the activity of his adored *Zeitgeist* in these words: " It twitches, rumbles, attracts, warbles, and ' Hambachs ' in me; it whistles shrilly in me like a quail, plays the war-trumpet on me, sings the *Marseillaise* in my entrails, and thunders in my lungs and liver with the drum of rebellion." Gutzkow greeted the rising generation thus: " Happy be ye, young warriors . . . happy, for so ye can know where in the poetic crowd others too are snapping their strings, their strings of philistine gut. . . . Let your spear strike its iron head into the earth so that after the heat of battle it may be to you a shady arbour." Smelling-bottles against foul air, champagne corks that jump from Paris to Petersburg, *Marseillaises* singing in the entrails, strings made of philistines' guts — this sort of thing we could scarcely find today even in provincial papers, while the shading spear is an obvious relapse into the very belief in miracles that Young Germany had just been at such pains to destroy.

Another of their slogans was the " emancipation of the senses," the ideal floating before them here being the Greek Culture. This conception of a " gay and sensuous " Hellenism is neither Classical nor Romantic, but comes out of operetta, with Dionysos turned into a public-house Bacchus, and the Muses of Apollo into ballet-dancers. Mundt devised the term " movement-literature," which in a way reminds us of the present-day activism. Now, there is nothing more active and actual than the politics of the day, and hence Young Germany soaked its art with politics to an extent that is hardly credible. They went so far as to assert that a poem that did not deal with the questions of the day had no justification for its existence, which was indeed a topsyturvy notion of the essence of art. One of the most admired actors of that period was Esslair. With reference to him, Börne said: " The true history of every day is wittier than Molière and nobler than Shakspere. A few lamps lit and the paper read — what better could Esslair give us ? " The sight of an Alpine glow instantly suggested to Herwegh the burning of Troy and evoked in him this chain of thought: " A sinking house of kings smokes before my eyes and I shout aloud to the land: ' *Vive la république!* ' " wherein (quite apart from the fact that Parisian republicanism was rather one of sentiments than of express acts) he completely forgot that the destruction of Troy was in no sense an anti-monarchical demonstration. The whole lyric of Young Germany is leader-writing, either Liberal or patriotic (in the latter case one is fairly sure to find " Rhine " associated with " wine," a rhyme that was worked beyond all limits of moderation) ; and the journals often went so far as to present their leaders in verse-form. Gutzkow, at any rate, had a sort of suspicion that this literature was one huge abortion; he said: " Börne accuses Heine of frivolity, but is it not the worst levity to reduce the century to nothing but the constitutional question? " This, however, was only a theoretical criticism; in practice Gutzkow never tackled anything save in a spirit of tendency and politics.

Gutzkow   The artistic products of this age, then, are of astounding triviality, unnaturalness, and impotence. They are, not to mince words, mere grease-paint drama, tinsel, toggery, for the sixpenny bazaar. Of these pieces some few maintained their position on the stage for a very long time. Gutzkow wrote a series of frosty celebrity-dramas: *Zopf und Schwert*, presenting Frederick William I and Ekhof, *Urbild des Tartüffe*, with Molière as its hero, *Richard Savage*, dealing with the fortunes of that poet and of Steele (the founder of the *Spectator*), *Uriel Acosta*, with Spinoza as a small boy, and *Königsleutnant*, in which figures a girl disguised as the young Goethe. Now, celebrities, for the dramatist, are very attractive subjects, but also very dangerous ones. They are attractive because they allow him to set numerous ancillary figures in sympathetic vibration which he can develop and with which he can work. They are dangerous because they involve obligations — to portray a genius it takes at least half a genius. But Gutzkow's great men are pure journalists and not first class at that. The effect is absolutely that of a parody when Steele as *raisonneur*, in presence of the corpse of Savage, breaks out at the end into the words: "Times and manners, behold your victim! Would that the fetters of every prejudice would burst; would that hearts dared to beat more bravely with the full breath of chests and did not in the turmoil of the world with its cold education and slavish legality," etc., etc. — there is more of it, but we need not listen to him any longer, but turn instead to the end of his box-office piece *Werner, or Heart and World* (a good sub-title this): "Julie, through that which befell thee thou hast looked into the history of hearts that vow themselves to love, peeped into the region that we would so gladly keep hidden from you women! In a thousand spirits of our time there slumbers the contradiction of heart and world, stilly and painfully concealed. Happy is he who can solve it as I can — through thee." The soubrette disguised as Goethe replies: "Quake, world, in thy corners, rage over the lands, grimacing Bellona, there must come a place wherein the seed of the soul comes to flower, and no shattered lance, no blood-stained banner, is tall enough to rear itself above the modest flowers of poesy." Manifestly this is not the way in which human beings talk to one another, but the padding of a third-rate newspaper writer. It is characteristic, too, that in several of his dramas, such as *Werner, Savage, Ella Rosa*, Gutzkow offered the theatre-manager the choice of various catastrophes. The physiognomy of his novels is similar; for example, *Wally, die Zweiflerin*, one section of which closes with the words: "See here a scene such as old times never witnessed! Here is something finicking, artificial, born of the disruptions of our time — but what is egoistic sex-love compared to

133

this enthusiasm of ideas that can throw two souls into the unhappiest inversions? "

Gutzkow is the first German dramatist to write star parts ("*Bombenrollen*"). Whole generations of actors have won laurels out of the Liberal tirades of Uriel Acosta, and Friedrich Haase for a whole generation played almost nothing but Chevalier Thorane in *Königsleutnant*. One readily understands therefore why Gutzkow was a vigorous champion of virtuosity. "The lamentable phrase 'ensemble,'" he wrote, "should be left in the mouths of the dullards. . . . It is not the decline of the art of acting but its regeneration that begins with Seydelmann," who was one of the earliest representatives of that type of actor who in poetry and gesture sees only instruments for personal success. He was the discoverer of the "character-mask," of touring, and of press publicity. As Shylock he unceasingly stroked and kissed his bond and sharpened his knife on the floor; as Antonio in *Tasso* he indicated by tendernesses and lecherous looks that there was an amorous relation between him and the Countess Sanvitale; in another part he should have threatened his partner with a knife and been checked by a pistol, but, reflecting that the ignorant public likes to identify the rôle and the player, he took care in his performances to mark himself as the winner by himself suddenly drawing a pistol. Mephistopheles he played in long claws, Struwelpeter wig, squinting eyes, and a nose that hooked over to his chin, and, as Immermann tells us, with continual " infernal croakings, puffings, and gruntings." In all this, his calculating rationalism, his serial-writer's making of points, his journalistic self-advertisement, and his very pronounced tendency to mercantilism, he was but the child of his times.

Laube and Heine Heinrich Laube, too, showed his liking for the literary-historical peep-show by putting on Gottsched, Gellert, and the young Schiller, and for dramas about favourites by presenting Struensee, Essex, and Monaldeschi — surely the dreariest genre that ever was. His pieces, too, are papers, though not so penny-a-linish as Gutzkow's; cheaply theatrical, sometimes to the point of unconscious bathos, crude, but well carpentered and in this last point foreshadowing the finished dramatist and producer that he eventually became. He not only directed several important theatres, with a rare capacity for finding and training theatrical talent, but in his histories of the Viennese Burgtheater and Stadttheater and the theatre of North Germany he so handled his subjects that these books are the best — indeed, almost the only ones — in which acting is adequately and helpfully discussed; moreover, in contrast to the rest of his works, they are splendidly written. But on the other hand, in the field of play-writing, his standpoint is practical but ignoble, and he looks exclusively at the wishes of the public, which he summarizes in these words: " Poverty succeeds because it can walk and stand, wealth is taken off the boards because it cannot do this, but wants to fly, and flying is not for the stage," the rejoinder to which is that a theatre that does not give us men that can fly has no justification for existing, for we can see people walking and standing on every military parade.

Heine participated in the misdeeds of Young Germany only during his very earliest period, and to reckon him in that group, as still happens again and again, is an ineptitude of professional history-writing. Gutzkow criticized his poetry, maliciously but very accurately, as when (for once, successful with his metaphor) he said that Heine's " flowers " are like scented artificial flowers; elsewhere, less maliciously and just as accurately, he calls them a mixture of laughter, nightingale-song, mountain and forest air, veiled satire upon veiled men, scandal, sentimentality, and world-history. The world as seen by Romanticism was never used by Heine save as pageantry, for inwardly he was a Rationalist, a Naturalist, almost — even thus early — an Impressionist. His poems are charming musical-boxes. His prose is pure, rich, delightful, rhythmic, and only occasionally a trifle too witty. What distinguishes him most definitely from all Young Germans is his musicalness. An actual world-outlook he cannot rightly be said to have had; such as it is, it consists (apart from his purely political and literary-polemical writings) in his half novelistic and unserious, half journalistic and democratic attacks on the surface of religious and philosophical transcendentalism, and in the preaching of a this-world gospel which in its erotic materialism rather looks towards the Parisian libretto. His lyric has proved more fertile for music than for poetry. The stylistic influence of his prose, on the other hand, must be set extraordinarily high; it extends even to Nietzsche, whom it misled into an overvaluation of Heine's personality as a whole. Apart from all this, he is in German literature the first creator of ambivalence. Tragedy and comedy, sentimentality and irony are related, in turn, not as two halves, but as the front and back of the same thing, and there is a corresponding ambivalence in the reactions that he has always evoked, for men have never quite known whether to regard him as intolerable or enchanting. The tragedy of his life was to be born into this utterly sterile time — a man full of thirst for reality in the midst of a world of tin-foil phrases and stuffed fair-puppets, a nature whose deepest yearning was to be allowed to revere, to worship, and to believe cast into a generation whose extreme of cleverness was to disbelieve, to strip everything of divinity, and to bury it in scepsis. And so he became a typical dual nature. Now, duality is the very condition of all men with any sort of artistic endowment, whether artistically creative or merely artistically receptive; very many women therefore have it, and indeed it is only the philistine that wholly lacks it. But it can take two forms. There are men whose two souls nervously flee from each other and when they meet, only cramp and confuse each other; these are halved beings. And there are men whose two souls attract each other like electricities of unlike name and hold each other in a sort of magic equilibrium that helps and intensifies them; these are doubled men. To the first category belong Heine and Byron; to the second, Goethe, Shakspere, Tolstoi, and Nietzsche.

Yet we must not be too hard on this group of souls disinherited by destiny — for that is what they all were, and in their outward life as well as their inward. After all, it is something great when out of a whole generation there suddenly bursts forth a blaze of passionate urge to truth; and to put honesty in place of political and religious hypocrisy, and plain sense instead of mystical and allegorical hocus-pocus, was the very intent of the whole movement. But sometimes the truth is appallingly banal and owes its life merely to the fact that the opposite truth is too utterly absurd; and so it was in the case of Young Germany.

Political painting   The German painting of this epoch is wholly literary. The view held in honour was that art should be educative and enlightening; consequently men painted not only history — which, when the motive is novelistic, is already bad enough — but historical philosophy and even politics. Karl Friedrich Lessing's pictures of the lives of Luther and Huss, which were sermons against Ultramontanism, were admired or detested according to the spectator's attitude to the Reformation; that is, in either case, for their *content*. Another favoured subject was the " story " of famous poems. " Realism " expressed itself in the historical canvases chiefly in the minute study of costumes, arms, furniture, implements, and architectural forms, and it was in all seriousness regarded as an æsthetic fault if a picture was " incorrect "; even the artist's conception of the situation had to conform to the latest researches of historical science. The highest reputation was that of Kaulbach, who was akin to Cornelius in philosophical ambition, and to Ranke in his conception of history, and yet, compared to them, was empty, stagy, tortured, and full of repetitions. Alfred Rethel, to whose frescoes at Köln we have already alluded, depicted Hannibal's passage of the Alps in six coloured drawings of freshness, power, and restraint, and in 1849 he illustrated the events of the past year in a grandiose and dramatic fashion under the title " One More Dance of Death." The genre painters chiefly portrayed, in an operatic style, popular scenes of all sorts, such as the smuggler, the poacher, the street life of Italy. In point of material Karl Spitzweg also belongs with them. It is significant that he began life as an apothecary, for his art has something spun-out, pedantic, crotchety. His favourite subjects were touching and farcical special types, the Sunday sportsman and the bourgeois general, the poetaster and the paint-actor, the amateur flautist and the serenade-singer, the archive-worm and the school pedant, the jolly bachelor and the timid lover, the nurseryman and the second-hand dealer, all framed in the weathered and angular, dreaming and tortuous German small town. The long-vanished poetry of the gala coat and peaked cap is preserved unforgettably in his tender and whimsical snapshots.

In this period before the German March Revolution three other geniuses lived within the frontier of the Federation, one unknown, one misunderstood, one masked by disguise: namely, Büchner, Grabbe, and Nestroy. Grabbe, who in spite of his conspicuous lack of concentration and stage-feeling often came very near to Shakspere, was all his life regarded as an idler and half an idiot; even Wilhelm Scherer calls him a simpleton and accuses him of " the most ridiculous bragging." Georg Büchner was only discovered in our own day. He was born near Darmstadt on the day of the battle of Leipzig and died so soon as February 1837, in his twenty-fourth year. He studied medicine, edited the *Hessische Landbote*, the first Socialist paper in the German language — which, however, only circulating secretly among the peasants of his home country, had almost no practical effect — and in 1834 founded the Society for Human Rights, a secret society for the promotion of radical republicanism which in reality was no more than a harmless political debating-club. He escaped the imprisonment

Georg Büchner

137

which threatened him by flight to Strassburg, where he continued his anatomical studies. The fruit of these was a treatise *On the Nervous System of the Barbel*, which brought to light certain quite new facts about the nervous system of the head in fishes and was declared by experts to be an unusual achievement; for this he received from Zürich University the doctorate of the Philosophical Faculty, and, after a highly applauded trial lecture, he was installed as a Privatdozent. His brother, the author of the world-famous book *Kraft und Stoff*, said of him that had he lived and pursued his scientific career, he would have " become the same great reformer of natural science that we now honour in Darwin," and indeed if one considers what a rare union of philosophical and scientific gifts is found in the monographs and sketches that he left behind, this assertion will not be regarded as exaggerated — nay, more, considering that on top of it all he was an artist, one must admit the possibility that he might have been even greater than Darwin. From another point of view, the gifted anatomist is true to himself, even in his art. In his fragment of a novel, *Lenz*, the hero says: " The good God has no doubt made the world as it should be, and we certainly do not seem to do any better with it; our own effort should be to create on His lines a little. . . . Men have meant to achieve idealistic shapes, but all that I have seen of these has been a wooden doll. This idealism is only a scandalous contempt of human nature. Make just the effort to sink yourself in the life of the smallest creatures and then reproduce this in twitching indications and play of feature so fine as hardly to be observed . . . none of them can be too small, none too ugly, for one, and only then can one begin to understand men." These sentences contain Büchner's own theory of art. In a world of shallow book-idealism and of paper journal-realism he was a Naturalist of that immortal and unanswerable species to which belong also Goethe and Gorki, Homer and Hamsun. He has been spoken of, consequently, as a straggler of the *Sturm und Drang* literature, but it might equally be said that he is the herald, already, of everything that there is in Wedekind, and that he anticipated and passed beyond all our Expressionism. There is in all German no grander people's play than *Woyzek*, and in the circle of post-Classicist drama no more full-blooded story than *Dantons Tod*.

Nestroy   For a whole generation Nestroy enjoyed in his native city an immense and uninterrupted popularity, due to the irresistible comicality of his endless dangling limbs and the tinny rattle of his voice, to his swift and telling extempores, his obstinate and droll battles with the censorship, and, lastly, the long series of his cleverly built topical farces. This was one half of Johann Nestroy, the outer husk which by the world, and especially the Viennese world, is so often and so readily taken to be the whole man. But there was another Nestroy, a Socratic dialectician and a Kantian analyser, a Shaksperianly struggling soul that with a truly cosmic fancy distorted the metric of human things in order thereby to let them appear for the first time in their true dimensions. This creative irony in Nestroy, wholly unrecognized by his contemporaries, condemned him to live posthumously; even now, indeed, he is for the majority of people an anonymous being. That this was his fate is due first of all to the fact that the supreme and radical sceptic has always a difficult position in this world; men do not readily emancipate themselves from the convenient and well-rounded relations of yesterday, and they regard him instinctively as an enemy, forgetting all too easily that the spiritual health, the capacity for evolution and progressive force, of an epoch depends on the quantity of spiritual dynamite that it has at its disposal. Secondly, there was the special reason in this case that Nestroy worked in a city that from of old has possessed an incredible virtuosity in the art of shaking off its teachers and degrading to the level of conjurer or mountebank everyone whose love of truth became uncomfortable to her. And yet it must be admitted that only in Vienna could there have arisen a genius like this, for whose essence there is no other word but Baroque. Vienna rose to its peak of cultural and artistic significance in the days of the Baroque, and in its most specific and conspicuous, richest and subtlest life-expressions it has remained a Baroque city to this day. And Nestroy is the greatest, even the only, philosopher that she has produced. That this fact is even now invisible to many is due to the widespread but fallacious notion that a philosopher must be what is called a serious-minded man, whereas one ought to say the exact opposite, that the philosopher only begins to take himself and life seriously at the point when the man ceases to do so.

Nestroy was a philosopher, too, in possessing no system. Hence he never possessed a political program and was regarded by Conservatives as an objectional subverter and by Liberals as a dark reactionary. But to be disliked by the Right and by the Left is ever the lot of the true actor-temperament, which is incapable of looking at things save from above, from the standpoint of an

139

Olympian good humour, for which Right and Left are but two halves (and usually rather ridiculous halves) of the same basic human being. Nestroy's flair for the complicated, the contradictory, the ambiguous, the intertwined and surging in human nature, and his gift of catching with his palette just the half, the mixed, the broken soul-colours, make him the heir and successor of Laurence Sterne and put his dramatic psychology by the side of the modern chromatics of Wilde and Shaw. He resembles these two Irishmen also in that he had an unabashed preference for the most commonplace categories of dramatic literature — the family melodrama and the farce — but ennobled them to the highest levels by implanting in them his ripe, sparkling, and many-sided spirit. He in fact took nothing seriously, not even his own work. Although he saw completely through the hollow void of all theatrical machinery, he nevertheless worked unconcernedly with the old traditional " props " and the immemorial gags that Plautus and Terence had employed to make audiences laugh. And he stole without shame — like Shakspere, Molière, and Sheridan. Another point of resemblance with Shaw lies in the fact that he was a destroyer of " romance," a pitiless torpedoer of all pathos and a tearer of illusions false to life. His *Lumpazivagabundus* was the dramatic annihilation of Romantic *form,* his later works destroyed Romantic *content* — a more killing parody of Byronism than his *Zerrissene* was never written. But it was a strange tragi-comedy in Nestroy's own life that his own generation never recognized in him the great critic of the times and satirist of society that it so badly needed. " Society comedies," said Laube, " are a gold-mine for the stage," and lamented that German production in this field was so far poorer than the French, oblivious of the fact that close by him there was an author who yearly and with the greatest ease produced society comedies that as far outclassed contemporary French work as a lava-vomiting volcano surpasses a firework display.

And, over and above all this, Nestroy absorbed into his comedies all the air of his city and his time — a time that with its peculiar poetry will never return — and thereby fulfilled the highest of all the comedy-writer's tasks. In this world there are no professions; most of the people are *rentiers,* or, as they said then in Vienna, " particulars." The professionists do not work, and that is (so to say) their " *faculté maîtresse.*" The activity of the engineers consists in falling in love with their pupils, the architects never look at a plan, Knieriem is a theosophical cobbler like Jakob Böhme, to whom he is scarcely inferior in " stupid profundity," and the tailor Zwirn is a variety of the genus illiterate snob — a genus that Thackeray forgot. Money is beer-money, and social questions readily reduce themselves to pieces of luck, dowries, and legacies. But the king of this country is the ever present manservant, a Hercules of laziness, armoured in a brazen will to vinous loafing, out of which he builds an all-embracing world-view.

Three months after the poet's death, however, the literary historian Emil Kuh wrote that a line of Halm made all Nestroy " æsthetically invisible." For decades thereafter the public, led astray by " expert opinions " like this, had only eyes for the crude forms that Nestroy used as deceptive wrappings in which to bring that forbidden article philosophy into the theatre. The " mimicry " of the American leaf-butterfly too is not detectable by the unpractised eye — but why should it be? It is precisely the impossibility of detection that gives mimicry its practical value. Nestroy's self-camouflage in the local farce was his weapon in the struggle for existence, by which he managed to get his pieces put on, talked about, and praised. Today, when it can no longer hurt Nestroy's theatrical prospects, it might as well be recognized that it was a vernal and living leaf-butterfly and not a dead leaf.

Strangely indeed, Nestroy had one contemporary who embodied the type of the poet in its highest purity, Hans Christian Andersen. The wide public's standpoint towards Andersen is more or less the same as that of the subaltern who thought that Julius Cæsar could not really have been a great man because he only wrote for the lower forms. Since, in fact, Andersen was so great a poet that even the children could understand him, the grown-ups regard him as not good enough for themselves. But the genuine poet is a King Midas : what he touches turns to gold and — there is about him, too, a trace of the ass's ears, of the child's simplicity.

Moreover, Andersen's works have a dual basis. Seen outwardly, they appear to be nothing but simple fairy-tales, and they can be read as such, as children do read them every day. But they *ought* not to be read as such, for in their innermost essence they are satires that have chosen the form of the fairy-tale. Andersen, it is true, gave himself out as a story-teller talking to children, but this is only an assumed standpoint; naïveté is not his condition, but his rôle, and this art-form can quite justly be described as ironic in the sense that Socrates gave to the word. It is given only to rude

Andersen

141

mankind and to genius to produce the impression of simplicity, but that does not mean that we should confuse these two, for they stand at the extreme opposite poles of human expressive faculty. And it was precisely through his plainness and artistic realism, which enabled him completely to vanish inside his objects, that Andersen was so profound and effective a satirist.

At bottom, indeed, every poet is a satirist. The poet looks on the world with unprejudiced and keen-sighted eyes and so naturally discovers a great many things that, it seems to him, are important, but have been insufficiently observed, or wrongly observed, or, for that matter, are false themselves. And so there awakens in him a need to remedy these evils by bringing them into the light with all possible distinctness. The best means to this end was, and is, satire. Deep ethical seriousness, reforming goodwill, and the gift of seeing correctly are the roots of genuine, vitalizing, poetic satire.

Andersen's fundamental theme is the eternal conflict of genius with philistinism, soulless materialism, sated complacency, intolerant narrowness, the inertia of habit of the average man. All shades of human limitedness, untruth, and egoism are mirrored in these tales, save that they are usually displayed, not in men, but in animals, plants, and domestic utensils, more or less in fable fashion. Nevertheless, no one would even think of calling these poems fables, for a fable is something that essentially speaks to the reason — when the fabulist relates to us the stupidity of the goose, the conceit of the peacock, the cowardice of the hare, we always feel that he is cocking an eye on us and asking: " Whom does that remind you of? " It is always too transparently obvious that he is talking allegorically. With Andersen, on the contrary, we forget entirely that the phenomena are really only carriers of human thoughts and feelings. The fox of the fable is at bottom nothing but the idea of wiliness, he is not a definite or individual fox, nor really for that matter a fox at all. Andersen's beings, on the contrary, are not personified virtues and vices, but living originals. We are firmly convinced that the cucumber is blasé, the weathercock is conceited, the money-box pig insolent, the necktie vain, the pen jealous, the garter prudish. All these fantastic creations condense to realities, become our personal acquaintances.

One of the chief characteristics of the philistine is that he regards himself as the mid point of the world, and his affairs as the most (indeed, the only) important thing in it. He estimates the value of his fellow-creatures merely according to the degree in which they are like himself and assumes that everything which differs from him is, by that very fact, worth less. Consequently we find professional futility a constantly recurring motif in Andersen. A second trait, related to the first, is that of professional arrogance; most of Andersen's creatures are pure bureaucrats, who start from the position that their job exists for them and not they for their job. The snail family is entirely convinced that the burdock is only in the world for the purpose of feeding it, and the rain to give it a little drum music, and when none of the family is any longer boiled and eaten, it concludes that the human race must have become extinct. The tomcat declares that a creature which cannot arch its back and spit fire is wholly unqualified to give opinions, and the muckworm has only one thought on seeing the tropics: what incomparable vegetation and how good it will taste when it decays. But the philistine character contains yet another trait, that no philistine is content with the place that Providence has assigned to him; every one of them pushes beyond his natural gifts, imagining himself to be more than he is. The darning-needle assumes from the very start that it is a sewing-needle, and in the end that it is a breast-pin; the smoothing-iron thinks it is a steam engine that can go on the rails and pull a train; the hand-cart declares that it is a coach and four because it runs on wheels; and the rocking-horse talks of nothing but training and breed. Every one has his pet life-lie, all want to live beyond their condition, cut a dash, throw dust in one another's eyes.

From these types, which taken together constitute a wide cross-section of everyday life, Andersen passes on to a still higher sort of satire that often contains a whole philosophy of human nature in a nutshell. For example, is not the situation of the Goblin in " The Goblin and the Shopkeeper " the situation of all men; do we not all oscillate between love of porridge and good butter and love of poetry, which one cannot eat? And " The Emperor's New Clothes," does it not contain a whole sociology? All maintain that they are seeing the Emperor's robes, although he has none on, for the word has been given that if anyone does not see them, he must be entirely stupid or unfit for his office. And the story of " The Ugly Duckling " is at bottom nothing more or less than that of the destiny and course of genius, for genius is marked before all the world precisely by its humility; because it is different from the rest, it regards itself as less, as particularly inferior, and the rest in turn mock it, hate it, and suppress it. " It is too big and uncommon," say all the ducks, " and so it has to be whacked," until it finally appears that the reason why it possesses none of the accepted virtues and beauties of a duck is that it happens to be a swan. Almost all Andersen's tales admit of an extended interpretation. One could even write fat books about them, just as the Chinese savants did about the nightingale — and about as usefully, for Andersen's poems, at bottom, tolerate no " elucidation." What gives them their high charm is precisely the apparently complete spontaneity of the narrative, which presents one impression after another, and the understanding love that only wants to show and no more.

The Blue Bird These qualities enabled Andersen to read all things. It is as though he possessed the magic stone of Maeterlinck's *Blue Bird;* he only needs to turn it to entice the souls of things, and out they come at once — the souls of cats and dogs and even dead things, milk, bread, sugar. And all became more beautiful and handsome. The hours leave the clock and become bright maidens stretching out hands to one another. Nothing is without soul or without life. The whole world is full of ideas and sensations, and all that is necessary is to know how to read. And the poet reads them. He reads the tender and loving thoughts of the nightingale, the false and cruel thoughts of the cat, the soft and modest thoughts of the rose, the noble thoughts of the hound, the proud thoughts of the poppy, the envious thoughts of the mole. But the humming-top too, and the ink-pot, the clothes-brush, the grandfather clock, the teacup, all have their various sensations that can be deciphered.

And, like Tyltyl, the poet needs only to twist his stone and he is in the realm of the past, among the dead. But they are dead no more, but sit contentedly in front of their doors and gossip. And he ascends into the realm of the future where the unborn souls are, and they become living and answer him. What he seeks everywhere is the Blue Bird, for to him who possesses this is revealed the last secret. And that, after all, is the one thing that Andersen could not discover, any more than Tyltyl or any poet before or after him. The poet for ever seeks that bird, for its sake alone he wanders through all the realms of being and touches the souls of things. True, he will never possess it. But that is probably a very good thing, for if he did, he would no longer be a seeker.

144

CHAPTER III

BUBBLE BUSINESS

> " *The idea that the only justifiable world-interpretation is that which allows counting, reckoning, weighing, seeing, and touching, and nothing else, is stupid and naïve, in so far indeed as it is not pathological and imbecile.*"
>
> *Nietzsche:* Fröhliche Wissenschaft

All thought is repetition, but repetition of increasing concentration. All higher levels of consciousness are reproductions of earlier series of ideas in an essentially compressed and crystallized form. Concentration is the hall-mark of increasing cultural development, and if there is such a thing as intellectual progress, it is to be looked for here. But these passages into closer and yet closer states of aggregation always involve qualitative changes also, and we can equally, therefore, say that thought is never repetition. Just as ice is the same in its components as water and is yet a phenomenon of quite different character, so also the process of thought-condensation involves a transformation: a stronger formation and clarification of spiritual life, but at the same time a stiffening, freezing, and ageing of it.

The refrain

A very distinct acceleration of the tempo of this recapitulation-process can be followed in the history of the last hundred years. In the Restoration period European mankind attempted to renovate certain sets of ideas, forms of art, and feelings about life belonging to the Middle Ages. In the period between 1848 and 1870, with which the present chapter is to deal, it worked over afresh the whole curriculum of the Enlightenment in tabloid lessons, under the name of *Positivism;* after the war with France a sort of neo-Classicism appeared in Germany and held its ground for a time, while the literary movement that came to the top in the Berlin of the eighties reminds one very definitely, in program and practice, of the *Sturm und Drang* (which itself was frankly an early Naturalism), and the contemporary painting was akin to the early Impressionism of the Rococo. And, for that matter, in

145

the most recent times we ourselves have been repeating the development of the first half of the nineteenth century at a still faster rate; while the turn of the century was marked everywhere by neo-Romantic currents, and the first decade harked back to the Biedermeier, in the second decade the Expressionists and Activists took up almost every position that Young Germany had occupied. We need only compare, say, a one-act play of Maeterlinck with a Romantic destiny-drama, or a post-war tendency-piece with a play of Gutzkow, to recognize at once that progress in concentration has been very considerable.

As to political history, Hegel laid it down that every political constellation occurred twice, and herein the great historical thinker was not showing himself merely as an " inverted prophet," for the two decades that followed the mid point of the century confirmed his proposition in a most conspicuous fashion. In this period France twice adopted the republican form — momentarily in the February Revolution, but enduringly after Sedan. The Italian people rose twice against Austrian domination, vainly in 1848, but successfully in 1859. The attempt to detach the German duchies of Schleswig and Holstein from Denmark was made twice; it came to nothing in 1848, and it succeeded in 1864. The latent conflict between the two leading powers of Germany became acute twice, producing the crisis of 1850, with the diplomatic defeat of Prussia, and the war of 1866, with the military defeat of Austria. The German crown found itself twice in the hands of the King of Prussia, who rejected it in 1849 and accepted it in 1871. Always, like a refrain, the same melody appears twice, but only on the second occasion does it strike home.

The February Revolution   The signal for the great conflagration that gripped Europe in 1848 was, as almost always, given in France. The immediate cause of the February Revolution in Paris was the opposition to Guizot, who, as baldly doctrinaire in his policy as principal minister as he was in his learned historical works, obstinately resisted the electoral reforms that were passionately demanded. The inward causes have been elucidated with admirable insight by Lorenz von Stein in the third volume of his *Geschichte der sozialen Bewegung in Frankreich,* in which he says: " The educated ruling classes of society *must* appropriate the power of the State, and not because they regard this as advantageous or prudent, not because it will be easy for them, but because it is their *unalterable nature* to do so. . . . Therefore, where there exists a social class

146

which really dominates, but which the power of the State eludes, conflict will and must ensue between them." The monarchy's only alternatives were either simply to give in or else to annihilate the possessing classes; the first course it would not, and the second it could not take. " But," continues Stein, " was the monarchy not secured from *political* overthrow by the possessing classes out of their fear of the *social* revolution? " And he answers very shrewdly: " It is *false* to believe that anything living forgoes that which is *unshakably* rooted in its nature for fear of the consequences, even to its existence, that the outcome might involve." In these words Stein lays bare the real knots in the almost insoluble tangle that we call " domestic " politics. In fact, in every state there is always but one single class that rules, and this means that it rules illegally. It is darkly conscious of this — its wisest heads, indeed, know it with entire clarity — and it seeks to justify it by clearer dialectic or fiery declamation, to soften it by brilliant deeds and merits, by private integrity, by mildness in practice; not seldom it even *suffers* under it. But it cannot help itself. Its members feel that this supremacy means their undoing — for in every injustice slumbers, maybe for centuries, the seed of its ruin — but it is far stronger than they. Deep-rooted in human beings, this heart's inertia and spiritual cowardice that never dares to acknowledge its own wrongdoing is the secret malady of which all societies perish. To it the philanthropic aristocracy of feudal France and the fraternal democracy of Revolutionary France alike succumbed. It is the common abyss that will swallow Liberalism and Clericalism, plutocracy and proletarian dictatorship. Salvation from the curse of injustice is possible only in a *Christion state*, but such a state has never yet existed.

Stein concludes with the words: " And there, in one stroke, in a single night, without great effort, without preparation, without (strange as it appears) any consciousness in the participants of the issue of their fight, it broke loose! Paris rose, and the work of eighteen years, the fine edifice of human wisdom, was seized as by a tempest and blown away. . . . If events are to be measured according to the degree of distinctness and decisiveness with which they affirm the great laws of human life, then the February Revolution is the most significant event in all the later history of Europe." The Citizen King did very ill when he set himself against the Third Estate — which had become the First — and its desire for power. But at the same time he did right, for a monarchy that

147

is content to give up the essence that nature put into it is unworthier than one which is beaten by the elemental force of facts.

In reality the three days' street-battle was decided before it began, for nowhere, not even in the army, was there a king's party. Louis Philippe fled to England, and abdicated in favour of his grandson, just as his predecessor had done and with as little practical result. The royal throne was burnt in the Place de la Bastille, and the National Assembly proclaimed the Republic. The hero of the day for the next three months was the poet Lamartine, who had already made himself very popular as the leader of the opposition to Guizot and as the author of the highly tendentious but bold and captivating *History of the Girondins* and now, as Foreign Minister, reached the climax of his reputation with his brilliant speeches and kindling proclamations. His republican ideology caused him to decline the presidency, which was offered to him, and thus he renounced a career that would probably have resembled that of Napoleon III in brilliance and collapse. The experiment of having a poet at the head of Europe would probably have had fatal results, but psychologically it would have been exceedingly interesting.

The National Workshops The risk that the political revolution might transform itself into a social one materialized in a very short time. The intellectual leader of the Fourth Estate was Louis Blanc, who in his *Histoire de dix ans* had dealt with the first decade of Louis Philippe's reign with plastic force and razor-keen polemic, and who tabled his economic program in his *Organisation du travail*. His principal proposal was for working and producing societies supported by the State. He was, as we have already remarked, one of the bitterest opponents of the Manchester school; in his view, free competition was the cause of all social evils, of the misery of the workers, of the crises of trade, of wars; and therefore men must have recourse to its opposite, association. The social "workshops" proposed by him are specialized, they group only the workers of the same profession. The necessary capital is to be found by the State, pay is equal for all, and the managers of the work are to be elected. The yearly surplus is to be employed in increased wages, old-age pensions, and extension of operations. In short, as Blanc himself categorically said, the State was to become the "banker of the poor." After the Revolution this project was taken up by the provisional Government, and "*ateliers nationaux*" were established which offered wages and work to every citizen. They were flooded with every sort of seeker for gain, but it very soon appeared that the State could not give them sufficient pay, still less offer them sufficient work, and in the end, in order not to have them completely idle, they were turned on to wholly unnecessary digging. The idea of National Workshops was in fact a pitiable fiasco, and all the bourgeois theorists of economics since have covered it with triumphant scorn. But it must be said, nevertheless, that the experiment in no way corresponded to what Blanc had intended. The workers were not qualified craftsmen, but casual unemployed, and the organization was not on well-considered principles of grouping, but a desperate expedient of the Government to divert the proletariat from revolution — which in fact failed, since after a few months the workmen rose in the " June Revolution," which Cavaignac, on whom the National Assembly had conferred dictatorial powers, stamped out in blood; nearly ten thousand persons were killed by the governmental troops. It is worth noting that Liberal bourgeoisies, in almost every case where they attain to power (that is, really, in France and in England), act against revolutionary movements with a brutality that reactionary absolutism seldom surpasses; but from the standpoint of historical necessity the victory of the bourgeoisie over the Fourth Estate was as legitimate as its victory over the King.

But how was it that the Revolution of 1848 ran so completely different a course in Germany and Austria from that which it took in France? Is this fact a " negative instance " telling against Lorenz von Stein's masterly analysis? The answer is no, for on German soil the monarchy won, not because it was the monarchy, but because there was no bourgeoisie which might have defeated it. And here as always we see that it is the spirit that decides and not the material power. In France, too, the monarch controlled the army, the police, the administrative machinery, but the spirit was in the possession of the bourgeoisie. One may despise the *Zeitgeist* as mean, banal, plebeian, unspiritual, but it was (and precisely on that account) the spirit, and the only spirit, of the time. In Germany the professors, lyric poets, and itinerant orators were not possessed of this spirit, and consequently they could achieve no revolution.

Even so, the year 1848 is for the whole constitutional life of Europe the most important in the century. We remarked in our first chapter that after the Congress of Vienna the State system of the Continent was based, not as previously on two foreign-policy fronts, but — unified by the Holy Alliance — on two domestic-policy fronts: namely, governments and peoples. Now the general front of the people arose in one outburst and in almost every country — save only in England, where it was already fused in the Government, and in Russia, where it was only just beginning a subterranean existence. And although the old régime was, in general, restored, it was in fact annihilated, for from 1848 absolutism, though remaining superficially a possibility, became inwardly an impossibility.

The March Revolution   The decisive month was, as everyone knows, March. Vienna made the beginning in driving out Metternich and setting up its National Guard. A few days later the barricades went up in Berlin. After indecisive street-fighting the troops were withdrawn from the city, at the personal wish of the King, who later remarked that " we all lay on our bellies in those days." A Prussian Parliament, an Austrian Reichstag, and a German National Assembly were improvised. The principal demands were: freedom of the press, right of combination, trial by jury, arms for the people, a new constitution for the Reich, converting it from an association of states to a federal state, which the " Little German " group in the National Assembly conceived of as led by Prussia and excluding Austria, while the " Great German " faction would have no Prussian hegemony and wished to bring in Austria. This Assembly, which met at Frankfurt in the Paulskirche, had amongst its assets much of Germany's best talent: the world-celebrities Jakob Grimm and Ludwig Uhland, the " Old Germans " Arndt and Jahn, and the " Young Germans " Laube and Ruge; the historians Droysen and Duncker; the literary historians Vilmar and Gervinus; the poets Wilhelm Jordan and Anastasius Grün; Dahlmann and Waitz, editors of the great *Quellenkunde der deutschen Geschichte;* the art-philosopher Vischer and the archæologist Welcker; Karl Vogt, the spokesman of neo-Materialism, and Ignaz Döllinger, the founder of Old Catholicism — one and all, men who were profoundly wise in their professions and profoundly ignorant of politics. Frederick William IV of Prussia, elected Emperor of the Germans, declared that he could only accept the crown with the consent of all the other German princes — which was a mere excuse, for he did not want it at all, since, as he expressed it, it carried with it the " tainted breath of the Revolution." Most of the more important sovereigns of the Germanic Federation refused it. In Munich, too, there were

March disturbances, which led to the abdication of Ludwig I in favour of his son; here the real cause of the " constitutional " conflict was the relation of the King to the dancer Lola Montez, a half-Creole, beautiful and eccentric, who in consequence of the scandal had to emigrate to America, where she put herself and him on the stage. The King, a highly original personality of an indubitably artistic cast, took the whole *coup d'état* with an unconcern that seemed to the Abderites of Munich most reprehensible; on the day of his abdication he wrote: " Now I am perhaps the gayest soul in Munich."

On Slavonic soil, the Poles revolted in Prussian Posen and Austrian Cracow, and the Czechs in Prague, whither Frantisek Palacky, the historian of Bohemia, who represented for his people the idea of the crown of Wenceslas, summoned a Panslavonic Congress, in which the Russian anarchist Bakunin figured with the rest. Even thus early there were demands for an independent " Czechia " in the north, and " Slovenia " in the south, as well as, of course, for the full restoration of Poland. The detachment from the Habsburg State which these Slavonic peoples envisaged, the Hungarians actually carried out; the assembly dethroned the dynasty and put Louis Kossuth as dictator at the head of the Magyar Government. On the same day as in Berlin, the capital of Lombardy revolted, with the King of Sardinia as leader, and Radetzky, the veteran of eighty-two, who had been chief of the Austrian General Staff as far back as 1813, had to retire beyond the Mincio; in Venice, too, the Austrian garrison was unable to maintain itself, and Italian irregulars appeared in the Trentino.

But with the autumn an ebb movement set in. Prince Windischgrätz at the head of Austrian troops reconquered Prague and Vienna, which were not supported in time by the Hungarian insurgents, and the victory of Reaction was dishonoured by the shooting of numerous citizens, among them Robert Blum, in spite of the immunity adhering to his position as a member of the Frankfurt Parliament. The reoccupation of Berlin was accomplished, so to say, patriarchally, General Wrangel — popularly called " Papa Wrangel " — marching in and disarming the National Guard without meeting with resistance. In Italy Radetzky burst forth from his quadrilateral of fortresses, defeated Charles Albert of Sardinia (whom his subjects called " *il re tentenna*, King Slowcoach ") at Custozza, Mortara, and Novara, and forced him to abdicate in favour of his son Victor Emmanuel. Against

The Peripeteia

151

the Hungarian revolution the Tsar gave his support with an unselfishness rare in international politics, his real motive being a pathological hatred of all libertarian movements: two Russian armies entered Hungary and forced the Magyar army to capitulate at Vilagós. The Austrian commander Haynau, nicknamed Hyena, distinguished himself, as he had already done in Lombardy, by particular and infamous cruelty towards the vanquished, on account of which, later on, he was roughly handled by the crowd both in Brussels and in London. Meantime Ferdinand I — of whom the popular wit said that it was not for nothing that he came to the throne on the Feast of St. Simplicius — had abdicated and been succeeded by his nephew Franz Josef, who was destined to sit on the throne almost as long as it was there to sit on. Austria was again governed absolutely, and the bureaucracy resumed its good old Austrian routine, that unique compound of malice and stupidity. All letters were read by the postal authorities (which led to the general adoption of code), and many simply suppressed. The censorship was so sensitive that the Burgtheater was forbidden to present plays in which nobles married commoners; the subversive beard might once more land its wearer in the guard-house, and official persons were permitted only moustache and whiskers, the latter "only of moderate length."

In Prussia the King gave his country a constitution, out of his own plenary powers and without the co-operation of a popular assembly — whence it was called the "granted" constitution. It stated that the legislative power was to be exercised in common by the King — represented by a responsible minister, but himself irresponsible — and the two Houses of the Landtag: namely, the Herrenhaus, whose members were nominated by the King and whose position was hereditary, and the Abgeordnetenhaus, which was appointed by the three-class system. Under this latter the primary voters designated electors, and these in turn the deputies; the number of electors stepped down in three stages according to taxable capacity, which resulted in the first and wealthiest class returning as many as the second or middle class and the third, with the smallest incomes. This franchise, which existed in Prussia right down to the establishment of the Republic, was thus neither equal, nor direct, nor secret.

Olmütz   As to Germany at large, the Diet of the Federation reappeared — a body that even so reactionary a politician as Metternich's

152

successor, Prince Schwarzenberg, described as a "torn and threadbare coat," a "clumsy, worn-out instrument, in no wise adequate for present conditions," a "thoroughly shaken, very rickety booth," which was bound shortly "to crumple up from feebleness." A constitutional conflict which occurred in Electoral Hesse in 1850 seemed as if it would bring this prophecy to pass. The Landtag refused the taxes, payment of which thereupon ceased all over the country. When the Government threatened the land with a declaration of a state of war, the officials ceased to function and almost all the officers resigned. The Diet declared that the refusal to pay taxes was illegal, and decreed "execution." This, however, was an intrusion into the sphere of influence of Prussia, Hesse lying between the two separated halves of that kingdom. As a breach seemed inevitable, the Emperor Franz Josef at Bregenz concluded with the Kings of Württemberg and Bavaria a military convention against Prussia; and even the Tsar, at a meeting with him in Warsaw, gave most satisfactory reassurances. The demonstrative invasion of Hesse by Prussian troops was answered by Bavaria with a like movement, and at Bronnzell, near Fulda, there was a skirmish — of which the only victim, however, was a grey horse. Austria deployed her forces in Bohemia and Moravia, while Prussia mobilized the whole of the Landwehr. The plan of Radetzky (drawn up for him, as in Italy, by his Chief of Staff, Freiherr von Hess) was to unite with the Saxons and then to risk a decisive battle before the gates of Berlin. This was not by any means a hopeless venture, since the armed forces of Prussia were divided between middle Germany and the north, though the Prince of Prussia (the later Emperor William I) told Beust after the crisis that the Austrians might have got up to Berlin, but that it was doubtful if they would have got away again. In the end the desperate political position of Prussia, who was faced with the possibility of war on two fronts and even three (the Russian attitude being very suspicious), led to a peaceful solution. At the Crown Hotel in Olmütz was made that memorable agreement by which Prussia declared herself ready to withdraw her troops from Hesse, to disarm completely, and to renounce for the future schemes for the reorganization of Germany. Thus of Schwarzenberg's program: "First humiliate Prussia and then destroy her," the first part was fulfilled. It seemed that Olmütz sealed not only the Habsburg hegemony over Germany, but, worse, the arbitral position of Tsar Nicholas over all middle Europe; for it was that which had decided Prussia to retreat, as it had decided the fate of the revolutions of the previous year. And again the motive was that of stark reaction, for he was not in the least interested in the settlement of the German question, but only in the circumstance that Prussia, even though merely on grounds of personal prestige, was supporting the refusers of taxes. " Under his government," says Bismarck in his *Gedanken und Erinnerungen,* " we all lived as Russian vassals."

Shortly afterwards, however, the hegemony of the West passed to another, a very clever man who, wholly unexpectedly and yet after full preparation, entered from the wings. His election to the French presidency was due to the possessing classes' fear of social upheaval, which impelled them towards a democratic military dictatorship; to the Church, with which he shrewdly kept touch; and to the Napoleon-cult, which put him above his only serious rival, General Cavaignac. This was the first stage of his advance to power; the second and third conformed exactly to the precedent set by his uncle. In his *coup d'état* of December 2, 1851 he took the 18th Brumaire as his pattern; he dissolved the National Assembly as Napoleon I had dissolved the Council of Five Hundred, and had himself made Consul for ten years. A year later, on that 2nd of December which was the anniversary of Napoleon's coronation and of the battle of Austerlitz (incidentally, the accession anniversary of Franz Josef also), he asked the French to confer upon him the dignity of Emperor, herein again following the great example with the skilfully staged comedy of a " plebiscite "; the people, said the proclamation, was, as sole sovereign, to express its will as to the Constitution. Practically, however, this sovereignty of the people consisted only in the right to give itself an absolute government. In truth, it was an alliance of the sword and money-bag; France was " saved by sharp practice and case-shot," as Victor Hugo said in a snorting condemnatory poem. The bourgeois party made no secret whatever of its view that the Empire was merely the lesser of two evils. The other states accepted the new régime without comment; only the Tsar made the slight reservation that he desired to address the parvenu, not as *Monsieur mon frère,* but as *bon ami,* and Frederick William IV boggled at the ordinal " Third " as contrary to the decisions of the Congress of Vienna, the powers having never recognized the Duke of Reichstadt as Napoleon II.

Napoleon III has often been compared to his uncle, but there was scarcely the smallest resemblance between them, or, if any, it was at most in their common contempt for all "ideology," and their miscalculation of the ethical forces that are the real motors of world-history. And even these points of resemblance came from different sources in them; the nihilism of the first Emperor was the result of his colossal stature and dæmonic contempt of men, while that of the nephew came from mediocrity and decadent undervaluation of men. Napoleon I was as amoral as an earthquake, Napoleon III as immoral as a stock-exchange *coup;* what discharged itself in the former was shattering primal forces that knew nothing about ethos; in the latter, disintegrating Late instincts that wished to forget about ethos. The one was an elemental catastrophe, the other an incident of civilization.

Bismarck, in one of those brilliant *bons mots* of his that hit the mark with devastating certainty, called Napoleon III a misunderstood incapacity, "*une incapacité méconnue.*" Where Napoleon differed from this opponent in his political game — considering both purely as politicians, for as human personalities they are wholly incomparable with each other — was that he was far more expansive, soaring, chameleon-like, and shifty in his plans and correspondingly far more hesitant, labile, viscous, dreamy in their adoption, execution, and manipulation. Cavour, too, the other great statesman with whom the Emperor had to deal, was his superior both in strength of will and in elasticity. Moltke describes Napoleon's outward appearance thus: "A certain immobility of features, and, I might almost say, an extinguished look in his eyes, struck me. A friendly and even kindly smile predominated in his physiognomy, which had little that was Napoleonic about it. He usually sits with his head slightly on one side, quietly, and it may be that this very quietness, which it is known does not desert him in dangerous crises, is what imposes upon the mobile French." Over his real self there lay the watery sort of veil of impenetrability and impassivity that one sometimes observes in captains of industry and financial magnates. Drouyn de Lhuys, who was his Foreign Minister and an ardent Bonapartist, but knew him at close quarters, said: "His inscrutability resides in the absence of considered motives for his actions." His technique of continually improvising projects of doubtful soundness, of skilful but temporary patching, and his astounding facility for staving off the latent bankruptcy by cooking the accounts at times of apparent boom — here, too, the type that comes to one's mind is that of the *chevalier d'industrie* and the bourse gambler — produced, in fact, the impression of secret and profound calculation. In the later years of his reign, moreover, his capacity for action was very seriously impaired by stone, the pain of which frequently caused fainting-fits.

He had given out as his watchword: "*L'Empire c'est la paix,*" but very soon satire turned this into: "*L'Empire c'est l'épée.*" He was probably at heart no militarist, but if even the godlike *Roi Soleil* could only maintain his prestige by great wars, this dubious "throne-stealer" was doomed in advance to a course of alternately exciting and satisfying the French thirst for glory. His foreign policy was a system of far-ranging half-measures, of large-scale rivetings; he would have Germany and Italy alike united, not as strong national states, however, but as impotent federations, where possible under an avowed or unavowed French protectorate. Towards these two peoples one or the other policy could have been pursued, either to help them to union and secure their enduring friendship, or to use their fragmented condition to keep them permanently impotent. But to aim at both policies at once was the over-clever idea of a reckless speculator. Politicians who looked deeper saw through this: Disraeli called the Second Empire a tragicomedy. What Napoleon lacked, as against Bismarck and Cavour, was the straight line. And this was equally missing in his home policy; on the one hand he sought to give his rule the appearance of a democratic régime — and in fact he supported it on the army, the masses, and the lower clergy — while on the other he kept down the social movement by harsh laws; freedom of opinion by rigorous supervision of the press, theatres, and associations; and constitutional rights by barefaced influencing of elections. After the Orsini attempt he even issued a "law of security" which gave the police the right to arrest any suspect without formality — just as in the days of the *lettres de cachet* by which Louis le Grand clothed his name with fear — and which it used with such rigour that a mere "seditious silence" was regarded as justifying action — here the ill-omened parallel is the Jacobins and the Reign of Terror. Publicists hostile to the Government were continually threatened with imprisonment and fine, which, however, did not prevent newspaper polemics from unfolding a splendid luxuriance of venom, above all in Rochefort's *Lanterne* and *Marseillaise*. "The system," says Treitschke in one of his careless but suggestive formulations, "was a monarchical

156

socialism." But the most untenable contradictions in which the Emperor involved himself were brought about by his Clericalism, to which he felt himself driven, partly because he hoped that the Legitimist party could be induced thereby to discard Charles X's grandson and to come over to his side, and partly because of the bigotry of the Empress Eugénie, *née* Countess Montijo, who for twenty years played the part of Europe's fashion-queen as Marie Antoinette had done in her time — more beautiful than Marie Antoinette, equally given to intrigue, and equally superficial. The protection which Napoleon was thus led to give the States of the Church crossed his policy of Italian union, and the power over schools and universities, literature and private life, which he conceded to the Church brought him into opposition with the Liberalism of the all-powerful bourgeoisie, which formed the very basis of his rule.

And in truth the modern plutocracy has never found more brilliant and grandiose expression than under the Second Empire. Napoleon III deserved even more than Louis Philippe the title of a Prince of the Bourse. Financial scandals in the courts were a daily sensation under his government. As early as 1852 the brothers Péreire, two Portuguese Jews, founded the first modern bank, the Crédit Mobilier, of which people said that it was the biggest gambling-hell in Europe. It speculated wildly in everything — railways, hotels, colonies, canals, mines, theatres — and after fifteen years was totally bankrupt. A new and permanent figure in public life was the *rastaquouère*, the word implying originally the rich exotic who tastelessly, insolently, crudely flung his gold about Paris, but soon (by a characteristic mutation) coming to mean the big showy business man who was " useful," and always a swindler. Taking everything together, society life under Napoleon III was more corrupt, cynical, and materialistic even than under the Citizen King, but it was far more temperamental, colourful, and witty; in the one régime there was still displayed a certain big-boned force and vitality, in the other there was already an interesting overtrainedness and a phosphorescence of decay; it was a sort of Rococo of the Third Estate.

The watchword given out by the Emperor that France must "march at the head of civilization " was first of all implemented by Haussmann, the Prefect of the Seine, who laid out fine street-lines, squares, and gardens, rebuilt whole districts, and put up exhibition buildings and so made a new Paris that was the true copy of the new régime, all façade, braggart, artificial, and parvenu. In 1855 the first Paris world-exposition took place — a *"revanche pour Londres,"* where four years earlier (on the suggestion of Albert, the Prince Consort, the "first gentleman in Europe") the very first of all such had been held; its "Crystal Palace," Paxton's pioneer effort in iron and glass, still stands to remind us of it. A second Paris exposition took place within the period of the Empire (1867), at which the great sensation was the newly-discovered art of Egypt and which was visited by nearly all the potentates of Europe; a Pole seized the opportunity to attempt the assassination of the Tsar Alexander II. The second London exhibition, of 1862, similarly laid itself out for Oriental art, but it led also to a much less welcome phenomenon in the shape of the first "International Working Men's Association," whose hidden head was Karl Marx. In 1869 the Suez Canal was opened, a triumph for French civilization; already in use three thousand years before, it had fallen into disrepair; restored by the Persians about 500 B.C., it again silted up; cleared a third time by Trajan, it became completely impracticable during the Middle Ages. Leibniz had indicated its importance in a memorandum addressed to Louis XIV, and Bonaparte had initiated preliminary works during the Egyptian campaign. Now the Compagnie Universelle du Canal Maritime de Suez, after buying the ground from the Egyptian Government and working for ten years, put it in condition again; it meant a saving of about forty per cent in the journey time to India, and through it the Mediterranean, hitherto an inland sea of south Europe, became a strait that united two of the world's oceans.

The Crimean War

Before he had reigned two years, Napoleon found the opportunity to stand forth in foreign policy. It was afforded by the efforts of the Tsar to achieve his long-intended expansion into the Balkans. Nicholas I was the most reactionary ruler that the classic land of Reaction has ever experienced. The Dekabrist revolt with which his reign had begun had convinced him that Russia could only be governed by iron terror. Under him the universities were supervised like monasteries, and books censored with the rigidity of the Inquisition, but the only result was to develop a technique of allusive writing far surpassing that of the Encyclopædia in refinement. In order to prevent as far as possible any infection from the poisonous material of Western Liberalism, he either forbade his subjects to travel abroad or else made it difficult for them by very heavy passport-taxes. He did not, indeed, go so far as his seventeenth-century predecessors who sent " book-readers " to prison, but writers and the Peter-Paul prison were closely cognate notions, and indeed an inseparable association of ideas. In a few centuries, perhaps all that will be known of Nicholas I is that in his reign Dostoievski was sentenced to be hanged. His hatred of everything that even remotely suggested popular rights was so great that when he visited Berlin, the Landtag was closed so as not to offend him by so revolutionary a spectacle.

It was he who launched that winged word that named the Sultan " the sick man of Europe." If he supported the Christian populations of the Balkans in their efforts for emancipation, it was self-evident that he did not do so from any interest in them — for they were a contradiction of his whole system — and that he was simply aiming at a Balkan protectorate. The fact that it was in 1853 that he came forward with fresh demands in this sense was partially accounted for by that year's being the fourth centenary of the fall of Constantinople — but world-history does not usually let itself be influenced by the dates of jubilees and suchlike.

When the Porte declined them, a Russian army crossed the Pruth and occupied Moldavia and Wallachia. But in a Russian victory France saw a threat to her Syrian and England to her Indian interests. Both powers therefore concluded an alliance with Turkey; later, by a shrewd political move of Cavour's, the little kingdom of Sardinia was brought in on their side. An Anglo-French fleet appeared in the Baltic, but did not risk an attack on Kronstadt. Austria, too, took up a threatening attitude, which compelled the Tsar " on strategical grounds " to evacuate the principalities, which were thereupon occupied by Austrian troops. The struggle concentrated itself on the Crimean peninsula in South Russia. The Russians were beaten at the Alma, at Inkerman, and on the Chernaya, but the main bulwark, the fortress of Sevastopol, held firm against attack by land and sea, thanks to the magnificent organization of the defence by the Kurlander Totleben; not until almost a year had passed was the Malakoff Tower stormed and the now defenceless city given up. On the one side, threats of war by Austria and Sweden and the bad state of the army and the administration, and, on the other, fearful cholera losses and the difficulties and insecurities of munition supply over a long sea route, brought the combatants to an accommodation, and the

Peace of Paris was signed in the spring of 1856. Little was changed thereby, and a French diplomat truthfully remarked that no one could tell from its terms which was the victor and which the vanquished. There were no war indemnities; the territorial changes consisted merely in Russia's ceding the mouth of the Danube and a small tract of Bessarabia to the Danubian Principalities. The latter, while remaining formally under Turkish suzerainty, were declared neutral and united in the Principality of Roumania; Alexander Cuza, a self-elected ruler, was invested in 1859, but his maladministration led in 1866 to his forced abdication and replacement by Prince Charles of Hohenzollern-Sigmaringen. The Straits Agreement was expressly renewed, and the Black Sea neutralized and closed to all warships. Turkey, which guaranteed equal rights to Christians and Mohammedans, was received into the " Concert of Europe " — by no means to the improvement of its harmony.

The diplomatic changes consequent on the Crimean War were, however, very important. Sardinia, by joining the Coalition, had made herself a political factor; she was admitted to the peace conference, whereas Prussia, thanks to the halting and hesitant attitude that she had observed during the war, only succeeded in getting a seat after — in Bismarck's phrase — " hanging around in the ante-room " for a long while. France replaced Russia as hegemon, 1812 was " avenged," Napoleon was the first man in Europe, and his throne seemed unshakably secured, all the more so because in the year of the peace a son and heir was born. Austria had brought herself into the most shameful and disadvantageous position; Radetzky, in a memorial to the Emperor, had proposed alliance with Russia on the basis of a partition of Turkey, but it was thought preferable to follow the policy of Schwarzenberg, who had said that Austria would once more astonish the world with her ingratitude. He was not destined, indeed, to bring this prophecy to pass, but his successor was the executor of his will: Austria, secured in the rear by an offensive and defensive alliance with Prussia — to which Bismarck agreed with the greatest reluctance — not only occupied the Danubian Principalities, as we have seen, but set on foot corps of observation in Galicia, Bukovina, and Transylvania, so that Russia was obliged to mobilize twice as many battalions against her neighbour as she put into the Crimea, and found her movements completely crippled. Justly angered, Tsar Nicholas said to the Austrian Ambassador: " Do you know

who were the two stupidest kings of Poland? Sobieski and I."
(Both had rescued Austria, and both got ingratitude for their reward.) Thenceforth the Russian motto became: " The road to
Constantinople lies through Vienna," and from this moment dates
that hostility of Russia and Austria but for which the World War
would never have happened, though on the other hand German
unity would never have been achieved.

Given, however, that a policy of perfidy (and the phrase is
anyhow a pleonasm at bottom) is to be observed, then at least it
should have been energetically pursued. But Austria's lukewarm-
ness put her in the bad books of the Western powers also; she had
not the courage to " stab in the back," but she fussed as though
intending to do so, ruined her finances with costly troop-move-
ments, and lost more soldiers by cholera than she would have done
in a war. " The good Austrians," said Bismarck in a letter of
1853, " are like Bottom the weaver in *Midsummer Night's
Dream.*" It had been her tradition and practice from the time of
Joseph II to try to put everything into her pocket, to make preten-
sions on all hands, but to concede nothing to her rivals; in this
case she did not want Russia to play the principal rôle in the
Balkans, or Prussia in Germany, or France in Italy, but desired it
for herself in all three cases.

One of the reasons why peace was reached relatively quickly
was the change which took place in Russia, in 1855 when Nicholas I died suddenly and was succeeded by Alexander II, the
" Liberator of the Serfs," one of the noblest and wisest rulers of
his time. He issued a general amnesty, reduced the army, promoted the development of a railway system, reformed the courts,
withdrew the upper schools from Church supervision, and granted
his people a sort of self-government through the Duma (an assembly of city deputies) and the Zemstvo (an elected council representative of the provincial circles). But his greatest deed was the
abolition of serfage, by which in 1861 more than twenty-one million peasants obtained their freedom; till then there had been on
an average fifty serfs to one " owner of souls." His motives were
from the head as well as the heart; " It is better," he said, " that
we should do it from above than that it should happen from below."
The exceedingly unwise Polish outbreak of 1863, however, brought
him nearer to the Old Russian party: on this occasion Prussia
earned the gratitude of Russia by closing her Polish frontier. None
the less, he planned to give the Empire a general constitution,

*The
liberator
Tsar*

161

and this would have come to pass, but in 1881 he fell a victim to a Nihilist bomb. That it was this one of all the tsars that Nihilism most continuously attacked gives one to think. It shows that terror is part of the *a priori* structure of Russian soul-life.

The Russian soul

This is one of the many traits that render the Russian soul so enigmatic to the Europeans. The fact of the matter is that the Russian is unable to look at the world with *two* eyes, to recognize that the truth is always the product of a double view. He lacks stereoscopic vision. He is entirely incapable of seeing things *in the round:* namely, from the front and the back. He does not know that every dogma requires its counter-dogma, as the divinely willed other half of its life, to be wedded with which is the beginning of fruitfulness. This is why, though Hegel long had a very great influence in Russia as elsewhere, the Russian is never a Hegelian. Spengler, in a foot-note in his second volume, makes the profound observation: " The idea of a Russian's being an astronomer! He does not see the stars at all; he sees only the horizon. Instead of the vault he sees the down-hang of the heavens. . . . Mystical Russian love is love of the plain . . . all along the earth, ever along and along." He cannot conceive the world as a vault, his eyes look always along the flat surface (which does not in the least mean that he is superficial), and hence he is not only no Hegelian, but no philosopher at all. Vladimir Solovyev says of the philosophical literature of his country: " In these works all that is philosophy is definitely non-Russian, and what has the real Russian stamp has no sort of resemblance to any philosophy, and sometimes indeed is quite unmeaning. . . . The authors either stop at brief thrown-off sketches or reproduce one or another over-driven and one-sided idea of the European spirit in a crude and caricatured form." And hence, also, the fact that in Russia almost everyone is an artist, with the result that there has developed there a novel-literature, a dramatic culture, and even a minor art of the cabaret that all Europe has failed to surpass. Precisely because he is so subjective, the Russian's thought turns itself at once into poetry, and if we wish to gain a firm and true picture of his world-outlook, we must look for it not in his speculative but in his narrative prose. Nay, the profoundest meaning of Russian Nihilism probably lies in Russian artistry. For what are they both but negations of reality taking the form of an impulse to hate and destroy in the one case, and an urge to love and create in the other?

For the poet too finds reality false, needing correction, ill scanned, and that is why he makes poetry.

The two main tendencies in Russia, which stood opposed and irreconcilable throughout the century, were that of the conservative Slavophils, who wished to maintain Orthodoxy, the old Russian culture, and the primitive peasant, and that of the liberal *zapadniki*, or Westernizers (also called *raznochintsi* or intelligentsia), who propagated materialism, enlightenment, and the culture of the great city. The position was: Church, Moscow, and Autocracy against Science, Petersburg, and Democracy. Only love of the " people " was a factor common to both, for it is a general and basic Russian character. The program of the Slavophil camp was laid down by Ivan Kireyevsky in an open letter: " On the Character of the European Civilization and its Relation to the Russian Civilization," which appeared in 1852 in the first number of the *Moskovski Zbornik*, founded by him. He distinguishes the Russian spirit and the " Romish," which rules the West and whose characteristic is that it regards the outer logical ordering of concepts and ideas of things as more important than the essence of the things themselves, and spiritual harmony as synonymous with an artificially balanced equilibrium of logical contents; hence theology in the West had got into an abstract rationalizing channel, whereas in the Orthodox world it was rooted in the "primal inward self-containedness of the human soul as an indivisible whole. . . . The west-European as a rule feels himself very contented with his moral attitude. The Slav on the contrary is perpetually accompanied by a definite consciousness of his incompleteness, and the higher his level, the higher the demands he makes upon himself, and the less contented he is with himself. . . . There we have the effort to participate in truth through logical concatenations of concepts, here the urge to get nearer to it by deepened knowledge of oneself, by sinking oneself in the primary foundations of the soul. There the highest truths are the object of rational school-teaching, here they are the rapturous content of one's most primary and individual life-feeling. There private property is the basis of all social relations, here it is merely the expression of the relation between persons. There outward correctness, here inward righteousness, there the rule of fashion, here the reign of tradition." The most important Westernizer who enunciated a theory was Vissarion Byelinski, who was regarded by his countrymen as their most prominent critic, a sort of Russian

163

Lessing. " The world has grown to manhood," he taught, " it needs no longer the variegated kaleidoscope of fancy, but the microscope and telescope of reason, which enable it to bring near the most distant things and to see the invisible. Actuality! That is the password and last word of our contemporary world." He despises the poet, who sings like a bird, for " only a mere bird sings just because it wants to, and without feeling itself into the sorrows and joys of its bird-folk." Dimitri Pisarev was still more radical in expressing this idea of actuality-poetry: " One can be a realist, a useful worker, without being a poet. But to be a poet and not at the same time a profound and conscious realist is quite impossible. One who is no realist is no poet, but simply a gifted ignoramus or a clever charlatan or a little jealous insect. From all these intrusive creatures the realistic critic must protect the souls and the pockets of the reading public." The first to make actual these demands of the " realistic " criticism was Gogol, the founder of the " natural school," of whose masterpiece, *The Overcoat*, Dostoievski said: "We all start from it." His *Government Inspector* (*Revizor*) may be called the best comedy in all the world's literature; it reveals, with devastating laughter, all the pitiful surfaces and horrible underneaths of a whole social sphere, a whole epoch, a whole nation, at the same time managing by a diabolical mechanism to clothe his figures in a ghostly marionettish unreality, somewhat like those in Molière's comedies, only that their psychology is to that of Gogol's figures as a logarithmic table to a calculating-machine. Another product of " Realism " was the " moujik-literature," of which Grigorovich was the bold founder, and Turgeniev the unsurpassable master; here the Russian extremism elevates to sainthood a being whom no one had hitherto regarded even as human. The counter-figure is the " repentant nobleman" who laments in self-reproach the centuries of injustice that he has done upon the serf. This chord of feeling is deeply rooted in the Russian, for he has in fact from of old regarded the peasant as something belonging to him, indeed, but not as distant from him — a domestic animal that one exploits, misuses, maltreats even, but yet feels as an intimate and indeed a loved piece of the family. Never in Russia have there been human beings of the first and second classes, or higher beings whose social position almost makes them members of another race, like the French chevalier, the Spanish hidalgo, the Japanese daimyo, the English gentleman, the Prussian *Junker*. And therein lies the immense superiority of the Russian over the European — he may have, he mostly has, lived contrary to Christianity, but he has never forgotten its teaching.

Nihilism, too, expressed itself in literature, in the politically harmless form of a despair about existence. A type cognate to that of the " repentant noble " is that of the " superfluous being." Herzen drew it first in his *Whose Fault?* and Turgeniev made it famous in his *Rudin*. In 1858 there appeared one of the most moving and singular works in Russian literature, Ivan Goncharov's *Oblomov*. In this he succeeds in achieving what had practically never before been done save in *Don Quixote* (and perhaps, though only if one stretches a point, in *Faust* and *Robinson Crusoe*) : namely, in presenting an entire nation with a national hero embodied in a poetic symbol. Oblomov is more than an immortal human being, he is the diagram of the race. He *is,* and the burden of this intolerable fact so weighs on him that it does not permit him to arrive at action. How profoundly this expresses the basic melody of the Russian soul one among a thousand evidences may be quoted, an essay of Tolstoi entitled *The Do-Nothing*. We read there: " They say that work makes men good; but I have always observed the opposite. Work and pride in work make not only ants, but men, too, cruel. And indeed in the fable it is only the ant, a being without understanding of, or impulse to strive for, the good, that holds work to be a virtue and pats itself on the back for it. Work is not merely no virtue, but in our falsely organized society it is usually a means of killing the capacity for ethical feeling. . . . The feast is ready, and the guests have all long been invited thereto, but one is buying land or wants to sell it, another is marrying, a third is building a railway or a factory, a fourth is missioning in India or Japan, steering a bill through or engineering its rejection, taking examinations, writing a learned work, a poem, a novel. All have no time, no time, to come to their senses, to retire within themselves and reflect about themselves and the world and ask themselves : ' What am I doing, and why? ' "

Here, in negative form, we have Oblomov characterized. He is the formula of a culture, but it is a formula that flowers and breathes. He is a grey average man and a luminous ideal type. He is — what only art can create, and that very, very seldom — a living concept. The things he does are as unimportant as they can be, but we entirely participate in them. He does nothing, but he does it in an unforgettable way. He is the most prosaic, the

165

noblest, the saddest and gayest of all our personal acquaintances. The aim of the book is the revelation of *Oblomovstchina*, Oblomovism, and the author means to warn us, shame us, and fire us, but he does not succeed. We love Oblomov, almost envy him. The overpowering ballad of Oblomovism closes thus: " One day at noon two gentlemen walked along the wooden pavement of the Viborgskaya; behind them drove, slowly, a vehicle. One of them was Stolz, the friend of Oblomov, the other a writer, stoutish, with an apathetic face and sensuous and at the same time sleepy eyes. ' And who is this Ilya Ilyich? ' asked the writer. ' It is Oblomov, of whom I have often told you. He has gone under, and that without any cause whatever.' Stolz sighed, and reflected: ' And he was no stupider than many another, his soul was clean and clear as glass, he was noble, gentle; and he has gone under! ' ' Why, then? What was the cause? ' ' Oblomovism,' said Stolz. ' Oblomovism? ' repeated the writer, astonished; ' what is that? ' ' I will tell you in a moment; only give me time to collect my feelings and my memories. And then write it down, it may be useful to somebody.' And he told him what is set down herein."

As with Falstaff, so with Oblomov; from a *bête noire* he becomes under the poet's hand the world's darling. But Oblomov is not Falstaff, although he works as little and eats and drinks as much as the fat knight. He is the Russian version of Hamlet. And as the soul of Shakspere, who has seen through the shallowness of all security in life, is not put into Fortinbras or into Horatio, but into Hamlet, so Goncharov's heart beats, not in Stolz, the active, kindly, helpful friend, but in Oblomov. And Horatio's words over the body of Hamlet:

" and flights of angels sing thee to thy rest,"
may well serve him, too, as epitaph.

Solferino This Russian literature was the modernest of the whole nineteenth century, the first in which the new content was made form. And, considering that the country was kept almost under seals, it is a very remarkable fact, proving once more that the spirit of a time is irrepressible, being, in truth, born with it. But it was long before the Russian Realism attained to its European importance, and, for the time being, Europe was oriented on France in politics, art, and world-outlook alike. Napoleon III capped his Crimean victory in a few years with another. In the same year in which *Oblomov* was published, Felice Orsini, a Mazzinist, carried out a fearful bombing attempt upon the Emperor as he was driving to the opera in his state coach; many persons were killed, but the intended victim escaped. Before execution Orsini wrote a letter to Napoleon in which he reminded him of his duty to Italy, and under the profound impression made on him by this incident Napoleon brought about a meeting with Cavour at Plombières, at which a provisional agreement was reached on the Italian demands for union: namely, the unification of northern Italy under the King of Sardinia, and the restoration of the dynasty of Murat at Naples. On January 1, 1859, at the New Year reception of foreign diplomats, Napoleon said to the Austrian Ambassador: " I regret that the relations of my government and the Austrian are no longer so good as formerly, but I request you to tell your Emperor that my personal feelings towards him are unchanged." That, in the diplomatic language of the day, was a declaration of war, and was immediately followed by a general fall on the bourses. Victor Emmanuel was still more explicit when he opened his parliament on January 10 with the words: " The horizon with which this new year opens is not exactly clear. We are not insensitive to the bitter cry that echoes to us from so many parts of Italy." Volunteers poured in from all districts of the peninsula, even from Milan and Venice, in defiance of the Austrian frontier-cordon. Even in this situation Austria displayed the brainless obstinacy and absurd pride that Paul de Lagarde — one of the clearest and shrewdest political thinkers in Germany — had characterized in these terms in a lecture delivered as early as 1853: " That Venice and Lombardy have not long ago been ceded to Piedmont shows as completely as anything can the political incapacity of the governing circles in Austria. For Italy will at no very distant date unite as a national state in one way or another; that is to me as certain as the fact that we are now in the Rannische Strasse at Halle. And then Italy will naturally claim Lombardy and Venice for itself. Some maintain that Austria will one day, indeed, give up these provinces, but that she cannot for honour's sake do so except after a war. But I say 'Rubbish' to an honour that regards itself as entitled to make an objectless war, to spill streams of blood, to kill hundreds of human beings, in order to be forced to do what it could have done, voluntarily and with advantage, beforehand." England and Russia proposed a congress, Napoleon agreed, and the Italian patriots were in despair, for it seemed as if it was all going to peter out. But at this critical moment the situation was

167

saved by the stupidity of the Austrians, who presented a three days' ultimatum at Turin, to which Cavour replied that he had nothing to say. On a smaller scale, it was just like what happened at the outbreak of the World War. The true Austrian touch in this tragic clowning, however, was the fact that the Austrian army did *not* thereupon advance; the reckless dash of the diplomacy was followed by the tame and circumspect manœuvring of the Austrian commander, Count Gyulai, a complete incapable, with as much brain as a ration loaf. He could have attacked the Piedmontese with superior forces, but he hesitated until they had united with the French. At Magenta the Austrian centre broke down, being so unskilfully led that a third of its strength never came into action at all; nevertheless it was only towards evening that MacMahon's victory over the right wing produced the decision, for which he was created Duc de Magenta. The Austrians evacuated all their positions up to the Mincio, and Napoleon and Victor Emmanuel made their triumphal entry into Milan amidst immense jubilation. Gyulai was recalled, and Franz Josef himself assumed the command, with Baron Hess, the best General Staff officer of his army, to advise him. In the eyes of the Austrians, Magenta had been an indecisive battle — and in actual fact it was in no way a crushing disaster, but merely a victory of French *élan* over Austrian clumsiness — and it was decided to make a new advance. This led to the most sanguinary battle of Solferino. Benedek at the head of the right wing hurled back the Piedmontese at San Martino, but the left wing failed completely, and the capture of Solferino, the key of the position, by the French Imperial Guard, forced the whole Habsburg array to retreat, accompanied by the double thunder of the guns and of a fearful storm. Yet here again it could not be said that an irreversible decision had been achieved. In Germany also, war enthusiasm had meanwhile been aroused by muddled patriotic phrase-makers who proclaimed that the Rhine must be defended on the Po. Bismarck, however, judged the situation more coolly and more keenly: " At the first shot on the Rhine, the German war becomes the main one, because it threatens Paris. Austria gets a respite; and will she use her freedom to support us in the more brilliant rôle? " In one of those telling metaphors of which he was a master, he warned Prussia not to let Austria make her drunk on an imitation of her 1813 vintage; and he considered the moment opportune for using the menace of war-preparations to force the house of Habsburg to give way in the German question.

Prince William (who since 1858 had been Regent for his now insane brother) mobilized, but against France. This meant for Napoleon a serious risk. He and Franz Josef, too, both now knew what it was personally to manage a battle, and both were deeply shaken by close acquaintance with the horrors of war; and so at Villafranca they came to an agreement on the basis of the cession of Lombardy and the creation of an Italian federation to which the sovereigns of Tuscany and Modena (who had meantime been expelled) and Austria herself in respect to Venetia would adhere, and of which the Pope would be the honorary head. These dispositions were ratified six months later by the Peace of Zürich, and the retired Emperor Ferdinand at Prague said: "That's what I should have done (*So hätt' i's a troffen*)."

When these decisions became known, they aroused profound bitterness throughout Italy. The posters that proclaimed them were torn down, Cavour resigned, Tuscany, Parma, and Modena united themselves to Sardinia by plebiscite. Garibaldi landed with his "Thousand" in Sicily. For a considerable time he was the most famous man in Europe, and the red shirt, *la camicia rossa,* became the fashion for ladies, even outside Italy. Volunteers and royal troops together occupied Naples and the States of the Church. Before 1860 closed, all the provinces save Venetia and the *Patrimonium Petri* — that is, the city of Rome and its environs — had been liberated. In 1861 Victor Emmanuel assumed the title of "King of Italy" and made Florence his capital. Napoleon could not well oppose these occurrences and contented himself — pursuant to his normal tactics, which Bismarck described as "pourboire politics (*Trinkgeldpolitik*)" — with annexing as "compensation" Savoy and Nice, the ancestral land of the Italian dynasty and the native place of Garibaldi; the latter never forgave him for it, though as a matter of fact the Niçois have always been strongly Francophil and speak a dialect of Italian that is very like Provençal.

Although Napoleon had thus won for France two fine and, strategically, most important districts, yet for his political system as a whole the war was only a half-success. He had not made good his proclamation: "Italy free right to the Adriatic," and the fact that the capital of the country was still in the hands of the Pope, protected by French troops, could not but seriously weaken his rôle as Italy's liberator in the eyes of the Italians. Nevertheless the Empire stood then at the head of Europe, and that not merely in

I Mille

Le genre canaille

169

the political field. The Empress Eugénie was the unchallenged queen of European fashion; one of the first acts of her government was the general introduction of the lace mantilla which she had imported from her Spanish home. Costumes were markedly and consciously plebeian. In the days of the Teutonic invasions it had been the custom of Roman ladies to wear large blond wigs; desiring to equal the interesting barbarians, on whom interest centred, in this much at least, they had their hair done, so to say, *alla tedesca*. Something like this took place in France at the period we are describing, except that the invasion came, not from outside, but from below. The *nouveaux riches* had forced their way into the salons, and the salons began accommodatingly to accept the ways of the conquerors. Fashion always bows to the rulers. The two goddesses which this age worshipped were Woman and Bourse. And the spirit of business mingled with the spirit of sexuality. Money-making became an almost sensual passion, and love a matter of money. In the days of French Romanticism the erotic ideal had been the Grisette, who made a present of herself. Now it was the " Rosette," who sold herself. As we said earlier, the style of life had been a sort of bourgeois Rococo; the place of the *genre rocaille* was taken by the *genre canaille*, an impudence and pertness of clothing and speech which made it almost impossible to distinguish the so-called respectable woman from the prostitute. A *gamin* element came into the fashions; ladies wore collars and cravats, paletots, coats cut like tail coats (the revived *" caracos "* of the Werther period), zouave jackets, military waists, walking-sticks, monocles. People liked sharply contrasted and violent colours, even in hair, fiery red hair being much admired. In the Rococo it had been *bon ton* to get oneself up as a shepherdess, in the age of the cancan and *La Belle Hélène* it was chic to copy the demi-monde. The fashionable type was that of the great lady acting the cocotte. The favourite materials were — besides silk and its modifications (some of which were new), such as taffeta, moire, gauze — airy, delicate, and scented fabrics like crêpe, tulle, mull, tarlatan, organdie; the bourgeoisie was playing at fairies. From about 1860 the hair was combed back *à la vergette,* and over it was worn the false chignon decorated with fruits, bands, artificial flowers, and gold-dust. Long curls, likewise false, fell like gigantic ear-rings down to the neck, and the crown of it all was the tiny hat with a veil that flowed almost to the feet; an Amazon hat with a towering feather, which had always to be worn aslant, was also for a time fashionable. At the beginning of the fifties the pagoda sleeve, narrow to the elbow, but very wide and open on the lower arm, made its appearance, and in 1856 the crinoline came up in a new form, invented by the Empress herself, in which the horsehair pads were replaced by spring steel insertions which made it very light. It was garnished with numerous flounces, which in turn were covered with ruches, ribbons, and lace. At the beginning of the sixties it was so enormously wide that the comic papers said that the broadening of the Paris streets had been undertaken on its account; it was, in fact, a standing target for satire. Friedrich Theodor Vischer demonstrated that æsthetically it was a monstrosity — naturally, without the least result. Like the hen-coop of the Rococo, it was everywhere, worn by peasant women and cooks alike, even by children on ceremonial days and in historical stage-plays — Clairon as Nausicaa had worn panniers, and now Christine Hebbel as Kriemhild appeared in crinoline. This grotesque piece of clothing has reigned in Europe in three different times and seems ineradicable; it is not at all impossible that it will reappear in our own, even if only for evening dress. To hide was no more its object in the Second Empire than in the Rococo; on the contrary, it was a matter of practised technique neatly to swing it so that the underneath could be seen, and the cancan fulfilled this aim to all desired excess. But what the Rococo did with graceful ambiguity, this age did with massive fleshiness. What the Rococo disengaged, the Empire engaged, and one can, without being any sort of a moralist, say that the insistent stripping of the breasts that prevailed was simply bawdy. In ornaments, the semiprecious stones were much admired; actually these are often far more beautiful and elegant than precious stones proper, but it was not for that, but for their bigness that this age chose them. For the stage star likewise it was obligatory to display as many ornaments as possible; Meyerbeer's peasant maiden Dinorah appeared, with her goats, in satin, diamonds, and gold-beetle spatterdashes. When real aristocrats like the Empress Elizabeth showed a fine taste by preferring the so-called "English costume" — namely, a trim and not overlong dress, blouse, and low shoes — it was regarded as an extravagance. As to men's costume, it differed but slightly from that of the preceding generation; in fact, from now on, it was practically stabilized — another consequence of the preponderance of a bourgeoisie that had other things to think about. The dominant features were the philistine Sunday

171

coat, the awkward elastic-sided boot, the ugly stiff collar, which, like the cravat, assumed a tighter form. Besides the top-hat, men wore the soft felt hat and the atrocious " melon " (bowler), and in summer an absurd round straw hat with fluttering velvet ribbons, which, because it recalled Czikós's headgear, was called a " Hungarian " hat. After the victory of democracy the full beard had the *entrée*, but in France Napoleon brought his " imperial " into vogue, and the " Kaiserbart " (moustache and full side-whiskers) of Franz Josef, Alexander II, and William I was also zealously copied. The clean-shaved face vanished almost entirely, and all male visages sported what Schopenhauer called " the outward symptoms of a masterful crudity, that symbol of sex in the middle of the face which affirmed that men preferred masculinity, which they have in common with animals, to *humanity*, and that one wanted to be first a man, *mas*, and only secondarily a human being."

Offenbach   Galop and cancan — the two wildest dances that there are — which had been invented earlier, now for the first time became supreme, though the waltz of Vienna was beginning its career of victory, thanks to Lanner and the two Strausses. On the cancan the Parisian dancer Rigolboche, who in her day was a world-celebrity, said: " One must, at a given moment and without knowing why, be gloomy, melancholic, and troubled, and then in an instant go mad, tear and toss; indeed, one may be required to do all this at the same time. One must, in a word, *rigolbocher*. The cancan is madness of the legs." Mankind was seized with a veritable mania for dancing; ballet dominated even on the stage, intensified to " *féerie* " by clamant arts of display and a bewildering employment of masses, and forced itself into opera in the form of big interludes. But the most genuine and first-hand creation of the age is the operetta. The term was originally employed for the play-with-song of the eighteenth century, called " little " opera in contradiction to " grand " opera, less ambitious in form and content than the latter, but really distinguished from this by its alternation of word and music; in effect they were comedies with interposed music. The new genre, of which the founder was Hervé, called itself *opéra bouffe*, from an older type, but was called by the public by the characterizing name of " *musiquette*." Its master magician is Jacques Offenbach, who began his career with one-act plays (the song-play had also begun as one-act). In 1858 he brought out *Orphée aux Enfers*, in 1864 *La Belle Hélène*, in 1866

Barbe-bleue and *La Vie parisienne*, in 1867 *La Grande-duchesse de Gerolstein*. In these works, choice bijoux of a complicated luxury-art, the scent of the *ville lumière* is distilled to a strong and retentive essence (as Watteau had distilled it for the Parisians of the Rococo), but an essence far more biting, saline, and pungent than his. They are persiflages ostensibly upon the antique, the Middle Ages, as well as the present, but at bottom they are essentially of the present, and — in contrast to the Vienna operetta (which only entered upon its reign a generation later) — it was wholly devoid of showiness, amoral, unsentimental, destitute of all *petite-bourgeoisie* melodrama, but on the contrary impetuously sceptic, exhibitionist in its sensuality, nay, absolutely nihilistic. The fact that Offenbach is regardless of psychological logic and artistic dynamic and really only produces detached solo-numbers is often made a reproach, but it, too, is the outflowing of a high (namely, an æsthetic) cynicism, a freedom of spirit and capacity for self-parody that laughs even at the laws of its own art. But to know that his heart was both deep and kindly we need only think of the Barcarole of his last work, the *Contes d'Hoffmann,* in which the German Romanticism of the subject, as ennobled and made artistic by the refining touch of the Paris Décadence, makes a strangely moving song. Here the Radicalism of the modern cosmopolitan laments its vanished love; woman is puppet or harlot; she who truly loves is marked for death. It is as though Offenbach for his swan-song chose to orchestrate that sentence from the diary of the Goncourts : " Ah, it is necessary to have made the tour of everything and believe in nothing. There is nothing true except woman." And even this last truth discloses itself as illusory.

It is less the period than the façade of the period that is mirrored — very expressively — in Gounod's *Faust,* which in Germany is more correctly called *Margarethe*. The work was first performed at the Théâtre Lyrique in 1859, and ten years later (a hitherto unheard-of thing) was promoted to the Grand Opéra itself, whence it started on its triumphal tour of Europe. Here Gounod, isolating the erotic episode of the Faust tragedy — in a way that for German feeling is grotesque, nay, almost obscene — and at the same time sugaring and sentimentalizing it to an extent only possible to a Frenchman, achieves one of those rare, and in their way marvellous, works that can fairly be described as first-class rubbish. He plays on a golden hurdy-gurdy, but that does not make it anything but what it is, a barrel-organ. A counterpart to

Gounod

Offenbach was the sculptor Jean Baptiste Carpeaux, sensual, witty, piquant, and full of sparkling vitality, who brought off the *tour de force* of making even marble melt and " *rigolbocher*." His anti-Classicism was so challenging that an attempt was made to destroy his principal work, the dance group on the façade of the Opéra.

*The comedy
of manners*

On the stage reigned the comedy of manners, a rich and high-coloured variant of the middle-class " emotional " play that, as we have seen, had flourished in France in the eighteenth century. Already in the thirties the elder Dumas had in many well-played dramas scarified the hypocrisy of society and preached the rights of passion; the hero was dæmonic and revolutionary in the style of French Romanticism, and usually illegitimate. And it was an illegitimate son of the author, Alexandre Dumas *fils,* who became the master of this genre; when, on the occasion of his first success, someone during the interval made the tactless remark to Dumas *père :* " No doubt you also contributed something to it," he replied: " Yes, I contributed the main thing, the author." The son's plays, too, deal almost always with a social problem, the kept woman, the unmarried mother, the " Kill-her! " or a thesis such as: Should a woman avenge herself, should a girl confess to a lapse, can the fallen woman be virtuous? His delightful knick-knacks are all of plaster, completely void within, tastefully gilded without, and show — at any rate the later ones — too clearly that they are all products of the same factory. A competitor to him grew up in Émile Augier, who created, amongst many others, two types of dramatic strength in Monsieur Poirier, the ambitious parvenu, and Giboyer, the venal journalist who nevertheless sacrifices himself for his family. He is also the discoverer of the Raisonneur, whom Viktor Klemperer in his *Geschichte der französischen Literatur* well describes as " a mean between the Classical chorus, the Classicist confidant, and the modern conférencier "; but this new figure only gets from the three others what is un-dramatic in them; from the ancient chorus its habit of dropping out of the picture and talking to the public, from the confidant its irrelevant scheming-ness, and from the conférencier the characteristic of not being a character at all, but a speaker of aphorisms. The Raisonneur had, however, a very long stage life, because the public identified him with itself and liked to see itself dramatized. Augier is, even more distinctly than Dumas, the descendant of the drama of the Enlightenment; he is at once a clumsier and a more artful Diderot,

174

but distinguished from him by the fact that his moralism is (although he was certainly unconscious of it in most cases) a lying one. In Diderot's time the bourgeoisie as a class was on the up-grade, morally and intellectually, but in Augier's it was a fat, high-coloured, predatory marsh-orchid, and efforts to ennoble or redeem it seem entirely misplaced.

But the most important phenomenon that in this period poured out its radiation from Paris over Europe was Comtism or Positivism. This philosophy is based on a remarkable belief, which Nietzsche, in the phrase which appears at the head of this chapter, characterizes as pathological — the assumption that there is only a world of the senses, a tangible, breathable, smellable, tastable world that one can inspect, listen to, touch, photograph, and nowadays film — in short, that Reality is the actual, and, indeed, only the actual. It is the necessary and inevitable world-outlook of the bourgeoisie, which manifestly could not tolerate the idea that this world with which we operate daily should not be solid, compact, and real. The hypothesis of Phenomenalism, that the activity which we call reality is nothing but a fiction, tacitly accepted as fact by all the shareholders in the concern — a "bubble business," so to say — was inadmissible for a society oriented on business. The difficulty was — apparently — got over by Positivism, which works with unchallengeable material, massive facts, evident conclusions, inclusive descriptions, exact experiments. Unfortunately this whole stock of real values has shown itself to be mere printed paper, and Positivism the biggest bubble-business that has ever victimized humanity.

Auguste Comte, whose influence did not become European till after his death, was a first-rate mind in which the Cartesian ardour for *clarté* and architectonic was the ruling passion. For him the basic principle of all thought and life was limitation to the positive, that which is given by experience. His orientation, therefore, is wholly anti-metaphysical and anti-religious. First causes and last aims are inscrutable and therefore do not concern science, whose business is not explanation, but the description of individual facts which, if they have been observed in a sufficient number of instances, one is entitled to sum up as "laws." Mankind accomplishes its cultural evolution in three stages. In the first, the religious, it believes in personifications of natural forces — in the successive forms of fetishism, polytheism, and monotheism. In the second, the metaphysical, it professes abstract principles which are

Comtism

only a subtler kind of anthropomorphism. In the third, the positive, science rules. There is, however, a sort of Positivist religion, which finds the object of faith in humanity and understands by immortality the continuation of existence in the grateful memory of posterity. This religion even possesses a cult, that of the *Grand Être* — which is Humanity — complete with a moral priesthood and a hierarchy of saints — men of merit to whom the Positivist calendar assigns, according to their rank, major feast-days, minor feast-days, and week-days. Of greater interest than this rather finicking form of diversion in Comte's hierarchy of the sciences. He orders the several disciplines according to their complexity. The simplest science is mathematics, which is a pure theory of quantities; then come astronomy, physics, chemistry, biology, and finally the theory of society, baptized by Comte with the hybrid Græco-Latin but now generally accepted name of Sociology. Increasing complexity involves also increasing uncertainty — it is far more difficult to establish biological or sociological laws than mathematical or astronomical — and this gradation coincides with the historical evolution of science along the line of Galileo, Newton, Lavoisier, Cuvier, and Comte. Sociology falls into two parts: static, which establishes the general conditions, and dynamic, which establishes the general laws and evolution of social life. This evolution discloses a progressive mastering of animal impulses by human, of warlike interests by industries, of oligarchic polities by democratic, of the theological world-view by the scientific.

Spencer and Buckle Contemporary English philosophy stood in close relation to this theory. James Mill described epistemology as " mental chemistry," which out of the elements — namely, sensations — constructed their compounds — namely, mental associations. His son, the celebrated John Stuart Mill, declared experience to be the only source of knowledge, and induction the only fruitful method; every general judgment is a résumé of individual observations, all knowledge is generalization, and the highest general judgment the law of causality, which is drawn from all prior experiences. A higher standpoint was that of Thomas Huxley, whose profession of faith was, to use the term coined by himself, Agnosticism: truth and reality are unknowable, and science has only to deal with phenomena. Spencer, too, admitted an unknowable, whereon Ludwig Büchner bitterly observed: "If fear or shame in the presence of the unknown dominated the crude primitive man and even to this day dominates the savage and the uneducated, this ought not to

176

hold good of the educated or culture-man. *Fiat lux!* " The criterion of truth, according to Spencer, is the inconceivability of the opposite; our *a priori* forms of knowing have been gradually acquired by the genus by adaptation; later came conscience, as the result of generic experience of the useful. The whole structure of his philosophy, which in essence is Comtism dovetailed with Darwinism, Spencer embodied in a vast series of amazingly learned and intolerably boring volumes, which is thus ordered: *First Principles, Principles of Biology, Principles of Psychology, Principles of Sociology, Principles of Ethics.* The basic idea of the " system of Synthetic philosophy " was the following: Nothing exists but matter and motion. These continually undergo two antagonistic processes, *evolution* and *dissolution.* Evolution is always at the same time integration of matter and dissipation of motion, while dissolution is identical with disintegration of matter and absorption of motion. Further, scattered matter is in a homogeneous, and concentrated matter in a heterogeneous, condition, and evolution therefore is always differentiation. Repulsion and attraction, which move the world of bodies, are an expression of this law, which governs the whole rhythm of the universe. Intellectual life is the continuous integration and differentiation of states of consciousness. In this leathern schematism which, for all the complication of its terminology, is yet exceedingly primitive, there speaks the typical English proneness to imagine things as far simpler than they are, a trait in which his eminently practical talent comes out, for nothing is more useful for living and for commanding the world than a handy A B C formula that ignores all contradictions, subtleties, and pitfalls.

Another such philosophy was produced by Henry Thomas Buckle in his *History of Civilization in England,* which we have spoken of in our first volume. As has already been indicated there, the work contains, not the theme proper, but merely a general program. " I hope," says Buckle, " to accomplish for the history of man something equivalent, or at all events analogous, to what has been effected by other inquirers for the different branches of natural science. In regard to nature, events apparently the most irregular and capricious have been explained, and have been shown to be in accordance with certain fixed and universal laws. This has been done because men of ability, and, above all, men of patient, untiring thought have studied natural events with the view of discovering their regularity; and if human events were subjected to

a similar treatment, we have every right to expect similar results."
And he arrives by this method at the following results: " 1st, That
the progress of mankind depends on the success with which the
laws of phenomena are investigated, and on the extent to which
a knowledge of those laws is diffused. 2nd, That before such investigation can begin, a spirit of scepticism must arise, which, at first
aiding the investigation, is afterwards aided by it. 3rd, That the
discoveries thus made increase the influence of intellectual truths.
. . . 4th, That the great enemy of this movement, and therefore
the great enemy of civilization, is the protective spirit. . . ." Will
it be believed that this is in fact the total philosophical content of
the two volumes — though to the author himself it seemed so
difficult or paradoxical that he needed some fourteen hundred
pages of text and over nine hundred foot-notes to illustrate and
establish them? In this heavy and crude, but human and good-
natured monster of a philosopher the valuable part is the equipment: he puts before us a most skilfully grouped and intelligently
developed wealth of data. It is a gigantic warehouse of historical
material. The English and the French Revolutions, the ages of
Louis XIV and Philip II, Iceland and Ireland, India and Mexico,
legal history and botany, meteorology and moral statistics, theology and prosody, food-chemistry and seismography — all is presented cleanly and plentifully, in order to show that when man
becomes cleverer, he becomes cleverer.

Darwin   All these English thinkers derive from Locke and Hume, who
in turn had their roots in Bacon. Their leitmotiv, which recurs *ad
nauseam,* is adoration of " experience " as a sort of Bible wherein
all truths are written, and " unbroken induction," which is nothing but a subtler kind of statistics; rejection of metaphysics as a
bogy or a *quantité négligeable;* explanation of all anthropological
phenomena on grounds of adaptation and habit, and of all moral
on those of rightly understood egoism. Hume expressed this once
with all desirable clarity: " If we take in our hand any volume; of
divinity or school metaphysics, for instance; let us ask, *Does it
contain any abstract reasoning concerning quantity or number?*
No. *Does it contain any experimental reasoning concerning matter
of fact and existence?* No. Commit it then to the flames; for it can
contain nothing but sophistry and illusion." This is the English
apperception-form; and in the second half of the nineteenth century it became the apperception-form of Europe, and it did so
through Darwinism, the importance of which for this period is

similar to that which Nominalism possesses for all the centuries of the Modern Age: namely, that in the fullest sense of the word it *made* the period, transformed it, steered it, penetrated to the most secret and remote channels of its spiritual and intellectual life.

Charles Darwin, to whom his followers gave the proud title of " the Copernicus of the organic world " — an admirable erudite and a pure childlike soul, who managed to combine a tireless urge to knowledge with the simplicity of a true gentleman and the humility of a true Christian — embodied his observations in a monumental work which appeared in 1859 and was entitled in full: *On the Origin of Species by Means of Natural Selection; or the Preservation of Favoured Races in the Struggle for Life.* His remaining works are only exemplifications, outworks, and supplements, and the whole basic idea is already indicated in the title of the book, which itself is only the demonstration thereof by a wealth of observational material. With a fine modesty, which came from wise self-criticism, Darwin never looked upon himself as a philosopher, but purely as a nature-researcher who collected facts and attached certain prudent hypotheses to them. His predecessors were Linnæus, Cuvier, and Lamarck. Linné, as we remember, had drawn up an exact classification of animals and plants in races, kinds, and varieties and had included Man among the mammals, but on the other hand he had declared that " there are as many species as the Infinite Being created in the beginning." Cuvier, already, went beyond this, in that although he held firmly to the Creation-dogma, he assumed that there were several Creations, which, conditioned by regular terrestrial catastrophes, brought forth in each geological age a new fauna and flora. Lamarck, on the contrary, in his *Philosophy of Zoology,* explained the evolution of the animal world by differences in the conditions of living, and principally by the use and disuse of organs. A similar theory was put forward by Geoffroy Saint-Hilaire, except that he assigned first place to the factor of the " *monde ambiant,*" the continually changing environment; in the controversy upon this which he fought out with Cuvier about 1830, Goethe took his part. But already towards the end of the preceding century Charles Darwin's grandfather Erasmus in his *Zoonomia, or the Laws of Organic Life,* had set up adaptation, heredity, struggle for preservation, and self-protection as principles of evolution — so that inheritance seems to have been at work even in Darwinism itself. But the decisive impulse for

Charles Darwin came from an author who had little to do with natural science: namely, Malthus, who had taught that the disproportion between the increase of available food, which followed an arithmetical progression, and that of population, which multiplied in geometrical ratio, imposed a continuous struggle for existence. And anyhow Darwinism, itself a product of adaptation to the *Zeitgeist,* was in the air: in 1858 the naturalist Alfred Russel Wallace had prepared an exposition the ideas of which coincided even in the details with those of the *Origin of Species;* further, Spencer had already, in the earlier fifties, sketched out a theory of descent, and a few years later Henry Bates formulated the theory of Mimicry. It was this general trend alone that brought Darwin to publish his work after more than twenty years of preparatory studies; otherwise, with his extraordinary conscientiousness, it might never have happened at all in his lifetime.

The thesis of Darwinism states that species are varieties that have become constant, and varieties are species in process of formation, and that the appearance of new races is a product of the struggle for existence, which was a sort of natural selection that favoured certain specimens, a process which Spencer had described as the " survival of the fittest." This view treats nature as an arrangement on *English* lines; it is, in the first place, *free trade,* in that competition decides; secondly, it is *correct,* in that only that which is least " shocking," the fittest, survives; thirdly, it is *Liberal,* in that " progress " rules, and there are ever novelties and improvements; fourthly, it is on the other hand *conservative,* for the battle for progress moves " organically," with slow transitions and majority victories. English, too, is the naïve equating of artificial breeding with natural selection — a colonial idea that conceives of the world as a great ranch and kitchen garden — and the incapacity to see the past as generically distinct from the present; everything must have happened " much as it does now," at least under similar forces of transformation — Darwinism here being the biological counterpart of Lyell's geology, with its reduction of everything to " actual " causes, causes that are invisibly at work today, a notion very characteristic of an unheroic age of learned myopia and microphilia, of political morning-prayers and world-commanding journalism.

All things considered, it is very easy to explain the immense effect of the Darwinian theory, but, further, it flattered certain æsthetic and logical needs of the human mind, in that it erected the highly artistic cathedral of a hierarchy of living things — from the unicellular first creature, through the co-ordinated but place-bound plant-animal, the mobile but soft worm, to the echinoderms, not yet possessed of limbs, the arthropods, which are still without a spinal column, the gill-breathing fish, the newts, which have both gills and lungs, the reptiles, which have only lungs, the warm-blooded birds, the mammals, with their milk-glands, the primates, with their hands and their reason, and the crown of all in Man, who is already capable of Darwinism. These fictions, so satisfying to the eye and the mind, are indeed pure poems of the intellect, " regulative ideas," but their fine clear architecture gives them a high charm of fascination; they make the world more luminous, more ordered, more rhythmical, more composed.

The reception that Darwin's work obtained immediately upon its publication has been described by Huxley with charming humour. " Everybody," he says, " has read Mr. Darwin's book or at least, has given an opinion on its merits and demerits. . . . Old ladies of both sexes consider it a decidedly dangerous book. . . . And the genuine *littérateur* is too much in the habit of acquiring his knowledge from the book he judges — as the Abyssinian is said to provide himself with steaks from the ox which carries him — to be withheld from criticism of a profound scientific work by the mere want of the requisite preliminary scientific requirement." Nevertheless, from the first there have always been some very weighty scientists who have refused their adhesion to Darwinism. Du Bois-Reymond called Haeckel's first great work, the *Generelle Morphologie,* " a poor novel," worked up after the manner of Homer's successors from fabulous genealogies; and the eminent Swiss zoologist Louis Agassiz called Darwinism " a travesty of the facts." The botanist Johannes Reinke declared, in his excellent *Einleitung in die theoretische Biologie:* " The phylogeny of organisms is not comparable in scientific value to the history, but only to the prehistory, of the human race," and Hans Driesch, a protagonist of " Neo-Vitalism," whose philosophical works have had a wide circulation in the last decades, even asserted that all Darwinists suffered from softening of the brain.

In fact, all Darwinism's positions are attackable from several sides. First, as to selection, the products of artificial selection are in no way better fitted for the " struggle for life," but even worse. The products that breeders aim at are either degenerate curiosities (such as, for instance, the Japanese gold-fish which has a four-

Anti-Darwin

lobed tail-fin, or the Japanese phœnix-fowl, which has six feet of tail-feathers), or hypertrophies incapable of fighting, like the numerous fattened species, or the domestic animals whose very name indicates that they are spoilt for life in free nature. Left to fend for themselves in the competitive struggle, barnyard fowls, geese, and ducks would without a doubt be at a disadvantage against the wild varieties, and this applies equally, indeed still more, to the thoroughbred products of domestication like the race-horse, the greyhound, the Angora cat, and the song-canary. Artificial selection is thus useless as an analogy with natural. Sexual selection, too, is far more of a puzzle than Darwinism assumes it to be. It is not true that the female always chooses the finest and strongest specimen for a mate, as we see in human beings themselves, where the erotic attraction seems rather to be governed by a polarity law, since very often beautiful women feel themselves attracted to ugly men, and strong men frequently prefer weak women. Further, if the evolution-theory were right, species ought to be continually fluid even today; at least one single case of productive adaptation should have presented itself within the space of time over which we have means of checking our data. But no such case has occurred — on the contrary, only regressions have been established. Darwinism, it is true, like Lyell's actualism, has recourse to the expedient of large spaces of time; but it is remarkable that the palæontologists' investigations into the earth's past, while failing, indeed, to establish numerous present-day classes, have also failed to find one single new class, as ought to have been the case had the species arisen out of one another, and the intermediate links died out. Huxley, one of the earliest and most vigorous champions of Darwinism, said in a lecture of 1862: " There are two hundred known orders of plants; of these not one is certainly known to exist exclusively in the fossil state. The whole lapse of geological time has as yet yielded not a single new ordinal type of vegetable structure. The positive change in passing from the recent to the ancient animal world is greater but still singularly small. No fossil animal is so distinct from those now living as to require to be arranged even in a separate class from those which contain existing forms. It is only when we come to the orders, which may be roughly estimated at about a hundred and thirty, that we meet with fossil animals so distinct from those now living as to require orders for themselves; and these do not amount, on the most liberal estimate, to more than about ten per cent. of the whole." And, what is most important, all these fossils are highly complicated and specialized. They are in no way simpler than present-day creatures; they are to some extent different, but they are equally enigmatic, and they are never ambiguous hybrid forms. It is true that this name has been given to some few discoveries. Apart from the poor amphioxus, a pitiful little fish, which according to the dogma of Darwinian ancestor-worship is the " progenitor of the vertebrates " (truly a peculiar one, for it is a vertebrate without a skull or a spinal column), there only remains, as the pride of the palæontological menagerie, *archæopteryx lithographica,* which is venerated as the prime bird; this is a climbing pigeon, with toothed jaws, not very efficient wings, but with a very long and feathered " saurian " tail, which it obviously used for steering and probably for parachuting — an odd sort of fowl, maybe, but, all the same, still pretty far from a lizard — and, whatever else it may have been, it was not an intermediate, but rather a quite sharply defined architectural form, presumably representative of a whole group of fauna that of old animated one of the scenes of the earth's drama. It is, in fact, simply the " bird part " in the age of the flying reptiles.

Natura non facit saltum is one of the falsest propositions in which men have ever believed. Nature makes *only* jumps. Wilhelm Fliess has shown by innumerable examples that in the life of the human individual all evolutionary pushes occur " with a rush," and it is the same with the life of our genus. Decisive historical events are always abrupt, immediate, explosive, and the " long previous preparations " that have been interpreted into them afterwards are but a round game indulged in by pedants. The Migrations, Islam, the German Reformation, the English and the French Revolutions happened *suddenly,* and for confirmation we need only look at our own present, for our New Age dawned in a flash. We do not propose to discuss whether it is better or worse than the " good old " time, but it is certain that it is completely different. We have a new outlook on art, a new form of society, a new state-life, a new world-picture, of which in 1914 there was not even a hint. The nebulous doctrine of " differential transitions " is an imagination of Liberal professors who are arguing from the undramaticality of their own minds and the sluggishness of their own metabolism to conclusions on the life of nature and history. But already at the beginning of our century the Dutch botanist Hugo de Vries had developed his theory of Mutation, which, on the basis of experiments with plants, showed that all variations occur " by leaps," that striking changes of habit happen spontaneously in " shocks." It is in the same way, De Vries supposes, that new species came into being.

Darwinism, in deriving the species from one another, tacitly assumes that they are interrelated; that is, the doctrine of descent already postulates descent, which is an unproved premiss. The Darwinian selection falls upon individuals of definite and already existing aptitudes that make them worthy of selection; that is, selection presupposes selection. Adaptation forms beings that have already evolved a predisposition to adapt themselves; that is, adaptation presupposes adaptation.

The actual facts of species now in existence stand in twofold contradiction with Darwinism, for if it were true, there would be too few and too many of them. Too few, for why are there only sharply distinguished groups, " specialisms," so to say? If all were interrelated, they could not be separated off by any such rigid and more or less intolerant class-differences. Too many, for why are there innumerable early, " unmodern," forms still surviving everywhere? If natural selection were really the determining principle, the types of higher development must long ago have triumphed in the struggle for existence and driven out the lower. The answer is in both cases that probably the discarded Cuvier is partly right after all, and that in animal and plant history, as in human, the different ages displace one another, each being a separate creation-thought, an epoch with its own character, structural style, costume, life-rhythm, all alike divine, all alike immortal. And as with the history of our own kind, so here too we can only contemplate the individual tableaux with wonder, never explain their coming and their going.

As has been indicated already in the first volume, it would be much nearer the mark to speak of a survival of the unfittest. For the vessel of evolution is never the " normal " organism, but the pathologically sensitive organism, unhealthily hypertrophied in one or another respect. In human history new historical varieties never appear as the result of adaptation, but of reaction against existing conditions of life; we need only recall the happenings that brought the Modern Age to birth. The " acquisition of new characters " is not a physiological and still less a mechanical process, but a *spiritual* one. Already in 1835 Schopenhauer had remarked in his essay *On Will in Nature* that every organ was to be regarded as the expression of a " fixed desire, an act of will, not of the individual, but of the species "; for example, the will to life " was seized with desire to live on trees, to hang on their branches, to eat their leaves, without fighting other animals, and without ever going to ground; this longing expressed itself, through endless ages, in the form (Platonic idea) of the sloth; what determined the structure of the animal was the way of life that it chose to follow in order to obtain sustenance . . . exactly as a sportsman before setting out chooses his equipment, his gun and shot and powder, his bag, knife, and costume, according to the game that he intends to kill. He does not shoot at a wild pig because he has a carbine, but he took out his carbine and not his fowling-piece because he was going after wild pig; and the bull does not gore because he has horns, but has horns because he means to gore." It is, we cannot too often repeat, the spirit that builds the body. If man really did descend from the apes, he certainly did not acquire his human qualities by being " better fitted " (for what?), but by the magic force of the wish. The apes can neither speak nor laugh, because obviously they have no room for dialectic and humour; but of mimicry and of the joke, which mean a great deal to them, they have an excellent command.

The innumerable disciples of Darwin have, for the most part, only compromised him. The wise, kindly miscellany of the master has been built up by limited and correspondingly conceited minds into distorted and wooden systems. Three examples among the many will suffice. The so-called " evolutionary mechanics," of which Wilhelm Roux is the chief representative, holds that only the " fit for the purpose " maintain and propagate themselves, and that the unfit languish and die, but (teleology being anathema to orthodox science) this is due to purely mechanical and not purposive causes; so, fitness for purpose, without purpose. Nägeli's " mechanico-physiological " theory of descent, on the contrary, attributes transformation, not to the Darwinian utility-principle, but to the " principle of perfection "; an organism perfects itself because a principle tending thereto is active in it; but this is the purest *a priori* scholasticism, taking one no further than Martinus Scriblerus's entertaining explanation of the action of a turnspit by its " meat-roasting quality." Weismann's germ-plasm theory, again, denies the inheritance of acquired characters; but, we ask ourselves, to what does selection refer if not to acquired characters that are heritable? Adaptations in the Darwinian sense can only be effected by external stimuli which modify the individual in the course of its life; and if these do not touch the germ-plasm, they must vanish again at the individual's death. For this Weismann hits on the absurd explanation that selection rests on "the latent presence or the germ-cell of tendencies towards useful qualities"; it is "the useful variations already contained potentially in the germ-plasm" that breeding turns to account. How the tendency gets into the germ-cell, and in particular this germ-cell, remains mysterious, so that according to this theory the function of selection is limited to this, that by it qualities become usefully modified because they are already usefully modified. Such are the empty straw-wrappings of tautology that haunt the "exact science" which describes theology and metaphysics as a barren ingenuity in word-spinning.

In fact, as we have seen, Darwinism, too, is a dialectical construction, nay, a sort of religion, with highly developed mythology and dogmatics. Its Paul appeared in Ernst Haeckel. Out of a typical English fad and *idée fixe*, the typical insistent largeness of English thinking had made a methodical lecture-room syllabus. It was Haeckel who gave this house of corners and personal tastes the convincingly clear, happy, and pleasing architecture that it needed, who made it accessible, light, and almost habitable. Vauvenargues remarked that " great thoughts come from the heart," but, in reference to Darwinism, one might equally say that great thoughts come from the bottom, for the ideas of English natural philosophy are obtained by sweating or by prescription. For Haeckel, on the contrary, the new doctrine was a sacred mission, which he nourished with all the juices of his strong heart, an evangel that he carried to the world, of which he was the preacher and ready at any time to be the martyr. This does not mean that he was merely a popularizer of Darwin; far from it. He developed the theory on his own account in new directions, applied it to new fields, and formulated it in new laws. And in these new developments (with most of which Darwin himself was in agreement) Haeckel revealed himself as a poet. Only a man of lively poetic instinct could, for example, establish the "biogenetic law" which states that every man recapitulates in his mother's womb all the stages that living organisms have traversed in the millions of years of their genetic history. Is there anything finer and more comforting than the thought that we are once more, for a brief moment, all that was on earth before we saw the light of the world — lowly progenitor, worm, fish, batrachian, mammal; that we carry within us, in a sense, every creature that breathes, that we know them all, are related to, nay, identical with, them all; that we are the heir of all the soul-stirrings that a being has ever experienced, even of all the sensations that a terrestrial being has felt since the spark of life first awoke on our planet? But, according to Haeckel, this very life did not happen by any sort of sudden event, but was in principle always there, it has merely freed itself more and more — becoming by degrees ever more master of itself, ever stronger to shake itself free, up to its final culmination in human consciousness — and it slumbers in all things, even in the apparently dead. And that again is the thought of a poet. In his last work Haeckel aimed at nothing less than to prove that even crystals — those astonishing forms that have ever aroused the wonder of mankind by their beauty and regularity — possess a sort of soul, that they take in nourishment and give off secretions, that manifest phenomena of poisoning can be observed in them, and that at a given temperature lively movements, and even a sort of copulation, occur in them. With amazement we saw mankind's immemorial childhood-beliefs that the wind and the cloud, the stream and the flame are vivified by mysterious spirits, confirmed by the most modern science, and there is something intensely moving in the picture of the old master thus coming before us in his eighty-fourth year and like a wise old Magus bringing to life with his wand even that which had been believed to be dead. And every one of the works with which he rejoiced the world was itself to be regarded as a crystal, just as viewable and transparent, just as clear-edged and finely angled. If only he had not occupied himself with philosophy! And yet even in his monistic catechisms, the *Welträtsel*, the *Lebenswunder*, the *Natürliche Schöpfungsgeschichte* (works that are in the hands of everyone), there is something touching in the childlike naïveté of their belief that the mysterious mechanism of the universe can be taken to pieces and put together again like a toy, and there is such a fullness of information, beautifully ordered, luminous and transparent as water, that we forgive their low philosophical quality in feeling them as works of art.

But, apart from this, the leading German natural scientists of the time were anything but Positivists. Helmholtz represented Kantianism with an orientation towards Johannes Müller. He did not hesitate to say in a rectorial address: " I do not see how it is possible to refute even an extremely subjective Idealism that

Ignorabimus

187

would regard life as a dream. One could assert as much as one liked that it is improbable and unsatisfactory — and in this connexion I would associate myself with the severest words of condemnation — but logically it is capable of being carried through without inconsequence. And it seems to me very important to bear this in mind. . . . There is more than one eminently useful and precise hypothesis for which we could not admit any realistic meaning and to which we dare not attribute necessary truth. . . . We have no better guarantee for the law of causality than its success " — for which he was clamorously denounced by the Büchner apaches as an " obscurantist." Still greater disappointment attended Du Bois-Reymond's famous address *Über die Grenzen des Naturerkennens,* in which amongst other things he says: " Motion can only generate motion . . . the mechanical cause comes out purely in the mechanical effect. Consequently the intellectual processes that take place in our brains along with the material processes lack the necessary basis for our reasoning. They stand outside the Causal Law, and thus by definition they are incapable of being understood. . . . It is entirely and permanently incomprehensible why it should matter, as it does matter, how a number of atoms of carbon, hydrogen, oxygen, and nitrogen are and were and will be so disposed, move and have moved and will move so. . . . One cannot in any way see how out of their co-operation consciousness could arise. . . . In presence of the enigmas of the world of bodies, the scientist has long been accustomed to say, with a manly resignation: *Ignoramus.* . . . But in presence of the riddle of what matter and force are, and how to think of them, he must, once and for all, resolve to make the much harder admission: *Ignorabimus."*

Gustav von Bunge, in his *Lehrbuch der Physiologie,* relates that his physics professor opened his lectures with these words: " Electricity and magnetism are those forces of nature with which people who understand nothing of electricity and magnetism can explain everything." To this state of things Du Bois-Reymond put an end, so far as concerned his own field of physiology. He said to himself: if human and animal bodies contain electricity, it must be just as discoverable and measurable as it is in other natural bodies; and only in so far as this is the case can science properly deal with it. This thought he applied to practical work with such minute care that in his experiments on muscular and nervous electricity he used a multiplier with five thousand turns, and he was the first physiologist to bring the exact methods of physics into that discipline — a fact of wide importance, for this application of strictly scientific experiment to the human body opened up an immense field of activity. Moreover, his experiments put it for the first time beyond dispute that the earlier scientists' suspicion that electricity is universally distributed in the animal world had a real foundation. We frequently observe in the history of the sciences that a certain piece of knowledge appears relatively very early, and that it is abandoned on the mere ground that the *explanation* of the newly-discovered phenomenon is found to be wrong; the fact itself, which is entirely correct, only obtains recognition much later. So it was in the case of animal electricity. We have told in our previous volume how Galvani observed that a freshly prepared frog's leg twitched in the proximity of an electrical discharge, and concluded therefrom that the frog's leg was electric. On the other hand Volta showed that the frog's leg had only played the part of a sensitive electroscope. This was correct, but so also was Galvani's contention, only his reasons being wrong. Moreover, eight years earlier, John Walsh had already made the striking discovery that the electric ray generated electricity in a perfectly definite organ, that it was thus enabled to impart powerful shocks, and that these could be conducted further by a wire. At this point Du Bois-Reymond joined in. He showed that this fish was immune from inductive shocks carried through the water, and he also demonstrated the existence of an " action-current," so-called, in the human muscle. He was equally successful in the case of the nerves.

Under the influence of these successes Du Bois-Reymond became the champion of what is called " Vitalism," the theory which finds the origin of all life-processes in a particular force, the *vis vitalis*. After the chemist Dumas had put forward the proposition that the true cause of all vital phenomena was to be sought in a *" force hypermécanique,"* practically every important investigator had adopted the same view in all sorts of individual variations. In his *Chemische Briefe* — a work eagerly read by the whole world of that day — Liebig said that it was impossible to build up a particle of sugar out of its elements, and that a separate life-force was required therefor. When, now, Du Bois-Reymond took up the position that there were no vital phenomena that could not be explained physically (a view that Lamarck also had held, but for which he had found no followers), he naturally went much too far, but in doing so he was merely obeying the physical law of reaction, for the natural-philosophers had been so outrageous with their mystic " life-force " that the come-back was only too understandable. Today, however, most physiologists incline to take a middle view, which is contained in the résumé with which Claude Bernard concludes his classic investigations into the phenomenon of life: " *L'élément ultime du phénomène est physique, l'arrangement est vital.*" Not a few researchers, however, have returned to unqualified Vitalism; for instance, Johannes Reinke, who supposes " dominants " endowed with intelligence to be the authors of the phenomena of life, and Karl Ludwig Schleich, who attributes a soul to every single cell. Bunge, too, adopts a completely sceptical attitude towards the mechanists. And Du Bois-Reymond himself, as we have seen, was a sceptic. Far from pronouncing a conclusive judgment on the ultimate questions of this science, he regarded every piece of knowledge simply as a new problem.

Spectrum analysis In other fields, also, natural science progressed, theoretically and practically. 1868 saw the synthesis of alizarin, the dye of the madder plant, in a much purer form than that derived from the natural sources. From the end of the fifties unwearying work was done on the problem of sending the electric spark oversea by means of a copper wire insulated with gutta-percha; the lines parted again and again, and it was only in 1866 that permanent cable connexion was achieved between America and England; whereupon the latter country proceeded vigorously to develop similar connexions with the Colonies. Photography, too, advanced rapidly, thanks in particular to the invention of the dry plate, which amongst other things benefited astronomy; the plate could gather and sum up many more light-impressions than the eye, and so astronomical photography became a sort of time-microscopy whereby many " invisible " fixed stars, comets, and nebulæ were caught in the plate. But the epoch-making development in the investigations of all the heavenly bodies was spectrum analysis. We have already noted Fraunhofer's discovery and accurate placing of the dark lines in the solar spectrum; and presently he was able to find other spectra for many of the fixed stars. In connexion with this, Kirchhoff and Bunsen in 1860 invented the method called " spectrum-inversion," which rested on the principle that every body absorbs precisely those rays which it emits itself. The sodium flame, for example, burns yellow, and if white light (which consists, as everyone knows, of all the colours) be sent through it, the spectral band that we get is continuous save that instead of the yellow line we get a dark one. In this way the chemical nature of both the simple and the compound gases was established, by the number and position of their lines, and to a high degree of accuracy — in the case of sodium, for instance, to a third of a millionth of a milligram. More, in the same year Bunsen by this means discovered two unknown elements, cæsium and rubidium — a discovery followed by numerous others of the kind — while Kirchhoff explored the solar atmosphere, wherein amongst other things he found gaseous iron — an experimental verification of previous hypotheses of the metallic character of that star. Similar confirmation was obtained of the theories that the moon has no atmosphere and no light of its own (by its being shown that its spectrum is identical with that of the sun), and that Venus, Mars, Jupiter, and Saturn possess envelopes of air very like the earth's. The fixed stars yielded differing spectra; in some cases lines indicating constituents unknown to the earth, and it became possible to arrange them in three groups — the so-called red stars, yellow stars of the sun type, and white stars of the Sirius type, with numerous intermediates. More, spectrum analysis made it possible to measure the movement of the stars by applying the Doppler principle, which rests on the following reasoning: if a source of light is moving towards the observer, then in a given unit of time a greater number of oscillations will reach his eye, and if moving away from him, a lesser number. The colouring in the first case shifts towards the violet, in the second towards the red end of the spectrum, violet rays having the shortest, and red the longest, wave-lengths.

In the same year in which spectrum analysis was discovered, Pasteur showed that fermentation and putrefaction, hitherto supposed to be caused by the oxygen of the air, were due to fissions produced by micro-organisms. He attempted also to solve the enigma of the origin of life. To this question Aristotle, who, as everyone knows, wielded scientific authority over Europe for about fifteen hundred years, had answered that it originated in nothing, declaring that every dry body becoming damp and every damp body becoming dry generated animals; for instance, flower-flies came from the flower dew, wood-boring insects from the wood, intestinal worms from the contents of the intestine. Classical poetry had taken up the idea, and Virgil describes in the *Georgics* how larvæ formed out of rotting flesh. The Humanists of the Renaissance period, too, who broke with so many other prejudices of the

The origin of life

191

past, reformed very little in this case; even van Helmont, one of the most distinguished investigators of the seventeenth century, maintained that in a vessel containing meal and a dirty shirt one could produce mice. Others produced evidences that frogs could be produced from the mud of marshes, and eels from the water of rivers. This was described as " spontaneous generation," life seemingly arising *sponte sua*. But in the second half of the century the Italian academician Redi proved that the maggots in rotting meat came from eggs laid in it by flies — and he showed this by a very simple method: namely, by wrapping the meat in fine gauze, under which it remained free from maggots. By degrees it came to be recognized generally that in all such instances the cause and the effect had been mistaken for each other — if worms appear in a rotten apple, the decay has not produced the worm, but the worm the decay. When, however, after the invention of the microscope, the fact was discovered that in every " infusion " (water poured on organic matter) innumerable small creatures appeared in a short time, the theory of " spontaneous generation " emerged again, and even a man of such extraordinary scientific genius as Buffon came out in favour of it. In order to refute it, the Abbé Spallanzani placed vegetable infusions into a glass vessel, sealed it, and put it in boiling water. After it had been left for a month, it was opened, and no trace of life could be found. This seemed to prove that the infusoria came from the air, since the boiling obviously destroyed the old germs, and the exclusion of the air prevented new ones from taking their place. Against this, however, Gay-Lussac argued that, as the vessel contained almost no air, the infusoria had lacked oxygen and that this was what had prevented their spontaneous generation. Throughout the first half of the century the majority of scientists still believed in spontaneous generation, and as late as 1856 Pouchet, director of the Natural History Museum at Rouen, published a work on the subject which opens thus: " Reflection and experiment have made it completely clear to me that spontaneous generation is one of the means which nature employs for the production of new living creatures." Even the more unprejudiced savants only got so far as to regard the problem as insoluble, and when Pasteur put forward his view, his teacher, the celebrated chemist Dumas, said to him: " I would not advise anyone to spend too long on that subject." Nevertheless, Pasteur succeeded by a series of extremely ingenious experiments in demonstrating beyond question that the infusoria came from the air, and since then no one has doubted that they come into the world in exactly the same way as all other organisms.

This did not, however, put the problem finally to rest, for the question remains: how did the *first* living beings arise on earth? The answer of a whole series of eminent investigators is that spontaneous generation took place somewhere and somehow, and opinions are just as sharply divided now as before. While Pasteur summarized his researches in the statement that " spontaneous generation is a fable," Professor Nägeli asserts that " to deny spontaneous generation is to proclaim a miracle "; and Du Bois-Reymond said that " the first appearance of living beings on earth is merely an extraordinarily difficult mechanical problem."

The lines on which a solution of the problem is to be imagined have been accurately laid down by the physiologist Eduard Pflüger. He draws a distinction between living albumen, of which, as is well known, all organic substance is built up, and dead albumen. The characteristic of living albumen, according to his view, consists in cyanogen (CN), a body made up of an atom of carbon and one of nitrogen, which does not exist free, but only in combinations such as the potassium cyanide of which everyone has heard. Now, it is of particular significance that all cyanic compounds that are made artificially in the laboratory can only be made at high temperatures, and it is known that the earth was once at these temperatures. Hence, Pflüger says, " life was born of fire." During the immeasurably long periods in which the earth's surface was cooling, cyanogen had ample opportunity to indulge its strong penchant for polymerization, and so, with the co-operation of oxygen, water, and salt, to pass into the albumen that forms living matter. It must be admitted that this theory solves at least one difficult question: namely, how life could have existed at a time when the conditions were so utterly opposite to what they are now. The process is in fact possible always and everywhere, and it is childish in the astronomers to assert the uninhabitability of most of the other heavenly bodies merely because they think that they would find themselves uncomfortable in them.

The further career of these hot cyan-compounds has been dealt with more closely by Haeckel. According to his hypothesis, there were first formed larger molecular groupings; these then tended to gather in still larger aggregates and formed homogeneous plasm-grains. These plasm-grains condensed to balls of plasm, in which, either from surface-tension or from chemical causes, there was set up a differentiation of wall and central body; and so the first cell came into existence. His suppositions as to the further course of development are Darwinian — though Darwin himself, we must not omit to observe, expressly declined to put forward any opinion whatever on the question of the origin of life.

Meantime other very eminent natural scientists had declared against spontaneous generation; for instance, Helmholtz, who maintained that inorganic and organic matter were alike eternal, and Fechner, who even set up the hypothesis that the organic is older than the inorganic. Latterly the brilliant Swedish astronomer Svante Arrhenius has developed a theory, also anti-spontaneous, which is known by the name of " transpermia "; according to this, seeds of life are scattered about the universe everywhere, floating hither and thither in infinite space till they meet a heavenly body that offers them the conditions needed for their further development. Arrhenius imagines these organisms as so small that the radiation-pressure of the sun suffices to drive them about in space. This, however, merely removes the question of life's origin from the earth to the Cosmos, and the only true position to take up towards this problem would seem to be that indicated by the great palæontologist Edgar Dacqué in his latest work: " Every attempt to answer this question that is really serious, and not outward and superficial, must lead into metaphysics."

Cellular pathology and psycho-physics Cell-theory was further advanced by Ernst Brücke, a pupil of Johannes Müller, who said: " I call cells elementary organisms in the same sense as we call bodies that cannot yet be chemically subdivided, elements," but prudently added: " Just as indivisibility of the elements is not proved, so also we cannot reject the possibility that cells themselves may be made up of still smaller organisms that stand to them in the same relation as they themselves do to the organism as a whole; but we have as yet no ground for this supposition." He regarded the cell as a " minute animal body " and established the fact that the contents of the cell have a " highly artistic structure." As to this aggregate state, he says: " If we are asked whether, as we do not admit that the cell content is a fluid, we believe that it is solid, we answer no. And if we are asked, is it, then, fluid, we say again no. The terms ' fluid' and ' solid,' as accepted in physics, have no application to the forms with which we have here to deal." And, strictly, after what has been established, we can no longer speak of cells as ultimate elements, but all the same the cell-theory has proved itself an extremely fruitful working hypothesis. The splendid proof of this is in the cellular pathology that Rudolf Virchow founded in 1858. Virchow saw the animal as "a sum of vital units, of which each carries in itself the full character of life, . . . a sort of social disposition, an organism of a social kind in which a mass of individual existences are thrown into each other's arms; . . . thus it is not an unfair demand that the major parts of the body as they exist in actuality, the 'Third Estate,' should receive their due recognition, and that, according this recognition, we should no longer content ourselves with merely considering constituents such as the nerves as wholes, as self-contained and simple pieces of apparatus, or the blood as a mere fluid, but should take account, even within the blood and the nerves, of the immense mass of tiny and effective centres. . . . In any case it seems to me to be necessary to assign to the specific action of the elements an overriding importance as compared with the specific action of the vessels, and to orient the study of local processes (so far as concerns their essence) towards this field of research." This democratic physiology, by directing attention to the individual "local societies" and "trade-unions" which decisively determine the life of the organism as a whole, has given an entirely new orientation to medical science and has produced most beneficent results — although, like every new dogma, it led to one-sided ideas through forgetting that from another point of view the organization of the human being is, after all, strictly monarchical and hierarchic.

In the domain of practical medicine the two most important achievements of the period were the ophthalmic mirror and antisepsis. Of the first, its inventor, Helmholtz, said: "It needed no more knowledge than what I had acquired in my optics course at school, so that now it seems to me absurd that other people as well as I myself should have been so hidebound as not to have discovered it long ago. It is a combination of glasses which lights up the dark background of the eye and at the same time permits all the details of the retina to be examined, seen even more accurately than one can, without magnifications, see the outside of the eye; for the transparent part of the eye acts as a reading-glass of twenty diameters' magnification." Antisepsis was an immediate consequence of Pasteur's discovery of the source of putrefaction. The English surgeon Joseph Lister concluded from it that careful disinfection was the most important requirement in the successful treatment of wounds. To this end he bathed the whole field of the operation in a mist of carbolic, for which he had devised a special atomizer, or " carbolic spray." In a short time " Listerizing " was accepted everywhere, and very many operations were robbed of their dangerousness.

This period also saw the coming of a new scientific discipline, experimental psychology. Its founder was Ernst Heinrich Weber, who was the first to carry out exact experiments on the differential sensitivity of the body-surface to adjacent touch-impressions; and who arrived at the following downward scale: tongue-tip, lips, finger-tips, palm, back of the hand, arm, thigh, trunk. He also measured differences of pressure and temperature and arrived at the general conclusion that the greater a stimulus is, the greater its alteration must be in order to be felt as such. If, for example, one lifts a weight of 40 grammes and then one of 41, the difference can still be detected; in the case of 400 grammes ten and for 800 grammes twenty are necessary to make the increase perceptible. The ratio between a stimulus and its sensible increment is thus in all cases a constant; that is, calling any stimulus s, and the increment ds, then $ds:s =$ constant. These investigations were further developed by Gustav Theodor Fechner, who in other fields also was an original philosophical thinker: he studied the soul-life of the plants and regarded the stars as conscious beings intermediate between God and man. In his fundamental work, *Elemente der Psychophysik*, he propounded the law of the " threshold-value of sensation," which states that every stimulus becomes sensible only when, firstly, it has attained the strength enabling it to pass the *threshold of sensation* and, secondly, when it is sufficiently differentiated from other elements and has passed the *threshold of difference*. The Weber law, in his formulation, is as follows: the intensity of sensations forms an arithmetical, while that of stimuli forms a geometrical, series, or, in other words, intensities of sensation increase as the logarithms of the intensities of stimulus; the sensation is proportional to the logarithm of the stimulus when the threshold-value is taken as unity. This formula, again, was improved by Helmholtz by the important correction that under very intense stimuli an upper limit is reached beyond which it does not increase.

The Marchese Corti discovered in the " cochlea " innumerable microscopic plates connected to the threads of the hearing-nerves; as the eye is a photographic camera, so the ear is built like a piano. On this Helmholtz built up his " theory of sensations of tone," the basic idea of which is that we never hear simple tones, but chords with a dominating fundamental; it is this vibration of the overtones that produces what is called timbre or " colour." Following on this, he worked out an elaborate physiological psychology of musical keys, of the æsthetic laws of harmony, of the different musical systems as conditioned by history and ethnography, the whole constituting the profoundest and most comprehensive study that this subject has ever had. An experimental psychology too, in its way, was Brehm's *Tierleben*, of which the six volumes appeared from 1864 to 1869, a work of such patience and accuracy, such love and fullness as only a German could have produced. Additions to the Darwinian stock were made by Ewald Hering, in his theory of memory — which he regarded as a heritable primary faculty of all organized matter and as the main cause of the birth of instinct — and by Pfarrer Mendel's plant-crossing experiments, on the basis of which he arrived at quite definite rules for the transference, suppression, and mixing of ancestral characters.

It was Hippolyte Taine who made Darwinism a literary power. In his first works, clever essays on La Fontaine and Livy, his new method was already foreshadowed with some distinctness; in another book, on the French philosophers of the nineteenth century, he attacked with many-faceted satire the prevailing intellectual eclecticism and its leader, Victor Cousin. In 1863 appeared his *Histoire de la littérature anglaise*, in three volumes, followed, a year later, by a concluding one on *Les Contemporains*. It is not a literary history in the ordinary sense, but a psychology of the English people, illustrated by splendidly coloured portraits of its great poets and writers. In 1864 he was appointed Professor of Æsthetics at the École des Beaux-arts, and the essence of his lectures in that capacity is embodied in his *Philosophie de l'art*, a program-work on the origins, nature, and values of the great art-epochs, demonstrated and illustrated by captivating panoramas of the Greek, Italian, and Netherlands cultures. His *Voyage aux Pyrénées* and his *Notes sur l'Angleterre* contain original and sparkling characterizations of the countries and their peoples; and indeed throughout his works he showed himself a gifted travel-painter. In 1875 appeared the first volume of his *Origines de la France contemporaine*: namely, " *L'Ancien Régime* "; others on the Revolution and Napoleon followed. In his preface he says: " In order to learn what modern France is, one must know how it came into

The Milieu-theory

197

being. At the end of last century it went through a metamorphosis, like an insect shedding its skin. . . . These three stages, *ancien régime*, Revolution, and modern régime, I shall attempt to exhibit exactly as a historical anatomist would do. I have no other object but this. I handle my subject as the naturalist would handle an insect." His model (whom, however, he far surpasses in magic power of revivifying the past) was the brilliant Alexis de Tocqueville, who in his *L'Ancien Régime et la Révolution* (published in 1856) — a work of marvellous socio-psychological judgment, clear sight, and richness of ideas — attempted for the first time to give an ætiology and diagnostic of the Revolution. "My intention," he said, " has been not merely to ascertain the malady from which the patient died, but to discover the remedy which might have saved him from death. I have done as the doctors do who seek to spy out the laws of life in a worn-out organ. My aim has been to make a picture which should be true and at the same time might be instructive." This is the feature common to Tocqueville and Taine: both have didactic aims, but they pursue them by means, not of rhetoric, but of biology and a kind of spiritual chemistry. " If," says Taine, " in psychological analysis one takes the pains to recognize the constituents of every field, one will discover that the various retorts contain elements that are similar to one another. . . . The natural scientists have observed that the different organs of animals are interdependent. In the same way the historians can establish that the different dispositions and inclinations of an individual, a race, an epoch, have a correspondence among themselves. . . . The natural scientists show that in a given group in the animal kingdom the same plan of organization appears in all the species, that the paw of the dog, the hoof of the horse, the wing of the bat, the arm of the man, the fluke of the whale are the same anatomical member, which has by certain alterations adapted itself to the most varied tasks. By a like method historians can show that in the same school, the same century, the same people, persons who differ completely from one another in situation, ancestry, education, and character all present a similar type, a nucleus of basic capacities and dispositions which, abbreviated, interlinked, and intensified in the most diverse ways, embody the unity of the group in its heterogeneity. . . . No one reproaches the heron for its long, fragile legs, its thin body, its contemplative immovable attitude, or blames the frigate-bird for its gigantic wings and pitiful feet; in the heron leanness and in the frigate-bird lack of even proportions constitute beauty. The one and the other characteristic disclose an idea in nature, and the business of the naturalist is to understand it and not to mock at it. He accepts her varied forms, rejects none and describes all." Taine makes up his cultural-psychological equations with four algebraic quantities, *race, milieu, moment,* and *faculté maîtresse.* " Vice and virtue are products just as vitriol and sugar are," so runs the famous sentence in the preface to his *Littérature anglaise,* which created such an uproar in France — quite unreasonably, for it was simply a formulation of the Gallic creed. In fact, Taine represents one of the highest intellectual triumphs of the race whose *faculté maîtresse* is Cartesianism; here once more is the whole Versailles of philosophy in its cold splendour; the spirit of analytical dissection and constructive architecture, whose tools — handled with hair's-breadth precision — are the scalpel of the logician and the compasses of the geometer. There is yet another reason why the " *Milieu*-theory " could have originated only in France; only there is there such an all-powerful social environment as in a measure to justify the theory. Leopold Ziegler says in a remarkable essay: " The Frenchman's conventional view of certain facts of actuality stands out sharply in contrast to our German selfness (*Eigenheit*). . . . This born talent for all actuality, in so far as it is conventional in origin, appears to have gradually sharpened the eye for the phenomena of sociability, in a widened sense of the word; namely, for everything that binds persons and things together, that is for them a foundation of life and a condition of community." At bottom, this too is a product of the Cartesian Rationalism; we need only remind ourselves how profoundly Descartes, both in his philosophy and in his private life, respected Church, State, and society as higher powers. In France the belief in, or superstition of, the uniformity of men and their origin in the same mint has always determined the life-feeling — herein Richelieu and Robespierre, Racine and Rousseau, were wholly at one. On the other hand it is this tacit inward consensus of a whole human variety that has given it the capacity for supreme cultural achievement. The Frenchman wears a uniform all his life, but it is a very fine one.

If Darwinism stripped nature of soul, Taine took the inevitable second step of reducing soul to a natural phenomenon, and morals to physics. The birth of a nation, a culture, an art-creation, a genius, is nothing but an involved problem of mechanical or geometrical calculation. If we know its parts, we can reconstruct the apparatus; if we know its equation, we can draw the curve. With any other man this ghastly scheme would have remained a dry and murky school-desk problem, but in Taine's hands it filled up with flesh and blood, sap and sun, colour and brilliance. He is not only the philosopher of literary Impressionism, but also, from the literary point of view itself, one of its most finished representatives. He was an event that would have been impossible anywhere but in France: namely, a doctrinaire and pedantic savant who was at the same time one of the most powerfully imaginative creators of men and magicians of words. In him, once more, we see that in art what matters is never the plausibility, but always and only the force, of vision. With his four rusty keys he opens for the astounded spectator imaginary picture-galleries of such fairy brilliance that doubt is perforce silent.

Flaubert   His poetic method, as we have said, is the Impressionistic; artful composition of innumerable " *petits faits significatifs* " observed with the keenest eye and the finest colour-sense. The same method was employed by Flaubert. The origins of Flaubert really lie still in the Romantic; his cosmic underfeeling is the " *désenchantement de la vie,*" only it is congealed into the atheism of worshipping only the " little facts." His gloomy thoroughbass is human stupidity, and his work is one gigantic glossary, herbary, bestiary, a comprehensive morphology, biology, œcology of every human limitation; in fact his last work (which remained a fragment) was even intended to put all these — and nothing else — into actual systematic form. But by that very token he is the opposite pole to Romanticism, for he rejects all stylization, transfiguration, and embellishment of actuality, forgoes all bright bits of mosaic-glass, and shows man in his insignificance, smallness, ordinariness, and indeed contemptibleness; his heroes are no longer heroes. He depicts his world with the same scientific thoroughness and coldness as an entomologist dealing with an ant-heap or a beehive; there is not a thread of the subjective in his whole fabric. He said himself that " the author must be in his work like God in the universe, omnipresent and never visible." But does not the author resemble God in this, too, that he lives in his creatures like a father in his children? Surely, and Flaubert is no exception to the rule. The unheard-of novelty of his scientific and unsentimental method deceived his contemporaries and himself alike; in reality, in him as in any and every artist an understanding love was the creative principle. His tender poetic soul is shut up in the sparkling ice-palace of his works like the fly in the glittering amber, the mummy-corn in the king's grave, the larva in the snow of the glacier. His pictures manage after all to be as little objective as those of his predecessors and his successors; they have only the relative objectivity that pure description has in comparison with frankly introjective lyrism. Nietzsche said of Flaubert that he "brought a sonorous and multi-coloured French to its climax," by which he meant to emphasize — in a polemical context, it is true — his high picturesqueness and musicality as the basic quality in his poetic powers. His prose is orchestrated with a subtlety and fullness hitherto unexampled; he is the first great *plein-air* painter in European literature. For example: "The dove-grey silk of the sunshade, shone through by the sun, illumined the white skin of her face with quivering gleams; she smiled under it in the tepid warmth, and one heard the drops of water fall, one after the other, on the stretched fabric." Or again: "In the avenue green light, softened by the foliage, shone on the rosy moss that creaked softly under the footfalls. The sun sank, the heavens flamed between the branches, and the towering parallel trunks of the trees, planted in a straight line, looked like brown columns set against a background of gold." His idol, to which he sacrificed daily and nightly, was the *impeccabilité* of his prose. He wrote every day a few sheets, often only a few sentences; on one occasion he worked for many hours on a single page, and then, wishing to savour it before going to sleep, read it over, only to think it so bad that he leapt out of bed and spent the whole of a cold winter's night, clad only in his night-shirt, in rewriting it. Unwearyingly he tortured himself in voluntary seclusion, a monk of literature, as Faguet has called him; he made preliminary studies like a specialist scholar (even where the material was contemporary) and research-expeditions to study his localities, he ploughed through comic papers, law reports, prints, fashion journals, laundry bills, address books, and street-plans. Filing and sandpapering were not sufficient for him; when a passage seemed to him to be sufficiently near being "impeccable," he read it aloud in order to test its sensuous sound-effect. Doubtless he exaggerated artistic fineness; he paid such attention to variety in expression that he never allowed a word to occur twice on the same page, nor a syllable twice in the same sentence, and this rigorous harmony and dynamic of his led him not seldom into an ornament of sound and mosaic of words that affects us like the glass splendour of Byzantine art. There was in him the same rage for work as in Balzac, but aristocratically toned, sublimated into self-sufficingness, sporting delight, and connoisseurship. He was to that genius of the plebs as a gliding luxury-car to a coughing steam plough; and he illustrates what has already been said as to the difference between the society of the July Monarchy and that of the Second Empire.

*The
immoral
poets*

His first work, *Madame Bovary* — the biography of a provincial woman who from discontent with existence becomes an adulteress — brought upon him, when it appeared in 1857, an indictment for indecency, although it is really, in its under moral, thoroughly *petit-bourgeois*. The uproar that it created therefore is only explicable on the ground of the novelty of its mode of vision. In this, and this alone, Flaubert's " immorality " consists. Every fundamentally new aspect of the world has a " subversive " effect, disintegrating compact solidarities and tearing asunder familiar linkages. Later ages, which no longer need him, are accustomed to pay high honour to the poet of the past; they make schoolboys learn him and they use him as a bludgeon wherewith to kill living poets; but his contemporaries, who do need him, call him subversive. And so he is, like all ferments. His sharp questions get into the holes and cracks of the spiritual ground on which the Present is comfortably living, loosen it, weather it down, split it asunder. In every sense of the word, the Poet is the salt of the time.

Manet painted a bunch of asparagus. At once there arose a spate of abuse, threats, curses. Admit, if you will, that it was a pretty poor asparagus, but does that explain the detonations of hate, rage, and contempt that it set off? Which among the sacredest possessions of mankind is damaged by the fact that someone does not know how to paint vegetables? Ibsen's plays were in some cases banned, though there is nothing " gross " in them — except perhaps the paralysis in *Ghosts,* and what is that compared with the brutalities in Schiller, Dante, and Shakspere? What comes out here is really the mysterious effect that the work of genius exercises upon everyone; some are attracted, others repelled, in both cases by the same magic force. Even the philistines were fascinated, they felt instinctively that evolution had just received a new and powerful jolt, but they only got the jolt, and it sent them backwards dazed and angry. If the Impressionist pictures had really been mere coarse and ugly daubs, as they asserted, they would simply have passed them by, instead of going for them as they did with their umbrellas. And if Ibsen had been a revolutionary of the stamp of Sudermann, he could have permitted himself anything and would have had the same momentary success as he. After the first performance of the *Enemy of the People* in Paris, Francisque Sarcey, the pope of Parisian literary life in those days, sat with Jules Lemaître in a café. Suddenly Sarcey said: "Yes, I find this Ibsen ridiculous and devoid of talent, and you regard me on that account as an old cow. *You* will only obtain that title after my death." The good old Sarcey spoke truth, more so perhaps than he suspected. The position of the " old cow," in fact, is that which the so-called leading critic and the public that he leads inevitably take towards the new. And the poet is probably already born towards whom we in our turn shall show ourselves to be a herd of old cows.

Still more unfriendly was the reception in 1862 of Flaubert's great historical novel *Salammbô,* dealing with the times of the Carthaginian mercenaries. Essentially, his method here is the same as in *Madame Bovary,* the only difference being that the "*exactitude documentaire* " is more obvious in the case of subject-matter that is so exotic. Others treated history from the view-point of present-day men, but Flaubert sees even the present with the eyes of the historian, the laboriously accurate chronicler, the reconstructor of lost linkages, the rediscoverer of forgotten life-sources, remote forms of being, and buried soul-curiosities. In his vivid novel *Éducation sentimentale* (1869), which is the history of a long unavowed love, with its beginnings in the forties, he achieves even the *tour de force* of fixing the slight modifications that the colloquial language underwent within a single generation, its transient catchwords and vulgarisms, verbal dynamics and emphases, the "pitch," so to say — and that with a refinement that frequently borders on pedantry. In *Salammbô* his keenness of vision sometimes becomes microscopy, and his stage a museum. But the climax of his analytical and picturesque psychology was his *Tentation de Saint Antoine,* which appeared in 1874. This is really an immense monodrama of St. Anthony's visions during one night. It is untrue to say that he meant it to symbolize the fiasco of religion; such a purpose would have been entirely unworthy of the pure creator that he was. Flaubert is as a matter of fact an atheist, but he does not say so; what he is concerned to do is simply to describe the " case," the psychosis. All imaginable tempting visions troop past the anchorite overstrained by fasting, vigils, and self-torturings — lust, cruelty, luxury, ambition, unbelief in every form, Bible-doubts and heresy, polytheism and pantheism. Finally one of the visions exclaims: " My kingdom is as wide as the world, and my desire has no limits. I go ever onward, freeing spirits and weighing worlds, without fear, without compassion, without love, without God. Men call me Science." But the Devil rises to something worse still: " Who knows whether the world is not merely an eternal stream of things and events, whether appearance is not the true reality, and illusion the only truth? " At last the night passes away, and between golden clouds the disk of the sun appears. It bears the countenance of Christ. The hermit crosses himself and returns to his interrupted prayers.

Flaubert died in 1880, mourned by almost nobody. People regarded him as a fool, many as a schoolmaster, many as a perverter, but all — in France, the death-sentence — as a bore.

Renan   A quite specific peculiarity of this new Positivist literature was that it worked out the frontiers between art and science. While Flaubert was a sort of historical investigator (his *Salammbô* even including scholarly annotations), Ernest Renan was a sort of romancer. His main work, like Taine's, deals with *origines,* but with those of Christianity instead of contemporary France. He says thereon: " A history of the origins of Christianity must embrace the whole dark and, so to say, subterranean period from the first stirrings of this religion to the point when its existence became a public and overt fact clear to everyone. Such a history would consist of four parts. The first, which I publish in this volume, deals with the event which served the new cult as starting-point; it is concerned only with the lofty person of its Founder. The second part would treat of the Apostles and their immediate disciples. The third would exhibit Christianity under the Antonines, its slow development and almost continuous fight against Rome. And, finally, the fourth part would deal with the important advance that it made with the beginning of the domination of the Syrian emperors, and show how the system of the Antonines collapsed and the ruin of the Classical culture set in irremediably." And he did in fact carry out this gigantic plan, following up the *Vie de Jésus* with *Les Apôtres, Saint Paul, L'Antéchrist, Les Évangiles ou la seconde génération chrétienne, L'Église chrétienne,* and *Marc-Aurèle et la fin du monde antique.* And to this structure he gave monumental foundations in his first volume, *Histoire du peuple Israël.*

His life of Jesus, which excited even greater attention than Strauss's, appeared in 1863, and within the year he was deprived of his professorship of Hebrew at the Collège de France. It was the fruit of a scientific research-expedition in Phœnicia which he had conducted in the two previous years. " And there," he says himself, " the old legends acquired form and body for me to an extent that amazed me. The astonishing agreement of the texts with the localities, the wonderful harmony of the Gospel ideal with the landscape that served as its framework, worked upon me like a revelation. I saw a fifth Gospel — which was certainly fragmentary, but still legible, and discerned, instead of an abstract being which we ought to believe never existed, a stupendous human form that lived and moved." And in fact the scene of the Old and New Testaments had never before been depicted with such purity and richness, such intimacy and colour. Withal, the book is not " belles-lettres," as the jealous inept maintain to this day, but highly scientific — far more so than Strauss's, because it is founded on a far more universal erudition. Renan was not a mere collator of textual fragments and argumentative Hegelian like the author of that product of study and candle, but an Orientalist in the widest sense of the word; he knew all the languages, confessional dialects, and life-forms of Asia Minor, he was an archæologist and geographer, an ethnologist and folk-lorist — and, above all, a psychologist. And on top of all this, there was his immense superiority as an artist. The Strauss work is a philological-dialectical sand-heap, Renan's a precious porcelain; the one is an obstinate pastor's growl, the other a piece of chamber music. His artistry protected Renan, too, from looking at the Saviour under aspects so crudely and incurably commonplace as we have seen Strauss did. All the world knows the beautiful conclusion of his chapter on the death of Jesus: " Rest now in thy glory, noble Pioneer! Thy work is accomplished. Removed from the dangers of frailty, thou wilt look down from the heights of divine peace on the unending consequences of thy work. At the price of some hours of sufferings, that did not even touch thy great soul, thou hast bought the completest immortality. Through millennia the world will look up to thee. Symbol of our contradictions, thou wilt become the banner about which the hottest of the battle will rage. A thousand times more living, a thousand times more loved, after death than in the days of thy pilgrimage here below, thou wilt so become humanity's corner-stone that the world must quiver to its foundations if thy name be wrested from it. Between thee and God men will no more distinguish. Supreme victor over death, enter into possession of thy kingdom, whither, by the royal road that thou hast shown them, the revering centuries shall follow thee." All the same, one can see, even from these sentences, that, for all his open-hearted receptiveness, Renan is far from grasping his subject, as, indeed, is to be expected of a Parisian salon-philosopher of the Second Empire. Out of the Passion story he makes a shimmering idyll, *"une délicieuse pastorale."* The magic of the happening is naturalized, sometimes to an extent that borders on frivolity. Jerusalem, for Renan, is the contested seat of a big bourgeoisie and a clericalism, of scholasticism and corruption, of scepsis and hedonism; in a word, Paris; and in place of the conflict of the two elemental worlds of Jehovah and the Son of God, which is something so vast that words can hardly embrace it, we are shown a conflict between stagnation and progress, reaction and freedom. The messenger of glad tidings who had said that one must lose one's life to save it, appears here as the teacher of an *improved* life, a reformer. The true Son of God, profoundest sharer of his secrets and highest mandatory of his will, who has changed round the poles of the world, turned everything upside down, and altered the face of the earth, is in Renan a kindly wandering preacher, a naïve pastor of souls, and a joyous friend of the people. " He laid the foundations for true liberalism and true civilization " — in this sentence is unmasked the real leitmotiv of the work, which appeals against Napoleonism to gospel truth — is in other words a mere negative-print of Napoleonism, Second Empire *versus* Second Empire.

The further Christianity gets away from its origins and immerses itself in the stream of the world, the more appropriate an object it becomes for the mundane brush-work of a Renan. His view of the Apostolic period is also somewhat singular: " Certainly, if Christianity had remained in the hands of these good people, imprisoned in the conventicles of the illumined, it would have been extinguished like Essenism, without leaving behind it any vigorous impulse to veneration. It was the intractable Paul who brought Christianity to honour and prestige and, defying all risks, boldly sent it out on the high seas. Protestantism existed already within five years of Jesus' death, and Paul was its noble founder. Jesus no doubt had not presupposed such disciples as he, but it is they nevertheless who contributed most to keeping his work alive and indeed to securing its immortality." Here speaks an opportunism that must hurt every religious feeling even though (or perhaps for the very reason that) it is expressed in so unrepellent a way. Renan is really in his element when he is describing interesting cultural phenomena like Nero, or Antichrist, or decadent Rome (which is Paris again). His personality as a whole is not unlike that of a highly cultivated prince of the Church in Renaissance times, whose feeling towards art and science is the intimate one of the gourmet and connoisseur, and whose relation to religion is non-existent, being not even one of doubting.

For thirty years Charles Auguste Sainte-Beuve wrote his weekly " *Causeries du lundi* "; " On Mondays at noon I breathe for an hour, then the iron bars close again and I sit in my prison-cell for a week." Evidently in the age of Positivism even gossip has to be a scientific robot. Sainte-Beuve has been called the " Prince of Critics," and in fact he possessed all the typical qualities of such; a stylistic goldsmith, testing every grain by the scales; master and devotee of the whetted adjective and minter of gleaming *mot*-medallions; subtle scenter of hidden beauties and defects, but completely without instinct for the whole and the essence of a personality, savouring the promising, original, and go-ahead with his fine nose, but never covering it with his body as a flag, drifting into pastel even when drawing characters already scheduled as great. Without the smallest feeling for the heroic in genius, which he always atomizes till it becomes genre; an almost inevitable succession of all over-intimate minor characteristics that, under such a microscope, appear no longer as fresh healthy skin, but as wrinkled bits of leather.

The work of Taine and Flaubert, Renan and Sainte-Beuve owe nothing to leisure and mood, everything to work and discipline. Like certain expensive sorts of hyacinths, they have a symmetry of form, a strength of scent, and a fineness of colour that are not found in nature — they are stuffed hothouse products.

This period witnessed the paradox of even lyric poetry wanting to make itself " objective," non-egoist, scientific, and atheistic — all characters antagonistic to its inmost nature. Consequently nothing remained for it but to make a cold cult of form, a virtuoso performance with golden word-piling. This tendency (which, further, was decisively pessimistic and revolutionary) was represented by " *Les Parnassiens,*" who were nicknamed so in contempt, but later adopted the label for their journal *Le Parnasse contemporain.* Their leader was Leconte de Lisle, who declared *impassibilité* to be the poetic ideal, who despised the *montreurs* who tastelessly exhibit their souls in chatter, and allowed, as worthy subjects for the lyrist, only philosophy, ethnology, cultural history, landscape, and portraiture — all to be treated strictly factually. The strongest talent of the school was Baudelaire, translator of Edgar Allan Poe, champion of Manet and Wagner, opium-smoker and alcoholic, dandy and masochist, the first great decadent of the New Age. His life consumed itself in ecstasies, excesses, exoticisms, depressions, and martyrdoms of love between his " black Venus " — a mulatto woman from a café chantant with " eyes like soup-plates," and a scent like " tar, nutmeg, and coconut oil " — and his " Madonna," Madame Sabatier, the gentle, mundane mistress of a banker. His only two works of any length are the collection of poems called *Les Fleurs du mal,* and the *Paradis artificiels,* which is a prose ode on the glories and terrors of hashish-smoking. His poetry is anything but objective; rather is it the height of subjectivity, in that it is pathological and perverse, but all the same a dizzying charm pervades its well-ordered unpleasantness and extravagance. With the Parnassian school must also be counted the *Contes cruels* of Villiers de l'Isle-Adam, fastidious luxury-products of a sadistic visionary, and Barbey d'Aurevilly's stories *Les Diaboliques,* which, with their intoxicating perfume, their excess of lighting, their Satanism at any price, their superimposed free-thinking and their worldly scepticism, are really a late after-crop from the eighteenth century. The draughtsman of the group was the Belgian Félicien Rops, whose abandonment and satyrism already today seem a little pinched and peep-show-like.

Ruskin   The artistic outlook of the Parnassians had a certain affinity with the theory of " Art for Art's sake." Already Théophile Gautier had heralded this : " What is useful is ugly and common ; the most useful part of a house is the latrines." Poe declared the object of art to be the " creation of beauty," the evocation of feelings of pleasure and happiness, even by means of terror, tragedy, uncanniness, and lunacy, but never by means of a truth. This creed found its clearest formulation in an essay of 1882 by Oscar Wilde : " In its primary aspect a painting has no more spiritual message than an exquisite fragment of Venetian glass. The channels by which all noble and imaginative work in painting should touch the soul are not those of the truths of lines. This should be done

208

by a certain inventive and creative handling entirely independent of anything definitely practical in the subject, something entirely satisfying in itself which is as the Greeks would say an end. So the joy of poetry comes never from the subject, but from an inventive handling of rhythmical language." Herein the younger generation placed itself in direct opposition to its former spokesman Ruskin, though they continued to honour him as writer and art-expert. Ruskin was a passionate opponent of cold Classicism (of which he regarded Raphael as the prototype), one of the earliest roadmakers of the modern technique of painting (of which he regarded Turner as the founder), and the creator of an æsthetic biology of animals and plants, stones and clouds (for these, too, for him were living things), a natural history for artists. But, for all his appreciation of the artistic factor, he insisted that art had to subserve moral ends. In his lectures on political economy, too, he taught ethics and æsthetics alike ; on the one hand he demanded that no one should be permitted to exist on the work that another, alive or dead, had done before him ; and on the other hand he insisted on the nobility of work — which ought once more to become artistic as in the Middle Ages, when craftsman and artist were synonymous — and therefore denounced machinery. Carlyle wrote to him to say that he now rejoiced in belonging to a minority of two.

Ruskin was the apostle of " Pre-Raphaelitism." Its "father" was considered to be William Dyce, the creator of the charming picture " Jacob and Rachel " ; in Rome Dyce was in relation with Overbeck, and thus a certain connecting link was formed between Pre-Raphaelitism and Nazarenism. But in reality the first artist of this kind had been William Blake (died 1827), a painter poet who illustrated his mystical poems with coloured engravings of a strange tired charm ; and it was Swinburne who, feeling this linkage, wrote his biography. In 1848 the " P.-R.B." (Pre-Raphaelite Brotherhood) was founded ; to it belonged, amongst others, Dante Gabriel Rossetti, Holman Hunt, John Everett Millais, and later Edward Burne-Jones and William Morris. The most distinguished representative of this school, although not a member of the Brotherhood, was Robert Browning. The love-romance of his wife, Elizabeth Barrett, is celebrated — her flight from her father's house and her secret wedding, her correspondence with her lover and the chaplet of sonnets in which she tells the story of her love. Although she suffered from disease of the lungs and was already marked for death, Robert cured her by a sort of spiritual therapy, and she died only after many years of wedded life. Browning wrote for the theatre, but his dramas are diaphanous, impalpable, and two-dimensional; he wrote many other poems also, mysteries that are strangely confusing and as unfathomable as dark fairy-forests. Wilde, who admired him immensely, said of him that he knew how to stammer through a thousand mouths. A love-destiny similar to Browning's came to Dante Gabriel Rossetti with the young Elizabeth Siddall, a consumptive milliner of royal beauty, with bronze hair, long eyelashes, and green eyes. In his set of sonnets *The House of Life* he depicted the spiritual history of their union; she was his eternal model, his Beatrice, whom indeed he painted in that character, in memory of the poet whose name he bore and to whom he felt himself linked by much more than a name. He is the one erotic among the Pre-Raphaelites; he sees his women with a delicate, connoisseur-like sensuousness. The splendid neo-Gothic canvases that his pupil Burne-Jones painted are, on the other hand, emphatically over-intellectualized, Gobelinish, ornamental, approximating to craft-art; the sweet spices that they breathe bring on headaches in the end.

The characteristic point in William Morris, as in the artificial side of Pre-Raphaelitism generally, is that in his pageant-poems he reshapes antique material under the aspect of the later Middle Ages; a capricious game of double-masking and of merely mystifying card-tricks. What was truly important was his influence in the field of the decorative arts, which he fundamentally reformed by his programmatic writings and by establishing a workshop of his own for glass-painting, tapestry, furniture, and tiles — to which later he added an art-printing works and a bookbindery. His principal collaborator was Burne-Jones, who designed marvellous tapestries, church windows, floral friezes, and cartoons. Another participant in his work was Ford Madox Brown, a highly original painter, an archaizer in drawing, colour, and perspective, primitive and piquant, wooden and hectic, and, in his urge to disengage and spiritualize, nearer to the Flemish Quattrocento than to the Italian. Holman Hunt, after pious studies in Palestine, gave himself up wholly to religious symbolism, therein resembling the Nazarenes most closely of all the Pre-Raphaelites — but a symbolism that, unlike theirs, was of a very late and conscious kind. George Frederick Watts brought off the rare *tour de force* of painting moral allegories without being either tasteless or undramatic.

Pre-Raphaelitism suffered from the inward contradiction of all Renaissances, in that it embarked on the suicidal enterprise of filling the only real life — namely, that of the present — into the perished vessels of an earlier life. Still, it entirely lacked the naïve blue-eyedness of Nazarenism, and the very fact that its infantilism was dressed up, powdered, and painted, a decadent bizarrerie, was in itself a real link with the time. In general the Nazarenes misunderstood the Quattrocento from the very outset; they regarded it as primitive, because they themselves were primitive, whereas in reality it had been a gracious and elegant, aristocratic and anæmic, sublimatedly sensuous and æsthetically distilled world. But the Pre-Raphaelites felt the genuine relationship, the common factors of an interesting unfitness for life and a flight from the actual motived by disgust of the massive reality triumphant around them. But the weariness of that earlier time four centuries ago was a spring dreaminess, whereas in their revivers, the children of the autumn, melancholy intensified to morbidity, high culture to overtraining, elegance to blasé-ness, artistic power to artistic cleverness. They made out of life a gold arabesque and out of art a silk tapestry.

The ideal of the school was the "painter poet," and they did not mean this in a merely external sense; it was demanded of the artist not only that he should be both painter and poet, but that he should be both in the same work. Every poem ought to be a colour-symphony, and every picture a poetic manifesto. Further, almost all Pre-Raphaelite creations were marked by high musicality. At bottom this was the old Romantic demand that all the arts should be mixed. But what resulted was only an artificial decoction. The Pre-Raphaelites only took the various precious essences into their hands and shook them together cleverly. Once when Rossetti was laboriously working on a picture and a sonnet at the same time, Whistler said to him: "If I were in your place, I should take the picture out of the frame and put the sonnet into it." Delacroix called the Pre-Raphaelites "*l'école sèche.*" Strictly speaking, they belong, not to the history of art, but to that of æsthetics; in spite of their ethical and religious tendencies they were not (using the phrase in its highest sense) in earnest, so little so as to verge on snobbery. And yet — so baffling and contradictory is the process of man's intellectual history — Pre-Raphaelitism dominated its time in an astounding degree. The Botticelli time, galvanically revived, reappeared in life. The women lost

211

their bosoms, their hips, their red cheeks, and one saw everywhere dreamy and fragile types whose pale heads mourned for their weary bodies like faded blossoms drooping on over-fine stems. How can a lie acquire such potency?

"Æsthete" is one of those words that can imply a flattery or an insult according to the way in which they are spoken. So far as we are concerned, the latter sense must prevail over the former. In truth, nothing is less æsthetic than an æsthete. For what is æsthetic? Surely, harmony with the laws of one's own organism. Hence Nature is always æsthetic. Humming-bird and emperor moth, lotus-flower and jelly-fish are beautiful not because they are pleasing, gaily coloured, elegant, but because they fulfil their own being. And therefore a bullfrog, a bog lettuce, and a crater spouting dirt and fire have each their own beauty. But the peculiarity of the æsthete consists precisely in his wanting to be something other than he is in the plan of creation. He is not that which God meant him to be. The divine thought to which he owes his existence does not coincide with his earthly functioning. He parades the form of a power that is not in him. He is a glass eye, a wax hand.

On the other hand, we have also to think of the æsthete, and, for that matter, the very snob, as the extremest imaginable type of the idealist. He has set up a picture for himself, and strives to be worthy of it with such fervour of wishing that in the end he actually becomes it. He is the "play-actor of his ideal." And just as we do not ask an actor whether he is lying, so the æsthete, if he has fire and versatility enough, causes us to forget that he is merely wearing an alien costume. If his imitation of that which it is his ambition to be is complete (and that, of course, is the presupposition), he incarnates, like all the rest of us, one of the many ground-plans of human varieties — in this case the Platonic Idea of the man who lives wholly in fancy. Nothing that he is or does or suffers is true, because he is *poetizing* with life. Reality does not affect him, for he makes his own reality. He is a petty sovereign, and often a very pitiful one, but at least we cannot deny him our tenderness. This problem of the life-lie that becomes the life-flame has, as everyone knows, been given immortal shape by Ibsen. But if we try to look right down to the bottom, we find that the real hero of that drama is not Hjalmar at all, but old Ekdal, as is hinted in the title. With the force of a craving he has transformed his attic into a mysterious forest, and the wild duck into a symbol of all hunting-adventures. Is not the difference between him and a " Nimrod " merely that between two aspects, that are just as equivalent before the soul as a body and its projection are in the mind of a geometer? Is he a king or a fool, a snob or a poet? Looked at in this spirit, even the wax hand and the glass eye can acquire life: namely, as soon as we put life into them. And therefore it is very probable that the Muses do not condemn the æsthete, but only laugh at him — and musingly, at that.

Beyond the ocean, too, Anglo-Saxondom produced new forms. *Whitman and Thoreau* The first to sing the world of America with its own harmonies was Walt Whitman, an untamed, gigantic, even barbaric shoot of Nature, that sprang up on the raw, rich soil of his country untended and, for a long time, unnoticed. Whitman like a true American had followed all callings and none — errand-boy, book-printer, village teacher, trader, lawyer's clerk, editor, and (in the Civil War) volunteer nurse. In 1855 appeared his *Leaves of Grass,* set up by his own hands and bound in green linen, a volume of barely a hundred pages, which laid the foundations of his future fame. Its title and content are explained in his words: " I believe a leaf of grass is no less than the journey-work of the stars." They are poems in the sense that the Psalms are poems, eruptions whose poetry lies in their force and elementalness: " Camerado, this is no book, who touches this touches a man." They draw their power from their wholly new tone and from a most refreshing uneducatedness that knows nothing of the restraints of form and logic. Their basic feeling is a sort of rabid pantheism and a trampling and trumpeting optimism: " I exist as I am, that is enough. If no other in the world be aware, I sit content. If the whole world be aware, I sit content." " To me every hour of light and dark is a miracle, Every cubic inch of space is a miracle, Every square yard of the surface of the earth is spread with the same, Every foot of the interior swarms with the same." It was said of him that outwardly he had the appearance and ways of an elephant, and so he was also as a poet, elemental as the forest, kindly, shrewd, humorous, colossal, useless in a room.

The intellectual centre of North America was Massachusetts. From there, as early as the first half of the eighteenth century, the clergyman Jonathan Edwards had given a lead to thought with a philosophy that, starting from Augustine and Malebranche, regarded all happenings as "God's actings "; we can, he taught, see all things only in God and through God. There also lived Henry

David Thoreau, first as a boy tending cattle, then as a maker of lead pencils, and finally, at Walden Pond, not far south of Concord, in a hut made by himself of white pine. Birds sat on his hand, squirrels fed on his shoulder, snakes curled about his legs, fish let him take them out of the water, and wild things took refuge with him. In these ways he reminds us of Francis of Assisi, whose brotherly love of the animals those very clever people who refuse to be imposed upon have relegated to the realm of legend; and yet here, full in the age of the machine-gun, the clearing-house, and vivisection, we have a verified case of the same thing, which would no doubt be multiplied were men somewhat less greedy and money-grubbing. The fruit of this two-years' alliance with Nature was his book *Walden, or Life in the Woods*, and his motto may fitly be the verse: " I cannot come nearer to God and Heaven than I live in Walden even." " I am," he said, " no more lonely than the loon in the pond that laughs so loud, or than Walden Pond itself. What company has that lonely lake, I pray? And yet it has not the blue devils, but the blue angels in it, in the azure tint of its waters. The sun is alone. . . . God is alone — but the devil, he is far from being alone; he sees a great deal of company; he is legion. I am no more lonely than a single mullein or dandelion in a pasture or a bean-leaf, or sorrel, or a horse-fly, or a humble bee." Marvellous is Thoreau's gift of penetration into the characterology of those of Nature's creatures which thus became his, nay, our, intimate acquaintances: ". . . the yellow birch . . . singularly allied to the black birch in its sweet checkerberry scent and its form, and to the canoe birch in its peeling or fringed and tasselled bark. The top is brush-like as in the black birch. The bark an exquisite . . . gold colour, curled off partly from the trunk with vertical clear or smooth spaces, as if a plane had been passed up the tree. The sight of these trees affects me more than Californian gold. . . . We have the silver and the golden birch. This is like a fair flaxenhaired sister of the dark complexioned black birch with golden ringlets. How lustily it takes hold of the swampy soil and braces itself — and here flows a dark cherrywood or wine coloured brook over the iron-red sands in the sombre swamp, swampy wine. In an undress this tree." " A kitten is so flexible that she is almost double. The hind parts are equivalent to another kitten with which the fore part plays. She does not discover that her tail belongs to her till you tread upon it. She jumps into a chair and then stands on her hind legs to look out of the window as much as any gossip. Ever and anon she bends back her ears to hear what is going on within the room and all the while her eloquent tail is reporting the progress and success of her survey by speaking gestures."

Thoreau despises all tradition: " Some are dinning in our ears that we Americans, and moderns generally, are intellectual dwarfs compared with the ancients, or even the Elizabethan men. . . . Shall a man go and hang himself because he belongs to the race of pigmies, and not be the biggest pigmy that he can? . . . It is not important that he should mature as soon as an apple-tree or an oak. Shall he turn his spring into summer? . . . Shall we with pains erect a heaven of blue glass over ourselves, though when it is done we shall be sure to gaze still at the true ethereal heaven far above, as if the former were not? " Herein he comes in touch with his friend Emerson, who himself had called his own thoughts " children of the woods." Concord, already renowned in the history of the United States from the fact that its inhabitants were the first to offer armed resistance and to give the signal for the War of Independence in 1775, was, besides being the birthplace of Thoreau, the spot which played the chief part in Emerson's life; he was not indeed born there, but his family came from there (his grandfather was one of the rebels) and he spent more than half his life there. Emerson, too, cared little for dogmas and traditions, and said that he would never assert of a fact that it was true or false; on the contrary, he would assert nothing, but stir up everything; and herein he links with Montaigne, with whom he has also in common his loose form of presentation, the realism of his language, and the passionate urge to penetrate the veil of superficial routine ideas and reach the true meaning of all life-relations. He said, indeed, after his first reading of the *Essays*, that it seemed to him as though he had written them himself in a previous existence. Yet we must not overlook the fact that Montaigne was in the highest sense what Nietzsche understood by " a good European," something unknown to Emerson even by hearsay. With Carlyle, too, he is often mentioned, and we need only compare his *Representative Men* with *Heroes and Hero-Worship* to recognize at once a likeness that applies even to their outward architectures. There are again, however, great differences. Emerson was the more harmonious and balanced nature of the two, but also the softer and more diffluent. Both took effect in the way natural forces do, but the elemental impetus of Carlyle is like that of a

215

wild flood that overleaps its banks and tears everything away with it, whereas Emerson's spiritual rhythm reminds one more of the gentle flowing-on of a meadow stream that hollows its bed slowly and peacefully. Something of the preacher was in both, but Emerson was not, as Carlyle was, the tempestuous and angry prophet, but rather the mild and persuasive pastor. His conciliatory optimism not seldom (and especially in his later works) contains some " moonshine," as Carlyle was accustomed to call it in his later years. Emerson, equally with Carlyle, was able to impart to everything that he said the character of infinity that opens out so many relations, but the boundless ocean in which we find ourselves with him contains in general too little salt, and we swim in a fresh-water sea. In the preface which he wrote to Emerson's *Essays* in 1841, Carlyle called them " a true soul's soliloquy," but not one of Carlyle's own works could be described as a monologue — he is always speaking to an imagined crowd.

It is purposeless, and indeed impossible, to reproduce or to comment on Emerson's philosophy, for, like a crystal or a landscape, it describes and comments itself. His propositions are there, unprepared, indisputable, like sailors' signals coming out of a misty deep. He appeared at a time when America was already confronted with the danger of becoming completely Americanized, and to the reality of the machine he opposed the reality of the heart. But a man who hales all our painfully won actualities before the tribunal of thought and faith can by no means afford to be a dreamer scholar, offering a few pitiful castles in the air as substitute for steam-milled corn and refrigerator-meat, telephone and linotype. It is from out of the midst of actual life's realism that he must develop his higher and richer world-views. This is what gives Emerson's physiognomy its special character. He is American, and he writes for a people of " self-made " men, he is the philosopher of the " New World." He holds his candle directly up to things and looks them straight in the face, like a healthy man who is not cowed by learned traditions and is thinking for young heads. He is never abstract, but takes his examples and metaphors from the wealth of the everyday life that he knows through and through. His language has the picturesque force of a man who is not seeking for pictures.

It is difficult to say whether Emerson was more of an idealist or of a naturalist. The general philosophical current that started from him is usually called " Transcendentalism," and we may accept the name, provided always that we do not give it the specific meaning that it has possessed since Kant. For into the epistemological problem Emerson in general put very little of his thought. Artist-natures in fact usually do pass it by; as is well known, even Goethe did not bother himself with it overmuch. Still, it can quite well be said that Emerson was a philosophical idealist, for he possessed what might be called the "transcendental organ." He knew and felt what all profound natures feel, that Reality is something that men can never reach. But he did not arrive at this world-view through scientific investigations, but by way of feeling. One of the finest passages in his essay on "Experience" runs thus: "Was it Boscovich who found out that bodies never come in contact? Well, souls never touch their objects. An innavigable sea washes with silent waves between us and the things we aim at and converse with. Grief too will make us idealists. In the death of my son, now more than two years ago, I seem to have lost a beautiful estate, — no more. I cannot get it nearer to me. . . . So is it with this calamity; it does not touch me. . . . I grieve that grief can teach me nothing, nor carry me one step into real nature. The Indian who was laid under a curse that the wind should not blow on him, nor water flow to him, nor fire burn him, is a type of us all. The dearest events are summer-rain, and we the Para coats that shed every drop. Nothing is left us now but death. We look to that with a grim satisfaction, saying, There at least is reality that will not dodge us."

Kant never spoke thus. He had given Phenomenalism such foundations as no one could overset, but after he had seen this task through with energy and thoroughness, he quietly turned to his scientific work like any Positivist. He had, as it were, only "salved" himself. Emerson, on the contrary, never had a thought of discovering theoretical foundations for Idealism. But although, as compared with Kant, he is a naïve empiricist, yet through all his writings there runs a note of deep phenomenalism, and a line of direct scepsis can still be detected in his epideictic statements.

He is an absolute Impressionist, in his style, his composition, and his thought. He never propounds his ideas in a definite logical or artistic form, but always in the natural and often accidental order which they have in his head. He knows only provisional opinions, momentary truths. He never sacrifices the truth of even a single word, sentence, or idea to the architecture of the whole. Things like "order of content," "introduction," "transitions," do not exist for him. He begins to develop this or that view, and we think he is going on to weave it systematically, elucidate it from all sides, entrench it against any possible attack. But then, suddenly, some alien picture or simile, epigram or aperçu strikes him, full in the middle of his chain of thought, and the theme thenceforward revolves on quite a new axis. He called his essays "Considerations by the Way," but everything else that he wrote might equally be so entitled. The form and connectedness of his thoughts were a matter of indifference to him — only the spirit-voices calling in him were important. We cannot contradict Emerson. His power of convincing resides precisely in this fact that he creates all under the inward dictation, and adds nothing to it. He stops still, listens to his heart, and writes as he listens.

Materialism   The continent of Europe lacked any personality of the Emerson stamp. In Germany in particular there prevailed a wholly thick-wired materialism. The desk-ideology of the men of " Forty-eight " had gone bankrupt — and in this crisis the *Zeitgeist* jettisoned all its older traditions: Romanticism, Weimar, Kant, and Hegel all fell into an undiscriminating neglect, only Schiller retaining a certain reputation — and that merely because he was useful to Liberal leader-writers. We have seen already that almost all natural scientists of more than momentary importance have rejected the purely mechanical interpretation of Nature, but the power over the public passed into the hands of feuilletonist semi-savants who took Darwin's, Comte's, Feuerbach's, and the Encyclopædists' most obvious platitudes and made out of them a philosophy of " healthy, human understanding " veneered over with science. Not for nothing is " materialist " the German word for a dealer in colonial wares; this materialism was in very truth a world-wisdom for root-merchants. In 1852 Jacob Moleschott published his famous *Kreislauf des Lebens; physiologische Antworten auf Liebigs chemische Briefe* — Liebig, as we know, being a decided Vitalist. Moleschott's refutation of Phenomenalism runs thus : " Is green anything but a relation of light to our eye? And if that is all it is, is not the green leaf so for itself precisely because it is so for our eyes? But this breaks down the dividing wall between the ' thing-for-us ' and the ' thing-in-itself.' " A sentence of such obscurity, of such striking obscurity when we consider that it occurs in a " popular " philosophy, should surely redeem its obscurity by its depth ; but if one paraphrases it, it is seen to be not merely shallow, but imbecile. Moleschott thinks, in fact, that the leaf could not be felt by our eye as green if it did not really emit green light, or, in other words, all that has the effect of green is green, a metaphysical assertion that has an undeniable persuasiveness, but hardly takes us further than the conclusion that everything that has wings flies.

In 1854 occurred the so-called " materialist controversy." The physiologist Rudolf Wagner had dared, in an assembly of natural scientists, to declare that science was not yet mature enough to answer the question of the soul's nature. Karl Vogt replied with *Köhlerglaube und Wissenschaft,* which was widely read, and in which he attempted to annihilate his opponent with a satire consisting of beer-mug jests and apodeictically presented schoolroom stuff. In it there occurs the oft-quoted phrase that the brain secretes thoughts, the stomach secretes gastric juices, and the liver bile; this Vogt borrowed from Cabanis, with, however, the tasteful addition of urine and the kidneys to the list, thus turning what, in the Rococo Frenchman, had been a capricious jest into a spun-out and humourless formula of belief. In 1855 appeared Ludwig Büchner's *Kraft und Stoff,* a form-master's disquisition — at once bald and coat-trailing, couched in crude brown-paper German — against " Hegel & Co." and the " Kantian swindle ": " The well-known proposition that all knowledge begins with experience, but does not spring from it, is obscure or inconsistent. . . . Kant's unfortunate division of knowledge into *a priori* and *a posteriori* follows necessarily from his having neglected to begin by forming an ordered idea of the concepts of experience and knowledge. . . . Nor can Kant's excuse be the times in which he lived, for Locke, Hume, and many another who lived before him had declared war on apriorism."

These materialist currents may be divided into three groups, none of which can claim originality, and all of which shallowed and coarsened their archetypes. The first variety, characterized as Materialism in the narrow sense, teaches the absolutism of *matter,* and proceeds from Holbach; the second, Sensualism, teaches the absolutism of *sensation* and has Condillac as its ancestor, and Feuerbach as its chief German representative; the third, marked by so important an advance towards spiritualization that it might almost be called a spiritualism with physical twinges of conscience, teaches the absolutism of *force;* it goes back to Leibniz and has been developed most logically in the " energetics " of the chemist Wilhelm Ostwald, for whom matter

" as a primary concept no longer exists," but arises " as a secondary phenomenon from the co-existence of certain kind of energy." This materialism-in-solution, however, only appeared a generation later; for " Büchner & Co." *only* matter exists, and force belongs to it as its property and expression, like blowing to wind, a world-view that is essentially no different from the fetishism that the medicine-man proclaims with similar fanatical noisiness.

Marxism   Economic development, which is so often an accompaniment to Materialism, was to be seen to a certain extent even in Germany, although far less so than in France and England. There were new railways, new steamship lines, new mines and factories, and, above all, big banks and joint-stock companies. Along with, and connected with, this came the expansion of Socialism, which appears in the world almost simultaneously with every genuine capitalism, and dogs its steps as the spirit of the beggar follows the insolent Flottwell. Its two most powerful exponents were, as all the world knows, Marx and Lassalle, both of whom came from an emphatically bourgeois *milieu*. Marx, next to Darwin, has had the most influence of any nineteenth-century thinker, although he was as little of a philosopher as Darwin was. His chief work, *Das Kapital,* of which only the first volume appeared in his lifetime, is an extremely involved, artistically and artificially joinered system of abstract definitions and conclusions, most of which is inaccessible not merely to the proletariat, but to the average educated man as well, so that (permitting oneself a certain exaggeration) one might say that a Marxist is a man who has never read Marx. And yet a certain mysterious spiritual radiation that they give off has enabled his doctrines to penetrate the whole world. The catechism of the new doctrine is contained in the " Manifesto of the Communist Party " which appeared in German, French, English, Flemish, and Danish in February 1848. Its authors were Marx and Engels, and it was directed against the bourgeois class, which has " replaced exploitation veiled in religious and political illusions by exploitation that is open, unashamed, direct and brutal," by abolishing private property for nine tenths of existing society, so that the proletariat is forced in turn to abolish it and " centralize all the instruments of production in the hands of the State: that is, of the proletariat organized as a ruling class." " Let the ruling classes tremble before a Communist revolution. You have nothing to lose but your chains. You have a world to win. Proletarians of all lands, unite ! " Marx rejected all earlier socialistic theories and declared himself the first representative of " scientific socialism," which in no way appeals to the feelings or to moral considerations, but merely takes the facts as they are and sets forth their inevitable development; it does not state what ought to be, but what will be. " As values," says Marx, " goods are nothing but crystallized work." They are worth precisely what they derive from this work, and their measure is quite simply the number of hours' work that has gone to their production. The cost of the work is determined by the quantity of subsistence that a worker needs in order to keep himself permanently in a condition of productive capacity. This is the " used-up " value. But the value that the worker produces is always in excess of this used-up value, and the surplus, which Marx calls the " plus-value," represents the profit of the undertaker. Now, the worker, as he receives only the wage corresponding to the used-up value, may appear to be getting what is due to him, but in reality is being cheated of the plus-value. He does plus-work, and the more, the longer the working hours; for if, for example, five hours' work is required in order to cover the worker's maintenance, a ten-hour working day yields more profit to the undertaker than one of eight hours. The obvious criticism, made by Karl Jentsch amongst others, that plus-value is far from being pure profit, in that the manufacturer has to pay the " ground landlord on whose soil the factory stands, the merchant who markets the product, and the capitalist who has lent him the money," is, from the Marxian point of view, irrelevant, since all these deductions — ground-rent, middleman's costs, interest on loans — go to benefit the possessing classes, and it is manifestly immaterial in principle whether it is himself or another capitalist, a ground landlord, a warehouseman, a banker, that he pays off with the plus-value.

Capital, according to Marx, is that which throws off a rent, an income attained by the work of others. Hence in the Middle Ages there was still no capital in the strict sense, since most workers were still owners of their means of production. During the course of the Modern Age it has come about through a number of causes, not only that Capital in this true sense has arisen, but that it has become more and more accumulated in a few hands, all the rest being expropriated. In earlier times the craftsman had sold his *products*, now he is forced to sell *himself*. This has led to the creation of a mass-proletariat; but in creating it the bourgeois has " produced its own grave-diggers." It lies in the nature of

Capitalism that it leads to periodically recurring economic crises, and of increasing severity. On each such occasion a great number of the possessing class are ruined, and capital is concentrated in even fewer hands, while the misery of the masses grows ever greater. Finally, the vanishing minority of the expropriators is itself expropriated.

The Class Struggle　　Marxism has two characteristics in common with Darwinism: firstly, that it is not a theory of catastrophe, but postulates organic transformations that come to pass almost of themselves — so to say, determining their course by their own laws of gravitation — and that it believes, as a general principle, that the laws of happening are scientifically controllable. Lassalle called Marx " Hegel turned economist," and in truth the essential character — and the essential failings — of the Marxian system lie in its Rationalism, which assumes it as self-evident that social evolution is a problem of logic, calculation, and deduction, or, in a word, that it goes according to Hegel. But man is distinguished from the animals in this way, amongst others, that he very often, and especially in his highest moments, acts illogically, supra-logically. And so far history has never in fact gone according to the Marxian theory; it is Russia, the country of lowest capitalistic development, that has seen the Dictature of the Proletariat come to pass, and it is in America, the country where capital is concentrated in fewest hands, that Communism has the smallest prospects.

Collectivism, the basic idea of Socialism, is a simple and a just one. It states that the earth and its soil, all means of production and communication, should be common possessions. That the earth, its products, the implements fashioned by mankind in common, should belong in common to the same mankind is a reasonable demand. In public parks, escalators, bathing-places and play-grounds, libraries and museums, schools and hospitals it had already to a large extent been actualized, and it is approximately so in such cases as letter-transmission and water-supply, which, in spite of the enormous installations necessary, function almost without cost, and in the theatres, which are now filled almost exclusively by " paper." The extension of this system to lighting and heating, transport, and housing is only a question of a few decades, and to apply it to clothing and nutriment is only a matter of organization and goodwill. But this Collectivism is not at all the same as equality of rights and duties, of labour and income, for these assume that all men are the same, which is blasphemous

222

nonsense. Marxism asserts that "the history of all peoples so far is a history of class struggles." If this is true, then class war is eternal, for there will always be within mankind groups of differing capacities and aims, and each of them will claim that it is the highest and most important. No one will ever convince a sailor that the stars are not exclusively intended to enable him to steer his course, nor an astronomer that they have any other purpose but to be seen in his telescope; a sailor or an astronomer who believes otherwise is devoid of *talent*. Between sailors and astronomers, therefore, there must always arise a class conflict, even if neither of them is drawing a plus-value. But this is wholly contrary to the view of Marxism, which asserts that the class struggle between bourgeoisie and proletariat will be the final one, since Collectivism "will cause the classes themselves to vanish." But how? By the dictature of one of them! This would be a most dishonest subterfuge were it not that it is unconscious. The ideal final State which Marxism not only aspires to, but exhibits as an inevitable and literally physical certainty, would be the tryanny, declared perpetual, of a single class, which would be still more unrighteous than any of the tyrannies of history, in that it would be the basest. The fallacy that proletarians alone exist is one that can only be maintained by unbridled force, by rooting out all the other classes or castrating them into proletarians. Here Marxism outbids even the inhumanly iron logic of the insect states, for even they do not consist of a single class — the bees have their luxury class in the drones; the Amazon ants their fighting class in the knights — whose food is not merely brought to them, but literally brought into their mouths by the workers — the termites have a hierarchized caste-state; and all three have queens or kings.

Marx was a professor without a chair, Lassalle on the contrary an artist, a mobile and superabundant spirit who reminds us a little of Heine; the latter, indeed, was one of the first to recognize his great talent and called him a new Mirabeau. The resemblance between that bronze Provençal seigneur and the hysterical silk-merchant's son from Breslau was, however, small enough, and at most consists in the fact that both regarded politics as a game in which they sought to satisfy their dramatic instinct and their desire to count in the world. Bismarck, in a Reichstag speech, said of Lassalle that he was one of the cleverest and best-hearted men with whom he had ever mixed and "essentially not a republican." But another saying of Bismarck's, that jealousy is a debt that weighs heavily on most political talents, may be applied to Lassalle with especial aptness. His chief practical demands were: general, equal, secret, and direct franchise and the creation of state production-societies, with profit-sharing for the workers. He satirized the "night-watchman rôle" of the modern State, which assures nothing but the protection of the exploiter. In 1863 he propounded his celebrated "brazen law of wages," but in reality only the name and the pregnant formulation were his, for it existed already in Ricardo. It states that "the average wage is always kept down to the level necessary to the sustenance that is customary among a given people for the prolongation of its existence and for its propagation; this is the point about which the actual day's pay for ever oscillates like a pendulum." In order to emancipate itself from the operation of this law, the working class must make itself its own entrepreneur. But evidently Lassalle never sufficiently observed that his "minimum for existence" is itself a variable quantity. A fairly well-off workman today, especially in England, has at his disposal more comfort and hygiene than a prince enjoyed in the days of the Migrations.

Mommsen   From Marxism derives also the "materialistic" conception of history, which, as everyone knows, assumes that the economic structure of society determines its "social, political, and spiritual life-relations generally." Now, this barbarous banality was not, even then, taken seriously by any real historian, and yet the materialistic spirit of the time so far influenced historical science that it went completely political, not only limiting itself narrow-mindedly to state history, but even putting itself at the service of party politics. Johann Gustav Droysen, in his anti-Habsburg *Geschichte der preussischen Politik*, attempted to show that from the Great Elector onwards Prussia had had in her hands the direction of German things, and that the history of Germany had for two centuries tended to the "Little German" outcome. Heinrich von Sybel sought to show from the history of the Middle Ages that the "Great German" empire was a mistaken idea and had been a misfortune for the country. In his *Geschichte der Revolutionszeit 1789–1800*, a long-winded array of political paraphrases based on a most industrious study of archives, there is no question of anything but constitutional struggles, military movements, and diplomatic shifts; it deals not only with France, but with all the countries of Europe, but, while purporting to exhibit a general view of all Europe, it in fact loses itself in endless details, so that its totality consists merely in multiplying the headings. While Droysen still admitted legend and anecdote as historical sources, Sybel mistrusted every oral report, burrowed busily through every available document, and worshipped realism of the archivist's sort; to his method we can well apply Nestroy's saying that men are so senseless that they take the truth to be that of which they can hold an illusion in their hands. Bismarck said once that there are two sorts of historians — "whereof the one makes the water of the past clear, and the other makes it muddy. Taine belongs to the first class, Sybel to the second." In Droysen's *Geschichte des Hellenismus* (in itself an excellent work) Macedon is obviously Prussia, and Demosthenes a German particularist corrupted by Persian (Austrian) gold. Yet this historiography "*ad usum Delphini*" is not so harmful in him as it is in Sybel, because he was far more of a living and human personality. Curtius's *Griechische Geschichte*, too, was tendentious in its way, with its pronounced defence of the dogma of Classical antiquity; it is the swan-song of Classicism, but a melodious and moving one.

Even Mommsen, whose *Römische Geschichte* began to appear about the same time, modernizes, and does so most emphatically, perhaps, of all those named here. Cato becomes a Conservative of the *Kreuzzeitung* party, Cicero a writer, advocate, and parliamentarian of the Thiers type, Crassus a bourse king after the fashion of Louis Philippe, the Gracchi are socialist leaders, the Patricians *Junker*, the Græculi Paris Bohemians, and the Gauls Indians. One might think from all this that Mommsen was a sort of scientific parallel to George Ebers, whose archæological romances were at that time very much the vogue. But here, as in so many other cases, we see that in art it is never the "what," but only the "how" — that is, the personality — that is decisive. Mommsen brings history into the present, whereas Ebers drags it down to the present; Mommsen's treatment brings it into relief, but Ebers by the same method manages to polish it till it is unrecognizable. Mommsen makes an art of professorship, Ebers a professorship of art. And all these differences simply come from the fact that these two historians had not *the same present*. The Mommsen present is graduated, full, and original, the Ebers monotoned, one-sided, and philistine.

From the first — as often later — Mommsen was reproached with journalism, which is a complete inversion of the true facts. For what is journalism? False ethos and passion not really experienced; routine empty of content, a coinage of clichés, a conventional looking through the eyes of " contemporaries," pretentious glossing from below; imposed choice of themes dictated by the demand; unintelligent overvaluation of " news." And all this, too, is just what is meant by " professorial." The common factor is uneducatedness. If from the products of average scholarship we abstract the philology (using the word in its widest sense), nothing remains but journalism made tedious, distinguished from other journalism only by its wastefulness of equipment, just as in the days before the war certain court theatres were merely richly endowed itinerant shows.

If on the other hand we take journalism in its best sense, as Bernard Shaw does, then Mommsen *was* a journalist. Shaw says in one of his essays: "Plato and Aristophanes trying to knock some sense into the Athens of their day, Shakspere peopling that same Athens with Elizabethan mechanics and Warwickshire hunts, Ibsen photographing the local doctors and vestrymen of a Norwegian parish, Carpaccio painting the life of St. Ursula exactly as if she were a lady living in the next street to him, are still alive and at home everywhere among the dust and ashes of many thousands of academic, punctilious, most archæologically correct men of letters and art who spent their lives haughtily avoiding the journalist's vulgar obsession with the ephemeral. I also am a journalist, proud of it, deliberately cutting out of my works all that is not journalism, convinced that nothing that is not journalism will live long as literature or be of any use whilst it does live . . . and as a dramatist I have no clue to any historical or other personage save that part of him which is also myself, and which may be nine tenths of him or ninety-nine hundredths, as the case may be (if, indeed, I do not transcend the creature), but which, anyhow, is all that can ever come within my knowledge of his soul. The man who writes about himself and his own time is the only man who writes about all people and about all time. . . . And so, let others cultivate what they call literature: journalism for me!" And in fact Shaw's picture of Cæsar is borrowed from Mommsen. Both authors provide new and brilliant illustrations of the eternal fact that genius is nothing but the most human humanity.

The literary seminar In the period of time which we are reviewing, the whole of German culture was dominated by the professor to an extent hitherto unknown. He heads the poll among politicians, painters, poets; he is the adornment of the salons, the typical hero of the novel, replacing the rake of an earlier generation, the schoolgirl's ideal like the lieutenant of a later generation, and in the person of the Bavarian king Maximilian II he actually ascended the throne. This remarkable dynasty of the Wittelsbachs has been characterized by a mixture of healthy, clear, reasonable, almost middle-class solidity and a complicatedness and obstinacy, a superabundance of imagination and sensibility, which bordered on the pathological. Now, this is almost the formula for genius: it is the same wood out of which the show-pieces of History's cabinet, figures like Frederick the Great and Goethe, Schopenhauer and Ibsen, Bismarck and Carlyle, are carved. Only, unfortunately, these two constitutional streaks were always distributed among different Wittelsbachs. The extreme of excitable, imaginative power was embodied in Ludwig II, the extreme of sober sagacity in his father, Maximilian II, who said of himself that he had nothing to fear from dethronement since he could any day earn his bread as a professor of history. It is said that he never laughed, and of course it would not have been seemly for a " full professor " to do so. He got together the great Liebig, the historians Sybel and Giesebrecht, the jurists Bluntschli and Windscheid, and tried to form a sort of literary seminar. A crowd of authors came to Munich by his invitation and met regularly for symposia, which, however, were anything but Dionysiac orgies. This literary group was known simply as " the Munichers," though also as " the Idealists." Their motto ran, in contrast to that of " Young Germany ": "Away from tendency, back to art "; by which, however, they meant simply an epigonism — " Classical " of hollow, polished, and pallid form, and " Romantic " of historicalism and sentimentalism. Their architectonic pendant is the " Maximilian style," which is highly cultured and ambitious, but impersonal and untemperamental, and was based on the belief that if all the precious things of all the ages are mechanically alloyed, something particularly valuable will come of it.

These " Classicists " differ from the genuine ones in that they had travelled along no road, that their works were not the products of development, difficult or hard-won achievements. They believed that they stood above their age, whereas they only stood aside from it. They believed that idealism consisted in ignoring reality, and beauty in eliminating the ugly. They were, unfortunately, Classicists from birth, and therefore not Classicists at all. Geibel

227

was a cultivated gallery painter, whose principal asset was his tasteful copying, an academician with " warm colour " and " fine studio tone." Bodenstedt's famous *Lieder des Mirza Schaffy* are the witticisms of a jovial *bel esprit* who goes to a Munich middle-class ball in Persian costume. Freiligrath's poems, aptly christened " janizary music " by Heine, resemble the panoramas which came in about that time: stuffed figures in front, flat scenery behind, but having nevertheless a certain picturesque charm. From Heyse's indefatigable pen there flowed sonnets, novels, short stories, epics, memoirs, proverbs, society plays, historical dramas, and *ottava rima, terza rima,* hexameters, and trochaics with the same ease as prose. His tragedy in iambics, *Der Raub der Sabinerinnen,* had, however, a far shorter life than the farce of the same name by the brothers Schönthan. Heyse was pretty well the model of a literary man as conceived by the middle classes: a soul with a velvet jacket, and always terribly interesting. Still, there have to be such writers. Heyse only becomes intolerable through a sour mixture of aunty-like moralism and luscious " sensual pleasure," an inquisitive toying with erotic problems under the governess supervision of virtue, which is immoral because it is not immoral enough. Wilhelm Jordan, again, was the " modern rhapsodist ": the singer of the Nibelungenlied, which he copied, and recited in person, in a manner that was both affectedly " old-time " and extremely real — that is, Darwinistic. His natural bard's mask added to the effect. Then there was Victor von Scheffel, the darling of maturer youth — that is, youth that has reached the stage of alcohol. His student songs are like the rousing wall-paintings in good old-fashioned inns, his epic productions like the " transparencies " which were then in great demand: clean and pleasant imitation paintings on glass in luminous coloured varnish. And what remains of all this Classical, Old German, Oriental poetizing in modern dress? The *Struwwelpeter* of Heinrich Hoffmann, a Frankfurt specialist for mental diseases.

Eugenie Marlitt

In the theatre the honours went to Friedrich Halm's pretty wax dolls and the comic masks of Roderich Benedix, which, although conventional and devoid of wit, showed that their creator, an actor who was also the author of excellent primers on declamation, had a good working knowledge of the stage. Another playwright, Bauernfeld, attempted to portray society and even introduced something like conversation on to the German stage, but he did it with a pale and timid pencil and lacked all plastic indi-

228

vidualization. His pieces are merely " well written " in successful feuilleton style, which, however, was already a good deal at this date. As for the feuilleton itself, it was now in Germany, as elsewhere, an instalment of a serial story, and the result was not only damaging to the art of narrative, but had a devastating effect on production, owing to the pronounced family tone of the newspapers. The character of this genre is sufficiently described by the word *Gartenlaube* (*Arbour*), for the name of this popular magazine has become a generic term. Its great exponent was Eugenie Marlitt, whose immortality is well deserved, since she was a natural growth in the midst of all the wise and worthy, would-be reformist and realistic novels of the day. She really believed in her rose-coloured lies, and her characters have something of the sweet stupidity of a water-lily or the convincing sheen of a gold-beetle. The same can certainly not be said of Berthold Auerbach. He was a Jew from a Neckar village, and the persons in his extremely popular *Schwarzwälder Dorfgeschichten* are Jewish strolling players (who have read the *Lichtstrahlen aus Spinoza*) disguised as Bavarian peasants. In Cornelius Gurlitt's *Deutsche Kunst des neunzehnten Jahrhunderts* we read that Schwind said with reference to Auerbach: " This extreme enthusiasm for everything that has the peasant touch, and the entire failure to see that all these social-communistic pictures are designed specially for the drawing-room of the banker and the fop are beyond my comprehension." From which remark it is again evident that the true Romantic is far closer to nature than the sham Realist. Richard M. Meyer points out, in his *Deutsche Stilistik*, that Auerbach depicts Rabbi Isaak (in his novel *Spinoza*) now as slender and red-bearded, now as well nourished and black-bearded, which is a discrepancy that by no means belongs with the group of justified and unavoidable inconsistencies that was mentioned in the Introduction to this work. For it is simply unpardonable when (as is here the case) the discrepancies are the result, not of too much perception, but of a complete lack of it, for it means that the writer simply does not *see* his figures. It is all of a piece with the unsound method which penetrates to nothing below the surface, but daubs away at the outer appearance. We see this in the contemporary illustrators of the classics, who draw Recha, Louise, and Gretchen differently in every picture. These are not trifles; they are either proofs of absolute lack of talent or of brazen contempt for one's public.

Gutzkow tried his hand at a novel of many threads (a "*Roman des Nebeneinander*," as he called it) in his *Ritter vom Geist,*
and it was actually nothing but loose threads, a mechanical hotch-
potch and no chemical fusion, let alone an organism. What he
really purposed was a cross-section of the whole intellectual and
social structure of the time, and this was, for a journalist, a hopeless undertaking. The aims which Gustav Freytag set himself in
Soll und Haben were more modest by far. In one of his feuilletons
Ludwig Speidel speaks of the " nourishing fragrance " which this
work exhaled to the whole German public, " as it came fresh from
the pan." It was an admirable dish, composed solely of pure and
sound ingredients, but, for all that, no more than a strong and
tasty culinary production. It is evident, both from his plays (almost all of which were failures) and from his *Technik des Dramas*
(which was the joy of all teachers of German, and the terror of all
upper forms for half a century) that Freytag was not at his best in
drama. The book in question might be called a guide to the construction of bad plays. *Götz von Berlichingen,* for instance, is
described as not an effective stage piece, Euripides is " quite un-
scrupulous," Parricida and the Black Knight are declared to be
superfluous. These three examples show that he treats dramatic
art as a pure handicraft which works with a mason's square and a
carpenter's pencil. Each drama must unfold itself in five parts and
three situations : " (a) introduction, (b) development, (c) climax,
(d) decline or reversal, (e) catastrophe " and " tense moment,
tragic moment, moment of final suspense." In one single instance
Freytag himself acted " unscrupulously," introducing superfluous
episodes and not worrying about his " moments," and the particular piece, *Die Journalisten,* was his only successful one, a fresh,
pleasant, and even original comedy, with characters so vividly
conceived that two of them, Bolz and Schmock, have become generic types. True, it is of a harmlessness which strikes us now as
incredible (his press corruption consists in nothing worse than the
concoction of a few canards) and should have been equally so to
the generation of Balzac. Freytag's most prominent defect, indeed,
is his untragic satisfaction with the world, which is in a sense
almost immoral, and his imperturbable common sense, which
borders on philistinism. That is why he never succeeds with figures, but only with picture pages, and his best and maturest work
is accordingly his cultural-historical *Bilder aus der deutschen Ver-
gangenheit,* a classic in its way. As a historical poet he was too

often a seminarist, as poetical historian he is one of the finest of pastel artists.

Taken as a whole, the German literature of that time is on a surprisingly low level compared with that of other countries. Two years before Spielhagen's *Problematische Naturen* there appeared the Russian vision of a problematical nature in *Oblomov;* two years before Ebers's *Die Ägyptische Königstochter* Flaubert produced his picture of the ancient East in *Salammbô;* two years after *Soll und Haben*, the psychology of the middle-class lives of the period, the same theme was brought forward in a French conception in *Madame Bovary;* and it was just as Baudelaire was writing his *Fleurs du mal* that Scheffel began to spread abroad his *Gaudeamuslieder*.

One must, however, not forget that *Der grüne Heinrich* was born about this time, though he, too, loses by the reflection that he was a contemporary of Raskolnikov. Keller's real domain was powerful miniature sculpture, and his novels are, similarly, on the short-story scale, even when they have not the outward appearance of it. He once said, in writing to Heyse, that an unwritten comedy ran through all his epic, and it is true that there is a streak of amused irony permanently embedded in his literary constitution. He resembles his countryman Burckhardt both in this and in other ways — in his unconventional psychological realism, which never accepts that which is said about things, but draws inspiration from direct intuition and the individual truth of his own heart, and in a certain cultivated humanism of form, which, however, remains sufficiently natural to relax frequently and easily into picturesque slovenliness. But he lacks the universal outlook which distinguishes Burckhardt. In his complicated cantonal turn of mind, which persistently shrank from the final abysses of life and knowledge, he remained ever the true Swiss. Zola he regarded as a low fellow, and Georg Büchner he admired only for his impudence. For many years he was town clerk in Zürich, and he was something of the sort in his writing too: the faithful, clear, well-informed chronicler of the detail of everyday life.

We still have Hebbel and Otto Ludwig to consider. In terms of literary history they are an inseparable pair, like Plautus and Terence, Fichte and Schelling, Raimund and Nestroy, Heine and Börne, all of whom are, so to say, called up to the blackboard in couples by the professors of literature. Although Hebbel and Ludwig had not much in common, certain similarities undoubtedly

Hebbel and Otto Ludwig

231

existed. It is a mere superficial incident that both were born in the year of the battle of Leipzig and that each left behind him an entirely unsuccessful *Agnes Bernauer,* but the lifelong antagonism that both felt towards Schiller, arising from secret rivalry, is definitely characteristic. Ludwig planned out a " Wallenstein " and a " Maria Stuart," Hebbel worked at a " Maid of Orleans " and a " Demetrius," of which he wrote four and a half acts. Ludwig's Realism, like Hebbel's Rationalism, was suppressed Schillerian Romanticism, but in their verse-form both followed Schiller's Classicism, and they developed in consequence a kind of Œdipus-complex. Identical features in their work were hard outline, inelastic intellectualism, want of atmosphere, a cold psychiatric predilection for the dramatic specimen-cabinet (quite unlike Schiller's refreshing appetite for thrills), and, in connexion with this, an excess of motivation — which from a theatrical point of view is really a defect of it, in that it causes the overstrained psychology to pass into pathology. This is particularly striking in Ludwig's *Erbförster,* although this character had what Hebbel never, and Ludwig only this once, succeeded in producing: namely, local fragrance and an impression of the magical working of destiny. *Die Makkabäer,* on the other hand, stands far below all Hebbel's dramas. The characters invariably become rhetorical in emotion, and in many places it is not Schiller that sticks out of it, but " Ersatz-Schiller ": namely, Gutzkow. From all these characteristics it will be clear that both men wrote their literary masterpieces on the plane of philosophical speculation, art-scientific analysis: Ludwig's *Shakespearestudien* and Hebbel's *Tagebücher* are real treasure-houses of knowledge.

Of Hebbel's outward appearance his friend Felix Bamberg, the writer on art, said: " His limbs appear to have turned out too delicately for the head and are merely there to support it." Here we have a symbol for his whole nature. There have been few men, perhaps, who, like Hebbel, were filled with so passionate a pleasure in thinking, and few indeed who suffered so much from the weight of their own thinking. There are dramatic thinkers just as there are dramatic poets, and Hebbel belongs to both categories. What is more, he was a tragic thinker. To reduce this conception to its simplest formula, one might say that a world-outlook is tragic that starts by regarding individual existence as a sin, every individuation as a deposit from the impure, and the whole world (in that its manifoldness is made up of individuations) as one single great Fall of Man. We find this world-picture unusually sharply defined in the one fragment of Anaximander that is handed down to us: "To the place whence things have come they must also return for their decline: thus the law wills; for they must do penance for the wrong that they have done by existing." Of this theory of the world Hebbel too, as poet and thinker, was the embodiment. Man is by his very existence a tragic creature. Every individual betokens a separation from the idea; he must be destroyed in order to be again absorbed in the Idea. Hebbel varied this gloomy theme untiringly; theoretically in his treatises, practically in his dramas.

After all, there can hardly be a philosopher who has not been preoccupied by this idea in some form or other. No thinker who penetrates to the metaphysical roots of human existence can pass it over. The only question is whether it hypnotizes him permanently or not. Hegel overcame it by his self-assured dialectic, Goethe by his reverent absorption in Nature, Fichte by his triumphant ethical feeling, Sophocles by Pagan, and Calderon by Catholic piety, Nietzsche by his belief in a future, Emerson by the irrefutable optimism of his happy personality, which was not that of a philosopher, but was a natural force, a thing in some way physiological.

There was something physiological, too, in Hebbel's pessimism. With this particular organic structure one is a pessimist. It is not a matter to be accounted for by adverse life-destinies — superficial reasons of that sort may be left for the theses of examination candidates. The world-picture of a poet is not to be constructed from the number of meals taken and manuscripts accepted. "You ask me of what mortal illness I should choose to die?" writes Hebbel, when not quite five-and-twenty, to his beloved Elise Lensing. "Dear child, there is but one death and one mortal disease, and there is no name by which they can be called. But the disease is that which caused Goethe's Faust to sell himself to the Devil, that which gave Goethe the power and inspiration to write his *Faust*, that which begets humour, that which heats and freezes the blood simultaneously; it is the feeling of the complete contradictoriness in all things, it is, in a word, the disease that your very asking about it shows you will never comprehend. Whether there is a cure for this disease I know not, but this I know: that the doctor (be he above the stars or at the central point of my ego) who would cure me must first cure the whole world,

The Anti-poet

233

and then I should immediately be cured. It is the flowing together of all misery into a single breast, it is the urge for redemption without the hope of it, and therefore it is torment without end." These are obscure words, which may well have puzzled wiser people than poor Elise, yet they illumine the core and the nature of this man who, stupidly misunderstood by his own age and inordinately admired by posterity, had no effect on either except as a disturbing element; who wrestled as fervently and doggedly as ever anyone did to become a poet, and yet was only the very opposite of a poet — as much a poet, one might say, as Lucifer was an angel. Because he did not love the world.

"The feeling of the complete contradictoriness in all things" is in truth the feeling from which art, philosophy, religion — in short, all that is creative — spring. It was certainly the root from which the young Goethe derived his questioning, and most probably the reason why Faust sold himself to the Devil, and it is undoubtedly correct to say that it begets humour. But it became disease, mortal disease, only when it entered Hebbel's soul. In him it did not beget humour. When Hebbel becomes humorous, it is as if a hyena offered to shake paws. Humour is an aroma, an act of grace — and both the one and the other were lacking in Hebbel's works. In a review on Stifter's *Nachsommer* he wrote: "Three fat volumes! We feel we may risk offering the crown of Poland to anyone who can prove that he has read them through, without being obliged to do so as a judge of art. . . . An inventory would be just as interesting." This lack of understanding is very understandable. Stifter possessed everything that was denied to Hebbel: music, the brush for values, union with Nature, faith, harmony, serene respect for small things. Hebbel felt this himself very definitely at times: "Are we not flames which burn for ever and consume all, all that they entwine and are yet unable to embrace?" But his fate was stronger than he.

If we examine certain of his poems in respect of the rhythm of their happening, we could suppose that he had been a dramatic Hegel. This is very striking, for example, in *Herodes und Mariamne,* where the scheme of thesis-antithesis is used, not once only, but a second time, for exactly the same constellation at a higher turn of the screw. But on looking closer we see that he was a Hegelian who never finished, who had not the force to repeat the whole dialectical process of his master, since he never blended thesis and antithesis into that synthesis known by the unphilosophical designation of love; in consequence of some intellectual dyspepsia or, more probably, of an inherent malice deeply embedded in his nature.

Otto Ludwig makes the very subtle remark in his *Shakespeare-studien*: "In Shakspere the characters have their moments of repose. Their real character shows itself only when it is brought out by the situation. Hebbel's characters are, day and night, in full war-paint; every one of his personages is perpetually chasing after his own characteristic features. Character is intensified to monomania in each of them. They all know that they are freaks, and for nothing on earth would they appear otherwise." This is most noticeable in the first great figure that Hebbel created: Holofernes. Here, in the process of "skipping the human being," of which Schiller set the precedent with his Franz Moor, the axis has swung round to "comic," even though it be by one degree only, and Schiller's theatrical instinct only just managed to stop short of it. Then again, *Judith* had the misfortune to be throttled at birth by Nestroy's brilliant parody. On the other hand, none of his dramas is without magnificent individual passages (take, for instance, the grand ending of *Herodes*) and amazing anticipations of our most recent psychology: there is a foretaste of *fin de siècle* in the decadence of Candaules, of Ibsen in the moral problems of *Maria Magdalena*, of Strindberg in the eroticism of Herodes, of Nietzsche in Golo. But he is greatest, as has been said, in his theoretical writings. It may be, therefore, that Hebbel's thoughts — his deep-boring, probing, strangely suggestive soul-analyses, his lightning ideas, flashing flame-like and gaining in mysterious effect by the darkness which immediately sets in again, his observations on art that cover so much ground — may yet some time live themselves, while his dramas will have only the historical attraction of Cyclopean structures.

A certain resemblance to Hebbel and Ludwig is seen in Feuerbach and Marées, who also are named always in pairs. Anselm Feuerbach was like an actor who comes on with "padding" to make his outward appearance more imposing. There was in him a ruminating, flickering ambition which defeated its own ends. He was a decorator (though in the most distinguished sense) and therefore, both on that account and by reason of the pallor of his ideas and his cultured superiority, the painter *par excellence* of his age, although regarded by it as its opposite. His grandfather and father, who both bore the same names as he, were famous

Feuerbach and Marées

235

professors, the one being the reformer of Bavarian criminal law and originator of the so-called " Feuerbach " or " Intimidation " theory, the other an archæologist and the author of an important work on the Apollo Belvedere. His brother, again, was the philosopher Ludwig Feuerbach, and there was even a fifth celebrity in the family, Karl Wilhelm Feuerbach, the mathematician, who gave his name to the " nine-points circle " or " Feuerbach circle." The youngest member of the family was, even as a boy, always surrounded by plaster casts, choice engravings, and Greek hexameters. During his callow years he copied with great virtuosity the works of Rethel, of the Frenchman Couture, and of the Belgian Wappers (who were the leaders of painting at that time) and also the Venetians and Florentines. In Rome he made the acquaintance of his Nana, a majestic Italian beauty who became his wife, his Medea and Iphigenia. Thus his Classicism was from the first a derivative one. His soul yearned no more for the land of the Greeks, but only for those who had sought it. He was a great colourist by nature, but came gradually to tone down everything to the colour of ruins, to joyless grey and the weathered red of Pompeii. He was the principal representative of that all too superior idealism of the connoisseur, which strenuously avoids " popularity " as well as " illusion " — as great art never does. Mozart and Weber, *Götz* and *The Robbers*, Andersen and Busch are understood by every human being. And as for the Greeks, the conception of popularity was entirely unknown to them, because they knew nothing of the opposite conception, which arose only in the Alexandrine age. The expert, the " esoteric," is always the vulture of true creativeness. And which of the high arts has ever scorned illusion? The Classical theatre, the Parthenon, the open-air Periclean statues, had an effect which probably was not far removed from that of waxworks. The fact that Classicism read out of its models precisely the opposite principles only shows that all art is self-presentation.

Hans von Marées also belonged to those fine doctrinaires, such as Carstens and Cornelius, who are always cropping up in Germany: the Germano-Romans who try to paint without the art of painting and in opposition to it. One of the last stalwarts in the hopeless rear-guard action of Classicism, he fought against all colouristic and luminosity and for pure form, adopting almost geometrical points of view in his composition. He aimed at reducing the whole art of painting to abstract motives (a sort of design of co-ordinates) and the construction of types (a proclamation of Platonic Ideas). What he could have achieved without this truly German bee-in-his-bonnet may be seen from the magnificent frescoes he did for the library of the Zoological Institute in Naples, though he himself had a low opinion of them.

The Piloty school went to the other, and equally false, extreme. It turned paintings into picture pages. Karl von Piloty, professor at the Munich Academy, painted heavy and ostentatious historical pictures, such as " The Death of Alexander," " The Murder of Cæsar," " The Triumph of Germanicus," " Galileo in Prison," " Wallenstein and Seni," " Nero Setting Fire to Rome," " Mary Stuart Condemned to Death." Schwind once asked him: " Well, Sir Colleague, what sort of a *malheur* are you painting this year? " On his giant canvases second-rate actors appeared in first-rate costumes. Of his pupils he demanded, first and foremost, " composition," by which he meant good mass effects and telling attitudes. Side by side with this, genre painting went placidly on. Its favourite subjects were amusing or touching situations in the child and animal world: The Village Prince, The First Cigar, The Overturned Bottle, Maternal Happiness, Child and Kitten, The Impudent Sparrow. Its most prominent exponent was Ludwig Knaus, who added comments to his drolleries into the bargain — a thing no good anecdotist should do. If we compare Piloty with Delacroix, and remember that by 1850 Impressionism had already set in in France, Germany's painting record looks decidedly unfavourable, and it will perhaps be evident that as a country she was at that time by no means " the heart of Europe."

The saying, quoted in and out of season, about that German nature which was to cure the world contributed not a little to the antipathies shown towards Germany in the World War. Nevertheless one does not need to be a chauvinist to find a certain truth in it. Obviously, it did not mean, as the war-mentality took it to mean, that Europe was to become a German colony. Germany must never rule over the other nations, for it could do so only at the cost of its soul. But the intellectual and moral future of Europe, if it has one, does indeed lie with Germany. Russia is chaos itself, and in any case does not belong to Europe. France is in a state of slow but inevitable decline. Italy's rise is merely economic and political. We will not explain again why England does not count in this connexion. Fichte's saying in his *Reden an die deutsche Nation* remains true: " Do we know a nation of

The two philosophers

237

whom the like expectations can be formed? I think everyone will answer this question in the negative." The section of time which we are now studying is a confirmation of this. For out of the dreary fog of those days two bright, clear-cut profiles appear: those of the two philosophers Bismarck and Schopenhauer.

Schopenhauer's principal work appeared in 1819, but it was the *Parerga* in 1851 which first made him widely known. By the middle of the fifties his philosophy was the height of fashion. It was in 1857 that Wagner wrote his *Tristan,* and in the same year Bonn, Breslau, and Jena gave courses in the new philosophy, Kuno Fischer of Jena being its most brilliant interpreter. The reason why recognition came so late to Schopenhauer, and was then of such extraordinary effect, lies in the change in the character of the time after 1848, which, in contrast to what had gone before, contained a curious mixture of voluntarism and pessimism. To the public at large Schopenhauer was the angel who throttled the suspect Hegelian ideology, and the mouthpiece of the political *malaise* of the Reaction period. It completely overlooked the fact that he was equally a pupil of the Kantian Idealism, like Fichte, Schelling, and Hegel, and that his pessimism was only an ornament, very distinctive, but secondary. It was a case therefore of a justified success based on a misunderstanding, much as in the case of Spengler, whose work likewise triumphed, not because of its rare originality and breadth, but owing to the mood of the postwar period, which saw in *The Decline of the West* a sort of desperate consolation for the fiasco it had suffered. Both instances show, also, that epoch-making systems of thought almost never come from the officially approved professional philosopher — a fact which may be traced right through the history of philosophy. The thinkers who left their mark in history were idlers like Socrates, Protagoras, Diogenes in Greece, statesmen like Bacon, Locke, Hume in England, *chevaliers* like Montaigne, Descartes, La Rochefoucauld in France, but never professors. The only exception is the period of the German Classics. This must have been either because the universities were so de-intellectualized or because philosophy was so deprofessionalized, and it is probably safe to assume the former. In any case, not only is true philosophy created by laymen, but it is they who first discover it and provide the recipe. Professional philosophy has always maintained an attitude of active and passive resistance against it for as long as possible, and then, when forced to recognize it, has used it only to discredit the newer philosophy that has arisen in the mean time. Even the admirable Kuno Fischer lost no opportunity of playing off Schopenhauer against Nietzsche. In 1791, ten years before the appearance of the *Critique of Pure Reason,* the Berlin Royal Academy of Science set the prize question: Wherein lies the real progress made by metaphysics in Germany since Leibniz and Wolf? A certain Professor Schwab of Tübingen demonstrated in a vast treatise that it had made *no* progress. He was awarded the prize.

Schopenhauer says, in his work on Genius, that all great theoretical achievements, no matter in what domain, are brought about by their originator's directing all the forces of his mind towards *one* point, at which he assembles and concentrates them with such strength, firmness, and exclusivity that all the rest of the world vanishes as far as he is concerned, and his subject fills out all reality for him. " Talent is able to achieve that which surpasses others' ability to perform, though not their ability to apprehend; it therefore immediately finds its appreciators. On the other hand, the achievement of genius goes beyond not only others' ability to perform, but their ability to apprehend; therefore these others do not directly perceive it. Talent is like a marksman who hits a target that the rest cannot reach; genius, one who hits a target which they cannot even sight: they therefore receive intelligence of it only indirectly — that is, late — and take even that on trust "; " the structure of the brain and the nervous system is the inheritance from the mother. This, however, is entirely insufficient to bring forth the phenomenon of genius unless, as an inheritance from the father, a lively, passionate temperament is added . . . when the condition which depends on the father is missing, the favourable structure of the brain coming from the mother will produce at best a talent, a fine understanding which is supported by the phlegm which then steps in: but a phlegmatic genius is impossible "; " every genius is a child, from the very reason that he looks out on the world as on a strange one. . . . He who does not remain all his life to some extent a big child, but turns into an earnest, sober, thoroughly settled and sensible man, can be a very useful and worthy citizen of this world, but a genius — never! " These sentences contain an exhaustive characterization of Schopenhauer himself. All the distinguishing marks of genius that he emphasizes are to be found in him: the concentration of his whole existence on a single object that to him replaces

239

reality; his late acceptance by the world, and even then only on trust; a certain infantileness, unreasonableness even, which pervaded his being throughout life and makes his works so enthralling. With respect to his own heredity, too, there is the same agreement. His mother, a well-known novelist in her day, obviously possessed a good understanding. His father was a man of great culture and character, but full of whims and, in his later years, mentally deranged — as a result apparently of a hereditary burden, for his mother had been insane and one of his brothers weak-minded. From him, obviously, the son inherited the touch of morbid sensibility without which no genius can exist. Schopenhauer stands out vividly from every page of his works, which are the incomparable self-portrait of a great writer. In his bizarre doctrinairism and choleric persecution-mania, his theoretical worldly wisdom and practical unworldliness, his touching caprices and crazy prejudices, his tragic solitude of genius and comic bachelor's absent-mindedness, he is an immortal type such as only Ibsen, if anyone, has succeeded in producing. We are reminded of Stockmann and how he struggled with contentious idealism against the "compact majority" of Borkman, waiting in unshakable confidence for the grand rehabilitation, and even a little of Doctor Begriffenfeldt.

Certain of these by-products of his empirical character have been exploited to the disadvantage of his personality as a whole, his "intelligible character," which was unusually great, profound, and pure. It was objected that he was not a fond son to his mother, and that he was very keen on favourable notices in the papers, enjoyed a good dinner, and once threw a waitress downstairs. Now, this is the good old headmaster's method. One collects "traits" and draws up the leaving certificate: work excellent, moral behaviour unsatisfactory. As if a "trait" did not with every person mean something different when seen in the ensemble of his character, just as a dab of sulphur-yellow or salmon-pink has a different colour-meaning in every painting. And as if this division of the report into two halves could take place anywhere in the world but in the brain of an ignorant pedagogue! Between life and creativity there is never a divergence. We have seen how Rousseau's ugly and sickly character found exact expression in his extremely talented, but dishonest, malicious, and unbalanced writings, and that Bacon, who chased after external honours and possessions in such unphilosophic fashion, was for this very reason only a philosopher of the second rank and created a system in which the earthly triumphed in precisely the same way as it triumphed in his soul. A certain self-importance mania which attended Wagner's earthly pilgrimage was discovered in the end and shouted from the house-tops, but it could quite well have been deduced from his operas at a much earlier date. Then, too, we hear that Ibsen was a coarse, reserved, and inconsiderate person. But why listen to this café gossip? Here are his works. Let those who want to see inside Ibsen's heart ask little Hedwig Ekdal. To eliminate the discrepancy between his own life and his moral teaching of which he was accused, Schopenhauer would obviously have had to join the Salvation Army instead of indulging in the leisure and research necessary for his noble works of edification.

Schopenhauer's true biography is contained in the words he used, at twenty-three, in speaking to Wieland: "Life is a dubious business. I have set myself to get as far as thinking it over." Seven years later he wrote to Brockhaus the publisher: "My work is a new philosophical system; but new in the complete sense of the word: not a new presentation of what already exists, but a succession of ideas, as closely connected as possible, which have never before entered the head of any human being. The book in which I have carried out the difficult task of imparting these intelligently to others will, I am firmly convinced, be one of those which eventually become the source and inspiration of a hundred other books. . . . The style is equally far removed from the high-sounding, empty, and meaningless flow of words of the modern philosophical school and the broad, smooth babblings of the period before Kant: it is in the highest degree clear and comprehensible, vigorous too, and, I may perhaps say, not without beauty: only he whose own thoughts are real has real style." Again a self-characterization, which could hardly be better put. That it is not " modest " is only because absolute veracity was perhaps Schopenhauer's most prominent characteristic.

His starting-point is Kant. He characterizes his merits intuitively and exhaustively in his *Kritik der Kantischen Philosophie* when he says that Kant took to pieces and exhibited bit by bit, with admirable circumspection and skill, the whole machinery of the faculty of knowing through which the whole phantasmagoria of the objective world comes into being. "We feel at once," he adds in another place (in his essay *Über die Universitätsphilosophie*), " removed and estranged in a marvellous way from the

241

whole dreamlike existence in which we are sunk, in that we hold the original elements of the same each in his own hand and can now see how time, space, and causality, linked together by the synthetic unity of the apperception of all phenomena, render possible the experiential complex of the whole and its course constituting our world, which is so greatly conditioned by the intellect and on that very account is only appearance." In his unqualified Phenomenalism Schopenhauer is in full agreement with Kant. "The world is my imagination": with these words his principal work opens. To be an object is to be conceived by a subject. The thing conceived is no other than the conception. In the closer doctrine of the transcendental faculties, however, he diverges from Kant. Of the twelve Categories he will allow only causality; the other eleven he calls blind windows. But causality is for him no category, no conception of reason, but a form of intuition, the one and only form of it, indeed, since space and time also are causality, in that through them things appear as if connected by laws, *causing* each other, in relation either to position or to succession: to be an object, to be conceived, is to be based, to be necessary; but this necessity has manifestly only a phenomenal character. The illusion of the world, we are told in *Über den Tod und sein Verhältnis zur Unzerstörbarkeit unseres Wesens an sich,* is produced by the apparatus of two polished glasses (functions of the brain) through which alone we are able to see anything. They are called space and time, and, in their reciprocal interpenetration, causality. Matter Schopenhauer defines with sublime simplicity as the "perceptibleness of time and space" or "causality become objective." As to the thing-in-itself, we naturally cannot arrive at this by means of imagination, but we do so by another way, which opens the window by treachery, as it were. The traitor is our self-consciousness. Our body is given us twice over: once from without, as a conception, and once from within, as will: the world is will and conception. The world is the *essence* of things and, in all its characteristics, the opposite of the phenomenon. Appearance is manifold, transitory, and subject to causality; will is indivisible, everlasting, omnipresent, free. The will is Being-in-itself, the substance of the world; the intellect only accident and secondary product. By the intellect we *apprehend,* by the will we *are.* The intellect is merely the tool. The unperceiving will stands to it in the relation of the roots of a tree to its summit or, to take a more comprehensive comparison, of the blind man to the lame one whom he carries on his shoulders. Nature is the visibleness of the will to life. It forms a graduated series of objectivations of the will: from the stone, which is the will to fall, to the brain, which is the will to think. The will appears at the lowest stage as the "mechanical, chemical, physical cause," in the plant as "attraction," in the animal as "intuitive motive," and in man as "abstract, thought-out motive." This will of Schopenhauer's is no Scholastic principle, no "*ens rationis*," no "word of uncertain fluctuating meaning," "but," says Schopenhauer, "if anyone asks me what it is, I refer him to his own inward self, where he will find it complete, and indeed of immense magnitude, a true *ens realissimum*. It will be seen, therefore, that I have not explained the world by unknown factors, but rather by the best known of all, which is known in quite a different way from anything else."

In this realm of the will there reign the gloomy powers of pain and death, disappointment and boredom, while pleasures and blessings are pure illusions. In the end death must win, for we were allotted to him at birth and he is only playing with his prey a little while before he swallows it. Meanwhile we go on living, with much interest and great care, for as long as possible, just as one blows a soap-bubble to last as long and grow as big as possible, although absolutely certain that it will burst. The life of the vast majority of people is a dull striving and torment, a dreamlike reeling through the four ages down to death, accompanied by a string of trivial ideas; they are like clocks and watches that are wound up and go, without knowing why. The wild ones devour one another, and the tame deceive one another, and this is called the way of the world. On the stage one man plays the prince or general, another the manservant or soldier, but the differences are only in externals; inside them all there is the same thing — a poor comedian and his worries and his poverty. In life it is the same. Most of the splendours are merely shams like theatre decorations. Our expressions of joy are usually but the hanging sign, the notification, the hieroglyph, of joy; they aim only at making others believe that joy has entered in, whereas it alone has declined the invitation to the feast. In the midst of this tragedy of emptiness and suffering we meet only one variety of happy people: the lovers. But why do they exchange glances so privately, fearfully, and stealthily? "Because lovers are the traitors who secretly try to perpetuate the whole misery and drudgery which would otherwise speedily come to an end."

There are but two ways out of this misery: the pure intuition of genius, and the abnegation of will by the saint. If we give up the ordinary way of looking at things, devote ourselves entirely to quiet contemplation, and " lose " ourselves completely in our subject — lose our individuality, our will, until we are nothing but a clear mirror of the object — then that which is thus perceived is no longer the individual thing as such, but the *idea*. The ordinary person, " that stock article of Nature's," is incapable of such completely disinterested contemplation. " To the ordinary man his power of perception is the lantern that lights his way, but to the genius it is the sun which reveals the world." " The degree to which everyone not merely thinks but positively sees in the individual thing only that thing, or else already something more general, and so on up the scale to the widest generality of genus, is the measure of his approximation to genius." And that which genius achieves on intellectual lines is reached by asceticism on moral lines. " A man who, after many bitter struggles against his own nature, has finally conquered is left as a purely perceptive being, an unclouded mirror of nature. . . . He can look back, peaceful and smiling, on the phantasms of the world, which once had power to disturb and torment his soul also, but now affect him no more than chessmen after the game is over or than the discarded masks and dominoes which piqued and intrigued us at the carnival of the night before."

The Classical Romantic The numerous " contradictions " presented by Schopenhauer's deductions, both in details and in fundamentals, have often been discussed. The most thorough and illuminating criticism comes from Kuno Fischer, who sorts them out and makes them file past us like soldiers, and Rudolf Haym, who achieves the result of not a stone being left standing. Eduard Zeller, again, declares, in his *Geschichte der deutschen Philosophie seit Leibniz*, that Schopenhauer transferred all the contradictions and whims of his capricious nature to his system. But this kind of denunciation is invariably a thankless task, since discrepancies of this sort occur inevitably and without exception in every genuine thought-structure, and it is particularly misplaced in the case of Schopenhauer, because his philosophy was only apparently a theoretical system, being in reality a work of art to be taken as a whole or left as a whole. Schopenhauer is, as Nietzsche at once perceived, an educator. His writings belong, as regards content, to the category of *The Imitation of Christ,* the *Confessions* of St. Augustine, and the self-observations of Marcus Aurelius and Montaigne, while in point of form they must be included among the masterpieces of prose painting. As a stylist Schopenhauer can be compared only with a Classical author : no one more recent is able to combine in the same degree suppleness with lapidarity, temperament with dignity, ornamentation with naturalness. In speaking of the professional author (by whom, naturally, he again means himself) Schopenhauer remarks that he *really* speaks to the reader and produces pictures, whereas the rank-and-file literary man gives us only set pieces. His own expression-form is in fact a live and highly personal talk with the reader. All his sentences are impregnated with his unique personality, in structure and rhythm and in the choice and placing of every individual word. Each metaphor, each antithesis, each quotation, indeed, is drawn from inward experience. His language — entirely un-Impressionist, " Classical " in the double meaning of the word — stands, like the Greek, beyond popularity and scholarship. His philosophy, on the contrary, approximates far more closely to that of the " windbag " Fichte and the " nonsense-scribbler " Schelling than to Kant and the Classics. In its irrationalism and pessimism, its æstheticism and aristocratism, its genius-cult and (underlying) Catholicism, it is the mature, rich bloom of Romanticism.

Bismarck also was half rooted in the period before the March Revolution, and even to some extent in the eighteenth century. In his era a politician had only the choice of being Liberal or reactionary, democratic or absolutist, Positivist or orthodox. Bismarck was none of these because he was all of them in one. He was really a Rococo seigneur, and that is why his soul could house impartially Legitimist and revolutionary, free-thinker and pietist, *citoyen* and feudalist, in a way that was possible for no other in his day. Yet this was only the one half of his nature ; the other half belonged to neither past nor present, but to the future : he had already conceived the idea of *democratic dictatorship* and a *pan-European state system* which dominates our century. Like Luther, he stood, a mysterious creative Janus, at the parting of the ways of two generations and waged all his life a sort of battle with the Devil (with his own personal devil too). But his closest relationship was to Frederick the Great. Almost all the characteristics which we pointed out in connexion with Frederick are found again in Bismarck. First there is that paradoxical medley of Realism and Idealism, adaptable elasticity and unshakable loyalty to principles,

245

which made the Prussian King so successful a statesman. Then the equally paradoxical relation in which both men stood to truthfulness: for apparently they lied from time to time (Bismarck very seldom, it is true), but this was only their professional jargon; inwardly they were the most upright men imaginable. The fact is, one can have spoken the truth consistently all one's life and yet have the soul of a damnable hypocrite, sham fighter, and false coiner; but we can also imagine the opposite. Only those who are definitely devoid of the sense of truth or deliberately close their eyes can read even a chapter or two of Bismarck's *Gedanken und Erinnerungen* without realizing that here is an elemental spirit whose basic feeling is the passionate desire to read the true face of all persons, things, and occurrences, and not only that, but to show them a true face also; that there is in these memoirs the reflection of a crystalline soul, as open and clear, though also as unfathomable, as a mountain lake. In this respect Bismarck stood higher than Frederick, just as he was also, and for that reason undoubtedly, the better author. His deliberately witty and invariably somewhat ironical method of observation, which indulges in unhackneyed epigrams, clear-cut, sparkling antitheses, and quotable *aperçus*, is quite eighteenth-century and has, like Frederick's, something French about it — paradoxical as this may sound to those who have the vulgar idea of him. Quite un-French, on the other hand, were his deep religiousness, his temperament, and his humour, and it hangs together with this last characteristic that he was one of the least vain of all the personages who ever possessed power on this earth. We were able to note this in Frederick also, and must add that Bismarck likewise was not a solemn person. Innumerable proofs of this might be brought forward, but one instance, more telling than all the anecdotes, will suffice. It is taken from the diary of the future Emperor Frederick, who, with Bismarck, Roon, and Moltke, had gone as far as Brandenburg to meet King William on his return to Berlin from Ems on July 15, 1870. On the way Bismarck gave the King a comprehensive account of the European situation and, the Crown Prince added, delivered it " with great clearness and dignified seriousness, without any of his usual favourite jokes." Imagine the situation: it is the moment between the Ems telegram and general mobilization; the Chancellor of the North German Federation is laying before the King, the Crown Prince, the War Minister, and the Chief of the General Staff the decisive opinion; he remains completely

246

serious, making not a single joke, and the Crown Prince enters this astonishing fact in his diary.

We might carry out the parallel in still more details. It seems to me particularly noteworthy that neither was Bismarck a militarist, often as one hears the contrary; he, likewise, looked upon war as an " emetic," although, once he considered it to be unavoidable, he sought to guide it towards a favourable moment, and this made him appear to be the aggressor; finally, he too was no monarchist. He was a royalist, emphatically, but that is not the same thing. His devotion to the dynasty was rooted in the feudal traditions of *his* house, and his attitude towards the Hohenzollerns had ever a touch of the Fronde below the surface. Must surprising of all is that he had even " physiological inferiority " in common with Frederick the Great. He was by no means the stony Roland that the people supposed him to be, but was the very type of a decadent. Above all, he was a really classical specimen of a neurotic, in that with him psychical attacks regularly turned into physical ones: for instance, vexation and disappointment turned into trigeminal pains. No *maléquilibré* of the *fin de siècle* surpassed him in irritability and lability of the nervous system. An " Iron Chancellor " who goes into hysterics when he cannot impose his will is really a very curious phenomenon, quite as curious in its way as a " German hero-King " who writes French alexandrines between two battles. Last of all, the two men had similar fates on their way to death and after death. They became so spiritualized in their last years as to be almost unreal, and have been the objects of furious discussion by posterity down to the present day, now worshipped as demigods, now branded as scoundrels and even criminals.

One may say that Nature really only produces her creatures to show, in each case, what a single organ can do when it reaches the extreme limits of its size and power. The tiger is all devouring jaw, the elephant nothing but a gigantic seizing and groping trunk, the cow a strolling stomach which chews and digests, the dog a " detective " nose on four feet. With the human race this process repeats itself on the intellectual plane in the creation of genius. Every genius is the amazing hypertrophy of a spiritual potency. Shakspere is all imagination, Goethe all perception, a vast inner eye. In Kant, as we have shown in detail, it was the capacity for *theoretical* understanding that developed to such superhuman dimensions, and in Bismarck *practical* understanding. What is meant by this is explained by a saying of Schopenhauer's: " The

The last of the heroes

247

talented person thinks quicker and more correctly than the others; but the genius contemplates a different world from that which any of them see, although it is only because he gazes deeper into the one which lies before them also, and because it presents itself in his head more objectively, and consequently more purely and distinctly." Carlyle says the same thing still more simply: " The crabbed old Schoolmaster used to ask, when they brought him a new pupil, 'But are ye sure he's *not a dunce?*' Why, really one might ask the same thing, in regard to every man proposed for whatsoever function; and consider it as the one inquiry needful: Are ye sure he's not a dunce? There is, in this world, no other entirely fatal person." If all men had a pure, clear natural understanding such as Bismarck possessed, they would be by no means free from vices and errors, it is true (for Bismarck was neither an infallible pope nor an immaculate saint), but their vices and errors would be harmless as regards themselves and others because they would dissolve in wisdom, understanding, and intelligence.

No one, probably, will deny Bismarck this understanding, but many declare that he was " immoral " with it all. As if superior understanding and immorality were compatible! A land-speculator, an exchange broker, or a theatrical agent may be a swindler and yet " clever " at his job, for the simple reason that his whole trade is a swindle; but take even a florist, an optical-glass-cutter, or an organ-builder, and a certain morality is indispensable. To be able to do a thing one must perceive it, and to perceive it one must look into its heart, which means that one must stand in a moral relation to it. The cowardly, selfish, or haughty person will never win the confidence of a thing, yet it is only by so doing that he can get at the truth of it.

The longer and more closely one observes people, the more one discovers how surprisingly little they differ in their principles. Most of them know, in general and in particular, what the " right " thing is, but they do not do it. To know and to act are with them two completely separated provinces, two chambers which practically never communicate with each other. Not that a man *consciously* denies his principles, it is not so simple as that. He does it with the best conscience, he simply *forgot* them when he was acting, and is therefore much surprised when he is accused of being so very different from what he always preaches. He is like the owner of a patent which no one can be found to take up — the idea, the model, the principle is all that there is. Nearly all human beings are in the possession of the secret of how they ought to live, but the magnificent and unique invention that each one of them embodies is hardly ever realized. This was precisely the great new meaning of Christianity: it taught men that the essential is not knowing, but being. A man who knows but a few truths, and yet lives them, will lead a godly life. A man who possesses all the wisdom in the world, yet only in his head as a dead program, may with it all have gone completely to the Devil.

In this sense Bismarck was a great Christian. He had wise and bold ideas; so had others. He, however, filled them with his strong *Junker* blood and *lived* them: the last hero that the modern age has seen.

To understand historically the origin of that which Bismarck brought about we must look as far as America. It was from there that the first powerful blow was dealt at the French Empire, on which fortune had smiled for half a generation. The new continent, which, ever since its emancipation, had been vigorously developing, made astonishing economic progress from about the middle of the century onward. The electrifying slogan was "Westward ho!" Contrary to European custom, railways were built before the new settlement areas were opened up. Thus at a time when communication between Munich and Vienna was still by coach, railway tracks were laid in the New World over immense stretches of totally uninhabited country. In 1845 Texas was brought into the Union, and in 1848 Mexico was forced to hand over New Mexico and California — about half of its territory — to the United States. In the same year a second alarm was sounded: Gold in California! An immense stream of immigrants now hurried westward. It was not the gold alone that enticed them, but the abundance of other treasures of the soil as well: minerals, oils, coal, and magnificent vegetation which produced fruit, vegetables, grain, and cattle-fodder in unheard-of quality. Meanwhile a strong opposition had developed between the Northern and Southern states. In the South a planter aristocracy lived on large and profitable plantations side by side with the "poor whites," who were almost as much slaves as the Negroes. The main products were rice, sugar, tobacco, and, above all, cotton. (The motto of the South was "Cotton is king.") The political and economic superiority of the South was based on its wealth, and that in its turn on slavery. In the North, where farming and manufactures predominated, the Negro was less needed and could probably not

The War of Secession

249

have been used to advantage for climatic reasons. The fight for Abolition was thus at bottom an economic affair. Three times in her earlier history America had begun a great war, and every time for money. For of what else was there any question in the glorious War of Liberation in 1775? The duty on tea. In the World War, too, in which, politically, they had no interest whatever, the United States only intervened in order to get back the money they had lent. It must not be overlooked, nevertheless, that there were Christian idealists who demanded the liberation of the slaves on moral grounds. William Lloyd Garrison — a native of Massachusetts, like almost all the great American divines of that time — had in 1831 founded a journal called *The Liberator* to that end, and he went on to found the American Antislavery Society in 1833. Emerson also approved of these efforts, although he as a free intellectual had no use for organizations. " It is high time our bad wealth came to an end," he wrote, and when his children told him they had been given " The Building of a House " as the subject for a school composition, he said: " You must be sure to say that no house nowadays is perfect without having a nook where a fugitive slave can be safely hidden away." In 1852 the whole world was shaken by Harriet Beecher Stowe's novel *Uncle Tom's Cabin,* which, though sentimental and oleographic, deserves mankind's eternal gratitude for its noble tendentiousness. The conflict over the slavery question became bound up with the opposition between the Republican and Democratic parties. The former, which predominated in the North, stressed the authority of the Union; the latter, all-powerful in the slave states, demanded all the extension possible for the sovereignty of individual states. The break came in 1861. The eleven Southern states announced their secession from the Union and formed a separate Confederacy under a president of their own — hence the name " War of Secession " given to the four years' Civil War which now broke out. Union and Confederacy, Washington and Richmond, stood in bitter opposition to each other. The war was waged for the most part on the territory of the Southern states, which had the advantages and disadvantages of the inner line, the most violent and stubborn fighting taking place in the border states of Virginia, which held by the South, and Maryland, which went with the North. Most European governments sympathized with the South. Both Palmerston and Napoleon III desired the downfall of the United States, Napoleon because he was trying to break through the Monroe

Doctrine by founding a Mexican empire dependent on France, Palmerston because he feared the rise of a transatlantic rival power and also because England was the chief consumer of cotton — added to which there still rankled the memory of the time when the American colonies had themselves broken away. Public opinion in Europe, on the other hand, was almost unanimous in believing the moral right to be on the side of the Northern states.

The War of Secession was the first pronouncedly modern war. It has considerable resemblance to the Franco-German and even the Russo-Japanese war, particularly in respect of the hitherto unheard-of mass of combatants engaged, the enormous extent and duration of the battles, and the great part played by the new technical means. The number of soldiers increased gradually to over three million, of whom more than half a million were killed or died. The cost of the war amounted to three milliard dollars. Steamships assumed strategical importance for the first time. Already there were armoured trains, light railways, and armoured frigates, the first of these being the Confederates' *Merrimac*, whose deck was cut down to the water line and ended in a ram, after the manner of the *rostrum* that the Romans employed in the First Punic War. The Union retaliated by building the *Monitor*, of quite similar construction, but which had in addition a revolving armoured turret with a heavy gun. This form of ship, called *Monitor* after the original model, proved so serviceable in war that it was immediately copied all over the world. The field telegraph was also in general use, and even the practice of reading the enemy's telegrams by means of inserted portable apparatus was already familiar. The Southern troops had the better leading and better military spirit, those of the North an overwhelming numerical superiority; but this advantage was impaired by the existence within the Union itself of parties with Secession sympathies, opposed to the war against slavery. Also, the Secretary of War had sent the greater part of the weapons and guns into the South before the outbreak of war. General Lee, the excellent commander-in-chief of the Confederates, operated very skilfully on the inner line and achieved some considerable partial successes, but gradually the superiority of the Northern troops made itself felt, the more so as they were better disciplined by their war experience and had at their disposal the terrible weapon of blockade. The first year of the war gave the Confederate troops the victory at Bull Run, a tributary of the Potomac, the boundary river between Maryland and Virginia. In the following year they were victorious once more in the Seven Days' Battle before Richmond, a victory out of which a threat to Washington itself developed. In the autumn they suffered a defeat at Antietam, but made this good before the end of the year by their victory at Fredericksburg. Lee then crossed the Potomac. On January 1, 1863, Abraham Lincoln, President of the Union, issued a declaration to the effect that all slaves were free. In the same year Lee was beaten in the battle of Gettysburg in Pennsylvania, the bloodiest of the war, lasting from July 1 to 3, and on July 4 a still greater catastrophe befell him: General Grant, in whom the Federal army had at last found an efficient commander, took Vicksburg and thus brought the Mississippi under the control of the Northern states. This had the effect of cutting off the Confederates in the West from Texas and from neutral Mexico. The blockade-ring, which had previously been several times broken through, now closed completely, for in the North the Southern states abutted on the Union, and in the East and South they were bordered by the sea. At once the pressure made itself felt. There began to be a lack of medicaments and dress materials, heating apparatus and building material, provisions and munitions. Neither could a grotesque manifesto of the Southern Government which offered freedom to all slaves who would participate in the war (for slavery!) turn the scale. On April 3, 1865 their capital, Richmond, was taken after three days' fighting, and on April 10 Lee capitulated with the remnant of the army. Four days later the noble Abraham Lincoln was shot by a stupid fanatic, the actor Booth (brother of the famous tragedian), as he sat in the beflagged President's box at the gala performance which was to celebrate the peace. He was a magnificent, truly American figure, an original and a doctrinaire, sober and kindly, a pathetic civilian in the midst of a murderous family war. He fell at the summit of his career through blind treachery, like Philip of Macedon, Cæsar, Henri le Grand. But these three found executors for their wills: Alexander, Augustus, Richelieu; Lincoln needed none, for his work was finished.

We Europeans regard this result with mixed feelings. That Negroes should be freed is a good thing; to regard them as human beings would perhaps be still better. That hostile brothers should be reconciled and unite afresh in peaceful efforts is gratifying; what is less gratifying is that the being born of this common productivity is a terrible and scurrilous Leviathan who threatens to swallow the planets, a chaos made up of economic elephantiasis, super-technique, megaphone-roaring, and psycho-analysis. Still, this only indirectly concerns the " crisis of the European soul."

Two years after the assassination of Lincoln another tragedy took place in the same quarter of the globe. The War of Secession encouraged Napoleon III to undertake a very risky venture. French troops landed in Mexico under a pretext of international law, pushed forward, and conquered the capital. A " national assembly " of paid creatures was summoned, and elected the Archduke Maximilian Emperor of Mexico. Brother of the Emperor Francis Joseph, he was one of the " Liberal " Habsburgs, a vague elementary idealist of the type of Joseph II, but still not Liberal enough to refrain from forcing himself on a population which did not want him. He, with the assistance of the French under Bazaine, fought against the " rebels " and the former President Juárez. The conclusion of peace in the North put an end to it all. The United States entered a protest. Napoleon, confronted with the eventuality of going to war with them, withdrew his troops, and Maximilian, as foolish as he was brave, disdained to flee and was tried by court martial and shot. This was a severe blow to the Napoleonic prestige.

Juárez and Maximilian

Before this, Napoleon had already suffered a more indirect weakening of that prestige through the Danish affair. The point of dispute was the two hereditary duchies of Schleswig and Holstein, which were bound to Denmark by personal union. As Frederick VII was childless, and as the rule of hereditary succession to the duchies was different from that of Denmark, they would have passed to another dynasty on the King's death: namely, to Duke Christian von Sonderburg-Augustenburg. Only Holstein belonged to the German Federation, and in consequence the " Eider-Dane " party (so called because they wanted the Eider to be the Danish frontier) engineered the incorporation of Schleswig. This was announced in the revolutionary month of March 1848. The answer to it was an insurrection in both provinces, assisted by Prussian and other German troops. But the blockade by the Danish warships, which commanded the sea and the mouths of the Elbe, Weser, and Oder, and the diplomatic pressure exercised by England and Russia, paralysed the war. Austria also came out on the side of Denmark and, with the vigorous assistance of the Tsar, forced Prussia in 1850, at that Olmütz conference of which we have already heard, to refrain from any intervention in the Schleswig-

Schleswig-Holstein

Holstein question. That after this there should still be people who ranted about a " German mission " of the Habsburg State is a puzzle. It would just as willingly have promised Schleswig-Holstein to the Fiji Islanders for no better reason than to keep Prussia out. In 1852 it was agreed in the " London Protocol " between the five great powers, Sweden, and Denmark that Prince Christian of Sonderburg-*Glücksburg* should inherit the whole Danish province after the death of Frederick VII. Duke Christian of Sonderburg-*Augustenburg* promised not to oppose the new order, but passed on his hereditary claims to Schleswig-Holstein to his son Frederick. A pretty sort of muddle therefore.

In 1863 King Frederick VII issued a decree which separated Schleswig from Holstein and united it with Denmark. The first act of his successor's reign was the confirmation of the joint constitution for Schleswig and Denmark. Thereupon Frederick of Augustenburg was proclaimed duke, and Prussia declared war. Austria joined in also, hoping either to obtain a kind of colony in the north — something like Belgium, although its experiences with that country had not been encouraging — or at least, by creating a new small state, to make trouble for Prussia in her sphere of influence. The allies had sixty thousand men, the Danes had only forty thousand, but excellent fortifications in addition. The Prussians were commanded by " Papa Wrangel," a strategist of the old school and actually more of a cavalry general, while Moltke had very little influence on the plan of campaign. His admirable plan of barring the Danish army's retreat on Flensburg and destroying it by envelopment was not carried out. The Austrians were cleverly led by Gablenz, well drilled in shock tactics and of great bravery in assault, but their success in tasks that were smaller than and different from those which confronted them later gave a false impression of their military strength as compared with Prussia's. After the famous storming of the Düppel redoubts by the Prussians, the allies occupied the whole of Jutland. But even this was not decisive, for the Danes could drag out the war to great length by retiring to their islands, which afforded excellent protection. It was therefore decided to advance on the island of Alsen. This was carried out with surprising rapidity by the Prussians under General Herwarth von Bittenfeld. After a few more small islands had been occupied, a truce was made, and by the Treaty of Vienna, Denmark ceded the duchies of Schleswig, Holstein, and Lauenburg to Austria and Prussia, who set up a common government in them. But this was obviously only a temporary settlement. Austria recommended that the Augustenburger should be put in, but Bismarck demanded a sort of Prussian protectorate if this plan were followed. To relieve the strain the two great powers signed the Gastein agreement in 1865, by which they reserved to themselves a combined supremacy over both duchies, but made over the administration for the time being of Holstein to Austria, and Schleswig to Prussia, while the duchy of Lauenburg passed definitely into Prussia's hands in exchange for an indemnity. Bismarck, who was made a count in consequence of this, was not exactly enthusiastic about the arrangement. He called it a "plastering-over of the cracks in the structure."

The situation was certainly untenable. The side-by-side government in Schleswig-Holstein proved immediately to be a practical impossibility, but this was only a secondary matter and merely an excuse for the rupture. The true reason of the war was the absurd Germanic Federation. As time went on, it became intolerable that a sclerotic state like Austria should arrogate to itself the supremacy over the German people and hamper the ordained German hegemon power in every act of energy, whether in internal or external politics. The break-up of this system was a historic necessity from the day on which it was created. History often takes its time about things, but nothing in the world can have duration which lives by a chimerical and crooked idea, an unnatural and fraudulent claim, a lie. Actually the German war of 1866 was not a settlement of accounts between North and South, but a German revolution, made, like most revolutions, from above and in this case by an individual man who possessed that combination of clear-sightedness and energy so rare in official life. " Every other Prussian war before the Austrian," said Bismarck, "is pure waste of ammunition." His superiority lay in the fact that, in contrast to Napoleon III, he never wavered, always wanted the same thing, and refused all semi-solutions, such as Bavaria's proposal to form a German Triad; with Austria limited to the Hereditary Provinces, South Germany under Bavarian, and North Germany under Prussian control. All his life long, Bismarck was supported by a single great idea, which was the inexhaustible source of his strength — here again is seen his likeness to Frederick the Great. Napoleon III, on the other hand, had only a crowd of "ideas," like an adventurer to whom a new *coup*

255

occurs every day, each overriding the one before it. The "royal idea," for him, consisted in keeping his firm's head above water at all costs and by every means available, irrespective of consistency. This simple idea was understood by Napoleon's nation, which, indeed, identified itself with it as long as business was flourishing. But Bismarck's countrymen did not understand his idea. In May 1866, when he escaped assassination only by a miracle, he was the best-hated man in all Germany.

Napoleon III displayed no political perspicacity, let alone long-sightedness, in this crisis. He promoted the conclusion of the Prussian-Italian alliance because he held Austria to be the stronger (partly from national vanity, since an army which had only with difficulty been defeated by the French must obviously be superior to all the rest in the world), because the liberation of Venetia lay in the line of his program for Italian unity, and because the "compensations," on which he definitely counted, would have restored his prestige: he hoped to gain Belgium, the Palatinate, and the Rhine Province (although these latter perhaps only as duchies under French protectorate), and at least the coal basin of Saarbrücken. All this was to come under the title of "*revendication*," for in France they consider that everything that was ever occupied by French troops belongs to the *grande nation* and can be demanded back at any time; further, even Napoleon believed in the possibility of a "*troisième Allemagne*," which, as a sort of Confederation of the Rhine — naturally, under French influence — would serve to balance Prussian hegemony in the north. Thiers, the opposition leader in the Chamber at that time, saw far more deeply into things. He declared, in a four-hour speech, that France could not but have dangerous rivals in a united Germany and Italy, and that the only possible national policy lay therefore in the line followed by Richelieu and Louis XIV. But while Napoleon was merely destitute of political genius, the diplomatic attitude adopted by the Austrian Government before the outbreak of the war was nothing short of insane. It might at any time have exchanged Venetia for the neutrality, and possibly the alliance, of Italy; instead of which it haughtily rejected all such offers, only to agree to everything suddenly when the menace of the Prussian attack was immediately impending. But it was too late. The treaty between Prussia and Italy had already for three months been agreed on. The same process took place exactly as in the beginning of 1915, when the Dual Monarchy hesitated so long over relinquishing the Trentino that Italy meanwhile bound herself to the Entente. Napoleon nevertheless undertook to negotiate the offer of neutrality in return for the making over of Venetia to the Government at Florence, which was now in a position to obtain without a war what it could only have hoped to obtain through one. But its sense of honour would not permit the breaking of the treaty, and, besides, popular feeling already ran so high that no going back was possible. Even that was not enough, however. On June 12 Austria concluded a secret treaty with Napoleon by which she bound herself to make or agree to no political or territorial changes without French consent, to restore the left bank of the Rhine to France in the event of a reconquest of Silesia, and to renounce her claim to Venetia in any case (even, that is, after a victory over Italy). One does not know whether to be more amazed at the stupidity or the perfidy of these conditions. A state that could abandon Aachen and Köln, Mainz and the Palatinate (these two belonging in any case to her allies), certainly proved its total unworthiness to be at the head of Germany. The Austrian minister Count Beust, who was at that time still in the Saxon service and remained all his life one of the most rabid Prussophobes, said likewise, on seeing the treaty later, that it was the most incredible document he had ever handled.

Hanover and all South Germany took the side of Austria without delay, and in Prussia itself the war was anything but popular. There were numerous petitions against it, and a Catholic agitation broke out in Silesia and the Rhine Province. Even the court was not whole-heartedly in favour of striking the blow. The Crown Prince was emphatically against the war, and the King, to say the least, pessimistic. He announced that, in case of a defeat, he would abdicate, and when his reader asked for permission to be taken in at headquarters, he replied: " Why? You can always ride over from Potsdam to Grossbeeren." Others spoke of a second Thirty Years' War. They were least in the right, for of all the great wars that one knows, this is the shortest. The decisive military actions lasted a week, and between the first engagement of the Prussians and Austrians and the armistice there lay exactly one month. In Austria the mood was optimistic. With the childish chauvinism typical of the country — born, not of incorrigible complacency, as in France, but out of imperturbable frivolity, which, when a débâcle ensues, turns into self-contempt — the word was passed round that the Prussians would be sent home with their tails between their legs. For this assumption there was no excuse. The Austrian soldier was brave, but illiterate, for all who had been through a middle-school course or could produce a "thousand-gulden-man" as substitute — which practically amounted to the whole middle class — were exempt from military service. The officer-corps consisted of conceited aristocrats and well-drilled cadets, neither class being distinguished by profound knowledge or breadth of intellectual horizon. In the Prussian army, on the other hand, elementary-school education was general and the intelligence of the commissioned ranks higher throughout, so that initiative existed even down to company commanders. As far as matériel went, the Austrian artillery was better than the Prussian; its guns were almost all rifled, while two fifths of the Prussian were still smooth-bores. To set against this, the Prussians had the needle-gun, which could be fired three times against the Austrian muzzle-loader's once. Consequently Moltke depended chiefly on rifle-fire, while the Austrians relied on the dashing bayonet attack which they had learned from the French in the Italian war, and against Austria's antiquated shock tactics of close-order units he pitted the loose elastic line of skirmishers which could envelop.

Germany was treated by Prussia as a secondary theatre of war. The first step was the occupation of Hanover and the Electorate of Hesse, which thrust themselves like a dangerous wedge into Prussian territory. This was concluded within two days by the Army of the West, which then proceeded to force the capitulation of the entire Hanoverian fighting forces at Langensalza, defeat the Bavarians, and enter Frankfurt. On August 2 hostilities were suspended.

Custozza   For the Italians Moltke had prepared the following plan of campaign : to envelop the Quadrilateral of fortresses and march on Vienna, and to land in Dalmatia and rouse a general revolt in Hungary. But to carry out these brilliant operations they would have had to have far more vigorous and prudent leading than they had. At the head of the Austrian Southern army was Archduke Albrecht, son of the Archduke Karl, who had been the greatest military talent of the Habsburg dynasty. His Chief of Staff, Freiherr von John, was the greatest and perhaps the sole real strategist of the Austrian army. It was he who evolved the plan of battle at Custozza, where the Austrians succeeded (though with heavy losses) in breaking through the enemy centre: a decisive victory,

258

which was in part due to the ineptitude of the Italian high command, which, though it had greatly superior forces, distributed them unskilfully.

In the main theatre of war the opponents were about equal in strength: Prussians and Austrians had each about a quarter of a million men. From various causes, however, the Austrians were from the very first driven to the defensive and forced to fight on their own soil. The mobilization of the reservists, who were scattered in all parts of the Empire, proceeded very sluggishly. Whereas the Prussians disposed of five railway lines for their concentration, the Austrians had to rely on the one between Vienna and Prague, and not only that, but marching on foot was greatly hampered by the neglected state of the roads. The commander-in-chief of the Northern army, Ludwig Freiherr von Benedek, had become popular as the victor of San Martino, but was only a dashing corps commander and no strategist; also he was at home only on Italian soil. His appointment was therefore a typical Austrian misfit. At first he flatly refused to take the high command, telling the Emperor that he knew every tree in Upper Italy as far as Milan, but not even the position of the Elbe in Bohemia, that he could play the fiddle, but not the flute. Thereupon Franz Josef's principal aide-de-camp appealed to his dynastic sympathies by intimating that public opinion expected it of him, and that the Emperor would have to abdicate if, under some other commander, the army were beaten. Ten days after Königgrätz, Benedek wrote to his wife: " Told them myself that I was no more use than a donkey for the German theatre of war." Being, as a simple working soldier, inadequately versed in the science of war, he was obliged for his rôle to choose a strategic adviser. Unfortunately his choice fell on a still greater " donkey," General Krismanič, who was recommended to him by Archduke Albrecht. The relation between them was very much that of Blücher and Gneisenau, but with the difference that Gneisenau was a genius. Krismanič was a position-strategist of the pre-Napoleon school, who believed in all seriousness that the art of war lay in taking up the right " positions." He had studied Frederick the Great's Bohemian operations with attention, and believed that all the principles essential to victory could be drawn from them. His method had been nicknamed " sausage strategy " at the War School because on his topographical maps all the positions in the Frederician campaigns were drawn in the form of sausages. This

259

system was truly Austrian in its reactionary worship of the past, its bureaucracy hypnotized by maps, and its lack of imagination which led to a faith in repetition.

Moltke thought otherwise. Strategy was, for him, " the application of sound human understanding to the conduct of war." Which says everything. His principle of " marching apart, striking together," was designed to secure freedom of operations for as long as possible, and in this he had the support of the new technical aids, train and telegraph, in the rapid and unexpected redistribution of troops. Correctly diagnosing the military weakness of Germany, he decided to send six sevenths of the Prussian force against Austria, causing them to march into Bohemia from three sides and move on Gitschin. The success of this plan meant practically that the war was won, for the Austrians were thereby thrown back on the inner line — a situation which has its advantages, but only when the army has a sufficiently large area in which to operate and can exploit it with the verve and presence of mind of a Napoleon or Frederick. Moreover, all great poets, from Shakspere to Busch, have long since realized that names are no casual externals, but the secret labels of destiny. Was it likely that a man called Moltke would be defeated by a man called Krismanič?

Königgrätz   At the outset the war seemed to promise well for the Austrians. On June 27 they defeated a Prussian corps at Trautenau, and their own defeat on the same day at Nachod was reported to Vienna as a victory. But during the two following days they were unsuccessful in actions at Soor, Skalitz, Trautenau, Königinhof, Schweinschädel, and Münchengrätz and finally driven back by the I and Elbe Armies, which had by then got in touch with each other, at the battle of Gitschin. Benedek telegraphed to Franz Josef: "Urgently beg Your Majesty to conclude peace at any price. Army catastrophe unavoidable." The Emperor replied: " Impossible to conclude peace. If retreat necessary, let it proceed. Has a battle taken place? " Translated from the Habsburgian, this reads : the prestige of the dynasty demands in any case a decisive battle.

The battle of Königgrätz on July 3, 1866, which brought larger masses into the field than the battle of Leipzig, was the greatest of the century and at the same time the first test of the new Moltke method, the most forceful envelopment battle hitherto known to history. Moltke intended even greater things than he achieved, his idea being a complete "mousetrap," as at Sedan, but he worked to some extent under handicaps. For one thing, the subordinate leaders did not quite grasp the originality and daring of his ideas and failed accordingly to execute them in entirety; further, his power was not absolute. He was only Chief of the General Staff, and the King could not bring himself to carry the war to extremes, partly from chivalry and conscientious scruples and partly, no doubt, from the prudence of old age and the narrower outlook of a former generation; thus he delayed mobilization, to his own great disadvantage, because he wished on no account to be the aggressor — a course of action inspired by his Protestant sense of responsibility, which, seen from the purely human angle, did him the utmost honour.

The battlefield extended from the village of Sadowa to the fortress of Königgrätz, the two being about three hours' walk apart. The fortress lay across the Elbe and was connected with the opposite shore by six bridges, to which six new ones were now added, for Benedek, who had gone into the war without confidence, had had this contingency of retreat in mind from the first. The troops were, as we have said, much the same in strength, but of the two hundred and thirty thousand Prussians available only about one hundred and seventy thousand went into the battle, so that the victory was actually won against a superior force. The Austrian centre had taken up its position behind the Bistritz, a tributary of the Elbe, and on the heights of Chlum, where they were covered by over five hundred guns, and had reserves in their rear. The Prussian centre, with its front towards the Austrian, was formed of the I Army, led by Prince Friedrich Karl, the right wing of the Elbe Army, under General Herwarth von Bittenfeld, and the left wing of the II or Silesian Army, under the Crown Prince. This last army was, however, still a day's march away on the night of July 3 and only began to move up in the morning of the battle. While the Elbe Army gained ground against the enemy's left wing, which was composed mainly of Saxons, the I Army made no progress during the fierce fighting at Sadowa. Consequently the situation about noon seemed favourable to Benedek, and he considered whether he should not launch an offensive at the Prussian centre. This would have meant the complete annihilation of the Austrians, for their preponderance rested mainly on their strong position. Had they ventured to leave it, all the points of Prussian superiority would have come

261

into evidence on level ground: the needle-gun, the skirmishing tactics, and the strategical envelopment. He gave up the plan, however, having heard, two hours in advance of Prussian headquarters, that the Crown Prince's II Army was already in the immediate vicinity. Its advance over rain-sodden ground—in itself an admirable achievement—brought about the decision. Arriving on the field at two in the afternoon, it overran the Austrian right wing, pushed on to the centre, and captured the village of Chlum, which was the key to the whole Austrian position. A counter-attack undertaken by Benedek with his reserves failed, and the simultaneous defeat of the left wing forced it also to retreat. The troops, already threatened in the rear, fled in confusion, but the Prussian pursuit was inadequate in spite of the available reserves. This was owing to the efficiency of the Austrian artillery and, still more, to the Prussian officers' non-experience of success and their failure to comprehend the magnitude of the victory. Possibly, too, the King's *noblesse* had some say in the matter.

The catastrophe of Königgrätz was a great surprise to all Europe. The Secretary of State to the Curia, Cardinal Antonelli, cried, on hearing the news: " *Il mondo cassa,* the world is coming to an end!" *The Times,* completely misreading the state of affairs, put it all down to the needle-gun. Napoleon III at once informed Prussia of his " pourboire " claims. The clearest summing-up of the causes of defeat was in the popular wit in Vienna: "The volunteers have got no buttons. The generals have got no head. The ministers have got no brain. And so we lose the whole concern." As Franz Josef drove along the Mariahilferstrasse to Schönbrunn, the crowd shouted: " Long live the Emperor Maximilian!" It is extraordinary that, in the case of the Habsburgs, popularity has almost always fastened on the younger brothers. This was so with Philip II, whose half-brother, Don Juan of Austria, was the hero of the day. Leopold of Tuscany, too, later Leopold II, was far more popular than the reputedly venerated Emperor Joseph, and Archduke Charles, brother of the Emperor Franz, was the idol of the army. To this very day, there is about Maximilian of Mexico a halo of romance, and Franz Werfel has caught it in a very interesting play.

Lissa   The scattered Austrian Northern army was more or less reformed at Olmütz, a large portion of the victorious Southern army was recalled from Italy to protect Vienna, and Archduke Albrecht took command of all the troops. The Prussians, now hotly pursuing, occupied Prague and Brünn and defeated Benedek at Tobitschau, in Moravia, forcing him to give up his line of march and diverge towards Hungary. At Blumenau, not far from Pressburg, on July 22, the Prussians sought to force the Danube crossing, and the action was already turning in their favour when, at noon, a five-day truce was declared, at the expiration of which hostilities ceased. Two days before, the Austrians had won a great and unexpected naval victory at the island of Lissa. The Italian fleet was far better equipped than its opponent's. It had not only more ships, but more ironclads, and also guns of heavier calibre and newer construction. The excellent Austrian Admiral, Tegetthoff, a Westphalian by birth, redressed the disadvantageous balance by the amazing skill and daring with which he slipped through the enemy's annihilating fire and by brilliant manœuvring brought his vessels close enough to ram the Italian battleships, two of which he sank, while two others were put out of action. He himself sank the enemy's flagship with his own. As a reward for this victory, which, in recent history, could be compared only with Nelson's feats, he was put on the shelf — though honoured, it is true, after his early death by a monument of sensational hideousness. The battle was won by the aid of numerous Venetian sailors, who were by then already Italian subjects, Austria having officially ceded Venice to Napoleon III on July 4, the day after Königgrätz. Here is one of those cases where the lightning of madness flashes brightly through the confused warclouds and reveals the fact that the war of men is at bottom a barbarous end in itself: a glorious naval victory, fought with the soldiers of the enemy, who already possesses that for which both sides are fighting.

The considerable weakening of the land front against Italy made it possible for Garibaldi to break through into Southern Tirol with his irregulars, who, although they were checked, formed a permanent danger to Trent. Benedek's troops had joined up near Pressburg with Archduke Albrecht's army, which had now arrived, but this fighting force, though by no means negligible, was nevertheless manifestly not equal to the Prussian — especially as Bismarck made no bones about commissioning General Klapka to raise a legion from the Hungarian prisoners of war with a view to promoting effective rebellion in Hungary. Austria's only hope lay in vigorous intervention by Napoleon. He did come forward promptly, but, in his short-sightedness, not to protect

263

Austria, but to make sure of certain bits of Germany at the prospective carving-up of that country. Without emphasis or precision in the indications he threw out, and changing from day to day as to the measure of his compensations in western Germany, he demanded Mainz, the Palatinate, Saarlouis, and Saarbrücken. He was modelling himself vaguely on his Italian policy in 1859, when he had raked in Nice and Savoy in return for his consent to Italian union. Bismarck managed to spin matters out by his "dilatory" method until the peace preliminaries at Nikolsburg were signed. For Prussia to consent to the annexation of German territories was naturally out of the question, for she would have forfeited all Germany's confidence by so doing. But Bismarck once said, years later, that Napoleon had made a bad mistake in omitting to occupy Belgium as a security during the war in Bohemia. Moreover, France was by no means in a position to oppose Prussia with any prospect of success. Weakened as she was by the Mexican adventure, she could not even set up as strong an army on the Rhine as she had had in 1859 in Italy, and would in any case have required weeks of preparation. The Prussian army, on the other hand, was mobilized and also recruited day by day by considerable new drafts. What was more, Moltke had definitely declared that he felt equal to a war on three fronts.

Yet there was much to be said for a speedy conclusion of peace. With every day the danger of intervention by neutrals — and not only France — increased. The Tsar was already talking of a congress. Cholera was making raids on the Prussian army, and Italy could not be relied upon much longer, after her defeats and the acquisition of Venice. How far Austria would pull herself together, if it came to a really desperate conflict, could not be estimated. More than once in the Napoleonic wars she had shown that she could be particularly dangerous as a beaten opponent. Even Moltke wrote to his wife: " I am strongly in favour of running no risks over the results obtained, if it can possibly be avoided."

The main consideration was that Austria's collapse, though quite conceivable, was not at all to the Prussian interest. But that it took all Bismarck's doggedness and circumspection to secure indulgent terms for the chief opponent — and they were the most indulgent terms imaginable — is common knowledge. The King's wishes were directed towards Ansbach and Bayreuth, the ancient seats of the Hohenzollerns, which Napoleon I had added to Bavaria; Austrian Silesia and the German north-west border of Bohemia, with Eger, Karlsbad, Teplitz, and Reichenberg; and, further, the annexation of the whole of Saxony — which Franz Josef, as a man of honour, opposed as strenuously as the handing over of his own territory. The King finally gave his consent to Bismarck's proposals in a pencilled marginal note with the bitter words: " Since my minister-president has left me in the lurch in the face of the enemy, and I am not here in a position to replace him . . . I find myself to my sorrow forced, after the army's brilliant successes, to bite into this sour apple and accept this most shameful peace." By this treaty Austria recognized the dissolution of the Germanic Federation and gave her consent to a reconstruction of Germany, withdrew her rights to Schleswig-Holstein in favour of Prussia, and agreed to the annexation of Hanover, the Electorate of Hesse, Nassau, and Frankfurt. Thus augmented by about one quarter, Prussia became the head of the North German Confederation, into which Saxony, Mecklenburg, Oldenburg, Brunswick, Upper Hesse, the Thuringian and all other states situated north of the Main duly entered.

The greatest advantages from the Austrian defeat were obtained by Hungary. In 1867 Franz Deák concluded a settlement with the minister-president Beust, on the basis of which an " Austro-Hungarian monarchy " was now constituted — Franz Josef was styled from now on: " Emperor of Austria and Apostolic King of Hungary." Hungary received its own parliament and cabinet, and all that remained common to the two were foreign policy, army, state debt, currency, and customs. The coronation of the royal pair took place at Ofen — with gorgeous and barbaric ceremony. The Hungarians, themselves so long oppressed, now proceeded similarly to oppress the minorities within their half of the Empire — the Germans, Roumanians, Slovaks, Serbs, and Croats — by trying to Magyarize them forcibly. On the other hand, the confessional minorities — Protestants, Greeks, Jews — received loyal treatment. The country, which was one of Europe's richest granaries, at once made great strides in her agriculture. There was, however, no equivalent social and cultural development; the system of large estates crushed the peasant class, and, as late as the turn of the century, every other Hungarian was illiterate. The capital, Budapest, rose to dazzling, though giddy and bazaar-like, splendour. The Cisleithan provinces also received a Constitution, and a " Bürger " ministry took charge of the government. This

The Hungarian Settlement

265

development Bismarck characterized in the Prussian Diet with these incisive words: "Austria's long years under restraint have placed her in the position to make a sensation today by the same Liberalism which with us is an outlook that we got over twenty years ago so far as concerns the main thing, and fifty as regards some of its parts."

The local-ized world-war

The same Bismarck said to Karl Schurz in 1867: "Now it is France's turn. . . . Yes, we shall have war, and the Emperor of the French will begin it himself. I know that Napoleon III is personally a peace-lover and will not attack us on his own initiative. But he will be forced to do so by the necessity of upholding the imperial prestige. Our victories have lowered it considerably in the eyes of the French. He knows that, and he knows too that the Empire is lost if he cannot rapidly regain his prestige. According to our calculation, the war will break out in two years' time. We have to prepare for it and we are doing so. We shall win, and the result will be exactly the opposite of what Napoleon is aiming at. Germany will complete its unity, with the exclusion of Austria, and he himself will find himself on the floor." This is exactly what occurred. Immediately after the end of the war the cry was raised: "*Revanche pour Sadowa!*" — for so the French designated Königgrätz, presumably because they could not pronounce that name. Napoleon realized that he had failed to exploit the situation, but that something must be thrown as a sop to the clamouring public, and, since Belgium had been let slip, he came forward with the, in many ways, far more modest demand for the incorporation of Luxemburg. He actually succeeded in obtaining a treaty of sale from the King of the Netherlands, but this was opposed by Bismarck, and the conference of the great powers (among which Italy was now included) held in London in 1867 ruled that Luxemburg should henceforward be an independent grand duchy, whose neutrality the powers would guarantee in common. This diplomatic success on Prussia's part brought the war alarmingly close. Meanwhile Napoleon had seen clearly the risk of a conflict *à deux*. "We can only face a war," he said, "if we have a handful of alliances." From 1868 to 1870, therefore, negotiations were carried on to that end. Archduke Albrecht visited Paris and held pourparlers for a military convention. Once more France was offered the left bank of the Rhine in the event of Austria's gaining Silesia and the hegemony over South Germany. Italy was also surrounded by suitors. Austria promised her Southern Tirol and the Isonzo frontier. France offered Nice and Tunis, to which was generously added the Swiss canton Ticino. The chief obstacle to a triple alliance was Rome, which both Austria and France desired to leave in the Pope's hands. In South Germany, too, there was sympathy for France, " in memory of the Confederation of the Rhine," as Bismarck said, but still more from an antipathy to Prussia that arose out of democratic feeling in Württemberg and clerical in Bavaria. On the other hand, Bismarck had contrived to turn public opinion in the south against Napoleon also by exposing his annexation schemes. By August 1866 he had already formed defensive and offensive alliances with Baden, Bavaria, and Württemberg, and these he published in 1867, doubtless with pacific intent. Nevertheless, Austria was arming and was playing with the idea of an alliance into which Italy might after all have been induced to come, while Denmark would certainly have done so. These possibilities grew increasingly more probable with every year that Austria was allowed for her regeneration. On the other hand, it was more than unlikely that Russia, which was well-disposed towards and under obligations to Prussia and had long been hostile to Austria and France, would look on passively while these two divided central Europe between them. Bismarck's firm but by no means provocative attitude did nothing, indeed, to prevent war, but it did localize the entirely inevitable struggle and prevent a general European conflagration.

Whereas with most great wars the question of responsibility forms an everlasting bone of contention, every unprejudiced judge can in this case answer it unequivocally. In 1868 the Queen of Spain had been driven out by an insurrection. The Cortes decided to offer the throne to the Hereditary Prince Leopold of Hohen-zollern-Sigmaringen. He was a Catholic, on the paternal side the grandson of a Murat, and on the maternal a grandson of Stépha-nie Beauharnais, adopted daughter of Napoleon I. Besides, the appointment of his brother to the Roumanian throne had been not only approved, but even protected by Napoleon III himself. There was therefore nothing insidious about the candidature. Bismarck supported acceptance because he saw in it commercial, political, and diplomatic advantages for Germany; this constellation, in fact, would be " a Spanish fly in the back of Napoleon's neck." The assumption cannot be lightly dismissed, however, that he saw in this complication a welcome opportunity for guiding the war towards a favourable moment and accounting for it by a

The Spanish bomb-shell

267

cause that would make France appear to be the peace-breaker. And indeed the "Spanish bomb" made a terrific din in Paris. The Foreign Minister, the Duc de Gramont, who was a typical diplomat, self-satisfied, uninformed, a hollow phrasemaker — in short, as Bismarck said, an ox — announced in the Legislative Assembly that France could not allow the balance of power in Europe to be disturbed by the elevation of a Hohenzollern to the throne of Charles V, and the honour of France imperilled. "In the event," he concluded, "we shall know how to do our duty without hesitation or weakness." Thiers, who entered the hall during this speech, cried in horror: "But this is madness!" But his protest was drowned in the enthusiastic applause. On July 9, at Bad Ems, the French Ambassador Benedetti demanded that the King should "forbid the Prince of Hohenzollern to accept the throne." The King replied that he could not exert his authority to make him go back on his word, but that on the other hand he would not restrain him from so doing, and should he be so inclined, would certainly give his approval. The Paris papers were furious at this calm attitude on the part of the King, which left Prussia unassailable. The phrase went round: "*La Prusse cane* (Prussia funks it)!" The *Pays* wrote: "The Caudine yoke is ready, the Prussians will bow beneath it . . . had Prussia spoken to us as we spoke to her, we should have been on the move long ago." And the *Liberté*: "Will Prussia refuse to fight? Very well, then we shall jab her in the back with the butts of our rifles and make her flee across the Rhine and leave us the left bank." Bismarck was well pleased with this outcry. "All that I care about," he wrote to Lothar Bucher, "is that we should be the ones who are challenged. Even as a student I was particularly keen on that point." But on July 12 Prince Anton von Hohenzollern renounced the Spanish throne in the name of his son, who, from a high moral sense of responsibility, did not wish "to plunge Germany into a war and at the same time bring Spain a bloody conflict as a dowry." The King thereupon wrote to his wife: "It is a load off my heart." And the French Minister-President said: "*C'est la paix.*" Napoleon thought so too, but he added: "I am sorry, for the opportunity was favourable."

But at this point France began to change into a lunatic asylum. Public, parliament, press, court clique — one and all felt they were not yet "satisfied." Gramont telegraphed to Benedetti: "If this renunciation is to have full effect, it seems to me essential that the King of Prussia should associate himself with it and give us the assurance that never again will he agree to this candidature." The King's bearing in the face of this piece of insolence is extremely affecting. When Benedetti communicated this imputation to him on the promenade on July 13, the King, although inwardly indignant, tried in a perfectly friendly and almost beseeching tone to make it clear to him that he was asking an impossibility. The course of this conversation he described to Bismarck in brief in the famous Ems telegram, leaving it to him to publish it. Only a crazy party opponent or an incurable French chauvinist can maintain that Bismarck forged it and transformed it into a challenge. He even softened it by leaving out the unfavourable introductory sentence: " Count Benedetti stopped me on the promenade to demand of me, in what became finally a very aggressive manner "; by substituting " challenge " for " imputation "; and by replacing the close: " that His Majesty has nothing more to say to the Ambassador " — which sounded like an ejection — by the more neutral phrase: " has no further information to give him." True, he shortened it by nearly a third, though without omitting anything of importance, but gave it thereby a sharper, more concentrated and epigrammatic form: he, so to speak, dramatized it. And although it had not in itself anything provocative, it was bound so to affect the French psyche — as Bismarck was well aware. He admitted it when he said it would " have the effect of a red rag on the Gallic bull." The formulation of the telegram was, then, nothing but a curtailed editing such as occurs daily in diplomatic and journalistic life. But that he published the telegram at all was what led to the war.

In the decisive sitting of the Legislative Assembly of July 15, *" A Berlin! "* which voted almost unanimously for mobilization, the exact text of the Ems telegram had not yet been communicated. The few deputies who wished to wait until it was laid before them were dubbed " traitors " and " Prussians." Worse still was another point. The King had, even after dismissing him, had a conversation with Benedetti in the reserved saloon of the Ems railway station, from which it appeared that he did not regard the negotiations as irrevocably broken off. Gramont knew this and adroitly suppressed it. France wanted the war and therefore was easily persuaded that Prussia wanted it too. In all Prussia, however, no one wanted it but Bismarck, and he only in a form that would put France in the wrong. And had not France been France, he would not have wanted it in any form. This is the apparently complicated but at bottom extremely simple truth.

The cause of the war, says the English Ambassador, was public feeling. The Chamber, wrote a French journalist, is like a Leyden jar. Commercial circles, industry, and finance were, as usually in France, against the war, and so likewise were the politically uninterested country regions. The Empress considered it essential in order to secure the throne to her dearly beloved son, and pictured it as a military promenade of a few weeks, on the analogy of Solferino. The Emperor wavered, as always. On the one hand, he realized the danger; on the other, he conceived optimistic ideas as to the attitude of Austria and South Germany. Military circles were eager to try out the chassepot and the machine-gun. The salons hungered for sensation. The press sent off its usual fireworks. Truly French was the way in which erotic imagination mingled with the cloud of megalomania, frivolity, and resentment — the *Gaulois* promised that the Turcos would bring back cart-loads of women to France. But it was only in Paris that the war was " interesting." France was once more the marionette of her centralization, the victim of the " *ville tentaculaire.*"

And from the Madeleine to the Place de la Bastille there rang the cry: " *A Berlin, à Berlin!* "

BOOK V: IMPERIALISM AND IMPRESSIONISM

From the Franco-German War to the World War

CHAPTER I

BLACK FRIDAY

" Unconstrained activity, of whatever kind it may be, goes bankrupt in the end."

Goethe

Who makes reality?

Who makes reality? Not the " realist," for he merely runs at its heels. It is certain that even the genius does not create out of nothing, but he does discover a new reality, in that it has been seen by no one before him and was, in a sense, not there until he did so. The *existing* reality, with which the realist has to reckon, is always at its last gasp. Bismarck transformed the face of central Europe by divination, by his Röntgen glance, by conjecture; in a word, by imagination. Imagination is needed and used by Cæsar and Napoleon just as much as by Dante and Shakspere. As for the others — the practical, positive men who live and work in the light of " facts " — they, if we look closely, are not in the world of reality at all. They move in a world that is no longer true and are in much the same strange position as, for instance, the inhabitants of a star which is so far removed from its sun that its light only reaches them after one or two days. The daylight which these beings saw would be, so to say, *post-dated*. And most people take a false illumination of this kind, the appearance of which carries conviction, for daylight. What they call the present is an optical illusion arising out of the inadequacy of their senses, the slowness of their apperception. The world is always of yesterday.

A genius lives aloof from these sense-deceptions and is accordingly called unworldly. It is the fate alike of the genius who observes and the genius who acts. Not only Goethe and Kant were regarded as fantastic dreamers, but, at the beginning of their careers, Alexander the Great and Frederick the Great, Mohammed and Luther, Cromwell and Bismarck also. And unworldly, " world-remote," was, after all, no bad label for them, since the sclerosed world of the present had in fact become remote to them. One is therefore tempted to say, generally, that all men live in an

273

imaginary, chimerical, illegitimate, invented world — except one, the poet.

Great men are a sort of axe applied to life. No sooner do they make contact with existence than it begins to clarify and divide, to refine and dissolve, disintegrate and become transparent. In face of their clear ecstasies life unveils itself, and all obscurities sink heavily to earth.

Bismarck's generation The penultimate section of the Modern Age, the double decade from 1870 to 1890, is Bismarck's generation. In the well-known opening to the first of his *Thoughts Out of Season* Nietzsche accounts for the German victory which ushers in this period by a series of exceedingly sound but entirely unspiritual qualities: " strict military discipline, natural bravery and endurance, superiority in the leaders, unity and obedience among the led — in short, elements which have nothing to do with culture, but by which we were enabled to triumph over opponents who lacked the most important of these elements." But surely we may also talk of the victory of the idea, for which we have to thank not only the new Germany of self-discipline and technical knowledge, but the old Germany of poets and thinkers. In the brain and heart of the man who created that work of art, German unity, everything that had ever brought honour to the German name was vividly present: the power to found churches as Luther did, the power to win intellectual battles as Lessing did, the power to construct historical systems as Hegel did. In Moltke, too, the spirit of classical German philosophy held sway. He had the same acumen in forming conceptions, the same sovereign methodology, and the same penetrating grasp of the objects in view. In his encyclopædic brain there was an exact topography, not only of all French military roads, but of all the highways of human thought and action. There was something, too, of the Kantian spirit — the categorical imperative, empirical realism, and transcendental idealism — in the nation that won that war. In the World War this national army still possessed the old discipline and precision, intelligence and informedness, only, having been infected meanwhile by the materialism of the West, it no longer had the same spirit. Otherwise it would have been invincible.

Yet had not Bismarck a share in building up that Germany which thirsted for gold and hungered for recognition, the Germany of self-glorification and self-indulgence, of flat façade and sham stucco, which was born of unity? The reply is ready to hand in Georg Simmel's remark: " Nothing ever happened in the world as the prophets and leaders wished it to do, but without prophets and leaders it would not have happened at all." We must remember also a point that was made in the Introduction to this book: that the age is the creation of its great man, but also that the great man is just as much the product of the age. The age is his breath of life, the sum of his biological premisses; he cannot emancipate himself from this medium. He belongs to it as does every living thing to its species: the structure of its spiritual anatomy, its intellectual metabolism, is his also. The philosophy of Socrates, wise and virtuous as it was, is nevertheless the growth of an age of sophistry. Shakspere, as an imperishable reflection of the Elizabethan era, is a barbarian; Luther, as the son of the Reformation world, a grand plebeian; and Nietzsche had no choice but to be a Darwinian and Antichristian.

The smoothness and precision with which the German war-machine functioned in 1870 was a great surprise to all Europe, and almost equally surprising was the complete failure of the French. Their relative positions were indeed paradoxical from the standpoint of national psychology. For whereas the soul of the German had, in the entire course of his history, been dominated by the brewing, the obscure, the world-remote, the formless — in a word, the cloud — the ideal of the French mind had ever been strict centripetality, order, *clarté, logique*. But it may occasionally happen that a specially tenacious and long-cherished habit of mind will suddenly swing to the opposite extreme on coming up against reality. We have shown in the preceding volume that the Rationalist trend towards regularity and clarity, which produced such admirable results in French art and literature at their highest peaks, may easily lead to pedantry, the mortal enemy of reality, akin to foolishness. On the other hand, it was inevitable that the German urge to the intellectual world-outlook should sooner or later express itself in actually mastering its objects. Edmond de Goncourt tells us in his war diary that Berthelot (a great savant, epoch-making in chemistry, particularly the chemistry of alcohols) once said to him: " No, it is not so much the superiority of the artillery, it is something quite different, and I will explain it to you. The state of things is this: when the Chief of the Prussian General Staff receives an order to send up an army corps at a particular time to a particular point, he gets his maps, studies the ground, calculates the time that each corps will require to

The French deployment

275

cover a particular portion of the route. . . . *Our* General Staff officer will do none of these things. He goes about his amusements in the evening, and next morning comes on to the battlefield and asks whether the troops have arrived and which is the best place for the attack. It has been so since the beginning of the campaign, and I repeat that this is the cause of our defeats." The mitrailleuse or "bullet-squirt," a sort of early machine-gun, on which in France the highest hopes were set, proved a failure. On the other hand, the chassepot, a rifled breech-loader, was definitely superior to the German needle-gun (which was being improved when the war broke out) because of its greater range and rapidity of loading, its flatter trajectory, and its force of penetration, particularly when medium and long ranges were in question. But the German command contrived to neutralize this sensible disadvantage by dissolving their company columns into loose, quick lines of skirmishers which presented no closed ranks as a target, with the result that the superiority of the chassepot was not effective in any of the major actions.

In France one army deployed at Strassburg under Marshal MacMahon, and a second at Metz under Marshal Bazaine. According to the French plan of campaign, both were to unite as the "Rhine Army," cross the river, and, by a swift and sudden attack on the Black Forest, separate south-west Germany from Prussia and compel it to be neutral, if not to join forces with France. Simultaneously one French fleet was to appear in the North Sea and a second in the Baltic, and these, by landing troops, were to tie up considerable portions of the Prussian forces. After the initial successes it was hoped, too, that Austria's intervention might be relied upon. In any case, Napoleon was expecting a short campaign. He wrote to tell MacMahon that he need only arrange for a temporary substitute as governor of Algeria, and that the war would be a little recreation for him. It was most probably his intention to offer Prussia the hegemony over South Germany after the successful preliminary battles and to receive compensations on the Rhine and in Belgium. In support of this theory, it may be recalled that he left strong reserves behind at Châlons-sur-Marne, not so very far from the Belgian frontier.

Of all the assumptions on which these military and political plans were based, not one came true. First, South Germany promptly sided with Prussia. On July 18 an Austrian imperial council took place, at which the Archduke Albrecht argued vigorously in favour of entering the war on the side of France, while Andrássy as energetically opposed it. The decision came with the definite announcement by von John, the Chief of the General Staff, that the army was not in a condition to fight. Then French landings were prevented by the vigilant North German navy, and in September both fleets had to withdraw. Most pitiful of all was the failure of the projected Rhine campaign. It proved that the French railway system was utterly inadequate to deal with such a rapid frontier concentration. Within a short time the railway stations were overcrowded and the lines blocked; half of the army had to set out on foot. The War Minister, Lebœuf, had said: "We are ready to the last gaiter-button." But not only were there no gaiter-buttons; there was a lack of everything: camp kettles and cooking-utensils, tents and harness, medicines and stretchers, forage and munitions. The commissariat broke down completely. The depots were in hopeless confusion. Many soldiers never found their cadres at all. Most of the divisions were without their baggage. The infantry had too much baggage and too little money. The artillery was in bad condition and never in the right place. It had been assumed as a matter of course that the war would be fought on German soil, and no French maps had been supplied to the staffs. Finally, the fortresses were in a very neglected state. Count Daru, Gramont's predecessor, said afterwards with true French sophistry: "The best proof of the peaceful intentions of France at that time was the complete absence of preparation on our side, the lack of all precautionary measures, even the most elementary and essential. Did ever one see the like?"

The German plan of campaign was superior to the French in that it rested on no preconceived scheme by which to stand or fall, but made allowances for every eventuality. Above all, it had the advantage of being really carried through. The Prussian mobilization proceeded almost without incident and according to a carefully worked-out military timetable. In the marching-tables every unit had its place of entrainment, day and hour of departure, length of journey, halt for refreshments, and point of detrainment precisely settled. On the evening of July 15, when Moltke entered the General Staff headquarters in Berlin, where the forms of mobilization lay in readiness, complete but for his signature, he merely said as he opened the cupboard: "*Also doch!* (So, then!)" And he told a friend at the time that he had "never had less to do than now." Roon also reports in his memoirs that this second

The conduct of the war on the German side

277

half of July was the lightest in worry or work of his whole official life. Nevertheless Moltke was prepared for the possibility that the enemy might get ahead of him in the deployment, and when the war broke out, he said: " If the enemy crosses the Rhine before July 25, we shall be unable to stop him and must try to force him back later; if he waits until August 1 to do so, we shall fight him on the left bank of the Rhine; and if by August 4 he has not invaded us, it will be on that day that we shall cross the frontier." It was the last of these alternatives which happened. On August 3 there were three Prussian armies concentrated between the Moselle and the Rhine: the I Army under General von Steinmetz, the II Army under Prince Friedrich Karl, the III Army under the Crown Prince. Moltke's intention was, broadly, to take Paris and force the enemy from the south of France up to the north. He says emphatically, in his *Geschichte des deutsch-französischen Krieges:* " It is a delusion to suppose that we can fix upon a plan of campaign far ahead and carry it through to the end. The first encounter with the enemy main forces creates a new situation according to the way it falls out. Much that one may have intended becomes impracticable, and many a thing becomes possible which could not have been forecast. To take in the altered circumstances and thereupon to arrange and carry out with decision that which is expedient is all that the supreme command can do." This elasticity secured for him the initiative throughout the war. On August 2 the French occupied Saarbrücken in the presence of the Emperor. This was reported to Paris as a brilliant victory: " Our army," said the official report, " flooded the Prussian territory." It proved to be a mere gust of air, for they had had to deal with only three companies. On August 4 the advanced guard of the German III Army crossed the frontier punctually according to Moltke's program and took Weissenburg; and on August 5 the same army defeated MacMahon in the battle of Wörth and forced him to fall back on the fortified camp at Châlons. On August 6 portions of the I and II Armies attacked Bazaine and stormed the strongly entrenched heights of Spicheren, which were considered well-nigh impregnable. Portions of the III Army, under General von Werder, bombarded Strassburg. Thereupon Bazaine decided to march to Châlons also and join MacMahon. But his retreat was cut off by the great battles of Vionville–Mars-la-Tour on August 16 and Gravelotte–Saint-Privat on the 18th, and his whole army forced into the fortress of Metz and there imprisoned. MacMahon for his part now left Châlons to relieve Metz. To prevent this, Moltke had recourse to the famous right wheel on the Meuse — the wheel of the whole front from west to north, a movement that is among the most difficult tasks that can be demanded of an army. At the battle of Beaumont on August 30 MacMahon was thrown across the Meuse, attacked in front and rear by two German armies simultaneously (the newly-formed Meuse Army and the III Army), and forced into the town of Sedan. A murderous bombardment then brought about the capitulation of this town on September 2 and with it the surrender of the Emperor, the generals, the whole fighting force, and great numbers of field and fortress guns. As Bazaine had not succeeded in breaking through the ring round Metz, this meant that France had lost almost the whole of her regular army. But the Frenchman, as Hermann Grimm remarked at the time, " is not so organized intellectually that he can regard himself as beaten." It was promptly announced that the imprisoned Emperor was dethroned, and a provisional "Government of National Defence" was formed which proclaimed "War to the last," and by its slogan: "Not a stone of our forts, not an inch of our land!" wrecked the peace negotiations between Bismarck and Favre, the new Minister for Foreign Affairs. The Minister of the Interior, Gambetta, an extremely energetic and alert Jewish advocate, left Paris in a balloon to organize the *levée en masse* from Tours and in a very short time had eight hundred thousand men on the move. Their fighting value was, however, considerably less than that of the German regulars. All the same, twelve more great battles had to be fought before peace could be concluded. In the west the newly-formed Army of the Loire took the offensive, hoping, with the assistance of a great sortie by the Paris Army, to raise the siege of the capital, which had meanwhile been completely surrounded. It actually succeeded at Coulmiers in forcing the Bavarians under General von der Tann to retreat and to evacuate Orleans. But at Beaune-la-Rolande its offensive went to pieces, and the Paris sortie also failed. Orleans was again occupied and the Loire Army practically annihilated in the winter battle in front of Le Mans. In the north a second French militia army was likewise put out of action by German victories at Amiens, on the Hallue, at Bapaume and at Saint-Quentin. In the east General Bourbaki had taken over the supreme command, and attempted to push back Werder's corps, but he was defeated in the three days' battle on the Lisaine, and his broken army forced to cross into Switzerland. Of the great fortresses, Strassburg had capitulated on September 27, Metz exactly a month later, and in December — again on the ill-omened 27th — the bombardment of the capital set in. The surrender took place in January. At German headquarters there had been two opposed parties, one advocating the method of starvation, the other that of bombardment. To the latter belonged Bismarck, who was supported by German public opinion; the former was led by Moltke, the Crown Prince, and his Chief of Staff, Blumenthal. Both Bismarck and Roon maintained, in their memoirs, that feminine influence played a part in the matter: that it had been conveyed to headquarters from England that the " Mecca of civilization " could not be bombarded as though it were an ordinary fortress (the Crown Princess and Moltke's and Blumenthal's wives were Englishwomen). If this was really so, then the women were probably right for once. Only the outer forts of Paris were subdued. The bombardment hardly touched the real fortifications. By January 7 Paris, it is true, was without meat, as de Goncourt notes in his diary; " neither can one rely on vegetables," he adds, " butter no one mentions now, and even fat, unless it be tallow or carriage grease, seems to have disappeared . . . cheese is a memory, and if you want potatoes, you will need protection." Lamp-oil and candles, coal and wood, were equally unobtainable. As a delicacy there were camel's kidneys and elephant sausage from the Jardin des Plantes. One jeweller displayed fresh eggs in jewel-cases in his window. The price of a well-nourished rat was one and a half francs.

The neutrals   Meanwhile the neutral states had begun to take part in the war in their own way. France having been obliged to withdraw her garrison from the Papal States for use in its own country, this territory was occupied by Italian troops on September 20 and Rome was declared the capital of Italy. The proud motto *" Italia farà da se "* has not really justified itself up till now in the history of the country. For Lombardy it had to thank the French victory of Solferino, for Venetia the Prussian victory of Königgrätz, for Rome the German victory of Sedan, for Trieste and Trent the Entente, while itself suffering defeats at San Martino and Custozza, on the Isonzo and the Piave. When Italy's delegates to the Berlin Congress requested compensations for the Bosnian occupation, a Russian diplomat remarked to Bismarck: " How can Italy demand aggrandizement? She hasn't lost a battle!" As regards Russia, Prince Gorchakov, the Imperial Chancellor, stated in a circular letter on October 3 that the Treaty of Paris had been broken several times and that Russia no longer considered herself bound by the decision which declared the Black Sea to be neutral. Thereupon, at Bismarck's instigation, a conference was called, at which Russia secured the passage of the Straits for her mercantile fleet, and the right to keep warships in the Black Sea and to build fortifications on it. This was a sort of acknowledgment on the part of Prussia for the diplomatic pressure that Russia had exercised on Austria at the outbreak of war. In England sympathy had at first been on the side of Germany, particularly as Bismarck had seen to it that the negotiations into which Benedetti had entered with him as far back as 1866 should become known there in good time. Then, when the unbroken string of defeats made the annexation of Alsace-Lorraine a certainty, more and more voices were heard asking for intervention on behalf of the vanquished. Public opinion veered round to some extent when Carlyle wrote his letter to *The Times* on November 18, in which he said that the Germans had only taken back what had once been "wrenched" from them, and that "noble, patient, deep, pious, and solid Germany" should be at length welded into a nation and become Queen of the Continent instead of "vapouring, vainglorious, gesticulating, quarrelsome, restless France." Soon after Sedan, Thiers made the round of the European capitals in the hope of persuading governments to intervene, but everywhere he received rebuffs. Gladstone told him that the Cabinet could only act simply as mediator. Beust said that Austria could only decide when she knew what Russia was going to do. Gorchakov could only promise to do his best to bring about an acceptable peace, Victor Emmanuel retired behind his ministry, which pointed out that without parliament it could take no steps —and parliament was not there. Beust, who politically was always on any side opposed to Prussia, summed up the position with resignation, saying: " I no longer see Europe." Bismarck was nevertheless full of fears. " The least shock given by one cabinet to another would have sufficed," he wrote. " The danger of Europe's intervention is a daily anxiety to me." And in fact Russia or England had only to summon a congress, and everything would have been in the melting-pot.

Neither was the union of the princes of the German Empire brought about without much anxiety on Bismarck's part. The form which he finally succeeded in imposing on those concerned was that of a letter which the King of Bavaria, as the sovereign next in rank to the King of Prussia, presented to that monarch in the name of all the German princes and free cities. Ludwig II put up a long resistance. His romantic mediæval reminiscences gave him visions of Wittelsbachers and Hohenzollerns alternately succeeding to the Imperial throne, and he was only brought to write the letter when he realized that the King of Saxony or the Grand Duke of Baden would do so if he did not. After the proclamation of the Empire, at which he was not present, he put on mourning. But neither was William I by any means satisfied with the course of affairs. "What good is a brevet majority to me?" To which Bismarck replied: "Your Majesty surely does not want to remain a neuter for ever: a presidency?" Finally the King signified his agreement to the new dignity, though only if he received the title "Emperor of Germany." But Bismarck, for constitutional and other reasons, considered "German Emperor" to be the only possibility. The King was so annoyed over this that he cut Bismarck dead at the proclamation festivities.

The Peace   As the majority of the fortresses and a third of the country were in the hands of the Germans, there could no longer be any question that the French had lost the war. To meet the situation Victor Hugo produced the formula: "Prussia has won the victory, France the glory." Thiers now entered upon peace negotiations with Bismarck. According to a map prepared by the Prussian General Staff, the original demands were considerably in excess of what was eventually obtained: included a much larger slice of Lorraine, with Longuyon, Briey, Nancy, Lunéville, and rounded off to the south by Belfort and Montbéliard. In the end it was agreed that Prussia should have the whole of Alsace without Belfort, and about a fifth of the former duchy of Lorraine. Of this, about a quarter, including Metz, is French-speaking territory, and this portion was added only for strategic reasons, based on the so-called "glacis argument." These conditions must be regarded as moderate. To renounce the famous "Gap of Belfort" was from a purely military standpoint inopportune, and that Bismarck's original demand for a war indemnity of six milliards was not excessive is proved by the astonishing rapidity with which the French nation raised the five to which he finally reduced his figure. And, after all, who in all Europe could have prevented Germany, with her nine hundred thousand war-trained mobile troops, from keeping the mineral area of Briey and the important junction of Nancy, seeing that her relations with Russia were good, that England was disinterested, and Austria and Italy impotent? On the other hand it is repeatedly claimed that it was the Treaty of Frankfurt which drove France to her radical policy of revenge. And here the question presents itself: how could any treaty have been drawn up that did *not* beget these feelings? To have limited the annexations to purely German provinces, or even to Alsace merely, would have made no difference. Even a complete renunciation of any conquered territory would still have left the thorn of defeat in the nation's pride. A people that could demand revenge for Königgrätz was obviously to be appeased only by victories of its own.

In the National Assembly, which had met at Bordeaux to discuss the peace conditions, Victor Hugo said: "Gentlemen, there are in Strasbourg two statues, one of Gutenberg, and one of Kléber. We feel within us a voice adjuring Gutenberg not to permit civilization to be suppressed and Kléber not to permit the Republic to be suppressed." And Louis Blanc cried: "Treat the Alsatians like slaves! The men who were our brothers! Hand them over like a flock of sheep, when there is not a drop of blood in their veins that they did not offer us, did not enthusiastically shed for us! Never, never, never!" Whereupon the peace preliminaries were accepted by an overwhelming majority.

Bismarck would have disarmed Paris, but Favre had opposed this to the utmost. The result was to evoke the *Commune de Paris,* which adopted the Jacobin principles of 1793. Well-to-do inhabitants were forced to agree to extortionate demands, numerous "hostages" — among them the Archbishop — were shot, the churches and certain public buildings plundered, the Tuileries palace, the Palais de Justice, the Treasury, the Hôtel de Ville, and the Prefecture of Police were set on fire. Only after two months' fighting did MacMahon succeed in entering the city at the head of regular troops. The "bloody week," in which he suppressed the insurrection in a savage war of barricades, was the most ghastly butchery of civilians in modern history. It was just at this moment that a Chinese embassy arrived in Paris. Excuses were offered, but the head of the mission replied: "No need for apology. You are young, you Occidentals, you have practically no history. It is always thus: siege and commune, that is the normal history of mankind."

The Commune

Germany, on the other hand, received her five milliards, a sum quite beyond everyone's conception at that time. Yes, Germany — the land of frugal lower middle class, of officers, dreamy professors, and musicians — had become rich! The consequence was a gigantic crash on the Exchange. That 9th of May 1873 on which it happened is known as "Black Friday" and is as terrible a memory to the financial world as was the battle of Kossovo to the Serbs and that of Cannæ to the Romans. But the years which preceded and followed it are called the "Founders' Years," for in that period everybody was "founding" something. Every week produced new partnerships, societies, syndicates, and joint-stock companies. The share — the absent employer, as it has been called — is the most modern and powerful form of capitalism. It is, according to Shaw's ingenious interpretation of the *Nibelungen Ring*, the helmet of darkness of Alberich, who was the "creator of capitalism." "This helmet," says Shaw, "is a very common article in our streets, where it generally takes the form of a tall hat. It makes a man invisible as a shareholder, and changes him into various shapes, such as a pious Christian, a subscriber to hospitals, a benefactor of the poor, a model husband and father, a shrewd, practical, independent Englishman, and what not, when he is really a pitiable parasite on the commonwealth." But occasionally it renders Alberich's hoard of gold invisible also.

The solid business man and the correct official, the exclusive aristocrat and the secluded scholar, even the army and the clergy, were all seized by the fever of speculation. This resulted in over-production, industrial crises, mass competition, the sinking in value of bills to that of the paper they were written on; the break-up of many private fortunes, the closing-down or reduction of numerous factories, the cutting of wages, and the dismissal of workers. And this, again, led to demonstrations, strikes, tumults, anti-capitalist propaganda on paper and at meetings. In May 1878 a tinker's prentice named Hödel made an unsuccessful revolver attack on the eighty-one-year-old Emperor. A proposal to increase the severity of the criminal law which Bismarck then put before the Reichstag was rejected. A few weeks later a certain Doctor Nobiling fired twice at the Emperor from a shot-gun, wounding him rather seriously — in fact, his life was only saved by his helmet. Bismarck now carried through his "Law against Social-Democratic aims which are dangerous to the community." The effect of this was the prohibition of all "leftward" societies and newspapers, the institution of frequent domiciliary searches, imprisonments, and evictions, while further developments included the introduction of the contemptible *agent provocateur* system, brutal despotism, odious chicanery, and a socialistic martyrdom by which the young party gained many friends. Bismarck was himself far too shrewd not to know that no intellectual movement can be suppressed by brute force, and his own scheme aimed rather at taking the worker's welfare in hand himself and so étatizing the whole movement. To this end were established such measures as the sickness insurance of 1883, the accident insurance of 1884, and the invalid and old-age insurance of 1889 — which, however, was rejected by the Social Democrats as a policy of " political almsgiving."

If Bismarck won but half a victory over the Red International, the outcome of the " culture-war " which he led against the Black International may almost be called a defeat. The name, invented by Virchow, who was a great scholar and a little politician, is misleading; for actually the cultural forces — religion, tradition, spirituality — were represented by the Church, while the civilization tendencies — education, statecraft, and material progress — were rather to be found on the opposite side. The original cause of the conflict is to be found in the dogma of Infallibility, proclaimed by Pius IX on July 18, 1870, the eve of the French declaration of war. Herein it was declared that the Pope, if he should speak *ex cathedra* and define any doctrine concerning faith or morals, was to be regarded as infallible. This caused dissensions among the Papists. The "State Catholics " recognized the pope's infallibility in the confessional domain, but disputed his competence in state matters; the " Old Catholics " refused to admit his primacy over any wider range than that defined by the Fathers of the Church and the Councils. One party formed a regular sect, which introduced the German liturgy, abolished celibacy, and elected its own bishop; others confined themselves to simply rejecting the new dogma. The differences became acute when the Curia made an unsuccessful demand for the removal of Old Catholics from the teaching profession. In the Reichstag Bismarck relied on the Liberals. Opposed to him was the Centre party, reinforced by Conservatives, Evangelicals, and all the secessionalists : Poles, Welfs, Alsatians. Great resentment was aroused by a series of government measures at this time. There was the " pulpit paragraph," directed against the misuse of the pulpit for political

285

agitation; the introduction of civil marriage, secular school-inspection, the " cultural examination " in German, history, philosophy, and the classics for clergy, and, finally, the dissolution of the Jesuit Order and other congregations. The clergy talked of Nero and Diocletian, and Bismarck delivered his famous *mot* on Canossa; in 1873 Kullmann, a Catholic cooper's apprentice, made an attempt on his life. The conflict reached its climax in 1875, when the so-called *Sperrgesetz* enacted that all parishes and bishoprics that did not explicitly bind themselves to obey the Government should be deprived of state aid.

Pio Nono had called Bismarck a Protestant Philip, but the Chancellor was neither an unpractical Habsburger nor a crazy Spaniard. He bowed to the force of the fact that (as he afterwards put it) the Centre was an " invincible tower " and that one could not govern contrary to the conscience of two fifths of the population. The change in the Papacy which occurred in 1878 made reconciliation easier. Bit by bit the anti-Catholic restrictions were removed, and all that remained unchanged of the essential rulings was state inspection of schools and obligatory civil marriage.

The Berlin Congress This same year in which Bismarck was forced to give way on questions of decisive home policy brought him a great triumph in the domain of foreign affairs. It was under his presidency that the Congress of the great powers met in Berlin in June 1878 to conclude the sixth Russo-Turkish war. In 1875 insurrection had broken out in Herzegovina. In an appeal to the powers the rebels proclaimed that the *rayah,* the Christian of the Ottoman Empire, had up till then been " a dumb creature," " lower than the animal, born to eternal slavery," and that they were now determined to fight for freedom or die to the last man. They asked for complete religious liberty, the right to give evidence in law-courts, a definite assessment of taxes, the abolition of the land-tax (which, as in pre-Revolutionary France, had led to great oppression), and the possibility of acquiring land of their own. The Bulgarians also revolted. The ghastly horrors that the Sultan's irregular troops practised upon them were exposed by Gladstone in fiery speeches and writings in which, after the good old English tradition, Christian humanity and political business instinct were the concurrent motives. For the British Eastern policy had undergone a very significant change: the principle of Turkey's integrity (at least in its former unqualified sense) had been given up, because the annexation of Egypt had now for some time been in prospect, this having become of incalculable value to England since the reopening of the Suez Canal. But when the insurrection, in spite of Serbian and Montenegrin support, looked like being put down, and Russia, having first mobilized six army corps in the autumn of 1876, proceeded to declare war in the spring of 1877, England's old anxiety about Constantinople revived. Many voices were heard to advocate a union of the Western powers with Turkey, such as had been arranged in the Crimean War. At these two critical moments Carlyle again addressed himself to *The Times*. He described the Turks as being the element of anarchy in Europe and declared that they deserved nothing more than an emphatic order to turn their face *quam primum* to the East. " The newspaper outcry against Russia is no more respectable to me than the howling of Bedlam, proceeding as it does from the deepest ignorance, egoism, and paltry national jealousy." It was in the first of these letters that there occurred the famous winged word: " *the unspeakable Turk*," usually, but wrongly, attributed to Gladstone. Before the commencement of hostilities Russia had assured herself of the neutrality of Austria, who in exchange had bargained for the occupation of Bosnia and Herzegovina. It was chiefly owing to Bismarck that all the other powers remained neutral; this he achieved by obtaining a statement from the Tsar that he would not touch Constantinople and would leave it to a European congress to settle the peace terms. After a military convention had been concluded with Roumania, a Russian corps crossed the Danube and occupied the Dobruja. The main army forced the Danube crossing at Sistova, took the Shipka Pass, which commands the Balkans, and pushed on still farther. Then, however, came a turn. The energetic Osman Pasha entrenched himself at Plevna and threatened the right flank of the Russians. Their counter-attacks were bloodily repulsed, and, with a third of their effectives killed or wounded, the Russians were then forced to proceed to a regular siege. This was conducted by General Totleben, the redoubtable defender of Sevastopol. Had the Turks taken the offensive and gone forward, the Russians might have been thrown back over the Balkans, especially as their rifles and guns were inferior and they had not even a numerical superiority. This superiority was attained only through the advent of the Roumanian auxiliary corps, and in spite of this, it took starvation to reduce Plevna. With the achievement of this, however, the war was as good as over. Without encountering further resistance worthy of the name, the Russians now took Philippopolis and Adrianople and pushed on to the gates of Constantinople. There the provisional Peace of San Stefano was drawn up. Bosnia and Herzegovina were declared independent, and Turkey ceded large stretches of Armenia to Russia, and the greater part of her European possessions to Serbia, Montenegro, and Bulgaria. Bulgaria, in particular, it was proposed to enlarge by the addition of Eastern Roumelia and nearly all Macedonia, reaching as far as the Ægean, which would have made her the premier Balkan power and limited the Porte's European possessions substantially to Albania, Constantinople, Adrianople, and the Chalcidic Peninsula, with Salonika. But both Austria and England protested against this, and a European war loomed on the horizon. The danger was averted by the Berlin Congress, at which Bismarck acted the " honest broker," as he put it. (Bleichröder, who, if anyone, should know, declared that there was no such thing as an honest broker.) After lengthy negotiations the Turkish losses were greatly reduced, though, even so, they remained sufficiently serious. Russia received (in Asia) Kars, Ardahan, and Batum; Roumania, as a reward for her services, was forced to restore to Russia the portion of Bessarabia that had been allotted to her by the Treaty of Paris, accepting in return the boggy region of the Dobruja; Montenegro was more than doubled in size, Serbia enlarged by the addition of Old Serbia. Bulgaria was created a principality, independent, but tributary to the Sultan, and limited to the area between the Danube and the Balkans, while East Roumelia remained under Turkish dominion, but was granted its own administration. The great powers advised the Porte to cede Thessaly and eastern Epirus to Greece, and this she in fact did in 1881. England received the important naval base of Cyprus. Austria was given the right to occupy Bosnia and Herzegovina — to the great disgust of the Italians, who claimed the Adriatic with its hinterland as their *mare nostro* and demanded as their indemnity Trent, whereas Bismarck proposed Albania for them. Russia's hope of turning the Balkan Peninsula into a protectorate of her own by autonomizing the Christian nations of the Balkans was not fulfilled. Roumania and Serbia (which soon afterwards were raised to the rank of kingdoms) relied on Austria, but Bulgaria conducted her own policy. The Sobranje had elected Prince Alexander of Battenberg as ruler, and in 1885 he took advantage of a rising in Philippopolis to assume the title of Prince of both Bulgarias and to incorporate Eastern Roumelia with his kingdom. This high-handedness aroused great annoyance in Petersburg, and Serbia even declared war on the ground of balance of power in the Balkans. But the Serbs were completely defeated in the battles of Slivnitza and Pirot and were only saved by Austria's intervention. Shortly after, Alexander was seized in the night by the Russian party in the corps of officers, who took him across the frontier and there announced his deposition. True, he soon returned and was enthusiastically received by the people, but he then resigned of his own accord, being of opinion that the pressure exercised by Russia made the prosperous development of the country impossible. In 1887 the Sobranje chose as their sovereign Prince Ferdinand of Saxe-Coburg, who in concert with his minister Stambulov pursued a strictly Bulgarian — that is, anti-Russian — policy. It will be seen that Russia's system in the Balkans was as illogical as Napoleon III's with respect to Italy and Germany. It aimed at the "liberation" of nations, with the object of bringing them under her own domination.

But in the west also Europe was in permanent danger of a new conflagration. The French elections of 1871 had yielded a large Monarchist majority, three quarters of which was Orleanist and the remainder "Legitimist" — namely, Bourbon. In 1873 MacMahon was elected President and took his stand openly as vice-regent of the monarchy. As Napoleon III died in that year, the chances of the Legitimist candidate, Count Henri de Chambord, a grandson of Charles X, were very favourable, particularly as a fusion with the Orleanists had been effected. For the Count was childless and had therefore recognized his rival the Comte de Paris, Louis Philippe's grandson, as his successor. " Henri Cinq's " accession to the throne fell through only on account of his refusal to accept the tricolour; he happened to be a genuine Legitimist — a fact that his partisans had not taken into consideration. According to the laws of historical analogy, it is practically certain that he could only have held his position by attempting to regain Alsace-Lorraine. But even under the republican régime war was ever perilously near. In April 1875 the Berlin *Post* published an article on the increase of the French army with the alarmist title: " War in sight! " This was generally believed to have been inspired by the German General Staff, and it is by no means unlikely that in that quarter a preventive war was considered desirable. On the other hand, it may be considered as certain that Bismarck shivered

War in sight

at the idea of such a war. In the following month the Tsar
came to Berlin with Gorchakov, who, after a conversation with
Bismarck, sent a circular letter to the Russian embassies beginning with the words: "*Maintenant la paix est assurée.*" This reflected double discredit on Germany and was deeply resented by
Bismarck. It implied that Germany had, in the first place, been
seriously contemplating war and, in the second, had only yielded
to the pressure of an all-powerful Russia. The war came danger-
ously near at the end of 1886, when General Boulanger, the French
Minister for War, who saw in it the promise of a Napoleonic
career, ordered preparations for mobilization on a large scale,
while the French press adopted a very challenging tone. Speaking
in the Reichstag in January 1887, Bismarck said: "No French
ministry has ventured to say: 'We renounce the intention of regaining Alsace-Lorraine.' Any moment a government may come
into power there which will start a war. It may break out in ten
days or in ten years, secure from it we can never be. Compared
with this war, 1870 would be child's play."

*Dual
Alliance,
Triple
Alliance,
and Re-
insurance
Treaty*
The avoidance of this terrible encounter formed the almost
exclusive aim of Bismarck's policy in the next two decades. Already in 1872, in the first "Three Emperors" agreement, these
monarchs mutually guaranteed each other's possessions. This
agreement offered the greatest advantages by far to Germany,
since only Alsace-Lorraine of her possessions was seriously menaced. In 1879 there came the Dual Alliance between Germany
and Austria. Its first article bound the two contracting parties to
stand by each other in case either should be attacked by Russia.
The second provided that if either of the parties was attacked by
any other power than Russia, the other should bind itself to observe an attitude of friendly neutrality; if, however, Russia should
assist the attacking power, whether by active participation or by
military measures constituting a menace to the one attacked, then
Article I should come into force. This second condition was obviously, although not expressly, directed against France. The agreement was made public only in February 1888, at a time when tension had again become acute. It was not concluded until Bismarck
had informed the Viennese Government of a proposal for the partition of Austria made to the German Government by Russia.
Bismarck intended it as a peace instrument which should ward
off, on the one hand, a French attack on Germany and, on the
other, a Russian attack on Austria; though it was also designed

to keep Austria from pursuing too vigorous an anti-Russian policy, for the *casus fœderis* was only to arise in the case of defence.

The extension of the Dual to a Triple Alliance was brought about by circumstances outside Europe. It was the age of general colonial expansion. In 1881 the Russian General Skobelev conquered Turkestan, and in the same year England established herself firmly in Egypt, which she annexed, not legally, but *de facto*. About the middle of the eighties, too, Leopold II of Belgium acquired the Congo State in central Africa as a sort of private colony; and Germany, by setting up trading companies under a state protection that gradually developed into sovereignty, secured Togo, Cameroon, German South-west Africa, and German East Africa, New Guinea, and the Bismarck Archipelago. Soon after 1880 France acquired the recognized supremacy over the immense empire of Annam, in Farther India, and the protectorate of Tunis, with the consent of Bismarck, to whom such a diversion of the French land-hunger was very welcome, and of England, who bargained in return for a free hand in Egypt. But Italy was greatly chagrined, for she had long coveted this much-disputed territory of ancient Carthage and Late Roman Africa, which had been one of the most flourishing countries of antiquity and, as Sicily's opposite coast, was of vital importance to her. Italy was thus driven into the Triple Alliance by the fear that, in her political isolation, she might lose even the expectation of Tripoli and be entirely crowded out of Africa, of which the middle of the northern edge is almost a part of the Apennine Peninsula. The new Roman empire was undoubtedly on the up-grade in every domain of civilization, by reason of the fruitful development of its industry and agriculture and the Liberal forms of its state and social democracy — which in this people spring from no political system, but are a natural growth of the soil and the race. Brigandage and illiteracy, ever the two principal evils, were also beginning to disappear. In the *Kulturkampf* the Italian Government went much further than the German: it introduced not only civil marriage, but the civil oath, and not only withdrew the schools from the ecclesiastical authorities, but made religious instruction optional and abolished the theological faculties. Moreover, far from there being any repressive " Socialist laws," freedom of the press and of speech was the rule.

" The Triple Alliance," said Bismarck to a deputation which

waited upon him on his eightieth birthday, " reaches back in origin almost to the age of the sagas. The dominion of the old German emperors of the Holy Roman Empire extended, remember, from the North Sea to Apulia." But the alliance had, as its text unmistakably indicates, a purely defensive character: it guaranteed to the three empires their possessions (in particular, the Vosges frontier to Germany, and to Italy the Papal State, whose re-establishment was always kept in view by Clerical circles in France); it was most definitely, so far as Italy's intention was concerned, not directed against England, and it was therefore practically non-existent in the event of a German-English conflict — which, of course, in 1882, was a wholly unlikely conjuncture. Not that Bismarck ever permitted himself any illusions as to the value of the treaty: it would satisfy him, he said, if an Italian drummer were put on the Alps to keep a part of the French army away from the eastern frontier in case of war. In 1883 Roumania was admitted to the Triple Alliance, and in 1887 Bismarck crowned the structure by his " Reinsurance Treaty," by which Germany and Russia guaranteed each other an attitude of friendly neutrality in case of attack from any other power. This covered Russia against Austria, for whom aggressive action was impossible without German assistance, and Germany against France, who, again, could not dream of striking without Russia; should Russia attack, however, the Triple Alliance would come into force. As we see, it was constructed on a most complicated system, which could only be maintained by constant, cautious, and clear-sighted moves of the pieces and was bound to crash from the moment that the inspired manipulator removed his hand. The calamity lay in the fact that the only available allies for the German Empire were Russia and Austria; if it turned to Austria, it drove Russia to a French alliance; if it turned to Russia, there was always the danger of being absorbed in its sphere of influence and forfeiting its independence as a great power. Yet it seemed better to choose Russia, for she was the strongest military power outside Germany with whom the Empire had no accounts to settle and whose political interests were practically identical with its own. A German-Russian bloc would indeed have been the firmest guarantee of European peace. There was, however, an important obstacle; a close alliance with the Empire of the Tsars would sooner or later have meant the liquidation of Austria, and this would leave Germany completely isolated between France and a Russia that had encroached far into Europe, and thus exposed to the constant danger of a war on two fronts.

It may be said without exaggeration that during the second decade of its existence the German Empire stood politically at the head of Europe. But as regards the intellectual outlook of its inhabitants, Nietzsche as early as 1873 spoke of the " extirpation of the German soul for the benefit of the German Empire." As to its spiritual condition, Lagarde said, in 1881: " The German of the new Empire is qualifying more and more for the state of mind described, not too elegantly, by its Chancellor as general parasitism; and it would be difficult to maintain that such a state of mind is favourable to the formation of character"; while as regards the moral structure, the one word " capitalism " adequately describes it. In 1875 Friedrich Albert Lange produced *Geschichte des Materialismus und Kritik seiner Bedeutung in der Gegenwart,* an important work, imbued with the finest traditions of classical German philosophy and far in advance of its age. In it we read: " The great interest of people in this period is not, as in Antiquity, immediate pleasure, but the *creation of capital.* The pleasure of our own times, for which we are so widely censured, looms by no means so large in a comparative view of cultural history as the work-mania of our industrial organizers and the work-hardships of our industrial slaves . . . to scrape together the means for enjoyment, then spend these means, not on enjoyment, but chiefly on earning over again: this is the predominant characteristic of our age." And, in truth, it was only now that capital had become an end in itself, a triumphant beast that devoured its own children: a senseless, paradoxical development-process of horribly grotesque uniqueness, which has never before existed and, in all probability, will never recur; a dark and terrifying riddle in the ensemble of world-history, which confronts us with the question as to whether so-called " modern man " is not in reality mad. Certainly his extreme (that is, pathological) Rationalism is a plausible collateral indication of it. To a later generation, at any rate, he will indubitably appear mad.

In another book emanating from the same decade: *Der Kampf ums Recht,* by the world-famous legal historian Rudolf von Jhering, there is a passage that is likewise very characteristic, though as a self-presentation and not a criticism of the age. Jhering says — and this is the basic idea which runs through the whole exposition — that opposition to any form of injustice whatever is one's duty: "the duty of the one who is in the right towards himself, for it is a law of moral self-preservation"; "the force with which the sense of justice actually reacts against an injury received is the touchstone of his healthy condition"; "law, though prose in the region of the purely material, becomes poetry in the sphere of the personal, when it is fighting for right and for the assertion of personality; the fight for the right is the poetry of character." We must admit that this standpoint of Ihering's not only shows depth and insight, but is also lofty and pure. At the same time, he shows what had become of the German ethos when so shining a light of abstract research could be so far converted to the "practical philosophy" of a sublimated rowdy or, more briefly, to Anglo-Saxondom, whose religion (as was shown in our second volume with reference to Milton and Cromwell) is no more than a relapse into the Old Testament under a mask of Christianity, if not, indeed, into the heathendom of Antichrist. For the fight for the right, which (as we should be the last to deny) may rise to the height of a "poetry of character," would, if it were taken as the main driving-force in the history of mankind, at best make a mere wild-Indian story of it. An outward expression of this changed world-outlook is the new speaking accent which came into fashion at that time. Nietzsche says of it in his *Fröhliche Wissenschaft*: "Something mocking, cold, indifferent, negligent in the voice: that is what now passes for 'superior' German . . . even little girls imitate this officers' German — for the officer, and the Prussian officer at that, is the inventor of these sounds." What we find in the written style of contemporary philosophers, of whom David Friedrich Strauss may stand as the representative type, is only a variation of this scale. In *Der alte und der neue Glaube,* a work of his old age, he combines in a strange fashion stolid narrow-mindedness and arrogant opinionated hectoring with a drab and sometimes uncanny detachment of delivery. The success of this book may have been owing to an effect similar to that experienced by the Inspector in Strindberg's *Am offenen Meer* after the conversation with the Counsellor's wife and her daughter: "the feeling that one has on visiting a mill, where there is a certain agreeableness in seeing everything covered with a soft whitish flour tone." Speaking of Genesis, he writes: "The sun is created on the fourth day only, although for three days previously the alternation of day and night, which is unthinkable without the sun, is supposed to have taken place. Further, the earth is created

294

several days before the sun, and the sun's relation to the earth, like that of the moon, is purely one of service, the stars being thrown in quite as an afterthought — an inversion of the true relative ranks of the heavenly bodies which is not very creditable to an inspired revelation. . . . On one day, the third, sea and land are supposed to have been separated and, in addition, all the vegetable world created; whereas our geologists can tell, not of thousands, but of hundreds of thousands of years that were necessary for this formative process." This kind of leathern argumentation, on the level of a people's educational institute, is found on almost every page. On prayer he writes: " The only true and genuine prayer is that in which the person praying hopes if possible to bring about something which otherwise would not happen "; this sentence — in form a classic case of the stilted phrasing of the law-book — is one of the many in which the author proves himself a crass dilettante and ignoramus on religious topics or, to put it bluntly at last, the perfect type of an intellectual ass.

Almost as successful was Eduard von Hartmann's *Philosophie des Unbewussten,* a skilful mixture of fashionable pessimism, Darwinism, " depth psychology," and " natural" science, which was at the same time a sort of synthesis from Schopenhauer and Hegel. And here Nietzsche's saying is appropriate: " he who tries to mediate between two determined thinkers stamps himself as mediocre." Hartmann's eschatology teaches that, as unpleasurable sensations must ever be in the majority compared with pleasurable ones, the day will come when the parliament of humanity, acting on the realization of this, will by a unanimous resolve do away with the Will and the world. Schopenhauer dubbed Hegel the clown of Schelling; one would be more justified in calling Hartmann the Simple Simon of Schopenhauer's pessimism. He even played the clown to Strauss, for what he writes about the Saviour goes far beyond Strauss or the most odious parody of him that could be imagined: " The contempt for work, for property, and for family duties are three points which were bound to be more abhorrent to the Jewish mind than to that of any other nation. Jesus learnt the carpenter's trade, but nowhere do we hear that he practised it, although this particular craft is universally in demand and of value. Then, too, he had absolutely no sense of the dignity of work. . . . With regard to property, all our moral conceptions were foreign to him; for he regarded any possessions as unrighteous Mammon, any saving as foolish and criminal. . . . The family feeling, that attachment to one's family which is one of the finest traits in the Jewish national character, he entirely lacked, and he proceeded logically to the destruction of all natural duties. In this respect he certainly cannot serve as a model. . . . If we sum up briefly the collective portrait of Jesus' personality we get the following result: no genius this, but a talent, which, however, through a complete lack of solid culture, produced, on an average, only mediocrity." Some very competent critics, such as Richard Müller-Freienfels, have declared it to be unfair to judge Hartmann by his earliest work, since he wrote many more important books later. I regret that I am incapable of adopting this attitude, as I most definitely refuse to read another line by a man who has written the sentences quoted above.

Dühring   But the real, though secret and uncrowned, king of philosophy at that period was Eugen Dühring. He wrote a critical history of the general principles of mechanics (his best work), a critical history of philosophy, a critical history of national economy and socialism — but criticism, to him, meant hostile rejection of almost all previous achievements. Although he possessed an astonishingly full and accurate technical knowledge in these domains, he revealed himself in his two volumes on the *Grössen der modernen Literatur* as an æsthetic ignoramus, lacking the most elementary understanding of the nature of literary creativity. In his most important — or, at least, most read — philosophical work he made an estimate of the " value of life " in which he, in contrast to Schopenhauer, arrived at an optimism of such frosty rigidity and leaden monotony that even as an affirmation of life one would definitely prefer the colourful spirit-world of Schopenhauer's world-negation. In his *Capucinades,* in which, unfortunately (and again in contrast to Schopenhauer), there is nothing amusing, he provides a running commentary of feeble and malicious sallies on the whole of spiritual history from Buddha to Einstein. Dante and Goethe, Shakspere and Ibsen, Plato and Kant: all these are immoral and at best but semi-talents. The discoveries in the domain of non-Euclidean geometry, made by Gauss, the greatest mathematical genius of our time, he calls: " the geometry not merely of nonsense, but positively of stupidity "; Helmholtz, the most lucid, stimulating, and witty writer on natural science in all German literature, he accuses of " dryness, confusedness, and philosophical drivel "; and of Kirchhoff's epoch-making scientific activities, with which we are already acquainted, he says (and this may serve also as a specimen of his style) : " The physical salad, or what was handed out as such, is here given a smear of psychology, physiology, and philosophical drivel; extreme unction, so to say." All religion is for him " cradle-mania," all philosophy, particularly of the modern order, twaddle " combined with deceit." For the rest, he teaches a philosophy of actuality drawn from Comte and Feuerbach: our reason is capable of comprehending the whole of reality; our thought and feeling depend upon objective truth: " The ideal system of our thoughts is the picture of the actual system of objective reality; complete knowledge has, in the form of thoughts, the same aspect as things have in the form of actual existence." This " complete knowledge " can very easily be acquired if one accepts Dühring's " ideal system " of shallow impertinences as a true reflection of reality. Again and again he insists that the only true philosopher is one who really lives his own philosophy; that for him there exists no gulf between philosophy and the philosopher; and here we cannot controvert him, for his private life was throughout as unjust and vulgar as his writings. One of the few historical personages to whom he does justice is Rousseau; and in fact he had a certain kinship with him in his capacity for resentment, due to persecution-mania, and his venomous arrogance. On the other hand, he differed from him in his absolutely impeccable life — which only made him the more unbearable, for there is no more detestable moral spectacle than the combination of morality and malice. On the intellectual plane, even the passionate coiner's sophistry of Rousseau stands miles above Dühring's sober class-room dialectics — we can enjoy picturesque lies, but never half-truths, which are the most worthless of all intellectual material. And these half-truths, in wearisome repetition and paraphrase, Dühring hammers mercilessly into the reader as if he were beating a monotonously discordant drum. Admittedly his style has clarity and a certain lapidarity; but the one has its origin merely in the strength of brutality, and the other in the unambiguity arising from poverty of nuance; here again he shows himself the complete opposite of Schopenhauer. He writes like a Morse key, which works clearly and energetically, but always with the same signs. Of one thing, at any rate, there is no doubt, and that is his pathologically bad taste, which not infrequently borders on feeble-mindedness and reduces his writings to the level and vulgarity of provincial comic papers. Almost on every page, particularly of his polemical carpings, we encounter the cheap pun, that revolting form of wit practised by comedians and commercial travellers, which Dühring obviously chose for its humourlessness — for he was without a doubt the most humourless person ever created. He makes up such words as " philoso-drivel " and " philoso-fudge "; talks of *Stielkunstler* (" stalk " or " handle " artists instead of " style-artists ") and *Mistik* (*Mist* = dung) for *Mystik;* accuses one of his literary opponents named Boerner of *Boerniertheit* (*borniert* = narrow-minded), and proposes that J. R. Mayer, the discoverer of the principle of energy, should henceforward be called " Irmayer " because he had led science astray (*irregemacht*). Goethe becomes for him " *das Köthchen* " (bit of dirt), Schiller " *der Schillerer,*" Nietzsche " *das Nichts'sche* "; Bismarck he calls " *Bisquark,*" Helmholtz " *Helmklotz* "; Tolstoy he writes " *Tollstoj* " (Crazy-toi), and Strindberg " *Rindberg* " or, still more elegantly, " *Grindberg.*"

Dühring had a great influence on his time, although an entirely subterranean one. That which was an *idée fixe* to Schopenhauer, that the philosophy professors were in a conspiracy of silence against him (whereas in fact they simply did not notice him), was in Dühring's case a well-founded suspicion; for, owing to his immoderate attacks on the whole body of scientists and his extremely tactless behaviour during his Berlin dozentship, he was in most scientific works either quite ignored or given only casual mention. He had, further, ruined his chances with the whole Liberal press by his excessive anti-Semitism, while his blunt denunciation of Socialism deprived him likewise of Radical backing. And, even apart from all these personal motives, the disagreeableness of his character and his manner ruled out any appreciation that he did deserve. His undeniable talent for throwing a vivid (if oblique) light upon wide spheres of human knowledge thus never achieved due recognition. Mankind does not distribute its laurels according to deserts alone, but only where sympathy adds its claim — and therein it is perfectly right.

The style of stylelessness In his extravagant want of style (in every sense of the word) Dühring was a very pregnant expression of his age. Now, a very strange thing happened at this time. The epoch appeared, both to contemporaries and to the next generation, to have no face at all. But suddenly its features began to appear: to acquire point, breadth, homogeneity; its manners, costumes, expression, and gestures revealed a large common measure; its people became figures, its objects symbols — until, as if by magic, the force of historical retrospect brought its hieroglyphics into the realm of visibility. And it became apparent that stylelessness is also a style.

It is perhaps worth while to reflect a little upon this remarkable fact. What a wealth of highly coloured and coherent associations appear before our inner vision when we hear the words: " Ramessids," " Punic Wars," " Crusades," " Reformation " ! But did the men of the time know all that we know? Very probably not. Yet they were " there," and not we. Is our picture imaginary, then? Yes, and for that very reason truer. Everything earthly is intended to be sublimated, as well as concentrated, in mind. Only then does it in the higher sense become real. But this process takes time, and it is this gain in time that gives us the advantage over the " contemporaries."

Men of the seventies and eighties were really touching in some respects. They were filled with a devouring hunger for reality, but had the misfortune to confuse this with matter — which is but the hollow and deceptive wrapping of it. Thus they lived perpetually in a wretched, padded, puffed-out world of cotton-wool, cardboard, and tissue-paper. In all their creations it is with the arts of adornment that imagination is concerned: with the art of the upholsterer, the confectioner, the stucco decorator; with an ingenuity of the smallest combinations.

The Makart bouquet

Their interiors irritate us primarily by their wearisome overcrowding, overloading, overfurnishing. These rooms of theirs were not living-rooms, but pawnshops and curiosity-shops. Simultaneously there is displayed a craze for satin-like surfaces: for silk, satin, and shiny leather; for gilt frames, gilt stucco, and gilt edges; for tortoise-shell, ivory, and mother-of-pearl, as also for totally meaningless articles of decoration such as Rococo mirrors in several pieces, multi-coloured Venetian glass, fat-bellied Old German pots, a skin rug on the floor, complete with head and terrifying jaws, and, in the hall, a life-sized wooden Negro. Everything was mixed, too, without rhyme or reason: in the boudoir a set of buhl, in the drawing-room an Empire suite, next door a Cinquecento dining-room, and next to that a Gothic bedroom. Through it all, the taste for ornament and polychrome made itself felt. The more twists and scrolls and arabesques there were in the designs, the louder and cruder the colour, the greater the success. In connexion with this there is a conspicuous absence of any idea of usefulness or purpose; it was all purely for show. We note with astonishment that the best-situated, most comfortable and airy room in a house (the "best room") was not intended to be lived in at all, but was only there to be exhibited to friends. We see, too, a number of things which, though costly, contribute nothing to comfort. There were portières of heavy, dust-harbouring material — rep, plush, or velvet — which barricaded the doors, and handsome flowered hangings which prevented the closing of the shutters; window-pane pictures, which kept out the light, but looked "romantic," and towels ill suited for drying purposes, but embroidered with the *Trompeter von Säckingen;* gorgeous arm-chairs, hidden all the year round with awful covers, and rocky thin-legged "occasional" tables littered with superfluous objects that are for ever falling over; splendidly bound volumes, impossible to read because one's hand goes to sleep in five minutes and uninviting because illustrated, and, as crown and symbol of the whole, the Makart bouquet of "everlastings" which, with great pretension and small success, poses as a bunch of flowers.

This brings us to one of the main features of the times: delight in the unreal. Every material used tries to look like more than it is. It is the era of a universal and deliberate swindling in the use of materials. Whitewashed tin masquerades as marble, papier mâché as rosewood, plaster as gleaming alabaster, glass as costly onyx. The exotic palm in the bay window is impregnated or made of paper, the tempting fruit in the epergne is of wax or soap. The rose-shaded lamp over the bed is just as much a "property" as the cosy log fire in the grate: neither is ever used. On the other hand, the illusion of a roaring fire is intensified by the use of red tinfoil. The sideboard boasts copper vessels, never used for cooking, and mighty pewter mugs out of which no one drinks. On the wall hang defiant swords, never crossed, and proud hunting trophies, never won. Should, however, any utensil serve a particular purpose, this must in no case be obvious from its shape. A magnificent Gutenberg Bible is discovered to be a work-box, and a carved cupboard an orchestrion. The butter-knife is a Turkish dagger, the ash-tray a Prussian helmet, the umbrella-stand a knight in armour, and the thermometer a pistol. The barometer takes the form of a bass-viol, the bootjack of a stag-beetle, the spittoon of a tortoise-shell, the cigar-cutter of the Eiffel Tower. The beer-jug is a monk, made to open, who is guillotined at every gulp; the clock is an instructive model of an express engine, a glass dachshund serves as cruet for the roast, the salt sneezes, and the gravy is drawn from a miniature barrel, carried by a nice little terracotta donkey. Cardboard antlers and stuffed birds suggest the ranger's lodge, suspended sailing-boats a seamen's tavern, and a still life of jockey-caps, saddles, and riding-whips the stable.

This period, supposedly so realistic, avoided nothing more fervently than its own present. The famous architect and teacher of architecture Gottfried Semper laid it down in his program that the style of every building was to be determined by historical association: thus a court-house should recall a doge's palace, a theatre a Roman arena, barracks a mediæval fortress. In obedience to these principles, there were built in Vienna, for instance, a town hall which appears to be modelled on a plan from a child's box of bricks; the Votivkirche, that looks like a gigantic iced cake; and, in front of the Parliament House, a monstrous Pallas Athene, believed by everyone to be made of stearin. As a home for the London Stock Exchange a veritable temple was chosen (and this time quite rightly). A town hall had always to be Gothic, as the result of a fallacious association between the Middle Ages and the City, and a Parliament building Classical because of an equally fallacious association between antiquity and a representative constitution; a city man's palace was Baroque, obviously because this (adulterated) style permitted of the most ostentatious ornament, and a bank was Florentine because of some (possibly unconscious) connexion between the modern condottiere of finance and the amorality of Renaissance man.

But the style most appreciated was that of, not the Italian, but the German Renaissance. Doors, windows, and ornamental cupboards were provided with pilasters and framework. And the favourite metal was " *cuivre poli,*" an alloy of copper and zinc that had been much used in the sixteenth century. The popular bull's-eye glasses and Luther chairs, chests and peasant stoves, lattices and ironwork, paintings on wood and mottoes, the mannikin of the fountain, and the little woman as candlestick: all these reproduce that period. For fancy dress the *Landsknecht* and the *Ritterfräulein* were in great demand. In our first volume we described the Reformation era as the age of repletion, and these decades might also be so characterized. The titular heroes of the two eras, Bismarck and Luther, were uncommonly hearty eaters and drinkers, and the thick pleasure-seeking of the " Founders' Age " was the more immoderate as to its food and drink in that the Romantic

301

ideal of ethereal man, which had reigned before the March Revolution, had long since yielded to an erotic conception that looked to Rubens. Four courses were the rule at the midday meal with the well-to-do middle class, and on festive occasions the number was raised to eight or twelve. The menu of a banquet in the year 1884 contains, for instance: hors d'œuvres, broth, sole, steamed chicken, spiced sirloin, ice with kümmel (to stimulate the appetite), roast pheasant, York ham, pineapple ice-pudding, pastries, dessert, coffee; and a " captain's dinner " consisted of: lobster cocktails, green pea soup, Rhine salmon, stuffed loin of veal with kidneys, oyster patties, strawberry sherbet, snipe with Russian salad, ox tongue with asparagus, loin of venison with compote, cream ices, a savoury, fruit, and coffee. There was definitely an inner relationship also between these two ages, which finds expression in a number of common traits: their philistinism and inertia, their love of fussiness and " Sunday best," of knick-knacks and ornaments, their lack of proportion and simplicity, rhythm and harmony. But the " Founders' Age " was completely devoid of that blissful naïveté, poetical narrowness, and playful craftsmanship which make the world of Hans Sachs and Dürer so attractive, and to which the *Meistersinger* has built a monument of such power as only vain yearning can inspire.

The Eiffel Tower   Entirely in the spirit of the age, too, are the great exhibitions, with their principle of bric-à-brac and the overwhelming mass effect produced by getting together all attainable curiosities. These were responsible for certain very characteristic architectonic creations: In 1873 we have the erection of the Rotonde in Vienna (though this exhibition was a dismal fiasco, not only because of the financial crash and the cholera, but also because the only preparation the city had made for the reception of its many guests was a firm determination to plunder them). Then, in 1878, when the rage for copying had begun to attack the West, Paris built the Trocadéro in so-called Oriental style. In Paris, again, in 1889, was built the Eiffel Tower, an iron construction, three hundred metres high and weighing nine million kilograms, which had on its first platform a variety theatre, a restaurant, and a café; in its highest public room, the main view-point, still space for eight hundred people, and above that, again, a large laboratory for meteorology and astronomy. In addition, there were originally facilities for optical signalling for military purposes, but these have since become objectless through the invention of wireless telegraphy. It is characteristic of this, the most famous building of its time, that, in spite of its prodigious dimensions, it yet makes a finicking impression. This is because the inferior artistic feeling of the epoch was only capable of thinking in the genre sense and in filigree technique; thus it was possible in fact to make miniatures of the structure that were used as knick-knacks. Now, with really great colossal buildings this is unthinkable: the Sphinx as nut-cracker would be impossible, similarly the Cheops Pyramid as a pincushion.

In women's dress the fashion in "Old German" style was started by the appearance of the Rembrandt hat at the end of the seventies. Puffed sleeves and Gretchen pockets followed in the early eighties. For men the velvet béret was much favoured; this was worn in the house and also, by those who fancied themselves as artists, in the street. After the fall of the Empire the crinoline vanished, making way for an even more grotesque article of dress: the *cul de Paris*. This was the rage in the eighties and was worn — though with intervals during which the princess dress, later so generally adopted, had its vogue — up till 1890. Over the whole period, skirts were so narrow and clinging as to hamper the wearers in walking — as did also the extremely high heels. From 1885 on, puffed sleeves began to widen into the preposterous " leg of mutton " type; to this period belongs, also, the bonnet. The hair was parted at the roots on the forehead and brought forward in a donkey fringe over the eyes. What with the suggestion of an abnormally developed seat, hitched-up shoulders, a Chinese hobble, a grandmother's cap, and hair dressed like a sheep's, it must be admitted that fashion had done her utmost to produce a hideous exterior. With it all there set in a reign of prudery that has perhaps never been equalled. Not the smallest glimpse of neck or arms was permitted to show. No " decent woman " might on any account show her calves, or even ankles; even when bathing, she went into the sea covered from head to foot. She was strictly forbidden to be alone in a room with a gentleman or to go out without a chaperon, and words such as " sex " and " drawers " were excluded from her vocabulary.

Men's costume had long given up the attempt to express the feeling of the age and showed only slight variations. From the end of the seventies trousers were wide from the knee down, falling funnel-wise over the boot with an elephantine effect; later they became as close-fitting as tights, and it was no small matter

303

for a dandy to get into his pantaloons. Army officers followed these fashions slavishly, and it is typical that even this class was carried away by the " faking " tendency of the time. It tight-laced, padded its chest and shoulders, wore high heels and wigs. Like the rest of middle-class domesticity, men's wear was made up of substitutes in almost every detail. Over the flannel shirt were worn the reversible cuffs and snow-white starched " dicky "; the made-up tie imitated the knotted one, the elastic-sided boots were provided with sham buttons. Elderly gentlemen wore their toupet almost as a matter of course, and it was the fashion to dye beards — which were universally worn except by priests, actors, and lackeys. Only the man of genius was able to hold aloof from the general swindle. Moltke, who was one of the few who went clean-shaven from choice, once received from an artist in hairdressing an excellent toupet. " What's this object you've brought me? " he asked indignantly. " I can't put that on, everyone would think it was real."

It was Moltke, too, who disposed of the " great " Lenbach's lying technique with the words: "The fellow always wants to make a hero of me." Lenbach was a pupil of Piloty, like Defregger, the inventor of the drawing-room Tirolese, and Gabriel Max, the theatre mystic, his equally famous contemporary. But it was a fourth pupil of Piloty, Hans Makart, who made his mark on the period. His fame as a painter faded as fast as his colours, to which he was able to lend a special ephemeral brilliance by a preparation of which he had the secret — this in itself being typical of the charlatanry of his art. In his pictures, which are well-arranged ceremonial processions (although the famous " Five Senses " are not even that, but pure bathroom tiles), he raked together everything good and expensive: jasper and marble, satin and gold brocade, glittering jewels, rosy female flesh. But as a side-line he filled the position of virtuoso " producer " of the great ballet of form and style which belonged to the age. He was a dictator of taste with a power equal to that of Bernini in Baroque Italy. There were not only Makart bouquets, but Makart balls, Makart rooms, and a Makart theatre. The Viennese critic Ludwig Hevesi wrote in his reminiscences of Charlotte Wolter's sixtieth birthday: " Amongst other things, Makart became director of the Burg Theatre . . . and the whole theatre was attuned to the key of Charlotte Wolter, that living fiery fountain of colour." This is very odd; for to a later generation she seemed the embodiment of marble coldness and pallor. Did they do her injustice, or did the whole Makart age imagine her fiery colour, when in reality she was grey and tepid? Obviously, no objective solution of this question is possible.

Of another famous tragedienne of the time, Klara Ziegler, Theodor Fontane gave it as his opinion that she "played Kaulbach." And Ludwig Speidel said of the Meininger players: "they stage themselves very much as Piloty paints." These players, who opened their tours with a visit to Berlin on May 1, 1874, represented a reaction from Laube's Spartanism, which laid small store by external settings as being liable to distract attention from the words of author and actor and allowed only such accessories on the stage as were essential to the action. (In this, Laube was not so far wrong; for, as everything on the stage is a symbol, only those objects which possess a meaning have any justification there.) Now, the Meiningers spent great care on the stage picture, which was not only richer and more brightly coloured, but also of an almost archæological correctness as regards the particular period. The "historical genuineness" went so far that the trellises, tapestries, chests, and door-handles used were actual "period" pieces. To make the events more dramatic they strengthened them with effects of every imaginable sort, not only optical, but "sound suited to the mood"; thunder-claps, the rustle of leaves, bell-ringing, and the rattle of rain. The principle of "genuineness" was applied also to "supers," who were drawn from the ranks of real actors — an innovation indeed! In the court theatres at that time, soldiers were actually paraded to go on as supers: for instance, in the *Miller and his Child* infantrymen were brought in to do the ghostly procession. Another day a soldier might find himself one of a Roman crowd or a Pappenheim cuirassier. The greatest effect was obtained in just those scenes where the mass-producer had the main part. The ensemble scenes in *The Robbers,* the Rütli scene, the forum scene, the banquet scene in *Wallenstein* — these were repeated whole, after a long interval, whereas it had been usual to play the second part only. The solo achievements never rose above the average; this is true even of the youthful and still quite immature Kainz and of Ludwig Barnay, who was never more than a shallow court actor of supposedly fine parts. One of the best things that the Meiningers have to their credit is their discovery of Kleist, who up to then had hardly been played at all. Their stage management was copied everywhere until, in

305

the end, every provincial theatre "Meiningerized"; then, in 1890, it was superseded by Naturalism.

The representative actor of the "Founders' Age" was Adolf von Sonnenthal of the Burg Theatre, knighted by Imperial decree and in actual fact a fine figure of chivalry, if only a chivalry of the acquired sort. At the same time he was the most complete, concrete expression of middle-class ideals: sonorous, respectable, and sentimental, he fulfilled all the requirements of an age which looked upon art as a fancy article and rejoiced in the glitter of glass tears. Those were days when all the world played at Humanitarianism and Liberalism; Sonnenthal repeated this game on the stage, making, as it were, double play with his democratic dukes, his noble upstarts, and his wise apostles of humanity. And yet — this is the paradox of the footlights — his tears looked real, his sweet persuasiveness had an inner ring, his pose was natural — precisely because it had become real to his own vision.

The "collective art-work"

But the mightiest theatrarch and at the same time the masterful smith who welded all the tendencies of the age was Richard Wagner. "In cultural history," says Bulthaupt, in his *Dramaturgie der Oper*, "the Empire and Wagner will one day be as inseparable as are the tragedies of Æschylus and Sophocles from the *floraison* of Athens." His "collective art-work" aims at producing, by the co-operation of all the arts — poetry, painting, music, miming — that real drama, the "music-drama," best defined by himself as consisting of "acts of music become visible." The centre of gravity lies, however, in the dramatic side of the task, to which the musical is subordinated: "Opera suffered from this mistake, that a means of expression (music) was made the aim, and the aim to be expressed (drama) the means." This signifies a harking back to the most honourable of theatre traditions, the Greek, which likewise aimed at a collective art-work of stage picture, text, gesture, song, and dance — with certainly a far more sparing use of the orchestra — as its ideal, and at the same time it marks a rude break with the opera tradition of the country, which was guided almost exclusively by musical considerations. We must remember that Gluck regarded it as his main reforming task to emancipate the text from the artificial and despiritualizing influences of music, and to restore to the drama its right of place; and that he did not fully accomplish this was simply due to the cramping effect of the Classicist prejudices of the age. Schiller, again, in his later dramas, was moving definitely in the direction

306

of the collective art-work, only he never found the composer who would have known how to supply the appropriate orchestration for his ensemble scenes, his dramatic climaxes, his lyrical intermezzi, and the finales of the acts — which all cry out for music. His own instructions to this effect are not infrequent: the opening of *Wilhelm Tell* is a complete opera, the coronation procession in *The Maid of Orleans* a musical intermezzo, and a note at the close of the Rütli scene says: " The orchestra comes in with a fine rush of sound." " I thought," said Gluck in the introduction of *Alcestis*, " that the music should support the poetry in the same manner as the bright colours and the pleasing harmony of light and shade animate the figures without altering their outlines and elevate the picture into a well-proportioned drawing." It might be Winckelmann speaking! And Wagner went very much further in this direction. Not only did he heighten the drawing by painting it; he veiled it in a precious web of colours which sparkled in all the shades of the rainbow. And not only did he support poetry by music, but he enticed it into a delirium of sound and bore it aloft into spheres to which pure speech has no admittance. This " curtain of tone " is the richest and most splendid theatre *décor* that has ever been used. The *Leitmotiv,* an invention which dates back over three centuries and was used by Gluck with great artistry, attains its full use only with Wagner, who with a wealth and refinement of ingenuity exploited it to the full, and even to excess. With his never-failing flair, he at once recognized the superlative stage-value of this expression-medium (for nothing is more effective in the theatre than the " significant," the symbolic reminder); at the same time, however, he thereby introduced into music a historical, dialectical, non-musical element. At its height this technique leads to the " unending melody," of which Wagner says: " As a man in the forest, who, overcome by the general impression, sits down to register that impression . . . and listens more and more keenly, he only hears more and more distinctly the everlasting varied voices awakening in the wood. . . . This melody will ever echo within him, but trill it himself he cannot."

As we know, Wagner took his theory of music from Schopenhauer: according to the philosopher, all the other arts are reflections of ideas, mere phenomena of the will, but the revelations of music are the reflections of the will itself; therefore its effects are more comprehensive and profound, more understandable and more mysterious. This high (and, for that matter, completely justified) estimate of his art turned Wagner's head. But he over-looked the fact that Schopenhauer had never thought of including opera in it, had even expressly separated opera from great music, placing it on a level with military and dance music and compar-ing it in its artistic value with utility-architecture. Mozart and Rossini, he said, had not infrequently treated their texts with mocking contempt, which was a truly musical attitude, and Gluck, who had aimed at making music the complete slave of bad poetry, had taken a false track. This point of view developed quite logi-cally out of his theory that, just because music was the direct expression of the will, it should not attempt to express the intel-lect, its phenomenon; what it stood for was our emotions, " so to say, *in abstracto*," not " as they appear, accompanied by various motives and circumstances, clothed and dressed up, as it were, in different sorts of persons." " Inasmuch as music — far from being a mere auxiliary of poetry — is an independent art, the mightiest, indeed, of all and therefore achieving its aim entirely through its own means, it is certain that it has no need of the words of a song or the action of an opera. Music as such knows only sounds and not the causes which produce it. Accordingly, the *vox humana* is, to it, primarily and essentially no more than a modality of tone, like the timbre of an instrument. . . . Words are, and remain, a thing foreign and supplementary to music — and of inferior worth at that, since the effect of musical notes is incomparably more powerful, unerring, and rapid than that of words." One passage in Schopenhauer's principal work sounds as if it were directed expressly against Wagner, although the composer was but a child when they were penned: it conveys a warning against allowing the text of an opera to leave its subordinate position and " make itself the main thing, and music a mere medium, which would be an exceedingly false step and sheer perversity. . . . If music tries to adapt herself too closely to words, and model her-self to suit events, she is trying to speak a language that is not hers." Yet on the very next page the " unending melody " seems to be foreshadowed: "Through this intimate relationship that music bears to the true essence of all things, it becomes explicable that when music is heard, suitable to a particular scene, action, event, or environment, it appears to unlock for us the inmost meaning of it and to be its best and clearest commentary "; and a sentence from the *Metaphysik der Geschlechtsliebe* sounds al-most like a paraphrase of the Tristan idea: "The species alone has everlasting life and is therefore capable of everlasting desires, everlasting satisfaction, and everlasting pain. But here these are incarcerated in the narrow breast of a mortal; no wonder, then, if this should feel like bursting and can find no expression for the endless bliss or endless woe which fills it." On the other hand, Wagner was wrong in thinking that he had dramatized Schopenhauer's idea of redemption; on the contrary, this idea, often and powerfully as it occurs to him, is always piquantly eroticized, drawn from the metaphysical-cosmic into the empiric-individual — one might say, the private. " Redemption through woman " is an idea which Schopenhauer, if asked for his opinion, would have rejected with insults and fury.

That clever cultural philosopher Houston Stewart Chamberlain says, in his fat Wagner book — a disconnected and unfruitful work of adulation, that can only have the effect of alienating one from Wagner, whose cardinal defect was, indeed, always the Wagnerians — that he was never merely an opera-composer; he was a poet from the outset, and the naïve astonishment over his having " written his own texts " would certainly be no less naïve but more logical if people should wonder that this poet had written his own music. The truth, quite obvious to everyone but Chamberlain the Wagnerian, is that Wagner was neither a musician who made poems nor a poet who made music, but a "theatricalist," who made both whenever he wanted them. The collective art-work consists simply in the subordination of all the arts to the theatre: to the will to magical illusion, which, whether it enhances or blots out reality, always dominates it; to the painted but picturesque scene and the artificially arranged but effective vegetation; to the gauze-veiled " atmosphere " and resinous flash of passion which, just because it is not real, is more suggestive than the natural form. Wagner is always first and foremost the stage manager. His prose is peculiarly unmusical; when he is deprived of the stage, he is as clumsy and helpless in his movements as a turtle that has left the glittering element in which it floats. Even his opera text, if examined apart from the music — which ought not to be permitted, though the Wagnerians do it — lacks musicalness in the higher sense; its effects are produced quite externally by rhyme, rhythm, and alliteration and are often spoilt by unpleasing cacophony, tortured phrases, and stumbling sentences. He has thereby provided the proof for the rightness of Schopenhauer's theory that word-language represents a form of expression

The theatre at its highest

309

that is quite particularly alien, and even antagonistic, to the real musician. Wagner appears to have felt this dimly (in his later works at least), for he cleared an extensive space for pantomime: his music-drama is not merely song and accompaniment, but movement also — and it is this last element that rounds it into a collective work of art. The actors' steps, gestures, looks are not left to chance or individual choice, but are definitely fixed by the music. Even the movements of dumb nature are regulated: the river in the *Rheingold*, the forest in *Siegfried* are both animate creatures, whose vital expression the orchestra attentively follows. In this Wagner once more shows himself a grandiose stage manager. And it is really more than probable that he is to be regarded as the greatest theatrical genius of all time. Dramatic moments such as the appearance of Lohengrin, the landing of Tristan in Cornwall, the close of the second act of the *Meistersinger*, together with many others, denote positive peaks in the art of the stage. If it be argued that the effect of these scenes is primarily due to the music, it may be said in reply that music is an integral component of every true drama, as is colour of all true sculpture, and that the pure spoken piece is a degenerate modern product. In each of his works Wagner gives us the last word, theatrically speaking. In *Rienzi* he reached the summit of perfection of the Spontini spectacle-opera, in *The Flying Dutchman* of the Marschner demon-opera, in *Tristan* of the love-opera, in the *Meistersinger* of comedy in music, in *Lohengrin* and *Tannhäuser* of all romance; the last-named in particular may without exaggeration be claimed as the most magnificent piece written for the stage in the world's history. Yes, Wagner's work for the theatre was the greatest imaginable; it only remains to ask whether the theatre is itself the greatest thing.

So unique a phenomenon could only arise, perhaps, in a world that was all coulisses and imitation. And Wagner is also a pregnant expression of his age in that he pushed the scientific side of art to extremes. Schopenhauer said that music, as the direct language of the will, can be understood by everybody, but this is no longer true of Wagner's " tone-poetry." For with it came an intensification and exaggeration of a general tendency which, as we have pointed out, set in with the Renaissance. It was then that the art of " refinements " arose, together with its correlate the appreciative connoisseur, who knows the premises of what he sees. This tendency towards the technical has, in the course of modern times, become ever more exclusive, tyrannical, and caste-proud, and at last everything in its turn became a speciality produced by organized experts for intelligent gourmets : painting and poetry, natural science and divinity, politics and strategy, even commerce and crime. Comparable to the highest finesse of mathematical calculation and the subtlest tricks of Impressionist painting, Wagner's harmony and chromatic, with their exuberantly shaded and interwoven allusions, their backward and their forward glances, is the musical technique that corresponds to the age of the virtuoso constructional engineer, the miraculous electro-dynamic engines, and the diplomatic Integral Calculus of a Bismarck. One might really in Wagner's case speak of a *genealogy* of leitmotivs, the complete knowledge of which would entail a life's work; the mere mastery of his mythological apparatus is a serious job, at least as wearisome to tackle as the Darwinian theory of descent, by which he was greatly influenced.

But if one were to try to fit Wagner (quite summarily, of course) into one of the great historical art-categories, he would perhaps be best described as a Baroque artist. He recalls that culture not only by the pomp and aplomb of his far-reaching, over-eloquent gestures and his mystificatory leaning towards rebus and twilight, but also by his sensualistic will to spirituality (for which incense is the opiate, and the Church the façade), by his spasmodic and yet bewitching artifice. And, most of all, by his superfine mixture of eroticism and asceticism, fervour of love and yearning for death, an oppressive metaphysic which in a certain sense — if a supreme sense only — is antichristian and frivolous. It is no answer to this that the secret identity of the two cardinal moments of earthly existence, conception and dying, is here given noble expression. Both man's entry into life and his farewell to it are *super*-temporal events; to couple his birth with the phenomenon of propagation is to see the secret of life biologically — Darwinism again.

No one recognized more clearly Wagner's imperfections and dangers than Nietzsche, but neither did anyone feel so deeply his unique significance and grace from God — which is what both Wagner's supporters and his opponents are apt to forget. Further, in praising him, he said the strongest, finest, and most illuminating things that have ever been said about him. No man had a more intimate — one might say, familiar — knowledge of the soul of this genius — a knowledge such as, in good and evil, only close

Wagner's curve

relations usually have. Who but Nietzsche, for instance, would have discovered at that stage that Wagner belonged to the European decadence, " as the Orpheus of all secret misery, greater than any other "? His significance in cultural history, again, could hardly be more tersely formulated than in the closing sentence of the preface to *Der Fall Wagner:* " Wagner epitomizes modernity. There is nothing for it, one has to begin by being a Wagnerian. . . ." In another place Nietzsche says that every really important piece of music is a swan-song: this applies absolutely to Wagner. His " music-drama " is the impressive funeral march, the pompous funeral ceremony at the grave of the nineteenth century; indeed, of the whole Modern Age.

It is the fate of all great dramatists to set up a wave-movement, and to this Wagner was no exception. First they are ruthlessly attacked and accused of being out of their mind, immoral, and murderers of art; the next wave then brings them enthusiastic recognition which places them at the summit of all that has been done before; there follows a reaction, as unjust as the previous overestimation, which declares them to be superseded, hollow, and dishonest; and after this, as often as not, comes a renaissance. Euripides, for example, was regarded by his contemporaries as a decadent phenomenon; yet in the Hellenistic period he was regarded with such respect that no other dramatist might even be named beside him, while all branches of the drama, tragic as well as comic, took their tone exclusively from him. To the age of Classicism, again, it seemed blasphemous to place him beside Æschylus and Sophocles: even Mommsen treats him as rather inferior; but now that dialectics, irony, and complex psychology have begun to conquer the stage, his star is obviously again in the ascendant. Shakspere, who in his lifetime was esteemed as a talented actor, if not as a great poet, was looked upon with the utmost contempt in the second half of the seventeenth and the first of the eighteenth centuries, only to rank unchallenged ever since as the world's greatest dramatist. Schiller was from 1830 to 1890 the established model by which every German dramatic poem in the grand style was judged: all the reputable dramatic authors who wrote in verse at that time — Gutzkow and Laube, Hebbel and Ludwig, Halm and Wildenbruch — derive from him. Then, with Naturalism, there set in (overnight, as it were) an extravagant contempt for, and even derision of, Schiller: his name became almost a term of abuse. Expressionism, however, went back to him. Ibsen, again, who was originally regarded as a cross between a knave and a lunatic, became at the turn of the century, by common consent of everyone in his senses, one of the most powerful figures of the world's international literature; but to the youth of today he is a prim old maiden aunt. Wagner's curve, which bears a likeness both to Schiller's and to Ibsen's (though of a more subterranean kind to the latter), reached its height when Schiller was still enthroned and Ibsen was only on the horizon; it began to descend when Schiller had risen again and Ibsen was on the wane: thus, paradoxically, the Wagner curve rose because the Schiller-world was still in power, and the Ibsen-world not yet, and drooped because Schiller was there again and Ibsen no longer. The explanation lies possibly in the fact that Schiller was an extremely emotional but entirely un-middle-class poet, while Ibsen was entirely unemotional, but very middle-class. It was therefore inevitable that the emotional Wagner should rise under the sign of Schiller and before the reign of the emotion-slaying Ibsen set in, while on the other hand it was Ibsen and not Schiller that went down with him in the collapse of that middle-class world-picture which stands in the background of all his poems. There can be no doubt, however, that, like Ibsen, he will one day return to power, though for quite different reasons and from quite different spiritual premisses; for the few genuine dramatic geniuses that humanity possesses are not to be killed.

The greatest share of credit for the triumph of the music-drama goes to Franz Liszt, whose encyclopædic mind embraced, in its disinterested and most warm-hearted discernment, Wagner and Verdi, Bach and Berlioz, Schumann and Chopin, Mozart and Meyerbeer. By his pianoforte transcriptions, his clever variations and fiery fantasias, he was able to introduce these masters to the widest circles in his travels all over Europe as the wizard of the piano and the darling of women and princes. Him, however, good fortune did not spoil, but ennobled. A sort of contra-Wagner was Johannes Brahms, who achieved his first success with his *German Requiem* (1868), but whose work was long known only to small circles. His art, again, attempts a sort of return to the Greek, but in contrast to music-drama, which emulated the Dionysiac side, its orientation is Apollonian, or, in other words, Protestant; there is something harsh and reserved, inflexible and puritanical about it. At the same time, its Classical self-limitation and integrity of form are, just as with the Greeks, an artificial palliative against

" Die Fledermaus "

latent Romanticism, the willed reaction of a self-curative experiment: music as a "banting cure."

Carmen, too, has often been played off against Wagner. Nietzsche was, of course, the first to do it: "May I say that Bizet's orchestral tone is almost the only one that I can still bear to hear? This music seems to me perfect. It has a light, flexible, courteous air; it is amiable and does not *perspire.* . . . And, lastly, we get love, love translated back into *Nature.* Not the love of a noble virgin! No Senta sentimentality, but love as fate, as *fatality.* . . . I know of no instance where the tragic jest, which forms the essence of love, is so rigorously expressed, becomes so terribly a formula." This work, in which popularity was combined with artistry, Spanish passion with French gracefulness, and elemental vitality with playful merriment, is in fact the ideal operetta. The greatest success in this genre in Germany was *Die Fledermaus,* which has a very good libretto and a fund of charming musical ideas; it has, however, no "atmosphere" and no point of view, and this places it at a wide distance from Offenbach and Nestroy: its figures have not, even musically speaking, any common origin in space, its bewitching melodies are gilt stucco, laid on. One must even admit that Konradin Kreutzer's naïve music to *Der Verschwender,* although naturally it cannot be compared with the *Fledermaus* for originality and bubbling life, is conceived more with a feeling of the whole and therefore stands higher than Strauss's work from the point of view of the collective work of art. But the main objection to Strauss is that he is completely domesticated, problemless, unrevolutionary; in contrast again to Offenbach and Nestroy, although the one flourished in the darkest post-March period, the other under the Napoleonic régime of the sword. No oppression, be it said, is so damaging to art as the lukewarm temperature of the rooms of Liberalism. It is therefore inexcusable to continue to speak of "Offenbach and Strauss." They are no more Dioscuri than Delacroix and Delaroche, Schopenhauer and Hartmann, Busch and Oberländer, Ibsen and Björnson, who until recently were always named in couples. All these are cases of genius being cleverly imitated by middle-class talent — and in the eye of an undiscriminating gallery, in terms of momentary success, surpassed by it.

Literature At the time of the French Revolution, Goethe wrote that although an outstanding national author could only be demanded of a nation, yet he would hesitate to desire for the German nation the upheavals which would pave the way for classic works. This remark shows that even a Goethe was not able to foretell history in advance. For the classic works came without the upheavals; and when the upheavals came, the classic works failed to appear. At the time of *Wallenstein* and *Wilhelm Meister,* of the *Phäno-menologie* and the *Farbenlehre,* there was no German nation; at the time of Baumbach and Brachvogel there was. The *floraison* of Gothic and Scholasticism had its roots in the wretched fiasco of the Crusades; the Italian Renaissance unfolded its superb vege-tation in the midst of the most desolating political conditions; Calderon and El Greco were contemporary with the complete overthrow of Spanish world-domination; Rome ruled the world, but had to draw every architectural motif, every drama-fable, and every philosophical idea from Greece. When Charlemagne revived the Roman Empire, he also attempted a spiritual rebirth, which was a complete failure. Is there, then, a state of antagonism be-tween the political and the cultural rise of a people? For, *per contra,* the era of Pericles was the fruit of the Persian wars; the English Renaissance occurred in the period of the victory over the Armada; Descartes, Pascal, and Molière were the subjects of Richelieu, Mazarin, and Louis XIV. Undoubtedly history has its laws; but they are so mysterious and complicated that they cease to be laws at all for us. We cannot, therefore, explain in so many words how it happened that Germany in her victory and unity forfeited nearly all her high cultural traditions, while France, after one of the most crushing defeats in her history, unfolded the bewitching flora of a totally new art-world.

The immediate effect of the war on German literature was the appearance of " victory " poetry, which was throughout second- and third-rate, unfelt, conventional, and coldly emotional. Even the two best-known poets of the time, Geibel and Freiligrath, failed entirely. The one produced such banal rhymes as: " Now throw away the widow's veil, now gird thee in thy wedding-dress, O Germany victorious! " while the other woke the echoes with: " Hurrah, thou pride of womanhood, hurrah, Germania! How boldly dost thou stand there, forward bending o'er the Rhine! " In the theatre the honours went to popular mendacities of the type of *Narziss* or pasteboard stories like Wilbrandt's *Arria und Mes-salina,* together with amiable stupidities in the style of the *Flie-gende Blätter,* such as *Der Veilchenfresser* and *Krieg im Frieden.* Halm's stale confectionery was still a great attraction, and that solid craftsman L'Arronge was taken seriously as a poet. But the main contingent of the repertory was of French origin, under which category are included the plays of Paul Lindau, the ingenious exploiter and adapter of Sardou. He even displaced his master in the favour of the German family public, with such clever cowardice did he de-erotize his works. The minor novelists of the Heyse class went on diligently writing, and it must be admitted that the most valuable product of the fiction of the day was Julius Stinde's memoirs of Frau Buchholz. This writer was himself as big a philistine as his characters, but his humorous attitude towards life enabled him to create a refreshing and faithful cultural picture of the eighties; it is therefore not surprising that Bismarck, with his unfailing instinct for what in wine is called " body," included the emotional outpourings of Frau Wilhelmine among his favourite reading.

For a decade Ernst von Wildenbruch wrote without meeting the slightest recognition. It was not until 1881 that the Meininger players admitted him to the stage with a performance of *Die Karolinger*. In his dramas we hear the creaking of the whole apparatus of the epigone drama. There are the gigantic villains, dæmonic viragos, feeble royal puppets, the explanatory monologue to the public, eavesdropping revelations, punctual entries of the essential figures, and meetings of the whole personnel in a central place as if in the hall of a hotel. On the whole the author expounds excellently, but then his breath fails him, and dimly feeling this, he overreaches himself. Usually he works up the scenes with great assurance to a trumpeting act-finale, which seldom fails in its momentary effect. In this, as in everything, he is Schiller's pupil. (There are, I may say, three sorts of finales: you may bring your act to a close with an exclamation-mark, like Schiller; with a question-mark, this being a method in which Hebbel excels; or with a dash — Ibsen's invention — which is the most thrilling, but also the most exacting in its demands on author and audience alike.) Wildenbruch's stage assurance had nothing to do with his profession, but had its source in a schoolboy-like instinct, which is why his works are a species to themselves and cannot be compared with others of the same style. He *believes* in his drunken tirades, his black-and-white technique, his psychological impossibilities; he is a completely unaccountable and irresponsible amateur, who plays with himself — and this excludes him from all criticism.

The same naïve passion for Bengal lights is seen in the otherwise quite differently constituted Ludwig Anzengruber, who made his first great success in 1870 with *Der Pfarrer von Kirchfeld* at the Theater an der Wien. Most of his pieces are anti-clerical, a sort of dramatized *Kulturkampf*. In them he fights celibacy, Catholic marriage, the doctrine of Infallibility, and testimonies favouring the Church in vivid colour-prints — often with much humour. There are individual scenes and charges, flashing witticisms, and clever streaks in which he verges on poetry, but in essentials he is melodrama. He paints the middle-class *milieu* with the eye of a provincial who has found his way up to town, and peasant life with the Defregger brush of the outsider.

What the middle-class German looked like in the second half of the nineteenth century posterity will learn with certainty from *one* master only, Wilhelm Busch, who has also in his way created a " collective art-work." Yet it is difficult to know what to say about him. Ludwig Speidel once said of the actor Fichtner : " Normally blame is the handle by which one seizes that which is at bottom excellent, but Fichtner is so thoroughly rounded-off a phenomenon that he is as difficult to grasp as a ball. The simplest would be to admire him in the lump, let oneself go in superlatives, and not be chary with the exclamation-marks." This is just the case with Busch. He is completeness personified, and all one really can do is to state the fact.

After his work had for decades been regarded as a harmless puppet-show, good enough for the nursery and afternoon tea, it has recently become the fashion to look upon him as a dæmonic pessimist and Nihilist. Both conceptions are equally wrong. The incomparable and indefinable effect that goes forth from Wilhelm Busch is accounted for simply by the fact that he himself does nothing, he lets life do it. True humour is the possession of life alone, and the only thing that humorists can do is to write down this humour. But they hardly ever do so. They think out all sorts of complicated situations and conflicts that are devoid of any real gaiety. All that they achieve is an imitated, constructed, pasted-up jollity that has nothing living and convincing about it, but is just a waxworks gaiety. Take, for instance, that poem of Busch's, the Haarbeutel cycle, which is probably his very best, though comparatively the least known. In it Busch describes a succession of typical forms of drunkenness. These are positively classical sketches, lifelike copies of reality to the last detail. The

*Wilhelm
Busch*

317

author adds nothing and takes away nothing. He simply copies down the complications which take place when a man is drunk. He allows the humour of life to flow into him without increasing it by anything coming from his own self — for that would only weaken it. He sits there and waits to see if life promises to be amusing; if it is, he merely notes it down.

But there are also a number of typical turns of speech and situations in his works which are bound to make the most cultured and sensitive person laugh in spite of being unwilling to admit that he thinks such things humorous or in good taste. If anyone misses his chair and sits down on the floor, it is undoubtedly funny, but still funnier is the effect if his trousers split in the process. If one man hits another a hearty box on the ear, it is undeniably most entertaining; and how much more so if he hits the wrong man! The actor who speaks broken Bohemian, Jewish, or Saxon can always be sure of cackling appreciation, whatever he may say. But with the exception of the very lowest type of theatre-goer, not a soul finds this amusing in our day. It is perhaps a case of atavism. Our coarse forefathers used to laugh with genuine heartiness at such things, and our diaphragm has duly noted these stimuli to side-splitting mirth. But as this kind is, so to say, a peripheral and vegetal laughter, which is as little under the control of our free will as our digestive activity, we afterwards feel deeply ashamed and annoyed. And this is why one observes that this kind of fooling causes much laughter, but very little applause.

As with all great artists, one is in a predicament to know where to put Busch. Is the primary thing in his art that wonderful gift for drawing which created an entirely new technique in caricature, inspired by art's highest rule: "*le minimum d'effort et le maximum d'effet*"? With six pencil-strokes he outlines a whole living type, a whole social sphere, a whole human destiny. An isosceles triangle as a mouth expresses delight, with the point downward, and genuine sorrow with the point upward; a pair of slanting lines over the eyes, serious doubts; a dot in the middle of the face, bitterness of soul. Or had he, from the first, that baffling ability to coax the most unexpected effects of speech from the simplest, most natural sentences? There is, for instance, the simple description: " He's very late again. His furniture waits quietly, till he comes stumbling along at last, and then it doubles itself." His supreme mastery of the treatment of sounds is shown also in the invention of names. Until then the comic name was produced by the conception of an association, but this was merely *witty*. Even Nestroy still had recourse to that when, for instance, he called a landlord " Paunch " or a thief " Grab." Busch's names, on the other hand, are psychologically descriptive, onomatopoetic; he paints, not with allusions, but with sounds, like the great poet and the small child. A mild, unctuous rector is called Debisch, a rough, flat-footed forester Knarrtje, a terrifying old hermit Krö-kel, a fat " vet " Sutitt, a dashing cavalier Herr von Gnatzel. At the very name Nolte the whole musty and yet homelike backwater of a little German country town rises before us.

We shall perhaps best do justice to Busch if we call him a great philosopher. In his pious nearness to Nature, his pan-psychism, he reminds us of Andersen. He has to perfection the art of making all creatures and things live. Is there, anywhere, a more touching and intimate biography of an animal than *Hans Hucke-bein* or *Fips der Affe*? The fat Brehm shrivels into a dry work of reference beside them. In the poem *Die ängstliche Nacht,* of which the first verse is quoted above, the furniture is positively organized as an opposition, and an anarchist one at that. Clothes-hooks, clock, and bootjack are in complete revolt; the impartial report of the battle with these malicious, cunning creatures makes one's heart go pit-a-pat. Also, as we have said, Busch's portraits have an extraordinary cultural-historical value. There he stands before our eyes, the German philistine, with his conventions and crotchets, his daily desires and opinions, his manner of walking, standing, eating, drinking, loving, living, and dying. Caricatured, and yet, strange to say, not in the least distorted; a collective por-trait, on which comprehending kindliness has worked as much as keen criticism. For the artist cannot indulge in polemics or alien-ate; he is a transfigurer and justifier of existence, and when people and things have passed through his heart, they come out into daylight again more beautiful than they ever were before. Goethe was only able to make so complete an art-work of his life because he recognized it as authentic in all its shapings. Hence his command of it. Shakspere could only reconstruct human passions so fascinatingly as he did because he allowed them all to have their way. Had he taken up a pharisaical and nose-in-the-air atti-tude about Falstaff and regarded him as an outcast from hu-manity, he could never have described him. But he loved him — in all his infamies, shams, and basenesses, and thus this despicable fellow became a darling for the whole human race. He loved his Macbeth too, his Iago, his Gloster; all these black villains were a piece of his heart. Now, Schiller's Franz Moor turns into a psychosis at every corner, and we cannot bring ourselves to believe in him. And why? Because his creator did not do so; he did not love him enough. Does the zoologist hate the mole? No, he leaves that to the gardener's boy. Busch makes merry without ceasing over the German bourgeois; yet we like all these people: his Tobias Knopp, Cousin Franz, Balduin Bählamm, even Pater Filucius. The counterpart is the conception of the Goethian Mephisto. Mephisto's irony is the true Satanic irony, which has its roots in malice and therefore cannot make us laugh. For malice is the most serious and saddest thing in the world. That is why Mephisto has always to succumb, he is doomed to everlasting sterility. For hatred is never productive, but love alone.

The tele-phone, the electric light bulb, and the bicycle

Leaving aside the two durable phenomena of Wagner and Busch, who are both rooted in an earlier period — Wagner in French Romanticism, and Busch in the Biedermeier — (Nietzsche was not then known to a living being outside a few Wagnerians), Germans of European reputation in that period were found only in the sphere of science, particularly in the applied sciences of chemistry (in which important new syntheses were established) and electro-mechanics. Gay-Lussac had already proved that the electric current was capable of magnetizing steel, and Faraday the converse: that magnetism could also induce electric currents. On the combination of electro-magnetism and magnetic induction was based the principle of the dynamo, discovered and developed by Werner Siemens, who hit upon the simple and brilliant idea that it was only necessary to let electricity and magnetism work upon each other to derive a permanent source of power. The current strengthens the magnet, and this in turn the current, and through this alternation the magneto-electricity develops more and more energy. From this basis there arose a wholly new type of machine which has altered the face of the earth. In 1870 the first great alternating-current machines were being built; in 1879 Siemens first demonstrated in Berlin the most important use of the electric motor, the electric railway-train, and in 1880 he invented the electric lift.

The principle of the telephone was also discovered by a German: Philipp Reis, a schoolmaster from Gelnhausen. The apparatus, which he named "telephone," made it possible to hear sounds sung into the transmitter, though the tone was subdued. The transmission of *spoken* words was only partially successful. Only with Graham Bell's instrument, first exhibited by him at the Philadelphia exhibition in 1876, did the invention come into practical use. It consists essentially of a magnet rod, an induction-coil, and a very thin iron diaphragm. This last is set vibrating by the sound-waves, which reinforce the magnet as they advance, and weaken it as they retire. By these magnetic charges alternating currents are set up in the induction-coil, which are led off to the induction-coil of the receiving telephone, where they produce analogous modifications in the magnetism of the iron core. As a result the plate, by alternate attraction and release, comes to have the same vibrations as the diaphragm of the transmitting telephone. The vibrations are transformed into audible air-vibrations. Through this process, however, the sound-waves have lost a great part of their original energy, so that the sound in the receiving station will be much weaker. This deficiency is remedied by the use of the microphone, which Hughes discovered two years later. In Bell's apparatus the sound-waves actually produced the electric currents; now it is only necessary to induce periodic fluctuations in the strength of a current which is *already flowing*. This is effected in the microphone by variable contact between two carbon pencils, since the current is very sensitive to changes in the resistance of a carbon conductor. The first German telephone system was established in Berlin in 1881.

We have also to thank a German — an Austrian, actually — for the invention of incandescent gas-lighting, named the " Auer mantle " after him. But of still greater importance is the electric lamp, constructed six years previously, in 1879, by Edison. This depends on the fact that heat is generated in every conductor carrying a current, and that the longer the flow of the current, the greater is the heat produced. In this way a carbon filament can be made to glow by passing a current through it. If, however, the glowing carbon were allowed to combine with the oxygen of the air, it would burn away very quickly. This can be avoided by enclosing the carbon filament in a vacuum glass bulb.

In the same year the first arc-lamp was made. This consists essentially of two points made of special carbon, the so-called porous carbon. A brilliant bluish-white light is produced when these two points are separated by a certain distance; this is the electric arc flame. The second half of the nineteenth century may be called the age of carbon in more ways than one, for in it were developed not only new methods of transport and manufacture, but also telephony and modern lighting.

Another great change in the urban scene was brought about by the introduction of bicycles, which were already being made on a commercial scale in 1870, but were not at all popular in their early forms; in England they were known as "bone-shakers." About 1880 the "velocipede" was in use. This was a wooden high bicycle and was always very uncomfortable. It was not until the introduction of wire spokes and pneumatic tires made convenient safety bicycles possible that the new method of progression came into its own.

In 1874 the foundations of stereochemistry were laid by van't Hoff. As we have already seen, Berzelius had tried to explain the phenomenon that substances of the same chemical composition can have totally different properties (the phenomenon of isomerism) by supposing that the atoms in them were arranged differently; this he called metamerism. For example, wine-spirit had the same chemical composition as wood ether; both contained two atoms of carbon, six of hydrogen, and one of oxygen. It was now assumed that in one case the two carbon atoms were directly connected (–C–C–) while in the other they were connected by the oxygen atom (–C–O–C–). Thus it was possible to construct for many substances formulæ which gave a picture of their "structure" or chemical constitution. It appears, however, that there were numerous substances which exhibited different properties even though the atoms were bound in the same way. The attempt was made to account for this by a new interpretation which represented the atom not as a point, but as a three-dimensional picture, regarded it as a body, and allocated to it a definite form. For example, the carbon atom was represented as a tetrahedron. In stereochemistry, then, the formulæ are represented in space.

In 1877 Hall discovered Deimos and Phobos, the two diminutive moons of Mars. They are about equal in size, about nine kilometres in diameter, and only visible when the earth is at her nearest to the planet. The inner moon, Phobos, has an orbit of about seven and a half hours, and the outer moon one of about thirty hours.

A year later the Milanese astronomer Giovanni Schiaparelli set the whole civilized world in a state of excitement by discovering the canals of Mars. In 1882 he noticed a second disturbing

322

and enigmatic phenomenon, the occasional double appearance of the canals. He himself regarded the canals as mountain formations of natural origin, although their remarkable regularity does not say much for this theory, unless indeed we are prepared to accept theories for the formation of the surface of Mars quite different from any that have ever been observed on the earth. Equally far-fetched seems the explanation put forward by contemporary astronomers, that the double appearance was an optical illusion, caused by double refraction of light. Camille Flammarion's hypothesis is much more plausible, according to which there is almost no rain on Mars, and only one sea (very shallow) in the south. Mars thus suffers from a lack of water. Flammarion assumes that the gigantic channels which run dead straight across the land were made by intelligent beings to drain the water from the polar cap when it melts in summer. The double appearance would then be due to the luxuriant vegetation growing on the banks of the canals. This theory, however, still suffers from a measure of anthropomorphism, in that it cannot bring itself to accept that the inhabitants of Mars may not have any resemblance at all to those of the earth, and that if they differ in build, body-material, or mind, they would have completely different vital necessities and completely different instruments for satisfying them.

Perhaps the Martians perceive the world by means of electromagnetic sensations; perhaps they feed on light; perhaps they themselves are gaseous. The assumption that Mars cannot be inhabited because the air is more rarefied and water is less abundant than with us represents a ridiculously " provincial " outlook. The significance of the canals of Mars we shall probably never understand; but there is no doubt whatever as to their existence; they have even been photographed by Percival Lowell.

Without telegraphs and telephones, locomotives and bicycles, photography and arc-lamps and all the other benefits of practical science, we cannot well imagine the rise and development of Expressionism; at the same time the new inventions were not the cause of the new painting, these are rather two different, but secretly interrelated, effects of the new outlook. The beginnings of Impressionism go back to Baroque. At that time, in a deliberate and emphatic contrast to Renaissance art, war was declared on outline, and " atmosphere " was created: that indefinable aura which envelops objects and, as it were, makes the language of

The Pre-Impressionists

323

the brush more inarticulate, while giving it, for that very reason, a mysterious suggestive charm and an enhanced naturalness. But, as we have pointed out, the Baroque only blurred contours without dissolving them. Light had still no independent existence; it was still bound to the objects around which it played like a shimmering astral cone or luminous courtyard. New attempts at Impressionism are found in the Rococo, with its predilection for delicate, broken, blended colours, for *chinoiserie* and *plein air*, and in the *Sturm und Drang* period, with its leaning towards Pointillism and analysis. Both these developments were cut short by the onslaught of Classicism. An almost complete anticipation of Impressionism occurs at the beginning of the nineteenth century in Goya (practically) and Runge (theoretically). But the father of the new manner in painting is usually considered to be John Constable, who lived from 1776 to 1837. He had already discovered that air was neither colourless nor entirely transparent, but rather a real body, which has to be painted like any other, and he therefore painted the sky in all the tints of the spectrum, as the dissolving palette that it really is, and the atmosphere just as it trails its azure over the landscape. The painter, he said, must forget, when face to face with nature, that pictures exist. Another time he remarked that, for him, painting and feeling were the same thing. This saying embraces practically the whole Impressionist program. Turner, who was a year older than Constable and lived until 1851, went still further. He dipped the visible world in a sparkling colour-bath, a flickering fire-sheaf of new tones. He painted damp steam, glistening leaden mist, fires, and snowstorms; tackled problems of double lighting, such as " Sunrise in a Storm " and " The Fighting *Téméraire*," and actually discovered the beauty of the steamer and the locomotive as it rushes through the damp fog with glowing goggle-eyes and steaming mouth. This particular picture is called " Rain, Steam, and Speed," and it is really made up of these three phenomena — considered until then unpaintable — and nothing but these. Another is called " Venice in the Twilight," and here again he paints only the twilight. No wonder that his contemporaries did not understand him; he was considered to have an eye disease.

From about 1830 on, a group of young artists, headed by Camille Corot and Théodore Rousseau, settled down to paint at Barbizon in the forest of Fountainebleau. Their strength lay in " *le paysage intime*." Rousseau is the master of trees, but he takes in only their skeleton; his tone is hard and dark — Muther goes so far as to compare him with Poussin. Corot was already aware of the trembling, melting lights in the water, the fog, the grey sky, the morning mist, the twilight. These two were not really Impressionists, but " tone-painters," who merely draw a transparent veil of colour over their painting. The Barbizon school sketched its pictures out of doors, an unheard-of innovation, and only gave the work its final finish in the studio. The first to complete his painting to the last brush-stroke outside with nature was Charles François Daubigny, who had a special delicate art of capturing the perfume of the seasons.

The chief (and really only) point in which the " Barbizons " were Impressionistic was their strong, fine feeling for Nature. In 1849 Jean François Millet joined them. He painted " *le cri de la terre,*" the brown ploughed field and its growths and, above all, its most characteristic feature, the peasant. Him he represented, for the first time, not from the townsman's outlook, but as from his own conditions of life. Unsentimentally, unanecdotally, he shows him as he is; not as socially stigmatized, but simply as a cultural-historical or, one might say, metaphysical phenomenon; as the primitive being and timeless species, as one of the great categories of humanity, land-cultivation become, as it were, an organism like the mole, which is the organism evolved from burrowing in the earth, and the fish, which is the organism evolved from water-wandering. Millet, therefore, still stylizes and in general is more of a sculptor than a painter.

The strongest personality among the Pre-Impressionists was Gustave Courbet. In 1855, when his pictures were rejected by the Paris Exhibition, he erected a pavilion of his own with the inscription: " *Le Réalisme. G. Courbet.*" His motto ran: " *Il faut encanailler l'art!* " He was the very type of the undismayed iconoclast, incapable of concession, but also himself a fanatic. This is meant quite literally, for during the Paris Commune he helped to demolish the Vendôme Column and was later reduced to great straits by the damages that he was sentenced to pay. Very probably he was inspired less by political than by artistic Radicalism: obviously he considered that this monument was fair game. On German Naturalism, in particular, he had great influence. In this connexion Menzel may also be mentioned, for besides his famous historical scenes he painted perspectives, gardens, and massed groups in the *plein air* style; he possessed a noble sobriety and love of truth, a witty but not loquacious penetration, and a genius for application that was inexhaustible. The attraction he so often felt towards the Frederician era had its roots below the surface: his whole manner of painting is derived from the Prussian Rococo. But his " *Théâtre Gymnase* " and his " *Eisenwalzwerk* " belong to full Impressionism.

What is Im-pressionism?

On this, Japanese painting was not without its influence. At the second Paris Exhibition, in 1867, it was made familiar to wider circles; and *japonisme* became the fashion. Above all, one learnt from it the art of leaving out: an art which deliberately constructs but a fragment in order to convey more suggestively an idea of the whole; which gives only the diagram, the cipher, the stenographic seal of objects, their strong perfumed essence, their nourishing extract — their point of reality, as it were. The name of the group was originally intended for mockery and only later became a title of honour, in which respect it resembled that of the Parnassians and the Nazarenes, the Gueux and the Quakers. It arose through Monet's having, in 1874, labelled a picture simply: " Impression." This aroused screams of laughter. So painting was to convey nothing but the mere " impression," to relate no more anecdotes, impart no more historical information, proclaim no ideas; in a word, to become meaningless! And this in fact was what these modern fools did intend. But the question at once arises: is the " impression " the extreme of objectivity or of subjectivity, of convention or autonomy, of reality or the ideal? Obviously this remains a quite undecided question, the manner of answering which depends upon the world-outlook. We can answer it Phenomenalistically and say that there are as many impressions as human eyes and brains, each of which can be valid only for its possessor. We can answer it Positivistically, to the effect that the bare sense-perceptions are received unfalsified and set down, forming an exact record of the actual, a piece of natural science of convincing integrity for all to see. We can interpret it Romantically, in which case the artist's impression is his personal poem of the world. We can interpret it Naturalistically, and see in the conscientious registering of the drawing, just because it is the artist's, the truest mirror of existence. We can give it a Collectivist meaning, and look upon Impressionism as a " social " art which proclaims the will of the species, the thing common to all, the great convention of humanity. Or, taking it the other way round, we can describe it as supreme Individualism, the effect of the genius's age, whose view becomes law. Reduced to the shortest formula, the question resolves itself into: is the artist's picture sight or insight, vista or vision?

Peter Altenberg used to grow very angry if one laid the accent on the " I " in mentioning his first book: *Wie ich es sehe* (*As I See It*). He wished to picture, not anything peculiar or personal, not *himself*, but things; and that, not as *he* saw them, but as he *saw* them. The book was, as it were, to contain only retina-pictures; he wished to do no more than record these optical realities. There can hardly be any doubt that the first generation of Impressionist painters took this view. They sought above all to render the pure sight-impression. It was chiefly for this reason that they were plein-airists. For room-lighting falsifies and " arranges." They tried systematically to accustom their eye to distinguish fine nuances of brightness, to make of it a sort of dry-plate which would absorb light-impressions even more patiently and permanently and keep them still longer. As a result of these methods they became able to distinguish " *des riens visibles*," as a French astronomer once described those most distant stars which announce their existence to the photographer of the heavens only after weeks of exposure. They thus discovered what are known as " values ": a world in which every gleam of light has its history, and shadows also help to determine the colour; in which the sun is ruler, modelling and tinting everything at once more delicately and more boldly than the dull, " tasteful " exhibitor's brush. They were the first to refrain from " posing " the landscape, projecting it instead on to the canvas just as they found it: as a mysterious bit of Nature carrying its laws within itself. They emancipated themselves from the frame and were not afraid of " over-placing," determined ever to sacrifice beauty rather than truth. And by that very means they discovered a new beauty. They opened up to painting the magic world of the metropolis, with its restaurants and cafés, theatres and music-halls, railway stations and canals, market-places and race-courses, ball-rooms and engine-rooms; a hundred-armed glittering polypus full of incessant greedy movement. And, just like the metropolis, these paintings of theirs have a compelling rhythm and powerful breath, but no harmony and no soul. This phase of Impressionism culminated in its initiator, Claude Monet — who conceived the brilliant idea of putting the colours straight on to the canvas in a series of " commas " instead of mixing them on the palate — and in Edouard Manet, whose work is almost exhaustively described in his marvellous saying: "*Il n'y a qu'une chose vraie: faire du premier coup ce qu'on voit. Quand ça y est, ça y est. Quand ça n'y est pas, on recommence. Tout le reste est de la blague.*" With Monet everything is dissolved in reflections, he is the magnificent painter of shifting light. But Manet, if it does not sound too contradictory, might be called the Classicist of Impressionism: he tries in every case to find the ultimate formula, to conjure into the realm of visibility the Platonic Idea of each phenomenon. Between the two stands Edgar Degas, the uncanny virtuoso of colour dissonances, who dealt so masterfully with the new problems imposed upon painting by electric light. Side by side with these, there appeared the beginnings of "absolute" painting, which restricts itself to symphonies in colour. Its main figure is Whistler, an American-born Irishman with a distinctive and sparkling talent for writing also, who in his bizarre, revolutionary, and definitely witty manner of painting proved himself a worthy fellow-countryman of Wilde and Shaw. His orientation is shown in the very titles of his pictures: "Harmony in Black and Grey," "Arrangement in Blue and Rose," "Fantasia in Brown and Gold," "Nocturne in Blue and Silver."

The "Ouvrier"   Examined more closely, Impressionism is a fresh triumph of French Sensualism, and of its reverse side, Cartesian Rationalism. It does with supreme virtuosity that which Descartes exacted of philosophic thought: it dissects the given reality into its elements, and the objects into their final components, then puts them together again in the "correct" way; it both analyses and constructs. Both are mechanical activities; but just as with Descartes, the subtlety and precision, power and abundance with which they are handled raise them to the rank of a spiritual process. Simultaneously, there established itself in Impressionism the new ideal of the "*ouvrier*," one half of whose talent consisted in the stupendous accuracy and doggedness of his work, for which he had models in Balzac and Flaubert. Impressionism thus took its place as the legitimate child of an industrial and technical age. In a *Speech to the Young*, made by Zola in the nineties, we have these words: "I had only one faith, one strength: it was work. I was only kept going by the immense work to which I devoted myself . . . the work of which I speak to you is regular work, a lesson, a task that I set myself so that I might progress daily, if only by a step, in my undertaking. . . . Work! Remember, gentlemen, that it is the only law in the world that counts. Life has no other

328

aim, no other cause for existence. We all exist only to perform our share of work and then to disappear." Which means: the earth is one vast workshop, and the mind a steam turbine. The principle of conservation of energy has now conquered art as its final domain.

The connexion between Impressionism and photography has often been pointed out; it is, however, a purely external one. It can only be sustained with respect to the Naturalistic component, and this indeed is of the essence of Impressionism; but at the same time Naturalism is not dependent on the invention of the camera. The Egyptian portraits of the Old Kingdom were markedly icon-like, and in the Hellenistic Age there existed a realistic mode of painting which the indignant bourgeois denounced as "dirty" art, just as with us in the eighties. The only close relationship is between Impressionism and *instantaneous* photography. The common feature is that in both cases the result is an isolated time-differential, a fragmentary lightning "snap," an abbreviation of reality, that is in a sense *false;* this is why instantaneous photographs are hardly ever considered good likenesses. There is a far greater affinity between Impressionism and the dynamo. The dynamo achieves the most powerful results by a summation of the smallest effects. It is much the same with Impressionism: it "interrupts" unceasingly, in the manner of the electro-dynamic current in which, though it alternates, there is set up a continuous and increasingly powerful effect of induction. As regards incandescent light and the arc-lamp, however, I would almost maintain that these were a result, and not the cause, of Impressionism: once the new painting had dressed the world in a sputtering shining cloak of heat and light, gas and paraffin were simply no longer to be borne.

Seldom have any artists had to fight so fiercely and almost hopelessly for their new gospel as the Impressionists. All their pictures were unsalable; the official exhibitions rejected them, and, in addition, they had in their own camp an enemy almost more dangerous than philistine stupidity: namely, *false* Impressionism. Shaw puts this excellently when he writes: " It is exceedingly difficult to draw or paint well: it is exceedingly easy to smudge paper or canvas so as to suggest a picture. . . . Plenty of rubbish of this kind was produced, exhibited, and tolerated at the time when people could not see the difference between any daub in which there were aniline shadows and a landscape by

Monet. Not that they thought the daub as good as the Monet: they thought the Monet as ridiculous as the daub; but they were afraid to say so, because they had discovered that people who were good judges did not think Monet ridiculous. Then, beside the mere impostors, there were certain unaffected and conscientious painters who produced abnormal pictures because they saw abnormally. . . . Some of the most able of the Impressionists evidently did not see forms as definitely as they appreciated colour relationship; and, since there is always a great deal of imitation in the arts, we soon had young painters with perfectly good sight looking at landscapes or at their models with their eyes half closed and a little asquint, until what they saw looked to them like one of their favourite master's pictures." It is a fact that Impressionism — and not only its impostors and hangers-on — went too far in its dissolution of contours. Form also is a component of the visible world, and the neglect of it by a section of the Impressionists (not all of them), either from instinct or with intention, had the result that their works were quite unintelligible to their contemporaries and appeared to later observers as experiments by ambitious but fettered researchers. The whole movement was " historical " in its deepest significance and in a special sense: as the strained expression of a great dying world-feeling, as the last gigantic stage in the tale of crises through which the European soul had to pass. In it the Narcissus-like atheism of the great cities and amoral nature-pantheism of the Modern Age reached its climax. It is Antichrist become colour.

The de Goncourts The founders of literary Impressionism are the brothers de Goncourt. They completed the work of Flaubert, surpassing him even in refinement of taste, precision, and nervous sensibility, but lacking his ruthless determination to overthrow and conquer. They stand to him in the relation of the great Diadochi to Alexander. They created the "*écriture artiste*," that language in which every line, every vibration, was a product of the most subtle and sovereign colour-mixing, the most expert artistic calculation. They brought Flaubert's " exactitude " to supreme perfection by relying exclusively on a science of "*documents humains*," and correspondingly they were painfully conscientious collectors, dissectors, and registrars of human spiritual emotions. In a far higher degree than their master they turned psychology into pathology, the novel into a clinical study. Their books are marvels of technique in infallibly sensing the faintest oscillations of the pulsebeat and blood-pressure of their characters, the soil and air-pressure of their *milieu* — in short, the ideal sphygmographs and seismometers of their generation.

The new movement in literature received its strongest impetus through Zola. He took over from contemporary painting the " comma " method and " *plein air*," the predilection for the city *milieu* and artificial light, for social problems and night-life, shapshots and mass scenes; where he differs from it is in his lack of musicality. From his exterior, any physiognomist would have said he was a famous advocate — and this he actually was: an ingenious, merciless, penetrating investigator of cases, who, having got together a stupendous mass of material with which only he himself could deal, proceeded to plead with icy logic and fiery eloquence. His own definition of art is well known: " *la nature vue à travers un tempérament*," and it was his own practice to lay the accent definitely on the " *nature vue*." He aims, quite unmistakably, at that greatest possible elimination of the ego which is the naturalist's ideal. This he seeks to attain through the " experimental " novel, which handles the phenomena of life more or less as laboratory material, testing their reactions in test-tubes and retorts. In the preface to his *Rougon-Macquart* series he says: " I intend to explain what happens to one family, one small group of people within the social structure; how it opens out, giving birth to ten or twenty individuals who, at first sight, seem not to resemble each other at all, but on closer examination reveal themselves as related. Heredity, like gravity, has its laws." This is almost word for word Taine's program, that was quoted in our last chapter: sociology becomes biology, the " family " a zoological category, Darwinism the Philosophers' Stone. Even less than the brothers Goncourt did Zola escape the snare of allowing purely analytical psychology to transform itself in every case into psychiatry. For they evaded the final consequences of their system by their still latent connexion with the belletristic culture of the pre-Naturalistic period: their feminine charm, gaming-table caprice, and decadent delicacy smacks of the *ancien régime*.

It has probably struck everyone, however, that even Zola was a sort of spiritualist. For while he describes society, with astonishing verve and accuracy, in the workings of its collective soul and its artificial and self-devouring monster creations, his exchanges and factories, markets and warehouses, mines and

331

railways, gin-shops and brothels come to be for him mighty symbols, living beings, indeed. There is the faint survival of grand epic in his " protocols " and " inquiries " (as, in legal vein, he called his novels), and at the same time of Romanticism, French pathos, grand opera, and Victor Hugo. Thus his Naturalism is reduced *ad absurdum* through his own secret mythology. But, for all that, he denotes, in his contempt for all things divine and his adoration of the mass and the machine, a peak of modern Paganism. To the four Christian gospels he opposed his own: " *Fécondité, travail, vérité, justice.*" They are, in point of fact, devil's gospels. (He was prevented from completing the last by his death — a quite irrelevant " technical " death, caused by accidental gas-poisoning, although in his case, since every man is the author of his own biography, there is nothing strange about it.) These modern false gods: *fécondité* (Darwinism), *travail* (Materialism), *vérité* (Rationalism), *justice* (Social Ethics), are one and all devices of Satan. As if " fertility " were anything but lust, " work " any different from Adam's curse, " truth " not the same as man's Fall, " justice " not identical with Jehovahism! Triumphs of Antichrist, every one. It is here that the first faint dawn of intellectual Bolshevism sets in, that final creation of the God-forsaken West by which it has brought upon itself a Mongolian scourge, a new spectre of the Hun. Before this was to be, however, Russia's art took another course.

Tolstoi and Dostoievski

Carlyle's essay on Dante and Shakspere, or " The Hero as Poet," closes with the words: " The Czar of all the Russias, he is strong, with so many bayonets, Cossacks, and cannons; and does a great feat in keeping such a tract of Earth politically together; but he cannot yet speak. Something great is in him, but it is a dumb greatness. He has had no voice of genius, to be heard of all men and times. He must learn to speak. He is a great dumb monster hitherto." Since then Carlyle's wish has been fulfilled: Russia has learned to talk and has found in Tolstoi her Dante, in Dostoievski her Shakspere.

The last of the Byzantines

It is not by chance that Dostoievski suffered from epilepsy, known from the time of the Greeks as the " sacred sickness," or that his death-mask revealed a striking resemblance to the head of Socrates. The truth is, both these men were latent criminals who purified themselves into saints; and it was Dostoievski's disease that turned him into a seer. The earthly form in which genius usually appears — that paradoxical synthesis of overwrought high-tension cerebration and pathological irritability, of non-viability and colossal size — is seen in him in its most fascinating and riskiest guise. He combines the dæmonic intuition of a somnambulist, bordering closely on insanity, with a trenchant dialectic of the utmost alertness and frigidity, analysis and logic. And, added to all this, his moral feeling was of a delicacy and force unparalleled in modern times; we should have to go back to Pascal, and perhaps even to the Middle Ages, to find anything like it. No other author gives in so high a degree the impression of a medium writing in a mysterious trance; one almost sees his books being dictated to him by invisible angels as in legends of the saints. Yet he often showed an all too human side in his writings: he was not free from the religious and political zealotism of his nation and he asserts repeatedly that the Orthodox is the only true Church and that Russia has a divine claim on Constantinople. But these conflicting aspects solve themselves if we agree to regard him as the *last great Byzantine,* the latest form in which the spirit of Eastern Rome became flesh — that eternal Eastern Rome which we cannot understand, but at best dimly imagine. He is a revival of the Great Migrations spiritually conceived as the chaos from which there bursts forth light; for him the great enemy and tempter is Western Rome: that is, all Europe; his Russianness is, like the Greek emperor-idea, both cosmopolitan and national, imperialistic and theocratic, conservative and subversive, humble and filled with the pride of the elect. In him, as in Byzantine scholasticism, original Christianity and theological sophistry are blended; he hates the world of cities even more profoundly and fiercely, perhaps, than Tolstoi, but in contrast to him he remains through all his hatred a Byzantine, a cosmopolitan. This is why in his works we have, for the first time in Russian literature, the best-seller in poetic form — for the works of Tolstoi and the rest were, as he called them, "squire's literature." His art is complex, "Late," ghostly, catacombish, and Byzantine in its very form — its dusky, gleaming mosaic splendour, its pale hieratic swarm of figures, its lack of ambient and aerial perspective, of landscape in any sense. His figures stand mysteriously in the void, and instead of offering themselves for observation they rather fix their torturing, searching glance on the observer. And like that sinking world, Dostoievski is shaken by the premonition of a great Decline: he is the monstrous trombone proclaiming an end and a dark impalpable future. But this new thing that his prophet's eye discerns is Antichrist, and Antichrist is revolution. His books are apocalypses and Fifth Gospels.

The justification of evil

In the *Brothers Karamazov,* Zosima, the Staretz, says: " The truth is that everyone is guilty of everything, only people do not know it: if once they did, we should at once have paradise on earth." Here Dostoievski touches upon the profoundest doctrines of the Gnostics. One of the greatest of these, Marcion, preached that man must be redeemed from *everything* that is natural, from all that he is and all that surrounds him: from the world, from the law, from sin, from his own ego, *and also from justice.* This is the gospel idea at its intensest, and it was also Dostoievski's. The Saviour raised up the adulteress, the idle Mary, the sinful Magdalen, the unclean Samaritan, to be his favourites. This is the main reason why Dostoievski felt himself so particularly drawn to criminals and, as their creator, loved them — loved them *more* even than the others. His grand conception was that the criminal stands *nearer to God* because he has taken upon himself a greater share of the total human guilt; and that means a greater share of atonement: for guilt and atonement are to Dostoievski inseparable, being merely two halves of the timeless event. In his unique doctrine of justification, therefore, crime is a kind of sacrifice, and evil, so to say, only a *dimension of goodness.* The common root of both is Christian liberty, the freedom of choice between good and evil, the Christian knowledge. This it is which is the supreme gift of the divine mercy and the most certain pledge of redemption. For only he can recognize the good who has known evil also; in the existence of evil lies the certainty of the good. In the Christian's freedom lies the true theodicy.

The Unveiler

Beside Dostoievski, who is a voice from the between-world in which spirits build the bridge between God and man, Tolstoi affects us merely as a great artist who has made the earth purer and lovelier. As such he did indeed reach the utmost perfection: the art of artlessness. There is a passage in the fifth part of *Anna Karenina,* on the painter Michailov, which is strangely applicable to Tolstoi's own work: " He had often heard the word ' technique ' without at all understanding what it was really supposed to mean. He knew that this word referred to the mechanical facility in painting and drawing which is quite independent of content. He had often noticed that technique was compared with the content-value, just as if it were possible to paint well what was bad. He certainly knew that much care and attention was called for in unwrapping a picture, if it were not to be damaged, but as for any art of painting, any technique — it simply did not exist. Had that which he saw revealed itself to a child or to his own cook, they would have known how to scoop out what they saw. But not the most experienced and skilful master of the technique of painting would have been able by mechanical dexterity alone to paint anything unless the sum of its content had been revealed to him. But he knew also that where it was a question of technique, he had nothing to boast of."

Tolstoi's art is of this same order. He takes off the coverings. The picture has been there for a long time, but no one can see it. The artist comes and unveils it. That is all that he does to it. His whole achievement lies in his power to see things as hardly anyone else sees them: that is, as they are. There are descriptive writers who at once become boring if they expand at all, and there are soul-painters who are diffusive from the very start. To this class Tolstoi belongs. It is not that he is loquacious: he never says anything superfluous, and repeats himself only where it would be a sin against realism not to repeat himself. The events that he describes are, when one comes to think of it, of secondary importance. His novels are immense magazines of observations which are an end in themselves. They are not, as it were, an extract of life, but, on the contrary, an extension and elaborate completion of life. Not one of the personages whom he describes could consciously have experienced as much as the author, who merely looks on. People live at a far quicker pace than Tolstoi writes, and just because they are not authors. He catches precisely the most unnoticeable and hidden things: things which no other observer would notice, things of which the persons whom he describes have themselves no knowledge.

The acuteness and exactness of observation is so strong that at times it seems almost like irony. He says, on one occasion, of Vronsky, who afterwards becomes Anna Karenina's lover: " A new sensation of emotion and love overcame him, the blissful feeling of a purity and freshness due in part to the fact that all the evening he had not smoked." Once Vronsky is moved to tears. This is described as follows: " He, too, was conscious of something rising in his throat and of a peculiar sensation in his nose." The most moving scene of the whole novel is that in which Anna, when the doctors have given her up, calls her husband and her lover to her bedside to reconcile them. She succeeds, and they all three feel themselves in that moment as belonging to a higher community in which all men are united by the bond of forgiving love. These are the closing words: " She said: ' Thank God, thank God! Now all is ready. Just my feet stretched out a little further. There, that is nice. How badly those flowers are made, so utterly unlike a violet,' she continued, pointing to the carpet. ' O God, when will it all be over!'" Tolstoi certainly never thought of showing his figures and their impulses in that twilight that is used by Shaw, Wedekind, or Altenberg; but it is instructive to see how absolutely inevitable this twilight becomes as soon as an art is subordinated to the principle of verism. " Instructive " is, indeed, perhaps the most apposite term for Tolstoi's novels. They bring to our knowledge a mass of things that are new and strange and instruct us, so to say, in the elements of microscopic vision. And yet — one day Tolstoi came to hate his own great art. How was this?

The hatred of the artist
Man's fundamental instinct is desire to dominate. He wants to rule over things dead and alive, bodies and souls, future and past. All the many and varied activities to which he devotes himself are oriented to that end. Domination is the secret force which helps him to outgrow the limitations of his animal nature, and to this passion he owes the increasing spiritualization of all his vital impulses.

But nature and life go their own way according to superhuman laws. On the one side is obtuse matter, with its passive and yet insurmountable resistances; on the other, the world of the soul, intangible and strange and inscrutably complicated. And above it all is destiny, that directional force innate in all occurrences, which never concerns itself about man. Everything evades him; he is surrounded by shadows and riddles. The physical and the spiritual world stand under the same law of impenetrability.

What is he to do, then? Ruling is his foremost necessity in life, and it lies in the nature of every organism to obtain its necessities in all circumstances either by force or, failing this, by cunning. Thus it came about that man thought out a ruse by which to satisfy the basic depths of will: he invented art.

" Reality " withstood him. The world of the body was too hard for him and too inert in its massive immobility, and the world of the soul too light and unsubstantial in its problematical intangibility. That is why the cry arose in him: Away from this rigid reality, away from the world of things as they are! He conceived the ingenious idea of leaving those intolerant and obstinate

336

realities to themselves and constructing a new world of his own above the other. This newly-created world was his property, his unlimited, sovereign domain, which he could shape and steer according to his will. In this kingdom, his own free creation, he might hope to be at last a complete tyrant. Art became the sublimest form of his will to power.

But at this point an odd thing sometimes happens with the artist. There is, after all, a something stronger than himself: that formative power which created this whole kingdom of his and dominates it. His art is more than he is: for he is a helpless individual organism, a man as other men, but *it* is a terrific natural force. And with horror he begins to realize that this curious ability to create has made him but the more dependent. His " births " stand there, released from his will. And gradually there grows up within him dislike and hatred of this art, and he fights against it. Then, when clever folk come and say to him that this is contradictory, since in fighting against art he is fighting himself and the whole meaning of his life, he might reply to them:

True, I hate art, just because I am an artist. You others may love and admire it, but I am bound to curse it. For you it is an " inspiration," but for me a doom. I wanted to achieve dominion and freedom through it, but it is this same art which has made me entirely unfree. It is the super-tyrant in me. Gradually, without my noticing, it has grown up beyond me and swelled into a powerful, terrible creature that is alien and hostile to me. I wanted to make images after my own wishes, and ideals after my free sovereign whim. But my art never inquired about my wishes and ideals. The people who come and go in my poems are not the creations of my will. I wanted to create a world of beauty, and there grew up before me a world of truth. I wanted to construct a world of happiness, and there arose a world of damnation. My figures were not subordinate to me, they were never my compliant creatures. They stood there like their own lawgivers, endowed with autocratic vital forces, and they frightened me, for that was not how I had conceived them. And therefore I now fling my curse at art. It is the hereditary enemy of my life. It has set itself above me and robbed me, destroyed me, split me in two halves. It is the monster in me. Lying is human, but my art will have the truth and again the truth. Faith is human, but my art brings doubt. Blindness is human, but my art is the power of seeing. I did not know that the gift of seeing was so terrible a thing. Everywhere the

337

artist bores passages, digs up subterranean things into the light. With his doubts he hammers at everything. He asks: but is greatness really great? and is goodness really good? and beauty beautiful, and truth true? Why has he, he alone, this frightful mission? He is, after all, a man like other men, with the instinct to believe, to wish to believe; why, then, was he given this horrible function of seeing, being forced to see? I cannot see that the artist has reason to love art. Far rather would I have been a simple peasant, who thinks that everything is equally big and good, equally true and beautiful. I will make haste and try to turn into one. But I fear it is too late.

But I retain my hatred. Who else, indeed, could hate art so profoundly, *have* to hate it, as we artists? Surely not you semi-artists! You amateurs and artists by accident. You may love art, for you have never suffered through it. For neither, for that reason, does it belong to you. For only the things through which we suffer most deeply, only these belong to us.

CHAPTER II

GONE TO THE DEVIL

*" Heaven and earth and all that is between,
dost thou think that it was created for a jest? "*
Koran

The turn of the eighties marks a rather sharp cæsura. 1888 is
the " Three-Emperor year ": on March 9 William I died at the
age of nearly ninety-one, and on June 15 Frederick III, after
reigning but ninety-nine days; and the Wilhelmine era set in.
The political tendencies of this era were plain to read from the
very first years. In 1889 the Reichstag sanctioned the first aug-
mentation of the fleet, and in the same year French capital began
to finance Russian industry on a large scale — already, in December of the previous year, the first Russian state loan of half a
milliard francs had been raised, to be followed immediately by
others. Then, on March 20, 1890, came Bismarck's retirement.
The Russian Reinsurance Treaty was considered " too complicated " by Caprivi, the new Chancellor, and was not renewed. The
same year saw the end of the anti-Socialist law — which the
Reichstag refused to extend — and, at the elections, a victory for
the Left. In the spring of 1888 Georg Brandes lectured at Copenhagen University on " The German Philosopher Friedrich Nietzsche," and thus for the first time drew Europe's attention to his
works. In January 1889 Nietzsche's mind gave way, and almost
simultaneously he began to be read in his native land; a year
later he already enjoyed the " excessive fame " which he prophesied in one of his last letters to his publisher. At the same time
Tolstoi and Ibsen were making their way triumphantly in Germany, England, and France. In the season of 1889–90 the *Freie
Bühne* was opened in Berlin, and the paper of the same name
founded. This decided the victory of the Naturalistic movement,
parallel with which came the break-through of *Verismo* in Italy.
In 1889 there appeared: Strindberg's *Father*, Hauptmann's *Vor
Sonnenaufgang*, Sudermann's *Ehre*, Liliencron's *Gedichte*, Richard Strauss's first great symphony, *Don Juan*, and Bergson's first

339

study, which already contained his whole philosophical program; then, in 1890, Hamsun's, Wedekind's, Maeterlinck's, Mascagni's remarkable firstborns saw the light: *Hunger, Frühlings Erwachen, Princesse Maleine, Cavalleria rusticana;* and Leibl, Liebermann, and Uhde, until then unnoticed, began to excite universal indignation.

The will to power as decadence

It is thoroughly symptomatic that the hero of the most powerful drama of this epoch, Oswald Alving, should become mentally deranged and that the philosopher, the painter, and the musician who are the most striking and representative embodiments of the age — Nietzsche, van Gogh, and Hugo Wolf — should suffer the same fate. In these four great life-destinies, world-historical symbols of the first rank, the spirit of the age, turning tragically upon itself, declared its bankruptcy.

For all that, the age, seen from outside, appeared to be filled with vitality. But this robust urge towards reality was in fact a phenomenon of disease, in that it was a one-sided and hypertrophied development of one characteristic at the expense of all others, and an unconscious attempt to compensate an incurable aimlessness, non-viability, and inward emptiness by spasmodic outward activity and almost maniac craving for movement. This paradoxical connexion between decay and the apparently vigorous working of the will to life was typified by Nietzsche in his philosophy: the birth of the Will to Power as the spirit of the decadence. In *Ecce Homo* he says: "Besides being a decadent, I am also the opposite." The opposite is the Superman. But — and this is the deepest meaning of Nietzsche's philosophy, of which he was no doubt aware although he usually chose not to see it — the Superman is the decadent over again! Thus does his thought-poem float like a noble paradigm over the dying century: as the deepest criticism of European Nihilism and as its loftiest incarnation — for a more extreme Nihilism than the sweeping and exclusive affirmation of life does not exist, since naked "life" (as Nietzsche himself pointed out times without number) is nothing but a complete absence of any kind of meaning.

Hegel and Halske

In the last act of the Modern Age, which rises with the immorality of the Renaissance and sets with the immorality of *Zarathustra*, Germany was the leading champion. Beginning with a survey of the most superficial manifestations of life — the bark and bast, so to say, of the body of the age — we see Germany at the head of almost the entire manufacturing world, leading the fashion in gun-construction, shipbuilding, and the optical, chemical, and electro-technical industries. In marked contrast to the old Germany, Berlin is governed, no longer by Fichte and Hegel, but by Siemens & Halske, and the brothers Humboldt are succeeded by Bleichröder Bros.; at Jena Zeiss succeeds Schiller as a world-famous personage; at Nürnberg Dürer's works are superseded by Schuckert's; Frankfurt am Main retires before Höchst am Main, and in place of the *Farbenlehre* we have the " Colour Company, Ltd." (*Farben-AG*).

One of the essential changes in the outward carriage of the period is the rise of a new tempo: hurriedly built light railways, omnibuses, tramways — horse, steam, and eventually electric — fill the town-picture; lightning trains, telephones improving with every year, and daily increasing telegraph facilities provide for distant communications. This system of communications, as complicated as it is centralized, gives man not merely accelerated speed, but the power of being everywhere: his voice, his writing, his body pierces any distance, his shorthand note, his camera fix the most fleeting impression. He is everywhere, and therefore nowhere. He embraces the whole of reality, but in the form of a dead substitute for reality. An impressive symbol of this state of mind is the sinking of the *Titanic*, the world's greatest luxury-ship, which on its first voyage out made a speed-record, but at the cost of death. The same motif, humorously treated, occurs in Jules Verne's *Round the Earth in Eighty Days:* Phileas Fogg, whose life has hitherto run its mathematically even course between club and home, tears round the planet to prove that it is possible to do so with the same mathematical precision in exactly eighty days: romance is supplied by railway accidents, missed steamer connexions, and the overcoming of these obstacles by presence of mind. And before the century bids farewell, it produces the two greatest transforming agents in outward reality that modern times have seen — the automobile and the cinema.

The world-picture of theoretical as well as practical physics underwent a decisive reorientation through two discoveries, in which Germany was again prominently concerned: they are known by the magic words " Röntgen rays " and "wireless telegraphy." It will be remembered that Huygens, as early as the seventeenth century, had already claimed in his undulatory theory that light was propagated by the vibrations of a particular elastic matter, the ether. He could not, however, carry his point

The new tempo

The electromagnetic light theory

341

against the authority of Newton, whose theory of light was that it was a fine substance flung off by luminous bodies. A hundred years later Euler, the great mathematician of his time, went back to Huygens in pointing out that in light-phenomena no material loss could ever be proved, and that they arose through vibrations, exactly as did sound, except that here ether played the part of the air. Then, at the beginning of the nineteenth century, Thomas Young accounted for colours by mere differences in the number of vibrations which hit our eye during the same unit of time. According to the speed with which the ether movement works upon our retina, we experience, in a descending scale, sensations of violet, blue, green, yellow, orange, red. In 1835 Ampère proved that the sensation of warmth does not differ from that of light in the manner of its origin. Light and heat are the same natural phenomenon: if a body reflects light-rays, we call it luminous; if it allows them to permeate, we call it transparent; if they are neither reflected by it nor let through to permeate, we call it warm. Ten years afterwards Faraday proved that electricity was also of the nature of light and heat, all three being movements of the same medium. Upon this, in 1873, Maxwell constructed his electro-magnetic theory of light. According to this, electricity is nothing but the creation of transversal waves in the ether, which can be of very different lengths, but have invariably the same velocity as light: namely, three hundred thousand kilometres a second. The correctness of this theory was proved experimentally by Heinrich Hertz, the brilliant but shortlived physicist, by the aid of a most ingeniously constructed apparatus, the "Hertz oscillator." He reported on his experiment in a lecture given before the Versammlung deutscher Naturforscher und Ärzte at Heidelberg in 1889. "My assertion," he said, " is precisely this: that light is an electrical phenomenon — light in itself, all light, the light of the sun, of the candle, of a glow-worm. Remove electricity from the world, and light will vanish; remove the luminiferous ether from the world, and electrical and magnetic forces will no longer be able to traverse space. . . . We no longer see currents flowing, electricities assembling, in the conductors; we only see the waves in the air as they cross, unite, strengthen and weaken themselves. . . . We discover electricity in a thousand places where before we had no certain knowledge of its existence. In every flame, in every luminous atom, we see an electrical process. Even when a body does not illumine, so long as it radiates

342

heat alone, it is the seat of electrical disturbances." Thus electricity lost its material status as Stahl's heat-substance and Newton's light-substance had done before it, but it was elevated instead into a force of all-powerful ubiquity. Electro-magnetic waves which have wave-lengths of four to seven and a half ten-thousandths of a millimetre affect our eye as light; from that point to, say, fifty thousandths of a millimetre we feel them as heat; and if they attain a length of from some centimetres to many metres, they reveal themselves as electricity. Electrical waves are light-waves of very great wave-length; both are altered conditions of the same ether. A direct consequence of Hertz's studies was the invention by Branly, in 1890, of the coherer, which reacts with the utmost sensitiveness to electrical waves, and in connexion with these came the experiments of Marconi, who in 1896 first made wireless telegraphy practical by the construction of antennæ.

In the same year Becquerel discovered the rays that are named after him, a few months after Röntgen's discovery of the X-rays which, in turn, bear his name. The Becquerel rays, like light-rays, are electrical phenomena; they differ from these, however, in that they are neither reflected nor refracted, but are deflected by electric and magnetic forces; above all, they possess the mysterious power of illumining opaque substances while they themselves remain invisible. In 1898 Pierre and Marie Curie discovered two new elements in pitchblende: to one of these Madame Curie — a Pole by birth — gave the chauvinistic name of Polonium; the other was very appropriately christened Radium by her husband. For its main characteristic is radio-activity, the ability to radiate Becquerel rays permanently. William Ramsay went still further with his remarkable discovery that radium, by breaking down the atom, generates perpetually a gas, the so-called radium-emanation, which after various complicated processes finally transforms itself into helium, an inert gas whose existence in the solar atmosphere had been proved by spectrum analysis as early as 1868, but had not hitherto been established on earth. If the "emanation" is kept in contact with water, a further gaseous element, neon, is formed; if brought in contact with copper or silver salts, a third such element, argon, is produced. Radium is therefore an element which perpetually transforms itself into other elements. The radium salts (the pure metal has not yet been isolated) have further the characteristic of making the air through which they send their rays a conductor of

343

electricity — of " ionizing " it — and also of rendering all bodies in their vicinity temporarily radio-active, endowing them, that is, with " induced radio-activity." Attempts have been made to explain this on the ground of the so-called theory of electrons : a sort of return to the notion of a " substantial electricity," the hypothesis being that electrons are the ultimate building-stones, negatively or positively charged electric units several thousand times smaller than the tiniest atoms. Induced radio-activity would thus be accounted for by the theory that all atoms come from electrons, which, in the case of radium, form labile systems, so that they can leave the atomic structure and move in straight lines as so-called corpuscular rays. Generally speaking, an atom was now imagined as constructed like a solar system, in which the negative electrons move planet-wise round a positively charged central body, according to the laws established by Kepler for astronomical movements. But the electron-theory, which in essentials goes back to Helmholtz, is obviously quite irreconcilable with the Hertzian wave-theory. This being so, the Dutch physicist Lorentz tried in 1892 to synthesize the two on the hypothesis that all electrical processes taking place *within* the body can be explained on the basis of the atomistic substance theory — that is, by accepting the electron — while, on the other hand, all *distant* electrical effects are obtained through vibrations — that is, only with the assistance of the ether. This settlement of the problem has been universally accepted; I must, however, regretfully decline to agree, since — like the demarcation of spheres of influence, so familiar in colonial policies — it is a pure compromise, amounting, indeed, to an unconscious admission of bankruptcy on the part of physical science, which (although it refuses to admit it) has been brought to an impasse by a clumsy, one-sided world-formula. The fact is, matter cannot be explained materialistically : the failure to realize this has been the fundamental mistake of the whole of modern science. In the theory of light, also, a hybrid hypothesis has recently been set up with a view to saving the electron at all costs. This is a return to Newton in disguise; it assumes that the atom sends out electro-magnetic waves as a result of the transition of the electrons from a higher to a lower energy state, and that these waves manifest themselves as light-rays. All such theories are no more than ingenious triflings, whose duration stands in absurd contrast to the eternity value on which they pride themselves. If it be claimed that they have been " experimentally proved," the reply is that *everything* can be experimentally proved: this depends solely on the dexterity and gullibility of the experimenter. The " phlogiston " was also experimentally proved, and although it was obviously a fiction, this did not prevent Lavoisier, Haller, and other great scientists from achieving by aid of it the most enlightening chemical discoveries and the most beneficial medical cures. On the basis of Ptolemy's system the eclipses of the sun and the moon were foretold with the same exactness as today — and this was the experimental proof of its accuracy. Theories are convictions; and convictions are proved by the fact of one's having them. The general axioms of physics and chemistry which are considered to be right are always implicit from the first in the initial equation; so it is no wonder that they come out at the end of the operation. The protest that Wundt once made (from the " scientific " standpoint, of course) against Zöllner's spiritistic experiments is applicable to all experiments, including his own: " He who believes in magic makes experiments with it and he who does not believe in it usually makes none. But as a man has, notoriously, a great inclination to find confirmation of what he believes and to this end even displays great perspicacity in deceiving himself, the success of such experiments merely convinces me in the first place that those who make them also believe in them." The amazing discoveries of radiology in particular should have brought *Ignorabimus* home to the scientist, for through it three of his most fundamental conceptions were discredited by the complete collapse of their definitions. One of the basic conceptions in chemistry had hitherto been the element, whose cardinal characteristic consisted in non-transformability; another, in physics, the atom, whose decisive mark is indivisibility; and the other, in optics, the opaque or dark body, whose existence depends upon its absorbing light-rays. All these definitions are now untenable, are almost, one might say, nonsense.

Still further inferences, however, followed. If, in the process of radio-activity, electrons split off from the nucleus, the hope arises that this may also be effected by artificial means. In 1911 Rutherford (a name already famous in the history of science in connexion with the discovery of nitrogen) actually succeeded in " breaking down " the atom, if only on a very small scale and in exceptionally favourable circumstances. There is therefore a theoretical possibility that those who persevere may one day be in a position to liberate and utilize the enormous but, in the ordinary way, bound masses of energy residing in the atom. It has been

The breaking down of the atom

345

calculated that by the " dissociation " of a single small copper coin some thirteen and a half milliards horse-power would become active. The release of "intra-atomic" energy would naturally result in a complete revolution of all earthly proportions. On the other hand, only the very naïve could suppose that this would also signify a solution of the social problem. As the so-called " normal person " — who is in fact not that at all, but the lord of our economic life — is born and dies an unimaginative knave, we may assume that such triumphs of technique would, like those that came before it, only lead to new forms of universal greed and injustice. One has only to imagine that two hundred years ago someone prophesied the extent to which humanity would succeed in utilizing magnetic energy, electric energy, solar energy, the energy in black coal, and the water energy that is stored up in " white coal " — and what perfectly natural conclusions as to a social paradise the philanthropists would have drawn from it all! Instead, everything has become much worse, and Europe is divided into capitalist states wherein most people are beggars, and Soviet states wherein all of them are. No, the " utilization of atomic energy " would merely make those on the top greedier, and those below poorer; both classes hungrier, therefore, and war still more bestial. The solution of the social problem calls for a *moral* emanation, ray-production, and atom-destruction.

Fabians and lecture-room Socialists

So thought the " Fabians," a society whose very open-minded and valuable work at the close of the century deserves particular mention. The Fabian Society was founded in 1883, and Sidney and Beatrice Webb, Wells, Shaw, Annie Besant (later so famous as a Theosophist), and many other fine and talented people were members; it put forward no particular creed in its Tracts, Essays, and News, which found their way to all parts of the world. Their motto was: " For the right moment you must wait, as Fabius did most patiently when warring against — Hannibal, though many censured his delays; but when the time comes you must strike hard, as Fabius did, or your waiting will be in vain, and fruitless." By Socialism they understood, in a general way, a plan to secure to all equal rights and equal possibilities. Socialism was to come noiselessly and without its victims' being aware of it. Sidney Webb, in one of his lectures, quotes the saying of a British minister: " We are all Socialists now," and follows it up with: ". . . That which has long formed part of the unconscious basis of our practice is now formulated as a definite theory. . . . If we look back along the line of history, we see the irresistible sweep of the growing tendency." A similar standpoint was adopted in Germany by a large scientific school which based itself on " historical " economics, as opposed to the dogmatic or classical type founded by Adam Smith and completed by John Stuart Mill. It was maintained that there was in economic life a series of " natural laws," since man's elementary needs remained always the same. The nature of this *homo œconomicus,* common to all countries and all ages, had therefore to be investigated and fixed in definite economic axioms. The most important of these have already become familiar: the law of population, the law of wages, the law of free competition, the law of supply and demand. But a quarrel arose among the scientists, who split into two schools: the " deductive " school, headed by Professor Menger, which declared the main concern of economic science to be " the general, the typical, the typical relations "; and the " historical " school, led by Professor Schmoller, which declared classical laws to be " abstract visions, completely devoid of reality," and political economy a purely inductive science, concerned solely with the concrete life of the past and present and the description thereof. The connexion between this anti-idealist, pro-realist tendency, which became dominant at the turn of the eighties, with the simultaneous Naturalistic movement in art, is unmistakable. Theoretical and practical relativism, declared the supporters of the historical school, must replace the existing absolutism; the laws of national economy were not laws at all in the sense of physical and chemical laws, that hold good everywhere and always, but were valid only under definite conditions which were changeable. The contention was correct in so far as political economy is always in fact only the product of the given historical condition at a given moment, and its laws of existence are as little permanent in character as that condition; it overlooked, however, the fact that this is the common fate of all human spheres of activity and the sciences drawn from them, and that the setting up of theoretical laws is precisely as justifiable and as unjustifiable here as in other domains. For the laws of speech, of nature, even of mathematics, are simple deductions from previous observations, and change at once when contradictory observations are recorded; not even a new empiricism is required to suspend them; a simple shifting of the general world-feeling, of which they are mere functions, is sufficient to do so. Sciences are no more than the shorthand notes of our preconceived opinions.

But the supporters of the historical tendency developed also a very remarkable practical efficiency. They taught that the State was " the organ of moral solidarity " and had therefore no right to look on with indifference at the distress of a portion of the population : the central power was bound to organize economic relations on a generally satisfactory basis. The preservation of private property was, they said, nevertheless indispensable to the increase in production, as this alone kept individual initiative on the alert. To the propaganda of the State Socialists, as they called themselves, we owe a string of laws and control-measures for the protection of workers. Their opponents in the Liberal camp dubbed them " lecture-room Socialists (*Kathedersozialisten*)," because of the many professors in their ranks ; but Bismarck declared that he was himself a *Kathedersozialist*. In France the " interventionists " stood for similar principles.

School reform

Another direct result of the Naturalistic tendencies of the age was an effort to reform education. The attacks directed against the humanistic gymnasia at the end of the eighties in Germany came chiefly from two quarters : from upper-middle-class circles with industrial interests and from the militarist Prussian court party. The first group raised the familiar objections of the practical uselessness of dead languages and argued in favour of substituting a so-called " realistic " education for the Classical — in other words, of approximation to the technical schools ; the second pointed out that a predominant interest in antiquity would be detrimental to patriotism, and it therefore demanded education on a " national " basis — something more or less resembling that of the cadet schools. It cannot be denied that school-teaching was still almost mediæval in character, and bore distinct traces of its origin in the monastic schools, and that it did not provide the really harmonious education, embracing equally all domains of human knowledge — which alone could fairly have claimed the title " Classical." In 1890 the " December conferences " were held. There were meetings of educationists at which, after long debates, a few mitigations were secured. In history the leaving examination was waived where classwork had been satisfactory ; in geography it was abolished altogether. Fewer hours were devoted to ancient languages, and both Latin prose and the *viva voce* Latin examination were abandoned. This satisfied no one. The adherents of the old school wept for the Latin prose (although this had never been anything but a travesty of colloquial speech, consisting as it did of the purely

348

mechanical permutation of a handful of Ciceronian phrases) and teaching in the Latin tongue, although this was a complete farce, for what could be more idiotic than a tradesman's son with curled hair and spectacles addressing his fellow-creatures in the manner of a Roman citizen? The radicals, for their part, would have kept no Latin or Greek at all. These people held the naïve point of view that the value of a language lay purely in its use as a way of making oneself understood. They forgot that every language, even a "dead" one, is the precipitate of a human soul-form which can never reappear; and that, in the case of the two Classical languages, this is of a very high order and can be approached by philology and no other way. But though we might conceivably resign ourselves to the loss of Latin and Greek, we should still be unable, without them, to understand not only Antiquity, but the whole of that modern culture which begins with Dante's *Divine Comedy*, the supreme "*Summa*" of Latin Scholasticism, and ends with Goethe's *Faust,* the tragedy of the "arch-humanist"; for all that lies between is Renaissance, reawakening, of the Classical. No philosopher, no writer of European rank, is thinkable without a knowledge of the Classics. Our whole Western science is from first to last fed from Classical sources; even the "realistic" disciplines — medicine, physics, technicology — are Classicist in the extreme, down to their most everyday terminology. Even one's mother tongue can only be thoroughly acquired by way of the dead languages. No one can write a really precise, clear, and fluent German without the drill of Latin, or philosophical German without a knowledge of Greek. There has in fact never been a classic German stylist who was ignorant of the Classical languages; and the far more general knowledge of these among the middle classes in former days is also the reason why, up to the beginning of the nineteenth century, one so seldom finds bad German in letters, diaries, and other writings, whereas since then this has become almost the rule in private correspondence — the newspapers also having a heavy responsibility in the matter. The value of our gymnasia is evidenced less in those who have attended them than in those who have not.

The December conferences were convened by Kaiser Wilhelm, who indeed invariably formed a shining nucleus for the crystallization of the *external* tendencies of the time — though for them only. Laugh, deplore, or curse as we may, we cannot deny the fact that the name of this monarch was, over a space of thirty years, for

Kaiser Wilhelm

349

millions a fiery signal, a rousing fanfare, an intoxicating catch-word. Since the days of " Fridericus " no one on German soil had ever seen a whole generation stamped with the seal and label of one prince.

If the word " tragic " is permitted to have any applicable meaning in life as well as in art, then Kaiser Wilhelm's fate must be called a tragic one, a Shaksperian one — which has only not yet found its Shakspere. For tragedy weaves its magic around every throne, and his was no exception. Thus, he was exposed to the temptation of estimating himself as greater than other mortals, because he had been raised above them by *external* circumstances, and to the dangerous conviction of a preordained rulership that might dispose of earthly souls and destinies at will, because he has *apparently* received the power to do so — whereas no single created being has the right to divert any other creature from his own divinely appointed way by so much as a hair's breadth. "Who should be emperor? He who is humble ": unfortunately this simple and striking formula of Langbehn, the " Rembrandt-German " (to whom we shall allude later), did not become flesh in Kaiser Wilhelm. Yet is not this delusion very human? Have we not all fallen into it, each in his sphere? And are we not less guilty merely because our sphere of authority is smaller and the opportunities to sin against the wills of others fewer?

Pride and fall, brilliance and blindness, the mystical fascination of the delusive " divine right ": these have ever been the poet's material, from Œdipus to Jarl Skule. The Shaksperian dramas of all the kings — Richard II, Richard III, Henry IV, Henry VI — turn on them. In the first act of his historic drama Kaiser Wilhelm had already laid the seed of all the fatal complications that were to follow, when, with the arrogance of the newly crowned, he thrust from him the wise sage who for decades had been the heart and brain and seeing eye of his country. From then on he moved as if under a secret curse, piling up mistake after mistake, failing in everything, carrying even good intentions to a bad end. He tried, as no Hohenzollern had done before him, to get in touch with the German working man, and was doomed to find himself more detested by the proletariat than any of his predecessors. He set Germany's future on the water, and the water became the grave of Germany's future. He raised German prosperity, and this prosperity became the poison of the German soil. He wanted to create a world-empire, and what he achieved was the World War.

350

His whole fault was at bottom no more than this, that he found himself occupying a post in human society for which he was not quite big enough. This post was the biggest that Germany had to offer, and Wilhelm II was unfortunately not the biggest man she had to offer: a case which, as we know, is fairly common where thrones are concerned. Being, therefore, not a legitimate ruler in virtue of supreme moral and spiritual force, he was (like almost all his colleagues) dependent for his legitimation either on the people's inherited belief in his divine appointment or on his luck. But this faith had been inherited by fewer and fewer in his generation; neither had he any luck. Vanquished leaders are brought before a court martial, victorious ones set on a pedestal. Both Frederick the Great and Bismarck were determined to commit suicide in the case of an Austrian victory; Bazaine was until 1870 the idol of France and from then on an infamous traitor to his country; Clemenceau, who throughout the war was " the Tiger " to his countrymen, would undoubtedly have been torn in pieces in the event of defeat; Tirpitz's beard would, after a victorious peace, have confronted the German nation at every street corner in marble, stearin, bronze, or chocolate; and it would have been difficult to discover a pipe-bowl or beer-mat that was not adorned by the portrait of Ludendorff.

One may even say that William II in a certain sense fulfilled completely the duty of a king in that he was almost always the expression of an overwhelming majority of his subjects, the defender and executor of their ideas, the representative of their world-picture. Most Germans of the Wilhelmine era were nothing but pocket editions, reduced copies, miniature impressions of Kaiser Wilhelm. This is his point of contact — the only one — with Napoleon, and this was distinctly felt, even abroad. He was known everywhere simply as " *le Kaiser*," " the Kaiser," just as Napoleon was " *l'empereur* " to all Europe.

While the " moderns " persistently attacked him as retrogressive, uninspired, and out of keeping with the age, they failed to see that in his whole spiritual structure he bore quite distinctly the marks of his epoch; for he was undeniably an " *homme du fin de siècle*"; that is, an Impressionist and a decadent. His much-censured recklessness, impulsiveness, and incalculableness were nothing but Impressionism; for this, if we reduce it to a very general psychological formula, is no more than overpopulation in ideas, an invasion by enormous multitudes of mass conceptions

351

before the dominants have been found for them. And as regards decadence, the nature of it, according to Nietzsche, is " exaggeration, disproportion, disharmony . . . when an exhausted man appears with a bearing of the highest activity and energy, one *confuses* him with the rich man . . . the most interesting people, the chameleons, belong here . . . their various states lie side by side. They change, they do not *become*." A certain neurotic foundation was possibly produced by the considerable cross-breeding of which the Kaiser was the product — as the son of a British mother who, on her side, was again half German. But whereas Victoria remained all her life an Englishwoman to the bone, he took over from her neither the obstinacy nor the unscrupulousness which secured so many victories for English politics. In the middle of the war Shaw made the impartial and witty remark that the Kaiser was a naïve suburban snob — which was " quite natural," seeing that he was the son of an Englishwoman. Neither did he inherit his father's almost philistine considerateness and his grandfather's unobtrusive *noblesse*, but, on the other hand, he derived a certain lack of delicacy from some of his forbears — and the most important of them at that: Frederick William IV, the Great Elector, Frederick the Great. As was said at the close of our previous volume, Napoleon's worst enemy was declared to be good taste. Alexander the Great seems also to have displayed Wilhelmine traits as an incompetent art-critic — or so we are led to suppose from the following anecdote: a marble statue of Bucephalus by a famous Greek artist was found fault with by the King, but acclaimed by lusty neighing on the part of the model, whereupon the sculptor is reported to have said: " This horse understands more about art than thou." Of Frederick the Great it is alleged that his tactlessnesses brought about the coalition of the Seven Years' War. Luther, again, was indubitably no very tactful personality. But then, for a genius it is hardly possible to excel in tact. It lies in his very nature to " butt into " everyone, live ruthlessly for his mission, and make himself thoroughly unpopular. Every man of any genius is bound to offend against good taste in that he incessantly, and without being asked, speaks the truth and for choice discusses things of which people usually avoid speaking, for all the world as if they had signed a secret contract to cut them out once for all. The two geniuses Hamlet and Tasso are always behaving tactlessly, in contrast to their opposites, Polonius and Antonio. Beware the tactful leader of men, therefore! He has nothing to do with reality. He will lead humanity to nothing whatever.

One will perhaps be able to say that William II had a lively mental activity and adaptability and was a man of talent, possessing originality and force; but the quality of genius can in nowise be attributed to him. For this consists in the combination of a curious sobriety, standing within and yet above things, and supreme daring, which, scorning and, indeed, ignoring conventions, hastens forward to the realities. Now, these two qualities he lacked completely. As a result the numerous troubles that he caused were just troubles that became distorted in size in the mirror of his powerful position.

The " zigzag course " of his policy — rooted in a spiritual mobility which swept him suddenly from depressions to a fierce desire for movement and back again to inactivity — had the effect in the glare of such a position almost of *folie circulaire*. The central motive in the Kaiser's soul was the infantile desire to be loved by everyone, to be ever in the centre: he wanted, as Bismarck said, to have a birthday every day. Hence arose his incapacity to bear hatred and attack: a neurotic supersensibility to wounds to vanity and an equally neurotic tendency towards *episodic* reactions, pseudo-vigorous counter-blows: something in the order of what Alfred Adler called the " masculine protest." Infantile, too, was his delight in processions, festivities, dressings-up (he would sometimes change half a dozen times in a day and he appeared at the *Flying Dutchman* in admiral's uniform; the Berlin wits quite expected him to put it on for the opening of the Aquarium also). His speeches, again, though not seldom of thrilling effect through their brilliant formulation, reflected this delight in glittering accessories and operatic tinsel — shining armour, the challenging glove, mailed fist, sharpened sword, Nibelung loyalty, King Etzel (and, as the last example shows, the metaphor sometimes ran away with him: for the comparison with the Huns was most successfully exploited by the Allies during the World War). All this had something touching in it; and would have been quite harmless had William II been a mere commoner — say, director of a big bank or theatrical enterprise — and not Emperor. In spite of everything, however, the German nation is positively bound to preserve a certain piety with regard to this monarch — out of piety, I should say, towards itself. For a civilized nation will observe respect towards everything that has ever had power over its life, will acknowledge its former guide-stars even if it discovers, one day, that they were only wandering ones. As such they were, after all, part of their heaven, and in these cases a nation will have the magnanimity to say: I made a mistake, and the widely conspicuous exponent of my error was no worse, no sillier, no more godless than I, but only more *exposed*.

Bismarck's dismissal

One of the few who were able to look through the glittering curtain of the present into the grey future was Bismarck, who prophesied in his memoirs that crises would be the more dangerous the later they set in; and he added, in that veiled key of his last years — which was all the more annihilating in effect for its apparent passionlessness — " the release from all responsibility was, given my view of the Kaiser and his aims, in many respects very tempting to me." The dissolution of the firm of " Bismarck and Son," as, to the young monarch's vexation, it was called, originated in a difference of opinion on the question of labour legislation. Bismarck thought the moment inopportune for direct state interference in favour of the Sunday rest-day, unless, indeed, the workman were to be paid as high wages for six days as formerly for seven. In any other case it would mean depriving him of a possibility of earning: this would be, not workers' *protection*, but workers' *coercion*, coercing them to work less. The possibility of unloading the burden of lower output on to the employers could only be admitted if the other great industrial states did likewise. The Kaiser stuck to his point (" Ideal of His Majesty seemed at that time to be popular absolutism "), and Bismarck decided to retire from the scene of the controversy — the Ministry of Commerce, to whose province the labour problem belonged. Further disagreements, particularly as to the attributions of the Minister President and the relations with Russia, led him to begin to consider complete retirement, but before he had come to a decision in his own mind he received through the Chief of the War Cabinet, General von Hahnke, the brusque demand for his resignation. The Kaiser took this opportunity to offer him the title of duke and a life-size portrait of himself, in return for which he received the following reply from the master of delicate irony: " I feel greatly honoured by the present of the portrait, which will be an honourable souvenir to me and mine. . . . I venture, however, most humbly to beg Your Majesty's gracious permission to continue to bear my own name and title in future also." Bismarck's departure at the station was attended by military honours — a first-class funeral, as he put it. His successor, Caprivi, made no attempt to gain the smallest information from him. He refers to the fact in his third volume of memoirs: " I have never known a case where the transfer of tenure did not demand some degree of understanding between the retiring and the incoming tenant. In the government of the German Empire, with all its complicated relations, there was, however, no sign of an analogous necessity." Two years later, when Bismarck travelled to Vienna for his son's wedding, his request for an audience with the Emperor Franz Joseph was answered in the affirmative; but the German Government raised an objection. This insult he felt so keenly that, for a moment, he considered challenging Caprivi to a duel. On his eightieth birthday, when the President of the Reichstag proposed to send him the official form of congratulation, the majority of the House had the shamelessness to refuse its consent. On this occasion the Kaiser telegraphed his " profound indignation." But Bismarck wrote to a woman friend: " I feel towards all these folk just as Götz von Berlichingen felt at his window, I make no exception even for the Kaiser." It was the same final feeling that the great Frederick also took with him to his grave.

A few months after Bismarck's departure the Zanzibar treaty was signed. By it the German Government acquired Helgoland from the English and in return gave up Witu, Uganda, and the right to Zanzibar, one of the most important of east African trading centres. That this was a very disadvantageous deal for Germany has been asserted by two first-rate experts on African affairs, one German and one English: Peters remarked that the Empire had exchanged two kingdoms for a bath-tub, and Stanley said that it had got an old brace-button for a pair of trousers. Bismarck also voiced his disapproval of the handing over of so large a territory, and the possession of Helgoland seemed to him to mean merely the obligation to make of it a Gibraltar: until then it had been protected by the English flag in the event of a French blockade of the German coast (there was then no Franco-English entente to consider, of course). His attitude to the question shows nevertheless that Bismarck was by no means — as has so often been assumed — without comprehension of the interests of colonial imperialism.

Like all great political " new orientations," Imperialism is an English invention. Empire and Extension were the magic catchwords of the eighties and nineties. Their singer was Rudyard

355

Kipling, their advertisement manager the newspaper potentate Lord Northcliffe. It was then that the idea of an immense trans-African empire, realized only later through the World War, first presented itself to the British imagination. The line of march was from the Cape to Cairo. As a first stage came the seizure of the Nile Delta. At the turn of the eighties Cecil Rhodes, one of the most powerful Conquistadores of the declining New Age, took possession of Rhodesia and other vast tracts in the south of the continent. Between 1896 and 1898 Kitchener, a sort of modern Cortez, conquered the Anglo-Egyptian Sudan, forcing his way in on collapsible boats, field railways, and improvised military roads with an equal degree of caution and energy. This led in 1898 to the conflict at Fashoda. Captain Marchand, who intended to forestall the English, had hoisted the French flag on the Upper Nile. Kitchener demanded the evacuation of the place. When Marchand refused, a British squadron appeared off Tunis. A warlike demonstration between the two greatest colonial powers seemed imminent. But France was not armed for a sea war, and she retired.

At the southernmost point of Africa England already possessed the Cape, which it had annexed during the Napoleonic Wars. To the north of it, however, were still large Dutch free states, in whose territory lay the gold and diamond mines. The inhabitants of the " Boer republics " were true peasants, with all the shortcomings and virtues of their class, and strict Calvinists into the bargain, with the courage and harshness of their confession. The war which broke out in 1899 opened, to the general astonishment of Europe, with great victories for the Boers. They were, however, too clumsy and untrained to follow these up by crushing offensives. All the same, they held their own in obstinate guerrilla warfare against the superior power for two and a half years. At the Peace of Pretoria they lost their independence, but received a general amnesty, advances (free of interest) for the reconstruction of their farmsteads, guarantees for the preservation of the Dutch language, and a promise of autonomy, which came into force in 1906. In 1910 all South Africa became a federated state with its own Parliament. England now reigned in the north and the south. But between the two lay the wedge of German East Africa.

Italy, too, had tried to make a niche for herself on Africa's eastern boundary by founding the colonies of Eritrea (on the Red Sea) and Somaliland. Between these two lay Abyssinia, without the possession of which this group of countries must lack any serious economic and political significance. In 1889 the Italians proclaimed a protectorate over Abyssinia, but in 1896 they suffered a decisive defeat at the hands of the Abyssinian Emperor at Adowa, and this brought about Crispi's fall.

Till now it had been a generally accepted axiom that only European powers had a right to colonies. But in the Spanish American War, fought in 1898, the United States came forward as an imperial power. Its objective was the island of Cuba, the "Pearl of the Antilles," whose rich sugar, coffee, and tobacco plantations the Union desired to possess. The struggle ended in a complete defeat of Spain, whose wretched guns and antediluvian vessels gave the enemy the opportunity of some very cheap victories on the water, though her total collapse on land was certainly unexpected. The United States not only "liberated" Cuba and Porto Rico, but also annexed the Asiatic Philippines, against the will of the inhabitants. This was a flagrant break with the Monroe Doctrine, the only reasonable interpretation of which must obviously be that America, just as she will tolerate no interference from non-American powers, so also refrains for her part from any intervention in other continents. It was in fact a parallel to the world-historical decision taken in 264 B.C. when the Government of the "United States" of Central Italy decided to stretch out a hand towards Sicily: one has only to imagine the Mediterranean scene geographically enlarged. Whether the analogy will hold good in future developments cannot be foreseen, but long and serious clashes in the nature of the Punic Wars will hardly be avoidable.

For on the horizon a new Carthage has already arisen. The entry of Japan into world-politics is one of the most important external incidents of recent times. Until 1868 she was a mediæval feudal state, whose population devoted itself almost exclusively to land-cultivation and domestic manufactures under the rule of a hierarchically ordered nobility. At the head stood the shoguns, or crown generals, whose power was very much that of the mayors of the palace of the Merovingian kings; immediately below them were the daimios, or territorial lords, whose power rested on the caste of hereditary warriors, or samurai. The tenno, or mikado, was a purely religious head, and exercised no influence over the government. In that year, however, the young Emperor Mutsuhito took into his hands the political power that the tenno had possessed a thousand years before, ere the régime of the shoguns set in. He

357

began by transforming the structure of the State, making it into a centralistic absolutism with an organized bureaucracy and a standing army such as Europe had evolved in the seventeenth and eighteenth centuries. In 1889 he granted a Constitution. Within a few decades the runner was replaced by the telegraph, the litter by the express train, the bark by the ocean liner. Coinage, the administration of justice, the calendar were Europeanized; compulsory vaccination and school attendance, industrial freedom, and universal military service were introduced, and commerce and the army completely modernized on the German model. Within one generation Japan has accomplished the transition from the Franconian feudal state, by way of the Bourbon police-state and the Frederician Enlightenment, to the democratic imperialism of Chamberlain and Roosevelt, from the curved sword to the machine-gun, and from illiteracy to linotype, a transformation of such rapidity as to rouse both admiration and misgivings. There is something feminine in this unlimited capacity for reception and adaptation, and one has the suspicion that the model performances of the Japanese are possibly worth just as much as the examination results of schoolgirls and undergraduettes, which also are almost always excellent. Hitherto the Japanese had copied China with an equal skill and fidelity.

It was natural that the Japanese nation, blessed with a numerous population, but none too rich in products of the soil, should cast an envious eye on the iron and coal treasures of Manchuria and the rice and cotton fields of Korea. The inevitable clash with China came in 1894. It began with the occupation of Korea, which, although in name an independent buffer state, had always been in the Chinese sphere of influence. The Chinese dispatched an army and a fleet, but as they were quite unable to compete with the Japanese in modernness, equipment, and training, they were thoroughly beaten and forced by the Treaty of Shimonoseki to sacrifice not only Korea, but also the large island of Formosa and Port Arthur, with the Liaotung Peninsula, the key to the Yellow Sea, besides paying a heavy war indemnity. At this point, however, Europe began to intervene. The cabinets of Paris, Berlin, and St. Petersburg raised a common protest and compelled the restoration of Port Arthur. The Korean question also remained unsolved. On the other hand, Russia obtained China's permission to construct and to provide military protection for a railway across Manchuria, and " leased " from her Port Arthur and the Liaotung Peninsula, while by a similar formula Weihaiwei, on the opposite side of the Yellow Sea, fell to England, Kwangchow-wan to France, and Kiaochow to Germany. Thus, not only was Japan deprived of the most precious fruits of her victory, but China suffered greater losses through her protectors than through the enemy. But the main burden of east-Asiatic hatred fell upon Germany, because the Kaiser thrust himself in the most unfortunate fashion into the foreground of this general game of pirates, complicating it with mistimed phrases about protection from the " Yellow Peril " and the " preservation of holiest possessions." Bismarck did not feel obliged to abstain from saying what he thought of these doings.

Popular fury against the " white devils " found expression in the " Boxer " rising. The Boxers, so called in derision from their efforts to harden themselves for the coming struggle with the foreigner, were a secret organization of fanatical nationalists which was spread over the whole of China. The insurrection was soon over, though again accompanied by emotional speeches of warning from the German Emperor, the tone of which was quite unsuited to the occasion. In complete contrast to this romantic wild-Indian type of policy was the cool and judicious attitude of England, who, taking practical advantage of the course of events, proceeded to form an alliance with Japan. This was England's first formal alliance since the Crimean War; in 1902 the two powers gave mutual guarantees to maintain their existing possessions in the East; in case the protection of these interests should lead either to war with a third state, they promised each other benevolent neutrality; in case of attack by two enemies, assistance. This pact was obviously directed against Russia, though also against France, who alone could be that " second power."

A warlike reckoning between Russia and Japan could now only be a matter of time, after the Government of the former had brusquely rejected a Japanese proposal by which Korea should go to Japan, and Manchuria to Russia. This madness can only be explained by unteachable Muscovite arrogance, for the undisputed possession of Manchuria would have been an inestimable boon to Russia, while Korea had a purely naval strategic importance as the link between the two main eastern harbours, Port Arthur and Vladivostok. From the Japanese point of view, matters were urgent, since it was only for so long as the Trans-Siberian railway, connecting Moscow with Vladivostok, had but a single track that there was any hope of their not having to deal with an

The Russo-Japanese War

359

overwhelming numerical superiority. In January 1904, therefore, they addressed to Russia an unacceptable ultimatum which demanded the evacuation of Manchuria and the recognition of Japan's supremacy in Korea. No actual declaration of war followed from either side.

The Russo-Japanese War had little in common with previous ones, unless it were perhaps with the American Civil War. Its characteristic marks were the long duration of the battles, and the digging-in tactics of which the Boers had already made use on a modest scale. The Japanese employed the spade even in attack, under cover of superior artillery. New, too, were the use of the machine-gun, advances by night-marches, which had previously only happened in particular emergencies, and, in siege warfare, the practice of mining, which had been in abeyance since the days of the Turks and was now revived in modern form : without this Port Arthur could not have been reduced. Japan's victory may be traced to the incompetence of the Russian General Staff, also to the fact that Russia did not seriously believe that the enemy would risk so dangerous a war, and was correspondingly unready, but, above all, to the heroic enthusiasm with which the Japanese entered this war on which their whole future depended.

The ethics of " Bushido," the " way of chivalry," which was really the code of honour of the old feudal warriors, whose chief commandment — " better to die well than to live unworthily " — had penetrated deep into the nation. For Russia, on the contrary, it was no national war, for the moujik had no notion of what it was all about.

The main strategical task of the Japanese was the landing of sufficient troops on Liaotung and Korea, the envelopment of Port Arthur, and the holding up of Russia's reinforcements. To safeguard the transports Admiral Togo surprised the Russian fleet in the harbour of Port Arthur, inflicting heavy losses and reducing the remainder to inactivity by floating mines. After the first Japanese army had been disembarked under General Kuroki, it forced the Russians back from the Yalu, the boundary river between Korea and Manchuria. The Russians then gathered their forces into a fortified position at Liaoyang, but were defeated in a ten days' battle by Marshal Oyama's three concentrically united armies. An attempt by the Russians to take the offensive led to the battle on the Shaho, which was indecisive. Meanwhile the sortie of the fleet from Port Arthur (by order of the Tsar) had ended in the loss of the escaping ships, some of which were disarmed in neutral harbours, while others fell into the hands of the Japanese. On January 1, 1905 Port Arthur fell, thus releasing General Nogi's siege army. But the Russians also had received reinforcements through Siberia. In the end of January it came to a decisive battle at Mukden, in which more troops fought than at Sadowa, and which ended with the retreat of the Russians, who had been outflanked by Nogi. Their only strategic chance now lay in the dispatch of the Baltic fleet, through the intervention of which they might hope to prevent any further sea transport of Japanese troops and of supplies for those already landed, which would then be exposed to be crushed by the overwhelming superiority of the Manchurian army, which meantime was receiving constant reinforcements. But the Baltic squadron had the immense voyage from Libau to eastern Asia to cover. A section of the ships took the Mediterranean route by the Suez Canal, but the main body actually sailed round the Cape of Good Hope; they met again at Madagascar. When they arrived in the Far East, they were completely unfit for battle and suffered an appalling defeat. Of the thirty-eight ships, thirty-five were sunk, captured, or disarmed. Further, the outbreak of revolution in Russia itself jeopardized the service of reinforcement and supply by land also.

However, Japan, too, was at the end of her resources, both economic and military. The oldest of the annual contingents had already been absorbed, and further war credits could hardly be raised. And so it came about that both parties accepted the mediation of President Roosevelt. Under the Peace of Portsmouth Russia paid no war indemnity, but ceded to Japan the Liaotung Peninsula and the southern half of the island of Sakhalin and recognized the Japanese protectorate over Korea. In Manchuria China's former rights were restored to her, and the railway was divided, the northern half being placed under Russian management, the southern under Japanese. In relation to the enormous sacrifices these were but meagre gains. But the moral impetus which Japan gained from the war was extraordinary. From then on she ranked as the eighth great power (external proof of which was seen in the setting up of embassies) and was regarded as the undisputed leading power of eastern Asia. England renewed the alliance under more favourable conditions, both parties now binding themselves to give armed assistance in the case of unprovoked attack even by a single power. By this means Japan obtained a free hand in Korea, where in 1910 the Emperor was forced to abdicate and the country was formally annexed. On the other hand, the treaty also protected England against any Russian attack in India. Had Germany adopted a somewhat more accommodating attitude after the Chinese war with Japan, she might easily have stepped into England's shoes and demanded a similar protection to her rear; for up till then the Japanese had been intensely sympathetic towards the German nation, which had been her military and scientific instructor. A war on two fronts against Germany and Japan would never have been attempted by Russia, any more than one on Germany by the Western powers alone — for had they tried it, the whole Entente would have been rolled up from the East.

The Russo-French military convention of 1891, in which the Dual Alliance first took tangible form, was directed almost as much against England as against Germany, for England was Russia's most dangerous rival in China and Hither Asia and France's in Africa. The latter rivalry in particular led, nearly every year, to serious friction. After the Fashoda incident, however, this was disposed of by the Sudan treaty of 1899, by which the western portion of North Africa was acknowledged as the French and the eastern as the English sphere of influence. This made Rome nervous, and her claim to Tripoli was renewed. This was recognized by France, in the following year, conditionally upon a " Tunisification " of Morocco, and the value of the Triple Alliance for Italy, who had entered upon it mainly in view of its African ambitions, was thereby greatly impaired. Close upon this, therefore, in 1902, there followed a reinsurance treaty between Italy and France on the lines of the German-Russian, by which strict neutrality was guaranteed to the Republic, not merely in the case of an attack upon it, but also " if, challenged to protect its honour and security, it was forced to declare war ": that is to say, in *any* case — and this made the Triple Alliance almost illusory.

Post-Bismarckian world-policy

An opportunity occurred during the Boer War for an advantageous regrouping and for breaking through the Franco-Russian embrace, but Germany let it slip. When the Boer President Krüger was travelling over Europe in search of aid, he was acclaimed on landing at Marseilles and most honourably welcomed in Paris. In Moscow and Petersburg, too, there were great anti-English demonstrations. As a result of this popular feeling, France and

362

Russia conceived the idea of exercising the combined pressure of all the European powers upon England, and with this in view sought an agreement with the German Government. Germany declined, however, and thus saved England from a crushing diplomatic defeat. How far the momentary friendliness was genuine, in the case of France at least, or how long it would have remained so, may be an open question. But Germany's attitude towards the perfectly honest and seriously meant proposals made by England is simply incomprehensible. Towards the end of the century England was beginning to retire from her "splendid isolation" and look about for a "continental sword" against Russia. For this purpose Germany seemed best suited. In 1895 Lord Salisbury proposed England's entry into the Triple Alliance and the division of Turkey, in which case Germany's share would have been the provinces of Anatolia, formerly the scenes of a most flourishing civilization and offering a gigantic basin for the reception of superfluous population. The treaty proposal was renewed by England in 1898 and 1899, with the Atlantic coast of Morocco mentioned in addition. In 1901 she approached Germany yet again, this time with the most advantageous terms, being able to hold out the prospect of Japan's very probable entry into the coalition. Now, an English-German-Japanese bloc would have meant a world-dictatorship and would have secured for Germany a supremacy in the Triple Alliance such as Prussia had possessed in the North German Confederation. But all four proposals were turned down. Chamberlain said that he had quite lost heart and would have nothing more to do with the people in Berlin. If they were so short-sighted as not to see that a whole world-constellation depended upon them, then there was simply no help for them. There can be no doubt that Bismarck would have held out both hands in acceptance, for he was always desperately seeking fruitful alliances. In the period of his chancellorship Russia alone was at his disposal and she was too preponderant and prepotent to be a comfortable ally, while Austria and Italy would have been unable to turn the scale in the European balance of power. But at that time England was not wanting alliances. Now the German Government hesitated, out of weak-sighted dilettantism and over-zealous bureaucratism. That England's offers were to be taken quite seriously is clear from the very fact that such a grouping would have been at least as advantageous for her as for Germany. There was of course, even at the turn of the century, already the commercial rivalry which later led to the "encirclement," but this Great Britain would willingly have endured as purchase-price for the almost complete elimination of the far more dangerous and expansive Russian imperialism and for the paralysing of France in Africa and Indo-China. As an ally a tsarist Russia (and no other was then thinkable) was far more expensive than Germany, even in the event of a successful war, for she would then certainly not have been content without all Poland and Constantinople, through which she would acquire an oppressive European supremacy and become a permanent threat to Egypt. But it should have been realized in Germany that for no power in the world was there a possibility of succeeding against England and Russia simultaneously; the failure to see this was the greatest — perhaps the only — political mistake of Napoleon. In principle Russia is altogether invincible. According to Clausewitz, the aim of war is to " overthrow the enemy and thereby render him incapable of any further resistance "; to this end it is not enough to destroy the fighting force, but the country must be conquered, " for out of the country a new fighting force might be formed." That this is impracticable in the case of this mammoth Empire, to which even the huge European part is but a glacis, must be obvious. Since her entry into world-politics Russia has nearly always suffered decisive defeats (the Battle of Poltava is the one large-scale victory in her modern history), and yet she has continually enlarged her boundaries. She was only to be brought low by internal forces. Even in the Japanese war the outbreak of revolution alone forced her to make peace. England, on the other hand, could only have been conquered by the close union of all Continental great powers, a constellation that she had always dreaded and always averted by setting up instead a European coalition against the strongest Continental power of the moment. But in the mean time the problems had grown from a European scale to a planetary one, and the firmest guarantee against the world's two land colossi, Russia and North America, embarking on the oceans was undoubtedly an alliance with Germany and Japan. From the standpoint of racial psychology, too, an alliance with Germany, so closely related by race, world-outlook, and form of civilization, afforded more prospect of permanency than liaison with the autocratic and reactionary Eastern power, which in case of revolution would be quite unreliable and was in any case culturally and ethnically alien. The permanent bridge would have been provided by Holland, which had already frequently considered a customs union with Germany. The hope of destroying such a "Germanic" front, which would have stretched from the Shetland Islands across the Rhine and Maas deltas to Basel, could never so much as have occurred to France, and the entry of the Netherlands into the German empire-federation would have solved the colonial problem for centuries to come. It would, in a word, have been *Carlyle's Europe*. Not only that, but the Italian question would also have been settled by a German-English alliance. It had never been a secret that Italy, on account of her exposed coastal position, could not fight except on the side of England, and indeed, under certain conditions, would be obliged to do so. To turn the Irredenta front round from east to west could only have been to Italy's advantage, for an anti-French league would have meant Tunis and Algeria, Nice and Corsica — possessions which considerably outweighed Trieste and Trent in value — and a sensible Austrian government might well have renounced the Italian Tirol, which could not in any case be held indefinitely, in return for suitable compensation in the Balkans. In any case Bismarck's "Italian drummer on the Alps" would have been in his place, and the Schlieffen Plan would not have broken down. For this was entirely dependent on the enveloping German right wing being of invincible strength. There were two moments when this failed: once when the Kaiser's emotional strategy led him to take out two army corps and send them to menaced East Prussia — where they arrived *after* the victory of Tannenburg and were no longer needed — and when Italy declared absolute neutrality, thus enabling Joffre to withdraw the observation corps from the south and employ them in a surprise counter-envelopment, whereby the "miracle of the Marne" was achieved. Had the British contingent also been lacking on the western front, a monster Sedan would have been quite inevitable. The Schlieffen Plan had always reckoned on England's neutrality; and a long-sighted diplomacy of alliances would have been careful to secure this.

The birthday of the Triple Entente is April 8, 1904, on which day the Franco-British agreement was reached. The understanding with regard to Africa was renewed in binding form, and France was given permission to "Tunisify," or (more euphemistically) proceed to the "peaceful penetration" of, Morocco. Germany was treated as a negligible quantity, and this led to the

The Triple Entente

365

Moroccan crisis a year later: the Kaiser made an ostentatious landing in Tangier, and at the Algeciras conference an arrangement was made which pleased no one. The St. Petersburg Treaty of 1907, in which northern Persia was declared to be a Russian, and eastern Persia (with Afghanistan) an English sphere of influence, cleared up differences between England and Russia in the same manner as the Anglo-French differences had been disposed of: the " cordial understanding " was complete. At a meeting that took place in the following year between Edward VII and Nicholas II some much broader dispositions in world-politics were made. It was agreed that Russia should receive Constantinople and the Straits, and England a free hand in Egypt, Arabia, Mesopotamia, and Persia: this meant that Russia would rule over the Mediterranean, while England, dominant from the Nile to India, would be in possession of the land bridge Cairo–Calcutta that was intended to be the eastern pendant to the southern line from the Cape to Cairo in the grandiose schemes of British imperialism. It was quite obvious that in these combinations Russia had taken Germany's place. Next year the Tsar and the King of Italy met at Racconigi, and there the one consented to the opening of the Dardanelles, the other to the occupation of Tripoli; equally obviously, then, Italy was falling away, now that she was in friendly relation with *all three* Entente powers — as she already was with France since the treaty of neutrality of 1902, and with England under an express reservation in the Triple Alliance treaty itself. In 1911 there occurred two Moroccan crises: France used a rising against the Sultan as a pretext for entering Fez. Once more a German vessel, the gunboat *Panther,* appeared threateningly off the coast. It seemed that England was determined upon war. General French inspected the fortifications of northern France, the English fleet was put on a war footing, English high finance staged a run on the German banks, and the landing of a hundred and fifty thousand British troops in Belgium was at least considered. But as Russia (which had just come to an agreement with Germany over Persia) adopted an attitude of reserve, a settlement was once more brought about: Germany received as compensation a considerable though marshy section of the French Congo to round off its Cameroon colony. Both German and French nationalists were disappointed, the French because they considered their central African possession to have been sliced into when it might have become a French Brazil, the German because they had hoped for western Morocco or, at least, the whole of the French Congo.

The annexation crisis of 1908 was a kind of dress rehearsal for an envelopment that did not quite come off. The Young Turks' " Committee of Union and Progress " had wrung a constitution from Sultan Abdul Hamid. The new nationalist régime envisaged a stricter interpretation of Turkey's relation to Bulgaria (which was nominally still a tributary state) and to the " area of occupation." It was proposed to issue writs for election to the Turkish Parliament for Bosnia and Herzogovina. As a result Austria-Hungary, without having previously sought the agreement of the signatory powers, announced the annexation of both provinces, while on the same day Bulgaria was proclaimed an independent kingdom. The Turks replied with the boycott of Austrian goods and vessels; Serbia demanded as compensation a " windpipe " to the Adriatic; in Italy, too, there was great excitement, and Austrian troops appeared in the Trentino. The Czechs organized sympathetic demonstrations which obliged the Emperor Franz Josef to threaten Prague with emergency government on the very day of his sixty-year jubilee. But Germany backed up Austria vigorously, and as France did not feel sufficiently well equipped, and Russia still felt too weak after the war with Japan, Serbia had to retire. This she did by recognizing the annexation in an official declaration and binding herself to " abandon the attitude of protest and opposition." On the other side, Austria withdrew her right to occupy the Sanjak of Novibazar and restored it to the Porte, which received besides a sum of money — thus not only throwing open the door to Salonika, but loosing the bolt which would have separated Serbia and Montenegro in the event of a combined attack on Turkey. The *régisseur des coups,* the Foreign Minister Count Ährental, acquired for himself the title of " the Austrian Bismarck," and in Petersburg the saying now went: the way to Constantinople lies through Berlin.

But with all this, neither at the Tsar's court, nor in Rome and Paris, nor in Vienna and Berlin, had a uniform and clear-sighted policy been arrived at, but only in London. The Modern Age, which opens with the laying of the foundations of English supremacy at sea, closes with its completion. Through the World War British imperialism obtained everything of which it had dreamed: the Cape-to-Cairo land-block, the removal of Russia from the Near East and of Germany from international commerce. The spirit of Bacon and Cromwell, the *true soul of the Modern Age*, triumphed over the earth. There was but one single slip in the reckoning — in the moment of its supreme victory the Modern Age was at an end.

Pragmatism   This world-picture achieved its most logical formulation at the turn of the century in Pragmatism. It arose out of Oxford, but its chief exponent is the American William James, who, besides his book *Pragmatism* and some religious-philosophical writings, also composed an excellent empirical psychology, the best that could possibly be written. According to the conception of Pragmatism, even our theoretical reasoning is only a practical activity, a form of doing and leaving-alone. The distinguishing mark of truth is its usefulness. " Objective " truth is the sum of that which has been recognized by the human community as useful. " But the richer insight of modern days," says James, " perceives that our inner faculties are *adapted* in advance to the features of the world in which we dwell, adapted, I mean, so as to secure our safety and prosperity in its midst. . . . In the main, if a phenomenon is important for our welfare, it interests and excites us the first time we come into its presence. Dangerous things fill us with involuntary fear; poisonous things with distaste; indispensable things with appetite. Mind and world in short have been evolved together, and in consequence are something of a mutual fit . . . our various ways of feeling and thinking have grown to be what they are because of their utility in shaping our *reactions* on the outer world." This conception is extremely Darwinistic, puritanical, and mercantile; further, it contains just a touch of cant, the essence of which consists in taking the opportune for the legitimate. The touchstone for the rightness of our ideas is their success — this is the tradesman's philosophy — and its success with the majority — this is the logic of democracy — and this success is predestined — this is the doctrine of Calvinism. In short, a thing is true because it suits me — and this is the metaphysic of the Englishman.

This is, if one will, supreme Realism; but one can also see it as extreme Idealism; and that is what happened on the German side. For Nietzsche, " knowledge " is nothing but a form of will to power, and " truth " that which contributes to life or seems to do so; " we never stumble against facts." And Vaihinger's philosophy of " As if," discussed in our previous volume, declares thinking to be simply an " instrument of self-preservation " which

368

subserves our orientation in reality, without being its reflection. The conception of three-dimensional extension, again, is "a fictitious auxiliary structure, slipped in by the psyche to bring order into the chaos of sensations," and the same is true, most of all, of our religious, metaphysical, ethical, and æsthetic conceptions. To express it more optimistically, one may say that the whole of human life is put together out of ideals. These are not real, but it is they which first consecrate existence. Our life is a semblance, but an intentional one; in other words, a game. This means seeing the whole world and also one's own self, one's doing and suffering, through the vision of the artist; and this, precisely, was Schiller's world-outlook. Seen thus, Nietzsche's agnosticism seems no more than the splendid counter-peak of German Classicism.

Vaihinger had gone so far as to admit that the success of our modern commerce pointed to a certain agreement between the imagined world and the real one, but Ernst Mach went much further. He was really a physicist and expressly declined to be taken as a philosopher, but he nevertheless exercised great influence as such. Already in his *Geschichte der Mechanik*, which is equal to Dühring's for clarity, thoroughness, and wealth of material, he proved himself — in striking contrast to the other — a sort of freethinker from the opposite end, in that he allowed the tolerance which the Liberal usually extends to irreligious ideas to apply also to the other side, to opinions that are condemned by the dogmatism of "enlightenment" — a lack of Zealotism that is seldom found among the priests of science. His series of essays on *Die Analyse der Empfindungen und das Verhältnis des Physischen zum Psychischen* appeared first in 1885. A second edition followed only in 1900, but three more appeared within the next two years. Mach's spiritual genealogy points towards England: towards Locke, who declared the whole of experience to be a complex of elementary ideas, and towards Hume, who said that the conception of substance arose from the habitual association of the same characteristics and that the ego was a mere bundle of ideas. "My total physical finds," said Mach, "I can dissolve into these *elements,* which *at present* do not permit of further analysis: colours, tones, pressures, heats, perfumes, spaces, times, and so forth." For him, therefore, even the Kantian "pure intuition-forms," space and time, are no more than sensations, since once they appear in our experience, they have already a definite place, a definite extension, a definite duration, and therefore compose naturally out of elementary impressions of sight and touch. Spatially and temporally united complexes of colours, tones, pressures, are described as *bodies* and receive special names; but such complexes are by no means absolutely permanent. As relatively permanent there is, further, the complex of memories, moods, feelings, which is called " I." The delimitation of the ego arises instinctively, becomes usual, and may even fix itself through inheritance. Because of their high *practical* significance to the individual and the species, the conceptions " I " and " body " stand out with elementary force. All bodies are but thought-symbols for complexes of " elements." From this standpoint there exists no contrast between " world " and " I," thing and sensation, physics and psychology. A colour is a physical object if we consider its dependence on the source of light, a psychological object if we observe its dependence on the retina. The material is the same in both cases, it is only the direction of the analysis that is different. There is no gulf between psychical and physical, between inside and outside, between inner sensation and outward thing; *elements* are of *one kind* only and are inside or outside according to the point of view. The elements of the *material* world are called sensations in the *psychical* world; it is the business of science to probe for the connexion, the mutual interdependence of *all* these elements. Mach speaks here, not as a philosopher, but as a physicist: " I wish," he says in a foot-note, " to take up in physics a standpoint that it will not be necessary to give up from the moment one glances across to the domain of some other science, since in the end all of them should form a whole. The molecular physics of today emphatically does *not* meet this requirement." In a completely logical development of this conception Mach substitutes for the conception of cause the mathematical conception of *function:* causality is the functional dependence of the elements upon each other. The functional conception has the advantage over the rigid causal conception that it can adapt itself to every new fact; which indeed, according to Mach, is the aim of natural science in general. For science is the adaptation of ideas to facts, or *observation,* and the adaptation of ideas to one another, or *theory.* The two cannot be sharply divided, for all observation is in some degree already theory, and all theory rests on observation; " the apparently wide gulf between experiment and deduction does not actually exist." As the result of this incessant widening and rectification, we have natural laws, which, however, as Mach points out in his latest work: *Erkenntnis und Irrtum* (and explains by many examples), arise only through the simplification, schematization, and idealization of facts.

In the history of philosophy Mach's world-picture ranks as an unsurpassable distillate of *Nominalism*, the theme which runs all through the Modern Age. The teaching of Nominalism was that our spiritual life consists solely in individual conceptions, which, however, as mere " signs " need have no resemblance to the things; that it is (as the English empiricists maintained in continuation of this doctrine) a mere game of in- and out-going, meeting and separating sensations. Our brain, in the vivid phrase of Locke, is nothing but an antechamber; and similarly Condillac and the French Encyclopædists state all psychic activities to be unformed sensations. Mach then puts the final touch by declaring that there are not only no conceptions, no substances, no *a priori* forms of intuition, but no objects at all, not even any " unlike the sensations," for objects are nothing but the sensations themselves. At the same time Mach is the classic philosopher of *Impressionism*, in that he recognizes no other psychic reality than the " elements," the isolated individual impressions which form, so to say, the A B C of an experiential world, as its final and only facts. There are here obviously two possibilities: one can stand still with the elements as a conscientious " Realist " and be content simply to register them; and one can try to spell, but with the full consciousness of practising an irresponsible imaginative activity, for the speller's *given* material consists no longer of the actual sensations a, b, c . . . , but only of their ideal memory-pictures, a, β, γ . . . , which he puts together " as complexes " (bodies, ego-feelings, ideas, moods, and all the other higher products of the spiritual life). Now, these, precisely, are the two polar possibilities of *Impressionism*, of which we spoke in our last chapter. It might be supposed that only the first of these forms belongs essentially to Impressionism, and that the latter is common to it and to all art; even so, there is the great distinction that Impressionism in its syntheses invariably remains fully conscious that the individual sensation is its sole building material and that the structure is a fiction.

The emphasis on the " world as fiction " is common to all the philosophical tendencies of the out-going century, however heterogeneous they were in other respects. In France, the eminent mathematician Henri Poincaré adopted the standpoint of Pragmatism for even that apparently most secure and universally valid science, geometry. In his book *La Valeur de la science* he says: "We know in space rectilinear triangles the sum of whose angles is equal to two right angles. But we know also curvilinear triangles the sum of whose angles is smaller than two right angles. To call the sides of the one rectilinear means that we accept Euclidean geometry; to call the sides of the other rectilinear means that we accept the non-Euclidean. . . . Apparently, when we say that the Euclidean rectilinear is a *true* rectilinear, and the non-Euclidean is not, we only wish to express our belief that the former view represents a more important object than the latter. . . . If the Euclidean rectilinear is more important than the non-Euclidean, this means principally that it differs only slightly from certain important natural objects, whereas the non-Euclidean does very greatly differ from them." The system of mathematics is a convention: "it is neither true nor false, it is convenient."

Bergson   By far the most influential French philosopher since Comte, however, was Henri Bergson, who may also be compared with Descartes in the national extent of the influence that he exercised in pre-war days on literature, art, and outlook on life. He places metaphysics in definite opposition to science. The activity deriving from positive science is analysis. The conduct of analysis consists in tracing back its object to already known elements: that is, it attempts to express a thing through something that is not this thing itself. Every analysis is therefore a translation, a development in symbols. The instrument of metaphysics is *intuition*. "Intuition is that description of intellectual introjection by means of which one transfers oneself to the interior of an object in order to hit upon that which is unique and inexpressible in it. . . . If there is a means of grasping a reality absolutely instead of recognizing it relatively, of placing oneself within it instead of adopting standpoints towards it, of grasping it without any sort of translations and symbolical representation, this is metaphysics itself. Metaphysics is accordingly the science which endeavours to do without symbols." There is, then, a way of reconstructing reality independently of thought, the way of direct experience. In intuition the soul experiences itself as a being that is not conditioned by bodily processes. It is dependent on these latter in its sensations; but the very recollection in which the sensation is reproduced is a purely spiritual process. The soul is not in space nor in time, for these relate only to matter. Space and time permit of quantitative measurement; not so the vital manifestations of the soul; in space the " side by side " predominates — in time the " one behind the other." The soul is the realm of *liberty*. There are no things, there are no conditions, there are only " actions."

This highly dynamic philosophy regards the central power as residing in the " *élan vital*," which, engaged in a permanent creative intoxication, makes perpetual attempts to achieve the triumph of mind over matter. In the human being this force has gathered itself together in thought, but this has to be paid for by the loss of instinct: " Everything happens as though the being, in seeking actualization, reaches it only by sacrificing a part of its nature on the way. It is these losses that are preserved in the rest of animality, and indeed in the plant world also." The instinct is not simply a baser form of reason, but a capacity which differs from it generically. Its means of knowing is " sympathy," " scenting at a distance "; in men, particularly in the artist, it expresses itself as intuition. Usually the reason contrives, on practical grounds, that only that which ministers to self-preservation emerges from the dark depths of instinct into the consciousness: reason is the " prison warder " of the soul. Only one who is without interest in the struggle for existence, a dreamer, a " distraught " person, grasps reality whole and without detractions or distortions. Living means receiving only the useful impression from things and responding to them by suitable reactions. " Between us and nature — no, what am I saying! — between us and our own consciousness there descends a veil that is close for the ordinary person, but tenuous and almost transparent for the artist and poet. What sort of a fairy wove this veil? Was it a good one, or was it a bad one? " We see from Bergson also that Pragmatism conceals within itself the possibilities of a radical artist's-philosophy.

In extreme contrast to Bergson and his irrationalism was the " Marburg school," whose members called themselves (with small justification) Neo-Kantians. But they are equally in antithesis with Mach. Where he taught that there were only sensations, they maintained that there were only conceptions, these being the sole realities. No one will confuse them, however, with the mediæval

"Realists," whose belief in universals was rooted in a rich-blooded piety, while theirs flowed from the shallow arrogance of reason. Their chief was Hermann Cohen. In his *Logik der reinen Erkenntnis, Ethik des reinen Willens, Ästhetik des reinen Gefühls* — instances of dialectical falsification, so cumbrous as to be accessible only to the inner circle of fellow-philosophers — he takes Kant at his word in a most sterile fashion, pushes him to extremes, and " goes one better." A bit of the system of the *Critique of Pure Reason* is quite arbitrarily broken off and elevated into a " universal " philosophy — the scholastic category-theory, namely, which is precisely the part of it that could best be dispensed with and is most open to criticism. Actually, the Neo-Kantians with their pan-logic were late pupils of Hegel, devoid of his creative, architectonic, and world-embracing richness of intellect.

Wundt   As a sort of professor's philosophy, but of a more sympathetic and fruitful kind, we have the comprehensive life-work of Wilhelm Wundt. According to his own definition, philosophy is " the universal science whose mission it is to combine the universal parts of knowledge provided by the individual sciences in one consistent system." This is as good as saying that the philosopher is only a sort of collector and recorder, elucidator and compiler: a brain that gives honest and careful consideration to all the apparent absurdities, makes wise and clear-cut decisions between alternatives, strings observations on to observations, connects facts, draws cautious conclusions, and finally evolves a handy catalogue, a survey-map of the intellectual condition in which we happen to find ourselves. That is a remarkably modest mission; and Wundt fulfilled it admirably. In his many fat books there is a protocol of the whole intellectual inventory of the second half of the last century; the whole scientific life of two generations is spread out like a model beetle-collection, with the exhibits pinned up without any gaps, professionally arranged, and provided with instructive labels. The world really asked nothing more of a philosopher in those days than that he should be a sort of cicerone and mentor, who could lead it through the packed store-rooms of its culture, so that it could survey at its convenience the stage of enlightenment and progress, the keenness of methods, subtlety of differentiation, breadth and solidity, to which it had risen.

There was in fact a certain well-defined stamp of philistinism about the whole of Wundt's work. This natural trait revealed itself first of all in the shy precautions by which he avoided every sudden, daring thought, for fear of " inconsistencies," so characteristic of the middle-class German — for heaven's sake, no paradoxes! — and in the preference on principle for the golden mean, along which indeed lie most of the practical truths, but hardly ever the discoveries of genius. And this good middle-class faculty of seeing the sensible, just mean in all transactions enabled him in fact to deliver a reasoned and uncorrupted verdict on most of the philosophical controversies of his day. He arbitrated — like a *bon juge* who condemns everything, but at the same time gives everyone the time to retrieve himself — in epistemology between Idealism and Realism, in ethics between apriorism and empiricism, in natural philosophy between atomism and Energetics, in biology between Mechanism and Vitalism, and in sociology between individualism and collectivism. There was a touch of pedantry besides in his whole instructional method, but this very quality enabled him to present his age with the most complete and serious text-books that it could wish for. Finally, and above all, the worthy-burgher mind manifested itself in his unreserved prostration before the world of facts that can be inquisitorially examined with levers and screws, unmasked by test-tubes, imprisoned in comparative tables, and held fast in a net of co-ordinates. This worship of reality pervades Wundt's whole thought, and it is not incompatible with his having set up, on the broad physico-physiological foundation of his system, a very airy and empty storey of semi-Kantian, semi-Leibnizian Idealism which leaves one inevitably with an impression of a quite superfluous luxury-structure, intended obviously not for living-purposes, but only for occasional festive receptions. But we must not forget that this realistic trend in Wundt's mind was also responsible for the building up of two great new disciplines: physiological psychology and national psychology, or that it was to his patient penetration and loyal devotion that we owe in the first place our more enlightened knowledge of these today. His most important discovery in these two domains is the recognition that in the spiritual life the law of purely mathematical summation does not prevail: each complex that arises from simple conceptions or simple feelings is not only quantitatively but qualitatively something novel, the national soul something more than and something different from the concept of a certain number of individuals. Another original idea

375

of Wundt's was the "law of the heterogeneousness of aims." He meant by this: " the general experience that in the whole compass of human willed actions the activities of the will always occur in such a manner that the effects of the actions extend more or less beyond the original motives of the will, and that thereby new motives arise for future actions, which in turn produce new effects." Expressed in the language of the ordinary mortal, this would amount to: you think you are living and you are being lived; you prepare with your brain, your nerves, your constructive power, for a certain experience in which the aim and meaning of existence seem to lie; but reality comes unawares in its self-glorification and distorts your concept: the events have, gently and unnoticed, turned on their axis while you were experiencing them — nay, because you were experiencing them — and have taken on a quite new, quite different point. This law will one day presumably be applicable to Wundt himself, as indeed may already have happened. For while his contemporaries regarded him as a raiser of tempests, Providence probably designed him only as a barometer on which one may read what the air-pressure was when it was functioning.

"Rembrandt als Erzieher" In the sphere of philosophy we must also include two more works of the essay kind, which made a great and justifiable sensation: *Geschlecht und Charakter* (1903) and *Rembrandt als Erzieher*, which appeared in 1890 without the name of the author, Julius Langbehn, and ran through forty new impressions in the same year. In his temperamental orientation towards concepts continually contrasted, such as civilization and culture, literature and art, democracy and nationalism, bourgeois and *Bürger*, the vote and liberty, politics and music, he reminds us of Thomas Mann's *Betrachtungen eines Unpolitischen* — although the latter are more colourful, personal, and differentiated — as also in the fact that both are emphatically polemics against the times: " Schiller superscribed his first book: *in tyrannos;* he who would direct a general address to the Germans today should superscribe it: *in barbaros.* They are not barbarians in coarseness, but in culture." This has a distinct ring of the " Culture-philistine " of the first of Nietzsche's *Thoughts Out of Season,* just as the title reminds us of the third, and one of the very first sentences in the book — " the whole culture of today is Alexandrine, historical, backward-looking " — of the second. The professor, it says, is the German national disease, the contemporary education of the

376

young a sort of Massacre of the Innocents; in an age that insists on "thinking servant-girls" one should also have the right to demand thinking professors. The German university should by rights be called a "speciality," since it contains only specialities. "The specialist has given away his soul; one may say, indeed, that the Devil is a specialist, just as God is certainly a universal-ist." The idealism of the previous century had seen the world with the bird's eye, the specialist of the present century was seeing it with the frog's perspective; the next would, it was to be hoped, see it in human perspective. In the criticism of Wagner we are again reminded of Nietzsche. "His feelings are ecstatic or else they melt; on the level middle heights, where really healthy feel-ing lives, they do not last, they are over-refined. Shakspere is Kaiser, Wagner is *empereur*." (There is no question of his having been directly influenced by Nietzsche in all these judgments, it is only an interesting intellectual double.) Rembrandt, we are told, is suited to be the German leader on account of his mixed nature: "Light and darkness, scepticism and mysticism, politics and art, nobility and people, are one . . . because they are not at one. Out of doubleness, singleness is born; that is the world's glorious course."

When *Geschlecht und Charakter* appeared, Otto Weininger was twenty-three; six months later he shot himself in the house where Beethoven died. The basic theory from which his inquiry proceeds is the assumption of two polar soul-forms, of man and of woman, which he calls M and W. They represent ideal limits, always appearing in reality as intermingled in innumerable grad-ings. The law of sexual attraction rests upon the fact that a whole man and a whole woman always try to come together, as, for instance, ¾M and ¼W with ¾W and ¼M; from which it fol-lows that the contrary sex feeling also represents only a special case of the natural law. W is completed, absorbed, in sexual life, in the sphere of begetting and propagation, while M is not ex-clusively sexual. Further, in M sexuality is strictly localized, in W it is diffused over the whole body. The fact that sexuality is not everything to the man permits him both to lay it aside psychologi-cally and to be conscious of it. In W two inborn contrasted dis-positions are found: absolute mother and absolute prostitute; between the two lies the reality. To the absolute prostitute the man, to the absolute mother the child, is the sole interest. Peculiar to every W is organic mendacity and, that which goes with it, soullessness: "it is quite incorrect to say that women lie, that would assume that they also sometimes speak the truth"; "Undine is the Platonic Idea of woman." The woman is no monad. She is never lonely, she does not know the love of solitude or the fear of it, she lives perpetually, even when she is alone, in a state of fusion with all the people she knows: all monads, on the other hand, have boundaries. Perhaps man, in the act of becoming a human being, managed by a metaphysical and timeless act to keep his soul. For this his misdeed he now atones by love, in which he desires to give the woman a soul because he feels guilty before her on account of his theft. The hopelessness of this attempt explains why there is no happy love. The only way out consists in the denial and overcoming of femininity: that is, of sexuality. Woman will live only until man has entirely eradicated his guilt, until he has really overcome his own sexuality. "Therefore it cannot be a moral duty to provide for the propagation of the species, as one so often hears it said. This subterfuge is one of an extraordinary mendacity; it is indeed so plainly so that I am afraid I may make myself ridiculous if I ask whether a man has ever performed the coitus with the idea of obviating the danger of the downfall of humanity; or whether anyone has ever felt himself justified in reproaching the chaste man for his immorality."

Weininger's work — one of those great confessions in which a precocious solitary spirit expresses and at the same time gives itself unreservedly — is much more the bold and logical conception of an arbitrary world-picture than a new and deeper groping psychology of the sexes, and leaves behind it no clear impression. For there is in it an uncomfortable mixture of Kantian ethics, Ibsenish mountain air, Schopenhauerish urge to redemption, Nietzschean soul-knowledge with moralistic arrogance, and intellectualistic Nihilism — these, and an underlying fascination exercised by evil, against which this tragic thinker set up his whole structure and to evade which (we may assume from his utterances in his last days) he took his departure from life. In *Geschlecht und Charakter* the self-knowledge of the man of the New Age is already entering its twilight, turning its dialectic, its poison, on itself, resorting, like the scorpion, to release by its own sting.

Strindberg   The dæmonic sculptor of this hellish introspection, in which woman is merely a starting-point, was August Strindberg, whom the literary generation of the Expressionist exalted as its patron saint in the same way as the Naturalistic generation had exalted Ibsen. Ibsen, they said, sets sums, Strindberg piles up visions, Ibsen is a dry doctrinaire, Strindberg confesses out of the fullness of blood; in short, the " Magus from the North " was dispossessed and unmasked as a mere apothecary. A countryman of Strindberg's formulated the contrast as follows: " Ibsen is sheer simplified connectedness, Strindberg lush chaos."

Now, even if one were prepared to admit this as it stands, it is in the first place by no means clear whether the chaotic is exactly the essence of creative man or whether, on the contrary, his main strength does not perhaps lie in systematic reasonableness, the artistic disciplining and embracing, ordering and harmonizing, of the spiritual raw material: in short, in clearing up the inward chaos. Otherwise there would be really no essential difference between a hysterical woman and an artist; for " lush chaos " is present in her also, whereas "connectedness " — of a highly simplified order, too — is just what we find in a few artistically quite important persons, such as Sophocles, Bach, Plato, Calderon, Goethe. But this is a controversial matter to itself, and in the case of Strindberg there is a question of something besides.

There are undoubtedly many poetical works to which one's reaction is: " But that is not at all what the world looks like! " This, however, proves nothing against these works. It all depends on the after-sentence which usually comes into one's mind involuntarily. One may add in one's mind: " Yet, after all, the world *might* look like that." The ability to call forth this impression we call the poetic art. But one may also say: " The world *should* look like that if things went right." And this effect is made only by really great works of art. And yet again there is a group towards which one's feeling is: " The world really *ought not* to look like that! " To this Strindberg's creations belong, and they must therefore be called pathological. It is not, of course, the poet's business to draw imitations of nature. His mission is quite different: he has to depict an ideal according to which existing reality has to adjust itself. Now, *every* variation from reality is an idealization — even caricature, in that it simplifies, abbreviates, concentrates realities into the absurd. And so one can idealize the world into something hostile to life or into the reverse, and the first is what Strindberg did. Therefore the fact that the world is not as Strindberg represents it is not in itself an objection to his works; the objection is that his poetical world is not a desirable one. Neither is Hebbel's world exactly a desirable one, for it is definitely not worth the struggle to have a humanity made up of ill-natured Hegelians. For a similar reason we must call Wedekind's dramas pathological, for if real life were like these plays, one would have to think the world was a single huge phallus. This also is an ideal, but, I think, a false one.

The atmosphere in which Strindberg's creatures dwell is that of an oppressive, paralysing, stifling spiritual eclipse. Hatred — blood-red, white-glowing hatred — is the fire by which the movements of his dramas are fed. Hatred drips from the walls of the rooms, whirls in millions of bacilli through the air, rises from the earth in suffocating vapour. And to enhance the horror of the impression, one has never the feeling that it is wilfully superimposed, one feels most definitely that these people *must* be as they are, *must* bring useless trouble upon each other until they are torn in pieces.

There are a few basic motifs which Strindberg repeats with almost insane persistence. For instance: someone drinks up the good bouillon in the kitchen and gives the other person the nonnourishing watered remainder; someone takes the cream from the milk in the larder; someone buys another person's bonds and presses him for the money; someone steals another person's ideas and produces them as his own; someone knows of another person's secret misdeeds and so holds power over his life. Even this would be no justifiable objection to Strindberg's works. The perpetual repetition of certain leading ideas is by no means contrary to the nature of genius; on the contrary, it is often the very essence of it. Neither will anyone seriously maintain that art should merely refresh. On the contrary, it ought to disturb, alarm, and shake us up; to be the uneasy conscience of its age is its very mission. But at the same time its handling should help make the world more beautiful, lovable, and godlike. The glance which it throws upon things should enrich and rejuvenate them. But Strindberg's glance is an evil glance. He makes the world ugly and destroys its enchantment, makes it vicious in the literal sense of the word by peopling it with vices which he alone has conjured into being and which, but for him, might have slumbered for ever. In several of his dramas there are characters who play the part of vampires: they feed on the mind and blood of their fellow-men. But then, Strindberg himself is just such a vampire: he sucks the blood from the heart and brain, the veins and bones, of the people who are so rash as to be tempted by his works, robs them of their vital juices and vital air, and renders them utterly anæmic. He is a devourer of souls, and that is probably far more dangerous than being a devourer of men.

The Fall of Man into sexuality, the fight and the Descent into Hell of the sexes: this is the gloomy theme of all the grandiose symphonies of hate which Strindberg has flung out of himself in that flaming, storming furioso and bewitching hurrying staccato, the like of which no one in the world's literature has achieved before or since. In these infernal and merciless duels and knifing-scenes the woman is invariably the cruel devil, the man the innocent victim. But is this a right point of view? If it is true, as Strindberg upholds in artistic guise, and Weininger in a philosophic system, that woman is created out of man and is at bottom nothing but a sort of shadow and projection of his mind, then it is the man who is Satan personified. But it is obvious that Strindberg's whole method of observation is a purely *mythological* one. Woman as devil, woman as witch: this idea belongs to the same rubric as the conception of the sky as a blue dome with stars embroidered on its fabric. Nevertheless, as we have said, it is the poet's enviable privilege to " restylize " life in simpler and more impressive forms; but that being so, why not turn woman into a fairy and an angel instead? Novalis loved the thirteen-year-old Sophie von Kühn, whom " historical research " proved to have been an insignificant little *Backfisch.* Are we to conclude, then, that Novalis was mistaken in her, saw her for more than she was, that he was a dupe? No, what we should say is: a woman whom Novalis loved cannot have been an insignificant schoolgirl, can never have been anything but an exquisite poetical work. See in a woman a negligible, low, malicious creature, and she will be just that and nothing more; see in her a mysterious superior being, a delicate magical figure and divine benefactress, the " star of your existence," and she will be that star to you. That which we "put into " things they render to us faithfully: a very simple law of Nature.

We must add to this that Strindberg's steel-hard hatred, which at its supreme moments has the force and colour-splendour of an act of nature, shrinks in the works of his old age to a feeble detesting. This hatred of the evening of his days no longer roars heroically, but coughs senilely, has become dulled, and no longer gets home. It has no more teeth, or, rather, only false ones.

Ought we therefore to say, in view of all this: it would have been better had Strindberg not written at all? Heaven forbid! For natures of Strindberg's brand are as important in the evolution of mankind as the great affirmers. The world needs both. We want harmonious spirits that uphold the world and make life appear worth living and justified; but we have need equally of those others, the dæmonic spirits who shake the world and make life appear dubious and unjustified. Mankind is a weighing-machine on which belief and doubt have for ever to be balancing themselves anew.

If Ibsen had been called the Messiah of the modern movement, Strindberg might be called its Prometheus. His was the more painful and thankless task. He belonged to the martyrs of history, to those who never reach their goal. And therefore one might choose as a motto for his life and work the words that his great opponent's King Haakon speaks over the body of Jarl Skule: "He was God's stepchild on earth. That was the enigma of him."

The petard Shortly before Nietzsche's intellectual collapse the two thinkers — whose intellectual relationship has already been remarked upon — came into personal touch with each other. Their correspondence (little known even now) happened through the intermediary of Georg Brandes, that agent-general of European literature. In the end of 1888 Strindberg wrote to Nietzsche: "Dear Sir, there is no doubt that you have given mankind the profoundest book that it possesses. . . . I close all letters to my friends with: Read Nietzsche! That is my *Carthago est delenda!* From the moment that you are known and understood, your greatness will inevitably be lowered and the sweet mob will "thee and thou" you like one of themselves. Better that you should preserve your dignified seclusion and allow us others, the upper ten thousand, to make a secret pilgrimage to your sanctuary, where we can draw sustenance to our heart's content. Allow us to guard the esoteric doctrine for you so that it may be kept pure and undamaged." Nietzsche wrote to Peter Gast: "It was the first letter with the world-historical ring that reached me." His last communications to Strindberg already bear the marks of mental overclouding: he tells him that he has convened a meeting of princes (*Fürstentag*) in Rome for the purpose of shooting the young Kaiser, and signs himself "Nietzsche Cæsar" and "The crucified one." But the oddest part about it is that Strindberg's reply was

382

just as crazy. It began with the words: "*Carissime Doctor!* Θέλω, θέλω μανῆναι! *Litteras tuas non sine perturbatione accepi et tibi gratias ago* (Beloved Doctor, I will, I will be mad. I received your letter not without profound emotion and thank you for it) " and is signed: " Strindberg, *Deus optimus, maximus.*" One has the impression that the poet accepted the gloomy cry of the deranged prophet as a friendly greeting from the underworld.

In the more modern course of European culture Nietzsche's figure stands like the formidable shadow of a herculean bomber and *pétroleur.* He was an explosive, a scientific one in which elementary natural forces were united to triumphant technique with a blasting effectiveness. The tunnel opened, forced by gigantic boring operations, and new vistas, new paths lay open. That is the kind of " destroyer " Nietzsche was.

But this makes him one of the most tragic figures in all literature. He was a mad and daring adventurer, the executant of a mighty invasion of enemy territory, hurrying on ahead, too far ahead; his mission was most difficult and dangerous: to " enlighten "; and his fate the almost inevitable one of the forerunner: to fall without seeing his victory. Nietzsche was killed by his philosophy, but that is not a reproach to it, but rather the supreme proof of it.

One might perhaps put it this way: where Nietzsche said that Schumann was only a German event, but Beethoven a European one, it might be said of himself that he was a *terrestrial* event which shook and left trembling not only his nation, not only his continent, but the earth. He may also be compared with a drowning man. He seeks deep places which swallow him up, and with the consciousness that they will do so. He is a warning which says: It is deep here. Out of each of his words there speaks the impressive warning: Do not follow me. He offered himself as a victim, as the most tremendous sacrifice to the Moloch of European Nihilism and Positivism. He was right in naming one of his principal books: *Vorspiel einer Philosophie (Prelude to a Philosophy)*; nevertheless (or, rather, for that very reason) his work might better be called a finale.

Nietzsche's inheritance is the saddest chapter in his history. " Strong waters," he said himself, in one of his earliest works, " tear away with them many stones and bushes, strong minds many foolish and confused heads." His books have been called poisons. And that they are. Therefore a great section of humanity must be kept away from them: the minors and mentally deranged, the debilitated tonic-seekers and overstrained sensation-gluttons, the suicides and poison-mixers; it is only to the quite cowardly and quite unconcerned, the immune and the doctors, that they will be entirely harmless.

The Wanderer

Nietzsche's total output falls naturally into three periods: the first, from 1869 to 1876, stands under the sign of the Classical, Wagner and Schopenhauer, and embraces *The Birth of Tragedy*, the four *Thoughts Out of Season*, and a few important posthumous writings such as the Basel inaugural lecture on Homer, the lectures on *The Future of our Educational Institutions*, and the fragment: *Philosophy in the Tragic Age of the Greeks*. The second period, from 1876 to 1881, represented by several large volumes of aphorisms, is emphatically Positivistic and Rationalistic. The first volume of *Human, All-too-Human*, with which it opens, was dedicated to Voltaire, " one of the great liberators of the mind," and bore as its motto a sentence from Descartes: " For a time I considered the different occupations to which men give themselves up in this life . . . enough to say that, for my part, these appeared to me to be nothing better than that I should keep strictly to my own preference: that is, that I should employ the whole span of my life in developing my reason." (In the new edition of 1886, it is significant that both dedication and motto were left out.) The most important section of his life is the " Transvaluation " period (1881 to the close of 1888), which opens with the *Fröhliche Wissenschaft* and closes with the giddily productive year 1888, in which *Götzendämmerung, The Case of Wagner, Ecce Homo,* and the *Dionysos Dithyrambs* appeared and in which he worked out, fully for Book I and in draft for the rest, the monumental *Will to Power* that was destined never to be finished. In the centre of this period, as to both date and content, stands *Zarathustra*. It is extremely remarkable that the last manuscript on which Kant was engaged had a similar title: *Zoroaster oder die Philosophie im Ganzen ihres Inbegriffs unter einem Prinzip zusammengefasst*. Kant is said to have remarked that this book would be his most important; and Nietzsche had the same feeling about his *Zarathustra*, as we know. The similarity goes further, for both were unfinished, not only in the sense of having no ending, but also in the intrinsic torso-character of the whole conception. To realize this, we have only to place *Zarathustra* beside the two works that alone can be compared with it in the world's literature: *Faust* and *The Divine*

Comedy. In 1883 Nietzsche wrote to Gast: "Where does this *Zarathustra* really belong? I almost think, among the symphonies." But it is enough to think of Beethoven to see that this symphony was never completely orchestrated.

We saw, in the first volume, that Luther's biography was an embodiment of Haeckel's "fundamental biogenetic law" in that he recapitulated in his own life-course the whole course of development of the Middle Ages. The same is true of Nietzsche in respect of the Modern Age. The product of a pastoral *milieu*, he starts from German Protestantism. He receives his early education at the Schulpforta Gymnasium, the seat of the finest Humanist traditions. He studies theology and ancient philology at Bonn and Leipzig under famous tutors, and teaches at Basel, the city of Erasmus, as Jacob Burckhardt's youngest colleague. The upper current of his life's stream runs through the intellectual world of the Reformation and the Enlightenment, of Pietism and Classicism. Upon this there follows a definitely Romantic epoch, and upon this, again, a definitely scientific and eventually agnostic one. Last of all, there are symptoms of a mystical one. In short, he ran through all the phases of the Modern Age from Wittenberg to the World War. He was a Lutheran, a Cartesian, a Wagnerian, a Comtist, a Darwinian, a Pragmatist, and (in passing) even a Nietzschean. If examined as to his position in the history of philosophy, he would undoubtedly have to be called a Schopenhauerite; his "system" can be reduced to the formula: the world as will to power.

In the memory of posterity he will doubtless always remain as he was in his last, most powerful metamorphosis: the figure, gloomy but bathed in magic light, of the lonely wanderer, who strays through the blue ice-world of mountain tops, descending at times to the valley, but always alone and alien even in the turmoil of gay cities; shaping prophetic words which come streaming to him from an underground spring; finally, alien even to himself, shuddering in puzzled wonder at the exuberant splendour of his created work and, one day, wandering forth from his own treasure-house — whither?

The whole stolidity of that generation revealed itself in its attitude towards the phenomenon of this catastrophe — which took it quite unawares: it tried in all seriousness to explain it *medically!* Looking back, it becomes manifest that this ending was stamped in advance on that life whose tempo was always prestissimo, leaping into furioso in those last years. True, we are being wise after the event, which is a very cheap form of wisdom (though still too " risky " for learned ignoramuses) ; but Nietzsche saw it coming. As early as 1881 he wrote to Gast: " I belong to the machines which may *fly to pieces*." The fact is, a productivity such as the year 1888 has to show is no longer capable of increase or even continuation: the manometer, as we have already said, stood at 100. But this does not apply merely in the external, extensive sense ; there were internal counter-forces at work too. Nietzsche's development had obviously reached a crisis ; to turn the handle right round and, after a life-work of such incalculable richness, to begin as it were a new intellectual æon was a task which defied even the strongest earthly mind.

Nietzsche's psychology

The mysterious casting of accounts that goes on between a genius and the world has as yet reached no preliminary settlement in Nietzsche's case, though the opposite is true with regard to Wagner. His artistic significance, which forms a pendant to Wagner's in so far as he performed a rôle for German prose similar to that of Wagner for the language of music, is all that, up to now, stands clearly outlined. Every author born after Nietzsche (and this may almost be applied to foreign countries as well) stands quite inevitably under his influence, provided he lays claim to the title of author at all. Thomas Mann himself, one of the most fortunate heirs to, and finished pupils of, this prose, acknowledged this with emphasis in his *Betrachtungen eines Unpolitischen*. Since those impetuous pen-thrusts of strategic sentence-building, so superior even to Lessing's, since the sound of that hypnotizing and inspiring rhythm of a liquid cadence never before heard in German, since that recklessly profuse and yet never oppressing wealth of floating, opalizing words coming to birth in the background, that purity and colourfulness in an art of expression shaded to a hair's breadth by a thousand brushes, the German language has possessed a new tempo, several new tempi indeed, and innumerable new values. Just as the sea at the keel of a ship incessantly takes on different colouring — now orange or flesh-pink, now purplish red or glassy blue, and again milk-white, poison-green, sulphur-yellow or varnished black — so does this prose restlessly and mysteriously change its colour ; yet one invariably feels that at that moment, in this situation or connexion, it could not possibly be tinted otherwise.

As style is itself psychology, it was Nietzsche's mastery of language that itself produced his completely new psychological methods, which betoken an immense progress that is quite independent of their more casual and often forced results. He once said himself: " On the whole, scientific methods are at least as important a result of research as any other." In *philosophy* it is only since Nietzsche that one knows what complex psychology is: he applied the stereoscope of Flaubert, the microscope of the Goncourts, the deep-sea lead of Dostoievski, to the sphere of pure thought, where they are far more difficult tools to handle than in a novel. Until then such an abyssal depth of knowledge of men, such a breadth of world-outlook, had been seen only in religious geniuses; and if we inquire to whom Nietzsche was related, we must not be guided *externally* by the *content,* and seek in the free-thinking world — amongst the Stirners, for example — but in the family circle of an Augustine or Pascal. His Positivism was no more than the costume of the times (from which, notoriously, no one can escape) and in addition a reaction-phenomenon, the attempt to cure oneself of Romanticism; it played the same part in his life-economy as did Classicism in Goethe's. All philosophy is of necessity " disease," in so far as it is possible only in a decadence-type; all lofty creations of thought — Buddhism, Taoism, Platonism, Gnosticism, not to speak of the newer systems — presuppose a Late world. Nietzsche was the sole decadent of his generation who saw this connexion with perfect clearness and out of this contrast developed his philosophy, although it thus becomes merely another symptom of decadence. His voluntarism, which he opposed to Nihilism, is the same disease-phenomenon with the sign inverted: the "hyperbulia" which forms a mere variant of the "abulia." It appears, however, as if he knew this, knew even that a mystical solution of the conflict was already ripening, deep down within him: certain posthumous sketches in particular, intended for the unfinished parts of *Zarathustra* and the fourth book of *The Will to Power,* bear out this indication.

Nietzsche felt himself, with full justification, to be the adversary of his generation. In this respect he might be likened to Savonarola, of whom he reminds us, above all, by the fanatical unconditionalness of his insistence on truth, and the cruel asceticism of his self-chastisement; but he was in equal degree the strongest expression of the " Founders' Age " in his adoration of life and his anthropocentric sophism. Sophistry, the world-picture

387

of which is contained in the saying: "Man is the measure of all things," is no Greek speciality, it should be remembered, but the inevitable philosophy of all intellectual periods of decline. There are also an Indian and an Arabian sophistry; the Late Scholasticism, with which we dealt in our first volume, bears definite signs of sophistry; the whole philosophy of the Rococo was sophistical in orientation. Nietzsche's "*Lebensphilosophie*" — un-Nietzscheanly insipid, a shallow tautology — life will have life, which it really did not need a dæmonic crusher of everything to tell us — can only be comprehended by the counter-imitation of the theologian in him.

And this brings us to the real kernel of his nature. As we have indicated, there can be no doubt that he belongs to the history of Christianity: as a sort of "converted" Christian, Antichristian in spite of himself and at the same time Christian in spite of himself — the last, and for his time the only possible, form of Christian. His Antichristianism is only a metamorphosis of Christianity, an "allotropic modification," as the mineralogists say: he stands to it in the relation of the dark, glowing coal to the diamond, unmistakably different to outward appearance, but in reality of exactly the same stuff. His father, his two grandfathers, and a great-grandfather were pastors. The cards which he sent out in all directions after his collapse bore mostly the signature: "The crucified one," but occasionally "Dionysos." This had always been the fundamental problem of his life: Dionysos or the Crucified One! To see in this a new Paganism, as shallow and aggressive Nietzsche-priests proclaimed for decades, was an abysmal misunderstanding, and one possible only in Germany, which has at all times possessed the greatest philosophers and the stupidest schools of philosophy. The very posing of the alternative between the Cross and Hellas was completely un-Pagan. For the true Pagan is no Antichrist: he does not see Christ at all. Therefore the Jewish religion is, of all European confessions, the only legitimate heathen one (which is quite natural, as it is the only *Antique* religion). To the other non-Christian sects like the Monists, Socialists, Freemasons, Illuminati, this does not apply: they have all an underground connexion with Christianity. But the fact that, just when the overclouding set in (which can equally well be regarded as an inrush of supreme illumination, though no longer, it is true, on a purely empirical plane), the figure of the Redeemer began to fill Nietzsche's soul — even to identity —

shows that at the life's end of this great apostate also there stand the words: " Thou hast triumphed, O Galilean ! "

These interrelations were recognized by Nietzsche himself. In *Ecce Homo* he writes: " I have a terrifying fear of being some day made into a saint. I will not be a saint, rather a clown than that. Perhaps I am a clown." Here he feels himself clearly as belonging to the noble trinity of fool, heretic, saint, of which the essence of all religious geniuses is made up. It appears already in the figure of Socrates, who lived as a fool, was condemned as a heretic, and died like a saint. In externals Nietzsche's earthly pilgrimage differs in no respect from the legend of a saint. Adored by the people, misused or misunderstood by his friends, living aimlessly the life of a hermit with no requirements, fleeing the world, never touching a woman, tormented by perpetual physical sufferings and spiritual temptations, wrestling day and night with his God, seeking tirelessly the salvation of his brethren, he trod the martyr's path down to self-annihilation. No one perceived the halo round his head — but that also is appropriate to the real saint. The world-spirit chooses to reveal itself in the strangest disguises: now in a beggar like St. Francis, now in a prince like Buddha, in a peasant girl like Joan of Arc, a cobbler like Jakob Böhme, a play-actor like Shakspere — why not, for once, in a mild German professor?

Nietzsche says in *Morgenröte:* " These serious, thorough, just, deep-feeling people who are still Christians from their hearts, they owe it to themselves to live once, as an experiment, for a good long time without Christianity; they owe it to their *faith*." His turning away from religion was only one of the forms of his asceticism; he denied himself it as he denied himself Romanticism, Wagner, Schopenhauer, all his sacred things. And indeed this turning aside from the faith was absolutely necessary to the new faith, one of the indispensable by-ways in the history of human salvation. Christianity has become too cheap, like the Papacy at the end of the Middle Ages. Herein lies the true meaning of the Nietzschean iconoclasm, and possibly the meaning of the whole intermezzo of the Modern Age.

Paul de Lagarde, one of the few Christians who lived in the nineteenth century, says in his *Deutsche Schriften:* " In the Gospel one loves men because, in all humility, one is more than they are; in Liberalism, because one has the same low value as they. In the Gospel, human kindness comes from above, out of joy and

The last of the Fathers of the Church

389

humility; in Liberalism, from below, out of fear and the consciousness of guilt. . . . Jesus tells us to love our enemies so that we may be the children of our Heavenly Father, who allows his sun to rise over good and evil. He is not concerned with human kindness as such, but with the striving after godliness, after perfection." From these and similar sayings of Lagarde's, written before Nietzsche (who for his part was not influenced by Lagarde), we see that the superman is at bottom a Christian conception, as amorality is an intensified form of the vulgar ethic. " If one has temperament," says Nietzsche in *Nachlass*, " one instinctively chooses dangerous things, as, for instance, the adventure of immorality when one is virtuous." Immorality is nothing but hypertrophy of virtue. Naturally only a man of the highest and lowest, strongest and most delicate morality can triumph over moral. Immoralism refers to people who have already passed through the whole school and development of moral, but not to people who are not yet even moral: that is, to Nietzscheans.

In sum, Nietzsche was the last great voice of faith of the West, as Dostoievski was the last out of the East; and having called him the last great Byzantine, and Luther the last great monk, we may call Nietzsche the last great Father. He is at the same time one of the most outstanding national figures that the written word of his country has produced. He himself, as we know, believed that he hated the German people, because he confused it with the German public. The three forces that he delighted to contrast with Germanism were Renaissance Italy, the Classical world, and the French. But his own vitality is of a quite different order from that of the Cinquecento, his this-sidedness is far removed from the Hellenic, his will to art anything but the " art for art's sake " creed of the French. He is the strongest and noblest peak of the idealist and sentimental German ethos — like Goethe, who also thought of himself as a realist, artist, and classic, and yet remained all his life a great German seeker. At the cradle of the peoples God gave to the English the talent for success, to the French the gift of form, but to the Germans *Sehnsucht*, aspiration, yearning. One of its most typical master-figures was Friedrich Nietzsche, the worthy brother in spirit of Rembrandt and Beethoven. But in his last writings this grand and powerful spirit grew confused. It became — or so at least one hears from many sources — seized with megalomania. For it thought it was Friedrich Nietzsche.

These last writings represent at the same time an attempt to overcome Impressionism, in which Nietzsche saw the germ of decadence. It was to be vanquished as a world-picture as well as a form. There occurred the paradox, however, that it was precisely Nietzsche who definitively legitimized Impressionism for Europe and was the first to introduce it to Germany. In the nineties everything succumbed to Impressionism, even those domains that by their most intimate nature and purposes seemed most recalcitrant to it. It took possession in Rodin of sculpture, in Debussy of music, in Kaiser Wilhelm of politics, in Alfred Kerr of criticism. In connexion with this Pan-Impressionism there is also a growth of feeling for Nature which repeats on a higher spiral plane the Rousseauism of the eighteenth century. "The gardens of our forefathers," says Maeterlinck in an essay on "Old Flowers," "were still almost empty. Man did not yet understand how to look around him and enjoy the life of Nature." This is very intelligible: men could not yet look at Nature because they themselves belonged to it. In the last chapter of *Plisch und Plum* there appears a "Mister" called Pief, who gazes continuously through his telescope and justifies this extraordinary behaviour by the following monologue: "'Why should I not, when out walking, look into the distance?' said he. 'It is beautiful elsewhere too, and I'm here in any case.'" One of Busch's many profound philosophemata: the "worth seeing" is always "elsewhere," "here" is never enticing, because we are here in any case. Therefore lyrical enthusiasm for Nature must always proceed from urban civilizations only. The earliest front garden arose simultaneously with the cities of the dawning Modern Age, the "English" park with the rise of London as a capital, and Alpine sports with the birth of the modern cosmopolis. A quite analogous development is seen in landscape-painting. Its florescence began with the urban culture of Italy and Holland and culminates with the emergence of the giant cities in the Second Empire, in the Victorian and the Wilhelmine generation. The Middle Ages knew only vegetable gardens, regarded mountains and ravines only with fear and horror, and never felt the need of copying, exploring, or hymning them.

Meanwhile Impressionism, particularly in painting, had entered upon its *second stage:* it became Phenomenalistic. We have shown in the last chapter how, besides its Realistic interpretation of the world, it also held the possibility of this alternative

391

interpretation. First came the " Neo-Impressionists," who, because they followed up Monet's commas with a radical technique of dots, were named "pointillists," or alternatively " divisionists," because they dissected the field of vision into its ultimate elements. In a word, they painted Mach. Then, again, they used only primary colours — this obviously, because in their view the phenomenon of mixed shades was due purely to a psycho-physiological process, whereas what we actually see is only the spectrum-colours side by side. These colours they tried to place on the canvas in such a manner that the eye should be forced to combine them in the desired way. In fact, they transferred the mixing process from the palette to the retina. With this, the rationalization and the scientific handling of art reached their climax: just as in Zola the author turns himself into a social statistician, a local reporter, a legal psychiatrist, a heredity-biologist, so here the painter becomes spectrum-analyst, chemist, and experimental psychologist. A pointillist painting makes the proper impression only at a distance corresponding to that of the real setting. This is apparently the peak of Impressionism, but actually its point of dissolution; for if one steps back far enough along this line, one arrives at the *contour*, and even, for that matter, the glass mosaic. And this is what actually happened in the case of the one really important Pointillist, Giovanni Segantini. He was claimed by Austria as her son because his birthplace, the little border town of Arco in Southern Tirol, did not then belong to Italy, but by descent, place of residence, and type of education, and even his material surroundings, he was entirely Romance, taking almost all his motifs from the mountains of Ladin Switzerland. He became a brilliant exponent of the " dot " method, placing his brush-points as close together as grains of mortar, and clothing the heights magnificently in a thick sheet of snow, a rich cover of plants, and a close, almost tangible, swathing of air.

If Pointillism aims at forcing the observer to undertake the composition of the picture by his own active participation, it demands of him an act of abstraction. And from there it is but a step to turning the creative process of the work of art into an abstraction again. This step, from analysis to synthesis, was taken by van Gogh. He " formulates," and very often too bluntly, in giving us, as it were, only the grammar of the vital functions of a human or animal body and the truer (because seen as the sum of all past impressions) dream- and memory-picture of a land-

scape. His paintings, in which El Greco, Goya, and Daumier —
the most uncanny painters of modern Europe — are reborn with
terrible effect, seem to us ghostly nightmares, devastating caricatures, painful misdrawings, diabolical experiments; sometimes
one thinks, with a shudder, a tapping ghost would paint just so.

For this Phenomenalist and synthetic phase of Impressionism
the superfluous and confusing new word " Expressionism " was
coined. But if van Gogh is an Expressionist, then Cézanne is already a post-Expressionist. He is the model for Claude Lantier
in Zola's *Œuvre,* the revolutionary artist who makes a radical
break with the whole past. To that past, so far as he was concerned, Impressionism also belonged. He has got back to painting
the vision, the Platonic Idea, but as one who has gone through
the whole of Impressionism and sees it behind him, under him.
What he paints is never the impression, the image, of individual
objects, but always the object as such, the sum of all the jugs,
oranges, trees, in the world. One would think that this would
leave only an abstraction; but what emerges is a supreme con-
cretion. He is, then, as one might say, a painting Realist, though
not in the Sensualist meaning of the term as used by the Modern
Age, but in the mediæval sense of " *universalia sunt realia.*" But
he paints colour, too, as itself, not as a component of the picture,
but an idea of creation, released from the service of form, leading
a majestic existence of its own.

Van Gogh was a Dutchman; and it is noteworthy that in general the strongest artistic impulses of that period had their source
in small countries: in Norway, Sweden, Denmark, Belgium,
Ireland. There is no *novum* in cultural history: great intellectual
revivals have, as was pointed out in our first volume, almost
always originated in dwarf states. According to our present standards, Periclean Athens and Medicean Florence were medium-
sized county towns, and Luther's Wittenberg and Goethe's Weimar provincial " holes " on a larger scale. It is all a question of
what we have had occasion to call the " creative periphery." Culturally considered, the Russia of Tolstoi and Dostoievski also
falls within the conception of the periphery and the small state:
for it was no more than a monstrous straggling peasant settlement, artificially inoculated with a few town buildings.

Confronted with the new phenomenon, the critic fraternity
failed in a peculiarly grotesque manner. To take one example out
of a hundred, the literary historian Hans Sittenberger described

393

the situation about 1890 as follows: " Bourget set the fashion with his psychological cogitations (*Spintisieren*). With this there was associated the influence of Maeterlinck, the weak-brained mystic. . . . Here and there, too, one hears echoes of the anæmic, ludicrous, puffed-up pseudo-scientificality of Strindberg's creations. . . . From Ibsen they learnt the padding of dialogue with ideas and allusions quite irrelevant to the situation, the insistent and hopelessly old-fashioned self-characterization of the personages. . . . Their dialogue reminds one, like that of their master, of the primitive mummers' plays before Hans Sachs, where the personages introduce themselves with great politeness: ' I am so-and-so and this or that is my kind.' " If one were awarding a prize for anti-characteristics, it would undoubtedly have to go to him who said of Maeterlinck that he was weak-brained, of Strindberg that he was anæmic, and of Ibsen that his technique was even more primitive than that of Hans Sachs. In 1893 Max Nordau's muchread book *Degeneration* appeared, an uninterrupted vilification, several hundred pages long, of all the leading modern artists, in which — to take again only one example — Ibsen is called a malicious twaddler, modernity-huckster, and " thesis swindler," while the closing sentence reads: " The only unity that I can discover in Ibsen is that of his distortedness. Where he really always remains the same is in his complete inability to think a single thought clearly, to comprehend a single one of the catchwords with which he adorns his plays here and there, or to draw the correct conclusion from a single premiss." Taking fright at these sorry exhibitions, literary-historical criticism has recently gone full tilt in the other direction. It conscientiously registers and nervously dissects any fashionable trash that has enjoyed half a season's notoriety, a method of procedure which, no whit less idiotic and innocent than the other, reminds one of the clown zealously copying the conjurer's tricks.

The singer of Thule

Ibsen's spiritual ancestors are to be sought in his own country: in the Norwegian Holberg and the Danes Andersen and Kierkegaard. Holberg has often been compared with Molière, whom he cannot touch in respect of philosophical culture and elegance of form, although he surpassed him in juicy satire and sharpness of delineation. The mention of the apparently innocent Andersen may at first seem surprising, but only as long as one fails to remember that this writer for the young was one of the greatest expounders of men and creative ironists in the world's literature. To Kierkegaard Ibsen stands very much in the relation of Wagner to Schopenhauer, Hebbel to Hegel, Shaw to Carlyle, Schiller to Kant: he took from him a portion of his outfit of ideas, and in so doing occasionally made use of the artist's delightful privilege of misunderstanding the philosopher. Of great importance to the Nordic poets of that generation, especially in what might be called " imparting technique," was the work of the Dane Georg Brandes. He was a sort of literary king-maker, with a keen flair for the driving forces of the time, who revealed to educated Europe the rich literature of his country and, inversely, directed the current of European culture towards Scandinavia. It is true that, with all his taste and power of adaptation, he only touched the upper strata of literary personalities, never rising above the level of belletristic essays that display deep-sea wonders in artificial basins. Norwegian literature can of course no more be separated from the Danish than Dutch painting from Belgian. Norway belongs entirely to the Danish sphere of culture, with which it was also politically bound up from the beginning of the sixteenth century until the Congress of Vienna. For many centuries Danish was, throughout the land, the language of the Church, the law, and the educated classes, and only in the nineteenth century were attempts made to revive the Norwegian national tongue by absorbing elements of it into the (Danish) written language. Ibsen and Björnson wrote a Norwegian-tinged Danish.

In *The Pretenders* the skald Jatgejr says: " No song is born in full daylight." Of this order were the songs of the skald Ibsen: born in the land of the midnight sun, strangely clear and gloomy, shaded by the stars, illumined by the morning, bathed in the ambiguous twilight, floating dimly *between the ages*. And thus the figure of Ibsen stands before the astonished memory of posterity as the dark flame of the North, the mysterious singer from Thule.

If we are to catalogue Ibsen, we must undoubtedly put him into the family of the classics. By a classic we do not mean a poet who creates in a particular form (in scanned feet, for instance) or prefers certain material (such as the Classical or the antique); we mean every poet whose works are not only products of *vitality*, of experience and suffering, but also of *rationality*, of schematic calculation and noble measure; every poet in whom passion has clarified into science is a classic. As classical works of such origin, familiar to all, we may take the Greek tragedies — those creations of the ripest artistic understanding, carefully *durchkomponiert*

The last of the classics

395

in all the parts and balanced like an ancient temple or altar-piece, thanks to a full and certain knowledge of the craft, the material, the laws and proportions. Such, too, are the dramas of Goethe and Schiller, Corneille and Racine, in which all the elements ennoble, elucidate, shade, and illumine each other until for each entity a complete stage perspective is achieved; and such, too, are the dialogues of Lessing and Molière, with their light and airy, ordered and finished architecture. The last classic of this kind was Henrik Ibsen, the most perfect because the most complicated. What Goethe said of Shakspere is true of him in a higher degree: " His people are like clocks with a face and case of crystal; they show in their appointed way the course of the hour; and one can see, at the same time, the wheels and springs that work them." Yes, Ibsen saw through people as if they had been transparent, discovered the hidden scaffolding that upholds our world, the quiet heart that beats untiringly within it; his eye sent mysterious X-rays through the earth's dark happenings.

Zenith of middle-class dramaturgy

Ibsen marks the zenith of middle-class realism: his psychology and technique correspond to the form of dramatic production which, coming into power simultaneously with the bourgeoisie, is characterized by the completely darkened auditorium and the sharply isolated, glaringly lighted stage, solidified by the ceiling, the " practical " furniture, and three closed screens. In the previous volume we saw that the technical difference between Goethe and Schiller was that, from the point of view of the psychology of staging, the one worked with only *three* walls and *painted-on* doors while the other chose complete reality, with four walls and real doors; the result being, however, that because of a super-dimensionality, the stage effectiveness was not enhanced, but diminished. In examining Ibsen as to his capacity for staging we should have to define his difference from Schiller the more precisely in that, though both were eminent theatricalists, Schiller was the theatricalist of the soffits, the wings, and the cut-out door, while Ibsen was the stage master of firm ceilings, " built " walls, and the massive door that is nevertheless an imaginary door. His is, in a word, the highest attainable *stage realism*.

Dramaturgy in small things

In the face of this inviolable and often involuntary realism all the discussions of rationalist psychologists seem highly irrelevant, both the sceptical who inquire suspiciously as to whether everything hangs together, and the positive who enthusiastically verify particular fine points. Both these points of view rest upon a completely mistaken idea of the poetical creative art. The Aristotelian maxim that the whole is prior to the parts applies equally to the products of art as to those of nature. The Greek was, as we explained in the previous volume, firmly convinced that " idea," " form," " concept " (these three conceptions meaning for him in some mysterious way the same thing) were the " primary " thing, and " reality," " matter," " unit," only the results. It is no different with the artist: the first, original, begetting part is " form "; out of it flow, inevitably and independently of him, all " features " and " actions." This " form " is an organism; it therefore develops, not in accordance with a mechanical causality, dirigible from outside, but with the " vital " causality, which is a law unto itself. Accordingly all things must " fit," and all in the same high degree, and consequently all psychological criticism of works of art is (not, so to say, " disrespectful," but) senseless, an exhibition of complete ignorance in æsthetic matters. No less banausic is the admiration accorded to " a genius for detail," for in a genuine work all details show genius, and no one more than another. They all bear the mark because they are natural. They are all natural because they are divine. Judgments which praise or detract are as stupid as the entertaining criticisms of the Creation by Baroque writers who distributed censure to animals and plants: of the caterpillar, for instance, they expressed their serious displeasure on account of its repulsive appearance, whereas its metamorphosis into a pretty butterfly called forth their unqualified approval.

There are in the life of every man two states in which he is a finished poet: dreaming and childhood. Children never have crooked, confined, lifeless visions of existence; all that is for grown-ups. In dreams we are all Shakspers. Unfortunately most people, in their conscious and adult state, lose this obviously inborn and entirely organic constructive power and become appallingly talentless, because their reason, that cowardly and impotent one who " knows better," interferes everywhere. Only the artist, that ever-dreaming child, retains this gift. Therefore a " badly drawn poem " is as much an impossibility as an " untrue " dream. On the other hand, just as with the phenomena of life, judgments of sympathy and antipathy are absolutely permissible. Here again children may serve as teachers of æsthetics. They hate the wolf and the spider: in nature, in human form, and in poetry. Similarly, it is quite conceivable that certain poems are

397

felt to be " evil " because their world is denied by us, but this must not be taken to mean that it is wrong. A world can never be wrong.

Against this theory that all figures and events in a drama (to keep for the present to this art-form) are equally perfect, three arguments present themselves : that there are in fact some entirely unsuccessful plays, that even the successful ones vary greatly in value, and that even the finest among them contain blanks. But these objections answer themselves in a very simple way. The " unsuccessful " plays are not poems at all, but differ from these as generically as a jointed doll from a human being. There are very rough dolls and very artistic ones ; but common to them all is the fact that they are mechanical productions. Now, how does one recognize them as such ? By " feeling," the same feeling which has never yet allowed us to confuse a show-case model with a shop customer, or a panorama with a landscape ; it lives, infallible, in everyone — though often not in the so-called professionals of the theatre : for by perpetually being among the waxworks they have forfeited the normal capacity to differentiate. This brings us to the explanation of the " blanks." They, by exception, do *not* originate with the poet, but with the " improvers " : the intendants, dramaturges, stage managers, actors, who nominally make concessions to the " exigencies of the theatre," but in reality pander to the needs of their own hostility to art and a fictitious public which they regard as stupid. All through the centuries rings the complaint of publisher, editor, concert agent, stage director : nothing new, nothing deep, nothing serious must ever be set before the public, its taste being always in the direction of shallow entertainment, trumpery, conventional stuff. Now, this is simply an inversion of the true state of affairs : the backward, vulgar, and superficial elements are the professionals themselves. The public is one gigantic open mouth, which slings down everything that is set before it. That it would rather swallow good than bad is beyond dispute. There is immediate and quite unequivocal proof of it if one casts a glance over extensive periods. How is it that all the fashionable novels and theatre " hits," so greedily absorbed in their day, are remembered now only by a few seminar students ? Why do the successful street-songs and sentimental ditties live but for a season, although on everybody's lips ? And, vice versa, is there a single celebrity over a hundred years old who does not deserve to be a celebrity ? Are not Homer and Dante truly the greatest epic poets, Plato and Kant the greatest philosophers? And if statistics were taken of the last few hundred years on the stage, the most played dramatist would quite certainly be Shakspere. Who, then, has with such unerring judgment assigned to these men their rightful place? Not, surely, the professors of literature? For they only take a genius seriously when the last post-office official has digested him. None but the public makes these truly artistic and intelligent decisions; it merely requires a little time to do it in. If it is offered inferior nourishment by the professedly competent "manufacturers," then it will accept it, but only because it cannot get anything better; and sooner or later it will still be guided by its instinct to the right source, in spite of all the obstructions put in its way by the people who presume to guide it. There are protista which unite in the form of "cell-unions" or "cell-colonies": these tiny creatures then possess two souls, an individual soul and a so-called cœnobite soul, which expresses the general feeling of the whole cell-stock. It is much the same with the human being " *qua* public ": in addition to his own soul he receives a second, the soul of the public, in which the wise will of the genus rules. And to Chamfort's question: " How many stupid people does it take to make a public? " the answer might well be: that one can of course decide according to the particular case as to how many are needed, but that every time enough of them are assembled, something is born that is far wiser than they.

It is an undoubted fact that there is a hierarchy of dramatic works, but this does not in the least negative the view that each of them does get its indisputable reality-value; for there is an order of rank in reality also, and among living people. How is their respective value decided? I believe it to be precisely by their hold on reality. If we compare Bismarck with Bethmann-Hollweg, for instance, or Goethe with Gottsched, we should (if reducing the difference to the briefest formula) have to say simply that Goethe and Bismarck were more real as personalities. That is why Nietzsche called Napoleon the *ens realissimum*. It is exactly the same in our daily life. Certain people seem to us more massive, authenticated, alive, than others because they reflect a larger section of the world, have, so to say, a heavier tonnage. But they all are "psychologically right."

I should like to give just one example of the fact that it is not possible for a true poet to draw a character badly, even with the best will in the world. In *Vor Sonnenaufgang (Before Sunrise)*

399

Alfred Loth is undoubtedly intended as a sort of mouthpiece for the poet, as the hero of the piece, who must be in the right, with whom Hauptmann definitely identifies himself. Actually, however, he is a barren and narrow-souled expounder of principles, who has absolutely no claim to our undivided sympathy. In the second act, speaking of *Werther,* he says to Helene Krause that it is a stupid book, a book for weaklings. When Helene asks if he can recommend anything better, he replies: " R-read — let me see — do you know the *Kampf um Rom* by Dahn? It paints people, not as they are, but as they one day ought to be. It serves as a model." And when Helene then asks whether Zola and Ibsen are great authors, he answers: " They are not authors at all, Fräulein. I have an honest thirst and what I ask of the poetic art is a clear refreshing drink. I am not ill. What Zola and Ibsen offer is medicine." Here speaks all at once, not the poet's soul, but a swelled-headed, coarse-grained schoolmaster. That the *Kampf um Rom* was to be preferred to *Werther* can never have been Hauptmann's opinion. What had happened? The figure had simply made itself independent.

Now if we compare the parallel figures of Hauptmann and Ibsen, we shall see that Ibsen's have more reality in them; their relation to the others is that of sculpture in the round to reliefs. Gregers Werle and Relling take exactly the same place in *The Wild Duck* as do Loth and Doctor Schimmelpfennig in *Before Sunrise.* But Schimmelpfennig is only a profile and a diagnosis: we learn of him only that he is a sceptical country doctor and that Helene's family is given to drinking. In Relling, on the other hand, a whole human destiny, full of inconsistencies, stands out, and at the same time a whole philosophy of life, which might bear the title given to four of Nietzsche's posthumous dissertations: *Über Wahrheit und Lüge im aussermoralischen Sinne.* And in Gregers Werle we have the whole martyrdom of the tragicomic apostle of mankind, who, unlike Mephisto, always desires good and always does evil. Or if we compare the treatment of the heredity problem in *Before Sunrise* and in *Ghosts,* the one is a matter of medical prescription and Monistic dogma, the other a point where the moral and social problems of the present day all cross one another. In the first, the most primitive solution imaginable; in the second, none at all. This is the relation of the simple multiplication table to the probability computation of the Infinitesimal Calculus.

The most imperishable thing about Ibsen's dramas, the point
in which Shakspere only occasionally equals him, is that he succeeds in reproducing the ambiguity and fathomlessness of life. His
people give one the impression of being really only on a visit to
him. They come from somewhere outside, walk about in the play
for a space, and take themselves off again. They were in the world
before the piece began and go on living when it is over. One is able,
too, to form a more intimate acquaintance with them by frequent
meetings, just as with real people. But one will never know all
there is in them. For instance, two such special and thorough connoisseurs of Ibsen as Paul Schlenther and Roman Woerner differ
entirely as to the parentage of Hedwig Ekdal; the one regards it
as proved that she is the daughter of old Werle, the other that
Hjalmar is her father. The first is the generally accepted theory,
resting on the assumption that Werle's eye disease was inherited
by Hedwig; the second is supported by Hedwig's talent for drawing
and the fact that Hjalmar's mother also suffered with her eyes.
According to the newest psychology, it would have also to be
indicated that Hedwig was in love with Hjalmar: that is, had a
" father-complex "; but it might equally be assumed that she had
created for herself a " father-substitute." All such controversies
would have been after Ibsen's own heart, for his aim is not clearness, but life. Once, when asked whether Engstrand had set fire
to the asylum, he replied: " Well, it's just the sort of thing the
fellow would do! "

Ibsen's realism once achieved the incredible by depicting an
obscure genius who rang true. Usually those tragedies that hinge
on a manuscript are in danger of turning out ludicrously, and, in
general, authors as dramatic heroes are a thankless proposition.
That Goethe's Tasso should have written *Jerusalem Delivered*
was quite beside the point, as we have already remarked, and we
have simply to take *Die Räuber* on credit in Laube's Schiller. But
in *Hedda Gabler* we are profoundly convinced that actually an irre-
placeable literary work has been burnt, although — to return for
comparison to Hauptmann — we definitely do not believe Johannes
Vockeradt's work to have been an outstanding achievement. But
Ibsen created something even greater and more incomprehensible: the Platonic Idea of the average man in Hjalmar Ekdal.

Nature, so wasteful in some respects, is in others uncommonly
frugal. She scatters forms by the thousand, achieves the most
bizarre shapes, is never tired of new departures, so that it

401

sometimes seems as if she were ruled by the insatiable play-impulse which makes the artist so restless a creature. But if we look closer, we find that all the time she is only carrying out just a few simple ideas. Among the almost incalculable abundance of forms which we group together under the name of mammal, for example, there is a single law of structure, easy to grasp; they are all created on one uniform plan: the neck is always formed out of seven vertebræ, in the case of the mole and the giraffe alike, and the heart of two chambers and two antechambers, in the elephant as in the squirrel. And Nature's procedure is exactly the same with human beings. For although there are no two human souls which completely resemble each other, the same types recur again and again in the many-graded vastness of the realm of spirits. Fundamentally there are but three types: the idealist, the realist, and the sceptic.

The greatest poets of the Germanic race have embodied these three forms of crystallization in three luminous figures. Shakspere created the figure of the sceptic in Hamlet, Goethe the figure of the idealist in Faust, and Ibsen the figure of the realist in Hjalmar. Hamlet is an aristocrat of the Elizabethan Renaissance, with that curious mixture of bigotry and free-thinking which marks the period: he still believes in ghosts, it is true, but he has also read Montaigne. He is infinitely more than this, however; he is simply the man who knows too much to be able to act — in plain words, the man that culture evolves. We might meet him in the street any day: in Paris, in Berlin, in London, in the garden of the epicure and in Thoreau's American forests, and in every age that is sufficiently ripe to produce human beings that look out on the mad and criminal world in which they live, with weariness and detachment. Hebbel called the tragedy of Faust the most complete painting of the Middle Ages, and he was right; but it is also the most complete painting of the eighteenth century and the most complete painting of the nineteenth. Faust is Abélard and Thomas Aquinas, but he is also Fichte and Nietzsche — in short, genius. And his opposite, Hjalmar, possesses the most complete ubiquity imaginable. He is the man who is blissfully satisfied with things as they are, never at a loss for a palatable explanation of painful matters, a virtuoso in overlooking tiresome responsibilities and always concerned to cover up life with cheap poetry, screening its light, as it were, by painting the glass — in a word, the complete philistine. Can we imagine any sphere of human civilization in which he did not exist, or that he has not, in all ages, formed the original stock

402

of humanity? He is ordinariness in the flesh, but the poet has shown him imperishable.

These are the three types of the human race. Or, rather, the three souls which dwell in every man build him up and are perpetually in a state of struggle and balancing. Who has not some time said: "What's the good, anyway? We are a lunatic asylum. Why interfere? It all has no meaning whatever." At that moment the speaker was Hamlet. Who has not some time said: " That's all very well. But now I should like a roll and butter and a bottle of beer." At that moment he was Hjalmar. And who, in spite of this, has not felt, again and again: " No matter. We must go on, and upward. That is what we are in the world for." At this moment he was Faust. And now what is the true meaning of life: mature scepticism, perpetual striving, or bread and butter? The poet replies: " We are men. We must doubt. We must strive. We must drink beer."

Strange to say, nothing so embittered the Norwegians as the fact that the greatest constructive mind of the dying century was a Norwegian. His very début on the stage roused the national indignation, which increased with each new drama. The *League of Youth* could hardly be played to the end at the original performance in Christiania, and the attitude adopted by the " compact majority " towards *Ghosts* gave Ibsen the idea for his *Enemy of the People*. The poet left his ungrateful fatherland and became a cosmopolitan in Rome and Munich. What happened next might be called Norway's revenge. All Ibsen's modern dramas have a Norwegian setting, not only as regards externals (which would not matter), but as regards internals. The problem of Nora, of Alving, of Stockmann, of Hedda, is only possible in that distance from Europe and in that peninsular narrowness, among those overcast skies and lonely fiords, in that fussy duodecimo and hole-and-corner society. Not that these conflicts between woman and marriage, individual and crowd, genius and the world, were not common to humanity, but in Paris they would have had other colours and perspectives, other atmospheric effects. And therefore, by way of paradox, Sardou has become the European dramatist, despite all the superficiality of his estimate of men, the cheapness of his philosophy, the brutality of his solutions, and the backwardness of his technique.

Attention has often been drawn to the links between Ibsen and the French comedy of manners. There is this much truth in it, that

Ibsen did actually take over — and greatly spiritualize — its technique, as being the proper, indispensable, and only possible one for the middle-class peep-show stage. All the standing figures of the Paris society drama appear again in Ibsen, ennobled by masterly character-masks: the *raisonneur* (Lundestad, Relling, Brack, Mortensgard), the false "good fellow" (Stensgaard, Bernick, Peter Stockmann, Werle), the confidant (Doctor Herdal, Foldal), the noble *déraciné* (Brendel, Lövborg), the man-eater (Hedda, Rita), the purified sinner (Rebekka), the *incomprise* (Ellida, Nora), the *ingénue* (Hilde Wangel). Moreover, we find him employing the unmasking technique, definitely in the *League of Youth* and *The Pillars of Society,* and less openly in *A Doll's House, The Enemy of the People, Ghosts,* and *The Wild Duck.* Even the "technique of metaphor" invented by the French was accepted by him, and it is here that we can see most clearly the many degrees by which he raised himself above his model. This technique consists in placing some allegory, picture, or *aperçu* in the centre of the action, and usually in the title also. The classical example is *Le Demi-monde.* Here the *raisonneur* says suddenly: "Do you like peaches? Well, go to a fruiterer's and ask for the best sort. He will bring you a basket of exquisite specimens, separated by leaves so that they do not spoil each other by touching. They cost, let us say, twenty sous apiece. You look about you and will certainly see, near by, a second basket of peaches, which are hardly to be distinguished from the others, being merely packed closer together. You ask the price; fifteen sous. Naturally you inquire why these peaches, equally lovely, equally big, equally ripe, equally appetizing, cost less than the others. Whereupon the salesman will show you a quite small dark spot, which is the reason of the low price. *Eh bien, mon cher:* you are in the basket of peaches at fifteen sous. The women around you have all a small blot on their name. They crowd together so that it shall be less noticeable, and although they have the same origin, the same exterior, the same manners and prejudices as the great world, they are no longer of it, and they form what is called the half-world, which is neither aristocracy nor bourgeoisie, but is like a floating island in the ocean of Paris." According to Dumas's technique, Relling would have said something like this: "Have you ever noticed a wild duck? Imagine that it has been injured and caught. For a time it will dream of the blue sky, of the deep pond and the thick rushes in which it used to disport itself. But gradually it will forget liberty and stay, fat and happy, in its dull box in the attic, which it takes to be the world. *Eh bien, mon cher, we are in a wild duck's box here.*"

If the parallelism between the French technique and Ibsen's only holds good with considerable reservations, the equally frequent comparison with that of Classical drama is completely misplaced. For while Greek tragedy merely developed, on artistic lines, a new way of reaching a result already known, with Ibsen the way itself was first revealed; there it was a question of an original route leading to an established cult-truth, here of an unClassical tension during the solution of an enigma. Both forms are analytical, but as different from each other as geometrical and chemical analyses; in the one a given rational equation is reconstructed in an obvious way, in the other a non-articulated state of things is first observed and established; the one reveals the motivation, the other the constitution. The development is dialectical in *Œdipus,* and an experimental process in the other. The relation is similar to that between the Hesiodic and the Darwinian cosmogonies, between the Platonic Idea, which is the generative foundation, and the Kantian, which is the sought goal.

To find the true model for Ibsen, one need look neither to Paris nor to Athens. It is the Icelandic and Norwegian saga of his native land, the ballad. He has in common with it all the features that determine his inward ground-structure; the oppressive straining towards the catastrophe, which is so certain that (although one only discovers it later) the drama works up with it; the everrecurring, more and more threatening refrain; the acute concentration; the double darkness of enigma and tragedy; the latent Romanticism. Who today would doubt that the story of Ellida and the stranger, of little Hilde and the big Solness, is a song? That the white horses of Rosmersholm and the "rat-mamsell" hail from the haunted chamber, or that *Ghosts* is a *real* ghost-story? They are nixies in cotton frocks, nightmares in holiday garb, legends by electric light.

The interpenetration of reality and symbolism in all this is quite beyond comparison. We have seen that even so probing a naturalist as Zola achieved great personifications quite against his will, and as it were in an underhand way. But with him these are mechanical products of summation, monster collective beings, which are therefore mere rational "omens" or at best cold allegories. With Ibsen, however, they have the full irrationality, dual basis, and uncanniness of magic fairy-tale. They become, in a series of increasing intensity, more and more mysterious and at the same time, strange to say, concrete. One has only to name them: the *Indian Girl* in *Pillars of Society*, the doll's house, Alving's burning asylum, the tainted baths in *The Enemy of the People*, the attic in *The Wild Duck*, Rosmersholm, the sea in *The Lady from the Sea*, the steeple in *The Master Builder*: all fantastic and everyday, unreal and tangible horrors.

The testament of the Modern Age

Like Nietzsche, Ibsen has three fairly distinct periods. The first, from 1863 to 1873, embraces in essence the great stories and poems in verse; the second, lasting until 1890, the revolutionary society dramas; and the last, the mystical poems. From 1877 to 1899 Ibsen brought out a new play with great regularity every two years, and this was always in some sense the continuation of a previous one. But all have at bottom the same theme, and this he sums up in a letter to Brandes: "There are really times when the whole of world-history seems to me one single big shipwreck — the thing is to save one's own self." The note that sounds through all the later works is struck in his very first drama, *Catilina*, whose hero passes for the type of the nihilistic enemy of society, but really (at least in Ibsen's conception) wished to be a revolutionary creator of the new. In Ibsen, the hypercritical fighter from the Northland, the Protestant spirit of protest again became flesh — the spirit of Luther and Hutten, Milton and Carlyle, and the spirit of the Kantian morality as it lives in Brand and Rosmer. "I received the gift of sorrow," says Jatgejr, "and so I became a skald. There may be others who need faith or joy — or doubt. But then the doubter must be strong and well." This uncontrollable, vital doubt, which struggles fearlessly with all, even itself, was Ibsen's "Kraftborn," his fountain of strength; from it he drew those dark songs of his which lit up the world. The evil spirits, though, which he went forth to fight were the "ideals" on which the overfed age had settled itself to rest. With untiring mockery he showed up their threadbareness, their emptiness, their mendacity, and pointed to the need for new constellations. But he never really arrived at these new ideals. It was on this score that Hermann Türck in *Der geniale Mensch* (not at all a bad book) was able to present him as the type of an anarchist and "misosoph," though without considering that it was just his immense moral feeling of responsibility which made denying easier for him than constructing. Doctor Allmers, the hero of *Little Eyolf,* works at a book on human responsibility that never gets finished. All his life Ibsen wrote at this book also, but it never appeared in complete form. This great wizard took his last secrets with him to the grave: out of shame, like Skald Jatgejr; out of pride, like Ulrik Brendel, who said of himself: "My most important works no one knows, man or woman. No human being — except me. Because they are not written. And why indeed should I profane my own ideals when I can keep them in purity and enjoy them for myself alone? " And a little, too, perhaps, out of malice. Above all, because he was a great poet. For the profoundest poems are recorded by the heart alone and shrink from freezing into letters. His last piece of revealed wisdom issues from the mouth of the hero of his last drama: "When we dead awake, we shall see that we have not lived." He himself called this work an epilogue, and it appeared, again with high symbolic meaning, exactly at the close of the century, in the last days of December 1899.

But there is also a sort of epilogue in the final scene of his last drama but one. Borkman's death strangely foreshadows Tolstoi's end. In both there arose, shortly before their passing, a secret craving to wander. They left the protection of their own roof and strayed forth into the inhospitable unknown. A kind of flight from reality.

" (*The landscape, with slopes and rising ground, changes slowly and continuously, becoming ever wilder in character.*) ELLA RENTNER's *voice:* But why need we climb so high? BORKMAN's *voice:* We must go up the winding path. (*They have arrived at a clearing high up in the forest.*) ELLA: We used often to sit on that seat. BORKMAN: It was a dreamland that we looked into then. ELLA: It was the dreamland of our life. And now the land is covered with snow. And the old tree is dead. BORKMAN: Do you see the smoke rising from the big steamers on the water out there? ELLA: No. BORKMAN: I see it. They come and they go. They make linkages all over the earth. And down there by the river — do you hear? — the factories are at work. My factories — the wheels whirl and the rollers glint, round and round, round and round. Do you see the chain mountains there, in the distance? One behind the other. They raise themselves. They pile themselves up. *There* is my deep and endless, inexhaustible kingdom. ELLA: Oh, but, John, it blows over so ice-cold from your kingdom! BORKMAN: It is the breath

407

of life to me. It is as if it wafted me a greeting from submissive spirits. I love you, you, dear life-craving things — with all your shining retinue of power and splendour. I love, love, love you. (*Screams out and smites his breast.*) Oh! ELLA: What was it, John? BORKMAN: An icy hand that gripped my heart. No, not an icy hand, an iron hand. FRAU BORKMAN (*comes through the trees*): Is he asleep? ELLA: A deep, long sleep, I think. FRAU BORKMAN: Ella! (*with lowered voice*) Did it happen — voluntarily? ELLA: No. FRAU BORKMAN: Not by his own hand, then? ELLA: No. It was an icy iron hand that gripped his heart. It was the cold that killed him. FRAU BORKMAN: The cold — that would have killed him long since. ELLA: Yes — and changed us two into shadows. FRAU BORKMAN: You are right. And now we can take each other by the hand, Ella. We twin sisters — clasp our hands over him whom we both loved. ELLA: We two shadows — over him who is dead. (FRAU BORKMAN, *behind the seat, and* ELLA, *standing before it, clasp hands.*) "

This finale (abbreviated here to allow the leading ideas to stand out more powerfully) forms the perfect counterpart to the close of *Faust*, which ends in the highest optimism. But its blissful vision of human energy and working power is just what causes Ella Rentheim to shudder; for what was once dreamland is now covered with snow, and humanity's tree of life is dead. Round and round go the wheels and rollers, always the same circle: they have become a senseless aim in themselves. Borkman takes pleasure in these tokens of an apparent power, they are his breath of life. But what he takes to be life is death. The icy hand of the cold at his heart grips him, the iron hand of matter. And above the dead man shadows are left standing. Borkman really went on from where Faust left off. The whole planet was to be subordinated to human power. He would have wrenched the earth's treasures from her — the sea, the mountains — would have turned the sky into a bridge, night into day, and all the land into an orchard. And the end of it all was the bitter wisdom of the Duke in *Measure for Measure:* "Merely, thou art Death's fool." We said in the first volume that *Faust* was a compendium of the Modern Age. *John Gabriel Borkman* is its testament.

In this connexion Ibsen's real significance stands revealed to us: he was, after Shakspere, the greatest poet of histories of modern Europe. Like him, he will only come fully into his own when the dresses of his characters have become "costume." To try to modernize him is as inartistic an amusement as to put Hamlet into dress clothes. Oswald and Hjalmar can only look right in velvet jackets and flowing ties, Bernick and Borkman only in old-fashioned frock-coats and white satin ties, just as Nora must have a bustle and a donkey fringe, and Hedda a princess dress and a chignon. Once these costumes seem as remote to the public as Lady Milford's *Adrienne* and Franz Moor's hair-bag, it will realize that it is in the presence of dramas written for all time, although — or, rather, because — the poet conceived of them as tendentious dramas of the day, like *The Robbers* and *Kabale und Liebe*. After all, were not Shakspere's "royal" dramas, Kleist's *Hermannsschlacht* and *Prinz von Homburg* equally tendentious, indeed frank partisan tocsins? We only do not notice it any more. For the "ideas," that were then the main thing, have blown over, but the men, who merely conveyed them, have stayed. It would be foolish, all the same, to regret that these poets did more than simply "construct," for it was just these perishable ideas which imbued their work with its imperishable impetuosity, the power to construct, the "cue to passion." At present we only feel, with Ibsen, that his problems are not the problems of *our* time, but one day he will be most admired just because he clothed the problems of *his* time in such overpowering plastic form. And here we have the clue to the peculiar curve of public recognition which, as was shown in the previous chapter, is to be observed in the case of nearly all great dramatists. First they are regarded as an alarming revolution, a murderous attack on all that has gone before, and are accordingly fiercely resisted. Then they are discovered to be spiritual liberators, and are hailed *ad nauseam* as Messiahs. Later the public turns away from them, regarding them — according to the degree in which the new world-picture they have fought to establish has "lived itself in" — as complete superfluities, megaphones of the washed-out commonplace. Finally they receive appreciation on the one appropriate score of their purely human and artistic merit. Their true worth is seen when they are recognized as the most powerful, clear, and pure mirrors of their time, as something like gigantic telescopes through which one can look into the past. And it is realized that they were the greatest men of their day. Even poets are not perfect; they are only fluttering, seeking will-o'-the-wisps, cross-breeds between wish and error. But the fact that they, alone among all the rest, were *whole* men is what can never be forgotten. This

409

one thing remains and will jump across from one Galaxy to the next.

Of Ibsen's dramas of the first period only one, *The Pretenders*, at first found its way to the German stage — and that, obviously, because it was confused in people's minds with the dusty dramas of chivalry so popular at the time. It was first performed by the Meininger players and at the Burg Theatre. The wretchedness of the translation began with the title. So modern a conception as " pretender " is completely misleading. (We have already said that the name of this piece is untranslatable: it is literally " Kings' material " or " Wood from which kings are carved "; the nearest would be perhaps " The king-idea," for this is the focus of the whole internal action.) The *Pillars* was performed in Berlin on three stages simultaneously in 1878, a year after its first appearance (as the literary productions of Scandinavia were not yet " protected "), again from a miserable translation in the Reclam edition. *A Doll's House* also appeared, a year after the Norwegian publication, in the Reclam edition and was played at several important German theatres, at Laube's in Vienna and with Hedwig Niemann-Raabe in Berlin. Both times the title-rôle in *Nora* was watered down and the author persuaded to make a false ending: Nora stays, on the children's account (which, if one cared to argue with such a view-point, amounts to upsetting the whole play in its very motivation, for it is just because of the children that she *goes,* realizing that, morally, she is not yet a mother). Here it once more becomes quite clear that Laube, whose flair for discovering talent in actors amounted to genius, never got beyond the stage carpenter's stolid outlook with respect to the drama itself. The fêted actress Francillon had declared that she must insist upon this ending because *she* would never leave her children: very interesting, no doubt, but really her own private affair; incidentally, she had not found the incongruities between her own biography and that of gay French ladies an obstacle to playing such parts.

Of *Ghosts* Paul Heyse said: " One doesn't write such books "; which, coming from him, was quite true. This play appeared in 1881, but was first played in German in 1886 by the Meininger players, who also gave it in Berlin in January 1887. Only the one matinée was given there, however, as the censor forbade further performances. *The Wild Duck* was likewise allowed only one afternoon performance, in the autumn of 1888. The Royal Court

Theatre opened its doors in March 1889 to *The Lady from the Sea,* although the performance was of the regular court type, only Emanuel Reicher as Wangel and Paula Conrad as Hilda being worthy of mention. But the opening of the " Freie Bühne " in the same year marked the break-through.

Nature, who only allows an infringement of her rights in passing, again assumed her sway, and a savage hunger for reality broke out and reared itself up as the banner of the times. And again, as so often before, the young generation thought it had discovered Nature for the first time. The whole movement was much over-estimated on account of its elementary vehemence. At bottom it was but a counter-attack, drawing its vital energy less from itself than from the force of the collision. It had, however, a most purifying effect. The beginning was made with the founding of the journal *Die Gesellschaft* (*Society*) by Michael Georg Conrad in Munich. "We propose," said the introductory note, " to restore to honour that manliness in discernment, authorship, and criticism which has been grievously imperilled by the speculative taking into consideration of precious drivel and the sentimental pet theories and moral prejudices of the so-called family . . . to make war on the embarrassment-idealism of Philistia, the white lies of morality, the old régime of party and clique." Soon after, the "Durch" society was formed in Berlin, to which, among others, Arno Holz, the Hart brothers, Bruno Wille, and Wilhelm Bölsche belonged. Its motto was: "Our highest artistic ideal is no longer the Classical, but the modern," and its insistent contempt for Classicism was directed against Schiller in particular. In Otto Ernst's comedy *Jugend von Heute* a representative of the moderns calls him a blockhead, and Gottfried Keller once flew into such a rage with a young stranger at the next table in a café who spoke of him in similar terms that he boxed his ears. Otto Julius Bierbaum gave a very plausible description of the change of front in the youth of the day in his novel *Stilpe:* Four schoolboys formed a society called "Spring (*Lenz*) " with a double meaning: it embraced the spiritual spring and was also the name of the revered literary light. In their debates they annihilated "Herr Schillinger" and discussed such themes as "Truth as the sole principle in art," "How far Naturalism and Socialism are parallel phenomena," "Émile Zola and Henrik Ibsen, the supporting pillars of the new literature," "Wherein lies the danger to the community of so-called idealism? " and they resolved " that

411

the mention of certain names — for instance, Paul Heyse and Julius Wolff — among members would entail a heavy fine, up to twenty pfennigs." The lyrical signal came from Hermann Conradi, who died in 1890, at the age of twenty-eight, as the result of an attempt at suicide. In his *Lieder eines Sünders* he writes: "The age is dead in which great heroes wrought. The age is dead — the age of the great souls, we are a wretched people all of pygmies. What we achieve we do according to pattern, and our hearts cry out but for gold and prostitutes. We *all* fall on our knees before the idols and sing the death-songs of our liberty." In 1889 there appeared *Papa Hamlet*, a strictly naturalistic, psycho-pathological sketch by Bjarne P. Holmsen, behind which (significantly, Norwegian) pseudonym Arno Holz and Johannes Schlaf sheltered; in the dedication of *Vor Sonnenaufgang* (removed from the later editions) Gerhart Hauptmann speaks " with delighted appreciation " of the " definite impetus received from the book." In 1890 there followed *Die Familie Selicke,* a situation-drama in rigorous Berlin jargon; it is Christmas Eve, as in *Friedensfest,* and the domestic picture is equally unedifying. The father, a drunkard book-keeper in poor circumstances and unhappily married, makes erotic advances, as in *Vor Sonnenaufgang,* to the daughter, who, martyr-like, sews half through the night and makes the sacrifice of giving up the theological candidate whom she loves, while the younger daughter, who is bedridden, dies. In 1891 there came a breach between Holz and Schlaf — two doctrinaires can never get on together, even when they are of the same opinion — and *Meister Ölze,* which appeared in 1892, was signed by Schlaf only. This was really a serial shocker, with murder by poisoning, motivated by the threatened alteration of a will, as the point of the plot. A study of phthisis and a study in dialect are other features, but the whole is tiresomely trivial. All the same, these two works had a liberating effect through their harsh unsentimentality, amounting to brutality, and their pedantically conscientious recording of observations.

The " Freie Bühne " On the 30th of September in 1889, the centenary year of the French Revolution, the " Freie Bühne " was opened — in its way also a storming of the Bastille. The prospectus stated: "We are united for the purpose of founding, independently of the activity of existing theatres and without entering into rivalry with them, a stage which is free from considerations of censorship and money-making. During the theatrical year there will be some ten per-

412

formances in one of the leading Berlin theatres, of modern dramas of outstanding interest which, being what they are, are not easily accessible to regular theatre-goers." The first performance was *Ghosts*, with Oswald played by Emerich Robert from the Burg Theatre, the most tragic and unreal actor of his generation, Manders by that splendid old veteran Kraussneck, who was still playing quite recently at the State Theatre in Berlin, Engstrand by Lobe, famous for his characterizations, Regine by Mme Sorma, and Frau Alving by Marie Schanzer, wife of Hans von Bülow. With the exception perhaps of the last-named, it was probably the best cast that could then have been conceived. On October 20 came the memorable first performance of *Vor Sonnenaufgang*. Fontane summed up his impression of this by describing the author, Gerhart Hauptmann, as " a realist with style: that is, the same from beginning to end." There were a few incidents which, though taken very seriously at the time, are merely amusing in retrospect. In the third act Hoffmann says to Loth: " I tell you, it's high time your doings were put a stop to, you're just popular agitators corrupting the people. Here you go, making the miner discontented and above himself, exciting him, embittering him, making him refractory, disobedient, unhappy, holding out visions of mountains of gold, while you sneak the last penny out of his pocket." This brought down the house, and Schlenther, in his pamphlet on the *Genesis der Freien Bühne*, remarks very pertinently: " In the heat of the moment Herr Gerhart Hauptmann has been identified straight away with his Loth; it seems to have been forgotten that the much-applauded Hoffmann is a child of the same poet's brain. . . . The brilliant success of his Hoffmann will encourage him to turn out his Loths also as whole, live men in future." In the fifth act a certain Dr. Castan created a diversion. He practised medicine as a secondary profession, his principal one being that of a fanatical first-nighter, in which rôle he now made for himself a permanent place in the history of the Naturalistic movement. At the close of the second act he had already gone so far as to shout: " Brothel! " — which, though abusive, could really only be interpreted as an unkind though justifiable comment on the Krause family. Knowing the book intimately, he was aware that, in the last act, the moaning of the woman in childbed should be heard from the next room. Although this was omitted at the performance, he was not to be deterred from carrying out his program, and at the appointed place he produced a large obstetrical forceps and waved it threateningly at the stage. This was the signal for a terrific uproar, which, in the gallery, ended in blows. The author's mild appearance, when he came forward repeatedly to acknowledge the applause and the hissing, moved Fontane to write: "Many of us will take pleasure in recalling that Geheimer Medizinalrat Caspar began his famous book on his experiences in forensic medicine with the words: ' My murderers all looked like young girls.'"

Early in 1890 the journal *Freie Bühne für modernes Leben* began to appear. In the introductory " *Zum Beginn* " was the passage: " The point of our endeavour is to be art, the new art which looks at reality and present-day existence. Once there was an art that shrank from the light of day, seeking poetry only in the twilight of the past. . . . Our art of today rivets to itself everything that lives. . . . We commit ourselves to no formula and make no attempt to bind life and art, which are perpetually in motion, to rigid rules. We are concerned with that which is still " becoming," and our attention is fixed rather upon that which is to come than on that everlasting past, which takes upon itself to tie up in conventions and precepts, once and for all, the endless possibilities of humanity." Otto Brahm and Paul Schlenther were the soul of the undertaking. They were both clever, thoroughly genuine, if slightly too matter-of-fact North Germans who, for all their keen judgment, devotion to the cause, and severity of outlook, were at bottom only very talented undergraduates who had " gone modern." (They were pupils of the excellent Wilhelm Scherer, who had made what is practically a record for Germany: namely, written an eminently readable history of literature.)

Naturalism   Naturalism was an error, but what a beneficent, full-blooded, fruit-bearing error! It was in its way a grand spectacle when the will to freedom and truth shot out from a whole generation like a fiery jet or a warm, healing spring. How bare, grey, glamourless, and crumpled, how insufferably futile do the Naturalistic plays appear today! And how terribly overwhelming, how positively magical, was their effect when they first appeared! An indescribable atmosphere of magic and terror emanated from them. One was literally frightened of them. It was like meeting ghosts in the street in broad daylight, who came towards you and held out their hands. Just because nothing but the most everyday, often the most vulgar, conversations and actions took place in these dramas, their effect was alarming and mysterious. In the place of art was set life, life in all its dangerousness and nearness : it was this grandiose inversion of things which made Naturalism so stupefying and so alluring. And today it all seems like a vast dustbin full of rubbish. The spring has snapped, the colour is washed out, and nothing remains but the cheap and common material : a few scraps and rags with which a heterogeneous suburban population once got up a meagre and tasteless wedding-eve carousal. At the time, the mystery of art seemed to have been unveiled : its mission was to reproduce reality, coldly, clearly, soberly, objectively, like a conscientious photographer; it had nothing to portray but that which had happened a hundred times and could at any moment happen again; impossible to comprehend why mankind had only just arrived at this simple and compelling idea. And today we again cannot comprehend how talented people could ever so have misinterpreted the nature of art as to assign to it a task which it was never meant to perform.

Arno Holz set up the theory at that time : " Art has the tendency to become Nature over again." One would be equally justified in maintaining that art had the tendency to *oppose* Nature. That art is simply Nature repeated is logically and psychologically impossible, for something else always enters into it: namely, man. That art has nothing to do with Nature is equally impossible, for there is something in it that is nature: namely, man. And what is Nature anyway? We do not know at all what Nature is, and shall never find out. Everything is art: that is, Nature that has passed through man. The eye is a subjective artist and so is the ear and every other sense-organ, and most of all, the brain. Nature is something that is constantly changing; only the name remains the same. For Classical man Nature was not the same as for us, and it was different again for the Roman from that which it was for his neighbour the Greek; different again for Cato and Cæsar respectively, and for young Cæsar and old Cæsar. The decisive word on Naturalism was uttered by Lamprecht, when he said : " All Naturalism has in it something of the nature of Curtius, who flung himself into the abyss — a dash forward, seen to be as essential, and a sacrifice." It is the historical mission of all Naturalism to establish the new Reality, record it artistically, drive it home to the universal consciousness: this is always pioneer work, absolutely necessary, but superfluous from the moment it is done. Naturalism is preparatory work, it provides a kind of sketch of the new Reality. It can never be anything but raw material, subject-matter, preliminary art. Naturalistic works are rough drafts and have all the desultoriness and unformedness, though also the charm and originality, of such drafts. This offers the best explanation of the overwhelming effect made by the dramas of the nineties. They announced at the outset a new spiritual content; the revolutionary technical, social, industrial, and political phenomena, the many unorientated perspectives, which modern psychology had brought to light, appeared now for the first time in visible concentration.

When I was still a thoroughgoing Naturalist, I once made the remark: " To invent is the business of children and savages. Imagination we may leave to the blue-stockings and the cooks." And, indeed, any cook may have imagination. But it will be a cook's imagination. How does her fibbing differ from that of a Dante or a Shakspere? Simply in the fact that these two present their phantasmagoria with such overwhelming forcefulness and corporeality that everyone believes them, or, more accurately, they condense into realities for everyone. Yet the whole is and remains an illusion, a fancy, an optical delusion, a sort of hypnotist's or conjurer's trick. This is so in both cases, only that in the one it does not work and in the other it does. But even if the poor cook did not bring it off, she still had a good idea of inventing. Only the result was, not a *Divine Comedy,* but a penny novelette. If she were asked how she came by all these stories she tried to make us believe, she would say she had " made them up." But then, Shakspere would have answered in the same way if asked how he arrived at *King Lear.* Is not this " making up " the general expression for all creative activities — of a Mozart and a Newton, a Leonardo and a Bismarck? That which comes of it is a matter of the combination of fullness and strength, spiritual courage, independence of tradition, and greater or less nearness to God; but the full determination at all events to achieve something that has not yet existed is to be required of all productive minds, for this is the first and last assumption of all creating.

And if we examine Naturalistic writings — the plays, for instance — more closely — with the microscope, so to say — it will be found that they are works of art just as their predecessors were: adaptations, interpolations, interpretations of reality. They scorned the monologue and the " aside " as unnatural, but they substituted for the one the carefully calculated pause, and for the other the exactly worked-out pantomime, which is simply another dodge of the same kind, only more subtle and therefore more effective. Naturalism was, like the culture of the " Founders' Age," a style of stylelessness. Maupassant spoke of the "*photographie banale de la vie*." But photographs may be as banal as they will, they are naturalistic for contemporaries only. To later generations they are antique, elaborate, highly stylistic woodcuts.

This comes out most strongly in the strongest Naturalist of the nineties, Gerhart Hauptmann. His dramas are folk-songs, strong and tender, bitter and sentimental, primitive and unfathomable, of the earth and remote from it. His greatest period embraced the seven years from *Sonnenaufgang* to *Florian Geyer,* during which he created and brought to their highest artistic level a whole number of new stage features: the family catastrophe in *Friedensfest,* the mass tragedy in *Die Webern,* the satire on modern times in *Der Biberpelz,* the naturalistic tale in *Geyer,* and *Hannele,* which has no counterpart in the whole world of literature and will live for ever in the hearts of posterity as the most realistic, imaginative, subtle, and thrilling soul-picture in German drama. As long as Hauptmann merely constructs, he has almost more atmosphere than Ibsen, but when he thinks, he becomes poster-like, undifferentiated, warped, and even amateurish and raw. In *Die versunkene Glocke* he descends to the pretty picture-book and to unsuccessful experiment with ideas and becomes a sort of oleograph of Böcklin and a cheap popular edition of Nietzsche. And many others of his later works, hurriedly written and uneven, are only weaker copies of his great early conceptions. Hauptmann is neither one of those slowly but continuously growing intellects who, like Goethe, gradually acquire everything, far and near, nor one of those which continually transform themselves and are always startling, alarming, and charming the world afresh by volcanic streams of lava like Nietzsche. But in every one of his characters a responsive heart beats triumphantly: in the big carter as in the school-child, in King Karl as in Beggar Jau, in the genius as in the village idiot. He is an organ of the whole conscious world around him, a human creature, creating without toil or intention, without " art," because of his inborn need to create: in short, he is a poet.

Sudermann's appearance was contemporary with Hauptmann's, almost to the very day. The two of them were at first generally regarded as " Dioscuri," even by professional critics. Brandes wrote in 1891 that it was not possible for the foreign

Hauptmann

Sudermann

critic to join the opposition to Sudermann which had arisen in certain quarters: " for he knows that a group reserves its bitterest feelings for another that differs from it by the finest nuance." Before the first performance of *Die Ehre*, Oskar Blumenthal, the then director of the Lessing Theatre, said to a housemaid who had been sent to exchange some first-night tickets for seats on the following day: " Tell your mistress she had better keep the tickets. Tomorrow is *Faust*. She will have plenty of chances of seeing that, but tonight will be her only one of seeing *Die Ehre*." He was to prove a bad prophet, however, for the play became one of the great successes in the history of the German theatre. It is written strictly on the lines of the French problem play. Trast is the classical type of the *raisonneur* who comes on the stage solely to enunciate aphorisms, and, at the same time, of the uncle from America, whose millions solve all dramatic conflicts. Abundant use is made of the stage " aside," sometimes with twofold effect, as when Trast says " to himself " in reply to a remark of old Heinecke: " Simplicity, thou speakest like a mother," and then adds, " recovering himself ": " For shame, Trast, that was not nice." The front house and the back one are painted not in the least as human *milieus*, but as two effectively contrasted coulisses and, to make things worse, the " witty " dialogue in the drawing-room is carried on in intolerably affected journalese.

No author of the last generation has been so much abused as Sudermann, and the abuse has come from almost every camp. The Naturalists decried his dramas as perfumed twaddle, while the Classicists accused him of dirty realism. The artists called him a tedious moralist, and the ethical group considered him lustful and frivolous. It was said that he stole intellectual property with the utmost impudence and deceived the public, inducing it to waste its time and money by unworthy subterfuges. Had there been a combine of box-office dramatists, it would certainly have ejected him for unfair competition.

Certainly purer and deeper notes have been sounded on the stage than those struck by Sudermann, and it is equally true that he always remained on the surface, that he, even in Ibsen's generation, still perpetrated plays which relied for their principal effects on paint and powder and, while Hamsun, Maeterlinck, and Shaw were enunciating their psychological Calculuses, contented himself with the coarse black-and-white technique which provided Scribe, Sardou, and Feuillet with their approved effects. But these, after all, are not capital sins. Everybody screamed: "He is no poet, but a lying faker (*Macher*)." Yet can one draw so sharp a line between *Macher* and poet? As we saw in the last volume, Schiller was in many respects a wily *faiseur*. And does not Wagner pile up effects by first creating suspense and then apparently breaking it, only to make it still more acute? Is not our attention first concentrated, then distracted, then led astray? Does he not hit out brutally and then restrain himself craftily; in short, use every means suggested by his intelligence and imagination to keep the audience in a state of absorbed expectation and excitement? And did not Euripides do the same more than two thousand years ago? The handicraft is, after all, the golden floor of every art, even if it is not the whole of the art. All stagecraft, for that matter, is in a sense "lying"; that is what it is for. The actor paints himself blue, white, and red like a Hottentot priest, he steps into a patch of light so bright and crude that he might be posing for an anatomical demonstration, he has to speak as loudly, as distinctly, and as pointedly as only a mentally deranged person would speak in real life, he has to underline everything four times by expressive glances, eloquent pauses, and carefully considered gestures — or it is all wasted. It is therefore natural that the text of a play should have something correspondingly artificial, over-bright, and loud-pedalling about it. And is it really so unpardonable a sin never to be boring? In spite of, or because of, his hollow mechanism, Sudermann did succeed in creating a whole series of figures that are impressive, clearly outlined, and able to stand independently on the stage; if they do not actually live, they are still capable of leading a robust and expressive existence on the boards for three hours together, and have accordingly tempted artists of the rank of Mitterwurzer and Duse to represent them again and again. He also succeeded, with the true stage insight that is given to so few, in producing a number of highly suggestive scene-pictures, such as the splendid close of *Johannes,* the studio scene in *Sodoms Ende,* the one-act cycle *Morituri* (a most picturesque conception, both as a whole and in its parts), and much besides. Whence comes, then, this fanatical contempt and indignation?

The answer is that nature equipped Sudermann lavishly as far as theatrical talent went, but unfortunately forgot to give him any other talent whatever, even the most modest and ordinary; and it was apparently this grotesque and revolting disproportion which roused such irritation. He possessed the language, the gestures, the

419

cast of brain, for keeping two thousand people spellbound. He had
no ideas, but only something that looked quite like them on the
stage; no passions, but fireworks that in the dark auditorium
might pass for them; no genuine struggles, but a machinery which
made much the same commotion: a multitude of sparkling, gilt-
paper-covered things which made a very good impression by artificial light. But he had not even the most primitive inhibitions. He
possessed practically no organizing, guiding, sifting intelligence.
In that he was like a strolling player who wants to shine, to show
himself, to turn Catherine-wheels without ceasing. This intolerable coquetry made him positively ludicrous at times, but it was
rooted — like all vanity — in defective intelligence. Some horrible
banality invariably occurs in the middle of his most interesting,
well-written and even clever speeches, some monstrous tactlessness, followed by a second, third, fourth, until we find ourselves
pelted by a rain of platitudes of the most idiotic arrogance and bad
taste. Bearing upon this is another of Sudermann's paralysing defects: he had not one spark of humour. Yet no one needs humour
more urgently than the dramatist, not only the comic, but the
tragic playwright, for his basic capacity consists in a talent for
seeing earthly happenings and all the human beings entangled in
them from above and from all sides; and to do this he must take
neither himself nor his characters too seriously. This is the common family trait of all dramatists from Kalidasa to Kaiser, and
the three greatest dramatists in the world (in our opinion, Euripides, Shakspere, and Ibsen) were at the same time those who took
their world the least seriously. Even if Sudermann had had but as
much humour as the leading comic character in a provincial theatre, as much taste as a superior upholsterer, and as much understanding as a professor of literary history, then his contemporaries
might possibly have been able to hail him as a dramatic star of the
first magnitude.

Fontane   Among writers of the older generation, only Theodor Fontane
joined forces with the new school as a recruit of late development
who produced his most succulent and mature work only in his declining years. This work was pervaded by a mild wisdom and
rarefied culture which occasionally degenerated into lack of temperament. The basic form of his art is the anecdote. The essence of
this lies in the single feature, which in the hands of genius yields
an almost exhaustive description of the character or incident, or
at least throws it into brilliant relief. His individual figures are

420

indeed measured and weighed as for a relief, with the finest instinct for their inherent proportions; and, as in the anecdote, the fundamental note is one of humour, irony, and smiling superiority. The point is often below the surface, but all the more subtle for that, and there is a tendency to treat everything earthly as a bagatelle and de-idolize it, but this is born, not of Nihilism, but of humanity. Fontane passed for a Naturalist; in reality he was the surviving type of the fine observer of the *ancien régime* which delighted in the close observation of man and his foibles; of *émigré* stock, he was a child of old Berlin and the Prussian Rococo. No wonder that he had a better comprehension of the Naturalist movement than his contemporaries: he had the eighteenth-century tradition. Diderot would also have understood Hauptmann straight away, and Lessing Ibsen — precisely up to the point at which Fontane too halted; for he, though according him full recognition, accused him of " splitting threads (*spintisieren*), playing the oracle, and propounding riddles," while Lessing would probably have put it something like this: " The poet must make us not so much examiners as lovers of his creatures, and while our reason admires these cold statuesque personages, our heart may well wish them smaller — what I mean is, more like ourselves and more human."

Frank Wedekind appeared on the scene at the same time as Hauptmann, but attracted no attention until a good deal later. He belonged to the Mannerists, a group which belongs to all ages and of which Goethe wrote, in his essay *Antik und modern:* "We . . . confess that even mannerists, if they do not go too far, give us much pleasure. . . . The artists who are called by this name have decided natural talent; but they soon feel that the conditions of the time or the school on which they have fallen leave no room for misgivings, that they must make up their minds and be ready. They therefore make a language for themselves with which they can both handle visible situations with ease and boldness and hang up before us, with more or less success, all sorts of world-pictures by which sometimes whole nations are pleasantly entertained and deluded through several decades, until finally this person or that returns to Nature and a higher way of thinking." Wedekind repeats in essence the positions of the "*Sturm und Drang.*" His realism often thrills us, though rather as a wild dream than an actual experience. The element of panorama attaching to all life has seldom been

Wedekind

421

reproduced with such point and colour. For all that, we never have the impression of reality, and this is because he fails to convey that continuity which is one of the basic principles of life. Real life may be illogical, irrational, and jerky, but a mysterious link runs through it. This link is lacking in Strindberg's dramas. Schiller once said that one must have plenty of guts to write dramas. But Frank Wedekind was abnormally short of guts. In his dramas the flight of thought — or, translated into dramatist's language, the flight of forms — is the rule. A most effective expedient for dramatists is that which we call " spacing out." But with Wedekind the empty patches do not represent artistic economy or even a refinement of virtuosity, but are perfectly natural rents and gaps caused by the looseness of his texture. As we said in the previous chapter, the technique of Impressionism reminds one of an alternating current which is steadily intermittent and increases in power for that very reason. With Wedekind, however, we get, every five minutes, simply a short circuit.

As regards his world-outlook, it appears, from what can be patched together out of old bits of aphorisms, to be the mere negative print of the accepted sexual morality. The philistine decrees that every person shall be " moral," by which he means that we should marry every one of our lady-loves. Wedekind decrees that every person shall be " immoral," by which he means that we should lay no value on such things as virginity, marriage, faithfulness. But the second standpoint is merely the more convenient and useful, and by no means the freer. It is only the dogmatic inversion of the other. For one may be an immoralist and yet a philistine. Everyone who starts from the point of view that laws which are good for him must apply to others too is a philistine. Freedom, on the other hand, consists in everybody's doing that which his individuality ordains. If anyone tries to force me into freedom in the erotic, when it is my nature to conceive of such relations as predominantly unfree and binding, he is *limiting* my freedom. If one insists that I should not be a philistine in moral matters, although this appeals to me, he is making a *philistine* demand on me. Wedekind's philosophy is nothing but inverted philistinism.

His plays belong definitely to the category of sensation-drama. The production is indeed brilliant and highly original, but this does not prevent the whole show from having the look of a grand circus performance (such as Wedekind himself, in a moment of self-recognition, has put before us in the prologue to his *Erdgeist*) ; of a monster performance by a brilliant clown, fire-eater, and mountebank. It is all there: philosophy and the grotesque, serial shocker and psychology; some of the scenes might come from Shakspere and some from an English melodrama. In this noisy fun-fair there is something for every palate.

In his inmost nature Wedekind is a dæmonic caricaturist of the stamp of Daumier. He has never created anything but wicked wax masks, grinning, grimacing, dangling puppets. The general characteristic of all his figures is the lamentable absence of Destiny in them. They are sheer *hommes-machines*, creaking mechanisms, flapping on rigid wires — albeit impressive and suggestive. They remind one of the " *Moritaten* " of the fairs, and the turns of knock-about clowns. House-fronts dance, lamp-standards collapse, one man turns into a bicycle, another into a clarinet, a third sends up a rocket from behind, and a fourth cleaves his head with an axe and asks sympathetically: " Did yer notice that? " The root of all this is in Wedekind's atheism, and the correlative of it is his amorality, which culminates in his two-part Lulu tragedy. The figure of Lulu has the same significance for Wedekind as Faust for Goethe, or Richard III for Shakspere. She is the extreme opposite of Richard, who is the supreme force of evil intended and planned in full consciousness, whereas she is the same, but entirely without her own knowledge or will. And then only is the final dissolution of Christian ethics reached. For the extreme of atheism is not the Devil, that dark angel who knows of his fall, but the *angel without a soul*.

That Nihilism hovered like a family curse over most artists of that time we see from the case of Maupassant, who had an entirely different class of mind. He was simply the embodiment of the eternal type which makes stories, the *raconteur* who tells his tale for the sake of telling it, with neither the philosopher's nor the soul-anatomist's ambition, but from sheer pleasure in description. All the things that ever happened, all the things that ever could happen, were stored in the warehouses of this impassioned collector: people, relationships, faces, passions, adventures, everyday incidents, everything tellable, without " criticism " or " selection." To him nothing is interesting and nothing uninteresting. Everything belongs to him, so long as it makes a story. His type is undatable. It is not " modern," it is not " old." He will

Maupassant

423

never grow old, any more than Boccaccio, because he was never new.

The clarity, sharpness, and delicacy of his contours is hardly to be surpassed. He uses the simplest means and yet sketches a figure or a situation in three or four strokes with such admirable certainty that they seem to hit us in the face. He was not an Impressionist like the rest, but a simple sketcher — with a magic pencil. And it was because he was so completely the sketch-book artist that he preferred the short story that could be dashed off in a moment. He differed, too, from most of his Paris colleagues in that there was nothing morbid about him; neither was there any of their dogged, almost pathological working capacity. He flung out his products, half for pleasure, half because it was, after all, his job. A happy blend of peasant and cosmopolitan, and enough of a gourmet and connoisseur to have an intelligent appreciation of all the tastes, colours, scents, and fluctuations of modern society, he remained at bottom ever the Norman, firmly rooted in reality, who has not yet lost touch with Nature and tackles art with a healthy hunger for facts and a straight glance; a taste for solid pleasures, too, in real life: for heavy wines, fat cigars, opulent suppers, and a " fine figure of a woman." This strong sensuality was invaluable to his art. Every sentence that he wrote is tinged with it, no matter whether he describes an idea, a love-scene, or a landscape.

One cannot really say, however, that his feelings go with the things he describes. That is, he feels with them, but through his nerves and not with his heart; peripherally, as it were. Herein he shows himself to be the complete epic poet, identical with Nature, who destroys without emotion. Maupassant's heart remains unmoved, never takes sides. He is not the victim of his poetic visions. He is of the same impersonal brutality as life itself, he exhibits people in the nakedness of their most intimate meannesses and uglinesses. The ordinary citizen, for instance, has never been more devastatingly portrayed in his greed and coarseness, his triteness and complacency, than by Maupassant. It is the same with the peasant, whom he sees as a malicious, sly, greedy semi-animal. His most famous novel, *Bel-ami*, is a huge arsenal of the infamies of all ranks, professions, and grades of society. He does not stop even at children, but shows them in all their perfidies and perversities. Love is often but a subtle form of human dupery, and vulgarity in married life has found in him its classic painter. Usually,

424

therefore, his stories engender a profound melancholy in the reader. It is the *désenchantement de la vie* at its worst. René is a Romantic, Flaubert a secret sentimentalist, Zola an emotional expounder of social ethics, but Maupassant is nothing but shrill Satanic laughter over the bungled human animal.

In one of his finest short stories: *L'Inutile Beauté*, Maupassant makes M. Roger de Salins hold a philosophical foyer-conversation with a friend in which he says: " Do you know what I imagine God to be like? A powerful creative force who sows millions of living beings in the universe just as a powerful fish spawns. He creates because it is his profession as God. But he does not know what he is doing, he has no idea what will become of all these scattered seeds. The idea of man is a little sport of chance, a local, passing, unforeseen event like a new chemical combination or the production of electricity by contact. A moment's reflection will show that the world was not created for beings like us." Here, in few words, we have the philosophy that forms the starting-point — or is it the result? — of Maupassant's art. It is a crazy philosophy, one of despair: God a monster herring, and we a mush of seeds in the ocean of eternity! One understands how the author, in spite of his apparently cool and clear objectivity, was one day bound to become the victim of his visions; his own characters became finally too much for him and settled like a heavy damp cloud over his senses.

German painting in that generation was in so far a pendant to German literature that it only advanced to Impressionism in quite few cases, most of it remaining faithful to Naturalism — with more than a sprinkling of sham Naturalism. The decisive event was the founding of the Munich " Secession " in 1893, which was followed, in the course of a decade, by similar societies in Dresden, Vienna, Düsseldorf, and Berlin. Its first president was Fritz von Uhde, who painted the Holy Family in a wretched carpenter's shop, the Apostles as plain fishermen and craftsmen, and the Saviour in the midst of peasants, school-children, and factory hands. The indignant conservatives forgot that the great Italian and Flemish painters had done just the same, and that it is precisely such sensitive modernization that first brings out the eternal, omnipresent, supertemporal in the Gospel message of salvation that is born anew in every soul. Leibl too was hailed and opposed as a modern, but he was not one. Rather was he a simple realist, such as there have been in all ages, and no more realistic

425

than Jan van Eyck, born nearly five hundred years earlier. He is dull, material, of a noble simplicity, and a thorough craftsman, a master in the old sense, like Peter Vischer or Hans Sachs. He never painted anything but what he had seen, and not only seen, but made a part of himself by faithful observation. It is characteristic of his artistic point of view that, when taken to see *Lohengrin*, he called out after the first act: " Lemme get out of it, I can't stick knights." And on another occasion, talking of a painter, he said indignantly: " Seems to me the fellow glazes."

In his little book on Jozef Israels, Max Liebermann writes: " The more naturalistic an art tries to be, the less will it be able to choose naturalistic means. The impersonator of Wallenstein who, as with the Meininger players, appears in a genuine jerkin and riding-boots of the period, does not necessarily make a more real impression thereby. The actor must play his part so that we believe that he is wearing the real jerkin and riding-boots. Israels appears to be a more naturalistic painter than our genre artists, not although, but *because* he paints less naturalistically than they." Liebermann was himself no Naturalist in the orthodox sense; rather did he hold by his own saying: " Drawing is the art of leaving things out." He arrives at nature from exactly the opposite quarter to Leibl. His landscapes are instinct with feeling and clarity as only the yearning of a clever cosmopolitan can make them. His art has a streak of old Berlin and Fontane. It is warm but quite unsentimental, sensitive but taciturn, unemotional but full of point and, in the portraits, of surreptitious humour. His way with the proletariat is neither to make heroes nor to excite sympathy, but to present his subject simply as a piece of painted life.

Böcklin　　Böcklin's fame came very late in the day, owing to the indolence of the German public (for he deserved to have outshone Piloty), and has now already faded. He might be called the last of the Germano-Romans, for he was the epitome of all that they strove for: the " antique " allegory of Winckelmann, the Germanizing Romanticism of the Cornelius group, the intellectual colourism of Feuerbach; in short, the whole development from Mengs to Marées. He often paints magnificently, but cannot resist putting in little metaphors and anecdotes on the top of his colour-poems. Nevertheless the latter are very juicy, and the former very solid. He has a feeling for Nature, but a literarified one, in contrast to Schwind, whose fairies and wood-nymphs are

426

natural products of a genuine (because naïve) fairy-tale mood and as such disturb nothing. Böcklin's pictures stand to Schwind's creations in the relation of grand opera to folk-songs, or *éditions de luxe* to children's picture-books. The Greeks painted and chiselled gods also, but these nymphs and Nereids, dryads and Tritons, Cyclopses and centaurs were *believed in* by them because of their remarkable gift for *seeing ghosts*. For them the river was *identical* with the river-god, the fountain with the fountain-goddess, Poseidon was at once the idea of the sea and the sea itself, Oceanos " a god " and " the ocean." This manner of conceiving things is unrepeatable in our time, and every such attempt at reconstruction is only cultured trifling, an artistic studio trick or triumph of archæological equipment, like the Meininger performances and Wagner's Germanic mythology. Böcklin, who was discovered as a " symbolist " in the nineties, belongs to the " Founders' Age " and is one of its most powerful figures.

On Austrian soil there has never been any Naturalism. Hermann Bahr was one of the first to proclaim its overthrow. Arthur Schnitzler raised the comedy of manners to a human and artistic level never reached by the French. His creatures consist no longer of one or two souls, but of a whole social state of souls engaged in ceaseless shifting and converging movements, who yet produce a regulated and symmetrical picture as in a kaleidoscope. And he has had, in intimate connexion with this, the courage and strength to descend into the mysterious dark-room of human subconsciousness and there trace those significant and contradictory inhibitions, counteractions, and polarities the scientific discovery of which is bound up with the name of Sigmund Freud. At a time when these doctrines were still in embryo, he had already dramatized psycho-analysis. And in his novels and plays he caught, and preserved for later generations, the *fin de siècle* Vienna. We hear and see a whole city in one unrepeatable stage of its culture, with the race that it bred and brought up and which lived itself out in a particular epoch of maturity and over-maturity. It was an achievement somewhat analogous to Nestroy's with pre-March Vienna.

Schnitzler and Altenberg

A similar topography of Vienna's spiritual condition about 1900 was provided, though by quite other means, by Peter Altenberg. He was the only perfectly consistent Impressionist of importance in German literature. The reader of his sketches will at first find himself in the position of a person who arrives late at a

427

public lecture and, squeezing himself into a distant corner, tries very hard to follow the speaker. In the beginning he takes in only indistinct, detached words and sentences, but in the end, having become accustomed to the acoustics of the hall and the speaker's voice, he is able to make sense of the separate phrases. Many do not give themselves the trouble to get beyond the first impression, yet this is misleading to the extent that what seems like disconnectedness is nothing but the extraordinarily concise and rapid thinking which skips so many connecting links. It is "telegram" style, typical of an age of fast trains, motors, and bioscopes. As an example of Altenberg's passionate straining after brevity we may take his "Five-minute Scenes," which, be it added, last not five, but at most two or three minutes. They fix one dramatic moment and leave the rest to the reader. For that one moment light is thrown upon some dangerous situation in which the soul finds itself, some arguable complication; then the curtain falls.

Even when Altenberg is emotional, it is in quite a new tone. His emotion stands in relation to that of the earlier poet as the noise of a steam roller or screw steamer to the blast of a trombone. Moreover, he treats language as if no one had ever handled it before him. Many passages in his sketches might equally well figure in an exhibition catalogue, a cookery book, or a fashion paper, and at times he sinks to the level of a newspaper advertisement. But no one had ever yet done such pointillist miniatures as, let us say, his description of summer in town and in the country with which the sketch: *Newsky Roussotine-Truppe* opened:

"A bit unhappy one feels on summer evenings in the capital. Like someone retired, superseded. For instance, I walk down the Praterstrasse at night. It is as if I and the passers-by had failed in the life-examination and — — —, while the good pupils enjoy their holiday as a reward. We may only dream:

"O sea-foam on the old wooden piles; O little lake in solitudes; O glades with the thin meadow bottom and brown marsh ponds, where the bailiff tells you: 'Look, this is where the stags come to drink at night.' O elderbushes, with your black capricorn beetles and little metallic mountain-beetles and lousy rose-beetles and light-brown mountain-flies, hard by the brooks which slip over big stones in such a hurry! And the elder feeds whole insect worlds! O seventy-two Fahrenheit spring in the open basin wherein lime blossoms swim; for the walk to the baths is full of limes; and everything is full of lime blossoms!

White sails in varnished yachts. The women are getting amber complexions. Everyone is banting. Who's going to win the regatta? Risa, give me a hand over the bridge. Mornings with ten thousand tons of sun heat, like the weight of battleships; afternoons with apricots, cherries, fine gooseberries; evenings like iced *Giesshübler;* night — do you hear the swans opening and shutting their beaks? And again the swans opening and shutting their beaks? And nothing more — — —

" But *we* are walking down the Praterstrasse in the capital. Eight in the evening. On both sides, decrepit-looking shops. Peaches side by side with pickled herrings. Baskets. Beach hats. Radishes. Bicycles gleam through everywhere. As if the air had sucked up all the smell of potato salad, the tar between the paving-stones, and the *millefleur de l'homme épuisé.* Arc-lamps, ambitious as glow-worms in summer nights, don't improve matters. Summer misery brought to light! Leave it in darkness, please, in silent shade. But the arc-lamps scream: 'Look there!' They bawl out the things of life, give away everything with their white glare."

Peter Altenberg was regarded as the type of decadence. Yet his feminism was not weakness, but strength: the capacity in a high and hitherto unrealized degree to live oneself into a woman's spiritual life. All the earlier authors had adopted the attitude of more or less successful interpreters of woman, but he experienced her himself in the most complete way. When he described her, he was not reading the soul of a stranger, but his own. Women are incurable dreamers and idealists, the great disappointed ones of life who wander through the everyday like enchanted princesses; melancholic because of their own imperfections, because of men's imperfections, because of the whole world's imperfections. And in their anchorless, exalted, hysterical, and, at bottom, impractical idealism, they have no more burning wish than that a man should idealize them completely, see them for what they are not, be himself a Romantic. Such a Romantic was Peter Altenberg. He discovered everywhere the fairy-tales of life, the Melusinas and Sleeping Beauties. And every modest cornflower was for him the blue flower of Romanticism.

In Italy Naturalism was called *verismo.* Its creator was Giovanni Verga, whose *novelle rusticane* inaugurated a new literary era. One of them, dramatized by the author, provided the libretto for Mascagni's *Cavalleria rusticana* and in its musical dress

Verismo

429

conquered the world. Two years later Leoncavallo's *Pagliacci* took its place beside it, and these two full-blooded dramas are of a triumphant brutality and dizzy verve such as possibly only Italy can provide. Parallel phenomena are found in the two brilliant stage stars, Novelli and Zacconi, who set out on their triumphal tour of Europe about this time. Novelli in particular was an immense force, comparable in his great moments to Mitterwurzer: one of the most uncannily complete impersonators, and yet with every trait stamped by his absolutely distinctive and dæmonic personality.

Dorian Gray   In Paris the focus of Naturalism was André Antoine's " Théâtre libre," which replaced the *comédie rose* by the *comédie rosse*. In London, William Archer was fighting against Sardou and English playwrights of his stamp; in 1891 Grein founded the Independent Theatre, which opened with a performance of *Ghosts;* and in the same year there was published Shaw's *Quintessence of Ibsenism*. Wilde's drawing-room pieces, again, are only apparently in the Sardou vein, being really veiled parodies. Wilde is one of those rare authors who face posterity in their works like familiar private friends (modern authors who belong to this group are Voltaire, Heine, Bismarck, and Schopenhauer), and yet his life-story is one of the most moving human tragedies that life ever wrote. He was most scandalously victimized by the selfsame English cant which built murderous concentration camps " for the protection of Boer families," and legalized eight-year-old child labour " to protect the children from dissipation." It would have been worth another India to the English nation not to have won the Wilde case. The overwhelming part of this tragedy is that he himself desired it. He thrust the possibility of flight behind him, quite like Socrates (to whom he otherwise bears small resemblance, being more like his opponent Alcibiades). His catastrophe was the self-crucifixion of the modern spirit of hedonistic scepticism and artist immorality: and this must have been the intention of his " Daimonion " when it urged him to the sacrifice.

There have certainly been few writers who hated ugliness so deeply and passionately, even morbidly, as did Oscar Wilde. His affection for the thousands of costly, fine, and useless things that surround the life of a man of position was extraordinary. He was never tired of describing them. But he was a poet, and a poet is more than a describer of beautiful things. Also, he undoubtedly loved vice. He loved it as an artist. Artists are always drawn with magical power towards the aberrations of life, the dark passions and their ensnarements. What frightful storehouses of human wantonness are Shakspere's dramas or Dante's *Divine Comedy*! The artist seeks out these things, for he knows that here are the instructive entanglements, the profound mysteries, the exciting movements that are as essential to him as stones to the builder. But at the same time the artist is the most moral of men, for he is full of sympathy for everyone and everything, and he yearns for the higher development of humanity. Thus Wilde was in love with sin while yet seeking only what was holy in his inner self, rushing from one gratification to another and in his aims a pure renunciatory ascetic.

And all this he poured out from his heart in *The Picture of Dorian Gray*. This book had itself a history besides that of the "picture" of which it treats; but its process of transformation was reversed. It confronted the world on its first appearance with an ugly repulsive grimace, and today it stands before us in complete flawlessness and beauty. When this strange vision arose, it was regarded as the work of a low-minded and vicious person, it seemed the very gospel of the Devil. Today we know that it is a gospel of purity, a deeply moral book, pulsating with the blood of a consuming yearning for kindness which attacks vice more sharply than a hundred abstention-sermons that are ignorant of life.

Wilde's countryman and contemporary Shaw was also mis-understood for a long time, and the misunderstanding exists to this very day. *Candida* closes with Marchbanks's departure and the embrace of husband and wife; but Shaw adds: "They embrace. But they do not know the secret in the poet's heart." Perhaps the attitude of the general public to Shaw is similar to that of the Morells to the poet Marchbanks. Perhaps Shaw has a secret that he jealously guards, perhaps he is other than what he seems, and, when the curtain falls, he goes softly away with a truth in his heart that he alone knows.

It is always harmful for a poet to be placed from the first under one rubric. For Shaw the label is: "cynic"; and the public is accordingly apt to take all his plays as puzzles labelled underneath with: "Find the hidden irony." Nevertheless, while it is of course true that one of Shaw's poetical characteristics is irony, that irony is not simple, but is a complex phenomenon, with at least three roots.

Shaw's irony

431

The one root is Shaw's inward contempt for the literary art. The dramatist is a demagogue; the novelist is a snuffler, who spies on strangers; the lyric poet is an exhibitionist. These activities are abhorrent to Shaw. He is of the opinion of Johann Nagel, the hero of Hamsun's *Mysteries:* "Do you know what a great author is? A great author is a man who is not ashamed of himself, who never blushes in the slightest at his own business of humbug. Other fools have moments when, all by themselves, they blush for shame. But not the great author." Or he agrees with his own Cæsar, who replies quietly, in response to the frenzied announcement of the learned tutor of Ptolemy that the library of Alexandria, "the first of the seven wonders of the world," is in flames: "Theodotus, I am an author myself; and I tell you it is better that the Egyptians should live their lives than dream them away with the help of books. . . . THEODOTUS: What is burning there is the memory of mankind. CÆSAR: A shameful memory. Let it burn . . . a few sheepskins scrawled with errors."

The second root is Shaw's Naturalism. Greatness is after all one trait among many. If I show a Bismarck or a Napoleon from *all* sides, the description must necessarily be ironical. This tendency in art, which has the most right to call itself Naturalistic, had its rise in Goethe and first took tangible form in Kleist (for instance, in the *Prinz von Homburg*). Here the characterization of the heroes and heroines already makes a breach in the "Nothing but greatness" principle. And Ibsen would have considered no drama that was *only* tragic in effect to be a real tragedy. It is the same with Strindberg and even Maeterlinck, as, for instance, in *Princesse Maleine,* where, after a night full of murder and horror, the old King says: "I should like a bit of salad." The point is that salad is just as much a part of the complete picture of human life as the great tragic upheavals.

From all this, however, one might still believe that irony was for Shaw an aim in itself. Yet in reality it is only a means, and an educational means at that. The people look upon him as a mere joker because he is a more amusing and witty instructor than most of his predecessors. *They* calmly turned the stage into a tribunal, never for a moment attempted to hide what they intended and whereunto they felt themselves called. Now, Shaw imparts his truths in an indirect way. He does not say them straight out by appointing his figures to be their mouthpiece and preacher, but he allows the ideals he is trying to teach to emerge from ambiguous destinies and turning-points in life, leaving it to the audience to abstract definite formulas and rules from what has taken place before its eyes.

Man almost always desires to be something different from that for which Nature intended him. He never stands in his own place, but must always be squinting across at his neighbour. But all men would be equal in worth if they obeyed the natural law. Some sort of grace and force, bestowed on him alone, works secretly in every man, even the most insignificant. It is this solely that gives him his existence, links him to life; without it he would never have become the unique and non-recurring individual that he is. But people usually have too little honesty with regard to themselves, too little love of themselves to be able to recognize this unique aptitude that is theirs. Together with this talent, given them by God, there is a kind of counter-dowry given them by the Devil in an unguarded moment: the fatal tendency never to want to be themselves. Actually Adam and Eve were victims of this peculiar mental derangement. Was there anything lovelier than Paradise? Yet it had just one fault for Adam and Eve, it happened to be their destiny. And people will insist on regarding only that as paradise that is *not* ordained for them. Thus the first human pair acted quite logically and consistently when they failed to obey God's commands — though their logic, it must be admitted, was an invention of the Devil.

Now, Shaw shows how most people wear a stranger's mask all their life, and that not only before others, but before themselves, until one day the fateful hour comes in which their real nature reveals itself. There is, therefore, in the majority of Shaw's plays a sort of *peripeteia* by which the whole action is swung through two right angles. In *The Devil's Disciple,* for instance, we have Richard Dudgeon, who is looked upon by all around him as a cynical adventurer, a coarse, impious fellow, and indeed holds the same opinion of himself. Beside him stands Anthony Anderson, the gentle and kind pastor who loves everyone and is loved by everyone in return. But there comes a moment when it is a question of life or death, and suddenly the parts are reversed. It turns out that Anderson's clerical dress was only drapery, and Richard's devil's grimace only put on. It is the same in *Candida*. There is Morell the clergyman, the petted, self-assured darling of fate and of the women, and the poor desolate poet Marchbanks, who has never been loved. The great decisive moment comes when

433

Candida has to choose. And she hits upon a truly feminine solution: she chooses the weaker. But this weaker one is Morell, who is the apparently stronger one. For he has been so persistently spoilt by life that he cannot live for a day without Candida. The other-worldly and homeless poet, on the other hand, is the true king of life. He needs nothing and nobody, for he has himself. And so he passes out, resigned to all appearance, but in reality the victor. This, if I read Shaw aright, is the secret that he carries away with him, the secret of which the Morell couple know nothing. But, remembering Düntzer's famous foot-note to an autobiographical remark of Goethe's: " Here Goethe was mistaken," I also should like to say, though without, I hope, making such a fool of myself as Düntzer: Here Shaw is mistaken, Candida knows the secret.

In similar fashion does the Serbian Major Sergius Saranoff appear in *Arms and the Man* as the type of a noble young hero, beside whom the dry and prosaic Captain Bluntschli cuts a poor figure. But in reality things are reversed: Bluntschli is the hero, and Sergius has nothing heroic but his costume, the outward gesture. A hero is not, by the way, a person who is never under any condition afraid of anything; that sort of person is simply a blockhead. No, a hero is a person who looks facts bravely and clearly in the face and is able to deal with them decisively and squarely. It is quite in this sense that Shaw set down his conception of the nature of genius in *Cæsar and Cleopatra*. The great Cæsar is the very simplest man of them all. The secret of his greatness is his naturalness, his conformity to the laws of his own organism. He is not the kind of man who does surprising and exceptional things in individual situations in life, but on the contrary the man who in all situations does what is obvious and appropriate. If we all lived and acted like Cæsar, the world would be chock-full of geniuses. It is their degree of naturalness that decides men's relative ranks. Unlying men are always great. Cæsar excels, not by being gigantic, but by the excellent proportion of his dimensions. And never has Shaw embodied irony more poetically than here, in the irony of the genius that sees through the world.

Shaw does not thunderously consign lying to the puddle of Hell, but shows how *absurd* any lie is. He does not say: every lying person is a reprehensible creature; but: every lying person is a caricature. And he goes further and proves that lying is extremely unpractical and sin extremely boring. But in order to bring the public to swallow these most unpalatable truths, he employs a pedagogic dodge. He puts his moral purgative in the sweet-tasting cover of a peddled drama, a burlesque, or a moving piece, just as a tamarind pastille is lodged in chocolate. Unfortunately the public is even slyer than Shaw. It licks off the good chocolate and leaves the tamarind. And that is why Marchbanks is so right when he says: " That is what all poets do: they talk to themselves out loud."

In an imaginary conversation Hugo von Hofmannsthal makes *Amor vacui* Balzac say: " About 1890 we shall see the mental diseases of poets — their exaggeratedly enhanced susceptibility, the nameless terror of their hours of depression, their disposition to succumb to the symbolic power of even insignificant things, their inability to be content with the existing word in expressing their feelings — all combining to form a universal sickness among young men and women of the better classes." And Oscar Wilde in one of his philosophical dialogues is made to speak of " *l'amour de l'impossible,* which falls like a madness on many who think they live securely and out of reach of harm, so that they sicken suddenly with the poison of unlimited desire, and, in the infinite pursuit of what they may not attain, grow faint and swoon or stumble." This sickness to which both allude was scepticism. Certainly the disease is old as the ages, probably as old as human thought, but it has its various forms and grades. There are dogmatic and critical sceptics, sceptics from a weakened and from a hypertrophied self-consciousness, through the play-impulse and from religiosity, from love of saying no and from the elementary urge to affirm, and from a variety of other causes known to us all. Yet this generation did produce a type that was perhaps new in its way. Former times taught and demonstrated scepticism, but these people lived it, they were the actual embodiment of scepticism itself. Doubt of every sort of reality was the secret prognostic which accompanied every one of their actions. A new human variety had, most threateningly, appeared: the sceptic of life.

We read the doubts of an Epicurus, a Hume or Montaigne, but these are powerful, self-glorious, and immensely positive compared with this scepticism. We have the impression with these philosophers that they only experimented with scepticism without ever taking it to be something corporeal that dwelt among men as an effective force. As long as one philosophizes over to be and not to be, all is well. But those modern sceptics had already ceased

435

to philosophize, and that is where the danger set in. They stamped themselves on the period, were to be found in all the streets and localities, in clubs and barracks, churches and counting-houses, lecture-rooms and ball-rooms — everywhere. They were no cynics. Nevertheless no one dared to be positive in their vicinity. Their strength was the *vis inertiæ*, their passion the *amor vacui*.

"No one," says Grillparzer, "is in so much danger of becoming dull as an extremely irritable person"; and indeed extreme irritability and dullness were the prevailing conditions of this generation. This particular type of interesting degeneracy and unstabilized intermediateness found its most vivid and expressive embodiment in Josef Kainz, the weary, richly laden, but also heavily burdened inheritor of a declining culture. He hacked or spluttered out his sentences, giving them a new and peculiar beauty, thereby, and his nervous gestures, his lightning play of expression, the flicker of his intellect playing in and through his body, amounted to a sort of stylized restlessness. In all his parts, whether from Shakspere, Ibsen, or Nestroy, he was the vibrant personality of the turn of the century: the typical *maléquilibré* from excess of mind, the overdosed intellectual in whom head and heart no longer form an organic synthesis, the provisional man who is made up of surrogates — reason, diligence, knowledge — and is predominantly a product of calculation, comparable to a subtle and efficient precision-engine. The time for "natural artists" was past. Men had forgotten how to play at acting with the ease of a Red Indian riding or an otter swimming. Kainz introduced the notion of work into his art — an element hitherto almost foreign to it. He worked under the pressure of ten thousand volts of self-discipline, drill, memorizing, and speculation. In the age of machinery he made his body into the most sensitive and responsive apparatus possible. Even his creaking, rattling emotionalism reminds one, like Altenberg's, of a mechanism: of artillery fire or a machine-gun attack. Although he undoubtedly raised the art of acting to a higher level in consequence, he lacked what may be called physiological mysteriousness. His effects had nothing baffling about them. Although one could not copy them, they were calculable. When Sonnenthal or Robert or Levinsky or Mme Hohenfels came on the stage, a vast gulf separated their art of the past from their younger contemporaries, yet no one could resist their magical influence. They affected one in a sense physiologically, like plants or animals, by merely existing. Here a tall pine rears itself blue and stern, or a fat snowdrop dreams in sweet stupidity; there hops a green-lacquered frog, flat-footed and goggle-eyed, or a steely ground-beetle runs along, full of importance — and one cannot say wherein the realistic and yet romantic effect of these mysterious creatures lies. Just so were the old actors bathed in an atmosphere of mystery which brought to one's mind forest, air, and earth and at the same time suggested unreal dreams and visions.

The turn of the century, which found the grandiose echo of its speaking voice in Kainz, had as its instrumental genius Richard Strauss, one of the greatest painters and thinkers, whose philosophy was not drawn from any other source (as even Wagner's was), but was evolved out of the orchestra buried within himself, a philosophy born of the spirit of music. He was likewise the creator of a completely new tone fashion, for (as Shaw so excellently puts it) he replaced Wagner's unprepared dissonances by unresolved ones.

In the great repetition-cycle of the styles it was the Biedermeier which had its turn round about 1900. Internal architecture displayed definitely simpler lines, sparer forms, less noisy colours. Yet this renaissance, which was only apparently in conformity with the spirit of the age, seemed as much an affectation as the preceding ones. In Wolzogen's *Überbrettl,* there was a revival of the tail coats and broad ties, velvet collars and waistcoats of the " pre-March " period, and these fashions also found favour with the frequenters of literary salons and with the dandies. The craze for slimness too, which began slowly to make its way at this time, was a link with the Romantic. The Biedermeier note was sustained in *Simplizissimus* by Thomas Theodor Heine, who like his namesake hid a melancholy susceptibility behind cynical satire. For a whole decade Gabriele d'Annunzio stood at the head of the European decadence. His productions, which are decrepit monster growths set in sweet overheated hothouse air, absorbed all the powerful suggestive forces of the epoch: the exuberant palette of Impressionism, the oppressive orchestra of Wagner, the studied morbidity of Pre-Raphaelitism, the brilliant effort dramatically to reproduce the life-philosophy of Nietzsche, d'Annunzio's works are (as Hofmannsthal so penetratingly expresses it) written by one who " had no footing in life ": " his were emphatically the experiences of one who had never had anything to do with life

437

but to look at it. This imparted something quite Medusa-like to his books, a suggestion of death by freezing."

The school of the decadents or symbolists arose in France in the eighties. Their founder and leader was Mallarmé, who played a part in the movement similar to that of Leconte de Lisle in the case of the Parnassians. His poetry is strictly esoteric, thoroughly artistic, sometimes deliberately puzzling, and in a sense " absolutely poetry," in that the words and their arrangement have their intrinsic value independent of meaning and connexion, description and logic. The Baudelaire of the group was Paul Verlaine. He also was entangled in tragic love-affairs, but he sacrificed to the Greek Eros, trailing the existence of an artist gipsy between night café and hospital — which is not in reality amusing. He was the first to find the picturesque word for the twilight between-worlds of the soul, he was the master of mezzotint.

One of the characteristic peculiarities of the Symbolists was their literary use of " synæsthesis " or the mixing of the senses: the hearing of colour, seeing of tones, tasting of odours. Everyone scoffed at them, quite forgetting that they were only consistently working out what had long been recognized in both art and science; for there had always been talk of colour-tones, sound-colours, and the like, and for decades it had been observed in experimental psychology that we never take in a single kind of sense-impression, but always several together, either blended or in opposition to each other. In reality it is all simply a consequence of Impressionism, a return to the real impression. We never see, hear, touch, smell, taste separately, but always simultaneously. The only thing we are entitled to call a real sensation is an inextricable mix-up of the most varied kinds of sense-stimulations, which in addition receives a special colouring from general feelings (situation, temperature, state of health) of which we are usually not conscious. The exclusiveness of a particular kind of sense — for example, hearing — is *pathological* and belongs to the repression phenomena. Why, two of the senses, smell and taste, are not even anatomically separable, for the *nervus trigeminus* discharges into the tongue as well as into the nasal membrane and is responsible for both sensations. We therefore speak of a violet taste, a rose taste, and of bitter, sweet, or sour smells. When we say that a thing tastes prickly or biting, it is sensations of touch that are called in. That the sense of sight comes into consideration every confectioner knows; that the sense of temperature contributes we can prove from lukewarm Rhine wine and ice-cooled Burgundy. Thus even this simple sensation that we call " taste " involves nearly all the sense-stimulations.

The new form created by the Symbolists was the *poème en prose, " l'huile essentielle de l'art,"* as Huysmans called it, " the sea of prose forced into a drop of poetry." As early as 1884 Huysmans had produced the classical novel of the decadence in *A rebours.* The story, which is practically a continuous auto-analytical monologue by the hero, has as its exclusive object irregularities and counter-regularities in every sense: the disharmonious, the morbid, the amoral, the non-social, the perverse, down to madness and crime. In language and composition, too, it is amorphous, asyndetonic, psychopathic. In Duke Jean Florissac des Esseintes an archetype is created as though in the *esprit romanesque* — he is René eighty years after.

Belgian symbolism has quite a different character. The first work to appear was an overwhelming little drama: *Les Flaireurs* by Charles van Leberghe, which describes the approach of death. Quite obviously it served as a model for Maeterlinck's *L'Intruse.* That author's first work: *Princesse Maleine,* had been proclaimed by Octave Mirbeau in 1890 in the *Figaro* as " by far the greatest work of genius, by far the most extraordinary, by far the most naïve creation of the age, comparable, even superior, to the best in Shakspere, an adorable, pure, everlasting masterpiece such as the noblest artists have occasionally dreamed of in inspired moments." And that was not too much to say.

Drama of the fourth dimension

Maeterlinck's figures float in an imaginary space, or perhaps in no space at all, since we see them, not bodily, but as gliding shadows. One might therefore be tempted to put him into the group of the " two-dimensional poets " alluded to in the previous volume, were it not that he differs from them in an essential something which makes his stagecraft unique in the world of literature. Whereas in that other group the trouble was a defect, an organic mistake, so to say, in their dramatic constitution, Maeterlinck quite consciously avoids the third dimension with full artistic deliberation, achieving thereby a something quite rare and unheard of, for he succeeds in bringing the *fourth* dimension on to the stage.

The general public, as we have shown in connexion with Shaw, possesses a very marked tendency to label every new spiritual phenomenon on the spot with some handy exclusive nickname and

439

considers itself relieved thereby of the arduous and responsible duty of really absorbing spiritually every such new phenomenon. This mass tendency, as deep-rooted as it is harmful — one might perhaps call it the " will to labels " — exercised its deadening and misleading effect in Maeterlinck's case also. It seized upon a phrase that he had used of himself to Huret and called him from then on " a Shakspere for marionettes." That is to say, a poet who, though not entirely averse from the abundance, colourfulness, and movement of life, nevertheless reduces them artificially to the primitiveness of a stiff, mechanical puppet-theatre. This universal epithet, which Maeterlinck has carried about with him now for more than a generation, is not only one-sided, like all catchwords, but has its very basis in crude misinterpretation. The point is not that some artistic freak led him to the decision to restore the childish and old-fashioned marionette theatre to life, which at best could only have been an amiable and witty bit of make-believe. He had realized that life is a dolls' drama and the marionette the deepest, most overwhelming symbol of our existence. If we step back ever so little, we shall see that the belief that we ourselves are the originators of our bodily and spiritual gestures rests upon an optical delusion. A great secret force which guides our whole exist- ence in all its movements, great and small — we might call it the invisible poet of our life — works itself out on this our earthly stage; and seen under such an aspect, everything begins at once to accomplish itself in a far more unemotional and impersonal way. Looking down from a high mountain over towns and fields, at the moving herds, the trees in the wind, the driving, riding, run- ning people in their noiseless activity, we shall immediately have the surprising impression of mechanical working, and it would be just the same if we took up a sufficiently distant mental attitude towards life. But, it may be objected, did not Maeterlinck, in seeing our destiny in this manner, put the soul out of communion with the world, as it were, and leave us richer in knowledge per- haps, but infinitely poorer in vitality? Surely, then, even with truth on his side, he would be no benefactor to the human race? But this is by no means the case. Far from thrusting the soul from its throne, he may be said to have discovered it and secured to it its true sovereign rights. For instead of being left to impotent beating of our individual soul-wings as hitherto, we are enabled to know the world-soul in its majestic timeless working. At the cost of that mean, uncertain, and, from the first, suspicious sensation which we call self-consciousness we have gained the all-consciousness. It will never disappoint us, for it is greater than we — never confuse us, for it is clarity at one with itself — never deny us, for it has given us birth — never forsake us, for it will outlive us and link us to immortality.

Who are we? Why are we? Are we steering towards anything definite? Do we rest on any certainty? Is there anything whatever that is certain? These and similar oppressive queries wail and moan from Maeterlinck's little dramas, repeating themselves constantly in endless variations, but always with the same mysteriousness, the same terror, the same unanswerableness. *One* great expectation alone causes these vague souls to thrill with pain and terror: something horrible is going to happen, something ghastly, unspeakable, incomprehensible, a misfortune that can never be made good. Against this misfortune there is no fighting. It will always come, it is invincible. Useless to seek protection, lay about one, arm oneself, calculate in advance. Life comes and takes us with her. To the fear of life, which penetrates and torments every living creature, Maeterlinck has given a form more impressive and annihilating than any poet before him. His creatures have altogether only two attitudes to life: either to be perpetually amazed or never to be amazed. To the first group belong the women, girls, children — all the beings who live by their feelings. They stand in a never-ceasing state of bewilderment *vis-à-vis* to all the movements of existence, the most tremendous and the most insignificant, and even the plain fact of life itself. Their organs are too sensitive for the brutality, meaninglessness, perversity of animal existence. Because they have to be always fleeing from something, thinking of and dreading a catastrophe, they never get as far as action. They never arrive at life, because they fear to expire at the first contact with it. They have already anticipated it with all its terrors in their instinct, imagination, nerves, and power of divination, and so they wander on like the helpless materializations of a powerful necromancer: as pledges of a higher existence, but with the power to *appear* only, being unable to get into practical touch with this world. They cannot, will not understand, because they have seen the incomprehensibleness of earthly things. "One must . . ." "one ought . . .": these are the limits of the vibrations that the approaching might of destiny is able to draw from these strangely bright and dull drifters. All about them there lie in wait the harshnesses, the abrupt transitions, the

441

complications to which none of them is equal. The other group, of the never surprised — the philosophers, the greybeards, the old nurses and mothers, the saints, kings, and beggars — know too much, on the other hand. And as they, covered like the angels of the Cabbala with a thousand eyes, see everything, all the manifold knittings and limitations of fate, they likewise never arrive at action. They have ties everywhere, but not one that they can trust.

Telepathic drama

In the first volume we said that the pictures painted by Maeterlinck's Flemish ancestors in the fourteenth and fifteenth centuries were painted mysticism. Of himself it might be said that he dramatized these paintings. His people, even if he transfers them to the present day, affect us as figures out of a grey past or as creatures of the future, never as beings of the present. He throws a magic light over them, the production of which is obviously his secret, and suddenly they are deprived of all sensual indication of corporeality, of all profane realism. Anatole France once said of Villiers de l'Isle-Adam that he went through life like a sleep-walker, seeing nothing of that which we all of us saw, while that which was hidden from our eyes he was able to see. Thus it is with Maeterlinck's figures. Real life — the daily, ordinary, practical side of things seen and felt — they do not see; they are timid and faint before it, helpless and dumb like children, almost like half-wits. But while they tap their way blindly through coarse reality, there reveals itself to a mysterious inner sense, which they alone possess, another world, as real as this one, more real indeed, the world of premonitions and dreams, of distant effects and distant storms, in which all minds and souls feel themselves to be undivided whole, a unity and harmony in which there can be therefore no mistakes, uncertainties, or struggles. They too are *flaireurs*, sensing the incomprehensible and invisible in which the true secret of our being lies hidden.

We say " secret," but, as has always been the case, we do not by that mean anything definitively insoluble and undecipherable, but only something from which we have not yet wrung the last word, something still becoming, arising, that is on the point of revealing itself to us. It still hesitates. Or is it we who hesitate? In a word, it is all a question of those energies and manifestations that we call occult. These are undoubtedly natural forces like all others, just as regulated and unfathomable, just as beneficial and dangerous, but they happen to be still hidden from us. Maeterlinck is the first dramatist of the occult, of the telepathic, of the " soul "-

sense. In his lectures on psycho-analysis Sigmund Freud says that man's self-love has up to now had to endure three great insults on the part of science: the first was when it learnt through Copernicus that our earth was not the centre of the cosmos; the second, when Darwin accused man of being descended from the animal world and of possessing ineradicable animal instincts; and the third, and most keenly resented, the discovery of psychological research that the ego was not even master in his own house, but had to rely on scanty news of what was going on unconsciously in his soul-life. This is in fact the knowledge that lives in the heart of Maeterlinck's dramas: "one says this, and one says that, but the soul goes its own way." But Freud, whose ingenuity has chosen merely to research into earthly things, without throwing one glance at the divine, overlooks or is silent about the immense moral gain that has come to us through this very knowledge — namely, that what psycho-analysis coldly and almost contemptuously calls sub-consciousness is nothing but the consciousness of a spirit infinitely superior, and therefore incomprehensible, to us, and that we were never so great as now, when, after the fall of the last bulwark of our self-glorious ego, we find ourselves in intimate and indestructible cryptogamy with the world-spirit.

All the methods by which the dramatist has hitherto most powerfully expressed himself and attained his most enthralling effects — distinctness and conciseness, forcefulness and home-thrusts, abundance of action and incidents, lively development, pressing forward to the climax, individuality and colour of the characters — are alien to Maeterlinck. His figures wander, fog-bound, under the shadow of a profound mystery, and their destinies are enigmatic to such a degree as hardly to be capable of interpretation at all. No character emerges from the dramatically fertile sphere of the will; nobody wills, nobody acts, and, even externally, little of importance happens. There are just a few narrow figures drawn with a peculiar spareness, who, as if crazy or bewitched, obstinately repeat the same sentences over and over and whose characterizations are quite homogeneous. They all have the same expression for the same sensation, and the same sensation for the same impression. Here is shadow-play in more than an outward sense. For what the author shows us is only the shadows, projected in advance, of the unborn and never-to-be-born deeds in the soul of men. Ibsen conjures up the shadows, of the past, Maeterlinck does the reverse; and actually it

443

all amounts to the same thing. Both of them will allow but *one* reality, the soul. Past and future are mere projection phenomena, reflections of the eternal, which is always there. This is either no action or the highest form of action, an entirely undramatic conception or the extreme of suspense — as when we are shown an apparently motionless body in the midst of whirling atoms, or the equilibrium of the stars in their monotonous course. It is a theatre without theatricality, a theatre of silence, of listening, of passive receptivity to the stream of cosmic harmony. The " suspense " in these dramas is not of the brutal material order to which we are accustomed, but the latent and therefore far more exciting form that a charged galvanic battery generates. Maeterlinck once expressed himself exquisitely on this point: " Does our soul open its petals only in nights of storm? . . . I am tempted to believe that an old man sitting in an armchair in the lamplight who, without comprehending them, listens to all the eternal laws that prevail around his house . . . lives actually a deeper, more human and universal life than the lover who strangles his sweeetheart, or the general who forces a victory."

Shakspere could not write any single one of his pieces again today. He would have to say to himself that Othello would never kill Desdemona just when he was *not* drunk, but would do or say something different, something apparently unimportant and secondary, something difficult to calculate in advance, but which might well wound more deeply than his dagger. For an Othello of the Shaksperian age the equation was clear and plain to see: he is to kill her. What else, just when he is not drunk, should he do? People of those days were, after all, much more comprehending, simple, and consequent. A clever and experienced student of souls could do astronomy with them as Galileo did with his stars. One had only to know the laws of the epicycles that one was going to describe. And Shakspere himself drew the fate of dramatic art in *Hamlet* as in a parable. It goes about tormented and pursued by faces out of the night, driven on to far-reaching, noisy actions, to murders and death-blows, battle and deed, and when it comes to testing all these manifestations of life, it realizes that they have no intrinsic right to exist, are nothing but concessions made to the *milieu* in which we live, the great madhouse of unwisdom and unkindness called humanity. And just as Hamlet in making these reflections decomposes himself and becomes unfit to

444

live, so does the dramatic art reach dissolution through the slow process of reflecting upon its image in a mirror.

I am ignoring here the noisy interlude of dramatic art that calls itself "Futuristic" although it belongs absolutely to the past. It is a last desperate struggle to arrive at artistic expression by means which have become historical. No, this expression does not depend on activism, on self-exertion and velleities, but on keeping still so that the new can work within us. This new thing is the soul. The soul has, of course, always been there, just as mouth and throat were there long before men used them for speech, but it is only today getting ready to speak. Maeterlinck is not, like nearly all his contemporaries, an end, but only a first beginning from which a new, immature and still uncertainly groping humanity is setting forth. He is not an estuary, but a source. In no other living thinker do we find the peculiar *coincidentia oppositorum* of supreme doubt and surpreme certainty which always form the presage to a new section in spiritual history — that intensity of concentrated, inwardly experienced, and profoundly moving dramatic expression — that we find in Maeterlinck.

The artistic emanations of the period between the turn of the century and the World War cannot be dealt with in the present work. It was laid down in the Introduction that our method was on principle to be unscientific. This was of course only an ideal, and to act up to it throughout is more than can be expected of the powers of an individual. Not infrequently the reader will have had to take the wish for the deed. This goodwill, however, no one with an objective mind will deny the author, who is consoled, further, by the hope that his sound instinct has led him to pseudo-scientific conclusions even where he did not intend this. But this method of treatment is not applicable to art since 1900, because in this domain (a confession which must not, however, be understood as an unfair *captatio benevolentiæ*) the professional scientists are just as much amateurs as the author is. His researches would therefore have been in danger from the outset of proving superfluous. Obviously, one can only deal unscientifically with that which has become an object of science.

These reflections may possibly arise from a certain over-conscientiousness. There is, however, a second and more decisive ground for the elimination of these phenomena, which is likewise to be found in our particular method. The standards of cultural

The gap

445

history are by no means the same as those of æsthetics. In the latter, a work of art or its creator is valued according to its absolute significance; in the former, with regard to its physiognomic character: the degree of strength with which, in the words of Hamlet, he shows " the very age and body of the time his form and pressure." Seen in this aspect, it may happen that works of eternal significance receive but a casual mention, and those that stand incomparably lower are considered in detail, or even that some which no history of plastic or literature or music could possibly ignore have received no notice at all. To mention only a few names, we are of opinion that poets like Ponsard, painters like Thoma, philosophers like Lotze, composers like Saint-Saëns, possess no tangible culture-historical significance.

Yet the last ten or fifteen years of the Modern Age have, strange to say, produced almost nothing but such " dateless " phenomena. They are all without any verifiable relationship to their epoch, they are not its diagram. Could not Thomas Mann be a contemporary of Wilhelm Meister, Heinrich Mann a contemporary of Stendhal, Max Reinhardt a theatre-wizard of the High Baroque, Hans Pfitzner an Old German master of Dürer's time? Stefan George has even been hailed as a Classical apparition by Gundolf. One might say that we lack the historical distance which would enable us to sense the secret link with the age. But, unfortunately for this idea, we do feel the link very distinctly in the case of the younger generation which had its say after the war. Its products, although far lower in value, are the unmistakable expression of a definite historical situation, and it is impossible to transfer them to any other. This applies even to acting. The alfresco art of a Bassermann and Werner Krauss, the water-colour art of a Waldau and Gülstorff (all of whom are from the pre-war period), would have been conceivable at any stage in the history of modern drama. But there have been, and are, actors who can with equal certainty be claimed for Expressionism: for instance, Duse or Yvette Guilbert.

In his history of the theory of colour Goethe occasionally employs the conception of a " gap." The period before 1914 was one such gap. The Modern Age was rolling on — to the World War. This might perhaps have occurred in any circumstances — perhaps! But that it came so unavoidably, so soon, and as it did was the work of European diplomacy.

Villainy, says the pessimist, is unfortunately more or less incarnate in the human race, as is only too often proved by the actions typical of us, both private and public. No, says the optimist, villainy is the lamentable exceptional case, otherwise it would not have conscience (both private and public) against it every time. Is there, for example, any single officially recognized, let alone state-managed profession of which villainy forms the content? Certainly, replies the pessimist, there is such a profession: diplomacy.

A whole class of people, belonging mainly to that rich and turbid upper stratum of do-nothings, women-hunters, and gamblers that is called the " cream," is sent by the government to particular schools, furnished with incomes, rewarded by honours and titles, to the express and admitted end that they should spend their whole lives in intriguing, spying, deceit, and bribery. That is, they are swindlers and wasters recognized and paid by the State: drones with a poisonous sting. They are the masters of lying, the mechanics of hell, the worst of the many varieties of villains: namely, villains with a good conscience, for do they not lie " for their country "? In the Renaissance they put poison in each other's chocolate, also for their country, and this rouses humane horror in us today. But the difference is quite small: they still go on poisoning, but with finer and more malign poisons.

Nothing of permanent value is ever achieved by lying. A lie is *nothing*, it is ever but the negation of some reality. How should one be able to construct anything in the least durable on a null, on a denial? Every lie is a boundless stupidity, a senseless attempt to achieve an aim by fundamentally unsuitable means. That is mainly why spiritually inferior persons feel particularly drawn to the diplomatic career. A life of constant dissimulation, bartering of secrets, and crooked, impure, and ambiguous relations to everybody and everything can only be endured, in the long run, by a hopelessly clever blockhead.

The assertion that lying is an indispensable of the diplomatic trade is a diplomat's lie. We have already shown that the triumphant basic strength of both Frederick the Great and Bismarck lay in their profound truthfulness. The greatness of Julius Cæsar was due to his having a soul that was crystal-clear in the midst of a turbid chaos. Napoleon's cardinal virtue, again, was the capacity to see into the heart of realities and stand in a straight relation to them. As long as he was the son of facts, he was the

447

acclaimed Emperor of Europe; when he began to deceive the world, his star began to sink.

Diplomats did not, of course, invent war, but they are its strongest auxiliaries and prolongers. Without them wars would not cease, but they would perhaps be rarer, and certainly nobler, more honest, and more reluctantly undertaken. And possibly, as they thus more and more lost their former position in the economy of our thought and feeling, they would, after all, cease.

The Balkan War

On September 9, 1911, the day of Italy's declaration of war against Turkey, there appeared over North Africa, in the constellation of the Lion, a comet which shone more brightly from day to day, and simultaneously a second streaming body which appeared to point northward like a sword.

Disturbances and bloody fighting in Armenia, Arabia, and Albania had encouraged Italy to establish herself firmly in Libya in this jubilee year of union. This in turn encouraged the Balkan states in their resolution to take up the struggle for European Turkey. In the spring of 1912 Bulgaria, Serbia, Greece, and Montenegro concluded to this end a quadruple alliance, which fell into a number of separate agreements. The Bulgarian-Greek agreement was directed solely against Turkey and contained no detailed stipulations for the partition of Macedonia. The Bulgarian-Serbian treaty allotted Old Serbia and the Sanjak of Novibazar to Serbia and about five sixths of Macedonia to Bulgaria, leaving the remainder to be disposed of by the Tsar. This meant, of course, that Bulgaria would still have an account with Greece to settle. But, besides this, the alliance was expressly directed against Roumania and Austria. Article 2 provided that if the Roumanians attacked Bulgaria, Serbia must immediately declare war on them; Article 3, that if Austria-Hungary attacked Serbia, Bulgaria should do her part and declare war. When the note by which Bulgaria, Serbia, and Greece demanded autonomy for the Christian peoples of the Balkans was answered by the Porte in the negative, the three Governments declared war on October 17. (Montenegro had done so nine days earlier; this — the war having of course long been decided upon — was simply a gamble on the fall of prices by King Nikita, who, with his Paris bankers, thereby raked in millions.) To relieve the situation the Sultan was driven to make peace with Italy, which he did by the Treaty of Lausanne on October 18. He thereby relinquished Tripoli and Cyrenaica, with the formula that "in virtue of his sovereign rights" he granted them full autonomy.

The Turkish army was in a pitiful condition. True, it was provided with Krupp guns, which were at least equivalent to the English and French pieces of its opponents, but had hardly any ammunition. Thousands of recruits were sent into the firing-line so untrained that they did not know how to handle a rifle. Since the Young Turk Revolution, Christians had also been enrolled for service, but they proved most unreliable. No transport or supply corps existed. As a great proportion of the troops had to be drawn from Asia, the mobilization proceeded far too slowly. The command also broke down completely. Towards the end of October the Bulgarians were victorious at Kirk Kilisse, and the Serbs at Kumanovo on the same day, and shortly afterwards the Bulgarians won the five-days' battle of Lüle-Burgas. It seemed as if Turkey was annihilated. Ferdinand of Bulgaria already had hopes of entering Constantinople and there being crowned Emperor Symeon of Eastern Rome. But the Chatalja lines completely cut off the peninsula on which the capital stands from sea to sea. They had been declared invincible by Moltke, when he was military adviser to the Sultan in the second half of the thirties. And here, in fact, the Bulgarian advance was brought to a standstill, the assaulting troops were bled to death, and whole regiments were swept away.

The great powers, who were all intimately concerned with the Balkan questions, had from the first, under cover of persistent assurances of peace, adopted a threatening attitude. Even before the outbreak of war Russia staged a "test mobilization" directed against Austria-Hungary and Turkey — in whose superiority everyone at that time believed. Then came the *status quo* formula: "Should war break out, the powers would allow no alteration in the territorial possessions of Turkey in Europe which might arise out of the conflict." Austria-Hungary proposed the following program: the "free development of Albania; Serbia's request for an extension of territory to the Adriatic to be dismissed *a limine;* Roumania's justifiable wishes to be satisfied; Austria-Hungary's important economic interests in the Balkans to be safeguarded, particularly as regards the railway connexion with the Ægean." These demands met with Italy's acceptance, though it can hardly have been sincere; for if Italy was to declare herself in principle disinterested in Albania, it would have to be for some better reason than leaving the road to Salonika open to Austria. In Austria an influential party led by Conrad von Hötzendorf took the view that accounts must first be settled with Italy. He had advocated an attack on this ally during the annexation crisis, and he now repeated his demand. Such a war would in all human probability have ended in the defeat of the Italians, always provided the Austrians had had to deal with them alone. This postulate was, however, utterly childish. The declaration of war on Italy would promptly have brought on the World War, with this difference, that the Central Powers would have had against them, in 1908 Turkey, and in 1912 the whole of the Balkan states as well as, in both cases, Italy from the very beginning. This would have made the south front simply untenable, while the French front would have been overwhelmingly reinforced.

After her defeats Turkey sued for peace, and the ambassadors of the great powers met in London to negotiate this. The victorious states not only wanted to keep their conquests, but claimed in addition the three besieged fortresses of Adrianople, Scutari, and Janina. These conditions were rejected by the Porte. In the renewed fighting, first Janina, then Adrianople, and lastly Scutari fell, the last-named being thereupon occupied by mixed troops of the great powers on behalf of Albania. In May 1913 the Treaty of London was concluded, which left the Porte, of all its European possessions, only Constantinople and a small strip of land within a line drawn from Enos on the Ægean to Midia on the Black Sea.

Meanwhile quarrels had broken out among the Allies. Serbia demanded a revision of the treaty, complaining that northern Albania, with the port of Durazzo, which had been promised to her, had not been handed over, owing to the representations of Austria, while Bulgaria had been given Thrace, on which she had not counted. Greece demanded Salonika and a considerable portion of Macedonia. Roumania also put forward a few originally quite modest claims, which the Bulgarian minister-president Danev, with a short-sightedness bordering on idiocy, rejected outright. Thus, in the summer of 1913 the Second Balkan War came about, in which Bulgaria was exposed to a concentric attack by all her neighbours (for Turkey also returned to the fray). The superior Serbian and Greek masses forced the Bulgarians to retire on pain of envelopment. Roumanian army corps crossed the Danube and marched on Sofia without meeting resistance. Adrianople had to be given up to the Turks for lack of troops to defend it. At the Peace of Bucharest the greater part of northern Macedonia fell to Serbia, of southern Macedonia to Greece, and the rich Bulgarian corn area of the Dobruja, with the strategically important fortress of Silistria, to Roumania. By the Treaty of Constantinople Turkey retained Adrianople and eastern Thrace as far as the Maritsa. While Greece, Serbia, and Montenegro emerged from the war at nearly double their original size, and Roumania by a mere demonstration march had rounded off her southern boundary most advantageously, Bulgaria, who had achieved the greatest feats of arms, had to be content with western Thrace and a small piece of Macedonia in the Rhodope.

The Balkan crises had greatly intensified the opposition between the Central Powers and the Entente, and a new feature appeared in the tension between Russia and Germany. Bismarck had never supported an aggressive Balkan policy on the part of Austria, but the German Government had entirely identified itself with Austria over the Albanian question; added to which Russia was being made nervous by such slogans as " Berlin to Bagdad," " The Elbe to the Euphrates," " The North Sea to the Persian Gulf," for Armenia was included in her vital sphere of influence. The German plans in Asia Minor, too, naturally impinged on the English idea of the " dry route to India." That, after Austria's attitude, the alliance with Italy would be anything more than a paper one, only the diplomats could imagine. In the winter of 1912–13 the two allies were in a state of permanent readiness for war with each other. Italy fortified Venice and Verona with modern armoured forts, strengthened the frontiers against Austria, and laid down railways for deployment throughout Venetia. The Austrian troop-concentrations against Montenegro and Serbia were directed equally against Italy. Her blundering diplomats had, further, alienated Austria's last friend in the Balkans, Roumania, her senseless demand for the revision of the peace treaty of Bukarest having roused the greatest bitterness in that capital. Demonstrations surged through the city with the cry: " Down with perfidious Austria! "

On June 28, the Greek St. Vitus's Day, in the year 1389, the Serbs suffered the catastrophic defeat of Kossovo. On that day in 1919 Germany signed the peace treaty of Versailles, and on that day in 1914 the heir to the Austrian throne was assassinated. The murder was committed by Austrian subjects on Austrian soil, and the deed was therefore an internal affair of the monarchy.

Sarajevo

451

In the *Vorwärts* next day the significance of the event was summed up in these words: " Franz Ferdinand falls a victim to a false, out-of-date system, of which he was the apparent supporter . . . the shots which laid low the heir to the throne have also punctured the belief in the continued existence of this old and antiquated state. . . . The ghastly event at Sarajevo is a serious warning to us likewise. Our bungling policy has bound up the fate of the nation too closely with that of Austria." Sektionsrat von Wiesner, who had been sent to study the documents on the scene of the murder, telegraphed after a fortnight: " Connivance of Serbian Government in the carrying out of the assassination or the preparations for it and provision of weapons entirely unproved. . . . On the contrary there are evidences tending to show this possibility as excluded." On July 7 the Cabinet decided to make " such far-reaching demands of Serbia that the rejection of these may be assumed in advance and there will be left no way out but the radical solution of military intervention." Tisza alone refused his consent. The ultimatum, handed in at 6 p.m. on July 23, was drafted accordingly. The very fact that its time-limit was twice twenty-four hours, and that the only reply allowed was a plain yes or no, made further negotiations and a diplomatic intervention by the remaining great powers impossible. *The Times* said that all those who had universal peace at heart must earnestly hope that Austria-Hungary had not said her last word in the note to Serbia, for if it were not so, we were on the verge of war. And the *Daily Mail* pointed out that if Austria rejected Russia's demand for an extension of the time-limit, the conflict would not remain localized, but the Triple Entente would be in opposition to the Triple Alliance. Sir Edward Grey, who undoubtedly did *not* want the war, declared that never in his experience had he seen such a note as the Austrian. Shaw, who was certainly neither a war-monger nor an Entente chauvinist, wrote: " The ultimatum to Serbia was the escapade of a dotard: a worse crime than the assassination that provoked it." The Serbian Government accepted all the demands of the note, with only inconsiderable modifications, except that which insisted that organs of the Austro-Hungarian Government should be present at the inquiry into the existence of a plot, as this would be an offence against the sovereignty, the administration, and the criminal law. The Austro-Hungarian Government's official comment on this was: " It was not our idea to have the Austro-Hungarian organs take part in the Serbian law-court proceedings:

they were only to attend the preliminary policy inquiry by which the material for the inquiry was to be got together and tested." Similar querulous and clumsy hair-splittings characterized the notes on the remaining points also. The Serbian reply closes with the words: "The Royal Serbian Government considers that it is to the common interest not to act precipitately over the solution of this matter and is therefore willing, as always, to accept a peaceful solution, should the Austro-Hungarian Government not consider this reply satisfactory, either by transferring the decision on this question to the International Court at The Hague or by leaving the decision to the great powers." On this the Austrian commentary is silent. Kaiser Wilhelm wrote under the Serbian reply: "A brilliant achievement for only forty-eight hours' grace! This is more than one could have expected. A great moral triumph for Vienna, but it does away with all grounds for war." There is no need whatever to raise doubts concerning Bethmann-Hollweg's assertion that the German Government only became acquainted with the Austrian demands after the event: the only reproach that can be made is that the Government should have given Austria *carte blanche* at all in the Serbian question. Moreover, only crazy party-opponents can question the fundamental will to peace of both Kaiser and Chancellor. We may take it as proved that France was by no means keen on war; whatever her attitude to war in general, she did not want war at this particular moment. Her two-years' service system had been extended to three, but as the contingent born in 1890 and called up in 1911 had refused to stay another year with the colours after the expiration of their two years in autumn 1913, it had been decided to dismiss them and call up instead two annual contingents of recruits, those born in 1892 and 1893. To justify this legally, the commencement of their term of service had to be set back a year. Thus in 1915 France would be able to count on four annual contingents for her standing army — those of 1892, 1893, 1894, 1895 — and similarly in 1916 on those born between 1893 and 1896. These two years were therefore the most favourable for the beginning of a war. Also, there was a scheme in hand for drafting far larger numbers of natives from Morocco, Tunis, and Algiers into the European army and replacing them in Africa by Negro troops. This, again, gave better prospects for a war that should begin in the next year or the year after that. In Russian Poland, too, the complete development of the railway network, on which work was being feverishly pressed with the aid of the French milliards, could not be expected before about 1916. Nevertheless the war party at the Tsar's court was very powerful, and, even apart from this, the fear of revolution urged the leading circles to an aggressive policy in the hope of averting internal conflicts by an outburst of Panslavism. There are evidences, indeed, of highly irresponsible efforts to bring about a break between Austria and Russia. Most complicated of all was the case of England, who was far too business-like not to know that a pan-European war must signify vast economic damage to all concerned. The "encircling" policy which had been observed for half a decade aimed therefore only at placing Germany into so unfavourable a position politically that resistance would be out of the question for her. If it then still came to war, England, with her gift of unfailingly correct prognosis, could not but divine that the Central Powers would win if they had only France and Russia opposed to them. She was therefore literally forced to "come in." Further, Italy adopted a greedy attitude towards not only her Austrian, but her French neighbour also and could only be regarded as safely neutral if England joined the Entente. The only reproach that can be raised against the British Government is that it did not define its standpoint towards Germany energetically and unambiguously. For, knowing it, Germany would never have risked the war. As President Wilson said, in March 1919, it was known with certainty that Germany would not have embarked upon this enterprise had she for a moment supposed that Great Britain would go with France and Russia. In November 1912 Sir Edward Grey and M. Cambon, the French Ambassador in London, had exchanged letters by which the Entente was made into a military and naval convention. These agreements, nominally private, but actually binding, came to the knowledge of the German Government in March, 1913. They were not taken seriously, however — as was right, up to a certain point, for the British Government was not itself quite clear as to how far it stood committed. And one cannot entirely reject the possibility that England might at least have hesitated had not the Belgian incident so extraordinarily simplified matters. There can be no question, here either, of Germany's guilt in the higher sense. She was under compulsion. The war could only be won by the Schlieffen Plan, which counted upon the rapid overthrow of France (whose mobilization would be quicker than Russia's), and this overthrow was only conceivable

by way of Belgium, owing to the extreme difficulty of mastering the barrier fortresses of France's eastern frontier. " Belgium," says Professor Rudolf Kjellén, the distinguished authority on the relation between State and space, " caps France like a hat that fits quite naturally; here, in the north-east, is the sensitive point of the Empire." This diversion was therefore a strategic necessity. But it can by no means be justified by international law; every attempt to do this can only increase the wrong, and it is therefore all the more unfortunate that, in a supposedly scientific work like Helmolt's world-history so honest and thorough a historian as Gottlob Egelhaaf should not hesitate to say (after the war, too) that Germany was not obliged to respect Belgian neutrality because Germany was not yet in existence in 1831. (To contradict this is presumably unnecessary.) No one in his senses can deny that the Central Powers began the war, not only formally by their " declarations," but actually by the unacceptable ultimatum which Austria conceived and Germany failed to disavow. But that takes us no further in the questions of war guilt. History is full of instances of offensive wars which in reality were defensive: for example, the Seven Years' War, in which, moreover, " neutral " Saxony played to a nicety the same rôle as Belgium in the World War. But as Frederick won in this struggle, Clio, the worshipper of success (whom Schopenhauer with reason calls a whore), crowned him with laurels. The reason for Germany's unconditional support of Austria is also to be found in a Nibelung Romanticism founded on reminiscences of historical picture-books. One may not give it political approval, but one cannot refuse it human sympathy. Speaking generally, too, the problem of this world-conflagration of the great twilight of a whole generation cannot be solved in terms of legal casuistry, but only on the higher plane of *mythological* observation. The position of the German nation did indeed recall the fate of the Nibelungs who, surrounded by enemies, became apparent peace-breakers in their sore distress.

The definite summing-up of the war was made by Lloyd George, when he said: " The more one reads the memoirs and books written in the various countries of what happened before August 1st, 1914, the more one realizes that no one at the head of affairs quite meant war at that stage. It was something into which they glided or rather staggered, or stumbled."

And here a black cloud falls over Europe. When it is once more   *The cloud* parted, the man of the Modern Age will be gone: blown away into the night of what has been, the depths of eternity; an obscure saga, a dull rumour, a pale memory. One of the innumerable varieties of the human race has reached its goal and is immortal: has become a picture.

EPILOGUE

The Collapse of Reality

> *"When we dream that we are dreaming, we are on the point of waking."*
>
> *Novalis*

The great leitmotiv of the Middle Ages was *universalia sunt realia*. But the finale of the Middle Ages was summed up in the sentence: there are no *universalia*.

And the swan-song of the Modern Age is the recognition that there are no *realia*. We are in a new incubation period.

This is only meant allegorically. Each historical generation is a definite conception of God's, a uniquely occurring light-ray between two infinities. In the progress of world-history there is nothing which is (in the geometrical sense) "similar" to it. Even to imagine that it could be reconstructed would be an atheistic conception; on the other hand, in the artistic sense there is analogy and even similarity. As in that period of change, so in ours we only see, for the moment, that a world-picture is dissolving. But this we see quite clearly: that what European man has for half a century called reality is falling to pieces before his eyes like dry tinder.

Even if we follow the idea of the infinity of the cosmos, with which the Modern Age set in, to its logical conclusion, we arrive at unreality; for infinity is nothing but a mathematical formula for unreality. Supposing we try to imagine that the Milky Way consists of more than a million fixed stars, among which are many with a diameter greater than the distance of the earth from the Sun; and that it does not form, as it were, the stationary pole in the cosmos, but is tearing along to somewhere or other at a speed of six hundred kilometres a second — that is, a thousand times as fast as a cannon-ball — the assumption that this could have anything to do with reality is reduced to a mere play of thoughts. Still, if one acquiesces in the latest hypothesis that the totality of the stellar clusters forms a closed finite system of the form of an ellipsoid of rotation, we cannot then out of hand reject the idea

The new incubation period

The cosmos as molecule

459

that this itself is nothing but one of the molecules out of which a larger body is constructed.

The molecule as cosmos Just as enormous and unfathomable as the dimensions upwards are the dimensions downwards as revealed in the atom. According to the latest calculation, the radius of an atom has the average length of 10^{-8} centimetres or a ten-millionth of a millimetre, and the mass of a hydrogen atom stands to the mass of a gramme of water in the proportion of the mass of a postal packet of ten kilograms to that of our planet. We must imagine each such atom, however, as a solar system, in which negative electrons describe large elliptical orbits round a positively charged central nucleus. The radius of one of these electrons is diminutive even compared with that of the atom; in fact, it is one three-billionth of a millimetre. An electron would appear by the side of a bacillus as would the latter by the side of the earth. The most important fact, however, is this: The positive charge is what determines the atomic weight; the mass of the atom is a function of the charge on the nucleus. This nucleus is something quite immaterial; it has neither weight, mass, volume, inertia, nor any of the other properties that are usually associated with matter. The mass of the atom is, then, only apparent; there is no substance there. Contemporary physics was forced to give up the hitherto accepted theories which dealt with empty space and corpuscular atoms in this space, and to introduce the principles of fields of energy and nodal points. But what the fields and the charge are, no one knows.

Positivism takes its last refuge in the consolation that all these differences in strain, potential differences, functions, paths, velocities, lines of force, and other symbols of embarrassment can be expressed by exact mathematical equations. We cannot be surprised at this, for all that has been said is not merely an equation, but an identity, or, in less formal language, all science is merely tautology.

Time as a function of position The same view with regard to matter is held in the theory of Relativity, which must be regarded as the greatest theoretical event of the present century. Time, which until now has seemed to be the deep azure bowl in which all being has reposed from all eternity — as in the Classical world-picture the cosmos rested in the blue bell of heaven — has now suffered the same fate that befell that earlier conception at the dawn of the Modern Age. European humanity, which during the last hundred years has been very liberal in its awards of the Order of Copernicus, bestowing it in turn on Cuvier, Comte, Darwin, Marx, Freud, and many others, can now talk of a Copernican Act with a vengeance; and it is not improbable that later generations will one day speak of our time as the age of Einstein. Let us imagine a train a hundred kilometres in length, travelling with a speed of one kilometre a second. (There is no such train in reality, for it would be about three hundred times as long, and thirty times as fast, as the longest and fastest trains hitherto possible.) At the front of the train is one person, A; at the back another person, Z. They send light-signals to each other at the same instant, which are checked by an observer, B, not on the train. All three have the most accurate precision-watches, which are capable of recording a three-hundred-thousandth part of a second. While the train is stationary, the signals will reach all three participants at the same time, in fact (since light has a velocity of three hundred thousand kilometres a second), one three-thousandth of a second after it is given. Even when the train is in motion, A and Z will receive the signals at the same instant. But from the point of view of B, the ray of light has travelled 101 kilometres from Z to A and 99 kilometres from A to Z, so that it will arrive at A two three-hundred-thousandths of a second later than at Z. In other words, contemporary events are only contemporary inside the same system; the time of occurrence depends on the state of motion of the observer, for every body, according to its state of motion, the time-reckoning is different, with every place there is a definite time associated; time is a function of position.

Mass is energy

As the place of every event only has significance through time, time is nothing other than the fourth dimension; in fact, there is a common measure for time and space. This unit is the *time-metre*: namely, the time needed for a light-ray to traverse a distance of one metre, one three-hundred-millionth of a second. Now, the energy of a body in motion, its "kinetic energy," is calculated by multiplying its mass (m) by the square of its velocity (v): this formula, mv^2 (or, to be precise, $\frac{1}{2}mv^2$), as we remember, was already discovered by Leibniz. The velocity (v) is obtained by dividing the distance travelled (s) by the time taken (t). If now we make our calculations in time-metres, we obtain the same units for energy and mass. For example, in the case of a shot travelling at 300 metres per second, applying the formula: kinetic energy $= \frac{1}{2}m\left(\frac{s}{t}\right)^2$, its kinetic energy is 300 *path-metres* (distance

461

travelled) divided by one second, or 300,000,000 *time-metres* (time taken), which gives one millionth, or, squared, one billionth, multiplied by its mass. Thus its kinetic energy is in this case one billionth of its mass, or, expressed the other way round, its mass is merely an immense quantity of energy, a phenomenal form of kinetic energy. The general formula for these conditions is $E = mc^2$, where c is the velocity of light; and it shows that " matter is not material," that there is no such thing as mass.

There is no simultaneity

From this new idea of time there came yet other foundation-shaking discoveries. Every motion is an alteration of distance. To get an idea of absolute motion we should have to imagine a body absolutely at rest, from which we can observe; this we cannot do. Thus all motion is merely relative. We cannot obtain on the one hand a system perfectly at rest, and on the other hand a system in motion; they are always two (or more) systems in motion relative to each other. Newton had already pointed out that there was no such thing as one-way gravitation, that the falling stone attracted the earth in the same way as the earth the stone. But the stone's mass is so small in comparison with the earth's that its effect is negligible. It is much the same when we say that the earth revolves round the sun.

It is because of the length or, rather, the slow tempo of our life that we do not notice the relativity of time, and for the same reason we do notice the relativity of space. If our power of conception had anything like the velocity of light, we should perceive that time moved, whereas we should never be aware — or at most we should deduce from " astronomical " observation — that a stone had fallen. As the movements and variations that are accessible to our senses would never bear even the most distant comparison with the velocity of light, our practical life is as little affected by the revelations of Einstein as it was when the geocentric system was dethroned by the heliocentric. Right through the Modern Age the sun rises in just the same way as it always had done and will do, but the world's consciousness had experienced a decisive reorientation. This consisted in the triumph of the scientific mind, which saw the cosmos for the first time, in its immense magnitude indeed, but at the same time as just a magnitude, something mathematical, and calculable. The theory of Relativity points in the opposite direction. It sees the cosmos as something finite, but entirely incomprehensible, evading the apperception-possibilities of science.

Conceptions of "before" and "after," which have meaning only in relation to a given station in time, are the same as space-conceptions of "over" and "under," which depend purely on the place of the observer. The assertion that two events are simultaneous, then, has only meaning if it is made in relation to a definite system of motion. An observer outside this system would think that they had happened sooner or later according to the place where they occurred. In themselves the events are *neither simultaneous nor non-simultaneous*. They only become so when fitted into the relativity of a system. Great and small, near and far, early and late, simultaneous and non-simultaneous are not even as much as "subjective" standards. They are no standards at all, for they cannot be referred to any absolute unit of measure. With the collapse of absolute simultaneity there falls also the absolute standard of measure for space-magnitudes, the notion, that is, of the *equality of two distances* and of *parallelism*: parallels do cut one another.

That all the "truths" of an age form a connected planetary system we see from Hanns Hörbiger's "World-ice theory," which appeared at the same time as that of Relativity. He himself more happily names it "glacial cosmogony," and in its sub-title, quite accurately, "a new history of the development of the cosmos and the solar system." He arrives at his results by practical observations which he made as a smelting expert. Ice-blocks, it seems, do not melt when thrown into the molten slag of a blast furnace, but the slag around them freezes into a spongy pumice-like isolated stratum. It is only gradually that the ice turns into water, which thereupon becomes heated up to a hundred degrees Centigrade and even higher in a "delayed boiling," and finally the "pumice bomb" explodes. On the analogy of this, Hörbiger imagines our Milky Way to have arisen somewhat thus. Somewhere in cosmic space, in the region of the constellation of Columba, there is the mother of the stars, a monstrous glowing star, two hundred million times the size of the sun. An "icelet," some forty thousand times as big as the sun, is caught up by this, penetrates into it, partially undissolved, and slowly begins to boil. If the gigantic explosion follows, the greater part of the spurting star-masses fall back again, but 0.25 per cent is shot outside the gravitation-field by the shock of the discharge, and also by the pursuing gases. This shot into the cosmos is our solar system.

Hörbiger's conception differs from previous ones on several

The shot into the cosmos

essential points, primarily in the infinitely bigger rôle given to ice as constructive material, but above all because of its *dynamic* form. The Kantian world-picture is static. The gaseous mists slowly take their course like gentle fleecy cloudlets, form into balls, warm themselves, and become encrusted, but the myth of the glacial cosmogony is, so to say, composed in a different key. Also, according to Kant and Laplace, the moon was a central knot left over in the gaseous whirl from which the earth had been formed. Other followers of Laplace believe that it broke loose from the earth through the effect of centrifugal force during the gaseous stage of the earth itself, as the earth had done from the sun. Against this "throwing off" theory two arguments may be put forward: that certain of the planets possess moons varying greatly in size, distance, and phase (the time of their orbits varies from twelve of the earth's hours to two and a half of the earth's years), and that the satellites of Uranus and Neptune even show a backward movement, which would be quite impossible if, as parts of a rotating gas-ball, they had been split off from it. The application of Hörbiger's theory to the moon-problem is far less strained; what it asserts, in this case as in others, is the direct opposite of previous explanations. The moons never have belonged to the mass of their planets, but they are all destined at some time to become incorporated with them, and the same fate awaits the smaller planets in relation to the larger. As a result of the resistance of cosmic space, which is not completely empty, the stars undergo a shrinkage of orbit, and in consequence of this the moons sink into the planets, and the planets into the sun. About ten "intermediate Mercuries" have already become united to the sun, and several "intermediate Marses" to the earth; these the earth first made into moons, then "hauled in." Our present moon was originally the planet Luna, between Mars and the Earth, and Mars will be our last moon.

There is an alternation, therefore, of periods with a moon with moonless "paradise," "lemurian" periods. The Flood was the catastrophe which accompanied the dissolution of the last moon but one, when this went down to earth in a gigantic hailstorm of ice and viscous iron. The equatorial flood-girdle, deprived of the moon's support, streamed away to the poles. Then the flood which, some four thousand years ago, was caused by the capture of our moon of that time — a sort of monstrously swollen flood-tide — made radical changes in the face of the earth. To it were sacrificed the continent of Atlantis between America and Africa, the Easter Island empire in the west of South America, and Lemuria, the broad bridge between East Africa and India. The picture presented by the earth just before the falling-in of a moon is extremely exciting and picturesque. The moon circles four times daily round the earth, enormous in size, hiding a third of the stars. It is never completely day or completely night. The sky is filled with thick ice-clouds and monstrous thunder-storms. Land and sea are covered with the drum-fire of rattling metal meteorites, writhing gas-discharges, and shrieking ice-bombs.

The glacial cosmogony is a catastrophe-theory. It follows from it that, in the biological domain as well, evolution has to be fulfilled in the form of explosive world-risings and world-settings that are quite incompatible with Darwinism. Neither can their thesis be reconciled with Newton's world-picture. No one can of course be forcibly convinced of the correctness of this ice-theory of the world (the art-category to which it belongs is that of didactic poetry), but it may at least have brought it home to us that the world-structure of so-called " classical mechanics " does not exist. In this respect it is in subterranean agreement with the Relativity theory.

What is more, the world of " saga " as a principle of nature-interpretation enters on a fresh lease of life. In the myths of every nation the tale of the " great water " recurs again and again like the refrain of a ballad: in the stories of Noah and Deucalion, among the Chaldeans, the Aztecs, and even the Eskimos. The coincidence of these historical reminiscences, tallying with the doctrines of astrology, is equally striking. There can indeed be hardly any doubt that our history-picture is — behind the historians' backs — preparing to orient itself astrologically.

According to the wisdom of the astrologers, which our time has merely revived, the course of the world's history runs in generations of 2,100 years each, which are determined by the vernal point of the sun and the state of the Signs of the Zodiac. The last era but one was the age of Aries: roughly, that which we call Antiquity. It lasted from 2250 to 150 B.C. At about 150 B.C. there set in the " Pisces " era, which is now drawing to a close. It corresponds to the "Western " epoch. And, in truth, before the end of the second century B.C. the coming of the Saviour began to be expected and the era of Christianity set in — Western Christianity, that is, which in all probability forms but the preparatory stage of

465

true Christianity. Speaking quite broadly, Imperialism and Impressionism, the two dominants which attained their complete and extreme development at the close of the Modern Age, have really been the decisive factors throughout this whole world-era. At the beginning we have the Roman, at the end the Anglo-Saxon domination, but through the whole of the Middle Ages also the leading idea was that of an ecclesiastical and political universal empire. And, similarly, the leading principle of men's conception of the world has always (though with many deviations) been the reproduction of impressions.

We are now on the point of moving over from the constellation of Pisces to that of Aquarius. Now, Aquarius means solitude, introspection, clairvoyance, depth — perspective. It means the end of belief in the primacy of the social, the importance of the surface, the convincingness of proximity, the reality of Reality. For the transition period astrology prophesies a new Hyksos domination such as existed at the turn of the third century B.C. in Egypt when the change occurred from Taurus to Aries. This can only mean Bolshevism.

The decline of history Spengler is certainly no believer in astrology. All the same, his theory of the culture-cycles can only be interpreted astrologically. The hitherto accepted system of the stages in world-history, which in essentials is a system constructed by the Renaissance generation, has certainly been completely shattered by it. The revolution that his new conception achieved is, however, of even greater import. It has shown us that we are incapable of understanding other Cultures at all, and that our own is only one possible form among many. That is why Spengler calls the picture of previous historians " Ptolemaic." The geocentric system was believed in by the Greeks, not because they were "backward," but because it corresponded to their inward life-form. It was on the same ground that the Indian, with his belief in Nirvana, became the inventor of zero, and " Faustian " man, with his urge to infinity, the creator of the Infinitesimal Calculus. For the Babylonians, astrological formulæ were as much a matter of " scientific " conviction as alchemy for the Arab and astronomy and chemistry for us. It is highly probable that the ruins of our wireless masts will one day be as hopelessly baffling as are the remains of Egyptian temples to us, and that our tables of logarithms will be the object of the same purely cultural-historical interest as that which we bestow upon the clay tablets by which the Chaldeans read the auguries of their liver-inspection. All our more modern historical research has considered history only from the standpoint of the Modern Age. From this standpoint we may indeed free ourselves, but from the European, never; we are unable to deal with even the Classical world. History does not exist. We are hopelessly imprisoned in a historical apriorism, which with luck we may comprehend, but never break through. As the Modern Age has just expired, this effort of ours has had the undeserved good fortune of enabling us to contemplate from a standpoint outside this Modern Age. Unfortunately, our faculties for so comprehending it are those of the Modern Age itself. It will therefore be tossed into the pit just as unceremoniously as the object which it describes, by the vast mysterious surge which in our helpless ignorance of its creative significance we speak of negatively as the " Collapse of Reality."

The most distinctive sign that our Rationalistic intermezzo is at an end is the tottering of canonic logic, the " Palladium of Modern Thought." Its creator is Aristotle. (Plato was no logician in the Western sense.) The two foundation pillars on which he constructed it are the *principium contradictionis,* which lays it down that contradictions cannot be thought of together, and the *principium exclusi tertii,* which establishes that there is only A or not-A, a third or intermediate conception being impossible; or, as Aristotle himself puts it: "It is impossible that, to one and the same thing, one and the same predicate both applies and does not apply." These propositions have only a paper validity.

The decline of logic

For all artistic as well as natural thought (indeed, almost all thought) is super-logical; that is to say, symbolic. Under " symbolic " we imply a conception which means something and also, at the same time, something different and (not infrequently) contrary. Entirely unsymbolic thinking is probably not possible even in science; here the scientists are merely deceiving themselves. For thought reigns unlimited only in the world of pure numbers and magnitudes, in the world of tautology, and (as in ball and card games) in the world of pure signs, the world of idiocy.

The Aristotelian logic, which simply confuses *thought* with *grammar,* was accepted without protest by the Romans — whose gifts lay wholly in the direction of jurisprudence and tactics — during the development of Alexandrinism and again during that of Late Scholasticism — products of the decay respectively of Hellenism and of the Gothic culture — and during the whole of the Modern Age. There were already traces of its dissolution in Hegel,

467

however, who was regarded as an extreme Rationalist on account of his misunderstood "*Panlogismus,*" but actually discovered truth in the union of thesis and antithesis; that is, in something irrational. His immortal contribution to epistemology was the establishment, or rather re-establishment, of the *synthetic form of reasoning.* This was in completest contradiction to Aristotle, in that it held that opposites *must* be thought of together, that to do so constituted the very business of thinking, and that between the two members of a contradictory opposition there *is* a third, there is, indeed, *only* this third. " A " alone and " non-A " alone are both wrong. Tertullian thought the same when he said of Christian tenets: " *Credo quia absurdum* "; they are credible *because* they are preposterous, certain *because* they are impossible. The acceptance of absurdity is not a departure from reason, as superficial opinion believed, but merely another form of it, which has the more abundant possibilities of development in that, whereas logical reasoning is only *one* form, the superlogical is a rainbow whose variety of colours is able to reflect all the forms of the mind. The sole supremacy of the syllogism is admissible only from the standpoint of the Positivist, who, whatever one may think of him in other respects, is only a historical speciality. The Twelve Tables Law of the Categories is a reality to the cultural historian only.

Dada   The historical limitation of Rationalism was instinctively recognized by Dadaism, which described it in a manifesto as " middle-class bluff." " Dada " in nursery language amounts to " hobby-horse," and anything more than that this new art-principle certainly was not. It found its classical formula in the saying of Moravagine, the hero of a Dadaistic novel: " *La vie est une chose vraiment idiote.*" This sentiment had, however, already been successfully documented by many an artistic achievement before Dadaism was born. And, generally speaking, one cannot really see in the whole of Expressionism any new tendency, in spite of the thick dust of tumult which it spread around itself. It was revolutionary only in its attitude. It simply replaced the " Im " by an " Ex." Just as Romanticism, for all its acrid polemics against Classicism, was really nothing but a variety of it, so was Expressionism really only a special case of Impressionism — not a birth, but the inevitable self-dissolution of Impressionism and, in the majority of its works, a slovenly caricature of it. It had this in common with Romanticism: that its strong point was its program. The crazy decision just to do everything the

468

other way round is, though undoubtedly entertaining, not of itself alone creative, and when a tendency starts off, not to revive poetry, but to revolutionize poetics, the dialectic of the art, all that emerges is — literature. In this noisy and sterile Opitzism it resembles the first Silesian school of poets; in its would-be spectacular substitution of noise for passion, the second. Further, in its journalistic method of obscuring art by politics and sociology, it reminds us of "Young Germany," and that it was short-lived by comparison with the last-named group is probably owing to its having been denied the martyrdom of suppression which had given the Young Germans a shimmer of picturesqueness. Never before, perhaps, has an intellectual movement which filled a whole generation of youth with enthusiasm flickered out so completely as to leave not a trace.

The terseness of form introduced by the military spirit of the World War was also but an external gesture. By the omission of the article, by inversions and neck-breaking ellipses, the Expressionists sought to achieve concentration, but actually only arrived at a sort of prattling telegraphese. To them, in the highest degree, was applicable what Nietzsche had observed long before: "the young speak, paint, blame, and write . . . too loudly, and at the same time with the dullness and indistinctness that sound has in a vaulted place, where the emptiness gives it such resonance"; "the fear that we might not believe from his figures that they are alive may lead the artist with a declining taste to construct them in such a manner that they appear to be crazy." They are as tiresome with their catchword "*Geist*" as Young Germany with its "*Zeitgeist*." No one talks more about intellect, however, than the unintellectual, no one more of Nature than those remote from Nature. Can one imagine Breughel or Rabelais calling himself a Naturalist, or Nietzsche *not* scorning intellect? On the other hand, Rousseau's "Back to Nature" was nowhere preached more enthusiastically than in decadent Paris salons, while the Naturalist movement of the eighties was born in Berlin beer-cellars and attics. And the infantile, undisciplined dilettantism of the Expressionists was as remote as possible from real intellectuality.

In the domain of the stage, Expressionism completed the catastrophe of drama. The impending was presaged already in the comedies of Bernard Shaw, who plays much the same part in the history of bourgeois drama that Euripides played in the

469

evolutionary history of Greek tragedy. In both it takes the form of dissolving strict dramatic form into philosophy, psychology, essay, discussion; into ambivalence, irony, tragicomedy, relativity. Euripides brings Socratic dialectics, the orator's tribunal, the emancipation of women, and the social problem on to the stage, quite in the Shavian manner. In the *Symposium* we are told that at the end of the feast all who were drunk fell under the table; only Socrates, Agathon, and Aristophanes remained lively, and Socrates proved to the two poets that the writer of tragedy and the writer of comedy must be one and the same person. They, however, were no longer in a condition quite to follow him and occasionally nodded off. But Euripides, who was not one of the party, did understand him and actually created this art-form. The break-up of the theatre is almost always accompanied by another tendency, moving in the opposite direction. It whittles itself down to a meaningless succession of pictures, a display of miscellaneous furnishings, a primitive show-piece. This feature too is parallel in both cases. In the Classical instance we find, corresponding to our cinema and revue, the gladiatorial displays and the " sea-fights," at which, on a stage placed under water, thousands of marines and rowers fought monster battles. As for ourselves, Reinhardt's instinctive genius discovered years ago that the circus is the form of theatre that suits us best.

Expressionism, however, is already beyond drama: it has passed into monodrama, where the scene of action is the soul of the hero — in other words, into pure lyric; nay, it has passed outside of art altogether, for in the main it produces just types, and that is what science is there for. *The* murderer is an object of investigation for jurisprudence, *the* lunatic a representative subject for psychiatry, *the* human being a theme for philosophy, just as *the* monkey belongs to zoology. But art never deals with types, and it individualizes even animals (take Busch or Andersen), although in its highest products it *raises individuals into types* — which is quite another matter. The cause of the break-up of drama (which also, in its way, is a crash of reality) is always to be found in its triumph over naïveté and childlike play-seriousness. One no longer plays *things,* but *with things.* José Ortega, Professor of Metaphysics at Madrid University, and the leader of Spanish youth, says in his very clever book *El Tema de nuestro tiempo:* " Never does art display its magic power more admirably than in self-mockery. For by the very gesture with which it crosses itself

470

out it remains art, and, thanks to its marvellous dialectic, its denial becomes its authentication and its triumph." That is finely put. All the same, it cannot be denied that decay sets in for art when it begins to see through itself. Here, again, Expressionism reminds us of Romanticism. But Ortega goes further still. He proclaims the principle of the "Dehumanizing of Art." "The moderns," he says, "have declared every admixture of the human in art to be tabu. What does this loathing for the human in art signify? Is it loathing for humanness in general, for reality, for life? Or can it be precisely the opposite: respect for life, and reluctance to see it confused with art, with so subaltern a thing as art?" Again very finely put. But from the "subaltern" standpoint of the artist it is art's admission of bankruptcy.

And indeed the deeper source of Futurism does seem to have lain in the effort to relieve a sort of suicidal instinct, and that in *all* domains of art. When the atonalists announced that melody was no longer bound to harmony, and the jazz band introduced cow-bells, motor-horns, and toy trumpets as musical instruments; when dancing turned into an idiotic walking; when "absolute plastic" aimed only at the rhythm of an object, and Cubism at purely geometric forms, when "absolute painting" would tolerate only "subjectless" pictures, and "constructivism" only engineers' buildings, and when the still life displayed in our exhibitions came to consist only of wire, wheels, wooden lids, rags of cloth, and newspaper cuttings (a symbol of the general "power"-izing of existence), the point was in every case the same.

We have pointed out on various occasions that painting is nearly always the earliest as well as the strongest expression of the feeling of the age. It was the same on this occasion also, and that is why Expressionism cannot be dismissed in painting as simply as it can in literature. What it wanted is fairly clear. In his program-pamphlet *Einblick in Kunst* Herwarth Walden says: "We feel music, but cannot understand it. It moves us, convinces us, but it expresses nothing, tells us nothing. And painting, too, can only be realized in this way. We have never heard these tones, this combination of tones, in the world of facts. Why must we have seen the combination of colour and form in order to be moved or convinced? So say the artists who produce expression instead of impression"; "the artist has to paint a picture and not a mood; further, the creation of an ox is a matter for oxen and

Suicide of art

471

not for the painter"; "the critic thinks a picture beautiful if it reminds him of Rembrandt, but a picture is only beautiful if it reminds one of no picture at all: otherwise what is it but a copy?" Perspective, too, succumbed to the iconoclasts, and, indeed, it is the fact (though it has been overlooked for centuries) that the laws governing the modern mode of picturing cannot by any means claim that character of canonic validity with which we used to credit them as a matter of course. They are only binding on the arbitrary assumption that a painting is there for the standpoint of a single observer, as his illusion. This is the optics of the photographic lens, the peep-hole theatre, and the realism of the theatre — the very art-form which, as we have seen, is most representatively bourgeois. Greek painting before Pericles still gave equal height to figures placed one behind the other. The Egyptians represented the sequence in *time* on their reliefs, and this, as we know, is what Expressionism tries to do; as absolute synchronization does not exist, it has no qualms about inverting this fact of knowledge and putting two non-synchronous events in the same picture. In a sense, therefore, it is painted Relativity. The peculiar doggedness, too, with which it gave the preference to slanting and crooked lines, so that its landscapes and town views look like photographs that have gone askew, has probably some connexion with Relativity and Relativity's triumph over Euclid's parallel axiom — hence the house-fronts are always on the point of collapse, and the whole of space in a state of insurrection against the plane and the straight. But for choice it paints split-off partial ideas, which lead a mysterious existence apart, and flings incomprehensible symbols into reality to burst; and it coordinates without scruple the concrete and the imaginary so that its pictures give the impression of a hunch-backed occult dream-world. In a sense, therefore, it is painted psycho-analysis.

The history of the development of modern painting crystallizes around one great principal theme: the conveying of movement. This problem dominates the whole art of painting from Rembrandt to Marc. The Renaissance did not yet seek movement, it did not even know of such a problem. It was the Baroque artists who first tried to portray movement, and that in the only possible way: by *indistinctness*. Classicism screwed itself forcibly back to the "rigid system," thereby proving itself retrogressive and a positive calamity to modern development. Impressionism took up the problem again with the greatest vigour. To us Impressionist pictures seem a matter of course, but people in the eighties felt literally their heads swim before a picture like Degas's " Rehearsal for the Ballet," for instance, just as we become giddy at the sight of a painting like Severini's glorious " Pan-Pan Dance " (a model work of Expressionism, or, rather, Late Impressionism). In Impressionism every new phase differs from the preceding one by a *plus* in the mobility of seeing. The optics of Impressionism's Monet phase, for example, stands in relation to that of the old régime as the theory of mechanical heat, which regards the phenomenon of heat as the lightning movement of minute masses, to the phlogiston theory of the eighteenth century, which explains the process of heating by the addition of " heating matter " — a doubtless more static and, so to say, more comfortable conception. But Expressionism corresponds to the new atomic theory, which no longer believes in masses, but only in dynamic — one might almost say, supernatural — charges. It need hardly be said that it is not by accident that Expressionism is the contemporary of the cinema, aviation, chemical warfare, and radium (of which one may say that it is perpetual motion actualized). Somewhere in all this — how this will and can happen we are not yet able to imagine — the dissolution of painting lies latent and waiting.

In the mean time, as everyone knows, Expressionism has been superseded by *Sur-réalisme*. One would rather like to know wherein the " *sur* " consists, for according to the program of this movement, the artist is to be nothing but a " registering apparatus," a " receptacle " of his impressions, and this is simply a reversion to the first phase of Impressionism, which we have described in the previous chapter. In painting, this school calls itself also the " new objectivity," and here again one wonders wherein the new consists, for its static is a pure inversion of the dynamic principle which embodies Impressionism and Expressionism alike, a doublet of pre-Impressionist Realism, say of Biedermeier. Occasionally " *Sur-réalisme* " calls itself " magical Realism." As a whole-hearted Impressionist, I for one fail to discover its magical quality. It attempts a compromise between the abstraction of Expressionism and the introjection of Impressionism. This sort of wisdom of the *juste milieu* has never yet made an epoch in art-history. It is a reaction in the fullest sense of the word: that is, not only a throw-back, but a step back — which, as we have seen, is no novelty in the development of modern painting. Carstens, Genelli, Cornelius signified a retrogression to behind Rococo, just

473

as Puvis de Chavannes, Moreau, and their pupils sought to put the clock back to Pre-Impressionism. The Nazarenes actually succeeded in wiping out the Cinquecento and wedging themselves back into the Early Renaissance — though a similar attempt by the Pre-Raphaelites did not succeed, as, fortunately, they were highly decadent and complicated cosmopolitans. The Sur-realists would naturally retort that they were neither reactionaries nor copyists of an earlier art-form, but that their Realism differed from all former Realisms in that it had gone through the stage of Expressionism. This certainly is so, and quite inevitably, for Haeckel's "biogenetic principle" applies also to art-history; everything that the human mind has wished, thought, or imagined is stored up within us, and we have to retain it whether we will or no. It remains true, nevertheless, that on all these attempts at forced archaization there lies the blight of sterility. Thorwaldsen wanted to emulate Phidias, and Schnorr Perugino. But the only effect of this "wanting" was to make them far worse artists than their models and not even as good as they might have been themselves. They had forgotten that these artists, instead of looking behind their age, had hurried on ahead of it; that the future spoke out of Perugino's brush, and that Phidias was so exasperatingly modern that the Athenians poisoned him. One cannot help suspecting that the "new objectivity" is yet another of those plaster Classicisms which return from time to time like a "White Lady" to pester European humanity. In his excellent book *Nachexpressionismus* Franz Roh says: "The newest painting seeks to achieve a model presentation, a picture of the absolutely finished, completed, constructed, through and through, in opposition to life, which is eternally fragmentary and forms itself only in tatters." Is this not a truly Classicist outlook? By this tendency to the round, the worked-out, the reposing in itself, Post-Expressionist pictures have a certain soothing firmness, a refreshing clearness as of glass, a cleanness of filigree, and in this sense remind us of masterly maps or first-class children's books. Here we have art completely degraded, or elevated, to a splendid toy — which agrees entirely with the above-mentioned theory of Ortega. As far as we can judge from its manifestations up to date, Post-Expressionism seems to be no more than the expression of an artistic state of exhaustion: the arts of all nations are copied, from that of the spry Japanese to that of the stodgy Ethiopians, and all the European styles from the Cretan to the Victorian are recapitulated.

The only legitimate style of the Modern Age — Impressionism — has exhausted all its possibilities, and for the first time in history, perhaps, man stands overwhelmed before the question: has art any meaning at all?

In the history of costume, too, one possibly unique event has taken place during the post-war period: a form of men's dress was created which was avoided by good society: no " gentleman " has ever worn a belted coat and padded shoulders. Here we have a small but speaking proof of the unreality of our incubation period: fashion, one of the most real of the earth's forces, does not exist.

We have already mentioned the cinema as a correlate of Expressionism. It was invented by the end of the nineteenth century, but only achieved world-supremacy a decade later. It has the same significance in our life as the silhouette for Late Rococo, and the panorama for the Second Empire. At first it looked as if a new art-form were coming out of it, but this illusion was merely the consequence of its dumbness. Imagination, even in the soberest and most limited of men, is a hundred times more thrilling and picturesque than all the spoken words in the world. The finest and deepest verse comes nowhere near expressing what the simplest of the " gods " feels *inarticulately*. As long as the cinema was dumb, it had other than film possibilities: namely, spiritual ones. But the sound-film has unmasked it, and the fact is patent to all eyes and ears that we are dealing with a brutish dead machine. The bioscope kills the human gesture only, but the sound-film the human voice as well. Radio does the same. At the same time it frees us from the obligation to concentrate, and it is now possible to enjoy Mozart and sauerkraut, the Sunday sermon and bridge. Both cinema and radio eliminate that mysterious fluid which emanates from artist and public alike, making of every concert, every lecture, a unique spiritual experience. The human voice has achieved omnipresence, the human gesture eternity, but at the cost of the soul. It is the Tower of Babel: " And the Lord said: Go to, let us go down, and there confound their language, that they may not understand one another's speech." We already have nightingale concerts and Papal speeches transmitted to us by wireless. Here indeed is the " Decline of the West."

There are no realities any more, there is only apparatus. It is a world of automata, conceived in the brain of a malicious and crazy Doctor Miracle. Neither are there goods any more, but only advertisement: the most valuable article is the one most effectively

The Tower of Babel

The two hydras

475

lauded, the one that the most capital has gone to advertise. We call all this Americanism. As well might we call it Bolshevism, for, alike in the political and social domain, the situation over the whole of our planet shows itself to be menaced on both sides by a Medusa-like will to annihilate, of which the executive forces in the East and the West merely bear different names. Both are embodiments of the same materialistic Nihilism, and both are doomed to perish by the nemesis of self-destruction.

In Russia and in America this same worship of technics and scorn of ideology prevail. Bolshevism speaks from out of the machine as the " visible God," preaches the " Imitation of the Machine " instead of the " Imitation of Christ," and regards outstanding individuals like Lenin as " especially powerful screws." It persecutes not only Monotheism in all its forms, but also every variety of teleology, psychology, Vitalism, indeterminism, and historical-philosophy; for any belief in aims, soul, vital spirit, free will, worldly reason, or anything with any sort of meaning it quite correctly regards as disguised religion. This is Positivism in the simplest and chemically purest form. In its foreign policy the Soviet Union is precisely as imperialistic as the West. One of its memoranda contains the words: " Persia is the Suez Canal of the Revolution." But it wants Afghanistan too, and Manchuria. Mongolia it has already swallowed up. It is very unlikely that the border states of Finland, Esthonia, Latvia, Lithuania, and Poland will not experience at the hands of Russia the same treatment as the buffer states of Lorraine, Burgundy, and Franche-Comté received in their day from France. As to home policy, Bolshevism is merely a " Left " Tsarism complete with Terror, Siberia, Tcheka (exactly corresponding to the former Okrana), a Draconic censorship, an Index, an extremely intolerant state religion (with Marxian Materialism replacing Orthodoxy), and a million-headed bureaucracy as idle as it is corrupt. And all this " for the good of the people," just as the " Little Father " Tsar used to say. In general the whole system is merely the logical continuation of Petrinism; a cruel experiment undertaken by a few Westernized Russians, which may be compared to the inoculation of unfortunate test-animals with foreign blood-substances. Not a single idea in Bolshevism is authentically Russian; everything in it is taken from the world-picture of the detested " bourgeois."

On the other hand the American monopoly system of gigantic trusts, syndicates, and cartels bears a notable resemblance to State

Socialism. There is a congruence also, in spite of apparent divergence, between the American and the Soviet economic outlook, in that both countries treat economics as, not a necessary evil, but an aim in itself and a thing of vital significance. Common to America and Bolshevism, too, are the elimination of the soul from social relations, the infernal device "Time is Money" (there is a "Time League" in Russia too, which sets before its members the duty of exploiting time to the utmost), and the absolute mechanization of work. In both countries the Taylor system prevails, in which the stop-watch is called in to settle the conditions in which a movement can be carried out in the shortest time possible. As this turns the worker into a replaceable machine-part, he thereby becomes even in peace time "human material" and, whether he is exploited by Capitalism or squeezed by Communism, an utter dependent.

The official Soviet philosophy is the "reflexology" which Professor Pavlov founded in St. Petersburg before the Revolution. It is completely covered by the American philosophy of "Behaviourism," whose originator is John Watson. One sentence comprises the whole of this: there is only doing, "mind is what body does"; and the conclusions that emerge are that consciousness = mechanico-chemical reactions; thought = language-habits; will = a chain of actions, a behaviour-cycle. Jacques Loeb, an admirable chemist, became interested in observing the "heliotropism" of the aphis (this foreign word is used to indicate the fact that it likes to get into the sun, a principle familiar to every child through the attraction of moths to light) and conceived the idea of making other varieties of lice heliotropic by the injection of acids. In this he was completely successful, and the only question is whether they would not have made for the sun even without the effect of the acids. In any case he arrived at the conclusion that that which we call "ideas" can be traced to internal secretions. The proof of this was completed to watertightness by Pavlov's demonstration that the reverse would also hold good. In his experiments on animals he induced saliva secretions by optical and acoustical signals and was able, by tireless research, to confirm beyond challenge that dogs, on being shown a ham bone, produced gastric juice and that their mouths also watered at the sight. On such scientific experiments does the Chicago school spend its time! If, as is said, Behaviourism and Reflexology are really the standard confessions of faith in their countries of origin, this sad fact would mean that in the Eastern and the Western hemispheres respectively a vast people has become mentally deranged.

The five possibilities There are just these five possibilities: that (1) America will triumph materially, which would mean world-domination by the United States and, at the end of this interim empire, the fall of the West through over-technicalization; (2) America will triumph spiritually by becoming sublimated, this implying the rebirth of Germany, whence alone this sublimation could be derived; (3) the East will triumph materially, bringing about world-Bolshevism and the interim reign of Antichrist; (4) the East will triumph spiritually, reviving Christianity through the Russian soul; and (5) the fifth eventuality is — chaos. These five possibilities present themselves, and no others, whether political, ethical, or psychological. It will, however, be clear, we hope, to the intelligent reader that none of these eventualities will materialize. For world-history is not an equation, not even one with several solutions. Its only real possibility is the unreal, and its only causality irrationality. It is made by a higher mind than the human.

Meta-psychology In our first volume it was shown at some length how Late Scholasticism so strained the mediæval principle of anti-rationality that its point was imperceptibly altered. Similarly Bolshevism has driven the world-conception of modern Positivism to such extremes that (in the very sense of the Marxian negation of negation in which it so fervently believes) this conception has been forced to turn itself into its opposite. For such an ultramaterialism would, if it held, amount to the utter and profound overthrow of reality. For, obviously, if there were only matter, there would be nothing. If there were no world of ideas, no soul, no world-meaning, then humanity, finding that its whole development had been on a basis of error, would have no course left but suicide. But even within the frame of our decaying forms of apperception — scientific experiment and rational syllogistic — it can be proved that the unreal soul is the true reality.

We allude, of course, to the facts of para- or meta-psychology, disputed now only by ignorant professors and hidebound freethinkers (the semi-educated world, that is). These facts shared the same fate in their day as the phenomena of hypnosis, which on its discovery was likewise denounced alternately as impudent swindling, blind self-deception, silly fashion, pretentiousness, and childishness; whereas today it already comes under the criminal

478

code — and what higher recognition could there be? The most important phenomena in this domain are: telepathy, which is the transmission of spiritual conditions without the agency of our organs of sense-expression; second sight, which is the gift of recognizing apparitions at long distances, and (as applied to time) of making it possible to read past and future; psychoscopy, which is the capacity to give the origin — one might say, the biography — of unknown objects; telekinesis, the movement of a body by remote control; apport, by which an object is made to move about of its own act, even to passing through closed rooms; levitation, or raising from the ground; materialization and ghost-phenomena. All these are mere provisional terms, inaccurate shots at a great unknown, none of them calling for explanation any more than the expressions "attraction" and "induction" in physics. In this connexion we may mention the school of Coué, which has built up a whole system of psychotherapy and biotics on a belief in the power of suggestion, and we may recall also Schleich's theory of the "thought-power of hysteria," which he sums up as follows: "To support Plato's assertion that the creative Idea of the world must have preceded its actual appearance, there is one and only one factual experience: namely, the symptoms-complex of hysteria. For here the diseased imagination — that is, an over-developed idea — leads to structural alterations in the body which signify a newly-created substance." Or, as Prentice Mulford very neatly puts it, according to the nature of our day-dreams we pile up gold or explosives in our interior. Surely that sounds like Freud. Is, then, Freud a metaphysician? Yes, but he does not know it.

The reckoning between *this* "poet" and his age is particularly difficult to decipher. It must, however, be said in any case that he belongs with the great transformers of reality.

Psycho-analysis has one catastrophal defect: namely, the psycho-analysts, whose elaborations represent a mixture of the Talmud and bachelor reading. The Americans call psycho-analysis, in contrast to Christian Science, "Jewish science." And indeed that *odium generis humani,* of which the Jews were already accused by the Classical world, seems to have become vocal once more. Its aim is quite undisguisedly the vilification and dedivinizing of the world. "With the Jews," said Nietzsche, "begins the Servile Insurrection in moral." And with psycho-analysis begins the Servile Insurrection of amorality. What should really

The Servile Insurrection of amorality

479

be done is to psycho-analyse psycho-analysis. Its conception grew out of the domination-desire of the neurotic, who seeks to bring humanity into subjection by assimilating it to himself. This he does because of a transference-neurosis, which objectifies its own hypertrophied libido-complex as " world," and because of an instinctive hatred of the content of religious consciousness which the adept of the " Jewish science " would like to eliminate in all his fellow-creatures, knowing that, as a Jew — which means, as a typical *homo irreligiosus* — he cannot compete with " the others " in this sphere. In short, it is, to borrow from Nietzsche once more, " a parasite's attack, a vampirism of pale underground blood-suckers "; a grandiose attempt at infection, a stealthy act of revenge by those who have got the worst of it: the whole world is to be neuroticized, sexualized, diabolized. Psycho-analysis proclaims the advent of Satan's kingdom. Perhaps the proclamation is true. Perhaps we are really in for an interim reign of the Devil, whose adorers, as the student of the Black Mass knows, worship his phallus and his posterior as the supreme sanctities. It is, to quote Nietzsche for the third time, " a Jewish transvaluation of all values."

The Orpheus from the Underworld   Psycho-analysis is in truth a sect, with all the signs and symbols of one — rites and ceremonies, exorcisms and cathartic consultations, oracle and mantic, settled symbolism and dogmatism, secret doctrine and popular edition, proselytes and renegades, priests who are subjected to tests, and daughter sects which damn each other in turn. Just as the whale, though a mammal, poses as a fish, so psycho-analysis, actually a religion, poses as a science. This religion is Pagan in character: it embraces nature-worship, demonology, chthonian belief in the depths, Dionysiac sex-idolization. This connexion of religion with therapy, hygiene, and the interpretation of dreams existed in the ancient world also, as, for example, the healing sleep for the sick in the temples of Asklepios. And we have here a seer and singer working for the powers of darkness in most enticing tones, an Orpheus from the Underworld: it is a new world-wide revolt against the Gospel.

That the founder of psycho-analysis has done a few extraordinarily useful things no one will deny. In the first place he knocked the bottom, not only out of Behaviourism, but out of the whole Positivist psychology, by revealing the enormous part played by the unconscious. Further, the decisive importance that he attaches to the power of the word — the creative Logos — is

480

an unequivocal admission of the supremacy of the spiritual over the physical. A new and extremely useful orientation is offered, too, by the discovery that the experiences of the infancy period of life are determinant of direction, as also by his extremely penetrating investigations into that mysterious linked system of suppressions, and particularly the failures — self-promises, self-interrogations, forgetfulnesses — which dominate our daily life. Of epoch-making significance, too, is the establishment of the fact that every person is a neurotic, and every neurotic a pervert and invert: that is, not only cultural man, but equally, or perhaps in an even higher degree, the " primitive " — this incidentally providing a refutation of Rousseauism. Here we have a complex of knowledge-elements, which serves as an admirable working hypothesis. But the futile, morbid, and disgraceful exaggerations of the school have degraded it from a blessing into a torment for the whole of that not inconsiderable proportion of mankind in which the neurosis never oversteps the latent stage and forms only a sort of " regulative idea " of the soul. Above all, Freud achieved a sort of therapy by liberation for a whole age by revealing the Œdipus-complex, the " core-complex of all neurotics." By making this complex manifest, and thereby almost harmless, he psycho-analysed a whole generation. As regards the interpretation of dreams, I am inclined to lay no very great stress on this particular piece of theoretical structure, though it has perhaps contributed the most to Freud's fame. For its few weight-carrying principles are weakened by overloading, and it tends to lose itself in a morose and abstruse scholasticism which sees more harm than good. In this I agree with Shaw, who said that he had always been greatly interested in his dreams till he made the acquaintance of psycho-analysis, after which he had attached no further importance to them. Meanwhile, though fully conscious that I am thereby exposing myself as the victim of a Freud-complex (a " negative transfer " of feelings to the doctor), I venture to raise one or two more objections.

The first of these is so obvious that it has often been made. That every person, including the so-called normal one, very often finds himself in a state of fear-neurosis we are all ready to believe: possibly the whole of life is a fear-neurosis. But that this arises purely from abnormal events in the sexual libido and is nothing but its transformation-product — bearing (as Freud himself with great intuition expresses it) the same relation to it as vinegar to

The dogmas of psycho-analysis

481

wine — is not probable. Keeping the metaphor, it may be said that not all vinegar is an offspring of wine. This pan-sexuality is simply an assertion that maintains itself because it cannot be refuted. But here we already have the false conclusion which is sustained all through psycho-analysis: the neurotic — and the exceptionally difficult neurotic case at that — is hypostasized as the archetype of humanity. Even more untenable in its sweepingness is the psycho-analytical dogma that every dream is a wish-dream, or (as Freud again very happily formulates it) that the optative becomes the present in a dream. Certainly, in his later writings, Freud has admitted other motives in a few cases which could obviously not be classed with the wish-dreams, as, for instance, the "repetition-compulsion" when a person dreams regularly of a railway accident. But it is probably not too much to say that quite half of the total of dreams are not wish-dreams at all: how, otherwise, could we account for the "school examination" dream, for example, or the dream that every actor has had of not knowing his part? The fact that one often dreams of the death of some beloved being is naturally explained by psycho-analysis as latent parent-hatred, but such an interpretation could be strained to include one's aunt or one's chief. But animal-lovers have such dreams too, and in the case of horses, dogs, and cats an Œdipus-complex is really rather a far-fetched notion. Then there are the thousand and one most undesirable situations in which our dream-imagination vies in malignant inventiveness with Wilhelm Busch (admittedly, psycho-analysis interprets them all by sexual symbolism). All of these are manifestly fear-dreams, and it is incomprehensible that Freud, who gives such a prominent place to the fear-neurosis in the spiritual life, should grudge it that prominence in this important domain. Nevertheless, here, as in all other questions, it is impossible to convict the psycho-analysts of a false diagnosis, as they are such adepts in refuting all criticism by means of the catchwords with which they make play — terms like "ambivalent," "inverted," "symbolic," "repressed," "transferred," "sublimated." The convincingness of the argumentation here rests on the assumption that the pettifogging verbal quibble is the organizing principle of all spiritual life, and that the dream-god is of the Mosaic confession.

The repressed thing-in-itself   But Wundt's law of the "heterogeneity of purposes" had already been applied to the founder of Mosaism, and it appears likely to fulfil itself in Freud also. Moses led his people for forty

482

years through the wilderness, seeking the promised land, without suspecting that it was just the purification by wandering that was the goal, and that that in itself was the promised land. With Freud it has been much the same, but the other way round. He set out on a pilgrimage of forty years, believing it to be the goal when it was only a wandering through the wilderness; then one day, involuntarily, he stumbled on the promised land. But he understood the ways of the Lord as little as Moses did.

At the beginning of the Modern Age stands Descartes, who recognized nothing but the *clara et distincta perceptio* and accordingly declared man, quite logically, to be an automaton. At the end of the Modern Age stands Freud, who, still by purely Cartesian methods, arrives at the notion of the soul as a mysterious, incomprehensible thing whose outlying spurs alone rear their heads in our three-dimensional empiricism. To Descartes, the life of the soul expresses itself exhaustively in those manifestations which lie in the day-bright cone of light radiated by *clara ratio;* Freud asserts that this sun-world of pure thought is only a minor fragment of our psychical cosmos. And here Leibniz, the inventor of "unconscious, dormant conceptions," speaks as a voice from the grave; here again that perpetual *revenant,* the spirit of Kant, reappears to tell us that this daylight is only apparent, the reflex of a real being that lies darkly hidden from our consciousness, the mere phenomenon of an irrational reality.

Psycho-analysis is a system of Irrationalism founded by Rationalistic methods; a Transcendentalism constructed by an extreme Bolshevist. In the centre of Freud's latest conception stands the theory of the " It." This is sent into consciousness as its representative by conscience, the exercise of moral censorship, the super-ego, the representation of our parental relation, the inheritor of the Œdipus-complex. That which we call a " sense of guilt " arises from the tension between the ego and the ego-ideal. " Besides the ego we recognize another spiritual domain, more comprehensive, magnificent, and obscure than the ego, and this we call the " It " . . . 'it went through me,' we say, or ' there was something in me that at that moment was stronger than I.' . . . Here the I lies between the reality and the It, which is the actual spirituality." At this point psycho-analysis penetrates deep into the occult. Can it be possible that this has escaped Freud? It has not escaped him; he has merely repressed it.

That which Freud calls the conscience-censorship is nothing

but Kant's " moral reason," the essential thing about this being that it holds the supremacy over our " cognitive reason." Freud's super-ego is the Kantian " intelligible ego," on which our empirical ego depends. This intelligible character of ours is, although the root of all empiricism, not in itself empirical, not capable of being experienced. It works deep down in the inward darkness and is of the essence of that mysterious power which reigns behind the external world also. The " It " is the Thing-in-itself. The " It " is not in time, not in space, neither is it subject to any physiological or physical causality. Our empirical ego is subject to coercion; our " It," our intelligible I, is free. The " It " or Thing-in-itself is the sole reality, just because it never appears and never can appear in reality.

The light from the other side
Experimental psychology and experimental physics arrive at the same result. The soul is super-real, matter is sub-real. Simultaneously, however, there appears a faint gleam of light from the other side.

The next chapter of European cultural history will be the history of this light.

CHRONOLOGY

1815   Decisions of Vienna Congress. The Hundred Days. Waterloo. The Holy Alliance. Birth of Bismarck

1817   Wartburg Festival. Byron: *Manfred*

1818   First transoceanic steamship

1819   Murder of Kotzebue; Karlsbad Resolutions. Schopenhauer: *Welt als Wille und Vorstellung*. Goethe: *West-östlicher Divan*. Guéricault: *Floss der Medusa*

1820   Oersted: Electro-magnetism

1821   Death of Napoleon. Birth of Dostoievski. Weber: *Freischütz*. Saint-Simon: *Du système industriel*. Seebeck: thermo-electricity

1822   Empire of Brazil. Beethoven: *Missa solemnis*. Delacroix: " Dante "

1823   Monroe Doctrine

1824   Death of Louis XVIII; Charles X. Death of Byron. Beethoven: *Ninth Symphony*. Delacroix: " Massacre of Chios "

1825   Death of Alexander I; Nicholas I. First railway

1826   Death of C. M. von Weber. Eichendorff: *Aus dem Leben eines Taugenichts*. Manzoni: *I promessi sposi*. Johannes Müller: specific sense-energies

1827   Battle of Navarino. Death of Beethoven. Heine: *Buch der Lieder*. Victor Hugo: *Cromwell*. Ohm's Law. Baer: the mammal egg

1828   Death of Schubert. Death of Goya. Birth of Tolstoi. Birth of Ibsen. Auber: *Muette de Portici*. Wöhler: synthesis of urea

1829   Peace of Adrianople. Rossini: *Guillaume Tell*

1830   The July Revolution; Louis Philippe. Separation of Belgium from Holland. Greek Declaration of Independence. Polish Insurrection. Comte: *Cours de philosophie positive*, I. Pushkin: *Eugene Onegin*

1831   Battle of Ostrolenka. Death of Hegel. Meyerbeer:

485

Robert le Diable. Hugo: *Notre Dame de Paris*. Faraday: magneto-electricity

1832   Hambach Festival. Parliamentary reform in England. Death of Scott. Death of Goethe: publication of *Faust*, II

1833   Frankfurt *Putsch*. Founding of German Zollverein. Bopp: *Vergleichende Grammatik des Sanscrit*. Raimund: *Der Verschwender*. Nestroy: *Lumpazivagabundus*. Gauss-Weber: telegraph

1835   Death of Francis I. First German railway. D. F. Strauss: *Leben Jesu*. G. Büchner: *Dantons Tod*

1836   Morse telegraph. Gogol: *Revisor*

1837   Accession of Queen Victoria; separation of Hanover from England. Death of Leopardi

1839   Schwann: cell-theory. Daguerre: photography. Stendhal: *La Chartreuse de Parme*

1840   Death of Frederick William III; Frederick William IV. Opium war. Schumann's "*Liederjahr*." Carlyle: *On Heroes*. Penny post

1841   Straits Convention. Feuerbach: *Wesen des Christentums*. Hebbel: *Judith*

1842   Robert Mayer: Law of Energy

1843   Wagner: *The Flying Dutchman*

1844   Birth of Nietzsche. Liebig: *Chemische Briefe*. Beginning of the Munich *Fliegende Blätter*

1845   Wagner: *Tannhäuser*. Stirner: *Der Einzige und sein Eigentum*

1846   Repeal of the Corn Laws in England. Cracow becomes Austrian. First submarine telegraph. The planet Neptune

1847   The Sonderbund War in Switzerland. Emerson: *Representative Men*

1848   The February Revolution in Paris. The March Revolution in Germany. Accession of Francis Joseph I. The Pre-Raphaelite Brotherhood. *Kladderadatsch*. Communist Manifesto

1849   Novara. Világos

1850   Olmütz. Death of Balzac

1851   Louis Napoleon's *coup d'état*. First World Exhibition

1852   Napoleon III. London Protocol. Dumas *fils*: *La Dame aux camélias*

1853   Outbreak of the Crimean War. Keller: *Der grüne Heinrich*. Ludwig: *Der Erbförster*

1854	Mommsen: *Roman History*
1855	Death of Nicholas I; Alexander II. Freytag: *Soll und Haben*. L. Büchner: *Kraft und Stoff*
1856	Peace of Paris. Birth of Shaw
1857	Baudelaire: *Fleurs du mal*. Flaubert: *Madame Bovary*
1858	Goncharov: *Oblomov*. Offenbach: *Orphée aux enfers*
1859	Magenta. Solferino. Darwin: *Origin of Species*. Spectrum analysis. Gounod: *Faust*
1860	Death of Schopenhauer. Fechner: *Psychophysik*
1861	Outbreak of American Civil War. Italy a kingdom. *Tannhäuser* in Paris
1862	Death of Frederick William IV; William I. Bismarck becomes minister-president. Hebbel: *Nibelungen*. Flaubert: *Salammbô*
1863	Renan: *Vie de Jésus*. Taine: *Histoire de la littérature anglaise*
1864	Danish War. Offenbach: *La Belle Hélène*
1865	End of the American Civil War; murder of Lincoln. Wagner: *Tristan*. Dühring: *Wert des Lebens*. Busch: *Max und Moritz*
1866	Custozza. Königgrätz. Lissa
1867	North German Federation. Execution of the Emperor Maximilian. Marx: *Das Kapital*. Dostoievski: " Raskolnikov." Ibsen: *Brand*
1868	Wagner: *Meistersinger*. Haeckel: *Natürliche Schöpfungsgeschichte*
1869	Opening of Suez Canal. Hartmann: *Philosophie des Unbewussten*
1870	Dogma of Infallibility. Ems telegram. Sedan. Third French Republic. Death of Dickens. Beginning of the excavations in Troy
1871	Proclamation of the German Emperor. Paris Commune. Peace of Frankfurt. Darwin: *Descent of Man*. Zola: *Les Rougon-Macquart*, I. Busch: *Fromme Helene*
1872	D. F. Strauss: *Der alte und der neue Glaube*. Daudet: *Tartarin*
1873	The great crash. Maxwell: electro-magnetic theory of light
1874	Van't Hoff: stereochemistry
1875	Culmination of the *Kulturkampf*. Bizet: *Carmen*. Taine: *L'Ancien Régime*

1876	Bayreuth. Indian Empire
1877	Russo-Turkish War. Gobineau: *La Renaissance*
1878	Peace of San Stefano; Congress of Berlin. "Socialist Law." Wagner: *Parsifal*
1879	Dual Alliance. Ibsen: *A Doll's House*. Birth of Einstein
1880	Death of Flaubert
1881	French in Tunis. Murder of Alexander II; Alexander III. Death of Dostoievski. Ibsen: *Ghosts*
1882	British in Egypt. Death of Emerson. Wildenbruch: *Karolinger*. Koch: tuberculosis bacillus
1883	Triple Alliance. Death of Wagner. Death of Marx. Nietzsche: *Zarathustra*
1884	Ibsen: *The Wild Duck*. Fabian Society.
1885	Serbo-Bulgarian War. Death of Hugo
1886	Nietzsche: *Jenseits von Gut und Böse*
1887	Reinsurance Treaty. Antoine: Théâtre Libre
1888	Death of William I and of Frederick III; William II. Sudermann: *Die Ehre*. Fontane: *Irrungen, Wirrungen*
1889	Freie Bühne. Holz-Schlaf: *Papa Hamlet*. Strindberg: *Der Vater*. Richard Strauss: *Don Juan*. Hauptmann: *Vor Sonnenaufgang*. Liliencron: *Gedichte*
1890	Dismissal of Bismarck. Zanzibar Treaty. *Rembrandt als Erzieher*. Wilde: *The Picture of Dorian Gray*. Wedekind: *Frühlings Erwachen*. Hamsun: *Hunger*. Maeterlinck: *Princesse Maleine*. Mascagni: *Cavalleria rusticana*
1891	Franco-Russian Alliance
1892	Hauptmann: *Die Weber*. Maeterlinck: *Pelléas et Mélisande*. Behring: diphtheria serum
1893	Hauptmann: *Hanneles Himmelfahrt*. Schnitzler: *Anatol*
1894	Death of Alexander III; Nicholas II
1895	Peace of Shimonoseki. Fontane: *Effie Briest*. Shaw: *Candida*. Röntgen: X-rays
1896	Altenberg: *Wie ich es sehe*. Bergson: *Matière et mémoire*. Marconi: wireless telegraphy
1897	Greco-Turkish War
1898	Death of Bismarck; *Gedanken und Erinnerungen*. Fashoda crisis. Spanish-American War. P. and M. Curie: radium
1899	Shaw: *Cæsar and Cleopatra*. Ibsen: *When We Dead Awaken*
1900	Death of Nietzsche. Freud: *Traumdeutung*

1901	Thomas Mann: *Buddenbrooks*. Death of Victoria; Edward VII
1902	Death of Zola
1903	Weininger: *Geschlecht und Charakter*
1904	Entente Cordiale. Wedekind: *Büchse der Pandora.*
1905	Separation of Norway and Sweden. Battle of Mukden. Naval Battle of Tsushima. Peace of Portsmouth. Einstein's special theory of Relativity. H. Mann: *Professor Unrat*
1906	Algeciras Conference. Death of Ibsen. Richard Strauss: *Salome*
1907	St. Petersburg Treaty
1908	Annexation crisis. Death of Wilhelm Busch
1909	Blériot: cross-channel flight
1910	Death of Edward VII; George V. Portugal becomes a republic. Death of Tolstoi
1911	Morocco crisis. Tripolitan War
1912	First Balkan War. China becomes a republic. Death of Strindberg
1913	Second Balkan War
1914	Outbreak of the World War

INDEX

xv

xvi

262, 264–5; II, 45, 165, 250, 353; III, 442

Nachexpressionismus (Roh), III, 474

Nachlass (Nietzsche), III, 390

Nachsommer (Stifter), III, 234

Nachtlage von Granada (Kreutzer), III, 53

Nägeli, Hans, III, 53

Nägeli, Karl Wilhelm, III, 185, 193

Nagler, III, 77

Nantes, Edict of, I, 312; II, 87

Napier, John, I, 327

Napoleon I, I, 13, 26, 62, 66, 192, 307; II, 9, 77, 90, 131, 136, 179, 180, 182, 213, 269, 286, 295, 330, 370, 371, 387, 389, 395, 429, 430, 431, 433, 435, 436, 438–49; III, 20, 23, 25, 26, 28, 54, 79, 86, 87, 155, 158, 264–5, 351, 352, 364, 399, 447–8

Napoleon II, III, 154

Napoleon III, II, 90; III, 89, 109, 148, 154–60, 166–9, 172, 250–1, 253, 255–6, 257, 262, 263–4, 266–8, 270, 276, 289

Napoleonic Wars, II, 4

Narbonne, II, 439

Narbonne (Schiller), II, 406

Narziss, III, 315

Nasmyth, III, 78

Nathan der Weise (Lessing), II, 238

Natural Philosophy (Hegel), III, 68

Naturalism, II, 289, 330, 434; III, 145, 306, 325, 329, 339, 347, 348, 414–17, 418, 421, 427, 429–30, 432, 469

Nature, return to, II, 278–9, 282

Natürliche Schopfungs-geschichte (Haeckel), III, 187

Nazarenes, I, 189; III, 56, 59, 209, 326, 474

Nebuchadnezzar, I, 85

Necker, Mme, II, 219

Nelson, III, 263

Nepomuk, John of, I, 115

Neptune, discovered, III, 116

Nero, I, 70, 236; III, 87, 207

Nero (Gutzkow), III, 92

Nervous System of the Barbel, On the (Büchner), III, 138

Nessler, II, 21

Nestroy, Johann, I, 71; II, 97, 135, 162; III, 137, 138–41, 225, 235, 314, 319, 427

Netherlands: revolt of, I, 310–11; suprem-acy of, in pre-Ba-roque period, II, 26–34

Nettesheim, Agrippa von, I, 208

Neuber, Friedericke Karoline, II, 161–2

Neue allgemeine deut-sche Bibliothek, II, 409

Neue Arria (Klinger), II, 287

Neue Zeitschrift für Musik, III, 129

Neunundzwanzigste Februar (Müllner), III, 43

New Principles of the Art of Gardening (Langley), II, 185

Newcomen, II, 265

Newman, John Henry, III, 112

Newsky Roussotine-Truppe (Altenberg), III, 428–9

Newspapers, II, 107, 284; III, 78–80

Newton, II, 109, 110–11, 127, 130, 184, 202, 205, 228, 304, 412; III, 176, 342, 343, 344, 462, 465

Newton (Voltaire), II, 206

Nibelungen Ring (Wag-ner), III, 284

Nibelungenlied, III, 38, 228

Nicholas I, Tsar, III, 28, 30, 153–4, 158–9, 160–1

Nicholas II, Tsar, III, 366

Nicholson, II, 429

Nicias, II, 336

Nicolai, II, 217, 232–3, 235, 245, 290, 417

Nicole, II, 95

Nicot, Jean, I, 325

Niebuhr, III, 35, 40

Niemann-Raabe, Hed-wig, III, 410

Niepce, Nicéphore, III, 121

Nietzsche, I, 16, 18, 25, 36, 37, 41, 58, 66, 69, 88, 129, 131, 168, 233, 237, 252, 254–5, 332; II, 17, 66, 150, 216, 239, 252, 303, 307, 324, 326, 333, 334,

Plato, I, 21, 24, 27, 45, 66, 77, 143, 173, 174, 175, 179, 212, 289, 338; II, 130, 171, 235, 268, 291, 304, 328, 342, 343, 344, 345, 350, 352, 353, 358, 447; III, 67, 226, 296, 379, 398–9, 405, 467, 479

Plautus, I, 224; III, 140

Plisch und Plum (Busch), III, 391

Plotinus, I, 174; II, 353

Plümicke, II, 298, 299

Plutarch, I, 46, 180, 212; II, 344

Podewils, II, 177

Poe, Edgar Allan, I, 66, 69; III, 208

Poggio, I, 174

Poincaré, Henri, III, 372

Pointillism, III, 324, 392–4

Political Testament (Frederick the Great), II, 178

Politique tirée de l'Écriture Sainte (Bossuet), II, 83–4

Polizei, Die (Schiller), II, 406–7

Poland: partitions of, II, 259–60; III, 20; Revolution of, *see* Revolution: Polish

Political conditions: at beginning of Modern age, I, 112–17; of Italian Renaissance, 157, 179–80; of Reformation, I, 265–71; of Counter-Reformation, I, 300–1; of eighteenth century, II, 157–60; of mid nineteenth century,

III, 146–62, 166–9, 245–93; post-Bismarckian, III, 362–7; to the World War, III, 448–55

Political economy, II, 263–5

Polo, Marco, I, 214

Poltava, Battle of, III, 364

Poltrot de Méré, I, 302

Polybius, II, 342

Polycletus, I, 38; II, 338

Polygnotus, II, 337

Pombal, Marquis of, II, 172, 245–6

Pompadour, Mme de, I, 63; II, 139, 146, 155

Pomponazzi, Pietro, I, 234

Ponsard, III, 446

Pope, Alexander, II, 192, 206

Porcelain, II, 138–9

Portsmouth, Peace of, III, 361

Portugal: annexed to Spain, I, 308

Positivism, III, 145, 175–6, 187, 387, 460, 476, 478, 480

Post (Berlin), III, 289

Postal service, I, 207; II, 106, 437

Potato, II, 22

Potato War, II, 255

Potsdam, Edict of, II, 119

Potter, Paul, II, 32

Pouchet, III, 192

Pour et le Contre, Le, II, 190

Poussin, II, 97–8, 328; III, 325

Powers, Congress of the, III, 27

Pragmatic Sanction, II, 158, 165, 176

Pragmatism, III, 368–9, 372, 373

Prague, Peace of, II, 14

Praise of Folly (Erasmus), I, 275

Praxiteles, II, 336, 338

Prehauser, II, 162

Pre-Impressionists, III, 323–6

Preller, III, 59

Pre-Raphaelitism, I, 189; III, 209–12, 437, 474

Presbyterianism, I, 300

Present, the, III, 3–4, 5, 14

Presse, La, III, 79

Pretenders, The (Ibsen), II, 220; III, 44, 395, 410

Pretoria, Peace of, III, 356

Prévost, Abbé, II, 190

Priam, II, 340

Priessnitz, I, 42; III, 120

Priestley, II, 183, 225

Primitive man, I, 203–5

Primitives, III, 60

Princesse Maleine (Maeterlinck), III, 340, 432, 439

Principles of Biology (Spencer), III, 177

Principles of Ethics (Spencer), III, 177

Principles of Psychology (Spencer), III, 177

Principles of Sociology (Spencer), III, 177

Printing-press, I, 163, 209, 210, 245; III, 78

Prinz von Homburg (Kleist), III, 24, 45, 46; III, 409, 432

xliii

xlviii

A NOTE
ON THE TYPE IN
WHICH THIS BOOK IS SET

This book is set on the linotype in Caslon, so called after William Caslon (1692–1766), the first of a famous English family of type-designers and founders. He was originally an apprentice to an engraver of gun-locks and gun-barrels in London. In 1716 he opened his own shop, for silver-chasing and making bookbinders' stamps. The printers John Watts and William Bowyer, admirers of his skill in cutting ornaments and letters, advanced him money to equip himself for type-founding, which he began in 1720. The fonts he cut in 1722 for Bowyer's sumptuous folio edition of John Selden, published in 1726, excited great interest. A specimen sheet of type faces, issued in 1734, made Caslon's superiority to all other letter-cutters of the time, English or Dutch, quickly recognized, and soon his types, or types modelled on his style, were being used by most English printers, supplanting the Dutch types that had formerly prevailed. In style Caslon was a reversion to earlier type styles. Its characteristics are remarkable regularity and symmetry, as well as beauty in the shape and proportion of the letters; its general effect is clear and open, but not weak or delicate. For uniformity, clearness, and readability it has perhaps never been surpassed. After Caslon's death his eldest son, also named William (1720–78), carried on the business successfully. Then followed a period of neglect of nearly fifty years. In 1843 Caslon type was revived by the then firm of Caslon for William Pickering and has since been one of the most widely used of all type designs in English and American printing.

THIS BOOK WAS COMPOSED, PRINTED, AND BOUND BY THE PLIMPTON PRESS, NORWOOD, MASS. · THE PAPER WAS MADE BY TICONDEROGA PULP & PAPER CO., TICONDEROGA, N. Y.